SEXUAL DESIRE

W9-ANT-653

Roger Scruton was until 1990 Professor of Aesthetics at Birkbeck College, London, and subsequently Professor of Philosophy and University Professor at Boston University, Massachusetts. He now lives with his wife and two small children in rural Wiltshire, where he runs a small post-modern farm. He has published over 20 books, including works on philosophy, literature and fiction, and his writings have been translated into most major languages. He is also well known as a broadcaster and journalist, and writes a weekly column on countryside matters for the *Financial Times*.

ALSO BY ROGER SCRUTON

Non-fiction
A Short History of Modern Philosophy
Art and Imagination
The Aesthetics of Architecture
The Meaning of Conservatism
A Dictionary of Political Thought
A Land Held Hostage: Lebanon and the West
The Philosopher on Dover Beach
Modern Philosophy: A Survey
The Aesthetics of Music
On Hunting
An Intelligent Person's Guide to Modern Culture

Fiction
Fortnight's Anger
Francesca
A Dove Descending
Xanthippic Dialogues
Perictione in Colophon

SEXUAL DESIRE

A Philosophical Investigation

Roger Scruton

PHOENIX
PRESS

5 UPPER SAINT MARTIN'S LANE
LONDON
WC2H 9EA

A PHOENIX PRESS PAPERBACK

First published in Great Britain
by Weidenfeld & Nicolson in 1986
Phoenix edition published in 1994
This paperback edition published in 2001
by Phoenix Press,
a division of The Orion Publishing Group Ltd,
Orion House, 5 Upper St Martin's Lane,
London WC2H 9EA

Copyright © 1986 by Roger Scruton

The moral right of Roger Scruton to be identified as the author
of this work has been asserted by him in accordance with
the Copyright, Designs and Patents Act 1988.

All rights reserved. No part of this publication may be
reproduced, stored in a retrieval system, or transmitted,
in any form or by any means, electronic, mechanical,
photocopying, recording or otherwise, without the prior
permission of the copyright owner and the above
publisher of this book.

This book is sold subject to the condition that it may not
be resold or otherwise issued except in its original binding.

A CIP catalogue record for this book
is available from the British Library.

Printed and bound in Great Britain by
Butler & Tanner Ltd, Frome and London

ISBN 1 84212 514 1

CONTENTS

PREFACE

The subject of sexual desire has been largely ignored by modern philosophy, and the biographies of the great modern philosophers suggest that they have tended to avoid the experience of desire as scrupulously as they have avoided its analysis. I leave it to others to offer theories as to why this is so. But the subject requires that I make a general remark concerning the trouble that philosophy encounters when it enters this domain.

Until the late nineteenth century it was almost impossible to discuss sexual desire, except as part of erotic love, and even then convention required that the peculiarities of desire remain unmentioned. This deliberate neglect also damaged the discussion of erotic love, which was made to appear yet more mysterious than it is, precisely because it had been deprived of its principal motive. When the interdiction was finally lifted – by such writers as Krafft-Ebing, Féré and Havelock Ellis – it was by virtue of an allegedly 'scientific' approach to a widespread natural phenomenon.

Such was the prestige of science that any investigation conducted in its name could call upon powerful currents of social approval, which were sufficient to overcome the otherwise crippling reluctance to face the realities of sexual experience. However, it was precisely this dependence upon the prestige of science that led to the continued neglect of the subject. It became necessary to assume that sexual conduct is an aspect of man's 'animal' condition – an 'instinct' whose expression exhibits the undiscovered laws of a complex biological process. But, as I argue in the following pages, no biological taxonomy could capture the lineaments of sexual desire. Desire is indeed a natural phenomenon, but it is one that lies beyond the reach of any 'natural science' of man.

By the time that Freud had introduced his shocking revelations – disguised once again as neutral, 'scientific' truths about a universal impulse – the language had been settled in which the details of human sexuality are now habitually presented. Freud described the aim of sexual desire as:

> union of the genitals in the act known as copulation, which leads to a release of the sexual tension and a temporary extinction of the sexual instinct – a satisfaction analogous to the sating of hunger.

Such language – which expresses a certain hatred of the sexual act and all that pertains to it – cannot capture what is distinctive in sexual experience. Its universal adoption by 'sexologists' has led, however, to a remarkable 'science', which purports to explain that which it has no language to describe. The *Kinsey Report*, like the pseudo-scientific literature which has followed it, merely continues, in more vulgar and more spirited form, the moralising enterprise of Krafft-Ebing: the enterprise of confronting our moral sentiments with an allegedly 'scientific' description of the facts which threaten them. The final outcome has been the establishment of the 'sexologist's report', as a new literary genre. The style is exemplified by the *Masters and Johnson Report*, with its repeated references to the 'effective functioning', 'adequacy' and 'frequency' of 'sexual performance', and its pseudo-experimental approach to matters which we can see in neutral terms only by misperceiving them: 'Subject C has vocalised a desire to return to the program accompanied by his wife as a contributing family unit.' The effect of this 'demystification' of the sexual impulse has been the rise of novel and unprecedented superstitions, and the growth of a new kind of pseudo-scientific mystery which it is one of the aims of this book to dispel.

Only occasionally has a writer addressed himself to the crucial question which this 'scientific' literature has contrived to ignore: the question of what a person experiences when he desires another. Desire is identical neither with the 'instinct' which is expressed in it nor with the love which fulfils it. It is, I shall argue, a distinctively human phenomenon, and one that urges on us precisely that restricting sense of 'decency' which once forbade its discussion. In this book I shall present a defence of decency; but in doing so I illustrate the truth of Bernard Shaw's remark, that it is impossible to explain decency without being indecent. I only hope that the benefit, in terms of moral understanding, will outweigh the moral cost.

Earlier versions of the text were read by Joanna North, John Casey, Bill Newton-Smith, Robert Grant, David Levy and Sally Shreir, and I am greatly indebted to all of them for their many criticisms and suggestions. I am particularly grateful to Ian McFetridge, whose painstaking examination of the first draft provided the indispensable support without which this book would not have been finished in its present form. Thanks to his generosity, broad-mindedness and philosophical penetration, this work has been saved from many errors and obscurities, and I only hope that he will not be too distressed by those that remain.

ADVICE TO THE READER

1. In this book I follow traditional practice, in using the masculine pronoun to refer indifferently to men and women, except where the context requires gender to be explicit. There are two reasons for this: first, that it is stylistically correct; secondly, that it is the most effective way of leaving sex out of it – as one must leave sex out of the discussion of desire. What I mean by that second reason can be understood, however, only in the course of my argument.

2. Because this is a work of philosophy it contains passages of difficult argument, designed to provide foundations for the central discussion. Most of these passages occur in Chapter 3 and in the two appendices. However, the reader who ignores these sections will be able to understand the argument, and appreciate my main contentions. In particular, anyone who finds himself obstructed by Chapter 3 should pass at once to Chapter 4, where the discussion of sexual desire is continued.

I

THE PROBLEM

Modern philosophers have described sexual desire and erotic love in surprising and paradoxical ways. For Kant, sexual desire can be understood only as part of the 'pathology' of the human condition.[1] For Hegel, erotic love involves a contradiction; for Sartre, the same contradiction is present in desire.[2] Schopenhauer regarded sexual desire as involving a delusion – the delusion, to put it simply, that it is the individual who is subject and object in our sexual endeavours.[3] Those romantic and post-romantic views exhibit an equal pessimism, and each contrasts with the discussions of the subject that have come down to us from ancient thinkers.

Perhaps the most famous of those thinkers was Plato, who introduced (in his own terms) a distinction that has caused considerable confusion in subsequent debate: the distinction between erotic love and sexual desire. Plato is the intellectual ancestor of a view which persists to this day and which conditions much of our moral thinking. According to this view, our animal nature is the principal vehicle of sexual desire, and provides its overriding motive. In desire we act and feel as animals; indeed, desire is a motive which all sexual beings – including the majority of animals – share. In erotic love, however, it is our nature as rational beings that is primarily engaged, and, in the exercise of this passion, altogether finer and more durable impulses seek recognition and fulfilment.

To Plato, it seemed that the two impulses are so radically opposed that they could not happily coexist in a single consciousness. Hence, in order to permit the full flowering of erotic love, it is necessary to refine away, and eventually to discard, the element of desire. The resulting love – 'Platonic' love – would be both intrinsically rational and morally pure. This pure love has, for Plato, a distinctive value, comparable to the value of philosophy itself. It provides a link with transcendent reality, a stage on the way to spiritual fulfilment and emancipation, which occurs only with the final release of the soul into that world of Ideas from which it descended and in which it has its eternal home. The subject of the erotic thus acquired, for Plato, a seriousness, and a pathos, rarely expressed in the writings of later philosophers. So seriously, indeed, did he regard it that he could permit his characters to discuss it fully only when drunk, in a dialogue which is rightly regarded as one of the great literary achievements of antiquity.[4]

Remnants of the Platonic view can be found in many subsequent thinkers – in the neo-Platonists, in St Augustine, in Aquinas and in the Roman philosopher-poet Boethius, whose philosophy of love was to have such a profound effect on the literature of medieval Europe and in particular on Chaucer, the Troubadours, Cavalcanti, Boccaccio and Dante.[5] It survives in the popular idea – itself founded in the most dubious of metaphysical distinctions – that sexual desire is primarily 'physical', while love always has a 'spiritual' side. It survives, too, in the theory of Kant, despite the enormous moral and emotional distance that separates Kant from Plato, and despite Kant's remorseless pessimism about the erotic life of mankind. It is one major purpose of this work to combat the Platonic theory. I shall argue, not against the distinction between the animal and the rational (indeed, I shall uphold that distinction as crucial to the understanding of our condition), but against the moral and philosophical impulse that leads us to assign sexual desire to the animal part of human nature.

In the course of my argument I shall try to explain why sexual desire has so often been regarded as mysterious or paradoxical; and I shall show that there is more than a grain of truth in these descriptions. I shall also give the philosophical grounding for a sexual morality, and argue that moral consideration cannot be subtracted from the sexual act without at the same time destroying its distinctive character. There is a modern prejudice (although it is no more than a prejudice) that there cannot really be such a thing as a specifically sexual morality. Morality, it is thought, attaches not to the sexual act, but always to something *else*, with which it may be conjoined. We may reasonably forbid sexual violence, say, but that is on account of the violence; considered in and for itself, and detached from fortuitous circumstances, the sexual act is neither right nor wrong, but merely 'natural'. Such a view may seem implausible when set beside the obvious immorality of child molestation or rape – crimes which seem to threaten the very existence of others as sexual beings, and to threaten also the sexual life of their perpetrator. But the precise reason for rejecting the modern prejudice is hard to discover, and it will not be before the end of this book that the reader will have my reasons for thinking that the sexual act is, and must always be, limited by moral scruples. And, although I shall be sparing in my moral conclusions – having neither the space nor the inclination to consider all that must be considered in order to present a comprehensive sexual ethic – I hope that at least some of the ideas of 'traditional' morality will no longer seem as strange after reading this book as they have seemed to many of the authors whom I have studied in the course of writing it. Whether or not the reader comes to agree with my particular conclusions, he will, I hope, agree that it need not be *absurd* to condemn homosexual intercourse, fornication, masturbation, or whatever, even though we all have an urge to do these things, and even though there may be no God who forbids them.

To begin a philosophical investigation into sexual desire is not easy. Not only is the subject encumbered by a thousand conflicting prejudices; it is also uncertain which method would enable us to broach it. Ought we to be engaged in 'conceptual analysis', sorting out the intricate connections of usage, and the deep connections of meaning, which link such terms as 'desire', 'arousal', 'love' and 'pleasure'? Or should we be engaged in an exercise of 'phenomenology', trying to give a specification of 'what it is like' that will fit the sexual experiences of those who have them? Or again, should we be attempting to locate and to solve the specific puzzles, in ethics and the philosophy of mind, to which reflection on our sexual experience gives rise? Finally, should we be preparing the ground for science, removing the initial muddles that stand in the way of a proper scientific account of one of the most important, and most misunderstood, of vital phenomena?

I believe that it is necessary to do all of those things, and indeed that they are all parts of a single philosophical enterprise. The main problem is one of description – description at the shallowest possible level. It is necessary to *locate* the phenomenon of sexual desire, to say what it is, as a human experience. It is this search for a shallow description that has been called, at various times and for various purposes, both 'phenomenology' and 'the analysis of concepts'.[6]

Like many 'analytical' philosophers, I am suspicious of phenomenology. I am suspicious, in particular, of the 'Cartesian' method of Husserl: the assumption that experience should be described from the first-person point of view. (My reasons for this suspicion are set out in Appendix 1.) At the same time, I am greatly indebted to another idea which has been of supreme importance in phenomenology, and which is

3

only belatedly gaining recognition among the practitioners of 'conceptual analysis'. The idea is older than phenomenology – perhaps as old as Aristotle, certainly as old as Kant. It holds that we must distinguish the world of human experience from the world of scientific observation. In the first we exist as agents, taking command of our destiny and relating to each other through conceptions that have no place in the scientific view of the universe. In the second we exist as organisms, driven by an arcane causality and relating to each other through the laws of motion that govern us as they govern every other thing. Kant described the first world as 'transcendental', the second as 'empirical', and steered a brilliant course between two exhaustive, mutually incompatible and, for him, equally impossible views of their relation. On one view the transcendental world is a separate realm of being from the empirical world, so that objects belonging to the one are not to be found in the other. On the other view, the two worlds are not distinct, but rather two separate ways of viewing the same material: we can view it either from the 'transcendental' perspective of the human agent or from the 'empirical' perspective of the scientific observer. In this book I shall defend a version of that second idea, in terms which owe something to Kant's disciple Dilthey, something to Husserl, and something to recent work in analytical philosophy of science, but which bear little direct relation to Kant.[7] I believe we must distinguish, not two worlds, but two ways of understanding the world, and in particular two separate conceptual enterprises, by which our understanding is formed.

The world is more than an object of scientific curiosity. It is compliant to our purposes: everywhere we confront the occasion for action and the means whereby to accomplish it. The world is also diverse, presenting variegated objects of desire and contrasting obstacles to our will. As practical beings we instinctively develop categories that will record and facilitate our commerce with our surroundings, and these categories bear the double imprint of human purpose and material variety – corresponding in part to our uses and in part to the natural condition of the objects described. Some categories do no more than record the purpose to which an object may be put: categories like 'table', 'swing' and 'shelter'. Others describe some recurring feature of the environment, and perhaps at the same time postulate an explanation of its unified appearance: such are categories like 'animal', 'vegetable' and 'rock'. Other categories seem to fit into either class, combining functional significance and explanatory power. When we describe something as hard, we situate it in the web of human purposes – it is something that will resist our attempts to transform it, and perhaps also hurt us. At the same time, we attribute a

4

physical character, a constitution, that allies it to a host of kindred substances in the world of nature.

Philosophers have paid much attention in recent years to the existence of these contrasting kinds of category, and in particular to the division between functional and natural kinds.[8] Given our dual existence, as active and as contemplative beings, it is natural that we should avail ourselves of the two kinds of concept, and that there should be so many notions situated in the hazy area occupied by 'hard' and 'soft'. We seek both to understand the world and to alter it; and usually to do both. Hence we equip ourselves with categories permeable to explanation (natural kinds) and categories permeable to purpose (functional kinds). But our relation to the world is vastly more complex than that implies: in addition to purpose and knowledge we have experiences, values, emotions and religious belief. These too dictate their own conceptual trajectories, their separate attempts to order the world as an object of our interests.

Classification may be compared to butchery, in which an object is divided, sometimes according to its nature and sometimes in defiance of it. The English butcher, motivated by a zealous disdain for the corpse before him, and also for the man who will eat it, chops the creature savagely into rough-hewn blocks, having little more than a tradition of fair-play to recommend them. An English 'joint' may consist of a scrap of dorsal muscle, a piece of backbone, a fragment of kidney, some skin and marrow, a few hairs, and the indelible mark with which Farmer Jones once branded his lamb. Sometimes – as in the kidney chop – the resulting combination of flavours gives rise to an interesting 'gustatory kind'. But this was no part of the intention. The French butcher, prompted by a native respect for *les nourritures terrestres*, endeavours to separate each natural texture and flavour from its competitors, detaching a complete fillet from the bone, fat, kidney and skin that encase it. He divides nature more nearly at the joints than does his English colleague; but his truth to nature is the result of interests that have no necessary relation to nature's laws. He still bears no comparison with the anatomist, who, forswearing all interest in appearances, explores nature's secrets in the order in which nature conceived them. For the anatomist, the real order of the carcase is that which explains, not only its taste, but also its structure, its former movements, its passing away and its coming to be.

In classification, as in butchery, we are often more interested in the relation of objects to ourselves than in their causality and constitution. For we seek, not merely for the causes of events, but also for their meaning – even when they have no meaning. For example, we group the stars into constellations according to fictions of our own, and in doing so we commit astronomical outrage. For the astronomer our concept of a 'constellation' displays nothing but the superstitious emotion of those who first devised it. For the astrologer it conveys the deepest insight into the mystery of things. For the rest of us this classification is a record of our familiarity with the world, a tribute to the human face which covers it. Thomas Hardy awakens us to much sadness when he writes, of young drummer Hodge, killed in the Boer war, that he 'never knew . . . / The meaning of the broad karoo': to die in surroundings that are opaque to our quest for meaning is to die unconsoled. And hence the bleakness of the 'strange-eyed constellations' that 'west / Each night above his mound'.

The example of constellations bears on matters to which I shall return in the final chapter. More useful to us at present is a category predicated on our interest in beauty: the category of the ornamental. Consider then the class of 'ornamental marbles'. The purpose of this classification – of great importance to sculptors, masons and serious-minded architects – is to assimilate stones that are the objects of a single aesthetic concern. An ornamental marble can be polished; it has a grain, a colour, a depth and a surface translucency which lend it to our decorative purposes. The classification includes onyx, porphyry and marble itself. Scientifically speaking, the classification is an utter nonsense. For onyx is an oxide, porphyry a silicate, marble a carbonate, while limestone – an isotope of marble – is expressly excluded from the class. A science of stones must aim to replace all such classifications – whose subservience to human purposes deprives them of full explanatory power – with other and deeper classifications, designed to capture the real similarities among the objects subsumed by them. Science aims, in other words, to discover natural kinds. For only a division of the world into natural kinds can enable us to penetrate below appearances, to the underlying 'laws of motion' which explain them.

A science of stones would therefore classify marble and limestone together, as different crystalline forms of calcium carbonate, generated by the decomposition under pressure of living things. Such a science would probably find no single explanation for the fact that the appearance and utility of marble approximates so closely to the appearance and utility of onyx and porphyry. Hence it would in all probability contain no classification corresponding to our idea of an ornamental marble. On the contrary, it is likely to dispense with all such classifications, which tend to dissolve just as soon as we reach below the surface of human experience to the underlying physical order which explains and sustains it.

Some concepts, therefore, including the concepts of natural science,

6

have an explanatory function. Not only do they provide the terms in which explanations are formulated; they are themselves explanatory, in that to subsume an object under them is already to provide an explanation of its empirically discoverable character.[9] Other concepts, including many concepts of common sense and intuitive understanding, are not (or not primarily) explanatory. Their function is to divide the world in accordance with our interests, to mark out possibilities of action, emotion and experience which may very well be hampered by too great an attention to the underlying order of things. Concepts of this kind often tend to give way before the pressure of scientific innovation. We feel this pressure in many ways, but most immediately as a kind of instability in our ordinary descriptions. It seems as though tables and chairs are not *really* as we describe them. They are not really coloured, not really solid, and so on. For the best explanation of these indelible appearances makes no mention of colour (at best only of the *experience* of colour), and postulates in place of the 'solid' table a discontinuous crowd of molecules, each separated from its neighbour by a distance greater than its own diameter.

There is no need for us here to enquire into the meaning of the word 'really' on the lips of the person who says that no table is *really* coloured. (I take up the point in Appendix 2.) What is important is the contrast between the 'thinness' of our ordinary descriptions and the 'rock-hard' solidity of the explanations which seem to threaten them, and which yield, if at all, only to better explanations than themselves. At the same time, the descriptions of ordinary thought and action cannot be forgone. Without them, we lack an essential instrument for the understanding of our world. The classification of stones as ornamental marbles indicates, not a structural, but a partly phenomenal, partly functional, similarity among the substances to which it is applied. And the purpose of marking this similarity is to enshrine in a classification the common purpose to which such objects may be put.

As our example shows, classification relative to purpose (classification in terms of 'functional kinds') is not the only example of the 'thin' descriptions generated by everyday human life. There is also classification relative to immediate sensory experience – the kind of classification that records 'secondary qualities'.[10] And there are more elusive examples: classifications relative to emotions (the fearful, the lovable, the disgusting), and classifications relative to aesthetic interest (the ornamental, the serene, the elegant and the harmonious). Such classifications record, not the varieties of material objects, but the varieties of human 'intentionality' – to borrow a useful technicality of the phenomenologists.

7

By 'intentionality' I mean the quality of 'reference beyond' which is contained in human consciousness: the quality of pointing to, and delineating, an object of thought. The 'awareness of the world' that lies at the heart of my experience, and which seems constantly to project my thoughts outwards on to a reality greater than myself, exists in many forms: belief, perception, imagination, emotion and desire. Each of these mental states marks out a space, as it were, before me – a gap into which an object may be fitted. My fear is fear of something, my perception perception of something, and so on. Sometimes I am myself the object of my thoughts; more normally, however, the object is something other than myself, something that belongs to the 'surrounding world' of my experience. (For an exact definition of the term 'intentionality', see Appendix 2.)

I shall describe this 'surrounding world' as the *Lebenswelt* ('world of life'), using a term popular among phenomenologists, though not exclusive to them.[11] The *Lebenswelt* is not a world separate from the world of natural science, but a world differently described – described with the concepts that designate the intentional objects of human experience. Intentionality implies that my consciousness is also a form of representation: my consciousness shows me a world, and also places me in relation to it. But not all forms of representation are transparent. The descriptions employed by science suppose that the nature of the objects identified through them is *to be discovered*. The representation identifies an object: but its nature is to be determined by further enquiry. The same is not true of the *Lebenswelt*, whose objects are identified by descriptions that are, or aim to be, transparent to our experience and purposes. The objects of the *Lebenswelt* are conceived under classifications that reflect our own practical and contemplative interest in them. These classifications attempt to divide the world according to the requirements of everyday theoretical and practical reason.[12] The classifications which define the 'phenomenological kinds' of the *Lebenswelt* are only partly responsive to the enterprise of prediction. They sometimes dissolve under the impact of scientific explanation, not because they necessarily conflict with the scientific world-view, but because they have no staying power against the standpoint of the curious observer, who looks, not to the interests of people, but to the underlying structure of reality.

At the same time, science may provide no substitute for the concepts which order and direct our everyday experience. A sculptor armed with the theories of chemistry, geology and crystallography, but without the concept (foreign to those sciences) of an ornamental marble, will not have that immediate sense of similarity in use which enables his less erudite colleague spontaneously to relate onyx to porphyry. His very perceptions will be different, for they will be deprived of a concept in terms of which such stones would otherwise be seen.

It is arguable that scientific penetration into the depth of things may render the surface unintelligible – or at least intelligible only slowly and painfully, and with a hesitancy that undermines the immediate needs of human action. (Such is indeed the case, I shall argue, with the crucial phenomenon of human sexual desire.) As agents we belong to the surface of the world, and enter into immediate relation with it. The concepts through which we represent it form a vital link with reality, and without this link appropriate action and appropriate response could not emerge with the rapidity and competence that alone can ensure our happiness and survival. We cannot replace our most basic everyday concepts with anything better than themselves, for they have evolved precisely under the pressure of human circumstance and in answer to the needs of gener- ations. Any 'rational reconstruction' – however obedient it may be to the underlying truth of things and to the requirements of scientific objectivity – runs the risk of severing the vital connection which links our response to the world, and the world to our response, in a chain of spontaneous human competence.[13]

Nevertheless, many of our everyday concepts waver precariously under the impact of scientific thinking, and one of them – the concept of the human agent, or person – will be the subject of much that follows. It is the duty of philosophy, as it is the need of religion, to sustain and validate such concepts and the human intentionality to which they give sense and direction. We are familiar enough with the dangers that attach to the scientific view of the human condition – the view which represents us, perhaps truly, as complex organisms, buffeted by the workings of a causality over which we exert no control. But it is important not to be hasty with remedies, not to seek either to deny the truths of science – taking refuge, for example, in some delusory metaphysic of human freedom – or to run impetuously to the protective sanctuary of religious faith, in order to provide dogmatic support for conceptions which are, in truth, our own invention, and which we alone have the obligation to repair. We need to show in detail that our spontaneous descriptions of the *Lebenswelt* – descriptions which make human agency into the most important feature of our surrounding world – are not displaced by the truths of science, that they have their own truth which, because it does not compete with the enterprise of ultimate explanation, is not rendered the less secure by the explanations which seem at first glance to conflict with it. Philosophy, which is the art of second glances, is burdened with a great task of restitution. Science has estranged us from the world, by causing us to mistrust the concepts through which we respond to it. I shall attempt to restore the concept of sexual desire to its rightful place in the description of the *Lebenswelt*, and to show in detail why a science of sex can neither displace that concept nor illuminate the human phenomenon that it describes.

The crucial concept for any philosophical attempt to provide the basis for human understanding is the concept of the person. It is a well-known thesis of philosophy – expressed in countless idioms and in countless tones of voice – that human beings may be described in two contrasting (and, for some, conflicting) ways: as organisms obedient to the laws of nature, and as persons, sometimes obedient, sometimes disobedient, to the moral law. Persons are moral agents; their actions have not only causes, but also reasons. They make decisions for the future, and so have intentions in addition to desires. They do not allow themselves always to be swept along by their impulses, but occasionally resist and subdue them. In everything the moral agent is both active and passive, and stands as a kind of legislator among his own emotions. He is also an object not only of affection and love (which we may extend to all of nature), but also of praise and blame, anger and esteem. In all such intuitive distinctions – between reason and cause, intention and desire, action and passion, esteem and affection – we find aspects of the vital distinction which underlies them and to the clarification of which Kant devoted some of his greatest chapters: the distinction between person and thing. Only a person has rights, duties and obligations; only a person acts for reasons in addition to causes; only a person merits our praise, blame or anger. And it is as persons that we perceive and act upon one another, so mediating all our mutual responses with the obscure but indispensable concept of the free moral agent.

I do not believe that we can accept Kant's majestic theory, which ascribes to persons a metaphysical core, the 'transcendental self', lying beyond nature and eternally free from its constraints. Nevertheless, his theory was derived persuasively from insights into human agency that we must not reject, and one of my major concerns in what follows will be to defend what is defensible in Kant's outlook, while avoiding the intolerable metaphysic which he – and, following him, Husserl, Heidegger, Patočka and many others – made into the central proposition of a theory of man. At the same time I shall reject any attempt to give a theory of human nature in merely scientific terms: in terms of the 'best explanation' of what we are. For we are mere appearances, and the best explanation of our nature will probably not employ the concept of the person, even though that concept defines what we are for one another and for ourselves. If this idea seems paradoxical, I hope that it will seem less paradoxical later – or at least, no more paradoxical than human experience itself.

I shall contrast two modes of understanding: scientific understanding, which aims to explain the world, and 'intentional understanding', as I shall call it, which aims to describe, to criticise and to justify the *Lebenswelt*. The second is an attempt to understand the world in terms of the concepts through which we experience and act on it: these concepts identify the 'intentional object' of our everyday states of mind. An intentional understanding, therefore, fills the world with the meanings implicit in our aims and emotions. The idea of such an understanding is a familiar *donnée* of Kantian sociology, underlying the view that the social world in which we act must be understood differently from the world of the disengaged observer, by means of an act of *Verstehen*.[14] Not only is this 'intentional understanding' indispensable to us as rational agents; it may also be irreplaceable by any understanding derived from natural science. Intentional understanding is concerned not to explain the world so much as to be 'at home' in it, recognising the occasions for action, the objects of sympathy and the places of rest.

Inevitably our intentional understanding must contain large explanatory elements – for you cannot act successfully without a system of belief. And to possess a belief is to be committed to the pursuit of truth, and hence to the construction of scientific theories, and to the consequent classification of the world in terms of natural kinds. Yet there is no reason to suppose that such a classification will provide sufficient basis for our rational conduct, just as there is no reason to think that the chemical classification of stones will provide a basis for the activity of the sculptor. In particular, this neutral, scientific view of things may be well adapted to describe the means to fulfil our purposes, but it must remain for ever incapable of describing the ends to which we aspire. The ends of life are also the meanings of our personal experiences, and the world of science is a world without meaning.[15]

Consider the most elementary human relations. The individual people I encounter are members of a natural kind – the kind 'human being' – and behave according to the laws of that kind. Yet I subsume people and their actions under concepts that will not figure in the formulation of those laws. Indeed, the hallucination of those laws (for so it must be described in our present state of ignorance) seems often to distract people from genuine human intercourse. If the fundamental facts about John are, for me, his biological constitution, his scientific essence, his neurological structure, then I shall find it difficult to respond to him with affection, anger, love, contempt or grief. So described, he becomes mysterious to me, since those classifications do not capture the intentional object of interpersonal emotion.

The point is a general one: the scientific attempt to penetrate to 'the depths' of human things is accompanied almost universally by a loss of response to the 'surface'. Yet it is on the surface that we live and act: it is there that we are created, as complex appearances sustained by the social interaction which we, as appearances, also create. The very same 'mystery' that veils the human person from the neurophysiologist veils human history from the Marxian determinist and human morality from the sociobiologist. The charm of those sciences is a charm of demystification; but they end by mystifying more profoundly what they intend to explain, precisely by enabling us to forget the purpose of explaining it. (As Wittgenstein put it, 'what is hidden is of no interest to us.')

However, the concepts of our intentional understanding are not easy to analyse. Their embeddedness in feeling and action makes it difficult to bring them into focus. The human world may not be 'deep' in the scientific meaning of that term, but it is dense.[16] Hence it is often easier to speak of the intentionality of an emotion as though it were a matter of perception rather than thought: the object of hatred is *perceived* hatefully. To understand the concept of the person might similarly require us to understand a kind of perception: to understand what it is to *see* human beings as persons. And this perception in turn may not be easily disentangled from the culture that is built upon it, or from the ultimate ends of conduct which it serves to focus.

This does not mean that our intentional understanding generates 'mere ideology' in the Marxian sense – a system of beliefs with nothing to recommend it besides its capacity to mystify the world, in a manner supportive of our ('bourgeois') endeavours.[17] The Marxists are indeed right to differentiate beliefs in terms of their explanation, and to point to the deviant epistemological status of a belief which is to be explained always in terms of some human interest other than the interest in truth. However, although many of our *concepts* are to be explained in functional terms, it does not follow that a functional explanation is appropriate for the beliefs in which those concepts figure. Thus the existence of the concept 'ornamental marble' is to be explained in terms of its utility in focusing our sculptural purposes. Nevertheless, the sculptor who judges some piece of stone to be an ornamental marble acquires this belief as a result of evidence. Such 'thin' beliefs are unscientific, since they employ concepts which are opaque to scientific method. But they may be true or false, and reasonable or unreasonable. For they are typically caused not by our needs but by our perception of how things are.

The same is true generally of the concepts which define the *Lebenswelt*. In particular, there are important concepts which inform our sexual experience, and which exist because they serve a human interest other than the interest in scientific truth (for example, the concepts of innocence and guilt, normality and perversion, sacred and profane). However, the functionality of those concepts does not imply the functionality of the beliefs which employ them. The objectivity of those beliefs may be as secure as the objectivity of science, even though they refer, not to the underlying structure of reality, but to the *Lebenswelt*. If the *Lebenswelt* is a bourgeois invention then we should praise and emulate the bourgeois mind, which is better fitted to perceive the human reality than the ordered consciousness of the 'demystifying' critic.

There are genuine, objective truths about the *Lebenswelt*, to be understood by philosophical analysis. Philosophy may therefore provide true illumination of the human condition, precisely through that 'analysis of concepts' which has seemed in recent years so often to deaden our human perceptions. An analysis of concepts *is* what is involved in the attempt to extend and deepen the realm of 'intentional understanding'. Nothing can serve to illuminate the intentionality of our natural human responses, save analysis of the concepts which are involved in it. This attempt to deepen our intentional understanding is an attempt to explore the realm of the 'given', but not that of the *subjectively* given. We are concerned, not with first-person knowledge of experience, but with the shared practices whereby a public language is attached both to the world and to the life of those who describe it. This is the idea captured in Wittgenstein's slogan, that 'what is given is forms of life', and in Husserl's own recognition (which failed to persuade him to reject the disastrous 'transcendental psychology' with which he encumbered it) that the *Lebenswelt* is given 'intersubjectively'.[18]

The foundation of our understanding of the human world lies in shared and publicly available practices, among which language – which defines the modes of representation through which we perceive the world – is the most important. Hence I shall make no further distinction in what follows between 'phenomenological' and 'analytical' conclusions. Two idioms are equally available to me, and neither need be thought to have a monopoly of the truth, since, as soon as we have accepted the import of the 'private language' argument (a version of which is given in Appendix 1), there can be no real conflict between them.

*

How then should we confront the problem of sexual desire? It needs little observation to recognise that our civilisation has suffered a profound crisis in sexual behaviour and in sexual morality. As I have already remarked, it seems to me inevitable that sexual conduct should be encumbered with moral scruples. I also believe that many of these scruples are justifiable, and that the failure to see this stems from a mistaken conception of the nature of desire. Hence my first task will be one of description: what is sexual desire as a phenomenon of human experience? I shall then try to sketch a sexual morality, whose basis will be located, not in religious belief, but in human nature, and I shall rely upon the general strategy explored by Aristotle in the *Nicomachean Ethics*, in order to pass from the facts of human nature to the morality which they imply. At many points in what follows, my discussion will make contact with religion, not only because – as has been frequently observed – erotic and religious sentiments show a peculiar isomorphism, but also because religious experience provides the securest everyday background to sexual morality. From the point of view of the subject, the complex and hardly manageable matter of sexual conduct is clarified and simplified by the root conceptions of religious faith, which give to the philosophical truths that I shall elaborate a concrete, immediate and practical reality. Religion rescues such concepts as those of the person, of freedom, of responsibility, of trust and commitment, of possession, surrender, personal union and personal separation, from all scepticism save that which attaches to God himself. Unfortunately that last scepticism is, for the philosopher, the hardest to vanquish. It is therefore a singular disadvantage of philosophy that it must bypass the appeal to faith, and so deprive itself of the most vivid symbols whereby our intentional understanding is focussed. Faith, which fills the world with meanings, leans too precariously upon an unjustifiable metaphysical claim. To justify those meanings the philosopher must pass beyond and behind faith, and look on the human condition with the uncommitted gaze of the philosophical anthropologist. He must attend, as the phenomenologists say, 'to the things themselves'.

But what things? I shall consider the three basic phenomena of human sexual feeling: arousal, desire and love. I shall contend that all are purely human phenomena, or rather, that they belong to that realm of reciprocal response which is mediated by the concept of the person, and which is available only to beings who possess and are motivated by that concept. The implications of this will be seen to be enormous.

In addition to the basic phenomena, there is the condition from which they derive: the condition of sexual existence, with its associated distinction between man and woman. There is also what might be called a 'realm of sexual experience': a realm of emotions and perceptions which are available to us, only because of our susceptibility to sexual desire. Much of this realm is mysterious to us. Consider, for example, sexual jealousy. It is impossible to deny the catastrophic power of this emotion, which leads us into the most desperate behaviour, and yet which starts up from the smallest circumstance. How do we explain this catastrophe? What is it in jealousy that proves so destructive to the one who suffers it, and why is jealousy so difficult to overcome? We shall find that the answer to those questions touches upon one of the deepest and most astonishing of facts about our nature as rational agents.

I shall consider the important expressions of sexual feeling: glances, caresses and the act of love itself. I shall try to account for the place and value of those dispositions – chastity, modesty and shame – which have provided a uniquely human obstacle to sexual indulgence, and I shall also describe some of the variants of the human sexual endeavour: the various 'perversions' and the often remarkable goals and strategies of which sexual union may form a part. I shall explore the important differences between homosexual and heterosexual desire, and between the sexuality of men and that of women. In conclusion I shall attempt to say something about the institutions through which sexual desire finds its safe conduit, and whose construction is all-important in creating the conditions of sexual fulfilment. Sexual desire, like the human person, is a social artefact, and can be built in many ways. But if it is to be properly built, so that its fulfilment is available to those who experience its normal forms, then it must be given the institutional conditions that it demands intrinsically. The problem of sexual desire becomes, in the end, a political problem, and the somewhat conservative moral conclusions that I shall defend must be seen as part of the larger political conservatism which they already imply, and for which they provide, indeed, one of the deepest justifications – a justification that stems from the inner quality of the most private human experience.

2
AROUSAL

Human beings talk and cooperate, they build and produce, they work to accumulate and exchange, they form societies, laws and institutions, and in all these things the phenomenon of reason – as a distinct principle of activity – seems dominant. There are indeed theories of the human which describe this or that activity as central – speech, say, productive labour (Marx), or political existence (Aristotle). But we feel that the persuasiveness of such theories depends upon whether the activity in question is an expression of the deeper essence, reason itself, which all human behaviour displays.

We should not conclude, however, that it is only as an active being that man displays his distinctive causality. Men are distinguished equally by the quality of their experiences and by a receptiveness – displayed at its most complete in aesthetic experience – in which their nature may be wholly absorbed in attentive enjoyment. Those who see the distinctive marks of the human in activity may try to discover the root phenomena of human sexuality in the stratagems of desire. I believe, however, that we can understand desire only if we first display the outline of a more passive state of mind – the state of arousal, in which the body of one person awakens to the presence or thought of another. Arousal provides the underlying circumstance of sexual enjoyment, and it contains the seeds of all that is distinctive in the sexuality of the rational being.

Sexual arousal – considered, for example, in the terms favoured by the *Kinsey Report*[1], and by other such exercises in reduction – is often represented as a bodily state, common to man and animals, which so irritates those subject to it that they can find relief only in the sexual act. The sexual act, it is thought, 'discharges' or 'releases' the tensions of arousal, and so quietens it. On this view the erection of the penis or the softening of the vagina are the root phenomena of arousal, and are to be observed throughout the animal kingdom. Their function in stirring the

16

animals to copulation is illustrated also by the human species. Sexual pleasure is then the pleasure, felt largely in the sexual organs, that accompanies the sexual act and which steadily accumulates to the point of discharge and release.

The attraction of that account is partly that it enables us to understand the localised nature of so much sexual pleasure. For sexual pleasure is not simply the pleasure of 'obtaining what you desire' – on the contrary, it is precisely a *part* of what you desire. And it is undeniable that similar physiological effects, and similar sensations, can occur in the act of masturbation and the act of love: perhaps they occur when riding a horse, or in all those chance circumstances of contact to which the Freudians draw attention in their theory of the 'erotogenic zone'.[2] It might seem reasonable, therefore, to suggest that sexual pleasure is fundamentally a pleasure of sensation experienced in the sexual parts. On the other hand, if matters were so simple, we should have cause to wonder at the widespread occurrence of sexual frustration. For it would be natural, in this case, to assume that sexual desire is desire for sexual pleasure: a desire that could be as well satisfied by masturbation as by the time-consuming stratagems of courtship and seduction. (Thus Wilde's ironical recommendation: 'cleaner, more efficient, and you meet a better class of person'.)

Moreover, whatever we say about the pleasure of masturbation, it has to be recognised that there is much more to the sexual act than its final stage: there is a desire to kiss and caress, and pleasures associated with those activities. A passionate kiss is both an expression of desire and a source of sexual pleasure. Once again, someone might be tempted to say that the pleasure here is no more than pleasure *in* the lips or mouth – thus giving credence to the idea of the mouth as an 'erotogenic zone'. But such a suggestion is, to say the least, incomplete. For only in certain circumstances is the pleasure 'in' the lips to be considered either as sexual pleasure or as part of such a pleasure. Consider two actors kissing – or in some other way going 'part hog', as Pinter might put it ('Joey: I've been the whole hog plenty of times. Sometimes . . . you can be happy . . . and not go the whole hog. Now and again . . . you can be happy . . . without going any hog' – *The Homecoming*). It is conceivable that these actors might feel pleasurable sensations in the affected parts – why not? To rule out the possibility would be culpable apriorism. But surely this would not be sexual pleasure. To be sexual pleasure it must be an integral part of sexual arousal. And that is precisely what is put in doubt by the supposition that the two participants are *acting*.

What then is arousal, and what difference does it make to the kiss? We should compare the kissing actors with a person kissing his friend in affection. It is true that in such a case there are strong proprieties at work, derived from our sense of permitted sexual relations. In the societies to which I and my readers belong, kissing has become too much a symbol of the sexual act to be regarded easily in other terms. Consider, however, a strict Islamic society, in which any such display of sexual feeling would be shocking, and indeed so shocking as not to offer itself as a possible interpretation. In such a society, as we know, friends kiss each other freely, and with evident pleasure. And the pleasure has nothing to do with any 'pleasurable sensation' located *in* the mouth or *on* the cheek, hand or brow. Such localised pleasures have little significance beside the act of attention with which the kiss is performed. While we may think of the pleasure of the kiss as focused in the mouth, this is largely because the *thoughts of the kisser* are focused upon his gesture, upon its tender meaning, and therefore upon the mouth only in so far as it is itself represented within the kisser's thoughts. The kiss is a recognition of the other's dearness, and its pleasure lies in the other's rejoicing in that. In such a case all idea of a 'sensation of pleasure' seems to evaporate. There may be such a thing, but it is of the least importance in explaining the act, or in accounting for its pleasurable quality.

Arousal transforms this pleasure into a sexual pleasure. But it is the pleasure of kissing – the pleasure which one person takes in another, when expressing his affection – that is transformed. It is not the 'physical pleasure' (whatever that may be) felt in the mouth or on the cheek, but what I shall call the 'intentional pleasure', involved in the recognition of the meaning of another's gesture. Arousal seems to affect, not so much the *sensation* of kissing, as its 'intentional content': although the sensation itself is by no means insulated from the thought which provides its context.

We must, indeed, always distinguish intentional from non-intentional pleasures. Some pleasures are essentially pleasures *at* or *about* an object; others (like the pleasure of a hot bath) are merely pleasures of sensation. It is not clear whether pleasures of the first kind can be attributed to the lower animals: *perhaps* they can. A dog may feel pleasure, we are apt to suppose, at the prospect of a walk or about his master's return. There are of course highly intricate problems here, and it is not enough to be guided by our common habits of speech. Description of the mental life of animals must depend upon an overall theory of animal capacities, and it would be inappropriate at this stage to make any unwarranted assumptions. A lion dozing in the sun feels pleasure at the warmth of the sun, but the 'at' here means only 'because of'. Clearly the case is quite unlike the manifold

18

pleasures which this situation can inspire in a human being. And it is evident that we could not begin to understand the structure of human pleasure if we did not recognise the predominance of the intentional component: of pleasure *directed onto* an object, about which the subject, in his pleasure, is concerned. Such is certainly the pleasure that expresses itself in the kiss of affection. Might the same be said of the pleasure which expresses itself, and the further pleasure which is anticipated, in the kiss of desire?

Non-intentional pleasures ('pleasures of sensation') share the defining properties of sensation: they are located in the body, at a particular place (even if that place may on occasion be the whole of the body). They have intensity and du.ation; they increase and decrease; and like sensations they lie outside the province of the will – a pleasure is never something that we *do*, even if we may do things in order to obtain it.[3] As I noted above, the sexual act, and much that precedes it, involves such pleasures – or, at least, it does so in the normal case. And they form an important part of the experience; in particular their capacity to 'overcome' the subject, so that he is 'mastered' by them, acquires an important role in the intentionality of desire. For the Freudian, these pleasures are the true source of sexual delight, which is entirely focussed upon occurrences in the 'erotogenic' zones. And Freud's attempt to base sexuality in sensation has an important philosophical motive: it is an attempt to incorporate the body into the stratagems of desire – to show exactly why our existence as *embodied* creatures is central to the phenomenon of sexuality. However, it is undeniably paradoxical to regard the localised pleasures of the sexual act as the aim or object of desire: so to regard them is to ignore the drama of sexual feeling, and in particular to ignore the fact of the other who is desired. Many pleasurable sensations accompany sneezing, for example, or, more appositely, raising one's voice in anger and exerting oneself in the pursuit of a quarrel. In the latter case they clearly do not constitute the aim, or even the gratification, still less the fulfilment or resolution, of anger.[4]

Procopius, in his *Secret History*, has many scandalous things to say about the Empress Theodora, wife of Justinian. One particular incident is of interest to us. Theodora, according to Procopius, had the habit of lying naked upon a couch, with millet seed sprinkled over her thighs and sexual parts. Geese would be placed on her body, and the birds would nibble the seed with rough osculations from her flesh. The contact of their bills apparently sent Theodora into ecstasies (or at least pretended ecstasies – for she was on stage at the time).[5] Suppose we were to say that Theodora felt intense pleasure at the pecking of the geese. This would surely imply that her pleasure depended in some way upon the thought that it was geese which were pecking her, rather than, say, carefully simulated automata, or any other device that could apply the gentle pressure of cartilage to her flesh. It *could* be so, but we should certainly find such a pleasure puzzling. Is she pleased *at* the pecking of the geese, or by it, or about it? (Those are not necessarily the same.) But then, why on earth? The correct description, I believe, is in terms of non-intentional pleasure. She feels a pleasurable sensation – a host of pleasurable sensations – which happen to be caused by geese. This is not necessarily abnormal, nor is it perverted, unless we suppose her to be aroused by the experience.

But it is precisely the supposition of arousal that would strike us as puzzling. For then it would seem that the geese play a constitutive role in her pleasure, that they are a kind of *object* of pleasure. Thus, in the normal case of sexual arousal, the physical stimulus cannot be detached in thought from 'what is going on': from a sense of who is doing what to whom. Tomi Ungerer has produced engravings of 'fucking machines' – machines designed to apply appropriate stimulation to the 'erotogenic zones' of those who 'consort' with them. I do not know Ungerer's purpose, but it is undeniable that the result is a vivid satire of a certain view of sexuality – the view which sees sexual pleasure and sexual arousal as purely 'physical', which is to say non-intentional, responses. Such a view corresponds to the picture of infantile sexuality given by many psychoanalysts, and indeed the theories of child sexuality offered by Melanie Klein have been favourably described by two of her followers as involving the recognition of the child's nature as a *'machine désirante'*.[6] Reflection upon the case of Theodora, and the idea of arousal that would be necessary to describe it, should cause us to recoil from such descriptions, which can be made to apply only by eliminating all reference to the intentional object of experience. They are, in other words, necessarily misdescriptions, and can derive their charm only from the covert recognition that this is so, from their character as 'demystification'.

Thus, in the normal case of sexual arousal, it would be quite extraordinary if the caresses of one party were regarded by the other as the accidental causes of a pleasurable sensation, which might have been caused in some other way. Sexual arousal is a response, but not a response to a stimulus that could be fully described merely as the cause of a sensation. It is a response, at least in part, to a thought, where the thought refers to 'what is going on' between myself and another. Of course, sexual pleasure is not merely pleasure *at* being touched: for that could occur when one friend touches another, or a child its parent. (There are countless ways in which we are pleased at human contact.) It is nevertheless (at least in part) an intentional pleasure, and if there is difficulty in specifying its object this is largely because of the complexity of the thought upon which it is founded.

The thought involves the following idea: It is *he* who is alertly touching me, intending my recognition of his act (or who is alertly kissing me, with a similar intention). The subject's pleasurable sensation is entirely taken up in this thought and, as it were, projected by means of it towards the other person. This is brought out vividly by the possibility of deception. Someone may discover that the fingers which are touching him are not, as he thought, those of his lover, but those of an interloper. His pleasure (in the normal case) instantly turns to disgust: it suffers, indeed, the same kind of reversal as is suffered by an emotion, when the belief upon which it is founded is shown to be false. Thus sexual pleasure, like an emotion, may be *in conflict with the facts*. The man who feels pleasure, mistaking another's touch for the touch of his lover, is to be compared with the father who feels proud, mistaking the boy who runs first past the winning post for his son. We find it no more puzzling that a lover's excitement should be extinguished by the discovery of unknown fingers about his person than that a feeling of triumph should be extinguished by the discovery that one has not, after all, won the prize. Similarly, the discovery that these fingers, while they are the fingers of my lover, are not alertly engaged in soliciting my attention – for he is asleep, say, unconscious, or dead – will extinguish my pleasure, even if it does not change the character of my sensations.

To some extent all pleasures – even non-intentional pleasures – can be undermined or compromised by a change of belief. The meat tastes differently when I discover it to be the flesh of my favourite dog. But it is important to see that the dependence of pleasure on belief is here much looser. I might have thought I was eating mutton, and learned in fact that it was moose or kangaroo. This does not automatically alter the physical pleasure of eating it; on the contrary, the pleasure will, in a reasonable being, reconcile him to the virtues (much misrepresented, if the newspapers are anything to go by) of moose or kangaroo. Similarly, although I would be a fool not to jump out of the soothing bath after being told that what I took for water is really acid, this is not because I have ceased at once to feel pleasurable sensations in my skin. In the case of sexual pleasure, the knowledge that it is an unwanted hand that touches me at once extinguishes my pleasure. The pleasure could not be taken as confirming the hitherto unacknowledged sexual virtues of some previously rejected person. Jacob did not, for example, discover attractions in Leah that he had previously overlooked: his pleasure in her was really pleasure in Rachel, whom he wrongly thought to be the recipient of his embraces (Genesis 29: 25 – and see the superb realisation of this scene in Thomas Mann's *Joseph and His Brothers*). If the belief changes, it is the persistence of pleasure, and not the *change* of pleasure, that needs to be explained.

Theodora may have fantasised that the geese-bills were the pecking kisses of some imaginary lover. And when one tries to imagine a 'pure' state of self-induced arousal – combined with undirected, or apparently undirected, sexual pleasure – it is really such a case that one is imagining. If that is so, however, then either sexual arousal, or sexual pleasure, or both, must be intentional. The function of fantasy is to *provide* an object for our states of mind, and, by making that object subservient to the will, to enable us to enjoy a magical power which we frequently long for but cannot possess. (Thus sexual fantasy is no more 'undirected' than is fear felt in response to the image of danger – as in a daydream.)

Of course, as I have recognised, there are non-intentional pleasures connected with the sexual act, which form an important part of what we seek in the sexual act. But they gain their importance for us partly because they can be taken up, as it were, in a state of arousal, borrowing the intentionality of arousal, and becoming incorporated into the drama of the sexual encounter. It is quite conceivable that these pleasures should occur – even the pleasure of orgasm – without arousal. For arousal is a 'leaning towards' the other, a movement in the direction of the sexual act, which cannot be separated, either from the thought upon which it is founded, or from the desire to which it leads. This may sound stipulative; but as we shall see, there are sound considerations in support of such a concept of arousal. In order to understand that concept we need to analyse, first the thought, and secondly the desire, to which it refers.

In speaking of 'thought' I am conscious of speaking somewhat loosely. The 'representational' nature of our mental states cannot always be comfortably described by this term: or rather, it cannot be assumed that any particular theory of 'thought' (such as that given by Frege, which argues that the identity of a thought is given by the conditions for the truth of a sentence which expresses it), will suffice to cover all the examples of intentionality. Nevertheless, for the purpose of this chapter, it will be sufficient to attempt to describe at least some of the thoughts which compose the intentionality of arousal, since, although the mode of representation that is intrinsic to arousal will not be exhaustively captured by this analysis, the analysis will provide what is required for an understanding of desire.

The first important component in the intentionality of arousal should be evident from the above discussion. Arousal is a response to the thought of the other, as a self-conscious agent, who is alert to me, and who is able to have 'designs' on me. The presence of this thought is evident from our understanding of those two all-important expressions of sexual interest: the caress and the glance.[7] A caress, when perceived under the aspect of arousal, has the character of discovery – of an 'unveiling', to use a somewhat Heideggerian idiom. A caress of affection is a gesture of reassurance – an attempt to place in the consciousness of the other an image of one's own tender concern for him. Not so, however, the caress of desire, which *outlines* the body of the recipient; its gentleness is not that of reassurance only, but that of exploration. It aims to fill the surface of the other's body with a consciousness of one's interest – interest, not only in his body, but also in him as embodied, in his body as an integral part of his identity as a self. This consciousness is the focal point of the recipient's pleasure. From the recipient's point of view, arousal, in these circumstances, is a form of permission, a silent utterance of the thought 'Go on! Make yourself familiar with what you seek to know.' Sartre – in what is perhaps the most acute philosophical analysis of desire[8] – speaks of the caress as 'incarnating' the other: as though, by my action, I bring his soul into his flesh and make it palpable. The metaphor is by no means inapposite. However, it is important to add that such 'incarnation' would mean nothing were it not for the element of familiarity, which is both offered and sought by the one who caresses.

The caress is given and received with the same awareness as the glance is given and received. They each have, so to speak, an *epistemic* component (a component of anticipation and discovery), which is also an important focus of arousal and desire. It is hardly surprising, given this, that the face should have such a supreme and overriding importance in the transaction of desire. And yet, on some views of desire, including the Freudian view, it is very strange that this should be so – strange that the face should have the power to determine whether we will, or will not, be drawn towards an act which gives pleasure in quite another part. Why do eyes, mouth, nose and brow transfix us, when they have so little relation to the sexual prowess and bodily perfection of their bearer? The answer is simple: the face is the primary expression of consciousness, and to see *in the face* the object of sexual attraction is to find the focus which all attraction requires – the focus on another's existence, as a being who can be aware of *me*. Much has been written about the glance of love, which seems so imperiously to single out its object and so peremptorily to confront him with an intolerable choice. In truth, however, it is the glance of sexual interest that precipitates the movement of the soul, whereby two people come to stand outside the multitude in which they are presently moving, bound by a knowledge that cannot be expressed in words, and offering to each other a silent communication that ignores everything but themselves. It is as true of the glance of desire as it is of the glance of love that it concentrates into itself the whole life of the human being, constituting a direct appeal to the other to recognise my embodied existence. The experience has been well described by Robert Grant:

> [The 'love-glance'] may be anything from an open, cloudless smile to a troubled, serious gaze, but it is instantly recognisable to a like-minded recipient. It differs entirely from Miss World's orthodontic grimace, the coquette's winsome leer, or the closed, resentful stare of the fashion model (which suggests nothing so much as a juvenile delinquent interrupted in the act of self-abuse). It is completely involuntary, the more obviously so the more it is fought down by modesty (the process is matchlessly and movingly depicted by Shakespeare in the courtship of Ferdinand and Miranda). What it announces is the fact of incarnation: I am here, my inmost self, in my face. The rest of my body, it says, my private parts, and therefore I myself, all are yours, if you will have it so. Being unguarded, like the naked body whose uncovering it foreshadows, it is a pledge of innocence, and an innocence not subsequently destroyed, but fulfilled, in the sexual act.[9]

It is a familiar thesis of the philosophy of language – and one which, thanks to the work of Grice, Searle and Lewis,[10] can no longer be easily disputed – that the act of *meaning* something is essentially interpersonal. It involves an intention to communicate, and also an intention that this first intention be efficacious in revealing the content of what is said. It involves, in short, an elaborate design upon the consciousness of the other, an attempt to enlist his participation in a cooperative act. Thomas Nagel has suggested that the complex intentionality exemplified by meaning is to be found also in the glances of desire, so that if we speak of those glances as 'meaningful' this should not be thought to be a metaphor.[11] If Nagel's suggestion were right, then, following the theory of meaning put forward by Grice, we should expect the glance of desire to involve, first, an intention to arouse sexual interest; secondly, the intention that this first intention be recognised; thirdly, the intention that, through being recognised, it play a part in precipitating what is intended. However, although there are grounds for thinking that the intentional structure of meaning may sometimes exist in the glances of desire, reciprocity is normally of a lower order. In the normal case, the intention is that the other's desire be precipitated, not by a recognition of my *intention*, but by a recognition of my *desire*. The intended reciprocity here is perhaps sufficiently like that of meaning to enable us to use meaning as a convenient metaphor for arousal, so long as we do not imagine that sexual gestures are fully 'articulate' expressions of cognitive mental states – so long as we remember, in other words, that sexual gestures cannot be 'translated.'

The experience of arousal may then be explained on the analogy with linguistic *understanding*: just as I understand your utterance by latching on to the intentions with which you thereby acquaint me, so do I respond to your glance or caress by recognising the desire behind them, and seeing, through the desire, the possibility which might otherwise have remained concealed. A caress may be either accepted or rejected: in either case, it is because it has been 'read' as conveying the message that 'we might surely make love'. In discovering this message through the language of your caress, I receive it, not as a raw image, so to speak, a shocking presentation of an outlandish possibility, but as a thought concealed within your gesture, which you too are discovering in the very act of discovering me. Ovid's instructions to the seducer (*Ars Amatoria*, book 1) are finely aware of this reciprocal intentionality. They illustrate the idea that the caress and the glance must not reveal premeditation: that truly arousing conduct is that in which the awakening of the woman seduced is made to seem like a mutual self-discovery, so that *she* seems, in her own eyes, to be responsible for what he feels.

The intentional structure just described, while clearly distinct from the structure of (linguistic) meaning, has much in common with it. But we should be misrepresenting the intentionality of arousal if we saw it simply in these terms, without considering the crucial element of 'bodily awakening', which each participant both feels in himself and seeks in the other. This experience is a crucial aspect of our experience of embodiment – and of our nature as embodied beings. It may be illustrated by an example, which will also help to emphasise the peculiar kind of representation that is intrinsic to arousal. Consider the case of a woman, who opens to her lover's explorations:

> Ile be a parke, and thou shalt be my deare:
> Feed where thou wilt, on mountaine, or in dale;
> Graze on my lips, and if those hils be drie,
> Stray lower, where the pleasant fountaines lie.
> [*Venus and Adonis*]

This opening (in the above lines, an importuning) is a fundamental gesture of arousal, and would be inconceivable without the idea of him, the lover, taking an interest in her as she is in her body. Venus' offendedness stems directly from her perception that this idea is no more than a fond illusion – having exposed herself to so much, she must then destroy the unfeeling witness of her humiliation. It is integral to the woman's thought that her lover is a conscious being, and also conscious of himself as an agent and patient in the sexual transaction. Moreover, she thinks of him as having a conception of her body, and of her in her body. Her sense of his caress is of an invitation: she experiences it as fundamentally *addressed* to her *through* her body, and *in* her body. Arousal is founded first in the thought of his bodily presence, as a source of interest in her, and secondly in a desire to address to him the equivalent of what he addresses to her.

In the first impulse of arousal, therefore, there is the beginning of that chain of reciprocity which is fundamental to interpersonal attitudes. She conceives her lover conceiving her conceiving him. . . . (Sartre argued that such infinite chains of response show sexual desire to be impossible. However, the regress is indefinite, not infinite, and certainly not vicious. For just such a chain of response is involved whenever one person understands another's meaning.)[12] There is also a specific experience of embodiment. My sense of myself as identical with my body, and my sense of you as identical with yours are crucial elements, both in the aim and in the reception, of the arousing caress. I am awakened *in* my body, to the embodiment of *you*. Underlying the woman's state of arousal is the thought: 'I, in my body, am something for him', and her response – the 'opening' to his approaches, and all that is entailed in that – must be understood in part as an *expression* of that thought, and of the interpersonal intentionality that is built upon it.

Although I am identical with my body, my experience of embodiment must be sharply distinguished from my experience of the body. In arousal the unity between body and person is immediately experienced, and forms the living focus of an interpersonal response. But the body is not the object of this response – as it is the object of a pathologist's examination or an anatomist's exposure. Arousal reaches through the body to the spirit which animates its every part. There are indeed 'bestial' inclinations, which seek to sunder the body from the spirit, and to present the first as the single focus of a sexual interest. But the interpretation of these inclinations is a matter of difficulty to us, precisely because their intentionality eludes our understanding. Consider again the female experience. In the 'normal' case of feminine bestiality the animal in question (a favourite dog, say) is treated *as if* he were a person. Not, perhaps, a very developed person, and not even a fully responsible person. But nevertheless a creature with at least one of the attributes that distinguishes persons: the attribute of the 'first-person point of view', which enables him to see the world as something other than himself, and to take an interest in it, not only as the repository of warm and welcoming objects, but also as the field of action of other beings like himself. For it is the sense of this in the dog's perspective – a sense which, however erroneous, is natural to our anthropomorphic way of seeing things – which permits the gestures of arousal. The dog, too, is perceived as an embodied person.

This is not to say that there is not true bestiality in women – an interest in the animal body *as such*. John Aubrey's description[13] of the voyeuristic Countess of Pembroke, who would watch the coupling of horses in order to prime herself for the lovers who were to mount her, is perhaps a case in point – although one can see at once how vast a shadow is cast in her desire by her own self-conscious perspective. Perhaps the Countess wished to see her lovers *as* animals, in order to be excited by the thought of herself as similar, indifferent to the human attributes and interpersonal demands of the creature who is mounting her. This is a refined case of true bestiality, in which the other both is, and is thought of as, an animal. True bestiality is perverted. 'Perverted' means turned from some 'normal' aim. In this case, the arousal is turned from a person to the caricature of a person – to a creature which either is, or is thought to be, stripped of that first-person perspective which gives sense to the intentionality of arousal. The bestial act, which abrogates the responsibility of the object, abrogates also the responsibility of the subject – and that is its point. It is an attempt by the subject to flee from the burden of interpersonality, to be *merely* an animal, in this encounter which could otherwise not be accomplished without intolerable disgust.

Of course, a person may take a distinctly personal pleasure in this – in the spectacle of his own degradation. But that it *is* a degradation should not be doubted. It involves a falling away from the normal condition of arousal, and a rejection of personal responsibility. No doubt there are physical sensations, and glandular transformations, that occur equally in normal human arousal and in its perverted counterpart (else there would be no call for the idea of 'perversion'). And if the *only* difference were to be found in the fact that, in the first case, the object is conceived as a person, in the second case as something essentially non-personal, and if there were no further difference that followed from this, then it would be arbitrary to distinguish them. But the differences between the attitudes, stratagems and satisfactions that arise from normal sexual arousal, and those that arise from its perversion, are so great as to justify the contrast between them. If you leave out the context, then you can always give arguments for assimilating states of mind, however different they may be.

You could, for example, assimilate love to hatred on the basis of their common fascination with another's well-being, or running to swimming on the basis of their common movements. My argument implies that the glandular transformations and physical sensations that accompany arousal stand to arousal much as the movements of the legs stand to running. They are an essential part of it, but may equally occur in its absence. And, as in the case of running, what makes them what they are is the intentionality of the state of mind which is expressed in them.

Furthermore, the sexual organs do not appear, so to speak, *neutrally* to us, at times of arousal. The sexual organ undergoes a transformation which is essentially dramatic, and not merely physiological. Both in one's own eyes and in the eyes of the other the sexual organ becomes the self. To be penetrated by a man's penis is to be penetrated by *him* (to be enclosed by a woman's vagina is to be enclosed by *her*). Suppose there were two such organs. Or suppose that a man could strap on his 'tool', remove it, replace it and exchange it. In this case there is a kind of depersonalisation of the phallus: it is, to use Hannah Arendt's useful term, 'instrumental-ised'.[14] It begins to lose some of its intrinsic personal interest, and comes to seem, instead, like the lurid dildos which are on display in sex shops, and which owe their appeal precisely to the fact that they are attached to no human body and no human will (and which therefore have precisely no *sexual* appeal to the person of normal inclinations). Even if, by some miracle, it would be possible to feel pleasurable sensations *in* the tool, rather than through it, it would cease to be the recipient of the kind of individualising attention which the lover normally craves. Caresses would direct themselves, not to the tool itself, but to the body to which it is attached, perhaps at the point of attachment, which would begin to gather to itself some of the magic of the phallus and some of its constant dialectic of modesty and pride. (There would be no point in concealing or revealing the thing itself, but much point in so 'dramatising' its mode of attachment.)

To be aroused by another is to incorporate that other into a sexual project, the project of love-making. We feel that there is something perverted, and perhaps inexplicable, about the man who claims that, being aroused by one person, he is able to perform the sexual act with another. Of course there are many cases here – the extreme example being perhaps the Empress Messalina, described by Juvenal (Satire VI), of whom we might wish to say that she was the victim of an insatiable appetite for sex, which, having been roused by one man, required her to proceed to others, and so on, *ad infinitum*. But notice that an important new element has been brought into the description: that of 'appetite'. The purpose is precisely to lift the phenomenon out of the realm of normal sexual arousal, and attribute to it a character, and an explanation, which are not otherwise exemplified. There is something very important in common to the Empress Messalina's desire and that of any other normal human engaged in the sexual act. But there is also something very different. The difference lies in the intentional content, and it is partly this difference of intentionality that is signalled by the idea of 'appetite'.

Of course there are less serious cases than that of nymphomania: the more normal case is that of someone who, having been aroused by one person, contrives to curtail that arousal, in order to engage in the sexual act with another. Here there are in fact two states of arousal, which may be closely joined but which can never be one. The first arousal does not *point* towards the second; it has no natural history of which the second is an episode. The anticipation that is invoked in it is not for the act which is intended, but for another which is denied. The case is to be compared with that of a man who whets his 'appetite' for paintings by contemplating, say, Poussin's *Golden Calf*. It may be that, after a period of visual 'starvation', such a project has much to recommend it. But we know very well that the terms 'appetite' and 'starvation' are here being used metaphorically. We cannot conclude that the man's real interest, in studying the Poussin, is one that might have been equally satisfied by a Velazquez, a Gauguin, or whatever object he may subsequently enjoy. On the contrary, he was attempting to revive in himself precisely that kind of interest in painting which compels him to treat each example 'for its own sake alone'. In other words, his interest in the Poussin cannot be satisfied by a Velazquez, say; if it could, that would only show that it was not the *Poussin* which interested him, but any painting that would 'do just as well'. In such a case we could indeed speak of 'appetite', but what kind of appetite this is, what are its meaning, value and rationale – all these would be highly mysterious. Likewise in the case of sexual arousal. The arousal must be understood as a response to a particular person. Even if it is possible to 'whet one's appetite' for such responses, this cannot show that they are 'transferable' from object to object, like the desire for wine which leads one to sip assiduously from every glass.

To the intentionality of arousal must be added that of excitement. The 'epistemic' intentionality that I have discerned in sexual arousal has an intrinsically cumulative character, and leads the subject constantly onwards with an effect of discovery. Each phase of arousal contains an anticipation of the next. Excitement can exist in both non-intentional and intentional forms – as a general state of heightened response, and as a particular state of excitement *about* or *over* some matter of interest. In the

29

latter case the element of anticipation and discovery – the 'epistemic' structure – is always paramount. Excitement is part of the dynamic character of arousal: and this dynamic character marks yet another difference between sexual arousal and physical hunger. At every point there is a pleasure of expectation and anticipation, which carries the subject forward, and which also forms an integral part of what is pleasurable *now*. Sexual excitement is responsible for the 'masterful' and 'urgent' quality of desire. It leads to the sense that desire 'overcomes' the agent, and deprives him of his freedom. (And therefore, according to some philosophers, notably Schopenhauer, it leads to the illusion that desire is an *exercise* of the will, and a peculiarly fruitless one, destined only to post-coital disappointment.) Excitement involves the thought of something happening, and not just a physical sensation – I am not excited in *this* way by the prospect of a cigar, a glass of ale or a hot bath. I am excited precisely by a cooperative enterprise, in which I and the other gradually evolve within each other's perspective, changing for each other and through each other, with a constant and reciprocal anticipation of our mutual intentions.

What, however, are we excited about? Although sexual excitement is a special case (a very special case) of the excitement to be observed in all friendly conversation, it has a focus which normal conversation lacks. This focus is our mutual embodiment, the other's 'being in' his body and I in mine. In our excitement we sense each other's animation, and become acquainted with the pulsing of the spirit in the flesh, which fills the body with a pervasive 'I', and transforms it into something strange, precious and possessible. The penis which hardens and the vagina which softens to the longed-for touch convey the whole person, just as he is conveyed in his laughter and his smile. (Hence, while you can 'possess' another in his body, you cannot possess the body alone: necrophilia, like rape, involves no fruition of desire.)

Sexual arousal has, then, an epistemic intentionality: it is a response to another individual, based in revelation and discovery, and involving a reciprocal and cooperative heightening of the common experience of embodiment. It is not directed beyond that individual, to the world at large, and it is not transferable to another, who 'might do just as well'. Of course, arousal might have its origin in highly generalised thoughts, which flit libidinously from object to object. But when these thoughts have concentrated into the experience of arousal their generality is put aside; it is then the other who counts, and his particular embodiment. Not only the other, also I myself, and the sense of my bodily reality for him. Thus Molly Bloom:

and how he kissed me under the Moorish wall and I thought well as well him as another and then I asked him with my eyes to ask again yes and then he asked me would I yes to say yes my mountain flower and first I put my arms around him yes and drew him down to me so he could feel my breasts all perfume yes and his heart was going like mad and yes I said yes I will Yes.

It can readily be seen why it is that, in so many cases, arousal seeks seclusion – seclusion with the other in a private place, where only he and his point of view are relevant to my intention. Moreover, arousal normally attempts to *abolish* what is not private – in particular to abolish the perspective of the onlooker, of that 'third person' who is neither you nor I. Milan Kundera describes an orgy in which two of the participants catch sight of each other across the room. The passage shows what an enormous effort is involved in sustaining true sexual arousal when the veil of privacy has been discarded. In effect, the consciousness of observation destroys the intentionality of the act:

> Both couples were in the same situation. The two women were leaning over the same way and doing the same things. They looked like enterprising gardeners working in a flowerbed, twin gardeners, one the mirror image of the other. The men's eyes met, and Jan saw the bald man's body shaking with laughter. They were united as only an object can be united with its mirror image: if one shook, the other shook as well . . . . The men were united by telepathic communication. Not only did each know what the other was thinking, they both knew the other knew. [*The Book of Laughter and Forgetting*]

Eventually laughter gets the better of them, and their hostess, partner of one of the men, is mortally offended. The laughter, however, is the expression of a particular perception of the sexual act. When witnessed from the third-person point of view, the focus of the act is no longer the embodiment of the participants, but their *bodies*. This being witnessed by the other tends to kill arousal in the subject. Clearly, neither man is responding to the woman who attends to him – only to the contact of her body. The two women might have been mechanical dolls; and indeed, they have become mechanical dolls, in the laughing eyes of those who suffer their attentions. The laughter expresses the incongruity of the act, when it is divorced from the sentiment of arousal. The personal has been made public, and in the act of public recognition, it has become impersonal and routine. The frenzy of the orgy might be seen, indeed, as a reaction to the futility of sexual experience, when the urge towards impersonality is elevated into its single goal (see Aldous Huxley, *Ape and Essence*).

The aversion from the public which is characteristic of arousal could also be described as a 'fear of the obscene'. The obscene is the representation or display of the sexual act in such a way as to threaten or ridicule its individualising intentionality, by placing the body uppermost in the thoughts of those engaged in it. If the desire for sexual stimulation is represented as directed indifferently towards, say, the penis, or towards anything possessing a penis, or towards a human body considered independently of its agency, viewpoint and will – if, in other words, sexual arousal is represented as an urge or appetite, focused on certain parts of the body, and satisfiable indifferently by anything with the right equipment – then the result (as in the ballad 'Nine Inch Will Please a Lady', attributed to Robert Burns) is normally obscene.

Obscenity is akin to bestiality. It standardly involves the attempt to divorce the sexual act from its interpersonal intentionality; from that epistemic 'directedness' that is contained within sexual arousal. But the divorce is effected by a peculiar shift of attention. In obscenity, attention is taken away from embodiment towards the body; the body rises up and inundates our perception, and in this nightmare the spirit goes under, as it goes under in death. Thus particular bodily perceptions – those which English children express in the sound 'ugh' and Yiddish-influenced Americans in the sound 'yuk' – play a prominent part in the experience of obscenity. The sense of the body as rotting, glutinous, adhesive – all that Sartre refers to in his celebrated analysis of le visqueux[15] – may dominate our perceptions, and nowhere more insistently than in our experience of sex, in which bodies adhere through their viscid and agglutinative parts. In the experience of the obscene the person is, as it were, eclipsed by his body, which, because it fits exactly to his shape and movement, creates an absence, a darkness, where he should otherwise have been. I no longer find the person whose embodiment enticed me: only the body which, in its frightful dissolution, its character as melting flesh, fascinates and also repels me.

In the eyes of an onlooker, someone not party to our arousal, our bodies invite obscene perception. (Hence there can be obscene representation of wholly innocent sexual acts.) The observer is not engaged in the delicate negotiations whereby we coax each other into our bodies, so as to experience that intense excitement which transforms the sexual union into a union of persons. The spectator of our antics sees, first and foremost, the agglutinating bodies. The thought of his interest is precisely an obscene thought, in which our embodiment is obliterated by our bodies, and rendered alien, impersonal, prey to the fascinated curiosity of the disgusted child. We see ourselves, so to speak, under the aspect of 'yuk!' (This is one reason that might be offered for the view that, whatever else they may be, masturbation and voyeurism of the kind experienced in the video booth do not involve the release and satisfaction of the impulses which more fortunate beings may release and satisfy in the sexual act.)

Sexual arousal can occur only between persons, and is an artefact of their social condition. An immense moral labour has gone into the construction of the intentionality of arousal, and while it is willing labour, constantly performed anew by each generation of consenting adults, it might not have occurred. The state of mind that I have described is one of those achievements of civilisation which it would be folly to discard and yet which can, like morality, be discarded at almost any time. There is, however, a temptation which wars against arousal: the temptation to free the sexual act from the demanding stratagems of personal communication, and to represent as appetite that which can become appetite only by losing its characteristic intentionality.

Before saying more about that intentionality, it is necessary to make a point about method. Questions about the nature of mental items are to be answered, not by scientific investigation, but by philosophical (which means equally 'phenomenological' or 'conceptual') analysis. Of course, scientific investigation of mental phenomena is also possible. There could be a science of sexual behaviour, which might show important similarities between human beings and the lower animals. It is likely that there are such similarities, since sexual behaviour is explained, in both cases, by a reproductive function. But such an investigation would not answer the questions that I have been considering. Those questions concern the perceived surface of things, from which our mental concepts take their sense. I believe that there is a significant phenomenon, to which I have given the name arousal, and that we single out this phenomenon – either by referring to it, or, more normally, by selectively responding to it – in much of our ordinary social behaviour. There may be other things that someone may wish to call by the same name – the sexual readiness of animals, or the titillations that occur in the bath. But, at the superficial level (which is the level that matters), these must be distinguished from arousal, to the extent that they lack the intentionality of arousal. I have been discussing a phenomenological problem: the problem of the intentionality of a state of mind. That such problems are (scientifically speaking) superficial should not lead us to discount them; still less should it lead us to look for a solution to them in the results of science. For persons too are superficial, as are their values, their projects, their griefs and desires. Better, however, the shallowness of persons than the unfathomableness of things.

Like every such shallow thing, however, arousal has a history. It is the descendant of experiences which we now only dimly imagine, and the ancestor of others which we cannot know. Much play has been made of our 'historical' nature. No human experience, it is argued, and no conception of the human being, makes sense outside the cultural context which generates and completes it. Conceptual analysis, which abstracts from this context, merely peels away the verbal skin, and preserves it in the formaldehyde of logic. If the result is sempiternal, it is because the human life has fled. Logic preserves, not the historical reality, but only our fleeting attempts to describe it: it gives us, not the 'real' but the 'nominal' essence. It may be a timeless truth that bachelors are without wives, but when has that been an obstacle to marriage?

At the deeper level, we are therefore told, there is no timeless truth about sex, only the endless reconstitution of our sexual experience from the fluctuating matter of human history. What can we conclude, therefore, from an examination of the intentional understanding contained in some given phenomenon? In what way does that lead either to a full description of the human reality or to a coherent prescription to which all of us might bow? A true 'genealogy of morals' would recognise no 'natural' sexual experience and no universal norm.

It is with such arguments that Michel Foucault, in his recent *History of Sexuality*,[16] would persuade us that there is no timeless 'truth' of sexual experience, and that sexual morality is the product of cultural conditions that have been eaten away by the worm of time. I am not persuaded by those claims, and hope to give reasons for rejecting them. When suffering their intellectual temptation the reader should remember two important observations. First, an experience may be historically determined and yet a part of human nature. For human nature too is historically determined, and an experience which belongs to the epoch of personality belongs to the human essence. Second, a description of human experience may – for all that has been written concerning the 'naturalistic fallacy' and the 'is– ought gap' – have prescriptive implications. The reader may doubt this, but he must recognise that his doubt is dogmatic. His duty is to keep an open mind for just so long as my argument requires.

So much by way of method. For the present we may draw an important conclusion, namely that a feature normally regarded as distinguishing erotic love (which possesses it) from sexual desire (which does not), is in fact present, not only in desire, but also in arousal, which is the surrounding circumstance of the sexual act. This is the feature of 'interpersonal intentionality'. The problem that worried Plato does not exist: there is no conflict or contradiction of the kind that he envisaged between sexual desire and erotic love, nor does the first belong to some

34

'lower' part of our nature than the second. Indeed, as I shall now argue, only a rational being can experience desire, and those sentiments that are so often slighted, as being indicative of our 'animal' nature, are sentiments that no mere animal has ever felt.

3
PERSONS

In choosing to discuss sexual arousal, which is neither the origin nor the aim of sexual desire, I have entered the subject *in mediis rebus*. My intention has been to describe the most distinctive sexual phenomenon, and the one which most readily seems to lend itself to the theory that desire is a 'biological' fact, rooted in the life which we share with animals. I have argued that sexual arousal is in fact an interpersonal response, founded in an epistemic intentionality. Hence only people can experience arousal, and only people – or imaginary people – can be the object of arousal. This does not mean that we should dismiss out of hand the similarities between the sexual behaviour of animals and that of human beings. Like animals we feel sexual urges; like animals we reproduce sexually; like animals we feel a need to unite through our sexual organs, and like animals we experience a compelling physical pleasure when we do so. But almost all comparisons besides those are apt to prove misleading. Animals are never sexually aroused; they do not feel sexual desire, nor do they have sexual fulfilment. Almost all that matters in sexual experience lies outside their capacities, not because they reach for it and fail to obtain it, but because they cannot reach for it.

To put the thesis so starkly is to invite scepticism. At the very least I must say something further about the meaning of 'animal' and 'person'. The concept of the animal belongs to both common sense and science; that of the person is confined to common sense alone. It denotes a part of the *Lebenswelt* that is more important to us than any other; yet it is a part that disintegrates under the enquiring eyes of science.

It is not certain that all persons are animals (for, on some views, God, who must be a person, cannot be an animal). But the fact that *we* are animals bears upon all the concepts – including, in the end, that of the person – through which we attempt to achieve a day-to-day understanding of our condition. We must begin, therefore, with a few remarks about the idea of animality.

An animal is a living thing, and has an individual life: it is born, it flourishes, it declines and it dies. Our perception of this process and our inner familiarity with it as the root of our own experience lie deeply embedded in our conceptual scheme. We perceive living things differently from lifeless things, and recognise in them a principle of self-government which marks them out from their surroundings. And animals stand apart from the rest of nature, as entities which are not only living but also in a very special way active. Their activity arises from their life, and is one with it; and, although we have only recently acquired any scientific understanding of the organic process, the life and activity of an animal are instantly recognisable to us. Our knowledge that some happening – a stirring in a hedgerow, a pattering on a roof – is the result of animal activity provides us with an extremely concentrated insight into it, and a rare ability to predict the most complicated sequel. The concept 'animal' therefore acquires an honoured place in our intentional understanding, embodying both a powerful insight and a spur to action.

There is another feature of animal existence that has made its mark upon the *Lebenswelt*. Animals are paradigm individuals. The vital spirit which generates the activity of the animal and preserves it in being establishes a unique unity and harmony among its parts. It is an inseparable part of our perception of animal activity that the animal appears to us as one and entire. And this has important consequences, revealed in our ways of describing, perceiving and counting animals.

The question 'How many?' presupposes a 'sortal' or 'count noun': a description which answers the question 'How many what?' The rabbit before me is one animal, two half-animals, 1270 cubic centimetre rabbit-parts, and so on. The rabbit may be dismembered both spatially and temporally, into parts and 'time-slices', and Quinean philosophers draw substantial and interesting conclusions from this, concerning ontological relativity and the impossibility of radical translation.[1] It is, however, worth pointing to a distinction between count nouns which the Quinean will dismiss as artificial, but which, in the eyes of common sense, is of the profoundest importance. Some count nouns, we believe, attribute a real, independent unity to their instances while others, we believe, attribute a unity that is merely relative to our passing interests. Thus there are countless inorganic individuals, which exist as unities within the frame of our perception. This field, this river, this stone – all these are unities: not two fields, but one; not two rivers, but one; and so on. But, in a certain manner, their unity is fragile; for it is an artefact of our devising. It so happens that we, for whatever purpose, choose to count this field as one.

But we could, without difficulty, count it as two or three: legal priorities may force us to make just such a choice. The river, too, is one, or two, or three depending upon our territorial conventions. If the stone seems to be more naturally a unity, it is partly because – unlike the field or the river – its parts may be sundered and removed from one another, so that their being together in one place, fastened by crystalline cohesion, is an interesting and additional fact, to which we refer obliquely in identifying this object as a single stone. But the unity of the stone, while firmer, as it were, than the unity of the field or river, is itself less substantial than the unity of a cat or a dog. The stone may be divided into parts, not only in the process of counting, but also physically. And when it is so divided, each part is itself a stone, existing separately from the whole from which it has been sundered. The stone removed from the block is an individual of the same kind as the block from which it was taken. At the macroscopic level, the noun 'stone' figures in the science of stones not as a count noun but as a 'mass noun'. The science of stones speaks, not of macroscopic individuals, but of the stuff from which they are composed – of porphyry, onyx and limestone. It is a science which employs, in the first instance, only mass nouns – nouns which answer, not the question 'How many?' but the question 'How much?' A stone is really (that is, scientifically) a lump of stone.

Real unities are those in which the whole is something more than a sum of its parts, in the way that a rabbit is more than a collection of rabbit-parts, or a car is something more than a collection of mechanical components. Modern physics recognises real unities at the microscopic level: atoms and molecules have a kind of 'substantial unity'. But, in ordinary (macroscopic) experience, only 'systems' present us with such real unity. And among systems two types predominate: the natural and the functional, illustrated respectively by rabbits and cars. The parts of a car are not a car, since they do not have the defining function of a car. This function emerges only when the parts are suitably combined. Hence our counting of cars is constrained by something more than spatial and temporal convenience. The function which this concept articulates determines a precise number of individuals that are subsumed by it. Each of these individuals is a substantial and indivisible unity, as a member of its functional kind. At the same time, the unity in question is an artefact. Cars exist by human fiat, and possess their unity only so long as we maintain them. This kind of unity is, in one sense, dependent on our purposes. To find natural unity, and natural individuality, we should look elsewhere. In particular, we should look to the animal kingdom.

Biology, unlike geology, cannot dispense with count nouns which range over macroscopic objects. For it is concerned with objects whose individuality is, in a sense, the most fundamental fact about them. This is to some extent true of vegetables. But it is much more obviously true of animals, whose individuality is also a form of *activity*. An animal is bound together by its activity, not only in its substance, but in its behaviour. An animal is not a lump of flesh, and cannot as a rule be divided into parts which exemplify the same natural kind as itself.[2] Of course, the parts of a stone are not themselves stones. But a stone can be physically divided into stones, while the attempt to divide an animal leads to the cessation of that activity which constitutes its being. A living part may be severed from an organism only when its laws of development permit division (as in the case of an amoeba). In the normal case, the parts severed from an animal cease to be pieces of living matter, and an animal, when divided, will surely die. Only while undivided does it continue to act, and that is the foundation of our belief in its indivisibility.

The individuality of animals is therefore no arbitrary device. It is not a grid which we impose upon them for purposes of our own. It lies in the nature of things. To put the matter in another way: there is an explanatory power in the idea that Fido is *one* thing, which cannot be reproduced by any rival way of counting him. The individuality of Fido is in no sense an artefact, but lies in the essence of Fido. Even if the two halves of Fido are subsequently joined together, so repairing the physical unity, the original object of reference – Fido himself, whom I loved or feared – has gone from the world.

It can be seen from those somewhat sketchy remarks that animals conform to some of the requirements contained in the rationalist philosopher's idea of substance.[3] And there is another interesting point of contact with rationalism. For Fido, while he lives, acts so as to conserve his life, to avoid injury, to sustain his strength. His individual continuity is generated from within, by the same vital force that compels all his activity. He has a large dose of what Spinoza called *conatus* – the innate capacity for self-preservation which in Spinoza's view was the sole foundation for that partial notion of individual existence (substantiality) which is the best that we (as mere modes of the one true individual) can, in our finite life, display.[4] Animals therefore provide one of the most vivid examples in nature of the active, self-preserving individual, whose individuality is not the arbitrary consequence of our ways of counting and classifying, but a deep and immovable part of its natural condition, to be acknowledged in any genuine explanation of its nature. An animal is an individual entity, not *de dicto*, but *de re*.

I dwell on this point since it will be of some importance later, when I come to discuss the individuality of the sexual object. The question will occur whether the individual object of desire is desired as animal or as person. Crucial to deciding this question will be the idea of individuality that is contained in the intentionality of desire.

Human beings are animals. They are also persons. The question arises whether the idea of 'person' is merely a qualification of 'animal' – denoting a biologically recognisable sub-class of animal life – or whether it is a concept of another kind, with some contrasting purpose behind its application. In other words, are persons something like a biological species? Or are they a class, all of whose members happen to be of a single species, but which is to be defined in terms of some other classificatory purpose than the explanation of animal peculiarities? I shall argue for the latter view – although the fact of our being animals of a certain species plays a crucial part in the development of the concept of the person. Consider dramatic music: is this a particular kind of music, with a musicological significance comparable to the classifications 'instrumental', 'symphonic' and 'operatic'? The answer is 'no': for although dramatic music is certainly a musical kind, it cannot be defined in terms of the intrinsic features – instrumentation and musical structure – which form the basis of musicological classification. It must be defined in terms of a pervasive *response* to musical sound. Dramatic music may belong to any musicological category. It could also be that it belonged only to one – say, to the operatic aria. The classification is not musicological: it aligns its object, not with similar musical structures, but with a similar human *response* towards structures which may, in themselves, be highly disparate. Likewise, the concept of the person aligns that which is subsumed by it with the other objects of a similar response. It is no accident that the objects of this response tend to belong to a single biological kind, but this is a fact about the response, and not about the classification.

It should not go unmentioned that the term 'person' comes from Roman law, which in turn borrowed it from the theatre. A *persona* was a mask, and hence the term came to denote the idea of a theatrical 'character'. Thereafter it was used more generally, to refer to the representation (in every sense) of the human being, his character, life and interests. In law, therefore, a *persona* denoted the collection of rights and liabilities which the law courts could adjudicate, on behalf of the subject who appeared before them. For Roman law, the individual human subject was nothing more nor less than the collection of rights and duties that attached to him: the person who appeared before the law, was, in a sense, himself the creation of the law.[5] Persons could therefore be either individual humans or corporations, since a corporation may also have legal rights and duties, and the agency and answerability which enable them to be confronted and enforced.

Were our concept of the person to be no more than an extension and refinement of the idea developed in Roman law, then of course it would be impossible to think of it as providing our main route to the understanding of the human individual. In the sense intended, however, men saw each other as persons long before the invention of Roman law, and – unsurpassed though the achievement of that law has been, in building institutions of government amenable to the individual life – it is wildly implausible to suppose that the concept of legal personality can be used to capture the real peculiarities that separate us from the rest of animal creation. We should bear the idea of legal personality in mind, however, since it is no accident that human beings exemplify it – no accident that they may bear rights and liabilities, and may be held answerable or aggrieved before a court of law. In what follows we shall often have to take note of this familiar, but in truth extremely mysterious, circumstance.

Traditionally the distinction between the human individual and the animal was drawn in terms of an idea of reason. Man alone, it has been argued, is a rational animal, and the idea of rationality is necessary, and perhaps also sufficient, to describe what is peculiar to him. Within limits, I believe, this ancient idea is correct. But the limits are severe. The concept of rationality is itself by no means clear, and – in the end – can be fully understood only in terms of the repertoire of thought, feeling and action that is available to the individual person. As Aristotle realised, reason exists in two complementary forms – the theoretical and the practical. Men reason about what to believe, but also about what to do – perhaps, even, about what to feel. This means that the transformation introduced into their nature by reason permeates all their thought, and also all their activity, perhaps even their entire emotional life. Nevertheless, it is worth exploring the ancient suggestion a little further. We shall find that it leads us directly to our theme.

A dog may have beliefs. But he does not form and amend his beliefs through reasoning, nor does he entertain the important ideas of possibility, necessity, probability and validity, which structure the mental processes of the fully rational being. Likewise, a dog may have desires, and in this sense he has reasons for his conduct. But in another sense he acts without *reason*, in that *reasoning* is not an additional causal factor in the explanation of his behaviour. He does not deliberate, make plans, weigh alternatives or make up his mind; he simply, and spontaneously, does what he is prompted to do by his present desires. In the case of the human agent, it seems to me (although there are philosophers who deny this),[6] belief and desire do not suffice to explain his repertoire of conduct. The reasoning being exists and acts on another plane, forming intentions, making plans, perhaps with some long-term and unlikely prospect. He may set himself to oppose his own desires, and, in all that he does, he is motivated – or believes himself to be motivated, which is itself to have a kind of motive – not merely by self-interest but by a conception of the good.

Those facts – which, to me at least, are evident – demand careful exegesis. What explains them, and how are they manifest in the detail of human conduct? Some philosophers argue that we do not, in the end, need to look elsewhere for an explanation than the existence of language, as a systematic device for representing the world. The rational being is a language-using being. He is able to store information about the world in symbolic form, and to retrieve that information for later use. The horse who was frightened by a shot while passing over Farmer Giles' territory may not venture there again. In this sense (the sense of 'learned response') he retains a memory of his past – but only in this sense. We say that his behaviour has been modified, but not that he now entertains some thought, of the form 'Yesterday something nasty happened here'. That particular ability, it has been argued – the ability to entertain thoughts which refer beyond the content of immediate experience, to the past and future, to generalities, particularities, possibilities and necessities – is the prerogative of the language-user, who can represent to himself states of affairs with which he is not immediately confronted.[7] To accept such an argument is not necessarily to deny the possibility of mental represent-ation in non-linguistic creatures, but simply to point to the limits of such representation, by arguing that the distinctive thought-processes of rational beings can be made available only by the deployment of a system of symbols.

That claim is indeed plausible. But we do not need to accept it in order to recognise the importance of language as an index of our mental activity. Nor do we need to discuss the intricate questions raised by theories of meaning, or the competing claims of the representational and expressive theories of linguistic understanding.[8] Nevertheless, there is a question in the philosophy of language which must here be raised, so that it will not impede our subsequent discussion. There are two broad approaches to the philosophy of language. According to the first approach, the distinctive feature of the language-using creature is language itself, and it is in terms of language that the complexities of his mental life – including such all-important features as intentionality – are to be explained.[9] He has intentions (in addition to mere desires), because he has the language in which to formulate his projects. He has beliefs about the past and the future, because he has capacities to represent past and future times – and so on. According to the second approach, language is itself nothing but an inert system of signs, which has meaning only because it is used. And what confers meaning upon it is the complex system of mental representation (thought, belief, judgement and intention) which it is used to express.[10] A sentence means that snow is white, on this view, because it is used to express the *thought* that snow is white. According to the first approach, the possession of language is the basic fact, prior to the possession of rational states of mind. According to the second approach, it is the states of mind that are prior, and which alone can explain the existence of a system of signs as a *language*.

It seems to me that we should not have to decide between those two views, and indeed that we perhaps could not do so. On either view, however, language is accorded a special importance in our understanding of persons, as the principal criterion of rationality. Whether language is the cause or the consequence of rational states of mind may be undecidable; language, and the states of mind expressed through it, being inseparable parts of a single 'moment of consciousness', to use the Hegelian idiom. If we are to study what is distinctive in the mental constitution of people, however, we must study the expression of that content in linguistic form. Even if there are rational beings without language, we could understand them only by postulating a language that *would* be theirs were they to have one (and, indeed, that is the way that we understand the thoughts and designs of the pre-linguistic infant).

The most basic application of rationality is reasoning itself, the linguistic expression of which takes the form of argument. Logic, which dictates the forms of valid argument, is surely nothing if not a part – perhaps the most fundamental part – of language. And logic gives insight into rational thought by *displaying* the relations between propositions, enabling us to understand the real distinction between the valid and the invalid inference. We can explain the unspoken reasoning of the rapid deducer, by displaying it as a series of sentences. We then suppose that the logical relations between those sentences are (we do not know how) causally efficacious in generating the reasoner's behaviour. If they were not efficacious, he would not be rational, even if he were, by some miracle, right.

In this book I am concerned with far more recondite manifestations of rationality – recondite because they do not, at first sight, seem to have anything to do with the power of reasoning, nor can they be evidently concentrated into overt linguistic habits. It is my belief (and one that I hope to vindicate) that rationality cannot be conceived as a simple addition to the mental life of an animal, which leaves the remainder of the mind unaltered. On the contrary, rationality is, so to speak, a condition of existence, which informs the entire content of the subject's mentality. Or at least, it informs every state of mind which contains some understanding of the world. (It could be that the *sensations* of men are like the *sensations* of dogs, since sensations lack intentionality. Even so, no man reacts to a sensation as dogs do.)

I do not deny that animals have mental states; indeed, it is essential to our idea of animal activity that we regard animals as sensitive in various ways, able to see things, hear things, suffer impulses of pleasure and pain, and undergo motivation by belief and desire. Moreover, it is essential to our idea of ourselves that we regard our mental life as permeated by animal experiences, which well up from the fount of organic life, and which are not *merely* aspects of the rational thought which overarches and sometimes incorporates them. Nevertheless, our mental life is through and through different from the mental life of animals, and not only our thoughts and projects, but our most inscrutable and seemingly irrational emotions, bear the imprint of our rationality. Indeed, it is only a rational being who can suffer the pangs of an irrational sentiment: nothing within the mental repertoire of an animal can rise to such a dignity.

What might lead us to assume that it is not only the thoughts and actions, but also the emotions and experiences, of the rational being that will be distinct from those of the non-rational animals? The most important part of the answer is to be found in a concept which rationality forces into the centre of our thought, and which will be, in a sense, the main subject of later chapters: the concept of the self. The rational being is also a self-conscious being, and this self-consciousness lies at the root of his existence as a person. It is this feature which enables us to adopt towards him (and he towards himself) the peculiar posture which underlies our use of the concept of the person. Of course, there is a use for the concept of the self in describing the behaviour of animals. A dog distinguishes himself from other dogs, and his own interests from those of his fellows. But he does not distinguish himself as a *self*, since he lacks what I shall call the 'first-person perspective' – a feature of consciousness that is distinctive of language-using beings. This point is of the greatest intricacy, but it must be understood at the outset, if we are to make any progress with the analysis of sexual desire.

One of the observed features of our use of language is the emergence of the 'first-person case'. I know about you and your state of mind, because I observe you; I also know about myself and my own state of mind, but not through any act of observation. The first-person case is characterised by certain highly puzzling features. When I am in pain, I know that I am in pain, without having to observe myself, or in any other way to embark upon a process of discovery. This is something that I just know, and it is even absurd to suggest that I might not know it. Likewise, when I believe that I am in pain, my belief is in some sense incorrigible: nothing that you can do, and nothing that I can discover, will show it to be false. Of course, I may be insincere in claiming to be in pain, and there are murky areas where insincerity borders on the hinterland of self-deception, and where my own mind is sown with the seeds of epistemic confusion. But, in the normal case, and barring accidents of usage, my sincere adoption of the proposition 'I am in pain' is sufficient to guarantee that proposition's truth. This is not a trivial consequence of my use of language. On the contrary, it is the root cause of much philosophy, and of the mystery that surrounds the human condition. It is precisely this 'privileged access' that I have to my own mind which gives rise to the sense that my knowledge of the world is forever doomed to imperfection. My beliefs about the outer world seem imperfect because there is something else – the self-guaranteeing awareness of my own inner condition – with which I can contrast them. And, stemming from this, is the well-known Cartesian thought, that what I essentially am is revealed not to you but to me, in the act of awareness whereby I grasp my inner reality, as a self-knowing, and self-motivated, ego. The thought (I shall argue) is founded on illusion, but it has a most important consequence – that the language-using creature can be identified, both by himself and by others, not merely as an animal, but also as himself.

We must resist the idea that the mind can be understood in terms of first-person awareness. It is particularly important to avoid the first-person perspective when it is itself the subject of discussion. For the privileges which that perspective contains are conditional upon its emptiness. As I argue further in Appendix 1, the incorrigibility of my first-person awareness is an indication, not of its foundational character, but of its flimsiness, of its inability to sustain any objective and substantial conclusion about what I am.[11] If we are to understand the first-person perspective then we must see it from the third-person point of view. We must ask for an explanation, not of *my* self-knowledge, but of yours. We must explain how it is that, when you utter sincerely the words 'I am in pain', your utterance is true. Why is it that here, as Wittgenstein put it,

45

truth and truthfulness coincide, so that the criteria of sincerity establish the truth of what is said?

The Cartesian view of consciousness, which is based upon this fact, does nothing to explain it. The idea of a special 'private' access to my own mental states can provide no explanation of my privileged awareness. At best it provides a *picture* of this privilege. The metaphor of an 'inner' state leads us to think of self-knowledge as a kind of permanent self-revelation of each mental item to its owner. The sensations, beliefs, desires and emotions lie as it were glowing in the mind like jewels in a case, each one visible to the surveying consciousness by virtue of its own peculiar radiance. Such a picture may seem to fit sensations: it certainly does not fit beliefs, which are not permanently 'present' to the mind. And yet it is arguable that beliefs are objects of incorrigible knowledge. If I *ask* you whether you believe that France is a monarchy, then in normal conditions you can answer with authority; but until I asked, you may never have thought of it. (Any doubt concerns the fact itself, and not whether you believe it.) An error has to be explained, not as a *mistake* (as though, inwardly peering at your belief, you had momentarily mistaken the belief that France is a monarchy for the confusingly similar belief that France is is a dyarchy), but in terms of some radical mental fault, such as self-deception. Not the least of the objectionable features of the Cartesian picture is that it makes the 'epistemological privilege' of a mental state into an intrinsic feature of it. It becomes a fact about *pain* that the victim is aware of it, so that whenever there is pain there is also consciousness of pain. It then becomes impossible to suggest, what is true, that there might be creatures with sensations, but without incorrigible knowledge: not because they have unconscious sensations, but because (being merely animals) they lack self-consciousness altogether.

We must explain, what no merely phenomenological (i.e. first-person) study *can* explain, the fact that whoever says sincerely 'I am in pain' speaks the truth – provided, of course, that he understands what he says. We are dealing here with necessities; the particular kind of absurdity involved in the suggestion that I should be mistaken, in my present belief that I am in pain, could be accounted for in no other way. It is the same kind of absurdity as attaches to the suggestion that there might be a non-spatial physical object, or a non-temporal experience.[12] No first-person study can explain such a necessary truth, since it is a truth that is expressed in a public language, and guaranteed – if at all – either by the rules of that language or by the 'real essence' of the objects to which that language refers, objects which (by the argument of Appendix 1) must be publicly identifiable if they are to be referred to at all.

We must explain what I shall call the 'rule of authority'. This holds that, whoever utters 'I am in pain' sincerely, and understands the words, is in pain: he is an authority concerning his own mental contents. From this rule we may derive that whoever utters 'I am in pain' sincerely, but is not in pain, does not understand what he says. The epistemological privilege turns out to be a rule of language – a condition upon understanding the sentence 'I am in pain'. A person understands such a sentence only if his uses of it are (with permitted exceptions) true. We can readily envisage the application of this rule: observing a child's behaviour we teach him to say 'I am in pain' only when he is in pain. When he gets it right every time we concede that he understands what he says.[13] Hence we may explain, first, how it might be a necessary truth that a person in pain knows that he is in pain; and secondly, how self-knowledge is a feature of linguistic performance.

In a similar way we might explain 'self-intimation' – the fact that, when I am in pain, I know that I am.[14] The failure to recognise the truth, in such circumstances, is a failure to understand the words that express it – which is why the remark of Mrs Gradgrind's (*Hard Times*, Part II, ch. 9), that there is a pain in the room somewhere, but she does not rightly know that it is hers, is so odd. For either she does not mean it, or else she does not know what it means.

The utterance 'I am in pain' contains four words; which, if any, has been misunderstood by the person who uses it to make a false assertion? Suppose that he ascribes pain accurately to others: that is surely sufficient evidence that he understands the word 'pain' – assuming that we accept the thesis (see Appendix 1) that such words get their sense from their third-person use. So is the offending word 'I'? Surely, someone understands that word just so long as he understands a certain application of the predicates like ' . . . is thinking', ' . . . is in pain'? Why should the occasional error show that he does not understand, what he has every capacity for understanding, a 'substitution instance' of an open sentence whose meaning he knows?

Some philosophers have argued that 'I am in pain' should not be regarded simply as a 'substitution instance' of 'x is in pain' – i.e. as a straightforward application of the predicate ' . . . is in pain'. Elizabeth Anscombe, for example, has argued that the sense of 'I' is not that of a 'referring' term: indeed, that 'I' does not refer at all,[15] so that 'I am RS' is not a statement of identity. Hence, although it is true that, if RS is in pain, I am in pain, this truth is not derived from 'RS is in pain' by substituting terms with equivalent reference. That thesis has come in for some fairly strong criticism;[16] but even those who reject it acknowledge that the function of 'I' is not like that of a proper name, say. It has been argued, for example, that 'I' is an 'indexical', like 'now' or 'here', whose function is to indicate something in the field of reference by marking its relation to the speaker. If this is so, then we should expect precisely what we find, which is that self-reference is 'immune to errors of identification'.[17] I can no more mistakenly identify myself as *I*, than I can mistakenly identify the place where I am as *here*. And this immunity to error may attach to 'I' even though the term has a referential use.

Those speculations are undeniably important, and promise to explain certain kinds of incorrigibility (or 'immunity from error') in the first-person case. But they do not provide a satisfactory account of what here concerns us, which is the certainty of first-person knowledge of present mental states. At best they explain the certainty of self-identification: of my belief that I am referring to *this* person, not that. But how they could explain my certainty about the mental *properties* of this person, I do not know. All the same, it seems to me that, even in this later kind of certainty, it is the concept of self that explains my epistemological privilege. An imperfect grasp of the rule of authority amounts to an imperfect grasp of selfhood. Both the word 'I' and, by implication, the word 'he', will then be used incorrectly. How can this be so? How can a rule so absolute and seemingly so arbitrary as our 'rule of authority' be adopted by fallible mortals? The answer is this: to justify the rule is to justify the concepts with which it provides us, and the functions which those concepts fulfil. The purpose of the concept that we are considering – that of the person, and its subsidiary, the self – is to identify the object of 'interpersonal reactions'. It can fulfil this purpose only on the assumption that those who use it obey also the rule of authority which determines its sense. For it is only on this assumption that we can 'take their word for it', when they speak their mind. It is that which is the cornerstone of interpersonal relations.

Wittgenstein asserts that, if a lion could speak, then we should not understand him.[18] Consider what would have to be the case if we were to accept the speech issuing from the lion's mouth as an expression of the lion's mentality. We recognise two possibilities from the outset. Either the speaker *is* the lion, or it is not. If it is not, it might yet appear to us to possess a mental identity of its own. In such a case, it would appear to speak *out* of the skin of the lion, inhabiting the lion as a dryad inhabits a tree. We readily imagine such spirits in the objects that surround us, and it is natural to primitive people actually to believe in them, to fear and to worship them. That is not to say there is any real possibility, either *de dicto* or *de re*, that there might be a spirit in the lion or the tree. But it is an idea that we can entertain and elaborate, and if there were not considerable emotional profit in doing so, half our literature would be without a foundation.

Now the lion, unlike the tree, has an independent mentality of his own. Whether or not the voice is his, the lion still has his own desires, sensations and leonine satisfactions. Therefore it makes sense to ask ourselves what would have to be true if the speech which issues from him is to be an expression of the lion's mentality, rather than of some spirit which possesses him. Consider the lion of Androcles. He roars, and a voice issues from his mouth saying, 'I roar. Moreover, there is a thorn in my paw. I seem not to be able to stand on the paw in question. Indeed, my behaviour exhibits the pattern of disorganisation which is characteristic of pain. Therefore, it seems that I am in pain.' Suppose too that all the lion's 'self-ascriptions' are of that nature, and suppose also that many of them are simply wrong, even when emphatically asserted. In such a case, the voice is clearly describing the mental state of the lion just as it would describe the mental state of any other thing, using the common public basis, and neither claiming nor achieving any special immunity from error or doubt. The lion's voice is therefore the voice of an 'observer' of the lion's behaviour, with the sole reservation that, where the observer would use 'he', the voice uses 'I'. But then, if that is so, 'I' in this use really *means* 'he' – the distinction between the two ideas (of self and other) has broken down. The voice's attributions to the lion are not the lion's own self-attributions, but rather the attributions of some other being. The lion is possessed, but not inspired.

How do we combine the lion with his 'voice'? We must grant to the voice just those powers of privileged self-attribution that I have been discussing. The voice must have a special kind of authority. It cannot, except occasionally and for very special reasons, make mistakes about the lion's mentality. And its knowledge must be 'immediate', based on no observation. In other words, the voice must obey the rule of authority. This is not just a rule that the voice follows; it is also a rule that it *obeys*. That is how the *voice* must understand its own 'self-attributions'. It must treat as absurd the suggestion that it might be wrong. As soon as it begins to do so, body and soul are united. The voice is beginning to express a self – itself – and not merely to refer to an animal organism with which it has no 'inner' relation. It now understands the word 'I': indeed, only a self can understand that word: only a self could understand, not just what is referred to by 'I', but also the use of 'I' as an instrument of communication.

Of course, it is a matter of fact that the voice, when it says 'I am in pain', does so only when the lion is in pain. Sensation reports may be incorrigible, but when true, they are not *necessarily* true. Only when the lion's voice does, as a matter of fact, obey the rule of authority can we allow that it understands the concept of self. As to what kind of 'matter of fact' this is, that too is an important philosophical question. We ought to give some detailed account of how things must be if there is to be incorrigible and immediate knowledge.[19] But that is not my present concern. I wish, rather, to consider the rule of authority that rests upon this fact. How is such a rule possible?

How is it that we can disallow the possibility of mistakes? Surely there must come a point when we have established that a child means what *we* mean by the expression 'I am in pain'. How can we then insist that henceforth he will make no mistakes in using that sentence? Here it is useful to refer to one of Wittgenstein's most celebrated observations.[20] No linguistic behaviour can logically determine its own sequel, since no past time can logically determine the future. A man may 'follow a rule' as we do, and yet, at some future time, diverge from us, insisting all the while that what he is doing is the *same* as what he has always done. We cannot establish, once and for all, and with no possibility of doubt, that another really does understand a word as we do – whether that word be 'he' or 'I'. The only point is that, if he begins to make *mistakes* in his use of 'I', this shows either that he has ceased to understand the word (and there are psychotics of whom this is true) or else that he *always* understood it wrongly (a most disturbing possibility). The problem of distinguishing between those alternatives is acute: but it is a *general* problem in the theory of meaning, and has nothing special to do with 'I'.[21]

Moreover, nothing in the rule of first-person authority requires that, whenever someone says that he is in pain, it must be *true* that he is in pain. It implies only that, if the utterance is not true, this is not because of a mistake, but because of an insincerity. Much now comes to hang upon the concept of sincerity. We shall have to be careful not to create all over again the absolute dichotomy between inner and outer, subject and object, that feeds the Cartesian illusion. Later in this chapter, and in Chapter 11, I shall introduce a concept of 'integrity' which will contain, I believe, the seeds of a theory of sincerity. One consequence of the emphasis on sincerity is that, if someone says falsely that he is in pain, we might reproach him. He cannot now withdraw what he said by pleading ignorance: his only excuse is that he did not mean it. We have, in effect, made him answerable for his declaration.

Nevertheless, it will be said, the original problem – or at least a major part of it – remains. How *can* we make another answerable for his first-person declarations? Is this not the same question as the one we started from: the question, why, when sincerely uttered, are such declarations true? Is an answer to be found simply by showing that we have a certain concept – the concept of the self – in which first-person privilege is immovably enshrined?

Ensuing arguments will suggest that I have indeed offered an answer to the question of first-person privilege. It must be conceded, however, that I have as yet given only a description – rather than an explanation – of the first-person case. If I am right, first-person privilege is embodied in our concept of the person. To understand that concept we must examine the forms of intentional understanding which it mediates, and which have human beings as their focus. It is in such a direction, I believe, that the full answer to the problem of the first-person will be found.

The direction will become clearer if we turn to another concept which is fundamental to interpersonal relations – the concept of intention. Our expressions of intention are also endowed with a form of first-person certainty – certainty about what we will do. If a man says that he will do something, understanding what he says and saying it sincerely, then – provided he intends what he says as an expression of intention – he will indeed do the thing in question, or at least try to do it, when the occasion arises. Or, if he does not do it, it is because he has changed his mind. The rule of authority here is of course vastly more complicated than the one given for sensations. It can be seen as a kind of elaborate limitation upon the explanations that may be offered for the falsehood of first-person statements about the future. They might be insincere; they might be misunderstood; they might be not decisions but predictions; they might have been superseded by a change of mind. Perhaps 'weakness of will' is a fifth 'escape route'; perhaps self-deception is a sixth. What is not permitted, however, is a sincere expression of intention which is neither cancelled nor fulfilled.

I shall concentrate on the third 'escape route' – the well-known distinction between predicting and deciding[22] – since it provides a vivid illustration of why a concept answering to the given rule of authority should be so useful to us. In order to form an intention, it is necessary to consider the future, and to see oneself as playing an active and determining role in that future. One must, to put it simply, 'identify' with one's future self. The attitude here contrasts with another – that of 'alienation' from one's future self – in which one sees oneself not as active and determining, but as the passive victim of external forces and of one's past, being driven along under the impulse of causes that are outside one's control.

What is involved in the first kind of attitude – the attitude of identification with a future agent? Intention involves a belief about the future,[23] but a sincere expression of intention cannot merely be the outcome of inductive reasoning. In Elizabeth Anscombe's words, intention and prediction differ in their 'direction of fit' with reality. In saying 'I will do it', I am taking it upon myself to ensure that it will be done; in predicting that I shall do it, I am, characteristically, putting forward a hypothesis as to how the world will be, without making myself in any way answerable for it. In the first case I must try to do as I say, and, in so far as I support my assertion, it is with practical reasons. Hence I have a peculiar certainty that I shall indeed try to do as I say: not to have that certainty is to be insincere. It is by virtue of this particular kind of certainty that expressions of intention can be understood as obeying their own rule of first-person authority.

It follows that, if I have intentions, I must also have a measure of practical reason. Suppose that someone expresses the intention to do x, and realises that the only way to do x is by doing y, and yet denies that he intends to do y. He must regard himself as committed to the truth of the following propositions: 'I do x'; 'I do x only if I do y'; 'I do not do y'. In other words, he is committed to contradictory beliefs. So that, if he has theoretical reason – which leads him to reject such contradictions – he has practical reason too. He is able to reason about the means to his ends. Since the ability to understand ordinary inferences is essential to understanding language, we can see that a connection has been forged between the possession of speech and the possession of rational agency. This is but one part of that chain of connection which links intention, rational agency, language, self-consciousness and the first-person perspective into a single idea, and which forms the full elaboration of the concept of the person.

The concept of intention, as I have characterised it, can gain application only because of certain matters of fact about the human animal. It is a matter of fact that those utterances about the future which are singled out as expressions of intention are generally followed by the agent's attempt to realise what they represent. But on this matter of fact rests an important practice. Given the general truth that a person will at some time attempt to realise his sincere expressions of intention, those expressions will provide us with a peculiar means of access to his future conduct. We can now, in effect, argue against what he plans to do. As Anscombe has demonstrated, it is precisely the possibility of 'argument against' that is the distinguishing mark, not only of intentions for the future, but also of intentional action.[24] We can change a person's behaviour by persuading him to change his declarations of intention, and he will change these just so long as he is rational and our reasons are good. Hence we have a direct means of access, through reason, to that core of activity from which his behaviour springs. When this means of access fails – either because the agent is unable to accept reasons (the case of irrationality), or because the matter-of-fact connection between declaration and performance breaks down (the case of insanity) – then we have no way of dealing with the person except through the manipulations of predictive science. The agent has become a patient.

In supposing someone to express intentions, we are permitting ourselves to trust his word, both now and in the future. Once again, we are holding him answerable – this time for his actions. It follows that reasons given to change what he says, will now also change what he does, and language becomes the means of access both to his present mental state and to his future activity. Our attitude to him may now single him out as the focal point in a network of intentions, as an agent, capable of committing himself to his future, and taking responsibility for his past, as a creature with a perduring 'self-identity'. Towards such a being I may reasonably feel gratitude and resentment, admiration and anger. He is the possible object of a whole variety of 'interpersonal' responses, through which our lives as moral beings are principally conducted.

When I am interested in someone as a person, then his own conceptions, his reasons for action and his declarations of resolve are of paramount importance to me. In seeking to change his conduct, I seek first of all to change *these*, and I accept that he may have reason on his side. If I am not interested in him as a person, however, if, for me, he is a mere human object who, for good or ill, lies in my path, then I shall give no special consideration to his reasons and resolves. If I seek to change his behaviour, I shall (if I am rational) take the most efficient course. For example, if a drug is more effective than the tiresome process of persuasion, I shall use a drug. Everything depends upon the available basis for prediction. To put it in the language made famous by Kant: I now treat him as a means, and not an end. For his ends, his reasons, are no longer sovereign in dictating the ways in which I act upon him. I am alienated from him as a rational agent, and do not particularly mind if he is alienated from me.

Just as we can take an attitude to another person which does not involve our giving special priority to his self-ascriptions, so can we take such an attitude to our future self. I may cease to regard my own assertions about the future as having any special authority in determining how things will be. In such a case, I cannot really be said to have intentions: all my statements about the future become predictions rather than decisions. They are founded on, and refutable by, the available evidence. And that is how *I* regard them. But if I have no intentions for the future, it seems that my attitude to my past must be similarly depersonalised. For how can I take responsibility for anything if I can have no intention to make amends for it, and no sense that it proceeded from any planned activity which has its origin in me? Attitudes like remorse, self-complaisance and pride become not just irrational but impossible. It can hardly be desirable to be like that, for, as I shall further argue in Chapter 11, this steady erosion of the will deprives us of the very capacity to value what we presently possess. And how can one rationally desire to be in a state which one cannot see as desirable when obtained? It seems, then, that we cannot, consistently with our rational nature, reject the habits of self-ascription that are enshrined in the rules of first-person authority.

The upshot of the above discussion is as follows:

1. There can be no genuine use of language without the privileges of the first-person case.

2. By virtue of first-person privilege, a man becomes, not merely a reasoning being, but also a rational agent, whose behaviour is changed by offering reasons for action (provided that the reasons are good, and he is rational).

3. Hence there is a public practice, among self-conscious beings, of reason-giving and reason-taking, which the agent incorporates into his own conception of what he is and does. He sees himself as one agent among many, answerable for his actions and called upon to act for reasons which might also justify his conduct. He *treats himself* as a person, and demands that others so treat him, where this means accepting his reasons and his self-confessions – his 'consent' – as the principal avenue to his conduct and emotions. It is upon this public practice of giving and taking reasons – which could be called (in the spirit of Oakeshott) [25] moral conversation – that our ways of dealing with people are founded.

The world contains, then, a class of entities, to which we ourselves belong, and which are the possible objects of a complicated pattern of response. They may be persuaded, educated and criticised; they can be met on equal terms; and each possesses a 'sphere of responsibility', within which he is answerable for what occurs. I shall use the term 'responsibility' to denote the fact that a rational being is both answerable and persuadable. I pass over the complexities that would be necessary in order to demonstrate – what I believe, nevertheless, to be true – that this idea is the root of the legal and moral conceptions of responsibility.[26] I shall also pass over the arguments for saying that, in so far as the concept of freedom has any real meaning, it is to be explained in terms of responsibility. In what follows, however, I shall often permit myself to use the word 'freedom': for it vividly captures the fact that *we think of* the responsible being, and *respond* to him, in ways which distinguish him from the rest of nature, and which crown him with a metaphysical halo. Resentment, anger, admiration and esteem – all attribute 'freedom' to their object. Indeed, towards the free being, we may feel responses which we could never feel, were it not for anthropomorphic imagination, towards animals. The concept of 'person' is used to single out the objects of these and similar responses.

'Person' does not denote a functional kind, since there is no specifiable set of purposes which guides and limits the employment of this concept. Nor does it denote a natural kind, even though all earthly persons are, as a matter of fact, members of the natural kind 'human being'. The person enters our *Lebenswelt* as the *target of interpersonal responses*. A scientific description of the tribe may very well dispense with such an idea, just as the scientific description of the table dispenses with the idea of colour. But that does not alter the fact that we perceive the world in personal terms, and indeed that our happiness totally depends upon our doing so. Of course, I have said little as yet about the many responses of which persons are the target. Suffice it to say that they are as far-reaching as the idea of responsibility – as the idea that a being might be answerable for something said or done. As we shall see, they include many emotions that we might, in our natural generosity towards creation, instinctively imagine that we share with animals.

The 'interpersonal attitude' casts, however, a strange metaphysical shadow, which lies across all our thoughts about one another, and which generates the idea of a wholly irrefragable individuality. As a result of the habit of self-reference, and the authoritative use of 'I', I come instinctively to believe that I am using the term to refer, not to this animal from whose lips my voice emerges, but to something else. I am myself, and what I am essentially, I come to believe, is the self that I am. Of course, it is easy to spot the *grammatical* illusion in that idea – the illusion that the reflexive pronoun 'myself' refers to a 'self' which is 'mine' – but it is no mere grammatical illusion that prompts us to subscribe to it. (Indeed, it is on the speakers of Latin and Slavonic languages that this illusion has had its most devastating effect, and for such people the reflexive pronoun is metaphysically innocent.) The idea is, in fact, an irresistible by-product of our day-to-day understanding of rational agency. As Kant perceptiently showed, it is an 'idea of reason', generated automatically by our need constantly to transcend the limits of legitimate thought.[27] Because the 'I' seems transparent to itself, through and through disclosed to itself, and because all my projects, all my rights and liabilities, and all my beliefs and feelings, are ascribed to this thing, the idea irresistibly arises that what I am essentially is this self-knowing I, this subject, who lies concealed within, behind or beyond the organism, but who cannot be identical with the organism, for the very reason that the bodily states and the substance of this organism remain obscure to me, while my mental life is thoroughly and completely known.

Moreover, it seems as though I am presented, in my inner experience, with an example of pure individuality that is both more immediate, and more metaphysically firm, even than that presented by the animal organism. The I cannot be divided, nor can it be in any other way supposed to be constituted from other individuals. This is shown most vividly by the cases of split personality, which rapidly compel us to speak, not of an I composed of several parts, but either of a single I in a state of turmoil, or of a plurality of I's, trapped within a single animal frame.[28] The I is a pure atom, with whose individual existence I am thoroughly acquainted, since at no point do I have to discover anything about it, in order to know it as it is. Out of such thoughts was born the Leibnizian idea of the monad – the soul-substance which is the only true individual, and which could never be divided or destroyed.

Furthermore, this I is an active thing. It is *I* who make resolves, on the basis of arguments and interests that are also *mine*. It seems, therefore, as though action springs from *me*, and not from the body through which I act – for *it* does not listen to reason, any more than does a car or a cow. So, along with the metaphysical idea of the self as the true locus of my individuality, comes the idea of the will and its freedom. I am essentially a free subject, whose individuality and freedom are complementary aspects of a single condition.

Those ideas have had a distinguished history, from Kant, through Fichte, Hegel and Schopenhauer, to Heidegger and Sartre. No subsequent discussion has improved on Kant's brilliant exposition, in which he shows that just such a metaphysical picture is implied, not only in our first-person knowledge, but also in our every moral thought. Just as Descartes had attempted to provide a metaphysical ground for first-person knowledge, by postulating the existence of an immaterial and indivisible – perhaps even indestructible – self, so did Kant (who thoroughly rejected Descartes' reasoning) attempt to provide a metaphysical ground for the first-person view of agency, by postulating the existence of a 'transcendental self' whose freedom lies beyond reach of nature's laws. As Kant recognised, such an idea is fraught with insuperable difficulties. How, for example, can this transcendental self act in the empirical world which is its only sphere of action? How can a transcendental freedom account for the wholly 'immanent' responsibilities with which, through our bodily presence in a physical world, we are everywhere encumbered? Just as the Cartesian ego proves powerless to explain the self-knowledge that supposedly justifies its introduction, so does the transcendental self prove unable to justify the practical reason which leads us indelibly to imagine its existence.

We should take a lesson from Kant. The transcendental self is an inevitable idea. Our self-conception as rational beings inflicts this idea upon us. At the same time the idea is powerless to resolve the metaphysical anxieties which prompt us to invoke it, or to show us what might really be meant by human freedom. We should look at the matter thus: we are animals, and have no securer individuality than animals have. Nor do we stand outside nature, or in any other sense possess a freedom from the bonds of causality which the animals are denied. However, language forces upon us two indispensable ideas, that of self-reference, which casts the shadow of the metaphysical I, and that of responsibility, which casts the shadow of a metaphysical freedom. We can try to justify these shadows, to uphold the belief that *they* are what *we* really are – and the first step in such a justification is to argue (with Kant and Sartre) that the two shadows are really one and the same, that I *am* my freedom, in something like the way that this lump of wax *is* the wax which composes it. Alternatively we may remain sceptical, as I shall in this work, and treat these shadows as nothing more than shadows. They wander with us everywhere, and to lack them would indeed be a terrible misfortune, far worse than the loss of one's real shadow (although that too, as von Chamisso demonstrates in the story of *Peter Schlemihl*, is bad enough), but they have only an illusory existence. These shadows loom large, and determine our interpersonal attitudes in countless ways. They provide the focus of much that is most real in human existence – including love, longing and desire – while remaining unreal. Through their very unreality, moreover, they promise always and at any moment to betray the yearnings which they guide. Little is more terrible than the discovery that your beloved is not a transcendental self – that, even in what matters most, he may be overcome.

Our 'I' thoughts, and our thoughts of other 'selves', contain, then, a new idea of unity, over and above the idea of animal individuality. This unity is immediately given in present experience. We suppose it to stretch unbreakably through time, since the very process whereby the rational agent takes responsibility for his past and future seems to record an indissoluble bond of unity between them. Perhaps there is no metaphysical necessity underlying the idea of responsible action. We are, as Strindberg expressed it, 'conglomerates of a past stage of civilisation and our present one, scraps from books and newspapers, pieces of humanity, torn-off tatters of holiday clothes that have disintegrated and become rags – exactly as the soul is patched together' (Preface to *Miss Julie*). Our projects and resolves do not *have* to have the kind of coherence implied in the idea of an enduring self. It has even been argued that there is no logical absurdity in the idea of a complete temporal fragmentation of the self over time,[29] a constant expiry of the subject and its motives. In such a case, it is suggested, it would be absurd to hold my present self responsible for something that this body, under some previous government, had done. (The analogy with changing governments might then provide us with the best means of understanding our situation.) Nevertheless there is an *ideal* of personal integrity which requires us to achieve continuity between past, present and future. Without this integrity, the moral conversation to which I referred is jeopardised, and our personal existence along with it. In all our interpersonal dealings, therefore, we hold each other to an ideal of 'integral action', which is to be something more than merely animal unity – something sanctified within, and generated by, the first-person perspective of the agent. It is this idea of individuality that serves to focus our most 'heartfelt' emotions, and which I shall consider further in Chapter 5.

Those first-person thoughts may, as I have said, be illusions. But they are (to mimic Leibniz) 'well-founded' illusions, which we may expose as such only from the third-person point of view, and never from the unalienated absorption in the first-person perspective, which is the natural condition of the rational agent. Persons are characterised by a subjective viewpoint, and also by individual responsibility. But, so long as they do not step outside that viewpoint or cease to respond spontaneously to the demand that they be through and through answerable for what they do, they cannot forgo the transcendental illusion which inspires them. They envisage themselves as pure, unified individuals, havens of possibility, located outside the limits of natural causality, capable of acting freely and integrally, so as to be responsible for the present action at every future time. This image may have no metaphysical grounding. But it is resurgent in our consciousness, and is never more dominant than in the transports of sexual desire.

4

DESIRE

Animals and persons

It may seem odd to say that an animal can feel sexual urges, yet not be sexually aroused. But this is largely because we read into the mental states of animals those complex social dispositions which generate our actions. We see the aggressiveness of the bull as a kind of irascibility, even though it is evident that anger – the disposition to exact a penalty for injustice – is an emotion no bull can feel. For no bull possesses the fundamental concept (that of justice) upon which anger is founded. Anger can be felt only by persons, towards other persons, or towards things held to account as persons are. In like manner we may see the randiness of a dog as a kind of lust, or the mating ritual of a bird as a kind of courtship, even though there is no possibility of attributing to such creatures the mental equipment that would justify so dense a description of their behaviour. To those philosophers – like Mary Midgley[1] – who repeat that we must look at the similarities, I answer that we must look at the differences. And the place where these differences are most telling is in the sphere of personal, and interpersonal, existence, into which the lower animals cannot intrude. Even the description of the herding animals as 'social', in so far as it implies a certain conception of 'self' and 'other' through which relations are mediated, is a false designation of their behaviour. That the organisation of the clan of gorillas *looks* social is obvious; but where are the laws and institutions, where the adjudications, where the disposition of rights, privileges and duties, which make up the social consciousness of man? Without rationality such things can never come into being, and while an ape may seem to possess them, he is in reality merely aping them. And likewise, all those attitudes which involve a 'feeding back' into the individual experience of the social activity which creates our sense of self lie beyond the gorilla's competence – sexual desire included.

I referred in the last chapter to a pair of attributes which I held to be closely connected, and peculiar to persons: the first-person perspective, and responsibility. Each has gone by many names in the history of philosophy, and each name reflects a different theoretical ambition, a different, but usually equally bold and tendentious, way of deducing from the language of self-reference a metaphysical theory of the human agent. The Cartesian ego, the Leibnizian apperception, the Kantian 'transcendental unity of consciousness' and 'transcendental self', the Hegelian *Fürsichsein,* and the Sartrean '*pour-soi*' – all these are different ways of describing and building upon the fact that I can attribute my present mental states with some kind of epistemological authority to myself.

A consequence of this authority – a theory of which I have given in Chapter 3 and in Appendix 1 – is that we can, in general, make the distinction between being and seeming. About some things – seemings – we have epistemological privilege: they are immune from certain kinds of error. About other things – beings – we do not have that privilege. The distinction does not exist within the realm of first-person awareness. My present mental states are as they seem (or if they are not, this is something that requires a very special kind of explanation, such as that proposed by Freud – an explanation which preserves my 'immunity from error'). It is also part of self-consciousness to be aware of the distinction generally, to recognise that, wherever we must *discover* the present truth, the truth is not 'part of ourselves'. At every point of my existence I am able to propose a distinction between how things seem to me and how they are. In making this distinction I am identifying within myself a *perspective* on the world, and identifying it as mine.

The same is true of you. I cannot consider you to be a person without also attributing to you just such a perspective, and an awareness of this perspective as yours. Moreover, your perspective has a crucial role in mediating our relations. It is through *it* that I approach you, hoping to cooperate by adjusting how the world seems to *you*: that is the crucial step in reason-giving, and, as I argued in Chapter 3, it is the element which transforms our responses to each other from animal reaction into interpersonal understanding. For it provides the foundation for all those conceptions – such as responsibility, free agency, right, duty and value – through which human beings perceive and act upon one another.

Thus persons are also distinguished from the rest of nature by the fact of their responsibility. Not only do they change the world; they can be praised or blamed for doing so. This feature of persons is intimately connected with their rationality: with the fact that they know *why* they are doing things, and can be dissuaded or persuaded by the presentation of nothing more substantial than a reason. They can make up their mind to do things, and those things which show 'how they are minded' are also things which are pinned to them and for which they must answer in the forum of moral conversation which rational beings spontaneously create among themselves. (Thus we are blamed not only for our intentional actions, but for those things which result from our negligence, or for anything else that shows a defect of character which we might at some time have been persuaded to change.)

There are many reasons, some of which I have already outlined, for believing that the first-person perspective and responsibility are systematically connected. And there are many metaphysical glosses which try to identify them – usually through some variant of Kant's idea that the 'transcendental self' is also 'transcendentally free'. I shall have something to say about these theories later, since they attempt to capture and solidify a dominating metaphysical shadow. This shadow lies across our inner perspective, and also across the landscape of sexual desire.

The first-person perspective and arousal

In sexual arousal the other appears to me, not merely as something affected by me, but as a perspective upon me. I am something *for* him, and he for me, and this thought is part of the foundation of what I feel. But we must distinguish two cases. It might be that some part of me, some quality of me, or some aspect of me, figures in his perspective. Or it might be that I appear to him. My hand, my arm, even my entire body, might appear to him either visibly or tactually, and yet I not appear to him, because he has not attached this appearance to a particular person – to a particular subject like himself. Suppose that you awake beside a strange body. You feel it, see its shape, hear its breathing, but for a long time it is no particular person for you, not even the person whose body it is. It may begin to exhibit those physical changes that signify arousal; and at the same time you may not know who is being aroused – you do not attribute this arousal to any particular person. And when you see this body as a particular person (you may even remember which person), there is a sudden and overwhelming change of aspect. Only then does this arousal come to have meaning *for* you, for only then does it become possible to respond to it as to another person. You are now seeing the body's condition as expressive of a particular perspective, and you might seek to be an object within that perspective, and the recipient of gestures that are expressive of another 'I'.

In Martin Sherman's play *Bent*, two men confined in a Nazi concentration camp are carrying stones, in a fatiguing ritual, beneath the eye of the guards. They may not touch each other or be seen to communicate. But they are commanded to stand to attention from time to time, some yards apart. One of them, staring before him, begins to describe to the other an imaginary act of love-making between them, representing the embraces that he would – were he allowed – bestow on his companion, and evoking the most passionate arousal. In this way, pathetically but convincingly, the two prisoners consummate their desire. The key to their emotion lies in the capacity for representation. Each man, through his words, is able to represent himself within the consciousness of the other, as a 'representing awareness', focused upon the other's perspective. The desire that they experience cannot be separated from their mutual understanding, and each figures within the perspective of the other, not as a body only, but as the embodiment of another point of view. Thus sexual arousal and sexual desire may exist and find consummation, just so long as there is the right reciprocal interaction between two embodied first-person perspectives. Embodiment is necessary, but bodily contact is not. Nor is bodily contact sufficient. Suppose two sleeping bodies lying in contact pass through all those physical transformations that are characteristic of the 'wet dream': this is not yet a case either of arousal or of desire. What would make it one or the other is the character of the *dream*, and the role played within the dream by the embodied presence of the other. Of course, there could not be desire between two disembodied minds: for desire requires thoughts of the body, and of oneself and the other as living, embodied creatures. Desire is through and through saturated, as it were, by *life*. But life would be nothing for us without the perspective that leads us to reflect on it. And sexual desire, which expresses life, also compels us to reflect on life, and take a self-conscious part in its drama.

It is partly by virtue of the prominence of the first-person perspective, as a component in the subject and object of arousal, that desire acquires its 'compromising' character. I cannot experience arousal without wishing to appear in a certain light within another's perspective. And the premonition of arousal is present in the first impulse of desire. The glance of desire as it were projects the being of one person into the consciousness of another. And this glance is compromising: for it seeks a response from a free being, who may withhold it indignantly, or who may return a glance of his own. And to return the glance is to acquiesce. The glance asks *you* to respond to *me*. I am inevitably held to account for it, and while I may excuse myself on account of the strength of my passion, the last thing that I want is for you to take that excuse seriously, to see me subdued by desire as by an alien force, rather than riding towards you triumphantly upon a crest of feeling that I also control. My very ambition towards you causes me to 'take responsibilty' for my desire, and to make it a part of myself. Thus we see – what we may also see throughout the realm of interpersonal emotion – that the first-person perspective enters into the intentionality of a feeling only by making the subject answerable for what he feels. As soon as I suffer such an interpersonal emotion, my responsibilities are engaged. It does not matter that the emotion is not something that I *do* – it matters only that it has the kind of interpersonal intentionality that leads me to 'have designs upon' another.

Involuntary revelation

Our existence as responsible beings is closely connected with our capacity to form intentions – with what philosophers have sometimes called 'the will'. And it might be thought that this fact suffices to explain all the 'compromising' and involving character of sexual desire. For desire expresses itself through patterns of deliberate activity, for which we might be praised or blamed. However, although that is of course part of the truth, it would be wrong to think that voluntary activity has the kind of supreme importance here that it has in other spheres of interpersonal communication, or that what is not voluntary is in some sense only a secondary and derivative expression of the self. On the contrary, we can understand sexual desire only if we recognise the central importance of the involuntary aspect of human behaviour, both as an expression of our mental states and as a crucial moment in what I have called the 'embodiment' of the subject.[2] It is an unfortunate consequence of the philosophical attempt to connect the 'self' with the 'will' – or with its freedom – that the connection has often been missed between the self and what is *not* willed, a connection which is in fact equally constitutive of our nature. Thus one philosopher – in what is perhaps the most profound recent reinstatement of the thesis of the centrality of the will – has argued that 'bodily action is *par excellence* an ego phenomenon', for it is through action that 'a man can feel that he himself as a distinctive entity is . . . making his presence felt in the world'. Thus a man can 'legitimately feel that he is represented in this event – as not in his sweatings and blushings and not even his laugh.'[3] On the contrary, however, a man is never so much represented to the perspective of another as when he blushes or laughs. The expression on a face is largely determined by involuntary movements; and yet it is the living picture of the perspective that 'peers' from it, and hence the true and dominant image of the 'self'. Its glances, smiles and blushes are the involuntary marks of a self-conscious perception. These reveal the other's perspective partly because he does not fully control them, and we desire him through them precisely when their movements are most involuntary – as in the closing of the eyes and the opening of the mouth in the kiss of passion.

Here we should notice a peculiar fact: that there are movements which are both *essentially* involuntary and yet confined to persons – to creatures with a self-conscious perspective. Smiles and blushes are the two most prominent examples. Milton puts the point finely in *Paradise Lost*:

> for smiles from Reason flow,
> To brute denied, and are of love the food.

These physiognomic movements owe their rich intentionality to this involuntary character, for it is this which suggests that they show the other 'as he really is'. Hence they become the pivot and focus of our interpersonal responses, and of no response more than sexual desire. The voluntary smile is not a smile at all, but a kind of grimace which, while it may have its own species of sincerity – as in the smile of Royalty, which as it were pays lip-service to good nature – is not esteemed as an expression of the soul. On the contrary, it is perceived as a mask, which conceals the 'real being' of the person who wears it. Smiling must be understood as a response to another person, to a thought or perception of his presence, and it has its own intentionality. To smile is to smile *at* something or someone, and hence when we see someone smiling in the street we think of him as 'smiling to himself', meaning that there is some hidden object of his present thought and feeling. The smile of love is a kind of intimate recognition and acceptance of the other's presence – an involuntary acknowledgement that his existence gives you pleasure.

The smile of the beloved is not flesh, but a kind of stasis in the movement of the flesh. It is a paradigm of 'incarnation': of the other *made* flesh, and so transforming the flesh in which he is made. Thus the smile of Beatrice conveys her spiritual reality; Dante must be fortified in order to bear it, for to look at it is to look at the sun (*Paradiso*, XXIII, 47–8):

> *tu hai vedute cose, che possente*
> *sei fatto a sostener lo riso mio.*

It is Beatrice's smile that recalls the poet to his heavenly purpose, and when Beatrice leaves him with a smile, she gives way to Mary, who appears as it were in the same lingering smile (*Paradiso*, XXXI, 92, and 133–5). Dante's symbolism is not forced: on the contrary, it captures the precise place of smiling in the perception of a beloved person.

A still more interesting (although increasingly rare) element in the sexual drama is blushing. This too lies beyond the reach of animal mentality. Charles Darwin wrote[4] that 'blushing is the most peculiar and the most human of all expressions. Monkeys redden from passion, but it would require an overwhelming amount of evidence to make us believe that any animal could blush.' Why overwhelming? The answer is obvious: no evidence that referred only to the changing of the animal's countenance could suffice. The evidence would have to persuade us to revise our description of the animal's mentality, so as to make room for embarrassment, shame, innocence, guilt and – of course – sexual desire. In other words, it would have to be sufficient to prove the animal to be a person. Hence the truth of Christopher Ricks's astute observation that:

> it is [the] calm and calmative unembarrassabilty in animals that makes them so frequent and delightful a feature within paintings of nudes, where they gaze good-humouredly upon the lovely nude or have their eyes elsewhere, in either case without the faintest tingle of embarrassment, and so make it easy and right for us to look upon the nude and upon them with the same equanimity.[5]

Blushing is a response, intimately connected with our sense of how we appear in another's perspective. It is therefore not necessary that the subject be observed by another: only that he believe himself to be assessed and judged by another. The point is well expressed by Mandeville (*The Fable of the Bees*, Remark (C)):

> let them talk as much Bawdy as they please in the room next to the same Vertuous young woman, where she is sure that she is undiscover'd, and she will hear, if not hearken to it without blushing at all, because then she looks upon her self as no party concern'd . . . but if in the same Place she hears something said of herself that must tend to her Disgrace, or anything is named, of which she is secretly guilty, then 'tis Ten to One but she'll be asham'd and blush, tho' no Body sees her; because she has room to fear, that she is, or, if all was known, should be thought of Contemptibly.

Precisely because it involves such thoughts of another's perspective upon me, my blush serves as a crucial index of myself. It is a kind of involuntary recognition of my accountability before you for what I am and feel. The thought of the blusher is: 'I, as a responsible being, am represented in your perspective.' It is for this reason that blushes are such important indices not only of guilt, but also of innocence:

> How she would start, and blush, thus to be caught
> Playing in all her innocence of thought.
> [Keats, 'I Stood Tip-toe']

And in the blush of modesty the subject is showing himself answerable for his own sexual inclination, making its expression, so to speak, a matter of policy, a negotiation with the other, and not a matter of instinct or release.

Christopher Ricks argues, in another context, that 'it is not only the obvious association of blushing with sexual attraction or the physicality of sensation, but also its strange relationship to the involuntary which makes blushing so important to erotic art ... for both love and desire have a strange relationship to the involuntary.'[6] Ricks has touched on something that will concern us frequently in what follows – the crucial role of involuntary change as the expression and also as the focus of desire. Such change owes its nature as the conductor of desire to the 'I'-thoughts on which it is founded. A blush is attractive because it serves to 'embody' the perspective of the other, and also at the same time to display that perspective as something essentially responsive to me. Mary's blush upon meeting John, being involuntary, impresses him with the sense that *he* has summoned it – that it is in some sense his doing, just as her smile is his doing. Her blush is a fragment of her first-person perspective, called up from whatever Cartesian regions it might otherwise seem to inhabit, and made visible on the surface of her face. In blushing and smiling, another is revealed in the life of his body. In our experience of these things, our sense of the animal unity of the other combines with our sense of his unity as a person, and we perceive those two unities as an indissoluble whole. That experience, I contend, is the foundation of our form of life.

Erection has been called 'a blushing of the penis'.[7] In one way the description is inept – for the meaning of blushes depends entirely upon the fact that it is the *face* that they suffuse. In another sense, however, the description is appropriate. For it reminds us that transformations of the sexual organs are exciting only to the extent that they are believed to be involuntary. When St Augustine complained that the penis is the only organ of the body that seems to have a will of its own,[8] he was, in part, referring to the involuntary nature of erection. Many sufferers from impotence have undergone 'penile prosthesis', which enables them to engender an erection by the operation of a discreetly placed pump.[9] (Perhaps one should speak here of a simulated erection, as one speaks of a simulated smile.) In such a case erection is no longer an unmediated response to the other, but a deliberate act. A man *erects* his own penis, and there arises at once the question of the profit and the loss. Is it worth it? Will I enjoy it? Will she? Most important, is there a risk that she might discover my secret? For one thing is certain: this artificial process must be concealed – my erection stirs her excitement only so long as she believes it to be *her* doing and not mine.

Such examples, while they illustrate the general importance of involuntary transformations in the transactions of desire, distract our attention from the more important transformations that occur in the face. Although glances are normally voluntary, and are in any case actions – indeed 'basic actions', in Danto's sense[10] – they too participate in this pattern of involuntary interchange whereby one person is 'revealed' in his body to the one who observes him. To turn my eyes to you is indeed a voluntary act; but what I then receive from you is not of my doing. As the symbol of all perception, the eye comes to stand for that 'epistemic transparency' which enables the human person to be revealed to another in his body – to 'look out' of his body – and in the act of revelation to summon the other's perspective, in the form of blushes, smiles or a reciprocated glance. Michelangelo asks his beloved to make of his body one single eye, so that it might become wholly transparent to himself, and wholly rejoicing in her:

> *fa del mio corpo tutto un occhio solo*
> *Ne fia poi parte in me che non ti goda.*
> [Sonnet XXIII]

This yearning for epistemic transparency involves a desire, not to make all expression voluntary, but rather to cause the voluntary and the involuntary to mingle inextricably on the perceived surface of one's body. The joining of perspectives that is begun when a glance is answered with a blush or a smile finds final realisation in wholly reciprocated glances: the 'me seeing you seeing me' of rapt attention, where neither of us can be said to be either doing or suffering what is done:

> Our eye-beams twisted, and did thred
>   Our eyes, upon one double string;
> So to'entergraft our hands, as yet
>   Was all the meanes to make us one,
> And pictures in our eyes to get
>   Was all our propagation.

Donne's lines convey one of the fundamental thoughts of desire, which is that, in this present experience of your body, I have in some way captured your perspective and united it with mine. The pictures that I get in my eyes I get from yours, and those in your eyes come equally from mine. Whether there is a coherent purpose here – one that is capable of fulfilment – is a matter to which I shall return.

Embodiment

It seems then that certain involuntary changes in another's body are important elements in the generation and directing of desire. I have been describing a crucial feature of interpersonal intentionality: the disposition to find the marks of another's perspective displayed on the surface of his body. A phenomenologist might refer to this as the thought of the 'incarnation' (Sartre) or 'embodiment' of the other; a Hegelian might describe it as the perception of the 'body as spirit' – the body transparent, so to speak, to mental interpretation. Such descriptions add no genuine *theory* to what I have indicated. Indeed, if the remarks of Chapter 1 are right, there can be no theory of such data which does not run the risk of abolishing them – the risk of replacing the concepts through which we experience the world with the more robust ideas that will explain them. The difficulty that now confronts us is that of 'staying on the surface', so to speak: of giving a description of sexual desire that is sufficiently shallow to capture *what is wanted* by the subject. In order to achieve this result it will be necessary to refrain from theory (from any attempt to give the causality of what is described) for as long as possible. In Chapter 7 I shall address myself to certain questions which might already have occurred to the reader, in order to show the errors that enter this subject, when scientific method is invoked prematurely.

Human embodiment is not a necessary feature of persons – for there are persons without human bodies and without corporeal identity of any kind, such as trading companies identifiable only by their books. (Ironically, these incorporeal persons are called 'corporations' in law.) However, if there are to be persons at all, it is necessary that there should be embodied persons. For how can we identify the agency and responsibility that attach to companies if we cannot identify the physical actions of the embodied persons who represent them? Moreover, embodiment is an essential property of whatever possesses it – a property that a person could not cease to have without also ceasing to be. Indeed, it is arguable that, from the material (scientific) point of view, a person is *identical* with his body.[11] All those features of him which constitute his personal existence – action, thought, speech and response – are redescribed by the scientist as states, movements and changes in the body and brain. Any tolerable metaphysic of the human person must take seriously the suggestion that, by all our normal standards of identity, the 'substance' from which human thought and action emanate and to which they ought to be ascribed is the human body. From the point of view of *material* understanding – the understanding of the objective structure and causality of events – self and body are one and the same.

From the point of view of intentional understanding, however, this identity seems to elude our grasp. I constantly identify myself without reference to my body, and in ways which seem to exclude the body. Moreover, I constantly react to you as though you were not identical with your body, but in some sense operating *through* your body, which is an *instrument* of your suffering and will. There arises, in our mutual transactions, the inescapable impression that each of us has a centre of existence which is not his body but his self. At the same time you are knowable to me only *through* your body and its effects, and when I attend to you, I attend directly and unhesitatingly to *it*.

In consequence, our experience of embodiment is incipiently dualistic. In a valuable study, Helmuth Plessner argues that I stand to my body in a relation that is at once instrumental and constitutive: I *have* my body, but I also *am* my body.[12] As a result I live in a state of tension with regard to my physical existence, while being at the same time wholly and completely bound to it.

Embodiment is a concept of intentional understanding; it expresses a feature of the human world that we instantly recognise and respond to, and all our references to one another are also, directly or obliquely, references to embodiment. It is doubtful, however, that any equivalent idea could feature in the *material* understanding of our condition. A science of man would refer to the human body as a particular biological organism. And often we need to see our bodies in that way – when injured, say, when speculating about exercise and diet, or as part of our contemplation of death. But, in doing so, we become estranged from our flesh, which ceases to appear to us as saturated with a first-person perspective. There is a tension between the scientific understanding of the human body and the intentional understanding of embodiment, which endorses the immediate tension contained within the experience of embodiment itself. We are 'at home' in our bodies, we feel, but only because we have the lingering suspicion that we might have been elsewhere.

The idea of embodiment helps us to understand why involuntary transformations – 'expressions' – have so important a function in mediating our interpersonal attitudes. In smiling, blushing, laughing and crying, it is precisely my loss of control over my body, and its gain of control over me, that create the immediate experience of an incarnate person. The body ceases, at these moments, to be an *instrument*, and reasserts its natural rights as a person. In such expressions the face does not function merely as a bodily part, but as the whole person: the self is spread across its surface, and there 'made flesh'.

Schopenhauer – whose view of these matters is a good example of the chaos that ensues from the premature attempt to explain them – argues that the face is the least important of all the indices of beauty, since it is the least relevant to the reproductive function which underlies and explains desire.[13] That is almost the opposite of the truth. Although a pretty face surmounting a deformed or mutilated body may indeed fail to arouse sexual interest, it is well known that a pretty face may compensate for much bodily ugliness. (Consider the crippled *femme fatale*, Signora Neroni, brilliantly portrayed by Trollope in *Barchester Towers*, or the eyes of the snake Serpentina, in Hoffman's story *The Golden Pot*.) A beautiful body, however, will always be rendered repulsive by an ugly face, and can certainly never compensate for it. It is in the face that our life is revealed – and revealed precisely in what is most involuntary. Moreover, since facial beauty is to a great extent a matter of expression, its attractiveness is the attractiveness of life itself.

In referring to the 'will' St Augustine was also drawing attention to a real distinction, between those involuntary changes that play a part in the expression of the first-person perspective (and therefore of the thing which has will) and those that do not. The erection of the penis (like the softening of the vagina) is of the latter kind: it can be *understood* only in the context of other transformations, and is itself opaque to interpersonal interpretation. Its doings are *outside* our concern, until attached to some interpersonal drama. (Hence, while I can fall in love on seeing another's portrait, I could not have the same reaction to a photograph of his sexual parts.) An excitement which concentrates upon the sexual organs, whether of man or of woman, which seeks, as it were, to by-pass the preliminary interest in face, hands, voice and posture, is perverted. It seeks to focus on the culminating act of gratification, while voiding that act of its distinctive intentionality – of its direction towards the embodiment of another perspective.

Reason is tolerant of mystery and seeks not to hide it or abolish it, but to live peaceably with it in a relation of mutual influence. For reason recognises, in the end, that mysteries arise only because of its own assiduous creation of the conditions in which they thrive, and that it can abolish them only by risking its own capacity for survival. (Thus, in its perverted forms – in the forms of rationalism and Enlightenment – reason wars against mystery, and prepares the conditions for its own eclipse.) Embodiment is a mystery for us precisely because, as rational beings, we understand ourselves from a first-person viewpoint. Reason therefore extends itself, in an attempt to mitigate the strange fact of bodily existence and to bestow on it the appearance of a social role. We play with our embodiment; we develop social norms which expand and limit it. We clothe ourselves, discipline our behaviour according to an idea of good manners, and steadily refine away the body's rough demands on us, confining them to a closet realm of dark and inscrutable imperatives. One of these stratagems of reason, in its close encounter with the body, is the transformation of sex into gender; in discussing this stratagem in Chapter 9 I shall try to show how the mystery of embodiment is both accommodated and neutralised in the sexual act, and the body transformed in our thinking from a prison to a home. Such transformation of the body is the *Heimkehr* of the self, and the final aim of sexual morality.

Discarnate persons

Not all our interpersonal attitudes require or focus upon the embodiment of their object – a fact which needs to be recognised if we are to understand the special role of embodiment in desire. We are political animals, and live in circumstances of corporate activity, surrounded and supported by 'artificial persons' whom we also create. I contract with companies, have rights against them and duties towards them. I take sides with one club against another. I recognise in a thousand ways the corporate activity of institutions and the rights and duties which are engendered by it. Nor are these rights and duties merely legal. I can be under a moral obligation to the firm that has looked after my interests, just as the firm can be under a moral obligation to me. Of course, the firm's moral identity is possible only because individual human beings make decisions on its behalf, and thereby take responsibility for its actions. But these decisions are not arbitrary human intrusions into the life of the company. Rather, they are natural – even inevitable – products of its own intrinsic energy and power. Not to make the decision to provide a parting gift to an old and loyal employee is an omission for which the company is rightly blamed. The moral choice *lies before* the firm, which, through its actions, has become answerable for the fate of its employees.

I can extend to corporate persons many of the attitudes which I extend to human individuals. I may love, hate, admire, esteem, despise and resent any kind of corporate agency, including firms, clubs, states and nations. Nor does the agency have to be a 'corporate person' in any legal sense. It is a principle of English law, for example, that unincorporated associations are not legal persons; nevertheless, they seem to have liabilities and rights, however difficult those liabilities and rights may be to adjudicate.[14]

It is a well-known human failing that collective entities may become the objects of interpersonal attitudes, even though they have *no* corporate activity, and no personality of any kind. Thus races and classes may be objects of love and of hatred, even though they perform no intentional actions, have no liabilities, no responsibilities, and no corporate rights: that is, even though they are not agents. Our disposition to extend our interpersonal responses here outreaches its competence. For where there is no agency, there is no person, not even a corporate person. It is the first requirement of political existence that people should submit to an impartial reign of justice, whereby rights and obligations are attributed only to agents, who can be made answerable for their deeds. The transition from the pre-political life of the tribe to the open, public life of the *polis* is the transition from confused ideas of guilt to clear ideas of responsibility – the transition, for example, from the blood feud to the trial for murder. There is much to be said about this transition – more even than Aeschylus expresses in the *Oresteia*. But I shall have to rely on an intuitive understanding. The aim of politics is to build a forum of responsible agency on the seething ground of agglutinative love and hate. The twentieth century has seen the partial collapse of that aim, as parties try to gain or retain their power through race hatred, class hatred and the love or hatred of abstract ideas. This pathological condition contains, however, a clear indication of the normality that it betrays: the normality of a state founded on corporate agency and corporate liability. Only such a state is a true person, fit to grant and to recognise the rights of others, and to lay claim to the obligation of its citizens.

Corporate persons may achieve a kind of 'embodiment'. A purely legal state may achieve a warmer, more appealing, more lovable aspect when embodied in a people who are bound together by unformulated ties: ties of race, language, culture and history, ties which are, in our perception, constituted from flesh. The nation-state is indeed the artificial person nearest, both in its agency and in its quasi-embodiment, to the individual human person, and it is not surprising that it is so frequently loved and hated. Nevertheless, it is clear that the 'embodiment' here achieved is not the embodiment of the human person, even if it borrows from the latter its major source of appeal. By and large, our feelings towards corporate persons do not require an individualised incarnation. Hence it would be nonsense to feel sexual desire towards a firm, a club, an office, a state or a nation. While all those things may be loved, none of them may be desired, for the simple reason that none of them has a human body which is uniquely its own.

In the opinion of many, there are also disembodied persons who are true individuals. God is the most important example. The Christians believe that only an incarnate God can inspire the warm and natural love that is the fount of earthly peace. However, the love of the Moslem for his discarnate God is of unrivalled fervour. It is sometimes argued that the fervour *towards* God is in this case less than the fervour against his enemies, and that it is only in Sufism – which addresses God in tones of such tenderness as to contain a covert recognition of his incarnation – that the warmth of a true human love enters the theology of Islam. But those are speculations; on the surface at least, God may be loved not in spite of, but also because of, his disembodiment, and not only with an *amor intellectualis*. And, if we extend our imagination to the realm of devils, spirits, angels and genii, we must instantly recognise that every personal attitude, with one or two exceptions, has been directed and continues to be directed to disembodied persons. One major exception, however, is desire.

People interest us primarily as agents, and it is to their agency that we normally respond. But we find this agency emanating not only from human bodies, but also from corporations, from institutions, and (we are apt to believe) from divinities and occult powers. If there were no such thing as human embodiment, there would be no special problem of personal identity. We should then treat people as we do other enduring sources of change, and determine their identity according to their continuity. (This is the conclusion reached by Derek Parfit, who could be reproached precisely for his disposition to overlook the intentional reality of incarnation.[15]) In desire, however, I wish to find a unity between your bodily and your personal identity, and to hold in your body the soul that speaks and looks from it.

Although people are essentially embodied for us, and although we always respond to them *as* embodied, it is only occasionally that their embodiment is *itself* the object of our interest, just as it is only occasionally that I am interested in the buildings of my university, rather than in its institutional procedure. It is only in desire, in certain tender forms of love, and in the tender hatred of sadism, that you must be, for me, through and through revealed in the flesh that harbours you.

The personal nature of the object of desire

By referring to embodiment as the focus of desire we have therefore identified an important differentiating feature – although one that is shared with other states of mind. To distinguish desire from these other states, it is necessary to say more about its aim: what is wanted of the embodied person in desire? What, to put it technically, is the intentionality of sexual desire? A simple picture, common to Freud, to the writers of the *Kinsey Report* and to other volumes of once fashionable nonsense, represents sexual desire in the following way. Sexual arousal is a localised phenomenon, a swelling of the glands. This physical alteration permits pleasurable stimulus and eventual climax (orgasm). These are, according to the picture, the root phenomena of human sexuality, and the principal phenomena which any scientific investigation must examine and explain. The most simple-minded of the proponents of the picture (e.g. the authors of *Kinsey*)[16] see orgasm as something like the aim of desire, the presence of the other person as its occasion. The picture can then be completed as follows: one person encounters another. This provokes arousal, which prompts the desire for stimulation of the gland, which prompts the pursuit of the other, and the engagement in the clinch which sets the subject on the road to orgasm. It so happens that it is the sight of another human being that sets this process in motion, usually a human being of the opposite sex. But it might have been one of the same sex; or a dog, or a caterpillar, or an expanse of water. The advantage of confining the response to human beings is that you can sometimes persuade them to cooperate.

It should be evident, in the light of all that has been said in the second chapter, that no such view is acceptable. As Nagel and Sartre have argued, its attempt to assimilate sexual desire to appetite misses the interpersonal component of human sexual responses.[17] Moreover, it is not simply that the object of desire – on this view – is no longer a person. It is also that the particular person enters only accidentally into the intentional structure of the desire that he occasions. It happens to be him, but it might have been another. This is one reason why it is so easy to derive from this picture an idea of sexual taste: some are 'turned on' by women, some by men, some by children, some by pigs, cartridges, ice-cream cartons or mangel-worzels. The other person may then drop out of consideration altogether. When sexual desire is represented as 'desire for an orgasm' or 'desire for pleasurable sensations in the sexual glands', the role of the other person becomes wholly mysterious, as do virtually all the complex stratagems of human sexual union.

If we attend for a moment to ordinary language (although it is a vacillating guide), we cannot fail to be struck by a singular phenomenon: the object of sexual desire is identified as the person himself. What you want is not this or that activity, sensation or release, abstractly described; you want Albert, or Mary, or Titania, or Bottom. There is, I believe, a truth conveyed by this common idiom which philosophical analysis must acknowledge and uphold. The comedy of Titania's desire depends upon the fact that Bottom has been translated into inappropriate form, so that her desire for *him* leads her to address her attentions to the most incongruous physical object — while at the same time being quite unconscious of the ludicrousness of her lover's costume:

> Come sit thee down upon this flowry bed,
> While I try thy amiable cheekes to coy,
> And stick muske roses in thy sleeke smoothe head,
> And kiss thy fair large eares, my gentle joy.

It is not that Titania has been 'turned on' by an instance of the species ass, but that she has awoken to a desire for Bottom, who is, however, an ass.

It might be argued that this habit of identifying the other person as the object of desire is no more than a manner of speaking, a convenient way of summarising the strategies with which the aim of sexual gratification is encumbered. In fact, however, it is very far from that. This is confirmed by a variety of observations. For example, it is very difficult to express sexual desire as a 'propositional attitude' (a 'wanting that') without seriously misrepresenting it. Normally, any sentence of the form 'A wants B' can be represented as 'A wants that p', where 'p' describes a change undergone by B. 'John wants the glass of wine' is equivalent to something like: 'John wants that he drink the glass of wine'. This translation is very hard to accomplish in the case of sexual desire. While there are of course occasions when one might wish to translate 'John wants Mary' as 'John wants that he make love to Mary', there are other cases where this is far from obvious. Mary might object sincerely and passionately to such a translation of the proposition that Mary wants John. There are two reasons for this. First, sexual desire is more like a vector which gathers momentum than it is like a definite project. The subject may be extremely confused, at first, as to what he wants, and then, only by degrees and through a process of discovery which is also a self-discovery, does his desire focus upon a specific aim. (Cf. *Daphnis and Chloë*, Bk 1, §22: *ēthelon ti, ēqnooun ho ti thelousi*).

Secondly, and more importantly, whatever one wants to do *with* the object of desire, his 'being who he is' (in some individualising application of that phrase) enters essentially into a description of what is wanted. It is Elizabeth or Albert who is wanted, and not just any person, answering to whatever description. If John is frustrated in his pursuit of Mary, there is something inapposite in the advice 'Take Elizabeth, she will do just as well.' Of course, Elizabeth can *console* John. But consolation consists precisely in extinguishing John's present desire in the flood of another. Likewise, John may make love to Elizabeth, while thinking all the while of Mary, whom he embraces in his imagination. But this 'congress of transferred love', as the *Kama Sutra* calls it,[18] is not a case of transferred desire: the desire was, and is, for Mary, and Elizabeth serves as an 'instrument' in its expression. In any account of what Mary would have 'done for' John (any account that is faithful to the intentionality of his desire) the term 'Mary' (or some term with equal reference) designates the individual object of desire. Its function is to pick out an individual person, by expressing an *individualising thought*. It is arguable that no proper name really can convey an individualising thought, and even that individualising reference is never secured merely by the content of our thought.[19] Names, it has been said, are 'rigid designators', whose reference is determined not by a mental content but by the world to which we refer. At the same time, however, we try to employ names as though the uniqueness of their referent *were* the product of thought – as though we ourselves, by our inner concentration, endowed names with their rigidity. Sexual desire involves a kind of mental fight against the flaccid designator: and the tragedy is that it is a fight which we are logically compelled to lose.

The phenomenology of proper names

I have touched upon a deep and difficult question in the philosophy of logic, and before pursuing the matter it is worth reflecting on the phenomenological basis for what I have said: the basis which leads me to imply that names are given a peculiarly individualising interpretation in desirous thoughts. This is most clearly revealed in the poetry of names, which acquire a role in erotic literature that they do not acquire elsewhere. Romeo, Juliet, Manon, Helen, Tristan, Isolde – these famous objects of erotic yearning are inseparably linked to their names, which are the stigmata of our imaginary desire for them. Verses which play upon the name of a desired object aim always to reinforce the sense that in the name is concealed a quiddity, an irreplaceable individuality, and that this is the object of desire. What is entertained in such verse is not the thought of the name itself (which denotes a million Marys, Juliets or Chloës), but the mysterious relation of reference, which enables the writer to see in this name the single individual who is picked out by it. This explains the poignancy of Juliet's situation when, having realised that Romeo bears the hated name of Montague, she attempts to separate him in thought from his name:

> What's in a name? That which we call a Rose,
> By any other word would smell as sweete,
> So *Romeo* would, were he not *Romeo* call'd,
> Retaine that dear perfection which he owes
> Without that title. *Romeo*, doffe thy name,
> And for thy name which is no part of thee,
> Take all my selfe.

As the tragedy shows, it is precisely this that Romeo cannot do. To doff his name is to doff his identity, as the child of these particular parents, heir to this particular debt of vengeance. As the two lovers are caught up in the web of disaster, their names begin to gather to themselves the resonance of their passion, and that which they strive at first to doff is at last engraved in marble on their common tomb. Thus before the end of the scene Juliet is already saying:

> Bondage is hoarse, and may not speake aloud,
> Else would I teare the Cave where Eccho lies,
> And make her airie tongue more hoarse than myne,
> With repetition of my *Romeo*.

In Act II, scene iii, Romeo's rejection of the claims of Rosaline is expressed in his forgetting of her name, and when Romeo later rages against his name,

> O tell me, friar, tell me
> In what vile part of this Anatomie
> Doth my name lodge? Tell me that I may sack
> The hateful mansion
> [III.iii]

his words show the futility of his effort to remove from his consciousness the focal point of Juliet's love. In all this play on the idea of naming, we see the record of sexual intentionality, which can be satisfied with no description of its object besides that which locates him irreplaceably. 'In the name,' Hegel argued, 'the individual as pure individual is "weighed", not only in "his" consciousness, but in the consciousness of all' (*Phenomenology of Spirit*).

Individualising thought

The individualising intentionality of desire might not surprise us. For sexual desire is as much an interpersonal response as sexual arousal, and it is part of our perception of another as a person that we do not, as it were, see him merely as an instance of his kind, replaceable by whatever substitute. In all our dealings with people, the attitude of 'respect for persons' – the injunction, in Kant's terms, to treat others as ends in themselves, and never as means only – leads us to attribute an irreplaceable value to those with whom we are brought into relation. An obvious contrast might be drawn here between sexual desire and the appetite for food.[20] My appetite for a dish of carrots is stilled by the possession of *any* (suitably arranged) dish of carrots. Someone who protests 'No, I want Elspeth (name of a particular dish of carrots)', protests too much, and incoherently.

However, an important objection here occurs. As Bishop Butler argued in his attack upon hedonism,[21] what I want, while it is before me is *this* dish of carrots. I might indeed accept a substitute – but then I do so by coming to *want* the substitute. So why is this case any different from that of sexual desire? Is it not merely a convention that leads us to say that, when I transfer my appetite from this dish of carrots to that, there is only *one* appetite, with two successive objects, while, when I transfer my attentions from Elizabeth to Jane, there are two desires, differentiated precisely by their successive objects? In either case, surely, I could say both that there is one desire, and that there are two – everything will depend upon the purpose of my counting.

The response to that objection is long and complex, and will occupy us further in the next chapter. But two things must be said at once, in order to dispel its immediate force. First, sexual desire is unlike my appetite for these carrots, in being *founded upon* an individuating thought. It is part of the very directedness of desire that a *particular* person is conceived as its object. Thus there arises the possibility – already discussed in relation to arousal – of mistakes of identity. Jacob's desire for Rachel seemed to be satisfied by his night with Leah, only to the extent that, and for as long as, Jacob imagined it was Rachel with whom he was lying. Likewise, I might reasonably apologise to my paramour's twin for mistaking her for her sister, not merely in the act of caressing her, but also in the impulse of desiring her. For in a crucial sense I did not desire *her*, but the other whom she resembles. The desire for a dish of carrots is not similarly dependent upon an individuating thought, and does not therefore give rise to errors of identity. To eat the wrong dish of carrots may be a social howler, but it is not a mistaken expression of desire – I really did desire the dish of carrots that I consumed. Of course I can make other mistakes in my appetites: I may discover that these are not carrots, say, or that they are carrots of a particularly nasty kind. But, in the relevant sense, these are not mistakes of *identity*.

There is an interesting contrast to be drawn here with the sexual behaviour of animals. Ethologists tirelessly remind us of the monogamous habits of wolves, swans and primates.[22] Why is this any different, they say, from the case of human fidelity, and what is it that would lead us to describe this behaviour in less elevated terms than those we apply to a human marriage? The principal answer, I believe, lies in the absence from animal mentality of genuine individualising thoughts. While a wolf may stay with his mate through all contingencies, this is not the same as a fidelity to the mate, based on a conception of *who she is*. Another mate might be found who is sufficiently similar to the existing one, to be accepted in place of her. Do we then say that the wolf continues his life on the basis of a *mistake*? Or do we say rather that he continues exactly as before, and in the same cognitive relation to the world? If we cannot (and we cannot) make the distinction, then we should, I believe, accept the second description, since it is theoretically simpler: it makes a less adventurous claim than does the first about the wolf's intellectual capacities. It allows us to see the wolf's 'fidelity' as – so to speak – fidelity *de re*. It does not need to be accounted for in terms of that 'fidelity *de dicto*', whereby a creature's dispositions are focused upon an individual, by virtue of the individualising tendency of his thoughts.

As I have already suggested, however, the idea of an individualising thought is far from clear. If a thought focuses upon an individual, surely this is by virtue of the surrounding circumstances? Names do indeed focus our thoughts upon individuals; but this is because they are rigid designators. Their reference *determines* their sense, and the uniqueness of their reference is a fact about the world, rather than an upshot of the thoughts in which they occur. Is the case not, therefore, exactly like that of the wolf, whose emotions are attached to his mate not by virtue of their intentional structure alone, but also because there is only *one* she-wolf who serves as their object?

The answer to that objection is contained in our discussion of the poetry of names. It is indeed true that names acquire their sense from their reference. They are nevertheless treated – in love and desire – as though their reference were determined by their sense. They are attached, in thought, to an *idea* of individuality, and epitomise our attempts to focus our thought upon the quiddity of another, and upon the indefinable 'sense' of his moral and emotional presence. Our interpersonal thoughts return us constantly to the individual, and to the need to grasp his individuality in an act of reference. Even our pronouns – and especially the pronoun 'you' – acquire this penumbra. Hence the helpless longing for revenge against a lost and barely remembered father finds persuasive expression in Sylvia Plath's use of the German pronoun:

> Daddy, I have had to kill you.
> You died before I had time –
> Marble-heavy, a bag full of God,
> Ghastly statue with one grey toe
> Big as a Frisco seal
>
> And a head in the freakish Atlantic
> Where it pours bean green over blue
> In the waters off beautiful Nauset.
> I used to pray to recover you.
> Ach, du.

The precise nature of the individualising thought contained in that last word, and of the (hopeless) enterprise to which it commits the author, will be the subject of the chapter which follows.

For the present, I shall offer an intuitive understanding of 'individualising thought', in order to consider its role in the intentionality of sexual desire. Consider the following: the desire to visit a particular place; the desire to visit my old school; the desire to contemplate a particular work of art. Are these not all ways of focusing on the irreplaceable individual? Suppose someone asks me *why* I desire to visit Nuremberg. Two broad answers may suggest themselves. First I may represent Nuremberg as interesting on account of some property that might equally have been exemplified by some other place – its atmosphere of a provincial German city, say. The second represents Nuremberg as interesting *for its own sake*

– on account of its *being* Nuremberg, with a particular history, culture and political identity, none of which can be detached from the town. In the first case one may legitimately refer to some other city that would 'do just as well'. In the second case, however, such a reference is, to say the least, problematic. The crucial phrase here is 'for its own sake': a device which serves to block the passage to purpose, and to focus all reasoning upon the thing itself. As we shall see in the next chapter, this phrase, which applies equally to the object of desire and the object of aesthetic interest, contains a clue to the idea of an 'individualising thought'.

The second example need not detain us. I am interested in this school because it is *my* school; no other school would 'do just as well' since no other school would be mine. But we can envisage, here, a kind of counterfactual substitution. Had another school been mine, then it would have been an object of just this interest. It is only the indexicality of the original identification – the identification of the school as *mine* – which blocks the substitution. Clearly the individuating attention to his beloved preceded the poet's ability to say '*Die geliebte Müllerin ist mein, ist mein!*' As I shall argue, sexual desire, aesthetic contemplation and certain forms of love are characterised by the fact that even this counterfactual substitution is ruled out. Any object that 'would have done just as well' as the object of aesthetic contemplation or desire would also be *identical* with that object. There is no possible world in which another object is the object of just *this* act of attention.

Study of those examples will, I hope, suffice to introduce the intuitive understanding of 'individualising thought' upon which I rely in arguing that sexual desire is the expression of such a thought. In order to defend that suggestion, however, a general observation needs to be made, and the point again concerns the relation between desire and hunger. It might be argued that sexual desire gains its individualising intentionality from the fact that it has a personal object. It is simply a feature of persons that they *demand* a certain kind of treatment: the respect which forbids us to look on them as replaceable by another. What distinguishes desire from hunger is therefore not the structure of the impulse itself, but an independent feature of those entities to which it is directed. Suppose that people were the only edible things. And suppose that they felt no pain upon being eaten and were reconstituted at once. How many formalities and apologies would now be required in the satisfaction of hunger! People would learn to conceal their appetite, and learn not to presume upon the consent of those whom they surveyed with famished glances. It would become a terrible crime to partake of a meal without the meal's consent. Perhaps, in the end, marriage might be considered, as the only

81

decent solution to an otherwise intolerable moral predicament. Why is this not a case of hunger – normal physical hunger – made part of an individualising project? And in which case, what is the difference between this kind of hunger and desire?

The answer is evident. In such circumstances hunger would certainly generate the courtesies that we currently associate with desire. But this is because of the absence of more appropriate nourishment. If there were anything non-human to eat, we should certainly eat it. The courtesies come, not from the internal structure of hunger, but from the indefeasible moral demand that people make upon each other. By contrast, the human being is the *normal* object of desire. The object of desire must have, not just human flesh, but also the first-person perspective which serves to individualise him in his own eyes and in the eyes of his pursuer. To put it another way: unlike hunger, sexual desire is interested in the *embodiment* of the other, and not in his body. The interpersonal intentionality lies therefore in desire itself, and is not imposed by the accidental privations of our existence.

The first-person perspective in desire

We may now put together our two major observations: first, that desire is directed towards the embodiment of the other, in the special sense of this term that I have tried to define. Secondly, that it has an inherently individualising intentionality. Both point in the same direction: both invite us to see the other's perspective as a fundamental part of the object of desire. For it is the perspective of the other that is made real to us in his embodiment, and which provides our most immediate image of his irreplaceable individuality. How things seem to him – we are apt to feel – they can only seem to *him*. For only *his* perspective expresses the self which he is.

Hence sexual desire is alert to every signal in which the perspective of the other is revealed: from this stems the 'compromising' character of desire upon which Sartre has commented.[23] Desire is not an action; yet it reveals itself in those gestures – both voluntary and involuntary – through which the self is disclosed to observation. In desire you are compromised in the eyes of the object of desire, since you have displayed that you have designs which are vulnerable to his intentions. Your desire does not excuse, but inculpates. 'I so wanted it!' may be an excuse for touching the cake; but it is never an excuse for touching the lady. On the contrary, it is the final condemnation. 'So that was it! He wanted me. How disgusting!' An accidental touch would have been blameless, even though it 'feels the same'. So too would a touch executed in the normal course of communication. It is the expression of desire in the fingertips that compromises. Likewise, when a woman is revolted by a man's desirous glance, her thought is something like 'How dare he!' – it involves anger at that man, who appears to her as accountable for the desire that is revealed in his eyes. (It is undeniable, however, that there are significant differences here between male and female experience. In Chapter 6 I shall return to these differences, so as to show that my emphasis on the female is not arbitrary.)

This sense of the other's responsibility may seem odd and unjust. But it is not confined to the recipient of sexual attentions. It is there in the first impulse of desire. The thwarted lover feels that he has been *disdained*. His being refused is not just a fact, like the cake lying out of reach. It is felt as a reaction to desire, which in turn bears the marks of his commitment. It is 'unfair' that the object of desire should be blamed for his refusal. Nevertheless, we must all learn the delicate negotiations whereby to disentangle ourselves from the unsolicited attentions of others, without offending their self-respect, and one of the most important features of moral education consists in the acquisition of the control implied by this transaction.

Kantian ethics – a digression

Not all philosophers have been prepared to recognise the personal nature of the object of desire. Kant, for example, insisted that 'sexual desire is not an inclination which one human being has for another as such, but is an inclination for the sex of another,' having previously argued thus:

> Sexual love makes of the loved person an object of appetite; as soon as that appetite has been stilled, the person is cast aside as one casts away a lemon which has been sucked dry. [Curious comparison!] Sexual love can, of course, be combined with human love and so carry with it the characteristics of the latter, but taken by itself and for itself, it is nothing more than appetite. Taken by itself it is a degradation of human nature; for as soon as a person becomes an object of appetite for another, all motives of moral relationship cease to function, because as an object of appetite another person becomes a thing and can be treated as such by everyone.[24]

Obviously Kant is arguing somewhat loosely in this passage, although the thought is the central thought – rephrased in the vivid terminology of the categorical imperative – of a tradition that begins with Plato. The consequence of Kant's view is that desire is never a *form* of love, but at best only 'combined with' love, just as an interest in someone's etchings might be combined with love. But if, taken by itself, desire is a degradation of human nature, why should it cease to be so when conjoined with a wholly different state of mind? Love is not an appetite, and has the very special intentionality of the interpersonal attitudes. The appetite for human flesh is scarcely redeemed by love for the person who is eaten; so why should love redeem desire? The way of thought is characteristic of Kant's failure to see that our animal nature is not just conjoined with, but also entirely transformed by, the aspect of self-consciousness which he calls 'practical reason' and whose workings he locates (ultimately) in a transcendental self. Or rather, it is not that he fails to see that, for he does see it, or at least he sees the need for a concept of 'embodiment':

> the body is part of the self; in its togetherness with the self it constitutes the person; a person cannot make of his person a thing.

But he fails to see the full consequences of such a thought, as is evident in the concluding phrase of that sentence: 'and this is exactly what happens in *vaga libido*'.[25] What is impossible cannot be exactly what happens.

Kant's thought is part of the attempt to criticise, from the standpoint of the categorical imperative, the motives of the fornicator. He wishes to show that the fornicator is using both the other, and himself, as a thing (i.e. in defiance of the second formulation of the categorical imperative, which forbids the instrumental approach to human nature). The fornicator uses his person as his tool, so to speak. (In traditional legal parlance, it was part of decency to refer to a man's tool as his 'person'.[26] Loss of decency has gone hand in hand with Hannah Arendt's 'instrumental-isation', a fact illustrated in the vulgar use of 'tool'. It is quite easy to see the connections that a Kantian would wish to make here.)

Kant's arguments fall short of the mark; but interestingly enough they exemplify the same unwarranted conception of human sexuality that I earlier dismissed. For Kant, sexual desire is a kind of appetite – it lies outside the realm of interpersonal feeling, and does not bear the intrinsic marks of responsibility or love. Kant dismisses desire as degraded, because he believes it to be an animal residuum (whereas in fact animals do not and cannot feel it). It only remains to wipe away the stigma of 'bestiality' – to argue, with the modern permissive morality, for the rehabilitation of our 'animal' nature – for the received libertarian morality to follow at once: sexual desire, treated in itself, lies outside the sphere of moral assessment. Morality attaches, not to the sexual act, but to its attendant circumstance alone. Thus one can see the philosophical basis for an observation that has frequently been made: permissiveness and puritanism (of the kind exemplified in Kant's downgrading of sexuality) are two sides of a single coin.

Kant himself did not draw that conclusion. But it has been drawn by many of his disciples, including the sociologist Roberto Michels (better known for his 'iron law of oligarchy' than for his immature reflections on the nature of sexual experience):[27]

> the sexual impulse is sharply distinguished from hunger in a matter of the first importance . . . the object of hunger is of animal or even of vegetable origin. The origin of the sexual impulse, on the other hand, is the possession of another human being. Abstractly considered, the sexual instinct has no moral value, either positive or negative . . . . But taken in the concrete, sexual love has to be justified in terms of the categorical imperative. In other words, sexual love, involving as it does the mutual activity of two individuals, must not consist in one's making use of the other simply for the purposes of the former – whereas a sexual act which injures no-one is indifferent, ethically speaking, and therefore cannot be immoral.[28]

Michels makes clear, I believe, the failure of Kantian ethics, when detached from a satisfactory theory of sexual desire. And since the Kantian ethic is, or has become, the prevailing ethic of our civilisation, the example is minatory. Two factors are missing from the Kantian account of desire: its individualising intentionality and its focus on 'embodiment'. It is the restoration of those factors, I shall argue, which enables the Kantian finally to present a persuasive sexual code.

The course of desire

Let us return to the discussion of the intentionality of desire. What is wanted by the person who desires another? I have already remarked on the difficulty in stating the aim of desire in propositional form. Although desire involves a strong sense of longing for another, there is no easy way of separating the longing from the individual person who is desired – no easy way of describing, in abstract terms, just what the other is supposed to do in order to satisfy me. The other *is* my longing – that is the immediate thought, captured in Rückert's poem '*Du bist die Ruh*':

Die Sehnsucht du
Und was sie stillt.

To some extent this impression is a compound product of simpler things: of the reciprocity integral to arousal, and of the dramatic moments which are implied by that. The lover seeks to overcome the object of desire, and as it were to compel his consent, by compelling his desire. This is the first movement in the direction of sexual reciprocity. In Machiavelli's comedy *Mandragola*, Lucrezia is 'seduced' by a complex stratagem, involving considerable deception, into believing that she must sleep with a stranger. The 'seducer', out of desire for her, represents himself as the stranger in question. The detail which transforms this nonsense into drama occurs with the retrospective description given by the lover (Camillo) of his success. He reveals himself, pleads with her from the strength of his desire, and elicits a confession of reciprocal desire. Only then does she surrender, and it is clear that what Camillo wanted was not to sleep with Lucrezia come what may, but to obtain the opportunity to bring Lucrezia to surrender willingly to her own, and his, emotion.

It is partly because the subject of desire puts himself thus at the disposition of the other's consent that, in a very important sense, his desire has 'its own course': it grows out of the mutual activity of the participants, and – while it may tend in this or that direction – its purpose remains partly veiled at the outset, by the opacity of the person who is desired. The object of desire becomes transparent to me only 'in the course of' desire.

At the same time desire has a recognisable sexual focus – a focus on the sexual nature, and sexual parts, of another person. Although the other is treated as a person in the act of love, he is desired *as* a man, or *as* a woman. This is as true of homosexual as of heterosexual feeling, and is an ineliminable part of the excitement and drama of the sexual act. This act of union, I recognise, might have occurred with another of the same sex, and I approach the other partly as a representative of his sex.

This does not mean that I necessarily have a very clear conception of sex as a biological category. I may be unaware of the role of sex in reproduction, or of any other scientific fact about it. I may even be unaware that there are two sexes. Suppose that Jane has been brought up on an island inhabited only by women. It is still the case that, when she looks upon Miriam with the eyes of desire, she sees Miriam as one member of a kind. Miriam begins to be liked for her bodily parts – her eyes, her mouth, her way of moving or standing. These are 'species-laden' characteristics, and bear the imprint of a biological kind, even though Jane's interest in them is an interest in the individual Miriam, and even though Jane may lack the concept either of species or of sexuality. When desire begins to focus, it is upon such things: it singles them out, and separates them from the thought that any other person's eyes, mouth or posture could have served just as well. In the very first movement of desire there is therefore a kind of paradox: the body of the other is interesting because it is one instance of a bodily kind; but the very interest which focuses upon it insists that it is no such thing, that it is unique, irreplaceable, the one and only object of this present emotion. This is yet another aspect of the tension that is present in our intentional understanding of embodiment.

Sexual interest in another has a natural tendency to gravitate, in the 'course of desire', to his distinctively sexual parts: those parts which have a special role in the transmission of sexual pleasure. We must distinguish two ways in which this gravitation of interest may occur: the way of curious pleasure, as I shall call it, and the way of desire. Sexual curiosity is wholly unlike most normal curiosity. If I am curious as to the anatomy of the garfish, say, my curiosity may be satisfied by an experiment in dissection or by reading a textbook – by anything, in short, that conveys the requisite information. The information that satisfies my curiosity here also brings it to an end. Sexual curiosity, by contrast, renews itself endlessly; for the object of curiosity is not the bodily region as such, but the region 'as inhabited by a pleased consciousness', and the pleasure is a dynamic thing, which has a constantly shifting significance in the experience of the person who feels it. Curiosity is in part directed towards his feeling, and therefore moves always onwards as his feeling evolves.

'Curious pleasure' rests fixated upon this experience: it is the essence of childish sexuality, and of the sexual stratagems of paedophiles, for whom the important sexual episode is one of 'exposure' of the pleasurable part, while soliciting an inexperienced interest in it. The 'dirty little secret' of the Freudians is, however, of no significance in desire, where the sexual part is interesting only on account of its dramatic role. A woman is interested in her lover's sexual parts because she wishes to be penetrated by *him*, and to feel him feeling pleasure inside her. The penis is the avatar of his presence, and the ground that it crosses in entering her is at once overrun and occupied by the man himself. All mere curiosity is dissolved in this experience; the excitement concerns the entire action of the participants and all that they are and mean to each other. The intentionality of arousal overcomes and abolishes that of curiosity, directing the woman's response towards the other, as the all-inclusive object of a personal concern. At the same time, however, crucial features of his embodiment – such as the thrusting motion of his sexual parts – stand out in the field of her attention, sharply etched and immovable in the enveloping cloud of pleasure.

The aim of desire

What, then, is the aim of desire? In order to answer this question, we must distinguish the various components in the intentional structure of desire. The desires of animals have a relatively simple intentionality, captured in the propositional attitude which denotes the aim or direction of desire. The desires that are indicative of our rational nature are very different, and do not as a rule have the simple goal-directed intentionality of animal desire, even when there is a recognisable goal. Consider that most goal-directed of human activities – football. Here the player's aim changes from moment to moment, but may usually be summarised as the aim to score goals. At the same time, there is an overriding project – that of winning – which might remain unachieved without the game being a failure. The players play, not merely in order to score goals or to win, but for the pleasure of playing – a pleasure of team-work, exercise and excited participation in a common enterprise. Finally there is an overall 'fulfilment' which may or may not be granted: the 'good game', in which enjoyment, achievement and beneficial exercise come together, providing an experience that is full of meaning to those who experience it. If someone asked, what is the aim of football?, he could be answered therefore in any one of four ways: there is the immediate aim (scoring), the longer-term project (winning), the motive (enjoyment) and the fulfilment (an experience of 'meaning').

Football is a sophisticated, rule-guided activity, and its structure is not that of the sexual act, not even of the act performed by the sexual athlete, anxious only to 'score'. However, the interpersonal responses tend to exhibit the same kind of multi-layered intentionality as social activities – which is not surprising, for they *are* social activities. Consider anger. This has the initial aim of punishment – of injuring another who has done you wrong. For many people anger does not proceed beyond that stage. At the same time, it is implicit in the very rational capacities that make it possible to be angry that the subject of anger will tend to proceed further along the road upon which anger sets him. From the initial aim of anger there emerges, as a rational continuation, the long-term project of vindication and repentance. The angry man who can vindicate his cause, and secure the repentance of the offender, has not only expressed his anger; he has also, in an important sense, fulfilled it. He has worked it through to its triumph, and given to it the form which it naturally demands. This long-term project is one that requires cooperation from the object. The angry man must persuade the other to see himself in the same light that he is seen in by the one who is angry, and thereby come to rue what he has done. A complete account of the intentionality of anger would go further still, and attempt to describe the 'fulfilling' anger – the anger which, being properly directed, and properly prosecuted, secures for the subject the best benefits that anger can confer. For this too, in a rational being, is a part of the aim of anger, even if it is an aim that can seldom be accomplished.

To return, however, to sexual desire. The full theory of its intentionality will not be complete before the end of this book, when I shall attempt to describe the fulfilment of desire. But we are now in a position to describe the initial aim, and to indicate some of the further, longer-term projects which that aim implies. In true sexual desire, the aim is 'union with the other', where 'the other' denotes a particular person, with a particular perspective upon my actions. The reciprocity which is involved in this aim is achieved in the state of mutual arousal, and the interpersonal character of arousal determines the nature of the 'union' that is sought. To put the matter shortly: the initial aim of desire is physical contact with the other, of the kind which is the object and the cause of arousal. No such quest for arousal enters into normal friendship or into the tender affection towards a child, even when these are focused on the embodiment of the object. Arousal is, therefore, the most important differential of desire.

In the light of our previous study of embodiment and the individualising intentionality of desire, we can see that the aim of desire, so described, must involve the other *essentially*. He cannot lend himself to my sexual purpose, without my purposes being focussed on him, as the particular person he is. It is he who is embodied in the creature whom I caress, and it is his perspective that is caught up in the compromising drama of arousal.

That is not to forbid the possibility of a sexuality that flits from object to object with orgiastic relish for novelty – the *Aphrodite pandemos* of unfettered lust. It is simply to point out, what is evidently true, that the 'novelty' that is sought is not that of 'new sensations', 'new positions', 'new contortions' or whatever – but that of *new people*. In other words, what is sought is a renewal of the *aim* of desire, with another person. And to renew the aim of desire is to begin again, with a new desire. Just how far this can be accomplished is another matter. Whatever the peculiarities of orgiastic desire, it is no exception to the rule that the other person enters essentially into the aim of desire.

Likewise with randiness, the state of the sailor who storms ashore, with the one thought 'woman' in his body. His condition might be described as desire for a woman, but for no particular woman. Such a description, however, seriously misrepresents the transition that occurs when the woman is found and he is set on the path of satisfaction. For now he has found the woman whom he wants, whom he seeks to arouse and upon whom his thoughts and energies are focused. It would be better to say that, until that moment, he desired *no* woman. His condition was one of desiring to desire. And such was his need that he took an early opportunity to gratify his longing: to exchange the desire to desire for desire. It is an important feature of sexual desire that it should arise in this way from a generalised impulse. Nevertheless, desire is as distinct from the impulse that compels it as is anger from the excess of adrenalin. One should think of 'sexual hunger' as one thinks of the hunger for conversation, not as an appetite, but as a predisposition towards an individualising response.

The aim of sexual desire does not stop short at 'union'. There is the further and developing project of sexual pleasure. Now arousal can be achieved without sexual pleasure, although pleasure requires arousal, both in the subject and in the object. Sexual pleasure is directed towards the arousal of the other, and a pleasure that does not require the other to be aroused – as when a man performs the sexual act on the body of a frigid witness – is perverted. The extreme case of such pleasure is that of the necrophiliac, and a man who is indifferent to his partner's pleasure is, in a sense, a disguised necrophiliac: if his excitement is in fact enhanced by the other's frigidity, it is because he can enjoy her only under the aspect of death. In his sexual behaviour, he in a sense wishes her dead.

Sexual pleasure carries the subject further along the path of arousal. It involves him still more deeply with the object of his delight, reinforcing his need for the other's response and for the other's increasing self-identification with the sexual act. But, someone might object, where does this all end, if not in orgasm or in some such pleasurable event? And why, then, does orgasm not feature as the *ultimate* end of this desire, the final fulfilling episode? Why should we wish to look elsewhere for sexual fulfilment?

Consider again the case of anger. The man who explodes in anger certainly relieves his feelings, and may afterwards feel pleasant sensations of relaxation, as the adrenalin ebbs from his system. But this temporary explosion is not part of the intentionality of his anger, since it bears no relation to the thoughts which motivate him. If *this* is what he wants, he would be as well fulfilled by an injection of adrenalin; why bother with the time-wasting search for an appropriate occasion and the risky perception of another's insult? Besides, is it not unjust to achieve relief by persecuting another, when an injection would have done just as well? Clearly, the pleasure of release is here of no account in the project of anger, even if it may feature in a scientific explanation of 'what goes on'. Similarly with orgasm. Although the experience is all-important, it is not part of the aim or project of desire. For it has no root in the thought upon which desire is founded, and plays no part in the continuation of the aim of union. In a very important sense, it is an *interruption* of congress, from which the subject must recover, as and when he can.

To see the orgasm as the aim of desire is as misguided as to see the exultation experienced by a player upon scoring a goal as the aim of football, rather than as a pleasurable offshoot of an aim fulfilled. But there is more to orgasm-worship than that: it is not *merely* the result of a false assimilation of desire to appetite. Spiritually speaking, it is also the sign of a peculiar and prevalent superstition: the belief that for every human activity there must be some single and evident experience which constitutes its success and which can be obtained not by virtue but by skill (to use an Aristotelian dichotomy). In other words, it results from the idea that sexual gratification is available to everyone, whatever his moral character, and can be achieved by technique. The roots of this superstition need not concern us – although Tocqueville's analysis of American democracy suggests that they may not be hard to trace.[29] But its consequences are of some importance. In order to be construed as matters of technique, human purposes must be sufficiently specific, and sufficiently circumscribed, to be the subject-matter of advice, in which end and means can be properly separated. The other person, on this view, cannot be described as the end of desire: he therefore figures as the means, as a substitute for whatever sophisticated appliance (*machine désirante*) might fulfil his functions better than himself. Such is the price of the ethos of 'available success' – the ethos that sees every human project in terms of an equally distributed achievement.

The orgasm could not be the aim of sexual desire, even if it is sometimes the aim of what I have called 'curious pleasure'. The other person is not the means to satisfy desire, but part of the end of desire. Suppose a man were to masturbate, entertaining a stream of disjointed fantasies, occasionally wandering to the thought of his tax bill, his child's future and the scandalous behaviour of his neighbour's cat. The process might lead to orgasm and presumably has orgasm as its aim; but it is not an expression of desire. Imagine now the same man performing the same movements, but with his eyes fixed on the woman who undresses in the neighbouring window. Now there is a fantasy object of desire. What would enable us to say that the man really desires the woman? The very least is that he should seek to gain her interest and complicity in his act, or that he should entertain fantasies of her participation. He wants not just to do this thing, but to involve her in it. Of course, nobody with any sense could imagine that he could achieve his purpose in *this* way; his motive is likely to be not desire but curious pleasure, and the woman herself enters as a mere instrument in the fantasy which helps him to achieve his aim. Indeed, it is a feature of all such immodest, self-regarding sexual conduct that it tends to regard the other, not as the object, but as the instrument, of sexual release, so that the other cannot be the object of desire. Being treated in this way the other feels outraged and degraded, and under most systems of criminal law indecent exposure is treated as a serious personal assault.

There are two further stages on the way of desire that we must mention: the project of intimacy, and the fulfilment of desire in erotic love. Intimacy is the point to which the unveiling gestures of love-making are directed, and it is a project that is disclosed already in the first glances of desire. The glance which sets lovers apart from the crowd speaks in an undertone of things which are outside the sphere of others' knowledge. The project of intimacy arises automatically, although not inevitably, from the bond of desire. It is the point to which desire naturally leads, by its own devices. Generalised lust can be sustained only by complex strategies of replacement, such as those of the orgy, which prevent the passage from pleasure to intimacy – which prevent the carnal 'knowledge' of the other. But it is a natural continuation of sexual pleasure to pursue such knowledge – to aim one's words, caresses and glances, as it were, into the heart of the other, and to know him from the inside, as a creature who is part of oneself.

Just as sexual pleasure tends to intimacy, so does intimacy tend to love – to a sense of commitment founded in the mutuality of desire. For the person who is compromised by his desire for another has acquired a crucial vulnerability: the vulnerability of one who has been overcome in his body by the embodied presence of another. This vulnerability is finally assuaged only in love (as Gilda, in *Rigoletto*, assuages her brief moment of arousal in the arms of the Duke of Mantua by sacrificing her life for him). It is through studying erotic love, therefore, that we shall be able to characterise in full the intentionality of desire.

92

Those remarks will be justified in later chapters. Before leaving the present discussion, however, it is important to see what they do not imply. In making erotic love into the fulfilment of desire, I am no more implying that all sexual desire leads to love than I am implying that all anger leads to vindication and repentance, or that all football leads to the 'good game', simply by identifying those conditions as the fulfilment of the two respective activities. The intentionality of interpersonal emotions varies from place to place and time to time. The fulfilment that we recognise in vindication may be attributed in some other culture to revenge. Intentionality in these complex cases is a vector that may be continued in a variety of ways by the admixture of other concerns. To some extent it will become a matter for moral argument that we should wish to construct the conditions which constrain desire in one direction rather than another. In using the term 'fulfilment' I am already implying that the intentional structure that I identify as a natural continuation of the aim and project of desire – the structure which leads first to intimacy and then to love – is also to be recommended. By the end of the book I shall have come clean (or as clean as I can) about my reasons.

This emphasis on intimacy does not imply that all sexual desire is cosy, gentle or faithful. Far from it. However, every developed form of sexual desire will tend to reach beyond the present encounter to a project of inner union with its object. For some this union can be secured only by the dissolution of the object, his conversion into the suffering recipient of one's will: such was the Marquis de Sade. For others, it can be secured only by seduction, in which the whole self is concentrated into the initial act of love and then afterwards withheld: such was Don Juan. For others still, it can be secured only by the total dedication of one's being to the other, so as to seek absolute possession and a removal of the other from the commerce of daily life: such was Tristan. I shall discuss these archetypes of desire in more detail in Chapter 6.

I have argued that desire focuses on the embodiment of the other, and upon the first-person perspective which that embodiment reveals. I went on to suggest that, as a result of this, the other's individuality – his individuality, not as animal, but as self – becomes inextricably entwined with the intentionality of desire. I then briefly sketched the aim of desire – the aim of 'union' with the other – and the various 'moments' which that aim contains. However, before filling out that sketch, and giving the necessary grounds for identifying the fulfilment of desire in the nuptial terms that I have ventured, we must pause to confront the difficult idea of individuality. For this idea lies at the root of the universally acknowledged mystery of sexual experience.

5
THE INDIVIDUAL OBJECT

In the previous chapter I gave a preliminary sketch of the aim of desire, which is 'union with the other', founded in a response to his individual embodiment. Poets and philosophers have thought of this aim as unfulfillable, because paradoxical. The nature of the paradox has, however, been a matter of dispute. Lucretius, mindful of his materialist metaphysic, believed it to reside in the desire for unity between two separate bodies. Because one may be tempted to agree with Yeats, that Dryden's translation of the relevant passage from Book IV is the finest description of sexual intercourse in the language, it is fitting to use it as a reminder of the familiar experience:

> So Love with fantomes cheats our longing eyes,
> Which hourly seeing never satisfies;
> Our hands pull nothing from the parts they strain,
> But wonder o're the lovely limbs in vain:
> Nor when the Youthful pair more closely join,
> When hands in hands they lock, and thighs in thighs they twine
> Just in the raging foam of full desire,
> When both press on, both murmur, both expire,
> They grip, they squeeze, their humid tongues they dart,
> As each wou'd force their way to t'other's heart:
> In vain; they only cruze about the coast,
> For bodies cannot pierce, nor be in bodies lost:
> As sure they strive to be, when both engage,
> In that tumultuous momentary rage,
> So 'tangled in the nets of love they lie,
> Till man dissolves in that excess of joy.
> Then, when the gather'd bag has burst its way,
> And ebbing tides the slacken'd nerves betray,
> A pause ensues; and Nature nods a while,
> Till with recruited rage new spirits boil;

And then the same vain violence returns,
With flames renew'd the erected furnace burns.
Agen they in each other wou'd be lost,
But still by adamantine bars are crossed;
All wayes they try, successless all they prove,
To cure the secret sore of lingring love.

Others have not seen the paradox in Lucretius' way, which takes the idea of 'union' literally, and suggests a project which no one in his right mind would ever embark on. The paradox is more usually derived from a tension between two things: between the subject's interest in the individuality of the other and his attempt to 'capture' that individuality in an activity of 'physical' contact. A high-flown gloss on this idea is Sartre's version of the paradox, which I shall discuss below. According to Sartre, desire aims to possess the other in his freedom – and therefore to hold as object that which can exist only as subject. On this view, the clash between the interest in the other's subjective identity and the attention to his body is glossed in terms of the metaphysical incommensurability between self and other. Similar ways of phrasing the paradox can be found in Schopenhauer,[1] in Hegel[2] and in Kierkegaard.[3] Sometimes the ruling thought is this: you can desire another only as an individual, and therefore only as a *subject*. And yet you can possess him only as an instance of his species – since you can possess him only as an object. Sometimes the paradox is expressed in terms of an idea of freedom: I am desired only as a free being, but enjoyed only in an act that renders me unfree. It is a singular charm of Sartre's theory that these two paradoxes become one and the same.

The paradox can only begin to seem persuasive, however, if we can uphold the first premise: that I desire the other *as* an individual and that the individuality of the other resides in his nature as a subject. The premise has two parts: one relating to the intentional object of desire, and the other to the metaphysical idea of individuality. It is claimed that I see the other *as* an individual, and also that his 'individuality' resides in his nature as a subject. It may be that the metaphysical thesis is false, even though it captures the sense of individuality that is involved in the intentionality of desire. In which case the paradox is with us immediately, in the form of a metaphysical illusion residing in the heart of sexual desire. In order to clarify this issue it is necessary to begin by noting some of the features of interpersonal attitudes which might lead us to speak of the 'individuality' of their object. I shall consider six such features, corresponding to six distinctions among attitudes.

Distinctions among attitudes

The universal and the particular

Some interpersonal attitudes are such that a universal (i.e. the sense of an n-place predicate) enters into their intentional object and provides the true object of attention. Such attitudes are directed towards the individual only as an instance of a kind. Among these 'universal' attitudes the moral emotions – indignation, admiration, contempt and so on – are paramount. If I feel contempt for James it is because of some feature of James: had William possessed that feature, I should have felt contempt for William as well. The object of contempt is the particular – James – as an instance of the universal (coward, selfish oaf or whatever). Of course, to rehearse a point familiar from the discussion of Hare's 'universalisability',[4] the universal may be so specific that, as a matter of fact, only James *does* exemplify it. But it must be possible to characterise it, without making 'identifying reference' to James. What I despise is James' cowardice or selfishness, and I would feel *just the same* towards anyone else who showed the same defect. If I did not feel just the same, this is because something has been left out of the 'description under which' James is despised, something that would make the distinction between James and those others towards whom I react differently.

The idea of universality must be disentangled from that of the 'formal object' of an emotion, explained in Appendix 2. The formal object is given by a description that the intentional object *must* satisfy if it is to be the object of the given feeling. For example, John can only be the object of contempt if he is thought to be inferior in some way. This 'formal' restriction states a necessary condition upon the object of contempt, but it does not provide the full 'description under which' any given person is despised.

Attitudes like love, hatred and sexual desire have particular objects. They impose on the subject no obligation to respond likewise on like occasions. Although there is, no doubt, some feature of James which is a reason (perhaps even *the* reason) why I love him, I am not obliged to love William as well, just because he shares that feature. (Imagine, if it were otherwise, the impossible love-life of identical twins.) Here we have a reflection of Kant's distinction between love and esteem, and the beginnings of an account of why he should have chosen to divide the 'pathological' from the 'rational' as he did.[5]

The reason-based, the reason-free and the reason-involving

The last paragraph draws attention to a second distinction. Some attitudes can be entertained only on the basis of 'justifying thoughts' – that is, on the basis of reasons which seem to support them. Other attitudes are, as I shall put it, 'reason-free', in that, while there *may* be reasons for them, their existence does not depend upon the subject's *having* reasons. Attitudes which are universal are automatically reason- based. Their being so admits of degrees, and it is a mark of the moral attitudes that the subject's belief in the existence of reasons is here unlimited.[6]

Attitudes which are particular may also be reason-based. An example is provided by resentment. My resentment of you depends upon the particular relation between us: I may therefore resent you for some act or quality that I would not resent in another. Nevertheless resentment is reason-based. If I resent you it is *on account of* some feature, which I also believe to justify my feeling. There are, however, particular attitudes which are not reason-based at all. I may just want something, for no reason (although perhaps not a saucer of mud).[7] Some animal desires are reason-free in this sense. A dog just wants to sniff another – for no reason (although of course there may be a perfectly good evolutionary rationalisation of his act). People sniff each other similarly (a child its mother, a man his wife). Those philosophers who argue (with Elizabeth Anscombe)[8] that all desire depends upon a 'desirability characterisation' of its object overlook the fact that the concept of desirability belongs only to the explanation of the behaviour of rational beings. The concept of desire, however, may be used in the description and explanation of behaviour that is merely animal. That is an *a priori* reason for thinking that there can be desire which is not founded on a conception of desirability. The reader should therefore have no difficulty in accepting what is in fact the most natural description of the desire to sniff.

Love, I have claimed, is not universal. But is it reason-based? Some philosophers have doubted that it is or could be.[9] However, there seems to be a definite tendency within love to find a *basis* in its object. I believe that there is a reason why I love James, and that, if I cannot now find the reason, this is because of a lapse of memory, a failure of expression or an epistemological fault. It is unclear, however, that love *is* really based in the reasons that are offered for it. It might be better to say that love *seeks* to base itself in reasons, and is liable to suffer reversals when its reasons are destroyed. A truly reason-based attitude – like resentment – is liable to *refutation*, by a demonstration that the object does not possess the feature for which he is resented. Love seems liable to be undermined, and to suffer every kind of catastrophic reversal, but not exactly to be refuted. It might be better, therefore, to describe love as 'reason-involving', so as not to obscure the real distinctions among states of mind that we are here considering.

It is possible to greet with a certain scepticism the view that an attitude can be reason-based or reason-involving and yet fail to be universal. Pascal held that love is based in reasons, and concluded that it could not, therefore, be construed (except paradoxically) as love of the individual:

> He who loves someone on account of her beauty, does he love her? no; for smallpox, which removes her beauty without killing the person, will cause him no longer to love. And if someone loves me for my judgement or my memory, does he truly love *me*? no; for I can lose these qualities without ceasing to be. Where then is the *I*, if it is not in the body or in the soul? And how can one love the body and the soul, unless on account of qualities which are in no way constitutive of the *I*, since they are perishable? For should one love the soul-substance of a person abstractly, and whatever qualities might reside in it? That could only be, and would be, unjust. One never therefore loves the person, but only the qualities; or, if one loves the person, it must be said that it is the totality of qualities which constitutes the person.[10]

Condillac rightly criticises this argument, for its dependence upon the 'perishable' nature of qualities: as though I were to say to the man whose foot I cut off: 'Since you have survived without your foot, then it was not *you* that I injured.'[11] But note the important metaphysical implications that Pascal draws from what is in fact no more than an argument about the intentionality of love. The argument collapses, just so soon as it is seen that reason-dependence and universality are logically distinct.

The difference is brought out most clearly by the important case of aesthetic attitudes. Aesthetic interest is interest in the individual object, not as instance of a universal, but as the particular object that it is.[12] A work of art may be a type with many tokens – as is a novel or a symphony. But to identify the type is to identify the individual, and any interest in the type is interest in the individual which instantiates it. My love of Beethoven's Violin Concerto may coexist with aversion towards every other work of music, without for that reason being inconsistent with itself. Aesthetic interest is nevertheless reason-based.[13] There has to be *something* that could be said or pointed to in answer to the question 'Why are you interested in that?' If there were no answer, we should be dealing with a case, not of aesthetic interest, but of torpor.

It might be objected that the examples – personal love and aesthetic interest – have been artificially created: I have done no more than stipulate that they are states of mind which are particular, while being based in, or while involving, reasons. It is true that there need not have been any states of mind corresponding to my two descriptions. But it is also true that the features I have described belong to the real essence of whatever possesses them. They define types of intentionality; moreover, it is in terms of their intentionality that states of mind are distinguished by those who enjoy or suffer them. There really is such a thing as personal love, and its involvement with reason is part of what it means to us, and explains why we should have noticed its existence in the first place.

Further theory as to the distinction between the reason-based, the reason-free and the reason-involving is a matter of considerable difficulty. It is worth remarking, however, that the three-fold distinction might be approached in the same spirit as Elizabeth Anscombe approaches that between intentional and non-intentional action.[14] We could say, as a first step (but it would be no more than a first step), that an attitude is reason-based if it admits application of (a certain sense of) the question 'Why do you feel that?' And here the answer may be a kind of place-holder for an answer, as in the case of intentional action: 'I am not sure why exactly' (to be distinguished from what Anscombe calls 'a rejection of the question'). The more one has to *look* for the reason – the more one has to 'discover why', for example, one loves a person, even when one is firm in the belief that, loving him, one has a reason – the more we should speak of love, not as reason-based, but as reason-involving.

If we were to take that approach, it would become as difficult to attribute reason-based and reason-involving attitudes to speechless creatures as it is difficult, on Anscombe's view, to describe their actions as intentional. It should be noted, however, that for the purposes of my argument it is quite unnecessary to decide these difficult questions of philosophical psychology.

The attentive and the non-attentive

Some attitudes focus on specific features of their object, and overlook others. Fear, for example, concentrates upon the present danger and all that causes it, while ignoring those features of the threatening object which might have been regarded with pleasure or awe. Such an attitude is 'non-attentive', in that it must necessarily overlook some part of what is presented to it. By contrast, attentive attitudes overlook nothing: no feature of their object is to be discounted, and no feature can gain prominence to the total exclusion of others, without the attitude changing. The most familiar example of an attentive attitude is aesthetic interest, every feature of whose object is relevant to the attention that embraces it. But it should also be recognised that certain kinds of love –

erotic love among them – are similar. The lover for whom every hair on his beloved's head is of individual significance is like the aesthete who ponders every note of a score. This kind of lust for detail is an inevitable dramatic continuation of attentive interest which, because it regards everything as relevant, tries also to find nothing insignificant.[15]

The attentiveness of aesthetic interest has been variously described; but in one form or another it has been acknowledged by most post-Kantian aesthetic theories. And it has given rise to a dangerous misunderstanding. Since every feature of a work of art is relevant to my interest in it, I am naturally disposed to look for connections among the features that will enable me to hold them in a unity before my mind. If I succeed in achieving this unity, this is a fact about me: I am able to hold together in my attention the totality of the object before me. Of course, it is only by virtue of the work of art that I *am* able to do this. But we should not deduce therefrom that the work of art itself possesses some kind of unity (whether or not organic), and that, in appreciating it aesthetically, it is this unity that I perceive. It is a further question to ask which features of a work of art facilitate the enterprise of unified perception. Perhaps there is no single answer to this question. Perhaps the question is to be answered separately for every work. Perhaps, in short, it is a question, not for the philosopher, but for the critic. And yet, how many philosophers have been tempted to derive, from the premise that aesthetic response is attentive, the conclusion that works of art are peculiarly unified objects, perhaps with a special kind of metaphysical individuality that sets them apart from the rest of man's creation?[16]

It is a like fallacy, and one that we shall have cause frequently to consider, that the object of love is endowed with a peculiar unity – a unity which binds all his features together in a totality that can be seized in a single intuitive act. And, since his physical presence so manifestly presents me with no such unity – for physically he has but the unity of an animal, from whom hairs and toenails may be removed at no cost to the whole – there arises the idea that his unity is of another kind, and has some other source. There arises, in fact, the great metaphysical illusion of love: the illusion that, in seeing another under the aspect of love, I am confronted with the underlying 'transcendental' unity from which all his actions flow. There are other sources of this illusion. But it is instructive to recognise its analogy with a major error of post-Kantian aesthetics – the fallacy of believing that the 'intentional unity' of an attitude is also the perception of a 'material unity' in its object. This, I shall argue, is an intellectual lapse of which no human being can, in his everyday existence, be cured.

The purposeful and the purposeless

The last distinction is sometimes glossed in terms of another, with which, however, it is not identical. Some attitudes approach (or retreat from) their object with an 'end in view'; some do not. To the first kind belong all our more practical emotions, such as aggression (which aims to hurt) and fear (which aims to avoid). Other attitudes – aesthetic interest again provides a paradigm – have no 'end in view'. They are, in Kant's useful expression, 'disinterested' (*ohne Interesse*), divorced from immediate practical concerns. When I approach some object with a particular end in view, my purpose determines a criterion of relevance – some features of the object have a bearing on it, others do not. Hence there is a tendency in the philosophy of art to explain the attentiveness of aesthetic interest in terms of its purposeless character, which deprives us of the ability to distinguish the relevant from the redundant.[17]

It is, however, far too simple to reduce the two distinctions to one. For there could be attitudes which are attentive, and yet also purposeful. Love is one of them, but a more vivid example is given by sexual desire. We cannot deny that desire has an aim; yet it would seem to have – or at least to tend towards – the attentive character of love: every feature of the object may enhance or threaten desire, and nothing can be dismissed *a priori* as irrelevant to the beholder's interest. It might be held that, if this is so, desire must be reason-involving – and perhaps even reason-based. But that conclusion is too hasty. Whether or not an attitude is reason-involving depends upon the *kind* of threat that new discoveries offer to it. A discovery which destroys a belief upon which the attitude is founded involves the refutation of a *reason*; it threatens the attitude by threatening its intellectual foundation. A discovery which simply draws attention to some new and unnoticed feature, and one about which one had no previous belief or unbelief, threatens, not the intellectual foundation, but the immediate focus, of the subject's state of mind. The difference here may not seem immediately obvious. But it will become obvious in the course of our discussion.

The distinction between the purposeful and the purposeless is far from clear. Consider friendship. In one sense this is purposeless: there is no 'end in view' which motivates the friend when he seeks the company of his chosen intimate. Yet it would be wrong to say that friendship is purposeless, if we mean that there are no aims or projects which are characteristic of a friend. A 'true friend' seeks the well-being of the other and actively pursues it, whenever appropriate. However, if there is some *further* purpose – for example, if he pursues the other's well-being in order to ingratiate himself or to seek a return in kind – then we should say that he is not motivated by friendship. Moreover, one may desire the well-being of another out of charity, out of disinterested concern for a well-ordered universe, out of religious duty or simply 'for its own sake', without being motivated by human affection. Concern for the well-being of a friend is a particular *kind* of concern, not truly detachable from the motive of friendship. The attempt to detach the purpose of friendship from the practice of friendship is therefore fraught with peculiar difficulties.

Here one might borrow a forgotten technicality of theology, and describe the purposes of friendship as *immanent*. That is, they lie in the practice of friendship itself, and could never be achieved by other means or from another motive. In a sense, this makes friendship purposeless – since it has no detachable purpose. In another sense, it makes friendship profoundly purposeful, since *all* of friendship can now be subsumed within a single ruling aim. Friendship, to put it another way, is the *description* of an aim. It denotes an activity that is a purpose in itself.

In most interpersonal attitudes the purposeless, the purposeful and the 'immanently purposeful' intersect and qualify one another. When I enter a shop and begin my transaction with the assistant, my attitude is an inextricable mixture of these three components. The immanent purpose of pleasurable conversation mingles with the purposeless contemplation of products that I have no wish to buy, and with the purposeful negotiations of the present purchase, to produce that spontaneous 'readiness for contract' which is the normal condition of economic existence. One can see much of the fashionable defence of market economies, in terms of the 'tacit understanding' which is integral to human cooperation, as a plea for the maintenance of arrangements in which economic purposes are always qualified by the immanent ends of social existence, and so pose no threat to them. Reflection on such discussions – and in particular on those of Hayek and Polanyi[18] – must certainly lead us to perceive how very difficult it is to effect a division between the purposeful and the purposeless in human conduct. Nevertheless, this distinction (which we have seen to be a threefold distinction) can be effectively employed when discussing the fundamental core of human intentionality. It will always make sense to ask of some basic intentional structure – that of fear, say, or anger, or sexual desire – to which category it belongs.

The transferable and the non-transferable

The above distinction leads us by natural steps to a fifth, and one which has already featured in the arguments of preceding chapters: the distinction between the transferable and the non-transferable. It would make sense to say to someone who was reaching for a glass of water, 'Take this, it will do just as well,' handing him a glass of beer or orange juice, or something else to quench his thirst. Here the desire can be transferred from object to object; or, if you prefer, objects can be substituted for one another, without precipitating a change of mental attitude.

Some interpersonal attitudes are transferable. Suppose someone, in a fit of rage at humanity, attacks another in the street. He desires to beat up this particular person; but his desire would be transferable to another. It would make sense (although it would not be sensible) to say, 'Take this man, he will do just as well.' Transferability is here a consequence of the generalised nature of the aggression underlying the original desire. Of course, a man may run amok, like the Ajax of Sophocles, under the delusion that each recipient of his blows has personally offended him. But the pathos of Ajax resides in the fact that his rage, although not transferable, is, by a divine hand, humiliatingly diverted.

It might be thought that, whenever the other person enters specifically into the intentionality of my attitude, the attitude is not transferable. But there are a variety of cases to consider. Suppose that I am looking for a companion to go with me to a performance of *The Wild Duck*. 'I was counting on Paul, but he is busy.' 'Take John; he likes Ibsen. He would do just as well.' The obvious contrast with that example is the case of love. It seems absurd to reply to the remark 'John, my beloved, has left me, what shall I do?' with the answer 'Take Paul, he will do just as well.' I say it *seems* absurd, because later I shall have to consider arguments which suggest that this sense of absurdity is no more than a well-founded illusion, to use again the Leibnizian idiom.

What (if anything) is the relevant difference between the two cases? In the first case there is a definite and non-immanent purpose for which I require my companion. Is this the difference? It is not obvious that it is. There are attitudes which are seemingly non-transferable, and yet which possess definite aims: sexual desire being the obvious example. Whether or not we wish to say that the aim is, in such cases, always to some extent *immanent* is another matter. Returning to Kant's discussion of sexual desire, we can see a clear tendency (manifest throughout his moral philosophy) to explain the non-transferability of interpersonal attitudes in terms of the fact that their object is seen 'not as a means only, but as an end'. (Precisely the same tendency can be seen in Kant's attempt to explain the individuality of the aesthetic object in terms of the 'disinterested' nature of the attitude which we direct towards it.) Presumably to see someone as an end is to have only immanent purposes for him (purposes into which he enters essentially).

However, it should be said at once that Kant's approach to these matters – commendable though it is for its ruling perception, that interpersonal relations generally, and morality in particular, are founded upon the irreplaceable individuality of persons – is far too sweeping. Consider curiosity. This is a thoroughly transferable attitude. A man curious about cows may pass quite freely from one to another, satisfying his curiosity on each. And yet his curiosity need have no purpose other than itself, and certainly no specific purpose comparable to a visit to the theatre. The object of curiosity is treated, not as a means, but as an end in itself.

It is better, I think, to approach the given example through the idea of relevance. The aim of the theatre-goer settles what is 'relevant' to his interest. He is well served by someone with the relevant properties, ill served by someone without them. His attitude is transferable because there are relevant properties which serve to focus it, even though he needs a companion (that is, an individual instantiation of those properties) and not just a Bradleyan set of quality instances (something which it would be very uncomfortable to take to the theatre). Of course you would be insulted to learn that you were wanted as a companion *merely* as the instantiation of a universal. It is quite important that I hide from you (and from myself) the idea that someone else might 'do just as well'. (Almost all of common courtesy can be seen as a stratagem for hiding that thought.) But the idea is nevertheless cogent. (Thus we are amused, or saddened, by the advertisement in *The New York Review of Books* which says: 'handsome, prosperous, male, bi-sexual, 39, seeks Jewish momma, into theatre, music (not pop), self-realisation, 30-35, Philadelphia area, own car and commitments, for meaningful erotic relationship.' For imagine the later quarrel, in which the woman says: 'But the description fits me exactly; what right have you to complain?' Maybe she should see her lawyer.)

We must distinguish here two kinds of transferability: the factual and the counterfactual. It is the latter which really concerns us. My anger at Alfred may be non-transferable, simply because it is bound up with the specific thing that Alfred did, and which no one else did. In this case it is not the fact of Alfred's being a person that makes my attitude non-transferable. For in a similar way I could be distressed at the particular meteorite that had made the crater in my garden. It would be absurd to take another catastrophe, however similar, and say, 'Take this, it will do just as well.' It was *this* meteorite, causing *this* catastrophe, that distressed me. In both cases, the identification of an individual object enters into the intentionality of the attitude. However, in another sense, the non-transferability of the attitude is here a trivial matter, for the reason that we can identify relevant features of the object that are the focus of what I feel. Had John done what Alfred did, I would have been just as angry with John; had another meteorite devastated my garden, I would have been just as distressed about that. These attitudes are factually, but not counterfactually, non-transferable.

The interesting cases are those of counterfactual non-transferability. I cannot say what properties of my Elizabeth would have to be possessed by another woman, for that woman to be an object of *this* present desire. If this is an illusion, it is nevertheless an illusion that we take most seriously, and by which we live. If the example of sexual desire does not seem plausible, then consider erotic love, the drama of which focuses almost entirely on a counterfactual thought: the thought that another person could not have been what this person is for me. That thought underlies all grief, all erotic bliss and every lover's suicide. (See the journey narrative, scene 3, of Chikamatsu's puppet play, *Love Suicides at Sonezaki.*)

The explanation might at once be offered that all these attitudes owe their counterfactual non-transferability to the simple fact that their objects are (or are thought to be) persons. It could never be the case, it might be said, that I should be so attached to or repelled by a mere thing as to be unable to envisage the counterfactual situation that would arouse in me a similar emotion. Could I be so attached to my piano that it would become impossible to say that another would do just as well?

Once again the example of aesthetic interest must cause us to hesitate. For we can have aesthetic interest in something that is not a person, and in doing so we regard it 'for its own sake', and without tolerating the idea that some other object might have done 'just as well'. It should not go unremarked that we commend as beautiful equally the object of aesthetic pleasure, the object of sexual desire and the object of love. And it is a plausible hypothesis that this language indicates a common intentional structure, which explains the enormous significance of these attitudes in concentrating our minds upon the here and now. Some philosophers have tried to explain aesthetic experience in quasi-personal terms. Taking their cue from Kant's idea that the aesthetic object is seen as purposive (although without purpose), they suppose that we see it as the expression of an intention, an idea or a character. The individualising intentionality of the aesthetic attitude is therefore merely a special case of the individualising intentionality of the interpersonal. But such suggestions are the result of theory, and the phenomena which they are invoked to explain can be understood without them. We can therefore suggest that counterfactual non-transferability is a separate property of an attitude from that of interpersonality.

Is sexual desire non-transferable? I have suggested that it is, and in order to defend the suggestion it is necessary to dispel certain possible misunderstandings. To say that desire is non-transferable is not to say that it is exclusive. Someone may desire several people: but not with the same desire. Nor does it follow that desire is not based in other states of mind (instincts, needs and so on) which *are* transferable. Consider Don Juan. The essence of his personality is seduction, and seduction is an interpersonal enterprise. You could not seduce an apple, a dog or a corpse, nor even a child (a problematic case about which I shall have more to say later), although all those can be put to sexual uses. Seducing is eliciting someone's consent, through representing yourself in a certain way. Don Juan is seductive because he feels passion for every woman that he meets, and yet his passion is not transferable. It would be absurd to interrupt his seduction of Zerlina with the announcement, 'Take this one, she will do just as well' (hence the pathos of Donna Elvira's interruption). The extraordinary feature of the Don (as Mozart depicts him) is not that he transfers a single passion to a succession of objects, but that his passion is constantly resurgent in novel guises. The sexual act is sufficient to annul (if not to fulfil) the previous desire, and to prepare the ground for another. Thus when Leporello reads from his catalogue, and tells us that '*in Espagna, son' già mill' e tre*', he is counting, not the objects of a single passion, but the diverse passions that they inspired. That is the source of Don Juan's mania, the 'demonism' which Mozart so brilliantly captures in '*Fin' caldo vino*'. This kind of desire is no more 'transferable' than is Tristan's for Isolde: it simply resurges in infinite forms. Like every sin, it is a form of unassuageable anxiety.

From the objective standpoint (outside the purview of human intentionality), we must recognise that sexual desire and erotic love are both manifestations of other things — of animal needs and emotional habits. These other things *can* be transferred from object to object and yet remain the same. Transferability is essential to the biological idea of a need, since a need is relative to a function, and a function can be fulfilled by any object with the relevant feature. However, although a lover may express his feelings in the words 'I need you', he does not mean 'I have a need which you happen to satisfy.' The emphasis is on the irreplaceable *you*. The need for sexual stimulation, and the need for companionship, can each be satisfied by infinitely many things. But this does not tell us anything about the intentionality of desire. A state of mind may not have the intentionality of the biological condition which underlies and explains it. To think otherwise is to imagine that you could derive the legal idea of a property right from a description of the territorial instinct, or the concept of authority from a description of the child's disposition to obey.

Mediate and immediate

There is another distinction which serves to align the sexual and the aesthetic and to set them apart from the moral. This is the distinction between attitudes which are founded upon the perception of their object (attitudes which I shall call 'immediate') and attitudes which depend only upon thought. Consider moral admiration. This is something that I may feel towards a person whom I have never met, simply on the basis of what I believe to be true of him. I may admire Cicero or Marcus Aurelius, without the least experience, whether literal or imaginative, of the men themselves. It is a received idea of aesthetics (received since Baumgarten invented the word),[19] that aesthetic appreciation is founded in the *perception* of its object, and cannot be based on thought alone. The point has been put in various ways. Some speak of the 'sensuous' nature of aesthetic interest; others refer to its 'concrete' or 'immediate' character; others argue that aesthetic judgement is distinguished by the fact that you must 'see the object for yourself'.[20] All these idioms suggest different ways of theorising a single observation.

It is evident that some attitudes are, like aesthetic interest, rooted in the actual experience of their object and cannot exist without that experience, while others (particularly those which are 'universal') can be detached from experience, since their intentionality is constructed from thought alone. Sexual desire belongs to the former category. It is awakened by an experience of embodiment – by the sight, sound or smell of its object. And it is as difficult to imagine a sexual desire which starts up from a mere description as it is difficult to imagine aesthetic appreciation 'at second hand'. We can indeed imagine a description that is so compelling that it serves to close the gap, as it were, between thought and experience – a kind of sexual equivalent of the descriptions which Thomas Mann gives us (in *Doktor Faustus*) of the works of Adrian Leverkühn. But such a description would provide an object for desire only because it would permit the subject to 'imagine what it would be like' to experience the embodiment of the person described. The example therefore simply confirms the point: that desire is dependent upon the experience which produces it. Hence the most plausible examples of 'vicarious desire' are those in which the subject is moved by a representation which enables him to create in imagination the embodied form of the object of desire. Such an example is provided by Mozart's *Magic Flute*, in which Tamino falls in love with Pamina upon seeing her portrait.

The immediacy of desire contributes in a way to its individualising intentionality. There seems, indeed, always to be a kind of nimbus of indexicality surrounding the object of desire: a sense of 'here and now'. The object of desire is identified by a physical presence which, even when merely imaginary, like the presence of Pamina in her portrait, is essentially 'perceived by me'. The beloved stands to me in an indexical relation. Or, to put the point in phenomenologese, he is always a 'this' for me. And this indexical element serves to concentrate my individualising thoughts, within the frame of an immediate perception. It seems as though I am presented, here and now, within the immediacy of my experience, with the individual other, whose nature could never be captured in a description, because it could never be translated from its 'given' sensory form.

Such thoughts are intoxicating, and it is as well to be aware of the consequence of giving way to them. Most importantly, the mystery of the 'substance' that lies behind its properties becomes compounded with the mystery of experience itself. An experience stands forever outside the concepts that would contain it. Hence, it is supposed, the irreducibility of a substance to its properties (the implausibility of a 'propertyless' description), is of a piece with the irreducibility of an experience to the thoughts which attempt to convey it. This confounding of mysteries may be observed both in aesthetic experience and in sexual desire. It motivates the neo-Platonist theory of love (see below), the idealist and expressionist theories of art and much of the Hindu philosophy of desire. It also lies behind Kant's otherwise unaccountable disposition to confound, in the *Critique of Pure Reason*, the distinction between individual and property with the distinction between intuition and concept.[21] I do not propose to unravel such confusions in their entirety. Rather, I shall allow them, in what follows, gently to unravel themselves. But, even without them, we can see strong reason to suppose that our disposition to describe the object of desire and the object of aesthetic interest in identical terms is no accident. The 'beautiful' is the proper object of attitudes that are attentive, non-transferable and immediate, and when someone refers to the object of some other attitude in these terms – when he refers, for example, to a beautiful machine, a beautiful proof, a beautiful case in law – it is because he has in this way surrendered himself to the immediate *experience* of something, so as to find order and significance in *it*.

The formal features of desire

The purpose of delineating the six distinctions to which I have referred is partly to disaggregate the highly complex claim that some of our attitudes are directed towards individuals *as* individuals, and others towards individuals only *as* members of some class. There is a sense in which universal attitudes may yet be directed towards individuals as individuals – for they may be without purpose (or with a merely 'immanent' purpose), and in this, somewhat narrow, sense, therefore may involve an interest in the individual as an end in himself. In fact this is exactly what is involved in the moral attitudes, such as esteem and contempt. Yet neither has the attentive character of love, and neither has the counterfactual non-transferability of aesthetic interest or desire. We have discovered therefore a nest of separate distinctions within the single distinction upon which Kant tried to found the morality of 'respect for persons'. And we should not be surprised, therefore, if we are now able to speak, both of love and desire, in ways which were forbidden to Kant by his own metaphysical ambition.

Sexual desire is particular: there is no 'universal object' which is its true focus, but only the particular object of pursuit. I shall later discuss this feature in more detail, in order to consider both its explanation and its real or imagined consequences.

Desire is not based in reasons, even though it could, on occasion, be justified, either from the first-person or from the third-person point of view. This matter of justification is one that I shall take up in Chapter 11. For present purposes it suffices to recognise that, while it is possible to argue against the pursuit of some given sexual object, there is something strange in the attempt to argue against desiring him. The best that I can do, in order to discourage your desire for Philip, is to draw your attention to features which you may not have noticed, and which you may find repulsive: 'How can you desire a man who greases his hair and picks his nose?' But is desire, like love, reason-involving? Does desire try to *find* the foundation which will also justify it? The question is difficult to answer.

For there seem to be two kinds of desire. The one is quite indifferent to the demands of reason, while the other tries – often unsuccessfully – to obey them. The second kind of desire, however, is already set upon the course of love, and if it is reason-involving it is in the way that love is reason-involving. This is the desire captured by Schumann, in *Frauenliebe und Leben*, which has no reality outside the need to love. Normally, when we refer to sexual desire, it is precisely to separate it from the love of which it can be a component. So identified, it ceases to be a part of desire, that it should be 'reason-involving'.

Desire has a purpose, although the purpose is partly immanent, inseparable from the particular object of pursuit. I have described this purpose as that of 'union', and given a partial characterisation of it, in terms of the aim of mutual arousal. As this book proceeds I shall continue to add to that description, until the full intentionality of desire is finally displayed.

Desire is attentive: any feature of its object may be brought within its focus, and all are relevant to its history and drama. Desire resembles aesthetic interest not only in that respect, but also in its immediacy: like aesthetic experience, desire finds its object in the immediate matter of experience – in the embodied form of the other, as he appears. Hence there can be no such thing as 'desire by hearsay' or 'desire by repute'. Finally, and most importantly, desire is non-transferable, and so, in Blake's words, 'binds another to its delight'.

Love is distinguished from desire, first in the actual content of its aim – which is immanent, but less specific than the aim of desire – and secondly in the fact of being reason-involving. Every love stands to be jeopardised by the new knowledge that will destroy the vital belief. The result of this knowledge may be catastrophic. Desire too has its catastrophes – the major one, jealousy, being closely connected with its individualising intentionality – but it is free at least from this one. And yet in that very freedom lies a further catastrophe. For desire survives the demonstration that its object is unworthy – and thus has a power to degrade the subject, by forcing him into intimate relations with a person whom he cannot esteem. Later I shall raise the question whether love, unlike desire, is mediate, able to live on a diet of thought alone.

It is now possible to rectify some of the misunderstandings, and uphold some of the insights, contained in Kant's two contrasts – between love and esteem, and between love and desire.[22] Esteem is universal, purposeless, non-attentive, reason-based, mediate and transferable. It is therefore different from love in every feature apart, perhaps, from its basis in reason and (perhaps) its mediacy. Desire differs from esteem in each of the formal features that we have discussed. And yet, paradoxically, it is love and desire which involve the full recognition of the other's individuality. Esteem, by its universal and transferable quality, passes over the individual case, and rests content with whatever displays the requisite qualities. To put it more immediately: esteem, unlike love or desire, is not a form of 'care'. It is hard to see how there could be a plausible morality which sets the individual before every abstraction, which recognises no value that is commensurate with the infinite value of the human person, and yet which regards care as no more than part of man's 'pathology'. It is only when we see love and desire as caught up within our moral perceptions that we shall be able to accomplish what Kant sought to accomplish. It is only then that we shall be able to give the grounds for a secular morality, in which the individual person is the final source of value. Kant mistakenly held that the distinction between seeing another as an individual and seeing him as an instance is to be captured in terms of the distinction between seeing as an end and seeing as a means. Hence he imagined that the purposeless character of esteem would secure its moral centrality. On the contrary, however; esteem is purposeless partly because it has *abstracted* from the individual object of care, and disentangled his moral worth from his individual existence. It is only in such purposeful attitudes as love, friendship and desire that he becomes, as an individual, irreplaceable.

The individual object

How can desire possess the intentional structure that we have described? How, in particular, can it be non-transferable? The obvious answer – that desire is directed towards the individual person, and not towards the type – is no more clear than the concept of the 'individual person' that is invoked in it. It is in terms of this concept that we must seek to understand, first the paradoxes, and then the fulfilment, of desire.

Individuum est ineffabile, says the scholastic tag. Many things are suggested by that utterance. Here is one of them: we make, because metaphysical necessity compels us, a distinction between the individual and the properties that attach to it. But how do we make this distinction? How do we separate, in thought, the individual from its properties? (I use the term 'property' loosely, so as to include relations: a property is determined by every meaningful predicate.) We seem to need some defining characteristic that constitutes the individual as *what* it is. But such a characteristic is a property, and how can a property be identical with the individual that bears it? Essential properties are still properties, distinguished only by the fact that their bearer cannot cease to have them without also ceasing to be.

Attempts have been made to circumvent this difficulty, through the idea of an individual essence – the *haecceitas* of Duns Scotus.[23] This is held to be an essential property, or list of essential properties, which is such that it can be instantiated by only *one* individual of a given kind, so that, in identifying it, one has also identified the individual which possesses it. Needless to say, the idea of an individual essence is fraught with difficulties. How can there be a property which, by its very nature, is instantiated only once? The most plausible examples are compromised by the paradoxes of theology (the property of being a god, for example, which seems to have at most one instance, but perhaps only because it has less than one). Other examples either smuggle in some covert reference to the single individual which instantiates them – the property of being identical with John, say – or else depend, for their unique instantiation, upon some accidental circumstance. Consider, for example, the property of being the tallest man in existence. It could indeed be said that this property can be instantiated by only one object: at the same time, however, it could never be an essential feature of any object that possesses it. It can always be said, of the tallest, the fattest, the cleverest man, that he might have been otherwise. The 'individual essence', construed so loosely, is not even an essential property – in which case, the idea that, in grasping the individual essence, one has truly grasped the *individual* becomes a nonsense. Hence only of some comparative properties has this ever been claimed: the most perfect, the most powerful, the most knowledgeable. And again this is because such are the attributes of God.[24]

The most plausible putative examples of individual essences are 'coordinate points'. Consider the universe of modern physics. It consists of spatio-temporal points and regions, variously modified by the distribution of energy. The individuals here are uniquely characterised by the spatio-temporal coordinates assigned to them. But what is it to possess a position within a system of coordinates? It is to possess a complex relational property. How is it that the mere possession of such a property suffices to individuate anything? Surely, only because we have some independent idea of what it is to occupy a spatio-temporal position. We individuate space–time points by relating them to the objects which lie in them. A point is not, for us, a true individual, but a place where individuals can be found. And although an individual may be uniquely identified by its place and time, it has neither position essentially, and might have been elsewhere and elsewhen. It is in any case rather a disappointment to be told that the ultimate 'substances' of our world have all their properties accidentally, other than their spatio-temporal location.

The now standard response to those difficulties is to reject the whole idea of an individual essence. It is said that we cannot possibly find the idea of individuality in a list of properties, for no such list can be attached essentially to only one thing. This cannot even be said of the complete description (the complete notion) of that thing. Any attempt to find such a property-description is an attempt to eliminate the distinction between reference and predication, between 'this' and 'such'.[25] A cluster of philosophical arguments, going back at least to Strawson's *Individuals*,[26] and having its ancestry in the discussions of medieval logicians, persuades us that 'this-ness' is not descriptive, but indexical, and of no indexical can there be a purely descriptive equivalent. If a coordinate system seems to provide us with a respectable way of identifying genuine individuals within it, it is because the employment of such a system is itself inherently indexical. No place has been individuated within any such system *for me*, until a 'here' and a 'now' (or, in the case of Kripke's coordinate system for persons, a 'me' or a 'him') have been picked out as belonging to it. Having identified one point as here and now, the rest falls into place. But until that identification we literally do not know what we are talking about.

But what is identified by such indexical 'identifying reference'? An old problem of Descartes' – that of the passage from subject to object – here re-emerges as a problem of reference. When I pick out a place in the spatio-temporal scheme, am I not picking it out either as being, or as standing in some relation to, the 'place where I am'? In which case does not every act of identification presuppose some prior act of identification of my 'point of view'? But then, why is my consequent description of the contents of the world a description of the world, rather than of my point of view upon it? Rationalist philosophy – and in particular the systems of Spinoza and Leibniz – can be seen as involving an attempt to provide a description of the world which involves individuation from no point of view.[27] Individuation would then be of what exists objectively, and not merely of what appears to the point of view which is mine.

Those thoughts bring us to a central and perduring conception of the 'human individual'. It is widely supposed that, in my own case, I have, by virtue of the privileged awareness of my own subjective condition, a kind of 'knowledge by acquaintance' of a pure individual, whose 'this-ness' is incorrigibly and immediately presented to the consciousness whose identity it shares. In short, a penumbra of 'individual essence' attaches to the first-person perspective. As I argued in Chapter 2, there is something about the basis of self-reference which gives rise to the idea of the *self* as a paradigm individual: I naturally come to believe that I am acquainted, in my own case, as an immediate *donnée* of consciousness, with a 'pure unity'. This unity is the Leibnizian 'point of view', which is both an evolving mental state of mine and a mirror on the objective world which contains me. It is this something that I automatically identify in using the word 'I'.

Many arguments have been given to combat that illusion – the illusion that the privileges of self-reference provide some special guarantee of my existence as an individual 'substance'. Kant's argument, given in the 'Paralogisms of Pure Reason',[28] is designed to show that, in identifying 'myself' I am identifying no *more* than a point of view upon the world, and not an entity within it. Whatever privileged knowledge may be associated with my self-identification, it provides no grounds for the belief that I exist as an individual substance. The 'I' is transcendental; it cannot be an object of its own awareness and retain its identity as the subject who is aware. How therefore can my transparent awareness as a subject give me any clue as to what I objectively am? Kant argued – with considerable plausibility – that the privilege of self-awareness (the 'transcendental unity of apperception') is compatible with almost any philosophical theory of human nature. I could as well be a property as a substance, for all that my awareness shows.

Some philosophers have remained unpersuaded by such arguments. Others have accepted their broad tendency, while insisting that there is nevertheless something true of the 'I' which is true of me as subject and which resists translation into the third-person point of view. Fichte, for example, accepted Kant's argument, as showing that the self is identical with no individual in the world. At the same time he believed that this simply showed the world to be 'posited' by the self, as a realm of objects whose nature is entirely subservient to the subjective point of view. The self becomes, for Fichte, the true subject-matter of philosophical enquiry, a thing-in-itself, an entity in which freedom and intellection are con-joined, an item with a structure and development that precede every objective process – in short, the true metaphysical substance, but one to which the category of 'substance' cannot be applied.[29]

Fichte's philosophy of the self is a paradigm of all such attempts to elevate the first-person perspective into a metaphysical principle. More modest, but no less rich in metaphysical implications, is the modern view that there are first-person truths, which cannot be expressed in any other way. Thomas Nagel has argued, for example,[30] that any purely 'perspectiveless' view of the world will necessarily leave out an important fact about it. For it will leave out all reference to the self – to the point of view from which the world is identified. Hence all identification of objects in this 'perspectiveless' universe will be crucially incomplete. Objects will be identified only in relation to one another, but not in relation to the speaker who describes them. As I shall argue, such views draw unwarranted conclusions from what is, in effect, the simple premise of indexical reference.

According to the view that we are considering, the individuality of the person is connected with the first-person perspective. The intimacy of my awareness of this perspective may be re-expressed as a 'transcendental unity' that obtains within it. I do not have to *find out* that this pain, this perception and this thought belong to a single consciousness: the fact is 'given' to me in the very act of awareness. Nor could I envisage what it would be for this unity to be sundered. There could be no 'point of view' upon a 'split consciousness', from which its divided nature could be observed. From 'outside' it is seen, not as a single consciousness which has been divided, but as two separate and mysteriously related 'unities'. From 'inside' it is strictly unobservable. If I am in a position to assign a 'given' mental state to one or other of two 'unities', this can only be because the mental state is presented to me as 'mine'; hence I know immediately that it belongs to a single unity which includes the other two.

Such facts might tempt a philosopher to conclude that the first-person perspective provides a model for the undivided individuality of the person, and also for the identity of the person, as the particular thing that he is. It might be thought that you could not have my perspective without being me, so that, if things seem to you *exactly* as they seem to me, then you *are* me: you are looking from my eyes, as it were, upon a world which makes room for me at precisely the point of observation which you occupy. Such conclusions are not warranted. Unless we adopt the Leibnizian principle of the identity of indiscernibles, there is nothing to prevent the conclusion that there could be two indiscernible points of view upon the same universe of objects. Nevertheless, as I shall argue, the emphasis on the first-person perspective contains a concealed appropriation of indexicality, and this lends a kind of spurious credibility to the view that it suffices to individuate that to which it belongs.

It is not only 'how the world seems' that is an object of my present awareness. The same is true of my present mental states generally ('how the world seems' being just one mental state among others). As I earlier argued, one way to summarise this privileged awareness is to say that, in the first-person perspective on my own mentality, the distinction between appearance and reality breaks down. (This is the idea of subjectivity: the absence of a distinction between being and seeming. And it is precisely this which characterises the position of the subject. To put the point in Hegelian language: the realm of the subject, and the realm of subjectivity, are one and the same.) It would be absurd indeed to think that we could transport this distinction into the first-person outlook. For 'how things seem' is equally a description of my mental state. If I can doubt its veracity, I can know only how things 'seem to seem', and that too may then be doubted. The subject dissolves in a pyrrhonistic regress of uncertainty.

Someone else can have knowledge of how things seem to me. And this knowledge could be complete. Presumably God has complete knowledge of how things seem to me. But he does not have my point of view, or indeed any point of view (to express the idea in Leibnizian terms). He knows this as he knows everything, neither mediately nor immediately, but as the working out of his own immutable will. (Thus Kant argued that God's knowledge of the world is like our knowledge of how things are (it is intellectual), and yet it has the certain character of our knowledge of how things seem (it is 'intuitive'). However, we can have no understanding of the idea of an 'intellectual intuition' except negatively.)[31] The difference lies, not in *what* I know, but in *how* I know it. When you know that I am in pain you know, as I do, that someone is in pain. If either of us has the advantage here it is you; for you could not *know* this, without having some idea as to who I am − that is, as to whose pain this is. Whereas I could know that I am in pain without knowing anything about who I am. Awakening from a brain-transfer operation which casts my identity in doubt, I may yet know with absolute authority that I (whoever I am) have a pain.[32]

Let us now return to our problem. Is the first-person perspective a genuine 'individual essence'? Is it, that is, a property that is both essential to, and uniquely instantiated by, whatever possesses it? It is hard to believe that my perspective is an essential property of me. It is essential that I *have* a perspective: without it, I should not be a person and therefore should not exist. But is it essential that I have the particular perspective that I have? Surely not. I might have viewed the world from another point of view. Moreover, it is not clear that the first-person perspective is individuating in the right kind of way. It contains, in its description, an ineliminable element of indexicality. It is 'my' perspective, precisely in being definitive of the 'point of view' which is mine. In identifying it, I am doing no more than to reaffirm the 'I', as a point of departure from which I identify everything else. It is as much a cheat to think of this identification as the description of a property of mine, as it would be to regard the sentence 'thing which is here now' as identifying an object by its properties. 'I' thoughts, like 'here' thoughts, are indexical thoughts, and owe their referential status to that. Some philosophers go further, and argue that the 'immunity to errors of identification'[33] which characterises first-person knowledge is of the same kind as the similar immunity exemplified by thoughts about the here and now. My abilities to refer to a place as here, and a time as now, are similarly immune from certain kinds of error.[34] Whatever epistemological privilege attaches to them attaches by virtue of the special position of the speaker. Since he does not need an act of identification in order to refer to himself, this simply reinforces the conclusion that he knows nothing special *about* himself, and in particular, that he neither knows, nor refers to, any special component of reality, such as a 'self', upon which to base the fortuitous certainty that is his.

The 'subjective essence'

As I have suggested in Chapter 3, such arguments, whatever their force, cannot entirely explain the phenomenon of first-person privilege. Nevertheless, added to the argument that I gave there, they must inevitably lead us to reject the notion of a 'subjective essence'. At the same time, there is something in our interpersonal attitudes which leads us to *think* of each other in this way, so that it may yet be the case that the 'subjective essence' features as the *intentional* object of certain mental states. We tend to think of persons as quintessential individuals, constituted by their inviolable subjective perspective, which lies enfolded within them like a kernel within the flesh. The thought seems to be affirmed in every use of 'I'; in every declaration of feeling, intention and commitment. And since I react to you as a person largely on the basis of your 'I' thoughts, I cannot avoid the impression that it is your 'I' to which I relate, and which contains the hidden treasure of your being. By conceding first-person authority to you, I confer upon your perspective a special status as mediator between us. Although there is no metaphysical ground for the thought that this perspective is what you essentially are, it is nevertheless true that I demand you to sustain it in existence, as the true invariable focus of my attitude towards you. The practice of reason-giving and reason-seeking, through which all our interpersonal communication is conducted, requires that we assume limitless responsibility for our acts, opinions and expressions, and also for our past and future acts and expressions. Hence, in the eyes of others, my present unity of consciousness is associated inevitably with the idea of my unbroken temporal continuity as an agent. I appear as a 'centre of responsibility' and an enduring 'initiator of change'. I live through my deeds, and in my deeds my unbroken perspective finds external reality. All this is incorporated into the idea of what I am, not only by myself, but also by those others who require me to be 'true to myself' if they are to enter into relation with me. Thus it is that our interpersonal attitudes become structured by a peculiar metaphysical idea.

In the perspectiveless eyes of science, we are no more than animals (although of course highly sophisticated animals), with the limited individuality which that implies. In our own eyes we are 'points of view', and what we are for ourselves we are for every other creature with a 'self' like ours. Hence the intentional structure of our interpersonal attitudes is built upon a conception of the individual which has no application in the world of animals. We are, as Kant persuasively argued, the victims of transcendental illusions, and of none more persistent than this one, of the Leibnizian monad which harbours our sufferings and our joys.[35] If we were to describe the world objectively, from no point of view within it, the 'self' and all its mysteries would vanish – as it vanishes from the impersonal metaphysics of Spinoza.[36] If, on the other hand, we try to construct the world, as Leibniz did, from an idea of individual existence which has the self as its model, then we shall effectively deprive ourselves of that single objective order into which individuals may enter as component parts. Leibnizian 'points of view' maintain no real relation with one another, but merely reflect, *ad infinitum*, the unpeopled spaces which forever sunder them.

We must, therefore, take the idea of the metaphysical individuality of the self both less seriously than those philosophers who would endorse it – for it is an idea that has no place in the scientific description of the world – and more seriously than those who would reject it out of hand – for it denotes an indispensable feature of the intentional understanding by which we live. It is, to put it succinctly, a 'well-founded illusion', which we could remove from our consciousness only at the cost of consciousness itself.

Individualising thoughts

What, then, should we say about the 'individualising intentionality' of desire? This kind of intentionality is by no means the simple thing that at first sight it appears to be. As we have seen, it can be 'disaggregated' into logically independent components, of which the most important for our purposes is the 'non-transferability' which desire shares with love and aesthetic interest. Non-transferability does not require the attribution to the object either of a non-arbitrary individuality or of a first-person perspective in which to locate it. This is established by the case of aesthetic interest in a heap of things. It is clear that, as individuals go, heaps are fairly arbitrary: they can be divided, destroyed and reconstituted at will; and they can be understood by someone who refrains from making any hard and fast decision as to how they should be counted (as one or as many). And of course it would be absurd to think of a heap as possessing a first-person perspective.

At the same time, aesthetic interest projects upon its object a unity and integrity which, materially speaking, it may not possess. As I argued earlier, the inaccurate philosophical description of this tendency is at the root of a prevailing fallacy. It is erroneously supposed that the work of art possesses, as a peculiar metaphysical property, the individuality with which our attitude endows it. As I pointed out, this fallacy parallels the 'well-founded illusion' contained within our interpersonal responses. Thus an aesthetically successful heap, such as the Süleymaniye Mosque in Istanbul, is *seen as* possessing an individuality which matches the attitude directed towards it. No stone can be removed, it is thought, without destroying its unity.

I might retain this attitude, however, while being under no illusions as to the metaphysical reality of the Süleymaniye. I know that it is a heap of stones, which bears no more unity than I am able to impose upon it. Something similar may also occur interpersonally. I may look upon my neighbour, and even upon my friend, with the eyes of disenchantment, aware that he does not, in his metaphysical heart, live up to the exacting requirements of my attitude. Nevertheless, there is an inevitable tendency to see him as a transcendental unity. And this perception of the other will be dominant in all successful 'moral conversation'. Furthermore, we have a basis for this attitude which we do not have for our attitude towards art. The other person exhibits the same unity of consciousness that I discover in myself. I see him as another 'I', and in that 'I' is summarised all his potential to support and damage me. It would be impossible for him to appear in my *Lebenswelt*, as the object of those responses which I cannot rationally withhold from him, without also appearing as a metaphysical individual.

In the case of aesthetic interest, I am often aware of the fact that the object owes its special individuality to my way of seeing it. Some even argue that it is integral to the significance of aesthetic response that it should permit this perception. We then step back from quotidian experience, so as to see that the world conforms to a consoling order, and that the origin of this order is in us.[37]

By contrast, the individualising intentionality of the interpersonal attitudes arises from a *belief* about their object. It is something in *him* – namely his possession of a first-person perspective – which gives grounds for my individualising attention. This attention is called forth from me automatically in the course of my dealings with him. I do not have to take up any attitude that would not spontaneously have governed our commerce. The frequently held view that desire and aesthetic pleasure are closely related – perhaps species of a single genus – is, as I shall later argue, not without foundation. But they differ markedly in the fact that the first, unlike the second, derives its individualising intentionality from the thought that it is focused upon a real, metaphysically integrated individual, who can also be identified and grasped in bodily form. We must now ask ourselves how this thought enters into the aim of desire, and how, if at all, it gives rise to the familiar sense of paradox.

Sartre's paradox

It is useful to begin from a consideration of Sartre's theory.[38] Sartre recognises that the principal problem for any theory of desire is to explain its individualising intentionality,[39] and he recognises too that no theory of desire which represents it as an instinct, with sexual pleasure (pleasure in the organs of procreation) as its aim, could possibly account for the phenomenological reality. For it could not explain how another *being* could be an essential component in the project of desire.

At the same time it is evident that the embodiment of the other is of fundamental interest in desire: at one point Sartre asserts that 'the full pressing together of the flesh of two people against one another is the true goal of desire.'[40] However, the two words 'flesh' and 'people' in this sentence need interpreting. I do not want to press against your flesh for the sake of whatever comfortable sensation this may provide, but for the sake of the consciousness with which your flesh is saturated. In my caresses, Sartre argues, I 'incarnate' you: that is, I summon your consciousness (your 'for-itself') into your flesh, so as to be able to possess you there. In explaining this idea, Sartre refers to the importance of 'involuntary' behaviour (behaviour that can be 'summoned') as an index of the other's consciousness. Thus he offers a theory of the phenomena to which I drew attention in Chapters 2 and 4 – the phenomena of arousal and of bodily transparency. The aim of desire is first to incarnate the first-person perspective (the for-itself) of the other; and secondly to unite with it as flesh.

There seem to be two forms which this uniting may take: the way of normal sexual desire and the way of sado-masochism. Sartre writes as though the first collapses into the second, and as though it is impossible in just the way that the second is impossible. In normal sexual desire, I want the other to appear in his flesh, and want him to want me likewise. Our energies are expended in this enterprise of mutual 'incarnation'. And, so long as the mutuality of desire is sustained, each summoning the other into the surface of his flesh, the aim of desire may be at least pursued, if not fulfilled. (Orgasm, on Sartre's view, as on the view defended in Chapter 4, is little better than an interruption of desire, and certainly no part of its aim.) In an important sense, however, I cannot really unite with your first-person perspective. All I can do is to summon it, and likewise to surrender myself. We do no more than *appear* to each other, making our flesh transparent, as in a longing glance. In desire we appear on the surface of our bodies like fish at the edges of adjacent tanks, so as to peer hopelessly across into the unattainable element where another has his being.

The real significance of this unassuageable condition is revealed in the 'two reefs upon which desire may founder' – sadism and masochism. Sadism, Sartre argues, is 'as a seed in desire itself, as the failure of desire; in fact as soon as I seek to take the Other's body, which through my incarnation I have induced to incarnate itself, I break the reciprocity of incarnation, I surpass my body towards its own possibilities, and I orient myself in the direction of sadism'.[41] In sadism, the other's body is used as an instrument; it is filled with torment, in order that the for-itself of the other will finally identify itself with its body, revealing its freedom in an act of self-betrayal. The sadist, however, refuses to be incarnated: he stands aloof from the process which humbles the body of his companion, for he wishes to retain the power to 'appropriate the incarnation of the other'.[42]

The thought of desire is roughly this: in my incarnation I am vulnerable, for I have been called forth by your action into the surface of my flesh. To retain my will as mine, I must either refuse or 'transcend' this incarnation. The first response is frigidity, the second sadism. In sadism I surmount my desire, by making it into an instrument of dominion over you. I embark upon a project, which is to possess (appropriate) the for-itself which I have compelled onto the surface of your body. But I can never succeed in this. If I succeed in compelling something from you, what I compel is not the expression of your freedom: and if I obtain the glance which expresses your freedom, it is a glance of pure alienation, in which I am revealed as an instrument of suffering, with which you will never freely unite. (I have put this in my own words, since Sartre's language is obscure and even contradictory.)

If we now look back at the aim of 'normal' sexual desire, we find that it importantly resembles the aim of sadism, and is similarly unfulfillable. What I wish to possess, in possessing you, is precisely that first-person perspective which I compel, in my incarnation, to incarnate itself. This perspective is nothing other than your freedom, which I cannot possess or appropriate but which I can only observe. I may engage with you in a cooperative endeavour – the endeavour of mutual 'incarnation'. But I can never 'take possession' of the freedom which is yours, or in any other way unite with the quintessential *you*.

The paradox of sexual desire is, according to Sartre, exemplified also by love and hate. Indeed, Sartre regards it as a fundamental affliction, which casts a shadow of impossibility over every attempt to bind oneself to another and another to oneself. All human relations exemplify the paradox of freedom. Sartre adapts Rousseau's famous apophthegm: I must always 'force the other to be free'. The intellectual structure of his argument is taken, however, not from Rousseau but from Hegel, whose parable of the master and the slave is the ancestor of Sartre's poetic invocation of sado-masochism.[43] According to one version of the Hegelian picture, it is not sexual desire that is fraught with contradiction, but lust. Lust is the form of bestiality that has the human body as its object: its extreme version is rape, but it is always, in some measure, tantamount to rape, since it regards the other instrumentally, and seeks to compel him to accept what is imposed upon him. The paradox could then be phrased as follows. The other, in becoming an instrument of my pleasure, becomes a thing. But the force of my passion arises only because I regard him as a person, who will respond to my violation of his freedom with hatred and pain. At the same time I fantasise that he consents to my deed, and that he responds with the same lustful impulse as myself. It is only on this supposition that I wanted him. Hence I both take away his personal nature in thought and return it to him in the form of fantasy. In some deep way I am at variance with myself, wishing him to be person and thing together.

The 'paradox of lust' will concern us at several points in ensuing chapters. But it clearly does not give sufficient grounds for Sartre's theory of desire. This theory involves the attempt to prove that the very individualising intentionality of desire contains the seeds of paradox. It is true that – at some metaphysical level – Hegel wished to assert that love and desire are contradictory. 'Love', he wrote, 'is a tremendous contradiction; the understanding cannot resolve it.'[44] For love requires total surrender of what is totally free, and absolute unity between what is utterly diverse. At the same time, this contradiction in interpersonal relations was, for Hegel, but one component in the 'dialectical' nature of reality; and it is the essence of dialectical contradictions that they are 'transcended' (aufgehoben). Sartre by contrast wishes to portray the contradictions of love and desire as irresoluble. He is therefore led to compare desire to hurtful sado-masochism, in which the body of the other is 'instrumentalised'.

Even without accepting Sartre's peculiar theory of freedom, we may discern a certain paradox in sadism. Desire is directed towards the individuality of the other. And yet, in seeking to 'appropriate' the other for uses of its own, desire no longer treats him as an individual. This 'appropriation' seems to be part of the sadist's aim. Hence sadistic desire involves the paradox into which we all must fall, according to Kant, when the categorical imperative is violated: the paradox of treating as a means what can only be treated as an end.

But, even if that is a consequence of sadism, it is a consequence of desire only on the assumption that desire leads naturally to sadism. As we have seen, the Kantian distinction between treating as an end and treating as a means is not the simple distinction that Kant imagined it to be. It is in fact a composite distinction, to be understood in terms of the six divisions among attitudes that I discussed in the first section of this chapter. To the extent that my purpose in desire is immanent, and to the extent that I seek for your consent, I treat you with as much respect as in any other transaction. Natural desire is in conflict neither with esteem nor with love, and leads not to sado-masochism but to 'mutual service'. Only a metaphysical theory of freedom lends plausibility to Sartre's claim that, because I want *you*, I want also to appropriate your freedom, thereby voiding your body of the perspective which I also wish to possess through it.

In Chapter 3 I suggested a more plausible theory of freedom.

'Freedom', I suggested, is a metaphor, through which we embellish the fact of our responsibility. The ability of persons to declare and take responsibility for their future actions lends profit to our 'moral conversation': it is to signify the profitable occasions of conversation that we announce that men are free. Men are free because they act for and are influenced by reasons. In soliciting another's consent to my desire for him, I respect his freedom, even in the final congress, in which we both are overcome by pleasure. So understood, the concept of freedom is metaphysically innocent. And so understood, it gives no basis for the theory that there is a 'paradox of desire'.

Sartre's theory makes contact with an idiom, the implications of which are now frequently questioned – the idiom of possession. The desirous man expresses himself in terms that imply a 'right of ownership' in the object desired. This language recalls the well-known tendency among warriors to claim both the land and the women who inhabit it. But it would be wrong to think that the language of 'possession' applies only to the activities of the human male. There is an intolerable egoism at the heart of every desire, which matches, and portends, the egoism of love:

> Love seeketh only self to please,
> To bind another to its delight;
> Joys in another's loss of ease,
> And builds a Hell in Heaven's despite.

Such observations are matters of wisdom rather than philosophical analysis. The desire to 'possess' may be a feature of love: it may even be a feature of desire. But it is not an essential feature of either.

We must be careful here to distinguish between the everyday metaphysical illusion generated by the first-person perspective, and the metaphysical gloss that endorses its claims. Sartre's theory is such a gloss: like Kant's theory of the transcendental self – from which it ultimately derives – it goes beyond what is 'given' in the intentional understanding. It proposes a theory of the individual essence (that I *am* my freedom), and then suggests that this theory captures what is thought by the man who sees himself or another as a person. In fact, however, our interpersonal understanding could never reach so far. It depends only on the sense that self-ascriptions proceed from the core of human individuality, and have a peculiar epistemic authority. This idea falls far short of a theory of the soul. Certainly, it does not imply that freedom is the substance of the soul. It implies only that each person is individuated within his own perspective, and that the authority of his perspective extends into past and future, so determining his responsibilities.

Thus, although it is true that the first-person perspective enables us to subsume another's actions under the concept of responsibility, and so to extend towards him attitudes founded in the ideas of right, duty, obligation and privilege, this does not entail that we should think of him as transcendentally free, in the manner of Kant or Sartre. At most it implies only that we should see his 'essence' as residing in a distinctive 'point of view'. If there is a paradox in our interpersonal attitudes it is the consequence, not of a metaphysical idea of freedom, but of another metaphysical idea, that of the absolute individuality which is 'given' to the individual in his consciousness of self.

The aim of desire

It is of course impossible for me to be 'united with' your first-person perspective – that would simply make me into you, so abolishing the separateness that underlies desire. If *that* were the aim of sexual desire, we could explain the individualising intentionality of desire in terms which also show its aim to be fraught with paradox. But compelling though the description may be, it is surely no more than metaphorical, in just the way that Lucretius' description is metaphorical. It is not *this* that we seek in desire, even if what we seek may be evocatively described in these terms.

Our first task, therefore, must be to describe 'sexual union' in more literal terms. The reader will recall that one of the major difficulties encountered in describing the aim of desire lies in the fact that desire, because it depends minutely on the reactions of another, 'has its own course'. We need therefore to know precisely how the other is conceived 'in the course of' desire; and in particular whether the well-founded illusion of his metaphysical individuality impedes – in some way analogous to that suggested by Sartre – the formation of a truly coherent purpose.

We must again turn our attention to the 'mutuality' of desire. The 'reciprocity' which is aimed at in desire does not in itself distinguish desire from countless other human attitudes. Cooperation is the core of social existence, and is based in mutuality – in the human disposition to desire that our desires coincide, so that our transactions may be governed not by coercion but by consent. In day-to-day business relations, this mutuality may be embodied in implied or explicit contracts; but this should not blind us to the fact that it is merely the normal condition of social existence between self-conscious beings, who seek to regulate one another's conduct by persuasion, and who therefore have a prior motive to align themselves with practices which command their common consent.

The reciprocity exemplified by *meaning*, to which I referred in Chapter 2, is more concentrated than the reciprocity of normal cooperation. It stems, not from a desire for a common purpose, but from a 'reflexive intention' – an intention that one's own intention be recognised by another. When the intentional structure characteristic of meaning emerges, there emerges also the possibility of, and the tendency towards, a progressive 'escalation' of reflexive intentions. The enormous concentration of human affect which every symbol contains can be seen as the result of the invitation that it offers to the observer, to recognise the manifest intentions that lie behind it, and to understand the symbol through understanding *them*.

In Chapter 2 I referred to the view of Thomas Nagel that the glance of desire contains a core of this heightened reciprocity – the reciprocity involved when another comes to share in my state of mind, precisely through the recognition of my intention that he should do so. I do not think that this idea captures the mutuality that is involved in the transports of desire. The look of desire has this quality partly because it *is* a case of meaning something – just as are the look of complicity and the look of anger. It is a symbolic, and even partly conventional, invitation, offered to another. In the ardour of desire, however, quite another form of reciprocity governs the intentions of the participants. And it is this which lies at the root of the individualising intentionality of desire.

This new reciprocity involves the *bodies* of the participants, and is known popularly, but appositely, as 'love-making'. It begins in glances and caresses, passes to kisses, and culminates in the sexual act. As I have argued, it is better described as a vector than as a simple purpose. It may be hard to deflect desire from its natural tendency; but this does not mean that sexual intercourse is the aim of desire. The aim is given by the intentional content of desire, and initially at least it resides in mutual arousal. However, concealed within this initial endeavour is a distinct and growing sense of what I want from the other. I want him to have knowledge of *me in my body*, and to delight in me there, as I delight in him. It is at the same time as crucial to my attitude that his attention be focused on *me* (me as an individual) as that mine be focused on *him*. In all natural desire, indeed, there is an element of narcissism. For I strive to see myself through his eyes. I wish to appear within his consciousness as overwhelming, and I respond to everything in him that conveys this impression.

There is clearly more to this than the reciprocity of friendly inter-change, and more than the reciprocity of meaning. There is the desire to be 'present as a body' to the other, and to observe one's presence through his eyes. There is also the desire that he should desire likewise: for he must respond to each of my desires with a matching mental affirmation. In the full ardour of desire, each participant is striving to be present in his body, and striving also to view his own striving from a point of view outside it. The excitement stems in part from the interplay of those two acts of attention.

It may now seem as though we have located both the paradox and its solution. For of course I cannot *in fact* view my presence with your eyes; in so far as I am attempting to do so, my aim must remain always frustrated. However, although I am indeed 'hungry' for you, and for that supreme closeness to you which is satisfied only in an act of mental identification, it is only a failure of imagination that would lead me to think that I must actually *share* your perspective before I can see myself as you see me – the kind of failure of imagination which leads some people to make love with the help of mirrors. All human intimacy requires an act of sympathy, an 'as if', which projects the participant into the mental landscape of his friend. It is difficult to describe such an act: but that should not cause us to dismiss it as paradoxical. For we must recognise that it exists, and forms the foundation, not only of personal intimacy, but also of representational art.[45]

This particular paradox, therefore, is no sooner stated than solved. But another and deeper paradox lies concealed behind it. For it is at this point – the point of imaginative identification – that the well-founded illusion of interpersonal emotion begins to take over. Our efforts are concent-rated upon making ourselves present and perceivable in bodily form. The body is tangible, seizable: I can touch it, squeeze it, bite it. It responds as a unity to my presence, and pleasure or pain in any part of it is also pleasure or pain in the creature as a whole. I rejoice in this unity, and in the fact that I have in my hands the single thing which is you. (Imagine some cunning device which enabled a man to penetrate Jane while kissing the face of Mary, concealing from him the fact that there are two bodies which receive his attentions. If he were to discover the truth, then, whatever the delight expressed by Jane and Mary, he should regard himself as *cheated*. He was not, as he thought, making love to another, but being strangely, and pleasurably, abused.)

The bodily unity that lies within my grasp is identified in my thinking with another unity, that of the perspective which 'peers' from its face. It is into the well of this perspective that all my desirous gestures are thrown, and I survey its bodily surface for the signs of my own significance. Thus there arises, within the kernel of that reciprocal arousal which is the natural 'course' of desire, a peculiar thought, and one that is peculiar to those interpersonal attitudes which focus on the 'embodiment' of the object. I seek to *unite you with your body*. I seek to summon your perspective into your flesh, so that it becomes identical with your flesh; I thereby at last *discover* your true individuality (your self) as a constituent of the physical world in which I move and act. I wish you to *be* your body, not in the straightforward sense in which this is always true, but in the metaphysical sense in which it can never be true, the sense of an identity between your 'unity of consciousness' and the animal unity of your body.

That, I believe, is the real mystery of incarnation. It is part of the genius of Christianity that it invites us to understand the relation between God and his creation in terms of a mystery that we have, so to speak, continually between our hands. The mystery that we confront in the sexual act, we can neither resolve nor abjure. No first-person perspective can bear the identity of a person, nor can it be united with the only thing – the body – in which individuality is revealed to us. And yet, so powerful is the paroxysm of desire that it seems to me as though the very transparency of your self is, for a moment, revealed on the surface of your body, in a mysterious union that can be touched but never comprehended. Those parts of the body which remain dark to me are dark only with the shadow cast by the flame of your self. This burning of the soul in the flesh – the *llama de amor viva* of St John of the Cross – is the symbol of all mystic unions, and the true reason for the identity of imagery between the poetry of desire and the poetry of worship.

The unity which I endeavour to elicit from you is one which I seek also to enact in myself. We are engaged in an impossible but necessary enterprise. We are attempting to unite our bodies with a non-existent 'owner', who is unable to possess the individuality for which he craves, but who sustains the illusion of his own existence, as a reflection in the glass of another's eye. In this resides the true significance of the 'involuntary' self-expressions which, I argued, form the initial focus of desire. The smile that draws me on is of flesh and blood. The desire to kiss it is the desire to plant my lips, not to a mouth, but to a smile: to a portion of the body into which I have summoned the other's perspective. A smile is indeed the food of love, while a mouth can be the food of love only for someone whose rage has turned desire to appetite – someone who, like the Penthesileia of Kleist, seeks to glut her intolerable yearning on the dead flesh of her beloved antagonist. In Dante's celebrated account of the eternal destiny of carnal love, Francesca recalls not the mouth but the smile of Guinevere, desired and kissed by Lancelot:

> *Quando leggero il disiato riso*
> *esser baciato da cotanto amante,*
> *questi, che mai da me non fia diviso,*

> *la bocca mi baciò tutto tremante.*
> [*Inferno*, V, 133–6]

By a fine transition, she then remembers Paolo kissing, not her smile, but her mouth, for she has been overcome by him and is, in her own eyes, no more than flesh for him. Francesca is a victim of the paradox of desire. Drawn by a smile, she becomes a mouth. Seeking to unite her perspective with her body, she is lost in her body. That which she wanted she cannot achieve. And that which she achieves is no more than the ash of her vanished purpose. This process – the '*Untergang* of the person in desire', as one phenomenologist has described it[46] – is a direct expression of the disparity that exists between the transcendent aim of desire and the merely immanent means through which we may try to achieve it. The punishment of Paolo and Francesca is that they should be swept along through the first circle of Hell, their bodies forever inseparable, their souls forever divided by the remorse which their bodies caused.

The paradox could be resolved only by abolishing the well-founded illusion from which it derives: the illusion that I am *essentially* what I am 'for myself'; that my first-person perspective contains the 'individual essence' which is me. We could abandon that illusion only by losing the capacity for moral conversation. For it is our trust in this picture that generates our commitments. Only those who suffer from transcendental illusions can be forthright in dialogue, for dialogue requires us to build our view of another from the data of his first-person declarations.

In comparison with love, esteem and admiration, desire has a 'troubling' quality. The trouble derives from the attempt to unite the illusory individuality of the other's self with the real but resistant individuality of the animal with which he is identical. It is as a body that I am able to perceive and understand his individuality. The Leibnizian 'point of view' lies forever beyond my comprehension; for me it is no more real, no more substantial an occupant of reality, than is the number 2. The long-term 'project' of desire can therefore be interpreted in terms of a 'trouble' which all rational beings have reason to overcome – the trouble of seeking to grasp in another's body the perspective which peers from it and which can never be grasped.

If those thoughts are correct, we may draw the following conclusions:

(1) The formal properties of desire – and in particular its non-transfer-ability – have a real foundation in the aim of desire.

(2) The aim of desire is individualising, in that it involves individualising thoughts about its object.

(3) These individualising thoughts identify the object in two ways: in terms of his real individuality as a human body, and in terms of his illusory individuality as a first-person perspective.

(4) Desire involves the attempt to unite these two patterns of indi-viduation, in a thought that is inherently paradoxical.

Thus while the term 'union' remains no more than a metaphor for the aim of desire, it captures the element of paradox involved, in the strategy which seeks to summon the perspective of the other into the surface of his flesh. The initial aim of desire, which is mutual arousal, is indeed far from paradoxical. For it involves no more than the desire to overcome the other, to cause him to reveal himself in those involuntary transformations which convey to me the picture of his interest in me. At the same time these transformations – which are the food of love – must leave desire unsatisfied. They are always less than that full revelation of the individual otherness that I seek to embrace. In my desire I am gripped by the illusion of a transcendental unity behind the opacity of flesh, the repository of infinite moral possibilities, and the promise of that perfect enfolding presence that would – if it could be obtained – justify the turmoil of sexual pursuit.

Original sin

I have listed four features of desire which together enter into the Sartrean paradox. But these features – it might be said – are also present in certain other sentiments, such as the tenderness towards a child. Why are these other sentiments not paradoxical as well? The proximity of desire to the love of a child – and their common emphasis on embodiment – is a well-known theme of literature. And the neo-Platonist theory of transcendence has been applied to both. In the Middle English *Pearl*, the poet is granted, through the holy vision of his dead daughter, the revelation that Dante is granted through the vision of Beatrice: and the terms of reference are almost the same. So what is it in Dante's vision which bears the mark of desire?

We must here return to the idea of embodiment. It is true that my tender concern for a child focuses on his embodiment, and is at every point dependent on the sense of his fragile body as the vehicle of a nascent consciousness, the translucent clothing of a spirit which, because it still develops with the rhythm of a human body, appears to me inseparable from the body in which it grows. I want to touch that body, to hold it, to kiss it, to press it to me – and at the same time there is nothing of desire in this, for there is nothing of arousal.

Why then does arousal make such a difference? The answer lies in the particular place of the body in sexual excitement. In this excitement I am in some sense *vanquished* by my body, which is in turn vanquished by yours (or by you *in* yours). (That is the lesson which Francesca learned so vividly.) It is not simply that I attend to your embodiment and cherish you in it. Our bodies are uppermost in our thoughts, and dominate us through the involuntary transformations of their agglutinative parts. I endeavour to unite you with your body in arousal, by inducing just *this* 'overcoming' of your will. I do not have recourse only to smiles or to the tender gestures of friendship and reassurance. I also wish you to engage in an act in which your self is thrown into disarray, fleeing before the body's violence, and unable to summon its habitual resources. The experience of your embodiment in arousal is also the experience of your subjugation to the body. It is the final proof, offered to me in the very moment of my attempt to unite with your perspective, that your perspective does not really define you. (For this reason many people find it precisely *difficult* to desire those whom they respect, and direct their attentions only to those in whom the disarray of the spirit is not also a threat to their 'dear illusions'.) Your 'transcendental' unity eludes me in the very moment of our conjunction, and I hold only the ashes from which it has been burned away. My attempt to unite you with your body, and to hold you *as* embodied, is jeopardised by the very experience which required it.

The paradox is not absent from the love for a child, nor is it absent from the tender forms of sadism. But it is only in desire that it also threatens me. Only in desire am I exposed to humiliation by the body. It is in some such way, I believe, that one should account for the traditional Pauline and Augustinian horror of 'concupiscence'.[47] The early Christian moralists clearly intended this term to refer to the course of desire in arousal, which condition they repudiated as a falling away from our spiritual fulfilment, a dangerous toying on the threshold of perdition. It is their encritic view of sexuality which has shaped the moral language of our civilisation, and which continues to peer darkly and mournfully from beneath the brilliant surface of Sartre's prose. And it is a view that we should take seriously.

Gregory of Nyssa argued that, if Adam and Eve had not sinned, they would have remained virgin, and the human race would have multiplied by whatever method is used by the angels, and not by 'that animal and irrational method by which they now succeed one another'.[48] On this view the most lamentable effect of the forbidden fruit of knowledge is not that we view desire in impure and self-regarding ways (although that too is true), but that we feel it at all. There is no doubt about the theological awkwardness of Gregory's view. (He is forced to concede, for example, that God distinguished the sexes only in anticipation of the Fall.) At the same time, Gregory speaks not only for a whole tradition of Christian teaching, but also for the morality that glimmers more darkly in the words of the Old Testament prophets, and in the words of the prophet of Islam, who repeatedly enjoins us, at all costs, to hide our private parts. For this morality, it is in the experience of arousal that our fallen condition is present to us, and also perpetually renewed by us. It is arousal that inspires the writer of the Anglo-Saxon homily, *Hali Meidhad* (*Holy Maidenhood*):

> that vice that begot thee of thy mother, that same
> improper burning of the flesh, that fiery itch of
> that carnal excitement before that disgusting work,
> that animal intercourse, that shameless togetherness,
> that filthy, stinking and wanton deed.[49]

Marriage, the monastic author insists, cannot save us, nor can any other companionship save us, from the uncleanness of sexual arousal. For in this condition we are tied to our flesh as we are tied by no other love or attachment. Arousal taints us with mortality, and feeds our souls with the poisonous delicacies of sin.

The thought here finds its clearest expression in *The City of God* of St Augustine, who argues explicitly, that we should see in the phenomena of arousal the sign of original sin. Alone among the external organs which implicate us in action, the sexual organs lie beyond our will. (Augustine was evidently thinking, not of action as such, but action for which we might be praised or blamed.) These organs impose their transformations upon us, and drag us along with them in a project that ties us to the mortal destiny of our flesh. Even if we excite ourselves voluntarily, it is not *we* who are the authors of the ensuing action, but the carnal lust which we have summoned.[50] It is for this reason, Augustine argues, that we wish to hide our sexual parts, which are the living testimony to our enslavement. At the same time, we surround the sexual act with shame and hesitation. Indeed, 'a man being in unlawful anger with his neighbour, had rather have a thousand eyes upon him, than one when he is in carnal copulation with his wife.'[51]

In such terms Augustine explained both the primacy of involuntary transformations in the transaction of desire and the puzzling phenomena of sexual conduct – shame, modesty, sexual compulsion and the genesis of chastity. In all of those phenomena he saw the signs of our war against the flesh. For the flesh is the vehicle of mortality, and therefore the true carrier of the contagion of original sin. He summarised his thought in a passage of great subtlety:

> This contention, fight, and altercation of lust and will, this need of lust to the sufficiency of the will, had not been laid upon wedlock in paradise, unless disobedience had become the punishment for the sin of disobedience. Otherwise these members had obeyed their wills as well as the rest.[52]

To put it slightly differently: our flesh disobediently binds us to its will, because our disobedient parents had sought to bind the will of God. And the will of the flesh is death.

It is undeniable that you can *see* arousal in that way, as you can see no other interpersonal attitude. Arousal is a critical interruption of our personal congress, in which we are forced, against the logic of our rational conduct, to dwell on and surrender to the incomprehensible fact of incarnation. The intentional structure of sexual desire represents a vast moral labour, whereby man has sought to overcome the trouble of his own embodiment. But desire is haunted, if not by the consciousness of original sin, at least by what I have called the 'fear of the obscene': the fear that the experience of embodiment may be overcome and eclipsed by the experience of the body.

We should not be surprised to find, therefore, that the sense of original sin in sex is associated, by Judaeo-Christian and Islamic writers, with precisely the same aspects of sexual arousal as dominate obscene representation: the dissolving, corrupting and 'viscous' character of that 'filthy, stinking and wanton deed'. The melting of the flesh in sexual excitement is a premonition of our final melting in death, and – by a compelling logic – the Christian writer finds in the sexual act the vivid reminder of death and decay, which are God's punishment for our original transgression. (Marvell both exploits this way of thinking, and also stands it on its feet, when he warns his coy mistress that 'worms shall try / That long-preserved virginity'.) Reflecting on this, we see the emotional significance of Sartre's horror of viscosity, of Leopardi's sense that his self and its 'dear illusions' are nothing but mud, and of Iago's negative confession (in Boito's *Otello*), in which all human joys are reduced to *fango originale*: original slime. The spiritual effort of humanity – to see itself as endowed with a transcendental identity and a transcendental freedom – is constantly jeopardised by the revelation of the flesh. The individual is not the pure observer that he longs to be. He exists only because born into the world, from the very slime of 'otherness' that he vainly refuses. The self is irreversibly tainted and defiled by an 'original' encounter with slime. For it was from one of slime's disguises – that of the mother – that the self was born. 'Man that is born of woman' comes into existence through original sin, which is, as Schopenhauer put it, the 'crime of existence itself'.[53]

Swift is sometimes rebuked for dwelling so assiduously on the noxious excrement of the Yahoos (in comparison with whom the Houyhnhnms, blessed with a horse's capacity to emit only fragrant excreta, seem to enjoy the incarnation that reason demands: an incarnation that is not a visible form of decay). But of course Swift's purpose was to renew the experience of original sin, in the face of man's constant temptation to forget it. This temptation is itself a sign of that which it denies. We should not be surprised to find that the utopian societies of our century, founded on the denial of original sin, have invariably established camps for the manufacture of human suffering, in which the 'enemies of society' are forced through every humiliation until – their identity with their suffering flesh having at last become disgustingly apparent – they can be despatched to eternity with no sense of belonging to the sinless order which expelled them. In the face of this great crime, we must recognise the need for Swift's vision of our nature. Even if we hesitate to adopt the monastic's sense of the vileness of procreation, we must recognise the dangers implicit in a morality that ignores the body, and offers no answer to the question whether the body should be disciplined and, if so, how. The very same Kantian morality that leaves us helpless in the face of sexual desire informs the vision of 'full communism', in which all of life will be conducted according to the transcendental requirements of a metaphysical freedom. In both cases the denial of original sin involves an attempt to rival the work of God. And in both cases original sin returns to exact its terrible penalty.

Animal and person

In the course of subsequent argument we shall again encounter the experience of original sin, as a moral fault within the structure of desire. The meaning of this experience is precisely the mystery of our embodiment: it is 'original' since we can no more escape it than we can escape our flesh. And yet the mystery always eludes our grasp, and prompts us to distinguish our rational from our animal nature in ways which offer some final redemption from a bondage which we can only pretend to accept, but which we never accept in reality. In *The Parliament of Fowles* Chaucer presents a vivid contrast between the mating of beasts and the mating of persons. The various birds are assembled for their diurnal rite of mating, and the goddess Nature presides over their parliament, as they severally come forward to declare their irresistible urge. In the character of the eagles Chaucer (borrowing from Grandson's *Songe Saincte Valentin*) represents what is distinctively human in sexual attraction, while the other birds give voice to animal instinct.[54] The lower birds assemble only as species, and mate only as species, with that transferable passion which displays the structure of a biological need. The eagles, however, assemble and mate as individuals. The three who desire the female desire *her*, and are in competition. Here there is more than an instinct of union; there is also a choice, and the choice becomes a choice of love. Nature rules that only he who is chosen by the female, by her 'choice al fre', shall have the pleasure of her. And the better to give grounds for this choice, she ordains that it shall be postponed for a year, the parties meanwhile remaining in a state of voluntary chastity. Thus the fervour of desire is incorporated into a rational project, and made one with the responsibilities of the individual.

Chaucer was of course not the only one to separate in this way Nature's 'governance' of the animals from the 'statute' by which she rules the free lives of rational individuals. The imagery of *The Parliament* draws upon a vital neo-Platonist tradition, running from Boethius to Alain de L'Isle (to whom Chaucer explicitly refers), which tries to give a metaphysical resolution to the problem of human sexuality. For the neo-Platonist, sexuality is elevated by reason from the realm of bodily appetite to the realm of choice. In making the choice, a person takes a vow, or what is tantamount to a vow. The significance of vows is eternal, since they engage the eternal part of our nature. Thus in sexual choice I am bound by a timeless loyalty. But what prompts my choice? It is a choice of union, with another *individual*, and the individuality of another can be grasped only in time, through his sensory embodiment (which, because desire is immediate, may be the object of desire). The occasion of my timeless choice is therefore the present moment. My ultimate freedom from the bondage of mortality is made real to me in the apparent unfreedom with which, confronted by the face of another, I am at once and forever bound to him in love. What binds me is the eternal part of him: the soul which confronts me through his features, and which may withhold or give itself of its own free will. The moment of desire is the 'point of intersection of the timeless with time', the display in earthly costume of an eternal spirit, and the occasion for a choice which, while eternally binding, takes place here and now. On this view the puzzles of sexual desire are explicitly represented as special cases of the mystery of embodiment. A neo-Platonist theologian might argue that our incarnation is necessary because of its epistemic opportunities; for it presents us with the opportunity to know ourselves and others as *individuals*, and so to feel the pathos of eternal loyalties. Similarly, he might justify the ardour of desire, as the most important moment in our need both to unite as individuals and to recognise the endlessness of the vow which springs from our union.

We, who lack that serene vision, must accommodate the trouble of desire in other ways. Or, if we cannot accommodate it, we must take steps to overcome it, to remove desire from the central place that it occupies in our lives. Some societies confine sexual congress to acts of ritual intercourse; in this peculiar stratagem can be discerned the *fear of desire*, and a consequent need to place sexuality outside the sphere of personal relations. In a similar way, the emancipated frolics of the 1960s, which sought relief from the pressure of intimate relations in the *partouze** and the orgy, can be seen as strategies for the elimination of desire. There are those who see this behaviour as 'childish' or 'immature'. More significantly, however, it involves severing a fundamental human attitude from its characteristic intentionality, so as to destroy the most powerful form of personal union. This may be a step on the road to another, and less exclusive, form of social bonding; or it may be merely another instance of the solipsism that threatens the life of over-emancipated man.

We regard each other as irreplaceable in arousal, just as we do in love, and individualising thoughts are in each case central to our endeavour. As I have argued, those thoughts have a large illusory component. Moreover, even in their most metaphysically blameless interpretation, they are, in a certain manner, false. Or at least, they correspond to no scientifically ascertainable 'fact of the matter'. In so far as we could give an explanatory account of what one person gains from another in love and desire, it is clear that he might have gained that benefit equally from someone other than the person to whom he directs his attentions. But it is imperative that we do not think of this. If we do so, our enterprise is jeopardised. By such thoughts we threaten the possibility of any lasting human attachment,

---

* A kind of party staged by left-bank youth in Paris during the late sixties, to which each person had to bring one partner in order to acquire the right to have sex with anyone present.

and therefore threaten the condition which alone can save us from the anxiety of false sentiment and lust.

Individualising thoughts are, in one sense, mystifications. But it is by such mystifications that we live. They are the necessary salve to the pain of incarnation: the pain that is forced upon us by our dual nature, as we see the self and its projects constantly swept away by the body and its needs. I look for the other *in* his body, for no other attitude can appease the fear of his otherness, the fear that he flits away from my grasp and that if I clasp him he is no more held by my arms than was the shade of Dido by the arms of Aeneas.

As we ascend into the territory of love we shall see more clearly that this confrontation with our embodiment is inescapable, and that, besides renunciation, there is no other salve than love and desire. At the same time, we shall see more clearly why it is desire and not love that forces us to stake ourselves upon the outcome of this confrontation. We shall then see why there is a morality which may forbid desire, but no morality which forbids love.

Before moving to that point, however, there are two tasks which remain, in order to complete the account of sexual desire. First, it is necessary to review some of the phenomena of sexuality, and to show their conformity to the intentional content that I have described. Secondly, it is necessary to answer the persistent – and so far neglected – question of the scientist, the question of the place of sexual desire (which stems from and focuses on our animal bodies) in our life as animals.

6

SEXUAL PHENOMENA

The description that I have given of sexual intentionality is the description of a *norm*. In due course the concept of the sexually normal must be examined, not least because of the widespread criticism of the idea as either arbitrary or covertly 'ideological'. I shall try to derive a theory of sexual normality from the concept of the person, so as to answer those criticisms. In the present chapter, however, I examine the intricacy and variety of sexual intentionality, in order to show that the features which I have identified are at the root of common sexual experience. I shall therefore be examining some of the phenomena of desire – its preliminaries, stratagems, varieties and obsessions. The account will be selective, and I postpone any attempt at a *psychopathia sexualis* until Chapter 10. My principal purpose will be to show that my theory of the individualising intentionality of desire can explain what we see.

Obscenity

A theory of the obscene is contained in what I have already written. Obscenity attaches, not to the things themselves, but to a way of seeing or representing them. If we say that certain parts of the human body are obscene, we mean only that, for whatever reason, we are compelled to see them so: their nature or function causes us to dwell on their fleshly reality, so as to eclipse the embodiment of the individual person. (Hence the idea of 'private parts', which must be hidden only because they invite obscene perception.) Obscenity involves a 'depersonalised' perception of human sexuality, in which the body and its sexual function are uppermost in our thoughts and all-obliterating. The copulation of animals frequently strikes us as obscene; so too does the copulation of human beings, when looked at from a point of view outside the first-person perspective of those engaged in it. Thus, in literary representation, the distinction between the genuinely erotic and the licentious is a distinction not of *subject-matter*, but of perspective. The genuinely erotic work is one which invites the reader to re-create in imagination the first-person point of view of someone party to an erotic encounter. The pornographic work retains as a rule the third-person perspective of the voyeuristic observer. In voyeurism a couple is viewed from a point of view which, as it were, enlarges their bodies: the perspective of the keyhole, used to such effect by Cleland in *Fanny Hill*. Cleland's device should be distinguished from the genuinely erotic and infinitely more exciting technique of Laclos in *Les Liaisons dangereuses*, where the point of view is always that of the participant to the act, and the sexual organs are no more than instruments in a game of psychological possession. A reader of Cleland might be tempted to agree with Lawrence Sterne that 'there is more sin and wickedness have entered the world through keyholes than through all other holes put together.' A reader of Laclos will know better – or worse.

Any part of the human body can be represented without obscenity: even the genitals. However, there is a great difference between the representation of a flaccid (and perhaps diminutive) penis and the representation of a rampant and enlarged one. The important feature of obscenity is normally the 'interesting condition' of the bodily parts, which bear vibrant witness to arousal. Equally the whole body might appear as obscene: as does the body of the tempting Basini to Musil's Törless. Having been displayed to him in its sexual availability, Basini's body threatens Törless's composure with its pleasure-sodden fleshiness.

A similar perception of the body may occur in violence and disease. It is only a minor abuse of language to describe certain displays of violence as obscene. For they too may dwell on the body to the exclusion of the embodied person. The body is shown in triumph, disintegrating under its own momentum, the spirit scattered in disarray by the pain which assails it, and replaced by the writhing, tearing, dissolving of the flesh. Here again we confront the mystery of incarnation, and here again we suffer that dangerous shift of attention which is the mark of original sin – the shift from the embodied person to the dominating and dissolving body.

Other situations also awaken analogous responses. A person slips on a banana skin: observing the way in which, for a moment, he is *all body*, I feel a strange embarrassment. I am pained and nonplussed; in my confusion I laugh, so distancing myself from the other's fate.[1] Laughter, in such cases, involves the recognition that a person has *gone under*, overthrown by the body's impersonal laws of motion (cf. the idea already referred to, of the person's *Untergang* in desire). There is, of course, a difference from true obscenity: for here I do not focus on the flesh as flesh, and do not enjoy the thought of its autonomous operation. From this embarrassment I recover at once, and extend to the object of my confusion the helping hand which restores him to the human world from which he was momentarily jettisoned.

Fear of the obscene is fear of the depersonalising quality of sexual curiosity. This tendency is an integral part of our interest in each other. At the same time, it is checked by the movements of desire, which focus on the individual and refuse to regard him only as a member of his sex, or to undergo that 'descent into detail' which is the mark of sexual curiosity. Peter Porter expresses the point with careful ambiguities ('Conventions of Death'):

> What I want is a particular body,
> The further particulars being obscene
> By definition

Curiosity and its pleasures can dominate desire. When that happens, we find ourselves suddenly irrelevant to each other, precisely at the point when we strove to be united. A collapse occurs in the heart of desire, and all its exploits and dangers seem, once the pleasure has ebbed away, worthless and even shameful. This is the phenomenon for which the Romans devised the phrase *omne animal post coitum triste*, which implies that coitus saddens by reminding us of our animal nature. (For obscene attention finds only the animal and never the self.) I shall argue in later chapters that it is intrinsic to desire that it should be subject to such an undermining. Some welcome this fact, believing that we need to 'release' our pent-up animal spirits. But we must not assume that, because our sexual desires are constructed upon a foundation of animal impulse, that it is the animal impulse that we need, and seek, to gratify.

Modesty and shame

Certain highly complex interpersonal emotions – embarrassment, shame and disgust – have an obviously important place in the sexual conduct of persons, and absolute candour in sexual matters is not commonly recommended or esteemed. Moreover, the recent decline in the practice of modesty, and the disposition to speak openly about the sexual act, has accompanied no heightening of the sexual passion, but, on the contrary, a relaxation – a 'decline', as Henry James once put it, 'in the sentiment of sex'.[2] It is nevertheless evident that embarrassment is no accidental consequence of desire. For the subject of desire is, in his very impulse, seeking a reciprocal response; he is therefore possessed by the thought of himself as a possible object of desire, and embarrassed by the inevitable conclusion that he may be no such thing. Moreover, he is seeking to elicit from the other a response which is deeply compromising. Only in special circumstances is it embarrassing to show friendship towards, or to receive friendship from, another. The reverse is true of desire: only in special circumstances is this emotion *not* embarrassing to either party. (And cf. St Augustine's comparison, referred to above, between arousal and anger.)

I suggest the following analysis of the intentional structure of embarrassment: the subject believes that he runs the risk of another's contempt, indignation, disapproval or other negative assessment. He fears this event, and believes that he can avert it only by his own conduct. Everything depends upon what he does and how he appears. Embarrassment is the expression of this fear, and its natural sign is hesitation – of which the extreme form is paralysis before the questioning eyes of the other. Embarrassment involves the dual sense of myself, as wholly individual and wholly social. In embarrassment I come before the other as an individual, and am understood, questioned, praised and condemned as such, so as to be held through and through responsible to others.

Shame is a special case of embarrassment. The man who is 'ashamed of himself' shares the attitude that he fears. He sees his own nature with contempt, indignation or disapproval, or he in some other way judges himself adversely. Hence his fear of the other's judgement becomes a fear of *discovery*, a fear that the other will know him, as he already knows himself. Thus, while someone may live with normal embarrassment, taking comfort in the prospect that he may persuade the other to view him differently, it is very hard to live with shame. For shame has no remedy. You cannot undo a discovery, nor render untrue a discovered truth. The first recourse, therefore, is to hide yourself, and it is an instinctive manifestation of shame that the subject should seek – like Masaccio's Adam as he is expelled from Paradise – to hide his face in his hands, to cover that part of him where his perspective lies exposed, as it were, to the fearsome gaze of another's judgement.[3]

It is a nice human touch that leads Masaccio to depict Eve as covering, not her face, but her sex and breasts. For in Eve shame is not the moral shame of a wrong acknowledged, but sexual shame. Moral shame is the peculiarly social form of guilt, but *sexual* shame is something else – the sign, not of sexual guilt, but of sexual innocence. In using the word 'shame' to denote this strange recoiling of the body, it might be said, we are speaking metaphorically, and what we have in mind has nothing to do with the idea of adverse judgement. However, this conclusion, tempting though it is, has long been thought to be unsatisfactory. Although there is something strange and even a little pathological in a person who feels that his sexual parts and functions are in themselves contemptible or evil, we sense that this *moral* horror of the body is but an exaggerated expression of a reticence and even distaste that seem to be present in all but the lewdest of humanity. In his classic study of modesty,[4] Havelock Ellis assembled impressive evidence to show that the disposition to withdraw the sexual organs and the sexual functions from the curious glances and unsolicited attentions of others is an almost universal human trait, however overlaid it may be with social and sartorial conventions. Moreover it everywhere accompanies the disposition to turn away from the gaze of the other – to hide one's face in one's hands, and to blush when one is not succeeding. Ellis himself offered various explanations of shame, seeing it partly as a survival of the animal instinct to avoid unwanted intercourse, and partly as a social product, the major element in which is the 'fear of being disgusting'. The first explanation does not concern us, since, even if true, it says nothing about the intentionality of sexual shame. The second, however, is more interesting, since it is an explanation in terms of the subject's intentional understanding. If true, moreover, it would establish that sexual shame is a genuine species of shame – the result of a prior belief in the disgusting character of one's sexuality and a fear of disgusting another by displaying it.

Naturally, we cannot reject such an account of shame out of hand. Havelock Ellis was not alone in thinking that the situation of the sexual organs *inter urinam et faeces* plays a determining role in our thoughts about them. There is a human impulse to recoil from dirt, and in particular from the dirt of human excrement. We need not speculate upon the origin of this impulse – whether it is innate or acquired, whether it is the continuation or the inversion of some infantile feeling, and so on – in order to recognise its great importance in the world of the child. The child thinks of his body as having 'dirty' parts. He also learns to conceal those parts, and, through the use of clothes, to subject his body to the drama of the revealed and the hidden. So important are clothes that many writers have wished to see them as the *origin* of sexual shame, which is created from the habit of concealing what may also be temptingly revealed. 'Shame, divine shame,' wrote Carlyle, 'arose there mysteriously under Clothes'.[5] To which one may add Montaigne's remark that 'there are certain things which are hidden in order to be shown.'

The explanation is, however, implausible. Anthropological evidence suggests that even those people who have no disposition to conceal their sexual parts suffer shame when those parts are exposed to unsolicited attention.[6] Nevertheless, there is much charm, for the modern intelligence, in the Freudian theory, which combines the scatological and the sartorial explanation. For Freud, shame is the survival of the childhood idea of a 'dirty little secret' which each of us carries about him, and which speaks to us not only of hidden dirt, but also of forbidden pleasures.

The hypothesis is further confirmed by the widespread use of words denoting dirt ('filth' for example) in order to describe obscene literature and lewd (that is to say, shameless) behaviour. Aurel Kolnai has argued, in a work which draws on phenomenology rather than anthropological fact, that the 'dirty' is the prime category of sexual morality, and that the dichotomy 'pure/impure' lies at the heart of all our moral feelings concerning the sexual act.[7] While times may have changed so as to render that hypothesis less than completely persuasive, it cannot be denied that it contains an important truth, and that thoughts of 'purity' are uppermost in the mind of a person subject to the burning sense of sexual shame.

However, the scatological theory of sexual shame is peculiarly inverted. The modest person does not think of his sexual parts as 'dirty'. On the contrary, it is part of modesty that such thoughts – which are truly the thoughts of a child – should be vanquished or put aside. (The Freudians argue, however, that these thoughts are not put aside but repressed, thereby suggesting that they continue to exert their influence, but in a secret way.) Moreover, a modest woman may feel shame focussed upon her breasts. These are in no way 'dirty', not even to a child; but they have in common with the genitals that they are the receptacles of sexual pleasure and the focus of sexual interest.

The normal occasions of shame are those of the prurient glance, the obscene gesture or the lewd utterance. These provoke shame because they dirty what is in itself not dirty. The thought of the subject is something like 'I am defiled by his glances'. The subject is *made to feel* shame, because he feels 'degraded' by the other's interest, by the tone of his conversation or by the implications of his gesture. It is not the other's disgust at my body which provokes this response, but, on the contrary, his pleasure in it. The woman who supposes that she is being undressed in the imagination of the man who watches her, feels, not that he is thinking of what is in itself dirty, but that he is thinking of her body in a way that dirties it. He is testimony to the living and corrosive presence of an obscene thought. Her response contains a small premonition of rape, the

143

victim of which may, like Lucretia, feel so defiled by the contact of her assailant as to be unable to live with herself. Her 'ontological condition' changes beyond hope of a remedy. She will never again be clean. She, against her will, has been forced to see herself as a partner in crime, and the victim of this crime is her own body, 'defiled', 'polluted' and 'rifled' – to use the words that occur most frequently to Shakespeare, in his unsurpassed description of Lucretia's mental anguish.

What is the nature of the degrading thought that induces shame? It is necessary to distinguish two possibilities. In the first case, the man watching her may entertain a certain *belief* about the woman, a belief that embarrasses her. (He may believe her to be a prostitute, for example.) She may be offended by this belief, but, by refuting it, she can overcome her embarrassment and reassert her right to his consideration. In the second case, the one which here concerns us, the man's thought is not a belief about the woman, but a way of seeing her. This 'way of seeing' is degrading partly because it is infectious. By recognising his thought, the woman comes to share it; her perception of herself is transformed, in a way that degrades her. She cannot regain her equanimity by refuting an unjust charge, for there is no charge. The thought itself besmirches her, and she turns away from the man who conveys it with an instinctive movement of revulsion.

It is not difficult to describe this thought, which so unjustly intrudes upon the mental life of the victim, so as to create the condition of which it also accuses her. What is difficult is to separate it from the other thoughts with which it is compounded, and which reinforce its penalty. There is an element in the Freudian account which I previously put to one side, but which should be mentioned here, if only because it corresponds to what has been the principal rival explanation to the scatological and the sartorial: the element of 'forbidden pleasure'. It is sometimes said that the ruling thought of shame is the idea of the sexual act – performed, perhaps, with the man whose stare prompts the present crisis – in the mind of someone who believes the act to be forbidden. The Freudians extend the concept of 'tabu' to describe this powerful sense of the sexually forbidden, meaning that it is something that is at once stronger and less questionable than any normal moral injunction. Having thought of herself as performing the forbidden act, the woman is ashamed to discover (but of course 'unconsciously') that she also wants it. Thus, wrote Restif de la Bretonne (an indisputable, if horrible, authority on these matters), 'it is the most modest girl, the girl who blushes most, who is most disposed to the pleasures of love'.[8] On this account, the degrading character of the thought lies entirely in the idea of being disposed to do what is forbidden.

But the theory is surely wrong. The woman in my example feels most ashamed before the desirous glances of the man whom she least desires. (There is a reason, which will shortly emerge, for concentrating on the experience of the woman.) It is her disgust at the other which awakens sexual disgust in herself: not because she realises that she wants him, but because she realises how much she does *not* want to do *this* thing with *him*. Why is such a thought degrading? It is here that we encounter the central component of the intentionality of shame. The woman is compelled by her thought to see herself as a 'sexual creature': as a creature who can perform the sexual act with 'men', and perhaps even with a man whom she does not know. In other words, she sees her sexuality divorced from the individualising intentionality of desire, and recast as a bodily impulse, an animal appetite in which she is at the mercy of her body. This thought degrades her, because it represents her as overcome by her body, without reference to her uniqueness as an object of desire, or to the comparable uniqueness of whomsoever she might desire in turn. In other words, she becomes the subject of an obscene thought. The lewd glance invites her to think in a way that menaces the interpersonal nature of her sexual life, and self-respect – respect for her own self, and for the self in general as the immanent object of desire – causes her to avoid the thought. She removes herself from its corrosive meaning, and from the eyes of the man who 'shares' the thought with her, and who therefore 'knows' her inner trouble.

Thus the occasion of shame is neither the thought of 'forbidden pleasure' nor exposure of the sexual parts. It is, rather, exposure to the desirous thoughts of another who is not desired, and who compels, through his interest, the degrading perception of oneself as partner to an obscenity. This is the true substance of woman's complaint, that she is treated as a 'sex object' by men. A. Duval, a pupil of Ingres, recounted that a model was once posing naked and unabashed at the École des Beaux Arts, when suddenly she screamed and ran for her clothes. She had seen a workman on the roof, who gazed at her pruriently through the skylight.[9]

Such a theory accounts for a curious occasion of shame: not the taking off but the putting on of clothes, after the sexual act. Again the experience is characteristically that of the woman, who feels herself no longer looked at with the eyes of desire and no longer fortified by the excitement of exposure. Suddenly everything seems flat, arbitrary and mundane; what was for a moment a glowing body, offered and accepted as an individual life, is now only a piece of human flesh, to be rewrapped and set aside for another occasion. At no point does a woman feel cheaper or more expendable than at this one, and hence, out of shame, she will wish to lie still with her lover, naked, talking out of her nakedness, until it becomes accepted again as her. (Sei Shōnagon inveighs, in *The Pillow Book*, against the intolerable vulgarity of the man who rises too early after love, and the strength of her contempt for him is a mirror of her shame. For in a sense her contempt is for herself, and is induced by the obscene perception of her own embodiment.)

Not every desirous glance inspires shame. On the contrary, so long as a gesture does not transgress the faint divide between sexual interest and obscene representation, a woman will welcome it. For the desirous gesture is a sign of her power, and of the manifold sexual possibilities which reinforce that power so long as she refuses to fulfil them. The change comes when, by some word or gesture, the man reveals an obscene perception of her body and compels her to glimpse, in imagination, what his interest really means. (Camille Mélinaud expresses the point in a nice definition of modesty: '*la pudeur c'est la honte de l'animalité qui est en nous*'.)[10]

Men welcome the desirous glances of women, which seldom display obscene perception, even when focused on the body. But only homosexual men welcome the desirous glances of men. To the heterosexual the desirous glances of the homosexual are in many cases *already* obscene, inviting him to acts which repel him, and placing him suddenly within the predatory perspective of the male – the perspective which a woman must confront from day to day, but against which a man has few social defences.

Sexual shame is a special case of a more extensive phenomenon: bodily shame – the shame induced by the perception of one's body from a point of view outside it, as an item curious in itself. Such shame is an overwhelming experience during childhood, when the power of the adult, who controls the objective world, gives added authority to the adult's perception. The child sees his body as an 'object in the eyes of the adults'. In the unequal encounter between his own sense of oneness with his body and the adult's moralising distance from it, he comes to experience the tension of embodiment in its acutest form. Hence the child's disposition to hide from adult glances: a kind of modesty which, because it has the body as its primary object, prefigures the sexual modesty of the mature human being.

We should not regret this modesty in children. On the contrary, it is the necessary consequence of a developing first-person perspective, and of a growing sense of responsibility towards the human world. It is the shameless child who should awaken our distaste. If he does not feel the tension of his embodiment it is because he lacks a crucial mental capacity: the capacity to entertain in a single thought the subjective and the objective view of his own condition. He has not acquired what the eighteenth-century moralists called 'moral sense'.

Shame exists, then, in a variety of forms: moral shame, which leads us to recoil before adverse judgement; bodily shame, which leads us to recoil before prurience and curiosity; and sexual shame, through which we avoid the obscene perception inherent in another's undesired desire. In each of these there is the same fundamental thought that structures embarrassment: the thought that I come before the other, and am judged, as an individual. Bodily shame, therefore, shows the deep recognition that I, as an individual, am present in the individuality of my body, and in a strange way answerable for it. Max Scheler saw shame in all forms as a 'protective feeling [*Schutzgefühl*] of the individual and of his individual worth, against the whole public sphere,'[11] and he derived from this the connection between shame and honour – a connection which, he argued, is closer in women than in men. With such a theory – which Scheler develops at some length – we may agree, and note only how significant a testimony, therefore, is bodily shame to our sense that the self and the body are identical, and that the individuality and apartness of the self are nothing else, in the end, than the individuality and apartness of the body.

An interesting ancillary phenomenon is that of 'word shame' – the universal human disposition to describe the act of love in terms exemplified by this sentence. Such a disposition is neither prudery nor euphemism, but merely modest reserve. It is part of the disposition to avoid the occasion of sexual shame. The phrase 'to make love', which uses the language of personal relations, avoids the implication that the participants are engaged merely as *bodies* in the act which excites them. The disposition to speak of 'love' and 'love-making' in describing the phenomena of desire is so widespread that no one has the slightest difficulty in understanding without further explanation the real meaning of a phrase like *faire l'amour*. Occasionally, the imagery is varied; occasionally all suggestion of an *act* is omitted, as in Turkish *sevişmek* (literally: 'to love each other mutually'); or the language for the kiss may be extended to denote the sexual act, as in French *baiser*. Some languages describe the kiss itself in the language of love, as in modern Greek *phili*, or Czech *polibek* (from *libit se*, to have a liking). The polite word for the sexual act may also be a variant of 'being together', as in ancient Greek *sunousiazo* (interestingly transformed in modern Greek to *sunousi-azomai* – as though only the passive voice could capture the right degree of reticence). Ancient Greek also had recourse to theology, describing the sexual act by means of the verb *aphrodisiazein* (or, for women, *aphrodisiasthenai*), a description which is also applied by Aristotle to the copulation of animals.[12] Some African languages have several different 'levels' of sexual reference, from the extremely circumlocutory to the obscenely direct – the use of each being dictated by the precise social context. But in all cases there is a definite distinction between the 'polite' reference to sex, in terms of personal relation, and the obscene emphasis on the body and its role. Those words which purport to denote the act 'directly', without further implications concerning the special relation between the participants, are shunned as obscene. Once again the Freudians try to explain this as a species of 'tabu'; but the explanation is no more than a repetition of the fact to be explained. Moreover, it makes quite incomprehensible that 'fuck' and 'cunt' should be used unashamedly as swear words, but only with immense reluctance, even by those for whom these words are a familiar part of everyday vocabulary, to refer to the act of love. D. H. Lawrence's attempt to redeem them (in *Lady Chatterley's Lover*), so as to cut through the 'hypocrisy' that shields us from the truths of sex, is partly responsible for one of the most striking of his many literary disasters. The result is unbearably coy, and in a strange way far more 'mealy-mouthed' than the honoured language of love which it is designed to replace. Lawrence is right in one thing, however, which is that the unembarrassed use of these words is reserved for situations of sexual intimacy; what offends in his book is the sense that this intimacy is too closely and too pruriently observed. With those who are not our lovers, we almost invariably (unless for effect) describe the act of love by means of circumlocutions. Aristide Bruant comments that 'almost all the expressions in *argot* to denote "coitus" are obscene';[13] meaning that, while most of them are elaborately circumlocutory (*battre le beurre, être sous presse, faire la bête à deux dos, manger de la soupe à la quequette, voire la feuille à l'envers* and so on), their circumlocution takes us precisely towards a bodily and depersonalised perception of sexual intercourse. (Perhaps the best example of this is the English punk description of love-making as 'squelching'.) The 'medical' terms, by contrast, are not obscene. But they can be used only because of their elaborate affectation of 'neutrality', of being outside human intentionality altogether; by using such terms we observe our actions from a point of view which renders them 'not our concern'. The 'modesty of words' which governs most of our reference to the sexual act has been described by Wayland Young as part of 'the denial of Eros'.[14] In fact, however, it is a mark of our respect for Eros, that we should describe the sexual act, not in the obscene language of curious pleasure, but in the language of desire.

The meaning of the sexual organs

Why, however, do shame and obscenity focus so vividly on the sexual parts – on the organs and the regions of the body that are activated in the condition of arousal? The scatological and sartorial theories purport to explain this fact, although neither succeeds. The first fails to account for a woman's attitude to her breasts; the second fails to recognise that shame over the sexual parts, unlike clothing, is a human universal. This brings us to a difficult question: that of the place of the sexual organs in desire. From one point of view, of course, it is easy to describe this place. From the point of view of biology the sexual urge requires contact between the sexual organs, which are the loci of pleasure and the channels of reproduction. But from another point of view – that of intentional understanding – the role of the sexual organs is obscure. How do we, and how must we see them, in the 'desirous thoughts' which motivate our sexual stratagems? Why, in particular, should the biologically based experiences that are 'delivered' to us by our sexual organs be incorporated into the intentionality of an interpersonal response? That last question is one of the most difficult of all, and I shall not be able to confront it until Chapter 9. But what I say here will foreshadow the solution that I shall later propose.

In a striking passage, Sartre remarks that 'no fine, prehensile organ provided with striated muscles can be a sex organ, a sex.'[15] He means, not that no such organ could take the part played by sexual organs in the activity of biological reproduction, but rather that no such organ could be *perceived* as we perceive the organs of sex. He comments cryptically that 'if sex were to appear as an organ, it could be only one manifestation of the vegetative life,' but his point is more far-reaching than that implies, and his subsequent reference to the 'organic passivity of sex in coitus' shows that he is not concerned with the distinction between the active and the vegetative. Once again, Sartre's thought is profoundly Augustinian. Sexual desire requires us to unite through organs which are in an important sense outside our will. These organs are not organs of 'doing', even if they undergo startling transformations (such as erection) as a consequence of things done.

We are impelled to distinguish between organs which are interesting to us all the time, on account of their ability to change things around them, and organs which are interesting only occasionally, and not because of their capacity to initiate change, but for their capacity to undergo it – to 'respond' to outside influence. The hands, which explore, seize and manipulate, have a vital role to play in sexual intercourse. Through them we go out towards the other, and when we clasp hands we express our will to be joined. But these organs which join us are full of movement, and of the readiness to depart upon another mission. They remain locked in contact, not from a pleasant sensation which compels them, but from a voluntary determination in us, of which our hands are avatars. Our hands rest together, but their resting is something that we *do* with them.

As I have already argued in the last chapter, our sexual organs are no such active purveyors of intention. They are hardened or softened, but not because we will them to be so. (Frank Harris contends (*My Life and Loves*) that Maupassant was able to 'will' an erection; if the story is true, Maupassant must be compared to someone who 'wills' a headache – i.e. who performs some mental operation which 'brings about' what is desired.) The transformation of the sexual organs is essentially a response, something that happens to them and in them. And we, in them, are overcome. The pleasure of their contact cements us with a force that is not of our own devising. This pleasure is not something that we do, nor is it the expression of our will, even though it is responsive to our thoughts and feelings.

That sexual intercourse should culminate in the union of these 'passive' organs, rather than in the union of hands or eyebeams, is of the utmost spiritual importance to us. For we are 'overcome' in these organs; their transformation represents the conquest of the will, and the absorption of the agency of each by each. It is only when we understand this point that we shall see both what is right and what is wrong in the scatological theory of sexual shame, and how near, and how far, are ideas of sexual 'purity' from those of faecal 'cleanliness'.

Yeats lamented that 'love has pitched his mansion / In the house of excrement'. But his regret is incoherent. For love could not (phenomenologically speaking) have chosen a better residence. The sexual parts possess a vital and regularly exercised function, which we can control, but which lies importantly beyond the reach of our intentions. It is our steady observation of, and eventual familiarity with, this function that prepares us for the drama of the sexual act. I come to see my sexual parts as overcoming me, in obedience to the natural and legitimate rhythm of my body. What happens to them happens to me, and as a result of what I have done – what I have eaten or drunk. They are therefore a symbol of the body's eventual triumph over the will; of its infinite capacity to 'have the last word' in all our alimentary transactions. This ability – which is at its most pronounced in death, when the body finally extinguishes all our resistance – is one that we learn to incorporate into our sense of what we are. It is precisely the body's obstinate dedication to the task of overcoming us, of imposing its iron law of motion, that forces us to recognise our unity with it. Excretion is the final 'no' to all our transcendental illusions – to the *cari inganni* of the poet who imagines with Leopardi, that '*sè stesso*' is something other than '*fango*', something other than mud or slime.[16] It therefore prepares us for the only union which is either available or conceivable – the union of selves in and through their bodies.

When I urinate, my life and activity are for a moment interrupted. (Contrast breathing, or the beating of the heart.) I allow the body to 'have its way', conscious that I cannot long resist its imperium, and that it does no more than commit me to the consequences of my previous action, when I raised my glass in a moment of hilarity. Hence, I come to see my sexual organ as the conduit of the body's orders, the instrument of its rule. Whatever happens to me through *it*, expresses the body's command. Excretion has a *daily* task of subduing me, and hence the organs of excretion acquire the nimbus of authority which is the body's ultimate due. Inevitably, therefore, they transform sexual excitement into a bodily imperative. The very fact that *they* are calling to me reminds me that, in this present arousal, I am overcome by my body. Nor can I regret the fact, for I *am* my body, and nothing more vividly reminds me of this than the organs through which the body expresses its lordship. Thus Rochester feels *betrayed* by his penis, which – despite its notorious habits – lies impotent with the woman whom he loves. He therefore wishes on it every bodily disease, and concludes:

> May'st thou not piss, who did'st refuse to spend,
> When all my joys did on false thee depend.

In other words, he wishes his penis to lose the capacity whereby it asserts itself, and through which it constantly reminds Rochester of their inseparable connection. The sense of the body's authority in sexual passion grows from the familiar call of bodily necessity which, like a daily parade, reminds us of the enduring authority of the sovereign. If it were not for this, the transcendental illusion of desire – the illusion that I unite with the other as a transcendental self – would threaten every project of intimacy that is presently available. It would constantly impress upon me the absolute disparity between my response to you and my body's response to your body. As it is, however, the sexual act is presented to me as the inevitable conclusion of a progressive process of 'embodiment', in which the body's sovereignty is affirmed, and in which I am aware of the fact that I *am* my body, and made real through it to you.

In the case of the woman there is a further and similarly imperative function which is served by the sexual conduit, this time one that cannot be controlled: the function of menstruation. This creates the woman's sense of being more at the mercy of her body than a man could be, of being subject to an added autocracy from her sexual part. While this fact has been sometimes regretted, and sometimes even fruitlessly opposed, it is a fact nevertheless, and no sexual morality can ignore it, just as no sexual morality can ignore the other and larger fact of which it is the regular reminder, the fact of pregnancy. It should not therefore be supposed, either that the above sketch of the intentional understanding of excrement serves completely to summarise the perceived sense of bodily dominion through the sexual organs, or that the perception is the same for either sex. On the contrary, men and women perceive their bodies differently. This has recently been made evident in the feminist claim that women have some special need, and some special right, to 'control their own bodies', as the only means of establishing equality with men. However, in neither sex is the excremental role of the sexual organs a cause either for regret or for added shame. Indeed, the process of education whereby we cease to share the child's fascination with, and horror at, his excrement is exactly what it appears to be: a process of understanding and repudiation. We come to realise that, if there is a distinction among our actions, between the pure and the impure, it has nothing whatsoever to do with excrement. Coprophilia and coprophobia are alike perversions; for they both attach the sexual act to a childish prurience, and at the same time attempt to replace its interpersonal intentionality with something animal. The very urge to construe sexual shame as a species of cloacal disgust is redolent of this perversion: for it shows the childish disposition to construe a moral relationship in merely animal terms. That which appeared so tragic to Yeats is no such thing, but one of the gifts of nature, which enables us to embark upon an elaborate social project: the cooperative construction of sexual desire.

At the same time, behind the scatological theory of shame and disgust, lurks the indelible emotion that I identified in the last chapter as the sentiment of original sin. The sexual parts are not only vivid examples of the body's dominion; they are also apertures, whose damp emissions and ammoniac smells testify to the mysterious putrefaction of the body. Hence Verlaine's deliberately satanic description of them:

Mais quoi! Tout n'est rien, putains, aux pris de vos
Culs et cons dont la vue et le goût et l'odeur
Et le toucher font des élus de vos dévots,
Tabernacles et Saint des Saints de l'impudeur.

The fact of being overcome through *these* parts enhances the tension of embodiment, and therefore imposes on us – as no other bodily contact could impose on us – the task of abolishing the separation that we experience between body and soul.

If we now combine those observations with our earlier remarks about sexual arousal, we can draw a simple, but important, moral conclusion. I have argued that arousal has an epistemic component – it is a response to an activity of discovery or unveiling. The observable facts about the anatomy of another are readily appreciated, and of no special interest, which is why people can be naked and not ashamed. But there is another kind of familiarity which is sought in the experience of arousal. In this experience, what is normally withheld (not perhaps from sight or touch, but from a certain kind of 'exploration') is now 'offered'. The disposition to offer requires the disposition to withhold. Only because the sexual organs are withheld (and in particular because they are not permitted openly to display the symptoms of excitement) is it possible to open them to the experience of arousal. This is not a cause of shame; nevertheless it is a result of shame that we should obey the edict which tells us to contain ourselves. Hence, to the extent that we value desire, we must also value the shame which safeguards its core experience – the experience of arousal. A functionalist anthropologist might seize upon this as an explanation of the universal institution of sexual shame; I shall later argue that, whether or not it explains, it certainly justifies, our habitual sexual reticence. What makes modesty a virtue is that modesty is the precondition of desire.

The sexual organs are like the face, in that they are subject to massive involuntary transformations which cannot fail to reveal and to compromise the subject. But they do not and cannot have the individuating function of the face: the role of presenting the perceivable index of me, here, now. You may recognise someone *by* his penis, but not *in* his penis. The face, as the locus of another's perspective, is the natural focus of all individualising attention, and it is to the depiction of the face that erotic art primarily addresses itself, so as to portray the sexual feelings of the subject as a kind of radiation in his point of view.

An art which concentrates upon the sexual organs will be, not erotic, but obscene: it will therefore be an art that negates the interpersonal intentionality of desire. It has been a mark of obscenity throughout the ages that it focuses on the organs and mechanisms of the sexual encounter, to the exclusion of all individualising representation of the subjects themselves. The rigmarole is familiar. First, there is the exclusive concentration on the organs, and a consuming interest in their physical peculiarities; secondly, the attempt to concentrate the sexual experience *into* the sexual organs, to make it a peculiar *sensation*, thus heightening the idea of the genitals as 'forbidden fruit' (the fruit of the tree of knowledge, from the tasting of which came shame, fig leaves and also – if Gregory of Nyssa is right – desire). This second feature of obscenity is used against itself, in order to condemn the meagreness of lust, in Lord Rochester's great animadversion against his penis:

> Worst part of me, and henceforth hated most,
> Through all the town the common rubbing post
> On whom each wretch relieves her tingling cunt,
> As hogs on gates do rub themselves and grunt.

Rochester's imagery in this passage recalls another condemnation of lust, attributed by Xenophon to Socrates (*Mem. i 229f.*):

> Then, it is said, Socrates, in the presence of Euthydemos and many other people, said that he thought Kritias was no better off than a pig if he wanted to scratch himself against Euthydemos as piglets against a stone.

The immediate consequence of those two obsessions – with the organs themselves and with the pleasures of sensation – is a collapse of erotic sentiment. That, indeed, is the underlying intention of obscenity. The result is 'masturbatory', because it has located sexual interest *there*, and severed it from the intentionality which provides its meaning.

In true erotic art it is usually the face and not the sexual organ that provides the focus of attention. The reclining Venus looks out from the picture or towards her lover, and the interest in her limbs moves always upwards to the face that surmounts them. A painting which conceals the face but exposes the genitals must inevitably verge on the obscene. (Courbet famously painted such a 'lower portrait' – which is now in private hands.)[17] At the same time, the 'straying' of the attention, from the individualising glances of the eyes, to the contours of the lower parts in which the body takes precedence over the embodied spirit, is a natural part of the drama of desire. The fine art of eroticism is to encourage the attention to stray, without rupturing the interpersonal intentionality that causes our emotions to be engaged, as we perceive the ideal conjunction of the beauty which is the object of aesthetic interest and the beauty which is the object of desire. Thus Velazquez, in his familiar transformation of the reclining Venus, turns his model away from us, in a posture that exposes her voluptuous haunches and conceals her face. An obscure image of her face appears, however, in the mirror which Cupid holds. The viewer's attention is caught between the real and sexual body, and the distant face, which is no more than the abstract idea of a face, sketchy, disembodied and without expression. We are brought back, in the midst of our depersonalised sexual interest, to the individual presence in this body, although we only faintly perceive it, and cannot engage with it, as we engage with the look of the Venus of Urbino. Our feelings reach the brink of the orgiastic, and are yet turned back to the woman, and the face, which are in part concealed. (The picture was once damaged by a prudish suffragette, who poked at Venus's rump with her umbrella. Asked to explain herself, the assailant said that she took against the rump 'because it is stupid!')

Modesty is the disposition to feel bodily shame (including sexual shame), and so to avoid its occasion. It is something more than the desire to cover oneself, or to conceal one's private parts, else we might agree with Madame d'Épinay's exclamation (*Mémoires*, vol. 1), '*Belle vertu! qu'on attache sur soi avec des épingles!*' We value modesty partly because we value desire, and look with suspicion on those habits which untie the knot of individual attachment. Havelock Ellis put the point tendentiously, but (as I shall argue) correctly, when he wrote:

> In the art of love ... [modesty] is more than a grace; it must always be fundamental. Modesty is not indeed the last word of love, but it is the necessary foundation for all love's most exquisite audacities, the foundation which alone gives worth and sweetness to what Senancour calls its 'delicious impudence'. Without modesty we could not have, nor rightly value at its true worth, that bold and pure candour which is at once the final revelation of love and the seal of its sincerity.[18]

The usual name for immodest desire – the desire which rides roughshod over the reticence of others, and treats every new object as an equivalent of the last – is lust. The above account of shame contains an explanation of what is shameful in lust. It also enables us to see why male and female modesty have traditionally been seen as separate (and perhaps unequal) virtues. Men have traditionally been the initiators of sexual union, women the recipients of their attentions. The modesty of the first consists in ardour – in a burning concentration upon the individual woman, of a kind that will appear not lustful but dependent. This modest ardour was held to undermine the woman's resistance, not by inspiring lewd thoughts – which in truth only heighten her shame and therefore her reluctance – but by persuading her to feel not demeaned but *valued* as the recipient of her lover's attentions. The woman herself will then (so Senancour and

Stendhal argue)[19] react accordingly. Her response, awoken by a sense of her value for the other, will concentrate on him, finding every excuse in his favour, until she seems unjustly to harm him by her resistance, and may therefore, without having entertained any but moral thoughts, give in at last to that which she desires.

The outline of the drama is familiar, and rehearsed in every work of erotic literature, courtly, ceremonial or profane. What is familiar in experience or in literature may, however, remain philosophically impenetrable. In later chapters, therefore, I shall endeavour to trace more accurately the course of love, and the moral and political consequences of the conflict between the bodily focus of lust, and the concentrated attachments of desire. One particular feature of this conflict has already been discussed: 'fear of the obscene'.

Prostitution

This 'fear of the obscene' animates the common view that prostitution is inherently shameful. Consider first the prostitution of the market (to be distinguished from 'holy prostitution' and from the 'prostitution of command' – see below). The essence of the market commodity is that it is transferable – exchangeable at any point for its price (or 'exchange value' as the classical economists called it). It is therefore replaceable by any simulacrum that will 'do just as well'. If the prostitute is humiliated, it is because she has divorced the sexual act from its project of sexual union. She is not the object of her client's desire, but the commodity which satisfies his need. Even if she responds with some kind of excitement, it cannot involve the burgeoning of reciprocity which is integral to the 'course of desire'. To desire her client would be to become intensely aware of her replaceability – of the fact that she, as commodity, is not desired. The perpetuation of her desire would then at once take on a perverted aspect, like the desire of the rapist, who seeks no reciprocity, and who indeed sets out to kill reciprocity, lest it prove too powerful an invasion of his self-centred perspective. Hence the prostitute must either refrain from desiring her client, or else invent for herself a fantasy object of desire. In each case the client is also used as a means: either as a means to earn money or as a means to satisfy her yearning for another. Hence the woman who 'sells her body' is forced to see her partner too in monetary terms, as someone who has no value besides that of the market. Any other who provided the money would 'do just as well'.

It is worth pausing to notice the power that money has to reconstitute human relations in its own image: a power that is the subject of endless moral commentary. Money represents a *quantifiable* transaction: one whose aim can be expressed in exact and finite terms. All monetary obligations are therefore obligations that can be discharged. As I have already indicated, the obligations that emerge in the course of desire are not in any simple way 'dischargeable'. Money is useful to the prostitute, in representing the sexual act as a fleeting transaction and in ending all question as to whether its obligations have been fulfilled. Inevitably, however, the act is transformed by money, which imposes the 'intentionality of the market' on conduct that cannot sustain it. Thus Simmel, in his impressive work, *The Philosophy of Money*, argues as follows:

> Money is never an adequate mediator of personal relationships – such as the genuine love relationship, however abruptly it may be broken off – that are intended to be permanent and based on the sincerity of the binding forces. Money best serves, both objectively and symbolically, that purchaseable satisfaction which rejects any relationship that continues beyond the momentary sexual impulse, because it is absolutely detached from the person and completely cuts off from the outset any further consequences. In so far as one pays with money, one is completely finished with any object. . . . Since in prostitution the relationship between the sexes is quite specifically confined to the sexual act, it is reduced to its purely generic content. It consists in what any member of the species can perform and experience. It is a relationship in which the most contrasting personalities are equal and individual differences are eliminated. Thus, the economic counterpart of this kind of relationship is money, which also, transcending all individual distinctions, stands for the species-type of economic values. Conversely, we experience in the nature of money itself something of the essence of prostitution. . . . Kant's moral imperative never to use human beings as a mere means but to accept and treat them always, at the same time, as ends in themselves, is blatantly disregarded *by both parties* in the case of prostitution. Of all human relationships, prostitution is perhaps the most striking instance of mutual degradation to a mere means, and this may be the strongest and most fundamental factor that places prostitution in such a close historical relationship to the money economy, the economy of 'means' in the strictest sense.[20]

I have quoted at length, since, for all its looseness of argument, Simmel's passage gives voice to fundamental intuitions concerning the nature of desire. But it also suggests a paradox. For how *can* the sexual transaction really be given a 'money equivalent'? How *can* there be desire which regards money as part of its goal? Clearly there *cannot* be such a desire; hence the old Spanish saying *el cuerpo de una mujer no es pagadero* – a woman's body is not merchandise. That which is wanted from the woman is precisely that which cannot be bought, and the money given must be seen as an oblation to the priestess of Venus, which she pays for her maintenance:[21] hence the institution of the brothel, in which, by paying to a third party, the client frees himself from the consciousness of what he is doing to the woman whom he chooses. For sex to be a genuine 'consumer product', the prostitute must be replaced by an impersonal object – a doll say – so that sex can be *manufactured* as a commodity. In a 'consumer society' one could expect the ideal of beauty to become 'dollified' and 'fetishised' – as indeed we see in the fashion models of today, and in the actual appearance of the modern prostitute.[22]

The paradox is illustrated also in the love of riches. While a man may be desired for his looks, his virtues, his power, it is difficult to make sense of his being *desired* for his riches. The paradox is enshrined in the myth of Danaë, who is said to have desired Zeus as a part of her desire for money, so that she welcomed his embraces when he appeared to her in the guise of a rain of gold. A couplet by Parmenion from the Greek Anthology (*Amatory Epigrams*, no. 33) tries to make sense of this, by referring not to the use of money in purchase, but to its symbolic form as a gift:

You rained as gold upon Danaë, Olympian Zeus,
so that the child should receive a gift, and not tremble before the son of Kronos.

But that also confirms the paradox: for what was given to Zeus was not given *for* money, and could not be given *as* money.

It is precisely this distance of the monetary transaction from the transaction of desire that is most liberating to the prostitute. The prostitution of the market frees the woman from every *moral* tie with her client, in just the way that the market undoes the ties of the 'moral economy' which bound the feudal serf to the feudal lord.[23] One should compare the prostitution of the market with the prostitution of command – prostitution which stands to market prostitution as slavery stands to the capitalist economy in the 'ideal types' of these arrangements that we owe to Marx.[24] The classic representation of this condition, and one that also shows it to be part of a 'depersonalising' strategy on the part of the enslaver, is given in the notorious *Histoire d'O*. The heroine is enslaved by a confraternity of violent men, who issue her with orders. The following is not untypical:

When we are in the costume we wear at night, that which I have on now, and our sex is uncovered, this is not for convenience sake; that could be otherwise assured. It is for insolence sake, so that your eyes should be fixed there, and should not be fixed elsewhere; so that you should learn that this is your master, to which above all your lips are destined. In the daytime, when we are ordinarily dressed, and when you are dressed as you are now, you will observe the same manners, and your only duty will be to open our clothing, if that is required of you, and to close it again when we have finished with you.[25]

The extraordinary success of this obscene book shows that it has captured a fundamental fantasy. The fantasy is that of a supremely achieved prostitution, in which the woman does not have even the liberty of refusal – in which the market economy has been replaced by an economy of command. In this achieved prostitution, the woman's spirit is wholly overcome by the force of masculine autocracy. At the same time, however, the command destroys the basis of personal relation, and compels her to attach her interests and her joys to the abstract penis, irrespective of who owns it or why he seeks her submission to it. This is the root fantasy of obscenity, and describes the content of the fear which underlies the paroxysm of shame. As it implies, its enactment involves the abrogation of all individualised feeling in the woman; her enslavement is merely, to use the Marxian language, the 'realised' and 'objective' form of this 'subjective' alienation.

The prostitution of command is at the other extreme from the prostitution of the market. Between them lies the 'feudal' system, represented by the *harem*. Here, the restoration of the 'moral economy' removes the paradox from the prostitute's desire. In effect, she is no longer a prostitute, since she is tied to an 'absolute sole lord of life and love'. Whatever the deficiencies of her circumstance, she is nevertheless restored to the realm of the erotic, by being required to perform the sexual act only with someone to whom she is also bound by an intelligible moral tie.

'Actually existing prostitution' is never as unmixed in its motives as the three cases I have considered. As Wicksteed argues, economic relations have a natural tendency to beget non-economic relations,[26] and from the ground of 'market' prostitution therefore may spring mutual friendship and concern. (Consider too the *geisha* and the courtesan.) Nevertheless, prostitution provides 'ideal types' of the sexual *transaction*, of sex removed from the realm of personal relation and made into a form of 'alienated labour'. The two main types that I have given involve the exploitation of others – their use as a means. Hence they provide paradigms against which to define an ideal of sexual love. In love the other is treated not as means but as end; his desires and pleasures are mine, and mine, I hope, are his. The desire for love, and the desire for money, each penetrate our lives, transforming the quality of every human relation, including those founded in desire. Love and money are felt as *cosmic* forces, and for this reason the prostitute appears to us as a symbol of transgression – of the possibility that, at any moment, we might give ourselves over to a force that wars with love. (Wagner distinguishes the power of Wotan from the power of Alberich, who, having renounced love, can obtain women only by paying for them. Alberich's world is poisoned by the absence of love, and, in taking the product of Alberich's labour, Wotan identifies with him, and so goes under, finding that his own world too is poisoned.)

Falling in love

In Chapter 8 I shall explore more elaborately the phenomenon of erotic love. But it is again necessary to anticipate later remarks, if we are to have a clear view of the problems which presently confront us. The most puzzling feature of erotic love is that you can *fall* in love – and, moreover, on the basis of the minimum acquaintance with the object, no more acquaintance than Tamino could obtain from gazing on Pamina's portrait. The recurrent image of the 'love potion' expresses the persuasion that this kind of love is a compulsion, which is in no way like esteem, and requires no knowledge of the other's character.

To understand 'falling in love' one must see that its intentionality is a special case of the intentionality of desire. The person in love sees his beloved's personality in all his acts and gestures, and is, as we might express it, spellbound by them. The person who *falls* in love makes the reverse assimilation: he sees gestures and features which awaken his desire, and, in order that desire should justify the effort to which it at once commits him, he imagines a personality to fit what he sees. This is the 'idealisation' of the object of desire. Thereafter all is discovery and deception, or, if his imagination triumphs, confirmation of the initial wish. Initially there is no distinction between love and 'infatuation': the difference is revealed when the lover is submitted to a 'trial' – and that is why true love requires a period of courtship, and why Tamino's love for Pamina must be subjected to ordeal. The person who falls in love wants the smile, the words, the acts of the other to be 'for him', in the sense of being done always in some measure for his sake. He feels, on perceiving the other, a premonition of 'home': of that which is 'mine by right'. Garibaldi describes his first meeting with Anita thus:

We remained silent and ecstatic, looking at each other, like two persons who do not see each other for the first time, and who seek in each other's features something which activates a memory.

At last I saluted her, and said: 'You must be mine.' I spoke little Portuguese, and uttered the bold words in Italian. Nevertheless, I was magnetic in my insolence. I had made a knot that death alone could untie.[27]

Garibaldi's egoism in that passage is integral to this kind of love. He who falls in love wants an elaborate recognition of himself. He needs the other's personality to live up to his requirements – requirements that he himself barely understands, except through the intimation contained in the face at which he stares. The subject 'falls in love' when he desires, and recognises in desire the possibility of love. He anticipates then the final consolation that will justify his trouble, and imagines the personality who will provide it. Love, here, is really an inspired guess: and it awaits what Stendhal called the moment of 'crystallisation'.[28]

There is a primitive experience upon which the lover frequently draws when entering this 'magic' realm. He remembers some human creature who once tended him, whose hands and features were marked for him with the imprint of safety, intimacy and home. Thus many a face in later life appears already to prefigure some future intimacy, and we see in it, perhaps rightly, perhaps wrongly, not merely the presence of a certain perspective, but also the trajectory of our days within its view. This experience combines with sexual desire to overcome the natural obstacles to passion – the embarrassment and distrust which accompany the thought of so intimate a union. It releases us for union, and for the consolations which our covert memory has already prompted us to seek. Hence the 'irresistible' nature of falling in love, which, by presenting us with the sense of something totally new and totally overwhelming, merely sets us upon a trodden path, down which we run with old and indelible expectations.

The above sketch of the genesis of love enables us to see that there is a peculiar ontological dependence which arises in the course of it, and that this dependence is rehearsed through a completely individualised desire. Fear of this dependence, combined with a dream of unobtainable sexual freedom, leads to flirtation and coquetry. In the half-closed eye of the coquette, the self is both offered and withheld. Coquetry is the vicarious enjoyment of a transaction which cannot be accomplished without catastrophe. Coquetry can come to a conclusion only by abolishing itself. Hence, argues Simmel, in a striking essay, coquetry is an expression of the 'Zweckmäßigkeit ohne Zweck' – 'purposefulness without purpose' – which for Kant is the core of aesthetic experience.[29] In coquetry the aim of desire is never pursued; all gestures are left hanging in the air, incomplete, and extinguished before any purpose could inhabit them. Coquetry, therefore, is a form of play: but while it only plays with reality, it is with *reality* that it plays. Coquetry is an oblique recognition of the dependence that is risked in desire, and a sign that the coquette, while less honest than the prostitute, is more sexually alert. For the coquette withholds herself, precisely because her impulse is one of desire: it is an impulse that can become a 'transaction' only in play.

Jealousy

The ontological dependence that lies within the erotic tie is acutely displayed by that most mysterious of sexual phenomena, the condition of jealousy. The experience of jealousy is an experience of rejection: not just rejection by another person, but rejection by the world which one had entered in joining with him. The victim of jealousy has encountered an ontological divide. He has ceased to belong to the world which contained him, and entered a kind of nightmare, prey to horrible thoughts and fantasies which he cannot shake off. Dryden describes jealousy as the 'tyrant of the mind'; but its tyranny has no real parallel in the world of politics: it is rather the tyranny exerted by the tempter over the mind of St Anthony. (Its nearest political equivalent is therefore not tyranny, but the burning envy of the underdog: which is no more than a negative tyranny.)

Jealousy begins in discovery – the discovery of a rival. Thereupon the victim falls, as the tragic hero falls, into an abyss of lonely suffering. He knows only one consolation, which is the reverse discovery. He must learn that it is not true. There are of course degrees of jealousy. In its extreme form (as with the jealousy of Othello) it may render its victim unrecognisable to himself and others. In its milder form it remains hidden, like a geological fault, which nevertheless gives way under the slightest pressure. Such is the jealousy of Swann or of Marcel himself, who lives haunted by suspicion. But in every form, jealousy is catastrophic. Why is this?

The jealous person typically wishes, not to possess what his rival possesses, but to abolish it – to abolish the pleasure and the triumph that exist without him. He is largely indifferent to his own advantage, and selflessly pursues the destruction of another's joy. Until that destruction is accomplished, his world is out of joint. It is almost as though he acted out of a sense of justice – towards himself and towards the scheme of things as he formerly beheld it. This impersonal 'rage for order' makes jealousy repulsive. At the same time *sexual* jealousy may stir our compassion, since the victim of sexual jealousy is also the victim of love.

The first feature of jealousy, therefore, is that it involves some degree of love. And the greater the love, the greater the jealousy. Jealousy is a catastrophe suffered only by those who have entered the condition of 'ontological dependence' that exists in erotic love – the dependence of one who has sought, in and through sexual desire, the consolations of a perfect intimacy. But the cause of the catastrophe is the discovery not that the beloved *loves* another, but that he *desires* another. The beloved's sexual desire is the pivotal feature of the jealous person's interest, and he may tolerate any favour granted to his rival, save this one. It is possible to be jealous even of the most casual encounter (and indeed, especially of the most casual encounter) provided only that it was the occasion of desire. It does not matter that your rival is not loved. Nor does it matter that he does not exist, that he is no more than the fantasy about whose body your beloved's arms close in his imagination, when they close in reality about yourself. Of course there is an element of insanity in this jealousy of phantoms. But it is no more than a distant point along the road upon which every lover embarks, just so soon as the 'green-eyed monster' catches sight of him.

The explanation of the catastrophe lies, I believe, in the same moral region as I have explored in the above discussions of shame and obscenity: in the clash between the individualising and the universalising elements in desire. Although sexual desire has an individualised object, it is bound up with interest in the other's sex. In the sexual act we cease to be merely John or Mary, and become the representatives of the common attributes of our sex. Moreover, this is what we want. It is true that the person in love wishes his beloved to want him as the unique irreplaceable individual that he is, and he wishes this to be the determining thought which underlies the movement of his beloved's desire. At the same time, however, he wants his beloved to focus on his body, and so to want him as a man, or as a woman, as an example of his sex: not as someone who might have been replaced in this act by another, but rather as *primus inter pares*, the best of the bunch. It is not that his desire is transferable; but rather that it provokes a sexual interest which, potentially at least, may reach out towards other objects. This element is integral to sexual excitement, and is part of what permits John to see Mary as 'giving herself' to passion, as 'surrendering' her individuality to her sexual impulse, which 'overcomes' her.

The happy course of love confines that conflict to the night, and so conceals it. Jealousy, however, forces it into the light of day, and so shatters the world of the lover, by destroying the myth of his uniqueness. It is to the act of love that he turns for confirmation of his irreplaceability; and when the act is poisoned by the thought of generalities, his existence is in some way jeopardised. That which is given to him might in this very way have been given to another – even, most horrifying thought of all, to another who was not loved. For when the element of desire is *uppermost* the betrayal is both obsessing and disgusting. The absence of love between the guilty pair is one of the most provocative features in the genesis of jealousy, precisely because it focuses the victim's thoughts on the body of his rival. Dr Zhivago, learning the truth about Lara's relation with the vile Komarovsky, acknowledges: 'I can only be really jealous – deadly passionately jealous – of someone I despise and have nothing in common with.' Such jealousy – unlike the jealousy inspired by a rival *love* – is naturally retrospective, fervently pondering episodes which preceded the present affair. Someone with a 'past' enters a relationship with the conditions for jealousy already fulfilled, and his wisest course is frequently one of concealment. (The situation is movingly and convincingly described by Alphonse Daudet in *Sapho*.) To reveal the past, as Levin did to Kitty when he showed her his diary (*Anna Karenina*, Part IV, ch. 16), is to assume a rare tolerance in one's partner, and a capacity to endure terrible pain. (It should be said, however, that there are crucial differences here between the jealousy felt by men, and that felt by women. I spell out some of these differences in Chapter 9.)

This ascendancy of sexual desire in the thoughts of jealousy has important consequences. Indeed, through jealousy, a lover may become suddenly and acutely conscious of the physical basis of his desire. Milan Kundera, in *The Farewell Party*, describes a familiar experience:

> He had to look into his tormentor's face, he had to look at his body, because its union with the body of Ružena seemed unimaginable and incredible. He had to look, as if his eyes could tell him whether their bodies were indeed capable of uniting.

In Act II of *Götterdämmerung* Brünnhilde encounters the faithless, unrecognising Siegfried. He swears before the company that he has not taken advantage of the night spent beside her, and mentions the sword which lay between their bodies. Incensed, Brünnhilde turns on him:

> *Du listiger Held*
> *Sieh' wie du lüg'st!*
> *Wie auf dein Schwert*
> *du schlecht dich beruf'st!*

Wohl kenn' ich sein Scharfe,
doch kenn' auch die Scheide,
darin so wonig
ruh't an der Wand.

'I know the sword; I know its sharpness. And I know too the sheath in which it lay.' Her words refer to the sword of Siegmund, and the music reinforces the reference, reminding us that Siegmund and Siegfried (and, in another way, Brünnhilde too) are blood relations. It was Siegmund who had first tempted her from her divine condition with the image of a carnal love; and it is Siegfried whom she desired, the reincarnation of that once pictured devotion. And now, victim of mortal love, she unites her wonderment at the virility of Siegmund, with her submission to that of his son, in an unmistakeable image of the sexual act. It is the final proof of Brünnhilde's mortal condition that she should feel the pain of love precisely in her sexual part.

Among the philosophers who have written of desire, only Spinoza seems to have attributed any importance to the fact that jealous thoughts turn always to the sexual act, and dwell morbidly upon it. He attempts to explain this in words which recall the scatological theory of shame:

> he who imagines that a woman he loves prostitutes herself to another, is not only saddened by the fact that his own desire is hindered, but also, as he is forced to unite the image of the thing loved with the parts of shame and excrement of his rival, he is turned from her.[30]

The theory is, of course, no more plausible here than in the discussion of shame. But it has the merit of recognising the core phenomenon of sexual jealousy, and the feature of it that is hardest to explain.

Because of this feature, jealous thoughts are frequently exciting. The jealous lover sees constantly unveiled before his imagination the scene of a sexual fantasy, in which the beloved is wrapped in desire and then given to another. He prostitutes his beloved in his thoughts, which are invaded, like Othello's, by a sense of the obscene – by the perception of the sexual act in its bodily terms, freed from the circumstance of love. The torment of jealousy is also an excitement. In order to heighten the fantasy, the jealous lover may become relentlessly curious. He may want to know every detail, even 'how it felt'. Proust writes of Albertine: '*je n'aurais pas voulu savoir seulement avec quelle femme elle avait passé cette nuit-là, mais quel plaisir particulier cela lui representait, ce qui se passait à ce moment-là en elle.*' And, after a paragraph of obsessive ruminations on this theme, he concludes:

> *dans la jalousie il nous faut essayer en quelque sorte des souffrances de tout*

165

genre et de toute grandeur, avant de nous arrêter à celle qui nous paraît pouvoir convenir. Et quelle difficulté plus grande quand il s'agit d'une souffrance comme celle-ci, celle de sentir celle qu'on aimait eprouvant du plaisir avec des êtres différents de nous, lui donnant des sensations que nous ne sommes pas capables de lui donner, ou du moins par leur configuration, leur image, leurs façons, lui représentant tout autre chose que nous![31]

It is significant that, in the paroxysm of jealousy, Marcel had come to think of the sexual act in these universalising terms – as a matter of 'sensations', which may be better provided by another than by himself. This is not morbid. It is, rather, a reflection of the secret workings of desire, which jealousy automatically diverts in the direction which we fear – the direction of the obscene.

The reference to Albertine makes clear the greatest source of Proust's imposture. For the experience he has just described is not that of jealousy over a woman's interest in another woman, but rather jealousy over a man's interest in another man. This is a topic to which I shall return in Chapter 10. But we should notice here that a man's jealousy of lesbian relations, precisely because it does not involve 'phallic' thoughts, escapes much of the wounding affliction of normal jealousy. It is often easier to live with the fact of your wife's desire for a woman than with the fact of her desire for a man. The former, unlike the latter, does not afflict you with the thought that precisely *you* are dispensable in your sexual part. Moreover, differences in the structure of male and female desire imply differences in the structure of male and female jealousy. The paradigm that I am describing should therefore not be taken to be an exhaustive representation of this complex phenomenon. If jealousy were a single unitary thing, identical for either sex, then it would not be possible for Proust to give himself away so easily.

In its extreme form jealousy leads to murder. But not as a rule the murder of the rival – rather that of the beloved. The rival is the mere replaceable instrument of a sacrilege which takes place within the body of the beloved. (These facts are again noticed by Spinoza.)[32] It is to the beloved that the lover looks for the confirmation of his existence, as the unique representative of the object of desire. In abolishing the beloved, he abolishes the disproof of himself. He removes from the world the secret proof of his unreality. Hence the avenging of jealousy (even of retrospective jealousy, as in Theodor Fontane's *Effi Briest*) has often been regarded as a requirement of honour. The requirement survives in the barbarous punishments for adultery in some Mediterranean and Islamic countries, and also, in muted form, in the legally sanctioned excuse of *crime passionel*. We should not imagine that these punishments, and this excuse (which sanctions, in effect, the private-enterprise form of the punishment) are merely arbitrary. On the contrary, they reflect the nature of sexual jealousy. It is as though, in the torment of utter insecurity, the jealous lover would prefer the finality of grief to the constant fluctuating terrors of a jealous love. Thus Racine's *Hermione* persuades Orestes to murder her beloved Pyrrhus, as the only cure for a suffocating jealousy. And at once she gives way to grief, and to a terrible anger against the unfortunate murderer, who had not foreseen that Hermione's indifference towards him could never turn to love, but only to hatred.

As I shall argue in Chapter 11, the power of jealousy is one of the most important facts to be taken account of in the derivation of sexual morality. In a world where sexual prohibitions are of diminishing force, we should not be surprised that so many people take refuge from jealousy in the avoidance of love. For where love exists, the price of sexual freedom is suffering.

Don Juanism

I shall conclude this chapter with a brief survey of three important variants in the intentionality of desire, all familiar: Don Juanism, Tristanism (as I shall call it) and sado-masochism. It is necessary to survey these phenomena, if only to show that the account so far given of sexual intentionality is not prescriptive, but simply descriptive of that with which we are all familiar. There are important phenomena – such as the sexual perversions and homosexuality – which I shall discuss later, but which will require the wider context that I shall by then have established.

The division of erotic passion into the fidelity which longs for death, and the fickle delight in successive conquests, is a familiar literary exercise. Stendhal identified the two poles as those of Werther and Don Juan: Denis de Rougemont altered the thought when, under the influence of Wagner, he exchanged Werther for Tristan.[33] But both writers were referring to varieties of erotic love. In what follows, I shall be describing not love but desire. If there is a similar division in love, it must be independently described.

Don Juanism is a widespread phenomenon, whose existence might be held to cast doubt upon much that I have said concerning the individualising intentionality of desire. In describing the phenomenon, however, we should beware of too simple a description. Don Juanism is not satyromania – it does not involve the urge constantly to quench the 'burning pestle' of lust. As Kierkegaard argues (following Mozart), the character of Don Juan is genuinely erotic, not because he transfers his attentions from individual to individual, but, on the contrary, because he concentrates them completely upon the present individual whom he is attempting to seduce.[34] His character is concentrated into the act of seduction, and this is what gives him the charm which awakens desire. The satyromaniac, by contrast, extinguishes the fires which he sets out to stoke, and does not so much desire women as seek to masturbate in their presence. (Satyromania involves a serious failure of the imagination.) Don Juanism is therefore the most time-consuming and indeed debilitating of all sexual addictions; it requires the constant re-creation of passion, and with it the strategies of seduction, towards an unlimited number of objects. The satyromaniac, who addresses himself to each woman concretely, but only as a member of her kind, is therefore the opposite of Don Juan, who, although he in a sense desires all womanhood, desires womanhood only as and when concentrated into the form and personality of each irreplaceable woman.

> But what is this force, then, by which Don Juan seduces? It is desire, the energy of sensuous desire. He desires in every woman the whole of womanhood, and therein lies the sensuously idealising power with which he at once embellishes and overcomes his prey. The reaction to this gigantic passion beautifies and develops the one desired, who flushes in enhanced beauty by its reflection. As the enthusiast's fire with seductive splendour illumines even those who stand in a casual relation to him, so Don Juan transfigures in a far deeper sense every girl, since his relation to her is an essential one.[35]

Thus Kierkegaard, who understands the Don not as the repository of some organic irritation, but as a great spiritual force, a boundless sensuous energy, a creature prodigal of desire. Yet each woman calls to him as the present object of an individualising impulse. He is not insincere when he addresses Zerlina, for example, with a promise of marriage. However, his understanding of marriage is an eccentric product of his present frenzy. His desire for Zerlina is an instinctive movement of sympathy, which causes him to see with her eyes, and to respond with her response, so accepting, for a moment, the absolute value of a marriage that will consummate and validate her access of desire. Of course, after the seduction, he will go his way. But for the moment he does not know this – he is intoxicated, attentive, utterly focused upon this individual person whose world lies open before him. Don Juan's heart is not split or deceptive, but fickle. His attention is engaged absolutely but always newly by every woman whom he comes across, and his aim is, not sexual excitement or physical pleasure, but conquest – the passionate invasion of yet another point of view, so as to compel it to surrender its embodiment to his own bodily prowess.

Don Juan's gaiety is one part of the seducer's necessary equipment: his immorality lies in his ability to persuade his victim that immorality is nothing more than a peccadillo. (The same immorality is discerned by Senancour in obscenity.)[36] At the same time, his gaiety conceals a deep anxiety, an inability to rest or to be consoled, some part of which is hinted at by Byron, in a letter:

> My time has been passed viciously and agreeably; at thirty one so few years, months, days remain, that 'carpe diem' is not enough. I have been obliged to crop even the seconds, for who can trust to-morrow? To-morrow quotha? To-hour, to-minute. I can not repent me (I try very often) so much of anything I have done, as of anything I have left undone – Alas! I have been but idle, and have the prospect of an early decay, without having seized every available instant of our pleasant years. This is a bitter thought, and it will be difficult for me ever to recover [from] the despondency into which this idea naturally throws one.[37]

The bitter thought against which Don Juan hopelessly rebels is the same thought that contains the promise of Tristan's consolation: the thought of death. Don Juanism and Tristanism are extreme responses to a perception that lies at the root of human attraction and human love: the thought of our common mortality. Herrick's measured lines show the true connection between death and desire. They also show the error by which Don Juan and Tristan are equally condemned:

> So, while time serves, and we are but decaying,
> Come, my Corinna, come, let's go a-maying.

Tristanism

Tristanism is one of the most puzzling of sexual phenomena, and a fine illustration of the catastrophe into which a rational being may be led by his rationality, and by the consequent commitment to a *personal* form of sexual union. Tristan's love for Isolde is implausible and obsessive. He is in the grip of a spell which binds him to this woman and from which he cannot be released. At the same time there seems to be no consummation for his desire short of death – only this will bring peace to him, for (such is the understanding) only this will make Isolde his. Of course, his love for

Isolde is a forbidden love, and therefore could not attain the normal forms of union. But Tristan loves Isolde for that very reason: it is the forbidden character of Isolde that causes him to be spellbound. But this forbidden character is itself no more than an 'objective correlative', so to speak,[38] of that sense of 'original sin' which, I have argued, lies so often dormant in desire. Tristan is therefore the type of all those lovers for whom the realm of sexual desire is the realm of the forbidden. While it is necessary to provide a dramatic expression of this in the marital status of Isolde, Tristan is as much indebted as is Werther to a situation which justifies the despair and futility which he would feel in any case. Another kind of forbidden love is described by Chikamatsu, in the puppet play *Love Suicides at Sonezaki*, and here too it can be seen that the forbidding of love is nothing but a pretext for love, and that the institutional obstacle to union is no more than the dramatic representation of an obstacle that is integral to desire. Tristan seeks death at last, for his desire seeks death. And death is the fulfilment of desire, only because it is the final obstacle to desire's fulfilment. In Freud's words, Tristan is possessed by an *élan mortel*.

Tristan is thus the victim of a self-defeating project, and he pursues his own defeat. How could such a project have its genesis in sexual desire? We can see with little difficulty how it is that the lover should seek to prove himself irreplaceable in the eyes of his beloved, and that he should subsume his desirous thoughts under a ruling idea of *himself*, as a transcendental centre of attention. At the same time, however, he experiences his own desire as an overwhelming, a subordination of himself to a bodily imperative. And he desires the same effect in the one he loves. The erotic significance of the sexual act lies in its *abandon*. The connection of our sexual organs with the body's dominion gives peculiar poignancy to this experience, in which I seem to be overcome by my body, precisely in that moment that I am overcome and invaded by you. It is as though you were present to me in my body, and overcoming me precisely through my body.

But of course you are not my body, nor could you be. The process of my overcoming has all the mystery and the inscrutability of the body itself: it is a darkness that wells up from within me and extinguishes the perspective which you endeavour to grasp. I vanish, and you vanish, at the point of union. This is the origin of that trouble to which Francesca gives such poignant expression in Dante's *Inferno*. And Francesca, like Tristan, is engaging in a forbidden love.

The example of Francesca helps us to discern the true source of Tristan's project. His desire is forbidden, not because of its adulterous character (which, as I have suggested, is only the outward symbol of an inner transgression), but because it has committed everything to the sexual act. It has divorced itself from all social norms, all forms of companionship, besides this one, of bodily union in the 'act of darkness'. The project of desire has become *concentrated* in the sexual act. But in the sexual act the Tristanian subject finds nothing beyond the body's dominion, which enslaves him precisely when he would be most free. He begins to yearn for another, completer, more possessing union with the object of desire. At the same time, because the subject does not look beyond the sexual act for his idea of a more perfect union, he envisages the fulfilment of his desire as another, but larger and irreversible, overcoming of the self by the body. Hence his thoughts tend in the direction of death. In death the body takes over entirely and forever, following a material imperative that I cannot control. And yet it is *I* who am dying.

To understand the thought here, we should reflect upon how a person is conceived after death. He remains with us in thought; we bury his body, respect all that belongs to him, and honour his memory. The triumph of the body in death seems therefore also like a kind of victory of the soul. The body is hidden and decays, while the self remains unaltered as an object of interpersonal feeling. Love is preserved in grief, and all other interpersonal attitudes survive until eventually they dwindle with the slow subsidence of memory. But the self persists only as an idea in the mind of the beholder. After death I am an intentional object without material reality. And it is this immaterial existence, this existence as a mere 'idea', which was mine before birth, when I lay, as it were, hidden in the womb of time. Thus Tristan, sinking into the torpor of his wound, finds solace in the darkness that overwhelms him. He is momentarily in that condition from which he came, and to which he must return:

> *Ich war, wo ich von je gewesen,*
> *wohin auf je ich geh':*
> *im weiten Reich der Weltennacht.*
>
> *Nur ein Wissen dort uns eigen:*
> *göttlich ew'ges Urvergessen!*
> [III.i]

The harmony here is based on a minor key version of the first two bars of the *Liebestod*; only in the relentless major cadence of the *Liebestod*, when this movement towards death has become mutual, can it be an affirmation, since only then does the thing that overcomes Tristan – Tristan's death – also overcome Isolde, and with the same finality. This death, which unites them spiritually, is the triumph of the soul over the body, at the same time as it is a triumph of the body over the soul, the final overcoming of all that the lovers individually are. Thus we see that the sexual aim, because it has been detached from every long-term social project, and is therefore confined to the sexual act, must take place outside the forum of the self, which now vanishes forever, exchanging the material reality of action, for an illusory persistence as memory.

From a single troubled sentiment arise the two contrasting projects of Don Juanism and Tristanism. In the first, the entire effort of the imagination is devoted to the sexual act, represented as a conquest. I put myself into the process of seduction, and the sexual act itself, when it is achieved, is the culmination of that process, which overcomes you, and, in doing so, removes the aim of my desire. I have no further use for you. Further desire will not now be for you, but for your successor, and, if you happen to *be* that successor (as at one point Donna Elvira, through mistaken identity, becomes successor to herself), this is no more than an accident, like retracing my steps around a maze. I hurry on from the scene of conquest, avoiding the question of what I am to you and you to me in the sexual act – for that question, and its answer, belong only to the process of seduction which is the prelude to my retreat.

In Tristanism, the effort of the imagination is concentrated similarly upon the sexual act, but conceived now as the sole vehicle of a spiritual union in which the participants are mutually overcome. I seek to extinguish the light which differentiates our separate forms, and so divides us. Only renunciation of bodily existence can fulfil a project which desires nothing more than mutual possession in the act of love. Only then does your individuality cease to trouble me, when I cease forever to be troubled.

Tristan is a morbid Don Juan – one who has perceived the catastrophe of a desire that cannot look beyond the sexual act. Rather than detach himself from the object of desire by the constant pursuit of novelties, Tristan seeks to accomplish in the sexual act itself what can never be accomplished without renouncing the absolute requirements of desire. He is obsessed with the knowledge that his desire is sinful (for his sense that his desire is forbidden is but a premonition of its catastrophic nature), and yet he can do nothing to steel himself against the moral insight which corrodes his imagination. Don Juan, who brushes all morality aside – or rather who postpones his final encounter with the moral law until it finally confronts him in the unbending form of a statue[39] – is able to sever his desire from every long-term attachment, and to transform his obsession with the sexual act into an obsession with woman. For Tristan, there is only one woman, and she has the all-extinguishing quality of death itself. For Don Juan there are infinitely many women, in each of whom, however, is seen the same occasion of desire.

Sado-masochism

I turn now to sado-masochism. A major task of any theory of desire must be to explain the presence in ordinary (that is to say, unperverted) desire of those components which have come to be described as 'sado-masochistic'. We must examine sado-masochism as we have examined Don Juanism and Tristanism, with a view to showing that it shares the intentionality of normal desire. Of course, taken to extremes, sadism and masochism may destroy their own intentional content, and become perverted, in the manner of bestiality. But behaviour which is perverted only when taken to extremes is not, in itself, perverted. As for the perverted form of sado-masochism, I shall discuss this more fully in Chapter 10.

Ever since Krafft-Ebing, in his celebrated *Psychopathia Sexualis*, suggested that sadism and masochism are intimately related, it has become a commonplace to adopt the term 'sado-masochism' to refer to both phenomena. There has also been a tendency to look for some biological instinct that will explain them. Thus Havelock Ellis, with characteristic erudition, amasses evidence from the 'courtship' rituals of animals and from the courtship behaviour of primitive peoples, to suggest that the origin of sado-masochism lies in the very structure of the sexual urge.[40] For Ellis, the paradigm example is the practice of 'marriage by capture' – in which a woman is pursued by her suitors and forced to yield by the strongest. He argues, in effect, that such 'marriages' are partly arranged by the 'victim' (as when the Kirghiz maiden, armed with a whip, flies on horseback before her pursuers). The girl therefore submits only to that force which she also desires. The aggression of the male, and the submission of the female, here combine to fulfil an archetype of sexual encounter: and the form of the archetype is sado-masochism. Ellis, Féré and other founders of sexology agree in the idea that it is pain, rather than cruelty, that acts as the stimulus to sado-masochistic feeling, and cite examples of animals whose sexual activity lies dormant until stimulated by physical violence.[41] (Cornevin refers to a stallion, which would not become potent, even when faced with a mare in heat, until a whip was cracked.)[42] All this might seem to suggest that we are dealing with a kind of sensory proximity. And indeed, the idea put forward by Ellis, that pain is itself a stimulant to sexual emotion, depends upon an analysis of sexual feeling as a sensory impulse – an analysis that cannot be accepted, for the many reasons already given.

In fact, however, as Ellis himself admits:

> The masochist desires to experience pain, but he generally desires that it be inflicted from love; the sadist desires to inflict pain, but in some cases, if not in most, he desires that it should be felt as love.[43] [For 'love', here, read 'desire'.]

In other words, sado-masochism seems to intrude into, and take its character from, the realm of moral relations, and not from that of physical sensation. This is strikingly illustrated by the case studies collected by Krafft-Ebing, all of which involve a distinctly moral thought, as the focal point of sadistic or masochistic desire: a thought of dominance or submission.[44] Sacher-Masoch's own initiation may perhaps serve to illustrate what I mean. One day, as a child, he was playing in the bedroom of a certain Countess, a relative in whose house he happened to be staying. Suddenly the Countess entered with her lover, and the boy hid in a cupboard, there to witness the passionate embraces of the adult couple. Within moments the Count, followed by two friends, burst indignantly into the room, confronted the guilty couple, and, stepping forward in anger, hesitated as to whom to strike. In that moment the Countess, with a well-aimed blow, sent him staggering backwards, blood pouring from his face; taking hold of a whip, she proceeded to drive all three intruders from her bedroom, so making the opportunity for her lover's escape. The Count returned, and, as he begged on his knees for his wife's forgiveness, the boy made his presence known. He was dragged from the cupboard and soundly thrashed by the Countess, at which he experienced a pleasure that he could never afterwards dissociate from the vision of her majestic power, from the feel of her fur coat, and the smell of her anger. From this experience derived all the hot passions of *A Venus in Furs*.

In that example is encapsulated a familiar experience. A person intrudes into my field of relationship with sudden overwhelming authority, focusing upon herself the whole force of my sexuality. Suddenly *this* is the preferred object; it is to her that I must submit; she is the one who deserves my slavery. And so on. It is surely not pain or cruelty, but what could, in other contexts, be *perceived* as cruelty, which is the operative factor. And this 'cruelty' is nothing other than punishment – the living hand of a coveted authority.

At the same time, there is a strange desire to inflict and to receive physical pain, which cannot be accounted for merely in moral terms. The masochist does not merely want to be punished or humiliated; nor does he *always* want that. To understand his attitude to physical pain we should look at the emotion of the sadist. What is the sadist doing, in inflicting pain? (A question about intentionality.) Consider the torturer. In the usual case, it is to be supposed, the torturer inflicts pain because he enjoys, not just the spectacle of another's suffering, but also the fact of being responsible for its infliction. His attitude is essentially one of 'me doing this to you'. Moreover, the victim must be aware of the torturer's agency. There is no joy — or at least not the same joy — in torturing an animal, because an animal has no sense of what is happening to him as a deliberate process initiated by a responsible being. The torturer wishes his victim to understand, not only what is happening to him, but the intention with which it is done and the fact that his suffering is wanted and enjoyed by the person who inflicts it.

Torture is, then, an interpersonal attitude. The torturer sees his victim as a person, and wishes himself to be seen as such, and to appear within his victim's perspective in a dominating light. Torture is therefore peculiar to rational beings, and has no more than a deep (non-intentional) resemblance to the cat's game with the mouse. Not surprisingly, therefore, torture can take on symbolic meaning; it can be used as punishment and as graphic morality.[45]

Pure torture, however, is not just punishment. It is the deliberate attempt to reduce another through pain, to vanquish him in his body, to force him to abjure himself for his body's sake, and so to be persuaded of his embodiment. Here is a part of Sartre's incomparable description of the phenomenon:

> The spectacle which is offered to the [torturer] is that of a freedom which struggles against the expanding of the flesh, and which freely chooses to be submerged in the flesh. At the moment of abjuration, the result sought is attained: the body is wholly flesh, panting and obscene; it holds the position which the torturers have given to it, not that which it would have assumed by itself; the cords which bind it hold it as an inert thing, and thereby it has ceased to be the object which moves spontaneously. In the abjuration a freedom chooses to be wholly identified with this body; this distorted and heaving body is the very image of a broken and enslaved freedom.[46]

Hence 'the moment of pleasure for the torturer is that in which the victim betrays or humiliates himself.'[47] The desire of the torturer is to enact for himself the spectacle of a human tragedy: to show the ease with which another's perspective can be invaded and enslaved by pain, to humiliate the other by compelling the self to identify with what is not-self, to 'go under' in the stream of bodily suffering. Christ had to be crucified, since it was necessary to overcome his spirit. His actual death had to be preceded by that other death, in which the spirit gives in to the flesh and identifies with its humiliation, under the mocking eyes of those who watch its writhings. That Christ cried out 'My God, my God, why hast thou forsaken me?' is no more a disproof of his godhead than is his death. To be fully human, fully incarnate, the spirit had to be subject to just such a final 'overcoming'.

In the passage quoted from Sartre, the word 'torturer' in brackets is in fact, in the original, 'sadist'. For Sartre, sexual sadism is continuous with the torture of the prison cell. I doubt that this is necessarily so. Nevertheless, there is a kind of sadism that is akin to torture, in which the subject wishes to appear as the inflictor of pain in the eyes of a helpless victim. Is there something in sexual desire that could lead to such an ambition? In discussing smiles and blushes I pointed out that the role of these transformations as a focus of desire stems from their ability to convey the embodied nature of a self-conscious perspective. In these reactions, the subject is fully himself and also, in the same instant, identical with his body. They are therefore the symbols of the 'other called forth'. Pain is in one respect similar: its symptoms are involuntary, and they seem to 'show the truth' about the other who suffers them. Emily Dickinson writes:

> I like a look of agony
> Because I know it's true;
> Men do not sham convulsion,
> Nor simulate a throe.

To elicit the response of pain, and at the same time to appear within the other's perspective as the agent of his suffering – this may seem like a substitute for the exchange of a lover's smiles. This may be the best that I can do, by way of compelling your perspective to show itself upon the surface of your body, and there to take cognisance of me. In the act of inflicting pain, therefore, the sadist may also be craving that very bodily recognition of his own embodiment which lies at the core of sexual desire. He 'overcomes' the other through pain, and extorts the recognition that he cannot obtain by a smile. (One should mention here that the visible signs of agony are hard to distinguish from those of ecstasy – a fact exploited by Bernini in his sculpture of St Teresa. In creating these signs, the sadist flatters himself with a perfect simulacrum of his partner's sexual *Untergang*.)

If that were *all* there is to sadism, we could hardly escape the conclusion that sadism is deeply perverted: for it seems so far indifferent to the other's pleasure and to the other's responsibility as scarcely to show any more recognition of his existence than that due to him as a 'sufferer of pain'. But one must distinguish the torturer from the sadist. The second borrows the motives of the first, but only because they fit into a strategy of sexual relationship. The true sadist does not want the other's pain *simpliciter*. He wants the other to want the pain inflicted, and to be aroused by it. In other words, he sees pain as an intermediary in the process of mutual arousal, and not as a gratification in itself. His impulse is an extended version of the love bite, in which one party administers to the other a wound that is both a mark of affection and an invitation to desire.

The masochist similarly wishes the pain to be understood as a sexual address, whose ultimate end is mutual arousal. The masochist, in his turn (assuming he is lucky enough to receive it), wishes to suffer pain, only because this is a sign of the other's interest in him, and because, responding to that interest, he finds himself embarked on the course of desire. (Cf. *Antony and Cleopatra*: 'A lover's pinch, that hurts, and is desir'd.') The pain is to be understood as an intermediary in the process of arousal. And it can be such not only because of its crucial relation to the body, but also because it is a vehicle for moral ideas: the ideas of dominance and submission. Those ideas form a fundamental part of the ordinary understanding of the sexual performance. Hence the sadist and the masochist, left to each other's devices, so to speak, achieve arousal, not despite the pain, but because of it.

The above brief description of the sado-masochistic impulse shows it to be a special case of sexual desire. But it does not explain why desire should choose such a channel. A variety of explanations might be produced in terms of the underlying biological need: such explanations are ever-present in Féré, Krafft-Ebing and Havelock Ellis. But to provide an intentional explanation – an explanation in terms of the thoughts of the participants – is far less easy. The first step in any such explanation must, I believe, mention the idea of inhibition. Pain permits the sado-masochistic couple to cross the barrier of inhibition. It enables them to do what they would otherwise be too embarrassed to do: to overcome the other, in the act of physical contact. Pain becomes the first move in what is, eventually, a fairly normal cooperative activity, which, once initiated, begins to flow in the familiar channels of sexual satisfaction.

Thus the propensity towards the infliction and suffering of physical pain in the act of love is rarely regarded as perverse, while the tendency to inflict and suffer sexual humiliation is almost universally condemned. Von Sacher-Masoch's desire to be trampled upon by ladies in furs arouses no more than mild curiosity; while his ardent (and eventually successful) attempt to persuade his wife that she must, against her will, betray him with a stranger (upon which occasion he devoted himself with loving attention to her toilet, anticipating the delicious pangs of jealousy that were to follow upon this panderous act) evokes the most vivid feelings of disgust. The pursuit of physical pain in sexual congress is not in itself a perversion of desire. Frequently, indeed, it is no more than an attempt to construct the intentionality of desire, in circumstances rendered un-propitious by inhibition – by the barrier which prevents one person from being 'overcome' by his body, and therefore by the other who affects it. When de Sade describes the desire for another's dissolution as the principal sexual impulse, he may be thinking in exaggerated terms of the first movement of sadism: to the sense that, because I cannot trust his smile, I must trust his groan. However, there is, in de Sade's particular obsession with dissolution, something more than this. He wants the *body* of the other to dissolve in pain and mutilation – and many of the horrible scenes described in *Justine* and elsewhere are scenes of simple murder.[48] The motive here is not the frustrated longing to hold the other in and through his body, but the obscene perception of the body as corrupting flesh. The *abolition* of the other, rather than his involvement in a cooperative project of desire – this is the real intention that festers in de Sade's appalling pages (whose literary reputation is a result of nothing more serious than their 'forbidden' quality). The sadism of de Sade stays locked in the moment of dissolution, seeking always to enhance it, to embellish it with further novelties, to achieve *there*, in the annihilation of another's will and pleasure, the glory of sexual release. Behind this perverted project lies also a remnant of Tristanism – of the sense that ultimate union requires the ultimate dissolution in death. But it differs from Tristanism in its obscene and solitary posture: the other is *reduced* to his body, becoming the mere instrument of my pleasure; while his death is required, I survive him, glorying in the release that my violence has permitted me. There is a complete indifference towards the other, or, if not indifference, then terror of his existence, of his ability to confront me with his demands and with the moral reality of his embodiment. Hence I must abolish him. De Sade's sadism is therefore sadism of the most deviant kind, and has little or nothing in common with the sado-masochistic stratagems that I earlier described. Despite the attempts by such thinkers as Bataille[49] to find the core experience of sexuality in this focus on dissolution (which Bataille rightly discovers in shame and obscenity), it seems to me obvious that de Sade's sexuality is wholly deviant. It has nothing to tell us about the elements of normal sado-masochism, let alone about the elements of desire.

In this chapter I have surveyed some of the phenomena and variants of desire. My aim has been to show that the account so far developed of the intentionality of desire displays the unity and variety of these phenomena, and associates them with a common human condition. There is no need to look below the surface of human consciousness in order to understand sexual shame, sexual modesty, obscenity and jealousy, or to understand how sexual desire may issue in such peculiar projects as those of Don Juanism, Tristanism and sado-masochism. All this can be easily accounted for, in terms of the conscious structure of desire, as an interpersonal emotion. At the same time we cannot doubt that desire is rooted in instincts that we share with the animals, and we must now confront the prevailing modern prejudice, that it is through a theory of the sexual instinct that we ought to understand all the phenomena to which I have referred. We must also consider the Freudian theory, which sees adult desire in terms of the sexuality of the child. Both theories have scientific pretensions, and both present a radical challenge to all that I have said. For both try to identify the root phenomenon of sexual desire outside what is 'given' to the subject, and both prove corrosive of the idea – which I believe to be fundamental to sexual morality – that desire does not exist outside the experience of persons.

7

THE SCIENCE OF SEX

The subject of this chapter is sex, conceived as a scientific problem. So far my discussion has remained (scientifically speaking) very much on the surface; I have tried to describe the phenomena, but I have given no explanation of them. It might be thought that little of what I have said can be of lasting value, since, not only does it stand to be completed by a proper repertoire of scientific fact, but it must also remain vulnerable to redescription, and therefore refutation, at the hands of any developed sexual science. In Chapter 1 I hinted at reasons for being sceptical towards such an objection. But it now remains to treat it more completely. I shall examine two approaches which, whether or not they succeed in being scientific, at least claim to be; whatever their merits, they serve to remind us of the tendencies that a science of sex must display. I shall discuss sociobiology and Freudian psychology, each of which is held to have revolutionised our thinking about sexual behaviour, and – whether or not justifiably – to have led to a greater revision in our moral attitudes than has accompanied any social upheaval or religious crusade.

The biology of sex

Men are animals, and none of their functions is more deeply rooted in their animal nature than is that of sexual reproduction. It is precisely in the day-to-day experience of sexual conduct that the idea of our 'animality' lies uppermost in our thoughts. We may condemn this or that act as 'bestial', but in doing so we are usually aware of its overwhelming resemblance (at least when judged from a certain light or from a certain point of view) to other acts which form the daily currency of sexual expression. And who could deny that, judged from the evolutionary point of view, the basic motor of all this elaborate ritual is reproduction, of a kind that occurs throughout the animal kingdom, and according to a rhythm that is common to almost all creatures who engage in it? It is salutary to reflect on the words of Montaigne:

> On the one hand nature drives us thither, since she has attached to that desire the noblest, most useful, and most pleasant of all her acts; while on the other she allows us to flee it and vilify it as insolent and of ill repute, to blush for it and commend abstinence. Are we not brutes to call the act which makes us brutish?[1]

Reflecting on such remarks, we are naturally tempted to conclude that our sexuality (when explored at the 'deep' level of biological science) is really 'nothing but' an animal phenomenon, obedient to laws exemplified by dogs, cats and horses, modified only by the peculiar evolutionary status of the human species. What I have described, it will be said, is not the reality of human conduct but only, as it were, a nimbus of thought and illusion by which it is surrounded, and which serves perhaps to conceal from the uninstructed the disconcerting facts of 'true human nature'. To think that my descriptions represent the nature of sexual desire is to mistake appearance for reality, and practical illusion for theoretical truth.

Of course, it is impossible to deny that there are close analogies between animal and human behaviour. All the movements of human sexuality, from courtship and rivalry, through modesty, jealousy and sexual congress, to marital fidelity and grief, have their analogues in the animal kingdom, and the temptation to describe animal behaviour anthropomorphically often leads to the overwhelming sense of the identity between our world and the world of the 'lower' species. Consider this description of the courtship of spiders (from. G. W. Peckham):

> On May 24th we found a mature female, and placed her in one of the larger boxes, and the next day we put a male in with her. He saw her as she stood perfectly still, twelve inches away; the glance seemed to excite him, and he at once moved towards her; when some four inches from her he stood still, and then began the most remarkable performance that an amorous male could offer to an admiring female. She eyed him eagerly, changing her position from time to time so that he might always be in view. He, raising his whole body on one side by straightening out the legs, and lowering it on the other by folding the first two pairs of legs up and under, leaned so far over as to be in danger of losing his balance, which he only maintained by sliding rapidly toward the lowered side. The palpus, too, on this side was turned back to correspond to the direction of the legs nearest it. He moved in a semi-circle for about two inches, and then instantly reversed the position of the legs and circled in the

opposite direction, gradually approaching nearer and nearer to the female. Now she dashes towards him, while he, raising his first pair of legs, extends them upward and forward as if to hold her off, but withal slowly retreats. Again and again he circles from side to side, she gazing toward him in a softer mood, evidently admiring the grace of his antics. This is repeated until we have counted one hundred and eleven circles made by the ardent little male. Now he approaches nearer and nearer, and when almost within reach whirls madly around and around her, she joining and whirling with him in a giddy maze. Again he falls back and resumes his semicircular motions, with his body tilted over; she, all excitement, lowers her head and raises her body so that it is almost vertical; both draw nearer; she moves slowly under him, he crawling over her head, and the mating is accomplished.[2]

The description is enchanting. It is also, in the Weberian sense, 'enchanted': it is a description of the world as it appears to one who still sees all movement in terms of his own, inner, apprehension of the human spirit. But why should it be the less correct for that? And if we must – for the sake of science – subject it to a cold and ruthless *Entzauberung*, why should we not do the same for human behaviour? To the extent that it is right to speak of 'glances', 'excitement', 'soft gazes', 'admiration', 'ardour', 'amorousness' and so on in describing the courtship of humans, so too, it might be argued, is it right to use those terms in describing the courtship of spiders. Conversely, to the extent that we should not use them of spiders, so should we not (when describing other varieties of the same sociobiological facts) use them of humans.

Later I shall have cause to compare the 'anthropomorphic' description above with what might be called the 'simiomorphic' or even 'ento-morphic' descriptions of human behaviour offered by such socio-biologists as E. O. Wilson and Desmond Morris. And we shall, I hope, see from the comparison the element of falsehood in each. But we must first remind ourselves of the standpoint from which my conclusions will be defended. The surface of human things is none the less real for being a surface: the *Lebenswelt* is the world in which we are situated, and how we perceive it determines the nature, direction and reasonableness of all our projects. To show that this or that feature of the *Lebenswelt* does not survive translation into the idiom of some explanatory science is not yet to prove its unreality – any more than we prove the unreality of colours by showing that they may be explained in terms of a physical theory that does not refer to them.[3] The position towards which I have been moving is the following: sexual desire and its attendant phenomena, while they are in an important sense rooted in our biological condition as sexually reproducing beings, are not reducible to any aspect of human conduct that is shared with the 'lower' animals. Desire, as I have described it, is a kind of social artefact, a pattern of response that is cooperatively achieved and, in the normal case, cooperatively enjoyed. There could be human beings without this response. But whether they could also be social beings may be doubted. Indeed, as I shall later argue, a race of beings without sexual desire would lack a vast range of interpersonal responses. They really *would* be animals, for they would lack the feature (personality) which causes us to describe ourselves as more than merely animal. The collective endeavour which transforms human beings into persons (which, as it were, paints this face on the blank of nature) *also* generates the conditions of sexual desire. These are the same process, under two separate aspects. The social construct of desire, which exists at the level of personal interaction, is to be described first and foremost as the object of a familiar and recurrent intentional understanding. The search for the deep biological determinants of that which we describe may lead us so far from the phenomenal reality as to miss what it purposed to explain.

That statement of position will not silence the scientific activist, for whom the important first step in any scientific investigation is the redescription of the phenomena in terms which belong to, or lend themselves to, theory.[4] He will be quick to point to the theoretical inadequacy of our intentional descriptions: indeed, we have already come close to admitting something metaphysically dubious in the concept which ultimately inspires them, the concept of the self. And he will argue that we must, in any case, confront the 'real truth' about the human condition, without the distracting illusions of everyday personal understanding. He is the equivalent for social understanding as a whole, of the Marxian in politics, who strips away the veil of 'ideology' and reveals (or at least thinks that he reveals) the hidden essence of society, which is its 'material' base. He will argue that the onus is always on the other side, to show that the surface of human conduct, as revealed to interpersonal understanding, is something *more* than a collective illusion, something more than a mystification of facts which must be understood from a point of view outside them.

Sociobiology

The most radical of all attempts at a science of sexual conduct is that of sociobiology, which, while recognising the existence of distinctively social phenomena, seeks to explain them in evolutionary terms, by showing their functional relation to the survival of the species. Consider the courtship ritual of spiders, described above. How would we explain such a phenomenon? There are two broad answers to the question. The first – the mechanical – describes how this particular stimulus (sight of the female) operates to produce this particular response. The second – the ethological – explains how spiders have acquired and retained such a mechanism in the first place. The two explanations are logically independent, although the hope is that they will be complementary. The first is not forthcoming: neurological science simply has not advanced so far. The second, however, is easier to provide – or, at least, it is easier to begin. The Darwinian theory of evolution enables us to venture a general explanation of all such phenomena, in terms of functionality. We explain the courtship dance by showing the function that it performs, in ensuring the survival of the spider's genes. The general theory of sexual selection emerges from the enterprise. The spider able to dance like Peckham's is clearly rather fit and active; his genes, preserved in his offspring, will contribute to the health and activity of his race. A female who shuns the weakling therefore enhances the genetic endowment of her children. Such an idea explains the fighting between males that occurs at breeding time, together with a host of other fairly complex-seeming facts. As E. O. Wilson puts it:

> Pure epigamic display can be envisioned as a contest between salesmanship and sales resistance. The sex that courts, ordinarily the male, plans to invest less reproductive effort in the offspring. What it offers to the female is chiefly evidence that it is fully normal and physiologically fit. But this warranty consists of only a brief performance, so that strong selective pressures exist for less fit individuals to present a false image. The courted sex, usually the female, will therefore find it strongly advantageous to distinguish the really fit from the pretended fit. Consequently, there will be a strong tendency for the courted sex to develop coyness. That is, its responses will be hesitant and cautious in a way that evokes still more displays and makes correct discrimination easier.[5]

Hardly a reassuring example for those scientists wishing to free their descriptions from anthropomorphic language. And the weakness of the explanation is barely disguised in the repeated use of the word 'strong'. Nevertheless, the principle is reasonably clear. Not only can we explain the sexual act; we can also explain such extraordinary phenomena as courtship, modesty, jealousy and monogamy, in terms of their functional relation to the gene's impersonal urge to perpetuate itself. Jealousy, for example, ensures that an animal will be less likely to devote his life's work to the perpetuation of another's genes. And so on. A small leap of the imagination (or rather, the leap of a small imagination) takes us to the human world. When the pride of Greek youth pointlessly spills its blood before the walls of Troy for a woman's sake, is this not the 'same' phenomenon as the clash of antlers in rutting time? If rejecting the analogy involves denying the application to human society of the Darwinian theory of evolution, then the philosopher may be reluctant to cross swords with the sociobiologist.

Sociobiology has not been without its critics, however. For example, there are those who object to its lack of rigour, and in particular to its failure to address itself to the fundamental question of ethnobiology – the question of genetic determination. Until we understand the *mechanism* of evolution, they argue, we should be wary of extending Darwinian theory to ever more complex facts. Without a clear answer to the question 'how?', such an extension does no more than commit us to functional explanations whose content may remain wholly undetermined. It is fairly evident – given the general truth of Darwinian theory – that dysfunctional behaviour will tend to disappear. But, offered as an explanation of the infinite variety of behaviour that remains, this is trivial. We need to know what additional factors push development in *this* direction rather than that. In the case of social behaviour, it is a huge and so far unwarranted assumption that these additional factors will be genetic.[6]

There are also those who criticise sociobiology (and social anthropologists are among the most vehement) for its impetuous description of human society, and its lack of sensitivity to the distinctions between the 'social' life of animals and the social life of man.[7] In particular, human social conduct is not sensibly to be compared to the conduct of bees in the hive or ants in the nest, for the reason that it is mediated by, and answerable to, a conception of itself.

Such criticisms, to which I shall shortly return, condemn not the enterprise of sociobiology, but the impetuous way in which it has leapt to its conclusions. After all, we are biologically determined beings, all of whose states arise from the organic processes which were initiated in us at our conception and which continue to govern what we are and do. Mental activity is activity of the brain, and the brain is as obedient to biological laws as every other part of the human body. How, then, can we suppose that our distinctively human mentality exempts us from the laws that govern the rest of nature? The theory of evolution and the science of genetics may yet be in their infant stages. But their success cannot be denied. Suppose we have to explain a complex feature of human society – monogamy, say. Surely, the first step will be to identify its ethnological *function*. Having done that, we are at least one stage nearer to providing the most satisfying explanation of its existence (which will be a theory of its genesis). Here again is E. O. Wilson's particular sketch of how the functional part of the explanation might proceed:

> Human beings, as typical large primates, breed slowly. Mothers carry fetuses for nine months and afterward are encumbered by infants and small children who require milk at frequent intervals through the day. It is to the advantage of each woman of the hunter-gatherer band to secure the allegiance of men who will contribute meat and hides while sharing the labor of child-rearing. It is to the reciprocal advantage of each man to obtain sexual rights to women and to monopolise their economic productivity. If the evidence from hunter-gatherer life has been correctly interpreted, the exchange has resulted in near universality of the pair bond and the prevalence of extended families, with men and their wives forming the nucleus. Sexual love and the emotional satisfaction of family life can be reasonably postulated to be based on enabling mechanisms in the physiology of the brain that have been programmed to some extent through the genetic hardening of this compromise. And because men can breed at shorter intervals than women, the pair bond has been attenuated somewhat by the common practice of polygamy, the taking of multiple wives.[8]

While we may deplore the immense simplification in that description of the facts (a simplification rendered necessary, however, by the author's polemical purpose), it would be as impetuous to argue that such explanations cannot be true as to assume, with the author, that they must be. For sexual behaviour, upon which the survival of the species depends, cannot be left by our species-nature to the vagaries of individual choice. So what if the explanation is true?

First, we should recognise that the very generality of the explanation makes it insensitive to the real distinctions between the phenomena explained. It cannot be doubted that our behaviour is – in its broad outlines – genetically determined. Nor can it be doubted that genetically determined behaviour survives only when it is not dysfunctional. If those facts were alone sufficient to solve the philosophical problems posed by human nature, then the problems would be quickly solved. But all we can conclude is that whatever exists, exists because it is not dysfunctional: what makes it true, however, that just *this* form of behaviour exists, here and now? The theory has no answer.

Moreover, the theory cannot really make contact with what is most puzzling in human behaviour. In the world of non-human nature, events and processes rarely present problems to our understanding that are not solved by scientific explanation – an explanation in terms of causes. But the human world abounds in phenomena that cannot be wholly understood merely by explaining them, because they are *themselves* forms of understanding. Consider mathematics – a social practice which no doubt has its genetic explanation. Mathematical understanding could not be generated through the sociobiology of mathematics. Certain mathematical practices (for example, that of deriving five from the sum of two and two) are indeed genetically dysfunctional, and must therefore disappear in the press of evolutionary competition. But this fact casts no light upon the nature of mathematical truth. It does not show what we understand when we understand that two plus two equals four. The evolutionary explanation of our mathematical habits depends upon our prior understanding that two plus two equals four, and therefore does not elucidate it. We can explain why we should have acquired mathematical understanding; but the explanation does not tell us what we have acquired. To understand *that* we must turn to logic and the foundations of mathematics, which are concerned with reasons, not causes, and which attempt to fix a standard of validity independent of empirical laws.

Of course, sexual conduct is not the same kind of thing as mathematical reasoning. But it is like mathematics in involving a kind of understanding that cannot be reduced to causal explanation, and which is therefore not necessarily enhanced by the causal explanation of its own existence. Our interpersonal understanding may be affected by our knowledge of sociobiology. But this is a peculiar fact, which does not follow simply because sociobiology explains what we are.

More broadly, we should not accept that the term 'social' used to describe, now the cooperative behaviour of human beings, now the instinctive agglomeration of the herd, now the totally cemented unity of the hive, is used unequivocally. As I earlier remarked, the social behaviour of human beings is mediated and transformed by a conception of itself. It may be rooted in instinct, but it is not reducible to instinct, not only because it exemplifies learning, but also because it involves rational response. In particular it involves cooperation, when one person joins with another, and acts from a conception of himself and the other as reciprocally involved and mutually answerable. The difference between rational cooperation and instinctive cohesion – between man and ant – is so great that it is questionable whether a single pattern of explanation could be applied to both.[9] Rationality, even when seen in evolutionary terms, is a capacity to *invent* solutions to problems, to work out individually an answer that may not have been contained in the inheritance of the species. The rational being therefore acquires behaviour and beliefs that are not the common property of the species, and could not be: in particular he acquires a culture, and his self and will are more responsive to this culture than to any species-laden imperative. No doubt evolutionary theory can explain why we have this capacity (that is, why, having acquired it, we were better fitted to survive). By virtue of possessing it, however, we rise above the level of 'species-being', and generate a new order of behaviour, the order of history. History is the collective order which we make ourselves, and which bears the imprint of our own self-conception.

Rational behaviour, like all behaviour, is biologically caused. But that does not mean that it has to be explained in terms of the evolutionary composition of the species. Rationality endows us with the capacity to modify our species endowments, in ways that can be predicted only from the laws which govern rationality itself. The prime mistake of sociobiology is to consider society as a *species* formation: to consider that, because we are, as a species, socially disposed, human societies will owe their ruling characteristics to genetic implantation. On the contrary, the structure of society is precisely *not* that of the species. Society is the outcome of cooperation, and cooperation is a rational act, mediated by a sense of self and other, as reason-giving and answerable individuals. In explaining social behaviour, therefore, we are explaining forms of *intentional understanding*. Some sociologists follow Weber in believing that such an explanation must be of a special kind: it must involve an act of participation in the intentional understanding that it seeks to explain (an act of *Verstehen*).[10] In which case, it is hard to see how the theory of evolution could be extended to cover social behaviour. However, it is by no means obvious that Weber is right: the fact that a form of behaviour is a *mode* of understanding does not mean that it is to be explained by means of the very understanding that it exemplifies. (There *could* be a causal explanation of mathematical understanding, and it would certainly not be a piece of mathematics.) At the same time, it is evident that a theory of social behaviour must include intentional understanding among its data. And this is precisely what sociobiology seems incompetent to do. For sociobiology wishes to explain social behaviour as the outcome of processes which are manifested throughout the evolutionary order, even by species who have no intentional understanding. In other words, it wishes to put intentional understanding aside, as a mere addition to behaviour that can exist without it and be explained without explaining it. This is to neglect the fact that intentional understanding is *constitutive* of social behaviour.

By way of disguising this difficulty sociobiology has embarked upon an elaborate redescription of human behaviour, in order to void it of its intentional content. The actual explanations offered by sociobiologists invariably begin from a misdescription of what has to be explained. The resulting 'simiomorphism' is not without considerable interest: in the hands of demagogues like Desmond Morris and Alex Comfort, it has proved highly destructive of human moral perceptions.[11] Before considering the sociobiology of sex, it is instructive to refer to the sociobiologist's account of another fundamental social institution – the institution of property. E. O. Wilson argues that 'the biological formula of territorialism *translates easily* into the rituals of modern property ownership. When described by means of generalisations *clear of emotional and fictive embellishment*, this behavior acquires new flavor' (my emphasis).[12] He proceeds to give evidence, in the form of a quotation from the sociologist Pierre van den Berghe, whose description of property rituals in Seattle shows exactly what this 'clearing of emotion and fictive embellishments' amounts to – a clearing of all that is distinctively human, of all that makes human behaviour hard for a sociobiologist to explain:

> Before entering familial territory, guests and visitors, especially if they are unexpected, regularly go through a ritual of identification, attention drawing, greeting and apology for possible disturbance. This behavioural exchange takes place outdoors if the owner is first encountered there, and is preferably directed at adults. Children of the owners, if encountered first, are asked about the whereabouts of their parents. When no adult owners are met outdoors, the visitor typically goes to the dwelling door, where he makes an identifying noise, either by knocking on the door or ringing a bell if the door is closed, or by voice if the door is open. The threshold is typically crossed only on recognition and invitation by the owner. Even then, the guests feel free to enter only the sitting room, and usually make additional requests to enter other parts of the house, such as a bathroom or bedroom.
>
> When a visitor is present, he is treated by the other members of the [vacation residence] club as an extension of his host. That is, his limited privileges of territorial occupancy extend only to the territory of his host, and the host will be held responsible for any territorial transgressions of the guests. . . . Children, too, are not treated as independent agents, but as extensions of their parents or of the adult 'responsible' for them, and territorial transgressions of children, especially if repeated, are taken up with the parents or guardians.
>
> The dirt road through the development is freely accessible to all members of the club who use it both to gain access to their lots and to take walks. Etiquette calls for owners to greet each other when seeing each other outdoors, but owners do not feel free to enter each other's lots without some ritual of recognition. This ritual is, however, less formal and elaborate when entering lots outdoors than when entering houses.[13]

A research grant that permits one to spend the summer in a vacation club, and call the resulting diary 'sociology', is clearly not to be sneezed at. It is evident, however, that the observer is either humourless or alienated.

The achievement of courtesy, whereby one person enters a house only when invited by the occupant, is described in language appropriate to the territorial ritual of birds: 'the threshold is typically crossed only on recognition and invitation by the owner.' The fact that people ask before using the bathroom becomes a peculiar aspect of the need for 'additional requests to enter other parts of the house'. Some of the behaviour can be described only in terms of a moral concept which informs the intentional understanding of the participants. The concept is then put in quotation marks, to indicate that, with the inevitable advance of sociological science, we shall soon be able to dispense with it. Thus an adult is not responsible for a child, but merely 'responsible'. A conversation is a 'behavioural exchange', a polite discourse is a 'ritual of recognition', a man announcing himself is 'making an identifying noise', and so on. At the same time, the description given is about as revelatory of what is going on as a description of a conversation given by someone who is both ignorant of the language and observing the speakers through the wrong end of a telescope. It is no more than a superficial glance at behaviour which, judged from the point of view of meaning, is intelligible to anyone, although intelligible in other terms than these – in terms of intention, courtesy, friendship, responsibility, recognition of self and other; in short, in terms which, while familiar from our intentional understanding of the human world, resist 'translation' into the language of sociobiology.

None of this would matter were sociobiologists content to admit their ignorance. However, they have shown no disposition to do so. E. O. Wilson, for example, has no hesitation in drawing moral conclusions which, despite their remoteness from everything that we know about the human condition, are asserted with the full confidence of someone who is at last bringing scientific clarity into a world of atavistic confusion. He argues that 'all that we can surmise of man's genetic history argues for a more liberal sexual morality, in which sexual practices are to be regarded first as bonding devices and only second as means for procreation.'[14] Not only does he thereby covertly admit that sexual conduct is not genetically determined, and therefore inexplicable by his method; he also shows the extent of his disrespect for the 'science' which guides him. If it is true that sexual practices are primarily bonding devices, they must inevitably be circumscribed by all the fears and jealousies of human affection – and hence will attract to themselves an 'illiberal' sexual morality, which sees value in fidelity, modesty and restraint, and danger in promiscuous dissipation. If, on the other hand, sexual practices are primarily devices for reproduction, we could liberalise them at once, simply by developing effective forms of impersonal nurture, perhaps on the model of *Brave*

New World. The fact that Wilson can draw, in so cavalier a fashion, precisely the opposite conclusion from that which his 'scientific' observations imply shows, I believe, the unserious nature of the 'science' from which he derives them.

A note on Schopenhauer

The idea that sexual desire is to be understood in terms of the long-term impersonal strategy of the species is by no means the invention of sociobiology. Schopenhauer, in a spectacular essay appended to *The World as Will and Idea*,[15] gave voice to the theory with a directness and psychological penetration which no sociobiologist has been able to match. Schopenhauer is interesting, too, in his attempt to reconcile a 'species' theory of sexual desire with a recognition of the individuality of the sexual object. He distinguishes love from 'sexual impulse', arguing that the 'passion of being in love'

> is directed to an individual object, and to this alone, and thus appears, so to speak, as the *special* order of the species. For the opposite reason, mere sexual impulse is base and ignoble, because it is directed to all without individualisation, and strives to maintain the species as regards quantity, with little consideration for quality. [Cf. the sociobiologist's theory of courtship rituals given earlier.] But individualisation, and with it the intensity of being in love, can reach so high a degree that without their satisfaction all the good things of the world and even life itself lose their value.[16]

How is this individualisation to be explained in terms of the needs of the species? Schopenhauer offers a variety of answers. At one point he seems to suggest that the individualisation of the object of desire is brought about by the individuality of its product – the new self that will be born from the act of sexual union. The union of parents brings about 'precisely that individual for which the will-to-live in general, exhibiting itself in the whole species, feels a longing'.[17] At other points, clearly unsatisfied with that fanciful, and in truth barely intelligible, explanation, Schopenhauer tries to give a functional characterisation of the individuality of the sexual object. Passion, he argues, will be 'more powerful in degree, the more individualised it is';[18] hence, by focusing on the individual, passion gains a greater chance of accomplishing the designs of the species. It overcomes the resistance that we (in our quite reasonable disgust at the idea that the whole wretched business will go on from generation to generation) naturally tend to offer to the workings of desire. (Again there is an analogy with the sociobiologist's explanation of courtship and contest.) However, it is also an idea of Schopenhauer's metaphysics that the individual is an ephemeral and in a sense illusory appearance. What I really am is not the individual I, but .the universal will, which, while manifest in me, survives my individual destruction. And, since sexual desire is a manifestation of the will, it stems ultimately from that in me which is *not* individualised. It is, Schopenhauer argues, the immortal part in me that longs to unite with you, and this immortal part is the will of the species which, as 'thing in itself', 'free from the *principium individuationis*',[19] is really the sum and the dissolution of all individual agents.

Schopenhauer's meaning is not fully explicable outside the context of his metaphysical system. Nevertheless, despite his vacillations, we can see here a brave attempt to reconcile the given facts of sexual desire – in particular, the fact of its individualising intentionality – with a theory that gives due prominence to our species nature and to the obvious fact that the species has interests which can be thwarted by too great an emphasis on the sanctity of the individual soul. Furthermore, behind Schopenhauer's reference to the *principium individuationis* lies an interesting theory of individuality. According to Schopenhauer, the idea of individual existence belongs purely to the world of 'representation': this is how we *see* the world, but not how the world is 'in itself'. It is precisely when I look into myself, and attempt to grasp the individuality that is me, that I become aware of the inner reality, the thing-in-itself, which is not appearance but will. This will, however, is not, and cannot be, individualised. I know it in myself, but what I know is not me, nor you, nor anyone. Only in the act of knowledge does it seem to be, for a moment, an individual I, but then neither the knower nor the known can, even in that moment, lay intelligible claim to the title. Hence the yearning for the individual, which is manifest in desire, is at the same time the surging of a universal and impersonal force, which governs our lives with the impartial law of the species, and dissolves our individuality in the very act of union for which we individually crave.

Schopenhauer's sociobiology, which aims at being true to the phenomenology of desire, saves itself only by stepping into those turbulent metaphysical waters. And while there is indeed a morality which floats like a mist above them (a morality quite at variance with the enthusiasms of Edward Wilson and Desmond Morris), its metaphysical undercurrent is so troubled that few can venture into it. Schopenhauer never hesitated to pay the highest possible price for his 'insights' – the price of an unintelligible metaphysics. But we cannot afford the cost, and

no 'science' of sex, however sophisticated, could follow in Schopenhauer's footsteps. It is salutary, therefore, to see what price has been paid
for the conclusions at which the sociobiologist aims, and which he has yet
to attain by the patient application of empirical science.

There are, however, two lessons to be learned from sociobiology. First,
we cannot ignore the fact that we are animals, and that in our sexual
conduct we conform to genetic laws which govern animal reproduction.
Crude though the existing literature of sociobiology may be, the
fundamental thesis cannot be rejected, and any theory of desire which is
incompatible with it must fall under immediate suspicion.

Secondly, the *scientific* truth of the evolutionary hypothesis has
implications concerning the intentionality of desire. Now that we know
the facts of human reproduction the irresistible impulse of desire seems to
us like a summons: the imperious demand of the future generation to be
born makes itself known to us in desire. When we look on our children,
and when we look on the person whom we desire, we hear the same
implacable demand, and submit, in the end, to a like impersonal tyranny.
At every point in our relations with those whom we love or desire, we are
addressed by something which is not ourselves, as the crowds who hover
at the threshold of existence call out to us with confused, supplicating
voices.

In the National Gallery in Washington, there is a painting by Poussin of
the nursing of the infant Jupiter, in which the swelling, commanding,
self-seeking energy of the new-born infant is portrayed as a quality of
flesh. The child sucks the goat's milk from a horn, and absorbs along with
it the energy of all who surround him. The anxious, puzzled face of the
nymph who holds the horn to the god's lips; the fervent attention of the
shepherd who has milked the goat; the glazed fixity of his companion,
made mindless by the infant's mesmeric self-absorption: all express the
utter tyranny of new life over existing life, of the god who is all future,
over the human present, which selflessly expends itself in the nurture of a
power that will never reward its devotion. The longing which causes us to
submit to the tyranny of an infant is prefigured in desire. Here too we are
made selfless, absorbed, even mindless by a force which draws us
inexorably towards another human being. In the call to sacrifice we feel
the premonition of death; for we have only this to do, in order to become
expendable. These aspects of our 'biological' predicament feed our
intentional understanding, and – however much we may embellish our
desire with Kantian story-telling – we know, in our hearts, that the thing
which overcomes us in desire works *through* the other, but not entirely
from him. Hence, as Schopenhauer recognised, we betray ourselves in

desire and, if we become furtive, it is perhaps in order to escape our own attention.

Wagner claimed that the philosophy of *Tristan und Isolde* derives from Schopenhauer. And we can see in the above remarks (far though they may be from the aspect of Schopenhauer which influenced Wagner) an avenue to the explanation of Tristan's melancholy. Tristan loves a woman from whom his children cannot be born. In their 'choice of love', which is also a destiny, Tristan and Isolde stand apart from 'species life'. Nothing justifies or fulfils their union save the intensity that compels it. No new life mocks the mortal apprehension of desire, and the I of Tristan loses itself in the gazing I of Isolde as in a bottomless pool. Tristan's race dies with him, extinguished by his own desire. The labour of his self-creation is in vain, and when he speaks in his delirium of the *Urvergessen* to which his soul is destined, it is not Tristan who speaks, but Tristan's seed, condemned by his own fruitless individuality to perpetual nothingness.

The unconscious

Sociobiology offers an explanation of the 'darkness' of desire – of the fact that I am gripped by this passion and led by a force that is stronger than me, larger than me, and in some mysterious way outside me. It is not the only explanation that has been offered for the fact that desire seems always to overreach its aim. In *The Symposium*, Aristophanes describes the situation thus:

> The partners cannot even say what they wish should happen between them. No one could imagine this to be merely sexual intercourse, or that such alone could be the reason why each rejoices so eagerly in the other's company: obviously the soul of each is wishing for something else that it cannot express, only divining and darkly hinting what it desires.[20]

Aristophanes offers his famous comic explanation of the enigmatic nature of desire: each of us, he argues, is bodily sundered from his other half, and led mysteriously by his body to unite with its missing partner.

Aristophanes' legend illustrates one of the perennial themes of erotic discourse. Because the aim of desire is so opaque to us, and because the immediate satisfaction of desire seems in retrospect so inadequate a recompense for the trouble of pursuing it, desire is provided with an *unconscious* motive – a motive originating outside the self, in the darkness of organic nature. The first major treatise devoted to the 'unconscious' – Eduard von Hartmann's *Philosophy of the Unconscious* – also addressed itself to Aristophanes' question, asking 'why the sexual instinct is concentrated exclusively on *this* individual and not on *that*', which is, Hartmann says, 'the question of the determining grounds of this fastidious sexual selection'.[21]

Hartmann, relying on Schopenhauer's arguments, claims that the question cannot be answered by reference only to the conscious aim of desire: there is nothing in conscious intentionality which explains the 'course of desire' in union and love. Hartmann therefore proposes an unconscious intentionality as the sole possible answer to the metaphysical question:

> The illimitable nature of the longing and striving spring, then, precisely from the ineffableness and incomprehensibility of a conscious goal, which would be absurd want of aim, were not an unconscious purpose the invisible spring of this powerful apparatus of feeling – an unconscious purpose of which we can only say that the sexual union of these particular individuals must be the means to its fulfilment.[22]

Hartmann offers a canny and vigorous description of desire; but he is no more successful than Aristophanes or Schopenhauer in explaining its intentionality. His conclusion – that the hidden purpose of desire is to 'beget such an individual as most completely represents the idea of the race'[23] – is also Schopenhauer's, and promises an explanation neither of the individualising intentionality of desire nor of its overpowering force. It is instructive to us largely because it shows the genesis of an important modern idea. For Hartmann the unconscious is a repository of motives that are organically constituted, and also, at the same time, endowed with a distinctively personal intentionality.

Freudian psychology: the general problem

The most important exponent of that idea has been Freud, who, like the sociobiologists, hoped to provide a theory of human nature and human sexuality that might eventually be given a biological base. This leaning towards biology determined much of the imagery and language which he used to formulate his ideas. The scientific claims of Freud's theories have been frequently questioned, and it is fair to say that few would now accept them quite in the terms in which they were originally proposed. Nevertheless, Freud's theories continue to be extremely influential, and to be accepted as something more than fanciful description. Whatever the defects of Freud's own presentation – which is widely admitted to be fluctuating, unsystematic and riddled with metaphor – his theories are held to represent genuine discoveries, and genuine explanations of otherwise mysterious facts. It is important to examine those claims. In the course of doing so I shall consider Freud not only for the sake of what he himself wrote, but also for the sake of his influence. And while there will not be space to consider the writings of his disciples, I believe that the substance of my criticisms will weigh equally against the sexual theories of Melanie Klein and, up to a point, against those of Wilhelm Reich – possibly the two most influential of the post-Freudian psychoanalytic writers on sex.[24] Freud and Freudianism have so entered the modern ways of thinking about sex that the reader may greet with unbelief my claim that Freud was neither an accurate observer nor a plausible theorist. Nevertheless, I believe this claim to be both true and of overwhelming importance for anyone concerned to rescue sexual morality from the morass into which modern ways of thinking have enticed it.

Freud's account of human sexuality – delivered in a variety of ways at several different periods of his life – is based in a metaphor of the human mind. For Freud, consciousness is a mere compartment of the mental, the division between conscious and unconscious mental processes being explained in terms of a dynamic analogy. The mind is structured by forces and barriers: mental states are pushed into the unconscious by repression, and retained there by defence; or else they break through, borne up on a crest of libido into the world of action. The conscious and the unconscious denote different regions of an internal space, one light, the other dark, and within this space great psychic forces contend for ascendancy. The region of light is dominated by the ego, actively engaged in defending itself from the contents of the id. At the ego's shoulder, barely visible but ever-present, stands the 'super-ego', who is both master and creation of the ego whom he persecutes.

The scientific value of the picture depends upon whether it can be translated into a literal, and explanatory, theory of the mind. Could mental phenomena be assigned a causal explanation, in terms that would render such a description apposite (if perhaps a little fanciful)? Could one, for example, envisage a neurophysiological version of the theory, which identified the 'forces', 'barriers' and 'inner spaces' in terms accessible to empirical investigation? It is probable that Freud eventually hoped for such a translation,[25] and at any rate that he would not have been averse to it. At the same time, it should be recognised that the imagery itself – of ego and id, of 'psychic force' and 'psychic resistance' – provided his principal inspiration, and his frequent references to an underlying 'chemistry' of the human psyche were accompanied by no serious theory. When faced with the task of making sense of some particular psychological phenomenon, Freud used the imagery, not as shorthand for some theory that had yet to be provided, but as a literal representation of the facts. It could therefore be said (and indeed has been said) that Freud's metaphor serves, not as theory, but as myth, and makes sense of human phenomena not in the way that science makes sense of them, but in the way that myth makes sense of them: by telling stories that reveal a consoling logic in what is otherwise strange to us and uncontrollable.

Moreover, it is doubtful that the Freudian metaphor could be translated and still retain its power. As myth, it belongs to the realm of intentional understanding, providing us with a redescription of our mental states, in terms of which to adjust and rectify our attitudes towards them. As scientific theory, however, it must step out of the intentional realm, and attend to that which underlies it. But how could it do this and still retain the ruling idea of a contest between ego, super-ego and id? At the same time that idea is highly anthropomorphic, and to retain it is to open the theory to a serious objection. The ego is construed as 'inner observer' of its mental states, a Cartesian Inspector, protecting himself from that which he does not want to know, and examining that which is permissible. Unless he acts to prevent them, mental states are propelled from the lower darkness into his realm of vision. The ego, therefore, is seen as a kind of agent, for whom the pronoun 'I' is indeed appropriate. We can make sense of the idea of one and the same mental state as, now 'in' consciousness, now 'in' the unconscious, only by means of some such theory of the 'inner observer', to whom things are alternately revealed and concealed. The states in the unconscious, being unobserved by him, are not really his – they are not 'in his mind'. Unless he too is divided into a conscious and an unconscious section – so opening the prospect of an endless *mis en abîme*, with no ultimate observer, and therefore no subject of experience at all – it must be true of him, at least, that his consciousness and his mentality are one and the same. But then it can immediately be seen that whatever prompts us to say of the ego that his mental states are all necessarily conscious ought to prompt us to say the same of ourselves. For he is envisaged precisely on the model of the human person – he is the 'little man inside' who is the real agent in all our acts, and the real recipient of all our impressions. There is no other way of retaining the Freudian metaphor. We must assume the ego to be a person, at war with another whom he can never see, and whom he knows only through the effect of those 'forces' by which the id attempts to subvert him. Only on this assumption can we think of the unconscious processes as *mental* processes: they are mental because they might at any moment *become* conscious, in the ego. If we dismiss the metaphor, and say that the 'ego' is not a kind of person but simply a 'region' of mental space, we lose all reason for thinking that the 'unconscious' forces are really *mental*. Why not say, now, that they are forces which influence the mental realm while not themselves belonging to it? In particular, why assume (as Freud assumes) that they retain, in their 'unconscious' form, the peculiar *intentionality* of the mental? Only if they do so, can the Freudian explanation illuminate what it purports to explain; for the influence of the unconscious is (supposedly) the influence of an intentional content. And yet there are no grounds for thinking that a *content* can be retained in the lower regions. Given the evident fact that neither I nor my 'id' can confess to an unconscious state it is hard to see how such an intentional content could be reliably assigned.

If we describe the 'unconscious' processes without using ideas of content, Freud's theory ceases to resist translation into empirical idiom. It gives way to a more ordinary and (from the intentional perspective) less illuminating idea, that the mind responds to events and processes of which it is not aware, and that some of these processes may be caused by experiences which have been forgotten. To return this explanation to its Freudian frame, we must argue that the forgetting was both 'deliberate' and, in a sense, unreal (since the id at least remembers). In other words, we must resuscitate the metaphor. A truly scientific account – one which eliminates the metaphor entirely – would have to dispense with all such language. But it would also dispense with any reference to the 'unconscious', and any attempt to attribute intentionality to states whose content is not represented in the behaviour which expresses them.

Of course, intentional content can be attributed to processes, even when this content cannot be expressed by the thing *in* which the processes occur (the mental states of animals, for example). But the attribution of content to events in the natural world is an exercise of intentional understanding, and one which we should naturally renounce in favour of mechanistic explanations, if we understood the true causality of things. Scientific explanation puts all ideas of content in jeopardy, and an explanation that depends upon such ideas is one that belongs not to science but to intentional understanding. Freud has attempted to complicate the idea of 'self', as this occurs in our everyday thoughts about ourselves, in order to bring within the sphere of self-understanding events and actions that erstwhile lay beyond it. The theory which justifies this extension is not science, but myth. Perhaps, therefore, the true criterion of its success is not explanatory, but practical – to what extent, for example, does it achieve the therapeutic success at which it aims?[26]

Freud: the specific theory

Let us suppose, however, that we can avoid those objections and can reconstruct the Freudian theory so as to eliminate all metaphorical components. Such an enterprise may be possible for those parts of the theory which concern us – the parts which deal with the psychology of sex. In any event, it is worth examining Freud's theory of sexuality in its own terms, in order to discover whether, if it were cured of its philosophical difficulties, it might at least deliver a correct description – perhaps even an explanation – of sexual phenomena. I shall argue that it can do neither.

The elements of Freud's theory are not easy to assemble, and the theory changed over time. I take it that the following sketch is not too great a distortion: Sexual experiences are rooted in an instinct, and 'the sexual instinct is in the first instance independent of its object.'[27] This instinct is further identified as a force (the 'libido'), represented as a developing principle, which structures both the sexual behaviour and the emotional character of the subject. The sexual instinct gradually *acquires* its objects, by a process of 'attachment', first to various excitations of the body, and secondly to the circumstances which arouse them. Principal among these excitations are the sensory experiences in the so-called 'erotogenic' (or 'erogenic') zones, and the main circumstances of their early excitement are connected with the family drama. The libido develops along with a developing response to family relations, and a child's feelings towards his parents come to exert a determining influence over his natural instinct for sexual gratification. The normal 'sexual aim' which results from the development of the libido is 'union of the genitals in the act known as copulation which leads to a release of the sexual tension and a temporary extinction of the sexual instinct – a satisfaction', Freud adds, 'analogous to the satisfaction of hunger.'[28] Sometimes the instinct will 'cathect' other objects (as in fetishism), or it will be 'sublimated', by which Freud means detached altogether from the sexual act, and transformed into a contemplative attitude which endows its object with a moral nimbus. Sexual perversion involves directing the sexual instinct towards an abnormal aim.

At times Freud tried to link his theory of the libido and its development with a general biological theory of instincts. Thus at one point he defines an instinct as a 'psychical representation of an endosomatic, continuously flowing source of stimulation',[29] while 'the source of an instinct is a process of excitation occurring in an organ and the immediate aim of the instinct lies in the removal of this organic stimulus'.[30] Sexual excitation is the result of 'chemical changes' in the 'erotogenic zones',[31] and the aim of sexual activity is therefore a return to normal, by reversal of those changes (an instance of the 'homeostatic principle').

Two further aspects of the theory should be mentioned: the concept of repression, and the idea of infant sexuality. It seems to be implied in Freud's approach that human sexual development, were it not for repression, would be similar to the sexual development of animals. That is, it would move towards a generalisable reproductive instinct, an urge to copulate which could be satisfied as hunger is satisfied, without evoking any interpersonal emotion. With characteristic hydraulic imagery, Freud speaks of the sexual instinct as obstructed by certain 'mental dams'; these obstacles to the free flow of the sexual instinct are 'disgust, shame and morality'[32] – and he treats the three phenomena as though they were, from a psychological point of view, on a par, being different species of inhibition. Each is to be distinguished, however, from the more basic *force* which explains them – that of repression.

The idea of repression is complex, and forms part of a theory which Freud himself never expounded in a systematic way, and which has only recently begun to acquire a canonical form.[33] We must distinguish primal repression (which occurs in infancy) from repression proper (which occurs in later life). The first ensures that certain infantile experiences and traumas are submerged in the id; the second ensures that they remain there. The first is a process, the second a force. Both may be more or less successful, and both may be more or less strong. In discussing the theory Freud tends to vary the metaphor, mixing the hydraulic and the overtly biological. He speaks of the 'protective' shield which the 'living vesicle' erects against external stimuli, and the further need for such a vesicle (the cortex) to protect itself from the destructive stimuli that assail it from within:

> Such an event as an external trauma is bound to provoke a disturbance on a large scale in the functioning of the organism's energy and to set in motion every possible defensive measure. At the same time, the pleasure principle is for the moment put out of action. There is no longer any possibility of preventing the mental apparatus from being flooded with large amounts of stimulus, and another problem arises instead – the problem of mastering the amounts of

stimulus which have broken in and of binding them, in the psychical sense, so that they can then be disposed of.[34]

Thus occurs the great 'anticathectic' force of repression, which serves to bind the invading stimulus and force it out of consciousness. The quotation shows the extent to which the theory has remained tied to metaphor. We can accept, however, that it has strong empirical content, and implies testable 'observation sentences'. (The theory implies, for example, that certain subjects will be unmentionable, or 'tabu', and that certain impulses, notably the sexual impulse, will be stifled by hesitations.) Some philosophers (for example Karl Popper and Ernst Nagel)[35] have argued that the Freudian theory does not have genuine predictive power, since it implies no testable observation: but I do not think that the objection stands up. The Freudian theory has both theoretical terms, and empirical content. The problem is that the transition from the first to the second passes by an ineliminable metaphor. In this it differs from all genuine scientific theories, which contain a core of meaning that tells us literally *how things are* (even though models and metaphors are often required if we are to grasp them). The forces and counterforces, cathexes and anticathexes of Freudian theory are described in irreducibly 'psychic' terms – not as physiological processes, but as mental actions. (This is what is meant by Freud's idea that the invading forces must be 'bound, in the psychical sense, so that they can be disposed of'.) The contents of the mind are described in intentional language, in the language of appearances, even though they denote events and processes which (because of repression) may never appear. If we attempt to find a 'mechanical' description of these forces – as currents, say, in the nervous system – we find that we can no longer explain what we seek to explain by referring to them. The crucial ideas of 'ego', 'id' and 'super-ego' now disappear. Such ideas do not survive the translation from the intentional idiom into the language of investigative science. Among physiological processes there is organisation, but no ego; force and counterforce, but no action. The ideas of 'defence' and 'repression' therefore disappear, and with them the theory which required us to see these forces in mental terms – as responses to a threat.

Once again we may put the objection to one side, and assume that the theory of repression and defence has all the explanatory power that it claims. In order to examine the resulting picture of the inner structure of sexual desire, we need to combine it with the Freudian theory of infant sexuality. For Freud, human sexual life begins at the breast and, unless impeded, exhibits a continuous development throughout childhood to the mature forms of sexual union. There are two currents in this development – the 'affectionate current of childhood' and the 'sensual current of puberty'. The sexuality of the adult is an outcome of the two movements, so that should they fail to converge, 'the result is often that one of the ideals of sexual life, the focusing of all desire upon a single object, will be unattainable.'[36]

As that remark indicates, Freud was aware of the facts of mature sexuality, and in various essays (notably in 'The Tendency to Debasement in Love'),[37] he ventured explanations of some of the most subtle features of human sexual response, in terms which are distinctly interpersonal, and which are attached to the theory of infantile sexuality by means of nothing stronger than dogma. Nevertheless Freud remained convinced that the social facts of sexual attachment could ultimately be seen to be natural outgrowths of an instinctual force.

The pivotal ideas of the theory are two: that of the libido, and that of the erotogenic zone. The libido is conceived as a force that may attach itself to various objects, and which also has a definite aim. The erotogenic zone effects the process of attachment between desire and object, by associating the object with the localised relief at which the libido aims. That the resulting theory is a caricature of sexual desire as I have described it goes without saying. Nevertheless, it may yet be an accurate account of the underlying physiological *basis* of desire; if so, it will clearly have important consequences both for the theory of desire and for the theory of sexual morality.

Criticism: the libido

It seems to me that both of Freud's pivotal ideas are incoherent. We are supposed to understand the libido both as instinct, which seeks the release of accumulated 'sexual tension' through sensory stimulus of some 'erotogenic zone', and at the same time as a passion, directed on to an object, whose aim and gratification are inseparable from the subject's conception of himself, of the other, and of the relation which binds them. (For how else is the prohibition of incest to be perceived as a prohibition of 'sexual release' with the mother?) Freud mentions the analogy with hunger – but either he had never been hungry or else (as he once half admitted) he was unfamiliar with desire. I may wish to sit down to supper only with those whose company I enjoy, and this will certainly give an important moral character to my eating habits, and provide me with a reason for abstaining until the moment has come. But my attitude towards my friend, and that towards my steak, are two quite separate things. I do not seek my friend's company out of hunger, or the steak out of friendship; nor does my enjoyment of my friend's company contain, as a component, my enjoyment of the steak. These two disparate attitudes could never combine into one, since their intentional structures are not congruous. Friendship is founded upon thoughts and beliefs about my friend, and is manifest in a desire for his company. It is an interpersonal attitude which crucially aims at reciprocity, and in which thoughts of self and other are integral to the aim. By contrast, the desire for the steak need involve no special conception of either self or steak (how else could animals be hungry?). It is not interpersonal; nor is it founded upon any thought besides the judgement that 'here, before me, is food'. The appetite that is stilled by the steak could equally have been satisfied by any other relevantly similar object, and the pleasure of eating it resides in localised sensations which can be experienced unthinkingly. It is inconceivable that this intentional structure should actually be embedded within that other structure I have described as friendship – not even in the imaginary case, described in Chapter 4, when nothing may be eaten except one's friends.

For Freud, however, the libido must possess both forms of intentionality. It is initially conceived on the model of hunger – a pursuit of bodily gratifications which we share with creatures who are not persons, and which has no object beside that of local gratification. It is this 'force' which, Freud believes, 'invades' our personal life, and re-emerges in the mature person as sexual desire. But how can this force acquire the intentional structure of desire? Once again, Freud has recourse to metaphor, arguing that the libido 'cathects' (besetze) a certain object, and so concentrates its energy in a certain direction. Sometimes this attachment of libido to object is described as an 'incorporation' of the object;[38] sometimes the libido is said to be especially 'adhesive'.[39] Similar metaphors have been used by Freud's disciples, notably by Melanie Klein in her theory of the 'part object', to which the child attaches his sexual leanings at the breast.[40] But what do such metaphors mean? *What is it* for the libido to be 'attached' to an object? This is surely precisely what a theory of desire must *explain*.

Freud grapples with the problem in the following way. He sees the major task for his theory as that of explaining how the generalised libido (the 'ego libido') of the child grows into the 'object libido' of true sexual desire.[41] It does this, he argues, by 'concentrating upon objects, becoming fixated to them or abandoning them, moving from one object to another and, from these situations, directing the subject's sexual activity, which leads to the satisfaction, that is, to the partial and temporary extinction, of the libido'.[42]

We can see in that passage the extent to which, when Freud wishes to argue for a conclusion, he begins by assuming it. He assumes that the satisfaction of the libido consists in extinction, like the extinction of hunger – and thus that the aim of the libido is to be compared to that of hunger. And he equally assumes that the intentionality of the libido is a form of 'concentration' upon an object, and that it 'directs the subject's sexual activity'. But the question was precisely how *both* of those could be true. How is it that a force with the first feature (an appetitive aim) can also have the second (an erotic intentionality)? Freud, under the guise of a theory, has smuggled in his conclusion: that the libido – that very instinctual force – might also be exemplified as a *desire for this person*, and in the *pursuit of this person*. But that is precisely what the basic moves of Freud's theory give us reason to doubt. For those moves situate the libido outside the realm of interpersonal attitudes; it remains wholly inexplicable how this appetitive force could acquire the intentionality of such an attitude, or even some other form of genuine object-directedness, and still remain itself.

If we return now to our earlier criticisms, we can see more clearly why Freud's metaphors were necessary, if his theory were to appear to explain what it seeks to explain. The relation of the libido to its object, while conceived in terms of a chemical idea of 'adhesion' or 'cathexis', is supposed to explain sexual intentionality. It appears to explain sexual intentionality, however, only because the metaphor of 'adhesion' is not literalised – only because we assume it to *be* an idea of intentionality. It seems as though we can explain a man's attachment to this woman, who is like his mother, by referring to a libido that has detached itself from one object, and then 'cathected' another. But in the 'intentional' sense of 'object', no state of desire could do any such thing. And if there is some underlying impulse which 'adheres' now to this, now to that, then the thing adhered to is not for this reason alone the intentional object of any particular state of mind. (To think otherwise is to confuse material with intentional relations: see Appendix 2.) The most obvious way of literalising the metaphor of 'cathexis', in terms of the proximate activation of nervous centres, deprives us of every reason for believing that the theory of adhesion is also a theory of intentional transfer.

Even if it could be shown that an instinctual force answering to Freud's 'libido' animates the sexual life of people, the very fact that the intentional structure of desire is one that this force cannot possess suffices to displace it from the moral eminence to which it has recently been elevated. In particular the hydraulic metaphor – the metaphor of a tide or surge of feeling, that becomes 'dammed', 'bottled up', 'blocked' and 'released' – this, the master-thought of modern libertarian morality (as exemplified, for example, in the work of Reich and Norman O. Brown),[43] ceases to have any bearing upon the question of sexual conduct. The fact that my libido is 'bottled up' is no more relevant to the question whether it is right to make love to this woman before me than the fact that my adrenalin is 'bottled up' is relevant to the question whether I ought to be angry with her. To think of sexual desire in these terms is to build a morality of excuses, but without a moral law.

Criticism: the erotogenic zone

Consider now the second ruling idea of Freud's theory of infantile sexuality – the idea of the 'erotogenic zone'. The term is taken from the French – *zones érogènes* – and was introduced by the physician Ernest Chambard in 1881.[44] Since then the 'doctrine of erogenic zones', as Havelock Ellis was to call it, has had a following both within and outside the field of psychoanalysis, and is comparable, in its influence as in its quackery, to alchemy, phrenology and structuralism. (The term 'eroto-genic' appears equally as 'erogenous', 'erotogenous' and 'erogenic'.) Freud's theory of the erotogenic zone is founded in precisely the same confusion as his theory of the libido. These zones, it transpires, must be both the place of sexual pleasure – a pleasure akin (for Freud) to scratching an itch – and also *for the very same reason* the place of sexual arousal, with the interpersonal intentionality which that implies. Freud tries on several occasions to define the erotogenic zone, but the definitions turn out to have a peculiarly tautologous quality: they can be understood only in terms of a prior idea of sexual arousal, and are never self-explanatory. The erotogenic zone is regarded as an 'apparatus sub-ordinate to the genitals and a substitute for them'.[45] It is then said to be 'a part of the skin or mucous membrane in which stimuli of a certain sort evoke a feeling of pleasure possessing a particular quality'.[46] The reference to the 'particular quality' of the experience (when it is a 'particular intentionality' that has to be explained) is reminiscent of Hume's account of the relation between impressions and ideas.[47] It is a clear index of the fact that Freud has phrased the problem of human sexuality in terms of the solution that he favours. His subsequent 'proof' that the infant's pleasure at the breast is a kind of erotic pleasure rests on a merely associative movement – a slip of the tongue or lip. The lip, he argues, is an 'erotogenic zone', because it causes pleasure of a 'particular quality'. The pleasure of sucking at the breast is also located in the lips. *Ergo* it is pleasure of that 'particular quality', and therefore 'sexual'.[48] If you require further proof, Freud offers the following famous, but not yet notorious, passage:

> No one who has seen a baby sinking back satiated at the breast and falling asleep with flushed cheeks and a blissful smile can escape the reflection that this picture persists as a prototype of the expression of sexual satisfaction in later life.[49]

(Why, one might ask, is the baby's expression not the prototype of a post-prandial doze? Thus Pope: 'Where Bentley late tempestuous wont to sport / In troubled waters, but now sleeps in port': *Dunciad*.)

If one protests at Freud's passage, it is not only because of its wholly spurious nature as empirical science, but because of its blindness to real distinctions in the things themselves. The intellectual movement is as follows: A is remarkably like B; B is more primitive than A; therefore B shows the essence of A. Only in this way can one arrive at the view that the tingling of certain mucous membranes constitutes the fundamental experience of sex. The absurd conclusions to which such reasoning can lead are well illustrated in Freud's view that the eye is an erotogenic zone. For after all, is it not the eye which is our source of pleasure when we gaze upon the object of desire?[50] But, as is immediately evident, the pleasures of sight are not pleasures of sensation, but pleasures of perception. They have precisely that epistemic dimension which belongs to sexual arousal. To think that pleasure at the sight of a desirable person is 'in the eye' (in the way that the pleasure of the infant at the breast is 'in the mouth') is to commit a grave philosophical mistake. It is to confuse perception with sensation, and the pleasures of understanding with the pleasures of the flesh. Yet, in another way, Freud is right. The eye is the vehicle of sexual arousal, precisely because arousal is an epistemic condition: it is a state of alertness toward the other, based in the perception of his embodied form. But the eye is not, as the vehicle of arousal, a 'zone of pleasure'. It is, rather, a 'channel of communication', through which the intentionality of arousal may begin to flow. What makes the eye 'erotogenic' is precisely what prevents it from being a 'zone' – a place where pleasure lies.

So great, however, is Freud's attachment to the concept of the erotogenic zone that he allows the hands too to fall within the category;

indeed, he asserts at one point that it is 'probable that any part of the skin and any sense-organ – probably, indeed, *any* organ – can function as an erotogenic zone'.[51] In other words, this pleasure possessing a 'particular quality' – the pleasure definitive of the sexual impulse – can be felt in any part! If that is so, one is tempted to add, it is because in reality it is felt in no part. It is not a localised, sensory pleasure at all, even though it is (at certain moments and for certain reasons) accompanied by such pleasures. It is an intentional pleasure, to be characterised, not in terms of sensations, but in terms of an intentional stance towards the sexual object.

Freud's blindness to the fact of intentionality – or rather, his reduction of intentionality to chemical 'adhesion' – gives rise to the most implausible descriptions. Touching in the act of love is explained in terms of pleasurable tactile sensations;[52] its role as an instrument of union and knowledge being totally ignored. In sublimation, we learn, sexual curiosity is 'shifted away from the genitals onto the shape of the body as a whole'.[53] Yet it is only Freud's disposition to believe the genitals, as the prime 'erotogenic zone', to be the true focus of desire that leads him to believe that this must be so. Common experience suggests exactly the opposite. Arousal, which focuses at first sight upon the whole being of another, is only gradually, and in the course of excitement, shifted on to the genitals. (And even that is a description which anybody, in the course of excitement, would recognise as a caricature of his experience.) Freud's theory displays a kind of phallocentric obsession, which describes not the desires of adults but only the curiosity of the child. By describing childhood titillation in *terms* of adult desire, Freud attempts to induce the belief that childish curiosity really is the root principle of sexual conduct. But the theory remains no better than a myth.

Freud's purpose in introducing the two concepts of the libido and the erotogenic zone is therefore to demonstrate what he believes to be a continuity between childhood and adult sexuality – between the 'sexuality' of sensation, as one might call it, and the sexuality of desire. In a way he recognises that he has not succeeded. For he introduces a distinction between two 'currents' in sexual development – the 'affectionate' current of childhood and the 'sensual' current of puberty. (See above, p. 202.) But this distinction is cast in the same hydraulic terms as the rest of Freud's theory, and again fails to account for the peculiar intentionality of desire.

The Freudian voice

Such is the character of Freud's writing – his ability to proclaim speculative nonsense in the tone of voice appropriate to meticulous science – that many writers have been disposed to accept him at his word, to adopt his factitious certainties as their own, and to suppose that the mystery of desire has been solved by his redescription of infantile pleasures as though they were the true basis of adult longing. Readers of Freud's papers are constantly reminded that 'science has shown', that 'the evidence has conclusively established', that 'there can no longer be a shadow of doubt'; and those who question are told that they are 'resisting' a truth that is uncomfortable to them. The inquisitive quack is 'the physician', and those 'patients' who permit themselves to doubt his diagnosis are looked upon with pity or irritation, as furnishing but further proof of their disturbance.[54] There is an almost grammatical refusal of hesitation; the 'observations' are reported as though they concerned matters as publicly observable and as incontrovertible as changes in the weather or the migrations of birds, while their language is that of the wildest fantasy. The following is not untypical:

> The object-cathexes are given up [in the normal solution to the Oedipus complex] and replaced by identification. The authority of the father or the parents is introjected into the ego and there forms the kernel of the super-ego, which takes its severity from the father, perpetuates his prohibition against incest, and so insures the ego against a recurrence of the libidinal object-cathexis. The libidinal trends belonging to the Oedipus-complex are in part de-sexualised and sublimated, which probably happens with every transformation into identification; in part they are inhibited in their aim, and changed into affectionate feelings. The whole process, on the one hand, preserves the genital organ, wards off the danger of losing it; on the other hand, it paralyses it, takes away its function from it. This process introduces the latency period which now interrupts the child's sexual development.[55]

The passage is remarkable for its combination of an unremittingly assertive tone, with statements that resist translation from the author's extraordinary idiom. Only someone initiated into the Freudian myth would be able to understand them, and yet such a person would not know how to justify them – how to justify, for example, the single occurrence of 'probably', or the absolute certainty with which the remaining utterances are affirmed. Well may Freud accuse the sceptic of 'resistance'; is there not a deal of resistance here too, resistance to the activity of cooperative confirmation that would require him to formulate his hypotheses in an idiom that was independent of his own conclusions?

But the passage introduces another theme: and one which has hardly been touched on in my previous discussion. Not only has the perception of adult desire been corrupted by Freud's 'infantilism'. So too has our perception of the sexuality of the child. No longer is the child innocent in our eyes: for the little pleasures which thrill him have been redescribed in terms of the strategies, triumphs and humiliations of adult desire. Far from removing the stigma of shame from childhood sexuality, Freud's influence has been to increase it, precisely by founding the myth that the child is motivated by forms (however 'primitive') of sexual arousal, sexual jealousy and sexual desire – that every little boy secretly contemplates the crime of Oedipus.

But we must acknowledge the power of Freud's imagery – and it is not only a power to disgust us. Despite (or perhaps because of) its unscientific basis, the theory of infant sexuality (and, in particular, the idea of the little Oedipus, forced by his dependence into a tragic love) has proved highly persuasive. People feel irresistibly impelled to see their predicament in the terms offered to them by Freud. We must try to explain why that is so.

Here it is necessary to distinguish the scientific theory of psychoanalysis from the therapy that has been associated with it. The first is a failure; but its falsehood and confusion do not prevent it from exerting an important influence on the therapeutic practice. In an illuminating discussion, Wittgenstein argues that, for Freud, the clinical criterion of the 'correct analysis' is not so much the success of the 'cure' as the patient's acceptance of the interpretation that is offered to him, and which contains, it is supposed, the *secret* of his cure.[56] The patient's acceptance must not be merely passive: it must not be of the 'I suppose you're right' variety. Rather, he must be brought to *adopt* the analyst's description, so as to see his own behaviour in terms of it: 'Yes, that *is* what I feel.' The patient is like the person who has been looking for a word (which may have been 'on the tip of his tongue') and who is offered it by another. He then uses the offered word with complete conviction: it is authoritative for him, the real expression of 'what he meant'. The process of discovery here is not like that of the scientist; it has rather all the spontaneity and immediacy of a *decision*. The subject takes hold of the word unquestioningly, and knows immediately and incorrigibly that *that* is what he meant.[57] He cannot be mistaken in this judgement, but only insincere. (Cf. the discussion of first-person ascription in Chapter 3.)

Likewise, the patient comes to see, in the analyst's description, an offered confession that he takes up and makes his own. The interpretation becomes authoritative. He believes with a kind of first-person certainty that *this* is what he feels. If what he says as a result of the analyst's persuasion is false, it is false not because it is mistaken, but because it is insincere. Freud explains this process as a 'bringing into consciousness' of a state that was previously unconscious. But there is no need to say as much. It could equally be called a process of mental persuasion, whereby the quality of the patient's experience is changed. For the criterion of the existence of the latent or unconscious content is precisely the (delayed) availability of that authoritative self-expression which is the criterion of consciousness. (A conscious mental state is simply one upon which there is a first-person point of view.)

The Freudian interpretation of dreams appears to use a similar criterion of validity. The criterion is what the subject is prepared to accept, not in the objective and hesitant manner of a scientific observer, but in the immediate and authoritative manner of the first-person perspective. As Wittgenstein put it, the analyst persuades the subject to 're-dream his dream'. He is brought to say, 'That is what I really dreamed'; if the analysis is 'successful', the resulting report will be a sincere expression of an (induced) memory. The various tests laid down by Freud for 'resistance' during analysis can be seen to denote ways in which an analytical redescription of the patient's condition may either fail to emerge or fail to be adopted by the patient as the authoritative expression of his mental state.

Analysis is of course not a simple thing. But it does seem that the process just described occurs in the course of it, and provides one of its major sources of authority. Note first that the process in no way depends upon the truth of the 'scientific' theory that I have examined – although it may be facilitated by the patient's disposition to believe in the theory. Note also that the main object of the process is not to provide an explanation of the patient's state of mind, but to induce him to change it, by understanding it differently. (The idea of the unconscious clearly helps him to do this. For it is easier to acquire a painful feeling, if you believe that you already have it 'unconsciously': for then you are not to blame. Psychoanalysis has a powerful capacity to dispense absolution for our criminal emotions.) In other words, analysis aims to change the patient's intentional understanding, by providing an alternative 'way of seeing'. That it can succeed in this points to important truths about human nature. In particular, the early experience of parental love seems to have a bearing on sexual development and upon the ultimate choice of sexual object. To admit as much is not to admit the fully fledged theory of the Oedipus complex: it is to recognise only that the intentionality of desire does not spring upon us unprepared, but is the outcome of a process and a history that determine its direction.

The Freudian approach also touches on a large problem in the theory of desire: the forbidding of incest. Perhaps there is no better way of seeing the ultimate divergence of Freudian theory from the canons of scientific enquiry than to compare the Freudian and the sociobiological explanation of the 'incest tabu'. The sociobiologist explains it as a species characteristic. A race without this tabu must degenerate through interbreeding; hence those with it are preferentially endowed in the struggle to survive. Such an explanation by-passes the mental content of the subject. It says nothing about the precise kind of aversion that he feels towards incest. (He might find it morally outrageous, aesthetically displeasing, unpleasant – or incest might simply never cross his mind as a real possibility. Each of these states of mind has an evolutionary bonus.) The Freudian explanation, by contrast, is concerned entirely with the intentional content of the revulsion. What is the underlying thought that turns us from this act? Who forbids it, and why?

The legacy of Freudian psychology, then, is not a science of sex, but a species of 'intentional revisionism'. The test of this revision will be, not the truth of the underlying science, but the cogency of the intentional understanding that shadows it. To some extent, it is a moral question, how far we should be persuaded to accept habits of thought that revise, in this radical way, the intentionality of our most personal responses. Freud's revisionism is, I believe, more harmful than helpful. For it leads naturally to a confusion of the sexual experience, by abolishing the barrier between child and man – the barrier of responsibility which we recognise in all other aspects of our personal life and which we ought also, I maintain, to recognise here. Moreover, Freud gives authority to a dangerous idea: the idea that human sexuality belongs in the depths of our organic nature. It remains, in its inner nature, a force of the deep, against which we protect ourselves by the erection of our 'mental dams', but which is always ready to overflow and invade us.

From this hydraulic picture arises a particularly seductive view of the human sexual impulse. It is seen as amoral, outside the sphere of personal feeling and relation, an appetite that is deflected from its inner purpose by the barriers of shame. We are charmed by the hydraulic image into a sense that this 'damming up' is intrinsically harmful – as though we hold back all that is most alive in us, impeding its development. When at last it bursts forth (as it must, the image tells us), it is in forms that are uncontrollable and destructive.

The image is a delusion. Sexual desire is not impeded by morality, but created by it. Attention to the human surface, in which this phenomenon exists, shows desire to be essentially interpersonal. It grows with the artefact of personality, and is shaped and nurtured by those interpersonal responses – shame among them – whereby we develop from animals into social beings. Shame impedes, not desire, but only its perverse expressions. And without shame there is neither desire nor any other form of personal union – only childish titillation, which fulfils itself easily, because it has nothing serious to fulfil.[58]

In this chapter I have considered two attempts at a science of sex. The first fails to cast light upon the nature of desire, because its explanations obliterate the distinction between desire and instinct. The second succeeds in casting light, but only to the extent that it revises our intentional understanding. When Freudian analysis stoops to science, it stoops too low. The result is naive, and also dangerous in its assumption that the exploration of what is 'hidden' is the exploration of what we really are. To the extent that the two theories remain scientific, they cannot add to the intentional understanding in which desire is founded. To the extent that they add to, embellish or undermine that understanding, to that extent do they fail to establish themselves as science.

We may therefore put aside the attempt to solve the problems that concern us through a science of sex. Philosophy alone can solve those problems, and it is to philosophy that we must now turn in our attempt to cast light upon the principal one among them, the problem of love.

8
LOVE

The subject of this chapter is erotic love, which I shall attempt to describe, first in relation to desire, and later in relation to the moral life of the rational being. The second part of the discussion will be spread over the chapters which follow. Since the topic is delicate and obscure, I cannot hope to do more than to provide guidelines. And much of what I say will depend upon an understanding of a crucial question which almost all traditional accounts of sexuality have either failed to answer or failed to pose.

The question is this: what place has sexual desire in love, friendship and esteem? Either it is a part of love, in which case erotic love is too purposeful, and too narrowly focused, to be a form of friendship; or it is not, in which case love is never erotic. Each answer gives a reason for thinking that there can be no such thing as erotic love – no state of mind that is both a form of love (where love includes friendship) and a form of desire. At best the two states may be conjoined, like ham and peas on a single plate. In which case they may taste better, or be better for you, when taken independently. Such was the argument of Socrates in Plato's *Symposium*, and I shall call the question Plato's question, in deference to the clever way in which Socrates first poses and then conceals it. I shall argue, against Plato, but in accordance with at least one neo-Platonic tradition, that erotic love is a form of desire and also a form of love. And I shall give reasons for thinking that the attempt to separate the two 'components' is ultimately destructive, not just of this love, but perhaps also of every love.

Discussion of the question is made especially difficult by the traditional misuse of the term 'love', in particular by those – the exponents of courtly love – who made it the name of their ruling divinity. Thus Andreas Capellanus, in his seminal work *De arte honeste amandi*, defines love thus:

> Love is a certain inborn suffering derived from the sight of and excessive meditation upon the beauty of the opposite sex, which causes each one to wish above all things the embraces of the other and by common desire to carry out all of love's precepts in the other's embrace.[1]

By 'love's precepts' Capellanus means what I have called 'the course of desire', and the definition is in fact a definition of desire, which corresponds at almost every point to the definition that I have given. At the same time Capellanus uses it to introduce a discussion of love. Thus he arbitrarily introduces the element of desire into his account of courtly love, first by defining love in terms of it, and then by ignoring the definition.

Still more misleading are the authors (and again the principal offenders belong to the tradition of courtly love) who entirely leave out the reference to desire and distinguish erotic love simply by its peculiar genesis – by the fact that its victim is *smitten* by love. Thus, in Dante's compelling redescription of his childhood encounter with Beatrice, nothing marks out this love from any other, beyond the implosive shock of its coming to be. Not only is the subject of this love a nine-year-old child; so too is the object. And the paroxysm is followed at once by a most exacting servitude, not to the girl herself, but to the tyrant love:

> At that point I truly declare that the spirit of life, which dwells in the most secret chamber of the heart, began to tremble so greatly that it appeared horribly in the slightest of my pulses, and trembling it uttered these words: *Ecce Deus fortior me, qui veniens dominabitur mihi.* . . .
>
> Thereafter I say that Love held lordship over my soul, which was so early given over to him, and he began to hold over me so much assurance and so much mastery, through the power which my imagination granted to him, that I was obliged to do all his pleasure perfectly.[2]

That a child should be addressed by his inner voice in Latin is, in a way, the least astonishing part of the experience. Dante was surely right in thinking that the most significant aspect of the phenomenon is also the one that is most familiar: the fact that someone is compelled to love by the mere sight of another person. Merely to note this fact, however, is to give no explanation either of the erotic nature of the passion or of our disposition to describe it as a form of love.

The philosophy of courtly love has an ideological motive. And, from the beginning of philosophy, love has been similarly connected with religious devotion, with redemption, with marriage and the rearing of children, by those who have wished to attach its excitements to some 'higher' cause. For those who have found this 'ideologising' of love implausible, it has still been customary, if not to justify, at least to explain, the trouble of love, by describing it as a cataclysmic 'passion'. From Capellanus to Denis de Rougemont, the emphasis has been, not on erotic love (love transformed by desire), but on the passionate constraint of love – Stendhal's *amour-passion*. For Capellanus, love exists only to the extent that it is hidden, forbidden and furtive. Furthermore, he insists, it is nourished on jealousy, destroyed by exposure, and cannot exist between husband and wife. Such is the love of Tristan and Isolde, both in the medieval romance and in Wagner's music-drama. Moreover, as de Rougemont has persuasively argued, passion-love continues to exist as a recurrent myth in Western literature, but only to the extent that new interdictions may be discovered, whereby to place intolerable obstacles before it – interdictions which will simulate the power and the authority of the ancient law against adultery. The most powerful invocations of *erōs* in modern literature therefore concern incest (Wagner, Musil in *Der Mann ohne Eigenschaften*), love for a nymphet (*Lolita*), or the no longer quite so forbidden love between woman and woman, or man and man (Proust, Genet).[3]

Such speculations, while comprising the mass of writing upon this subject, are irrelevant to the theory of love. Passion may indeed require the stern interdiction of a King Mark, or of the moral law that he personifies; but this is a fact about passion, and not about love. Some, including Denis de Rougemont and C. S. Lewis (in *The Allegory of Love*), have argued that passion-love exists only locally. Many go further, subscribing to the view that 'romantic love' was invented only with its name, and that, whether or not the outcome of 'Ovid misunderstood', it did not exist before the twelfth century. (Thus J. Huizinger in *The Waning of the Middle Ages*, and Bertrand Russell in *Marriage and Morals*.) I doubt that any such thing is true. Japanese and Persian literature provide abundant evidence to the contrary; our own classical literature too is replete with stories – Orpheus and Eurydice, Daphnis and Chloë, Dido and Aeneas, Haemon in Sophocles' *Antigone* and Apuleius' allegorical presentation of Cupid and Psyche – which are as 'romantic' as anything in Chaucer or Boccaccio. But even if it were true, this would only show how little *amour-passion* matters to our subject, how very much it is a localised constraint upon love, rather than love itself. If love between mother and child were forbidden – as in *Brave New World* – it too would be a vehicle of the most troubled passion. The interest in passion is part of a dangerous tendency to assume that the central example of a phenomenon is the one in which its effects are most vivid or extreme. This search for the pathological is also an unphilosophical distaste for the normal. It is important neither to share, nor greatly to respect, its intellectual motivation. The romantic movement did not invent erotic love; but it did invent the corrupt perception of love, which seeks for love's essence in love's disease, and mistakes the flush of fever for the glow of health.

Plato's question

What is it that lends such force to Plato's question? Love implicates the whole being of the lover, and desires the whole being of the beloved. The beloved's embodiment may be a crucial object of the lover's interest, but love cannot be satisfied either with the contemplation or with the possession of that embodiment in the act of desire. A mystical re-description of the two phenomena provides the easiest way to unite them – as when the neo-Platonist describes the aim of love as 'spiritual copulation',[4] or the aim of desire as 'physical union'. Love has an aim which is separate from that of desire. Love seeks companionship, in which mutual well-being will be the common purpose; it is nourished on counsels and conversations, on gifts and tokens, on affection, loyalty and esteem. Moreover, love involves dependence. It is not a commodity that can be received, now from this provider, now from that. To love is to acquire a need for another individual, and to wish for one's solace there, with him. Hence, where love is, there too is the certainty of grief.

Plato's answer to the question is well known. Desire, he believed, could have no place in love. For desire is a physical urge, belonging to man's baser nature, a bodily appetite that we share with the animals. Its connection with love is at best accidental. Erotic love is the peculiar form of love which appears to be *born* in desire, but which can remain love only by transcending desire. The conclusion is highly paradoxical, for two reasons. First, how can erotic love – the poignant attachment to the soul of another, which contains, for Plato, the premonition of every human good – start up from so base an origin? And secondly, how can desire, on this account, be an *expression* of love?

Plato answered those questions in the following way. First, erotic love starts up, not from desire, but from the perception of another's beauty. Beauty is the visible form of his immortal soul, which is revealed to us sensuously in precisely this apparel. Secondly, desire is not an expression of love, but a derogation from love, which impedes love's development, and must be transcended if love is to survive. True *erōs* exists only in the conquest of desire. Sexual attraction is nothing more than a premonition, which may be diverted into lust, but also refined into something higher. And its refined form – *erōs* – exists primarily between persons of the same sex, since only then does sex have nothing to do with its aim. Those two answers form, between them, the premises of the most influential of all theories of the erotic, according to which love is by its own nature set on the path of renunciation. Love's ultimate aim is either *amor intellectualis Dei* – the intellectual love of God – or else spiritual union with the other in a bliss that has much in common with religious devotion (cf. Dante and Beatrice). Desire is never more than an impediment to such a love, and can be wrongly taken as a sign of love, only because we confuse it with the sense of beauty.

Platonism is the other side of Kinseyism. Each is based in the same misdescription of desire; the first extends a universal frown, the other a universal smile, towards an activity which, in truth, is too integrally bound to the totality of our moral choices to be the proper object of either attitude. In each case, the impoverished description of desire makes it impossible to see how desire can be an expression, or a form, of love. (The same is also true of the Augustinian tradition described in Chapter 5.) Yet surely, while not all desire expresses love, some does; and this is an important part of its intentional structure. Furthermore, Platonism, which offers to explain the nature of erotic love, in fact does no such thing. All love, on this view, becomes reduced to a single kind, and the peculiarity of erotic love consists merely in its origin – that it begins in the perception of beauty – an origin, moreover, which the theory makes quite unintelligible.

It is useful to compare Plato's theory to another, which also describes sexual love as a kind of 'composite' state of mind, in which the sense of beauty, the sexual 'appetite' and an interpersonal regard are incongruously stewed together. This theory is that of Hume:

> 'Tis plain that this affection, in its most natural state, is deriv'd from the conjunction of three different impressions or passions, *viz.*, The pleasing sensation arising from beauty; the bodily appetite for generation; and a generous kindness or good-will.[5]

Hume then has the problem of explaining how the sense of beauty and the 'bodily appetite for generation' may be related. His argument suffers from the well-known limitations (transparently displayed in the phrase 'impressions or passions') of his philosophical psychology. Nevertheless, it is sufficiently curious to deserve quotation, if only in order to show how mysterious the facts of love become when sexual desire is given the structure of a bodily 'appetite'. Hume begins by arguing that parallel desires may become mentally 'connected':

> Thus hunger may oft be consider'd as the primary inclination of the soul, and the desire of approaching the meat as the secondary one; since 'tis absolutely necessary to the satisfying that appetite. If an object, therefore, by any separate qualities, inclines us to approach the meat, it naturally increases our appetite; as on the contrary, whatever inclines us to set our victuals at a distance, is contradictory to hunger, and diminishes our inclination to them. Now 'tis plain that beauty has the first effect, and deformity the second: Which is the reason why the former gives us a keener appetite for our victuals, and the latter is sufficient to disgust us at the most savoury dish, that cookery has invented. All this is easily applicable to the appetite for generation.[6]

The general explanation is of course absurd, implying as it does that someone with a scientific interest in excrement is on that account more likely to eat it. The particular application is yet more absurd. For what sense can we make of an 'appetising morsel', whose savoury preparation competes with her lack of beauty? No such idea could capture the special relation between the sense of beauty and the movement of desire. Desire is the tribute paid to beauty, and the judgement of beauty is an expression of the intentional content of desire. These are not two states of mind, but one. Most intolerable of all, however, is the assimilation of desire to appetite – an assimilation which indeed necessitates this 'disaggregated' analysis of love, but which also makes it impossible to represent desire as love's expression. On Hume's view desire is no more the expression of love than is the propensity to boil and eat the beloved. There may be a 'connection' between the states of mind, but only as there may be a connection between a pain in the chest and the thought that I must give up smoking. No one imagines that the pain expresses the thought, even if (as might happen) it is caused by the thought. In the same way, sexual desire, on Hume's account, could never be an expression of love, even when caused by love.

Clearly, if we follow in the footsteps of Plato and Hume, we shall never establish a coherent category of 'erotic love' – love expressed in, and modified by, desire. We shall arrive either at the amalgam described by Hume or at the mystery disclosed by Diotima to Socrates, in which one and the same love somehow ascends from the desire for boys (*paiderastein*), to the contemplation of the divine beauty itself: *auto to theion kalon dunaito monoeïdes katidein*.[7] This divine beauty is unique and irreplaceable; but only because it is the hypostatised universal, lying outside time and change. Hence erotic love, for Plato, realises itself only by ceasing to be love of a human being.

The account that I have offered of sexual desire avoids the immediate difficulties which confront both Plato and Hume. Nevertheless, the mere fact that desire and love each have an individualised and interpersonal intentionality is not sufficient either to prove that there can be erotic love (else it should prove the existence of erotic hatred, erotic anger and so on), or to show how desire narrows and transforms the focus of love, so justifying the idea of *erōs* as a separate species of it. We must show that desire can be, in itself and by virtue of what it is, an expression of love, and that love is modified by that very expression. Only then shall we have given a description of the erotic. And without that description we shall be one step further away from a sexual morality, whose outline is determined, I shall argue, by the needs of love.

Levels of friendship

A discussion of erotic love must begin from a discussion of love. But 'love' is an uncertain category, and one in which rival theories of human nature, and rival moralities, stake their conflicting claims. In Shakespearean English 'love' means both love and friendship, as does the word *philia* in Greek. And yet there is an abiding intuition – reflected in the distinction between *erōs* and *philia* – that love and friendship are not quite the same. To clarify this issue, therefore, we should first give an account of the intentional structure of friendship.

In a famous discussion,[8] Aristotle distinguishes three kinds of friendship, those based in utility, in pleasure and in virtue. In Aristotle, and in many of his successors, this distinction derives not from a study of friendship only, but from a theory of practical reason, which divides reasons for action into three distinct kinds (roughly, the useful, the pleasant and the good). For our purposes, however, the theory of friendship may be discussed independently of the larger theory.

The first kind of friendship, exemplified in friendly relations between those engaged in a common enterprise, is of a circumscribed nature. As Aristotle argues, such friendships expire just so soon as the purpose is fulfilled (or, if they seem not to expire, this is because friendship of another kind has arisen meanwhile). Such fragility is peculiar to the first kind of friendship, which, in its minimal form, need be no more than common courtesy. Friendship of the second kind is exemplified in the 'jolly companion', who is enjoyed like Falstaff for his company, but, like Falstaff, rejected at the call of higher things. It is tempting to distinguish the two kinds of friendship in Kantian terms: the first treats the other as a means, and what it contains by way of 'friendliness' can be seen as a special case of efficiency: people are more amenable, and business more swiftly accomplished, when you behave in a friendly way. Thus *'l'intérêt parle toutes sortes de langues, et joue toutes sortes de personages, même celui de désintéressé'* (La Rochefoucauld). If we were to be strict, we might consider this to be friendship only in a derivative sense – for it lacks an element that is crucial to friendships of the 'higher' kinds, the element of 'liking'.

Even so, however, it is by no means obvious that the Kantian language is sufficiently exact to distinguish the first kind of friendship from the second. While it may be said that Prince Hal treated Falstaff as an end – for he laughed with him, and at him, and sought his company with no thought of the abstract companion who would 'do just as well' – in another sense he treated Falstaff as a means to enjoyment (as he admits, indeed, in the soliloquy which closes the second scene of *Henry I V Part 1*). Hence the speed with which he rejected Falstaff, once the time for enjoyment had gone. Falstaff was at once no more to Hal than a foolish old man, 'the tutor and feeder of my riots' (*1 Henry IV*, V). At the same time, the purpose with which Prince Hal approached Falstaff was, at least in part, an 'immanent' purpose. (See above, Chapter 5, pp. 101-2.) Hal's enjoyment was enjoyment *in*, and not simply *because of*, Falstaff.

There is a prevailing error in aesthetics, typified by Collingwood's diatribes against 'amusement art'[9] and Croce's rejection of the *estetica del simpatico*,[10] according to which attitudes like amusement, sympathy and so on can have no place in the true appreciation of art (or the appreciation of true art). To be interested in something 'for the sake of amusement', Collingwood argues, is to be interested in it for something other than itself; it is not to be interested in it 'for its own sake', in the quite special sense of that phrase manifested by aesthetic interest. The argument is of course fallacious. When I laugh at something, I laugh at it for its own sake, and not for the sake of laughing. (Contrast eating.) Amusement is a species of interest in an object 'for its own sake'. The same is true of the second kind of friendship. And this enjoyment *in* a person, while it is 'particular', in the sense defined in Chapter 5, is also reason-based. I enjoy John *for* his qualities, which are the grounds of my enjoyment, just as I enjoy a work of art for its qualities, which might be offered as reasons in a critical appraisal. Thus I enjoy John for his humour, absurdity, good nature or intelligence. But – if we are to be true to the spirit rather than the letter of Kant's distinction – we can hardly call this kind of friendship a case of appreciating John as an end in himself. (Cf. Tolstoy's description, in *Anna Karenina*, of the quickly exhausted, but endlessly renewable, charm of Oblonsky.) There seem to be cases of interest in a man 'for his own sake', which yet do not deserve quite so dignified a label. The least that can be said is that Aristotle's tripartite division promises a finer understanding than Kant's dichotomy – a dichotomy which we have, in any case, already seen reason to question.

I may enjoy John's humour. Presumably I may also enjoy his virtues. (Indeed, humour is a part of virtue.) Why then does Aristotle set aside the special case of friendship founded in virtue, as friendship of a higher kind? One answer is that I do not merely enjoy my friend's virtue; I also value it. Someone who merely enjoyed the virtue of another would not be classed by Aristotle among his third category of friends. (One who sought the company of another simply in order to *laugh* at his virtue is certainly no friend. Nor is the person who takes an aesthetic interest in the virtue of another: as Gilbert Osmond in the virtue of Isabel Archer in James's *The Portrait of a Lady*.) The third category of friend is distinguished by the fact that the qualities found interesting in the friend are also valued. Friendship based in valuing the friend is clearly a different thing from friendship based in enjoying him. If I value you for your moral qualities, I have towards you not merely affection, but the attitude which features in the Kantian morality as 'esteem'.

Kant would no doubt have agreed with Aristotle in setting the friendship of esteem apart from the friendship of enjoyment. And he would have argued that only in this third kind of friendship is the other *really* treated as an end in himself. For only in the attitude of esteem do I reverence that in my friend which *constitutes his nature as an end*, which is his reason, as displayed in obedience to the moral law. For the Kantian, therefore, Aristotle's tripartite distinction must be reconstructed in the following terms: First, there is the friendship of utility, in which the other is treated as a means. Secondly, there is the friendship which treats the other as a means to enjoyment, and for that very reason appreciates him 'for his own sake'. Thirdly, there is the friendship which treats him as an end in himself, in the positive sense of that expression. This third friendship is based not in enjoyment but in esteem.

Friendship and esteem

I propose to adhere to the Kantian language, despite its unclarity, and despite the need to amend Kant's dichotomy in the direction suggested by Aristotle. The reason is this. Aristotle's moral theory is couched in objectivist terms, so that, when he speaks of loving one's friend *for his virtue,* he has quite specific qualities – courage, wisdom, justice and so on – in mind, and believes not only that these *are* the virtues, but also that all rational beings would instinctively perceive them to be so.[11] Although Aristotle is right (see Chapter 11), it is question-begging to assume so. Moreover, his distinction between kinds of friendship does not require his objectivist morality. It is sufficient to distinguish the *attitudes* of enjoyment and esteem, in order to make the distinction. And this involves no commitment to any objectivist moral theory.

Furthermore, although the Kantian language is associated with a theory which, by confusing important distinctions, has frequently threatened to damage our subject, it alerts us at once to a pivotal problem in the theory of love. Amusement (an attitude which may be taken as illustrative of the second level of friendship) is a particular attitude. Esteem, however, is universal. I cannot esteem you without basing my attitude in respect towards some quality which is the universal object of my esteem. (Hence Kant's view that esteem is a kind of reverence for the moral law.) But if that is so, it might appear as though esteem is less narrowly focused upon its object than is amusement, less clearly *appreciative* of the individual upon whom its gaze currently rests. (One should note here that the contrast between the 'universality' of moral attitudes and the 'particularity' of aesthetic interest is frequently used to define the distinction between them, and to clarify the sense in which an aesthetic interest is interest in an object 'for itself'.)[12] Why, then, is the friendship of esteem a form of friendship, when it is based precisely in an attitude that detaches itself from the individual, and respects him only for those features which it may equally respect in another?

This question occasionally troubled Kant, who was by no means happy with a theory that seemed to assign all love to the 'pathological' part of man, and all esteem to the rational. He found himself struggling with an analogue of Plato's question, since he wished both to unite those states of mind and to insist on their categorical distinction.[13] We see here another reason for disaggregating the idea of the 'individual object'. Aristotle's distinction between the lower and higher kinds of friendship corresponds to something that we all instinctively recognise. And yet it would become nonsensical if the object of esteem were not truly an individual, but merely the universal attribute which provides such a good reason for loving him. To return briefly to Plato: what is most intolerable in Diotima's revelation to Socrates is the suggestion that erotic love, which begins in warm enjoyment of the human individual, ends in dispassionate contemplation of the divine universal. Love is transformed from a live passion into an abstract reflection. Such love might look with complete indifference upon the destruction of the person who originally inspired it, and yet remain itself. For Plato, the process of seeing value in the beloved is the process of forgetting him, in favour of the universal value that his contingency can only conceal. The Platonic paradox emerges, then, in the theory of friendship. (Nor should this surprise us, since sexual desire, like amusement, involves a move towards the friendship of enjoyment. Plato's question – how can desire be an expression of erotic love? – relates to a more general question: how can the friendship of esteem be a form of friendship?)

Evidently the true friend, who is valued for his virtues, is also valued for *himself*. To put it another way: while I esteem his virtues, it is also *he* that is esteemed. In what way is this esteem part of, and a foundation for, friendship? In other words, how does it enter into, and qualify, an attitude of affection and enjoyment, the object of which is, in some non-trivial sense, 'individual'?

We must here introduce a notion that is crucial to Aristotle's theory of virtue – the notion of character. A certain kind of philosopher, asked to define 'character', might offer the following: a man's character is the sum of his dispositions to intentional action. Actions that are involuntary do not stem from character, nor do those which, while voluntary, express no abiding disposition. The purpose of this definition is to identify what another abidingly *is*, as a person.

As earlier discussions have shown, such a definition must fall short of the mark. If our aim is to focus on the moral reality of another, we must cast the net more widely. For, as Aristotle himself pointed out, and as is assumed by almost every sensible code of law, we are blamed, and also praised, for our dispositions to involuntary action. These too may be the product of education, and these too may be corrected, in the long run, by an understanding of what we do. (Only where that is not true – as in the case of epilepsy, say – do we withhold all praise and blame.) On the other hand, if our aim is to focus upon those actions of another which reveal him as he is – which reveal the perspective from which he acts and suffers – then again we must pay attention to involuntary actions. As I argued when considering smiles and blushes, involuntary conduct is here of paramount importance.

223

In Chapter 3, I discussed two closely connected, but initially distinct, features of an individual that form the basis of his existence as a person. The two features are the rational disposition to modify one's conduct in response to reason, and the first-person perspective. The idea of the individual person, as a centre of agency, who acts from himself and suffers in himself, is composed of those two conceptions, together with the crucial notion of embodiment – of existence *in* the world, as one material entity among others. We may therefore summarise the concept of the person, as presented in this work, in three complex ideas: responsibility, perspective and embodiment. The connections between these ideas are deep and obscure, and it is a subsidiary purpose of this work to cast light upon them. This purpose is furthered by considering a feature of persons which is already implied in those three ideas, but which has been of interest to recent philosophers for more specialised reasons: the feature of durability. People are extended in time, and what they are at one moment bears upon what they were or will be at another. This fact is of fundamental importance in the understanding of rational agency. A rational agent has a special attitude towards his own duration. The ideas of time, and of his own extension in time, form, indeed, part of the 'given' of his experience.[14] The attitude of 'taking responsibility' is revealed equally in decision and in remorse. Although our durability as persons is dependent on our durability as bodies, 'personal identity' through time is not, it seems, reducible to bodily continuity.[15] Moreover, persons are essentially capable of learning, and of responding at one time to information and arguments received at another. A person therefore *develops* in a way that has little or nothing to do with the development of his body. Hence, parallel to the metaphysical idea of the self, as an individual distinct from the bodily organism that he inhabits, there emerges a metaphysical idea of self-identity – of our duration as persons. This idea represents our history in terms that do not apply to the history of our bodies, and implies that self and body obey different laws of development.

From the third-person point of view, nothing is revealed of you and your perspective, save that which is displayed in your embodiment. The same is true of your 'self-identity': this too can be real for me, only through its overt embodiment in the world of agency.[16] The correct way to understand the idea of 'character' is, I believe, in terms of self-identity. Your character is that in you which endures through change, but which is nevertheless *you*, and which develops as *you* develop. It includes dispositions to intentional action, but also those other dispositions in which your enduring nature as a responsible being is revealed: clumsiness, negligence, half-heartedness; energy, wistfulness and serenity. It includes the disposition to blush with shame or flush with anger, to smile with affection or laugh with joy. For all these are critical revelations of your nature as a responsible being, and all, in their dispositional continuity, create for me the presence of the embodied and enduring you, the real object of my distaste or affection.

Friendship is crucially interested in 'what comes next': in the surprises and the unsurprises of companionship. Hence friendship is an attachment to what is durable in the other. The more lasting the friendship, the more durable the features in which it is founded. Furthermore, friendship is an interpersonal relation, which focuses on the embodied personality of the other. While I may enjoy the companionship of an animal, this is not friendship in any normal sense of the term. An animal cannot be my counsellor, the object of my raillery, the butt of my jokes and observations – even though I may prefer him to any such. Friendship seeks the self of the other, and is absent when there is no self to be sought. It follows that in both kinds of friendship – the higher and the lower – character must be the prime focus of attention.

The lower kind of friendship, the friendship of enjoyment, is, like amusement and aesthetic interest, essentially individualising. But there is a sense in which it leaves the real individuality of the other to one side, as does the sexuality of *vaga libido*. My friend is appreciated for what he is. But what he is *for himself* need scarcely enter my calculations. I may have little concern for his joy or well-being, and only a casual interest in how he envisages his own destiny. His reasons need not be reasons for me, and his self-image may be something with which I entirely fail to identify.

This is the real basis of the felt contrast between the lower and the higher form of friendship. While this higher friendship is based in the universal attitude of esteem, focused on the character of the other, it engages intimately with his individual existence as a self-conscious being. It is useful to return briefly to Aristotle's theory of virtue. Aristotle argued that the real distinction between virtue and vice is not between actions, but between the characters from which actions spring. What we admire in the other is not the action (which could equally be performed from some base or indifferent motive) but the virtue which is expressed in it. A virtue is a disposition, characterised by a specific motive; virtues and vices are alike in that, when acting from them, we act from, and reveal, ourselves. The distinguishing mark of virtue is that actions done from virtuous motives are actions in which rational agency is not overcome but dominant. In virtuous action, *I* am the originator of what is done, even though my motive derives from my embodied, emotional existence, and not from the prompting of some Kantian moral law. Thus I can be overcome by fear but not by courage; by rage but not by justice – and so on. Only the vicious man is repeatedly overcome by his passions; the virtuous man, on the contrary, expresses himself in and through them, as reason demands. The Aristotelian idea of virtue is, I believe, the idea of a disposition in which rational agency is in the ascendant, and through which it is fulfilled. (This parallels Kant's view, that what I esteem in you is the 'transcendental' freedom revealed in your practical reason.)

If that is right (and I shall spell out the argument more elaborately in Chapter 11), then esteem is more truly focused than is enjoyment upon the individual you. For esteem seeks out the centre of activity, which is at once the locus of your responsibility and the sign of your perspective. And your virtue is not something external to your own sense of what you are and what you intend. On the contrary, it is the very heart of you, the origin of all those reasons which you present to yourself in determining the value of this or that course of action, the desirability of this or that response. Thus my interest in your virtue is an interest in your character in the deepest and most intimate sense: it is an interest in what defines you, both for yourself and for me.

We can now see how to resolve the difficulty that we encountered earlier. The higher form of friendship is in fact interested precisely in the irreplaceable individuality of the other – in the self, obedient to reason, defined by its enduring character, through which learning and responsibility assert their own peculiar principles of development. The instinctive respect which I feel towards virtue expresses itself in my affection for you. No obstacle stands in the way of this transformation, for both attitudes focus on what you *really are*. Indeed, esteem focuses more nearly on your self-identity than does amusement, and hence founds a more deeply personal affection than could ever grow from enjoyment alone.

Of course, there are differences between mere esteem and friendship. I may esteem someone for whom I have no friendly feelings. The higher form of friendship involves an additional concentration on the individual – a desire for *his* well-being, together with that familiar and complex desire for a reciprocity of motive that we have already encountered in sexual desire. Nevertheless, esteem has a role to play in founding and transforming the intentionality of friendship, which ceases as a result to be a mere desire for companionship in pleasure. We esteem another on account of features which we value, and in which he is revealed as responsible agent. We confide in him, by esteeming him, a peculiar trust – the trust that he is, and will be, *true to himself*. We seek to rely on him, being provided thereby with an additional guarantee of continuity in change. In short, by enacting before me the spectacle of a being motivated by *himself*, the estimable person promises redemption from the shoddiness of my condition. He has authority for me, since in him I see strength and conviction expressive of the triumph of reason. Hence I instinctively tend to identify with him, to feel threatened by what threatens him, and consoled by what consoles him. *His* reasoning becomes mine. This is the insight captured in Aristotle's belief that the friendship of virtue is of a different kind from the friendship of enjoyment. The insight resurges in the Kantian theory that esteem confers upon its object a peculiar authority – the authority of reason; and it is present too in Sartre's idea that love seeks out the freedom of the other and seeks to make itself one with that freedom. (All these ideas are ways of glossing the fundamental human illusion, that what *you* are for *me* is given by your 'self-identity'.)

No actual friendship is based purely in enjoyment or purely in esteem. Always there is a mixture of elements, and the higher friendship would be incomplete if it did not stoop to the enjoyment that characterises the lower. The two forms of friendship define distinct but intermingling currents of intentionality, and all actual friendship can be seen as some idiosyncratic mixture of the two. One may here see foreshadowed the moral basis of another distinction – that between comedy and tragedy. The comic character is displayed as the natural object of the friendship of enjoyment, the tragic character as the natural object of the friendship of esteem. The comic character can be humiliated without abolishing our affection for him, but he cannot be tragically disposed of, without at once surpassing our capacity to find logic in the drama. (Hence Falstaff's death is shown to us only through Mistress Quickly's moral malapropisms (*Henry V*, II.iii).) The tragic suffering of a comic character is disgusting; our feelings are outraged by the demand that we sympathise with this character in a predicament that he lacks the virtue to bear. Our attention is taken away from the dramatic meaning, and directed towards the suffering itself: this alone now interests us, but with a horrifying force. It was famously argued by Lessing in *Laocoon* that poetry is not competent, as painting is, to represent in aesthetic form the dreadfulness of human pain.[17] Whether or not that is true, it is difficult to conceive a *dramatic* portrayal of a comic character subjected to terrible suffering, that could succeed as Raphael and Titian succeed in giving aesthetic form to the flaying of Marsyas. And a character who appropriates to himself a tragic suffering which he cannot truly feel – or which he feels only in the self-centred manner of the sentimentalist – may appear almost farcical, like Hjalmar Ekdal in *The Wild Duck*.

The tragic character, who is represented always as the natural object of a higher friendship, is brought down by a tragic 'flaw'. This defect, which would (like Falstaff's lechery) be inconsequential in a comic character, is the echo of an anxiety that inhabits every serious friendship. We know that, in endowing another with the authority that stems from our esteem of him, we overstep the limit of any possible justification. We know that – in this or that particular – he will deeply deceive us; and in doing so, he threatens what we promise, through this friendship, to become. The downfall of the tragic hero is a kind of propitiation offered to friendship – an exemplary punishment placed before all who would threaten the transcendental illusions in which friendship is nourished. This is perhaps what Schopenhauer had in mind, in arguing that the tragic hero expiates original sin – the sin of existence itself.[18]

The intentionality of friendship

What is the aim of friendship? Or does it have no aim? I have argued that friendship contains two currents of intentionality – that derived from enjoyment and that derived from esteem. Neither of these attitudes has a transcendent purpose, although there is, perhaps, an 'immanent' purpose involved in enjoyment. In friendship, however, there is an aim – that of mutuality – which transforms these attitudes into lasting projects. The purpose is again immanent: it cannot be specified without making essential reference to the immediate object of interest, the friend himself. But it endows friendship with a more 'purposeful' character than we may find in enjoyment or esteem. I may suffer from the full transcendental illusion that I have described as the natural consequence of esteem, and confer upon the other the task of redeeming the contingency of my existence. And yet I may not be 'friends' with him. Thus a whole nation may feel its destiny to be inseparably bound up with a redeemer. The people may be willing to die at his command; they may suffer grief at his death, and bitterness at his treachery. But this would not be friendship. It becomes friendship only when set within the context of mutuality. I wish not only to make my friend's reasons mine; I want him to make my reasons his.

This desire for mutuality is familiar from the analysis that I have given of desire. But it must be distinguished from another element, an element which distinguishes the higher from the lower friendship. Both forms of friendship involve pleasure in the company of the other, together with a desire for his reciprocal pleasure. But only the higher friendship includes the desire for the other's well-being, together with the desire that this desire be reciprocated. I may be largely indifferent to the fate of my 'boon companion'. But I cannot be indifferent to the fate of my 'true friend'. Although I may miss my companion, and long for his return, this is not necessarily the expression of a state of mind that informs my dealings with him while he is by my side. I do not necessarily show consideration for him, or include him in my practical reasoning as I include my true friend. It is for this reason that people sometimes dismiss the lower kind of friendship as not being a 'true' example. The higher kind of friendship, it is thought, must inevitably transform the life and character of the man who feels it, by forcing him to take account of another's existence and well-being. It is necessarily unselfish, in the manner of Montaigne's friendship for Boëtie:

> Our mindes have jumped so unitedly together, they have with so fervent an affection considered of each other, and with like affection so discovered and sounded, even to the very bottome of each others heart and entrails, that I did not only know his, as well as mine owne, but I would (verily) rather have trusted him concerning any matter of mine, than my selfe. Let no man compare any of the common friendships to this.[19]

Love and friendship

But this brings us to love. For is that not the correct description of Montaigne's affection for Boëtie? Montaigne even asserts that there can be only *one* true friend, supporting his contention with arguments that might equally be applied in defence of sexual monogamy. The implication of this, and of many similar descriptions, is that love is the limiting point of friendship – the point at which the highest union of interests is achieved.

Against that one must place the authors who have discerned in love a principle that wars with friendship. La Rochefoucauld, for example, asserts that love (by which he means erotic love) often seems closer to hatred than to friendship. Is this a special feature of the erotic, or is it characteristic of all love? Or is La Rochefoucauld exaggerating?

No philosophical account of the many things that have been called love can hope to achieve the kind of order which all philosophy must seek. Neither common usage nor literary artifice have been sparing of paradox in describing the human passions, and no theory could ever be produced that would not be immediately objected to on the grounds of this or that real or imaginary experience. In what follows, therefore, I shall postulate a norm, which I shall call 'love' largely because it justifies the trouble that is expended in love's name, but which by no means corresponds to everything that every writer has meant, or would want to mean, in the use of that description.

Consider, first, the love described by Montaigne: the love between friends, who seek each other's company not for *erōs*' sake, but for its own sake. The friendship of esteem becomes love just so soon as reciprocity becomes community: that is, just so soon as all distinction between my interests and your interests is overcome. Your desires are then reasons for me, in exactly the same way, and to the same extent, that my desires are reasons for me. If I oppose your desires, it is in the way that I oppose my own, out of a sense of what is good or right in the long run. The mere fact that you want something enters the forum of my practical reasoning with all the imperative character of a desire that is already mine. If I cannot dissuade you, I must accept your desire, and decree in my heart 'let it be done'. To dissociate myself is to withdraw my love: hence such love is *fed* by esteem, which causes me to have confidence that what you want, I shall want also. Contrast the tragic collapse of love, as between Macbeth and Lady Macbeth, when conscience increasingly withholds its sanction. There are degrees in this, of course. I can dissociate myself from some of your desires, and to some extent. But that is only because there are degrees of love. The tendency of love is towards the identity of interests described by Montaigne. My demand for your virtue is the demand that, in identifying with you, I do not enter into conflict with myself. You must be what I endorse.

Thus he who loves aims at the other's good, in just the way that he aims at his own good. This idea of a person's 'good' is not to be simply described. We may return again to Aristotle's tripartite theory of practical reason, and make a preliminary division among goods, between the useful, the pleasant and the virtuous (that which is good in itself). I want all of these for myself, and also for my friend; but to the extent that they conflict in my ambitions for myself, so do they conflict in my reasoning on behalf of my friend. Just as, in my own case, my sense of what I ought to be and do is constantly balanced against my wishes and interests, and tends, in the long run, to live a life of uneasy compromise with the vacillating requirements of utility and pleasure, so too, in the case of my love for you, my conception of your good is the outcome of a fluctuating compromise between competing claims.

This aim of love – which is a continuation and completion of the aim of friendship – is no extinguishable project, to be fulfilled and cast aside. On the contrary, it is part of what I am. I can no more think forward to its cessation than I can contemplate the cessation of my own practical reasoning, based in the present apprehension of my interests and values. While I love, I can have no plans for the extinction of love's purpose; to have such plans is to have ceased to love. Hence the death of someone loved *necessitates* grief. It is not merely that we happen to feel grief on such an occasion, as we happen to feel merry after drinking a bottle of wine; it is rather that we must feel grief. Grief is a kind of death itself: it is the response to a perceived calamity, in which the basis of one's action is suddenly shorn away, and one can only long helplessly for its return. Friendship, unlike the special case of friendship which is love, may require only that I be saddened by my friend's death. Grief is more than sadness. It is a state of disability, in which both thought and intention are fatally impaired.

It is clear from the above account that love cannot do without information. The lover is relentlessly curious as to his beloved's sorrows, joys and desires, which concern him as his own. Hence love seeks companionship – that 'being with' the other, in which what he thinks, feels and desires 'go without saying', since they can be perceived immediately in his face and gestures. If I am separated from someone whom I love, I am impatient to be reunited with him, so that my epistemic hunger can be appeased. This hunger is not only for propositional knowledge: it is also for that imaginative and immediate acquaintance with the other's mentality, which comes from looking into his face and hearing his voice. Hence all love shares, to some extent, that emphasis on the other's embodiment which dominates the love that springs from desire.

Erotic love

I have argued that the friendship of esteem may *become* love: in doing so it acquires the distinguishing features of love: the desire to 'be with' the other, taking comfort from his bodily presence, and the 'community of interests' that erodes the distinction between *my* interests and *his*. Love involves a transition (as Martin Buber would put it)[20] from I and he to I and thou. Two consequences follow. First, while friendship develops naturally into love, it does not do so *inevitably*: hence there can be friendship without love. Secondly, love could arise in some other way. Hence we should take seriously the possibility that there might be love without friendship. Love grows not only from friendship but also from companionship. Arranged marriages are not more loveless than marriages of passion – indeed, being founded in an acceptance of destiny, they are less frequently torn asunder by the dream of an unreal freedom. The community which unites husband and wife in such a marriage may unite companions in danger, workmates in a common enterprise, and a thousand others who have been thrown together by circumstances beyond their immediate control. It did not need Durkheim to show that 'solidarity' is as multifarious as human community, that it can exist without a common purpose, or that it is never stronger than when it *has* no purpose beside itself.

But the love which responds to destiny grows, in a sense, from nothing. No quality, no achievement, no virtue in the object need inspire the first movements of regard. It is enough that he is there, another warm human body, trapped beside me in the predicament that is ours. What need there be, in this, of friendship or esteem? And what is erotic love, if not just such a response to an inflicted destiny – the destiny of desire?

This peculiarity in the genesis of love has led some writers to deny that love has the structure of friendship – and, in particular, to deny that it is reason-involving. McTaggart argues that this emotion springs from a sense of pure and immediate union with another self. Hence, although love may arise *because* of certain qualities in the beloved, it is never held *in respect of* those qualities. Love may survive the qualities which first inspired it, and is not founded in the belief in their persistence, as fear is founded in a belief in the persistence of danger. Hence love is 'more independent than any other emotion of the qualities of the substance towards which it is felt',[21] and it is this which explains why 'a trivial cause may determine the direction of intense love. It may be determined by birth in the same family, or by childhood in the same house. It may be determined by physical beauty, or by purely sexual desire. And yet it may be all that love can be.'[22]

McTaggart's theory has a metaphysical motive, which is to show love as an approach to the 'pure individuality' of another 'substance'. As we have seen, a state of mind may have such an 'individualising intentionality', and yet be reason-involving – as in aesthetic interest. McTaggart seems to deny this, but only because his argument concentrates on the *cause* of love and ignores its intentional structure. It is true, in a sense, as McTaggart observes, that love may provide its own justification. But that is precisely because love is reason-hungry, searching always for a foundation in its object, and stepping always on shifting sands.

Consider the love with which the erotic is most vitally connected: love for a child, and in particular for a child of one's own. In this case it is evident that love normally precedes friendship. It is this body – fragile, dependent and unformed, in which a soul grows visibly – that awakens my emotion. I want to be with it, to cherish it, and all its interests are my interests. My child compels me to love, long before he arouses either my friendship or my esteem. By the time such interpersonal emotions are possible, I am already trapped by love. Not that I loved his body only. From the beginning my love was conditional upon the thought of a distinct, and distinctly personal, life, expressed in this body and growing with it. I loved my child's *embodiment*, but not his body. And yet this embodiment also provides my love with its ground. I love my child's smile, his eyes, his face; I love his energy and character; I am proud of him, and cannot quite believe it when someone other than myself speaks frankly of his imperfections.

It is a brute fact that such a love grips us more intensely (even if not more profoundly) than the love that stems from friendship. Such 'brute' facts are facts about our brute condition: they remind us that we are animals, governed by the implacable requirements of the flesh.

Erotic love, like the love of children, is compelled by the embodiment of its object. We may retain, as Chaucer tells us, our 'choice al fre', even in the encounter with the object of desire. It may even be that, in some sense, our ability to suffer precisely *this* compulsion is – as it was for Dante and Boccaccio – the highest expression of our original freedom. But it is also true that we are subjected by erotic love, and that our freedom suffers the impact of an external necessity. Erotic love is experienced, not as a decision, but as a destiny. The hope of the traditional moralist has been to rescue human freedom from this predicament – to restore it to itself, by showing us how to transform erotic love into an expression of virtue. This is the motive behind Kierkegaard's defence of marriage:

> [first love] is the unity of freedom and necessity. The individual feels drawn to the other individual by an irresistible power, but precisely in this is sensible of his freedom.[23]

Through his eulogy of marriage (which is in truth rather more tedious than the eulogy of sensual passion which precedes it, and which it aims to counter),[24] Kierkegaard defended the theory encapsulated in Chaucer's great invocation of the vow of love. Freedom may yet be retained, such thinkers argue, just so long as the expression of love is withheld until it may be released in a lifetime's commitment.

It is well to remember Plato's own reasons for being suspicious of *erōs*. Desire, by virtue of its fixation upon the body of the other, seems to limit itself to what is finite, temporal and sensory – to the 'embodied individual'. Hence desire defies the essential nature of reason, which is to attach itself only to what is universal, infinite and outside space and time. Man's destiny is to transcend the erotic, discarding in this act of transcendence the element of desire. However, to love is to love an individual. It is only in his embodiment that the individual is revealed, and only in his embodiment that he may be individually known. For love to be an act of free choice it would have first to be rescued from this attachment to what is immediate and concrete. Love could obey reason only if it had the structure of esteem, and would have the structure of esteem only if it grew from esteem. Erotic love, which focuses on the embodiment of the other, is therefore not a rational response, even if it is a response which only rational beings may experience.

Nevertheless, erotic love, like other love, is reason-involving. It is true that in erotic love I may rejoice in your faults, which may be, for me, the precious sign of your dependence, the emblem of a lifetime at my side. However, we must be careful how we understand such feelings. In one of his thin protestations against the human normality, Nietzsche exhorts us to despise our friends, so as the better to love them.[25] The real meaning of such an exhortation is this: abolish the friendship of esteem and replace it with *erōs*. For, bonds of kinship apart, it is erotic love alone that can survive the awareness of another's depravity, without declining into that weaker, more vacillating friendship, from which nothing serious can be built. At the same time, this is not the happiest form of erotic love. To the extent that it is cherished, it is from an abundance of desire. Thus, when Genet's anti-heroes wax tender over the vices of their paramours, the effect is of a supreme sensuality, outside the reach of normal human emotion. Interestingly enough, however, their sensuality is represented as a kind of moral virtue, which, through an inverted admiration for what others despise, becomes an act of defiance towards the moral norm:

> [*Culafroy*] *aima Alberto pour sa lâcheté. En face de ce vice monstrueux, les autres étaient pâles at inoffensifs, et pouvaient être contrebalancés par n'importe quelle autre vertu, surtout par la plus belle. . . . Abolir ce vice – par example, par sa negation pur et simple – il n'y fallait pas songer, mais détruire son effet amoindrissant était facile en aimant Alberto pour sa lâcheté. Sa déchéance était certaine, si elle n'embellissait pas Alberto, elle le poétisait. Peut-être à cause d'elle, Culafroy se rapprochait de lui. Le courage d'Alberto ne l'eût pas surpris, ni laissé indifferent, mais voici qu'à ce lieu il découvrait un*

autre Alberto, plus homme que dieu. Il décrouvait la chair. [Notre-Dame-des-Fleurs].

We can see in this passage a peculiar inversion of the mythology of 'passion-love', in which everything is negated, save that which 'overcomes' the subject of desire: the quality of Alberto as flesh. This reflects Genet's desire to build a 'wholly inverted love': love in which all values of community, and in particular those which deny the validity of homosexual passion, are systematically negated. However, in that very negation, there is a reaffirmation of value. It is true that Genet's love seems focused upon vice, but then so is his esteem. His love, like his esteem, is an exercise of what Sartre calls '*la morale du Mal*':[26] an attempt to rebuild, through that very erotic passion which society denies, the inverse of a normal love. Culafroy's inverted love is in fact moralised into a kind of inverted esteem.

Tensions in love

Erotic love seems, therefore, to defy the demands of reason only to influence reason towards its own point of view. (Which is why McTaggart says that love is 'its own justification'.) Love 'moralises' its object, so that it conforms to an ideal. When the object cannot be moralised according to the old ideal, love favours a new one – even an inverted one – in order that its object may seem worthy of its care. Love brings esteem within its orbit, often causing it to travel along unfamiliar paths.

In love at first sight, therefore, the other is seen as a 'total moral presence'. Desire is experienced as a moral demand, and also as a moral right, both of which seem, in imagination, to precede the first encounter. The experience is captured in Florizel's words to Perdita, in *The Winter's Tale* (IV.iii):

> What you do
> Still betters what is done. When you speake (Sweet)
> I'ld have you do it ever: When you sing,
> I'ld have you buy, and sell so: so give Almes,
> Pray so: and for the ord'ring your Affayres
> To sing them too. When you do dance, I wish you
> A wave o'th Sea, that you might ever do
> Nothing but that: move still, still so:

> And owne no other Function. Each your doing,
> (So singular, in each particular)
> Crownes what you are doing, in the present deeds,
> That all your Actes, are Queens.

The poet expresses the sense of the beloved suspended before me, ineffably there in the beam of my desire. She is poised – 'move still, still so' – and yet absorbed in her actions. And in this moment all her nature and character is concentrated – her buying and selling, her giving of alms, her ordering of her affairs, and also her dancing and singing. The language here is the language of desire, which caresses its object with a palpitating tenderness:

> When you do dance, I wish you
> A wave o'th Sea, that you might ever do
> Nothing but that: move still, still so.

At the same time, the thought encapsulates the mystery of Perdita's incarnation – 'so singular, in each particular' – and the intimation of a moral life that is entirely hers. It is hard to find a better representation of the way in which love, when expressed in desire, focusses upon the bodily presence of the other.

It is desire, and not love, which gives this *immediate* sense of the other's necessity to me. But desire transforms the whole perception of the object – the heart is commanded, as the eye is commanded, to obey. (Thus Guinevere, as she rises to leave, pulls after her both 'the eyes and the heart' of Lancelot: Chrétien de Troyes, *Lancelot*, ll. 3987–9). The experience of 'love at first sight' is really nothing more nor less than the experience of an intense desire, which commands through the physical embodiment of the other. It becomes love at once, but only because it is so interpreted. The subject, being vividly aware of the personal nature of the object, is moved to think always of the perspective that is prefigured in the forms before him – as Perdita is prefigured to Florizel. There follows the 'idealisation' of the object of desire. The lover casts his ambitions in moral form; for this alone justifies his sense that he *must* be united with the person before him. The physical attractiveness of the other is seen as an expression of her virtue – her 'conscious heart', which 'glows in her cheek', as Byron phrases it (*Don Juan*, CVI) – and the lover begins to moralise his desire. Desire becomes, for him, a way of appreciating the real and imaginary merits of his companion. There is thus conceived the secret stratagem of valuing the other, so as the better to desire him. The lover may even (in the extreme case) deceive himself into thinking like Plato, that desire is not the meaning of this experience at all, that it is aimed, on the contrary, at some infinitely higher thing. Such a thought may also be useful, in granting secret permission to desire.

> Oh Plato! Plato! you have paved the way,
>   With your confounded fantasies, to more
> Immoral conduct by the fancied sway
>   Your system feigns o'er the controlless core
> Of human hearts, than all the long array
>   Of poets and romancers: – You're a bore,
> A charlatan, a coxcomb – and have been,
> At best, no better than a go-between.
> [*Don Juan*, CXVI]

Stendhal – in a misleading image – describes this moralising of desire as a 'crystallisation': one has only to think of a virtue, in order to see it at once in the other's face and conduct.[27] (As though one dips the image of the beloved into super-saturated liquid, and withdraws it with the bright sparkle adhering all around.) More appositely, the process may be described as a *commentary*. Just as you see meaning in the work of art which you love, so do you see meaning in your beloved's gestures. That which focusses your attention on his body also disturbs you with the sense that this experience *must* have a meaning, that it *must* be morally significant. Desire obliges you to find value in its object, and so to 'see him as' the embodiment of virtue.

As the example from Genet showed, the process of commentary goes two ways. A critic, in assigning meaning to a work of art, sees the aesthetic experience as qualified by its meaning. He also sees the meaning as qualified by the experience. No meaning is critically significant, unless it can enter into the aesthetic experience.[28] Hence the moral content of a work of art is always described, by the persuasive critic, in terms adapted to its aesthetic rendering – it is a content that can be fully appreciated only in the act of aesthetic attention. In the same way, the lover experiences the virtues of his beloved as clothed in the garments of desire. They wear, in his mind, a bodily form, as though he could kiss and hold them. Thus Cleopatra conjures, in her tribute to Antony's virtues, the beauty of his body and the sexual presence that was the occasion of her desire (*Antony and Cleopatra*, V.ii):

> His legges bestrid the Ocean, his rear'd arme
> Crested the world: His voyce was propertied
> As all the tuned Spheres, and that to Friends:
> But when he meant to quaile, and shake the Orbe,
> He was as ratling Thunder. For his Bounty,
> There was no winter in't. An *Autumn* it was,

That grew the more by reaping: His delights
Were Dolphin-like, they shew'd his backe above
The Element they liv'd in.

(The first folio has 'Antony' in the place of 'Autumn' – which is in a way more expressive, even if a trifle absurd.)

Thus, just as desire is moralised into love, so is love demoralised, so to speak, into desire. This explains the principal features of courtly love. The plaint of the courtly lover to his mistress involves always an extended tribute to her virtue, and the declaration of a loyalty that will justify her love. The poet invites the mistress first to love him. But he then – in his language and the movement of his verse – pleads for her desire, as a sequel to, and expression of, a love which she cannot withhold. Thus the lover rises to the point to which the mistress declines, the first having sanctified his desire by attaching it to virtue, the second having humanised her virtue, by clothing it in desire. *Frauendienst* is primarily a cooperative strategy, to generate the greatest desire, and then to fill that desire with the greatest virtue, and so generate the greatest love. It is the poet's desire which begins the process, and desire has its origins in the compulsion which overcomes him at the sight of another form. But this form is understood by the poet in terms of its spiritual possibilities. By praising the mistress, he exacts from her the moral regime that will turn those possibilities into actuality, and so justify his love. He then, acquiring her virtue, justifies, and so permits, her desire. Thus Cavalcanti, in his famous *canzone*, '*Donna mi priegha*':

> *Egli è creato*
>   *e a sensato*
>   *nome*
> *D'alma chostume*
>   *di chor voluntade*
> *Vien da veduta forma che s'intende*
>   *Che'l prende*
>   *nel possibile intelletto.*[29]

'He (love) is created, and has a sensory name, takes his costume from the soul and his will from the heart; comes from a form seen, understood so as to include latent spirit (*intelletto possibile*).' The terms are scholastic, and it is not easy to understand the higher reaches of Cavalcanti's thought. But it is clearly a neo-Platonic attempt to 'discompose' the knot of erotic love, and to give a metaphysical description of the interpenetration of love and desire. The core experience is the body seen, and seen as an embodiment: a revelation of 'latent spirit'.

Desire does not imply love; but it provides a motive to love – and this fact is crucial in understanding the intentionality of desire. 'Falling in love' is not to be seen as a transition from the absence of love to the presence of love, but rather as the sudden acquisition of this motive. Your self-esteem requires you to love, so that, while being overcome by the other, you can believe yourself to have preserved your inner freedom. In such a case (and according to Robert Solomon, in every case),[30] love has the character of a decision. By calling our passion love, we commit ourselves to that which makes it love (and therefore 'love', according to Solomon, is a 'political word').[31] The metaphors with which we embellish our passion also transform it: they endeavour to literalise themselves, so that you become my life, my heart, my happiness, by virtue of the fact that I describe you so.

If we talk of 'decision' here, however, this too is a metaphor: an attempt to capture in words something that lies beyond our intellectual horizon. We are 'drawn' to love by the mysterious transparency of a human body, and if we idealise the person who is there embodied, it is because we idealise ourselves. Everything that bears for us the mark of destiny we moralise into the expression of spirit. In our eyes, as in the eyes of our lovers, we are self-made men. The bodily presence of the one whom we desire is decked out for us in spiritual meanings, so that its allure – which in truth is irresistible – will seem like the allure of virtue. The other's desirable body is made to seem no greater an assault on our freedom than is the appeal of virtue to our esteem. We speak of 'soft' lips, 'tender' expressions, 'innocent' eyes, a 'passionate' mouth and so on; and while some of these descriptions foreshadow the delights of love-making, others bear the mark of love. We find ourselves, in the very beginning of desire, already seeing the body of the other in terms that suggest the possibilities of a fully justified union. And this is what makes our love seem like a decision.

Love and indolence

Love in all its forms involves a desire for another's good. But I too am implicated in that good; I identify myself with it, and act to secure it as though it were also mine. Implied in this motive is the overriding desire to be with you, profiting from your company, recognised by you as part of your good, as you are recognised by me as part of mine. Hence my project is intrinsically self-limiting. My desire for your good is limited by my desire to be with you, and to be received by you as an object of an equal love. This is the dual variant, so to speak, of a self-limitation that exists within my own self-seeking projects. All such projects are limited by what La Rochefoucauld called '*la paresse*' – by the desire to be undisturbed and at ease with myself, possessing and possessed by myself, according to known and existing conditions. Love is intelligible only on the assumption that it too has a state of 'rest': an unchallenging 'being with', in which I know that you know that I know that you know that neither of us seeks from the other any more than he can willingly give.

Love is therefore essentially 'interested', and never more so than when it is disinterested. If a conflict arises between your good and our companionship, I can sacrifice the second to the first only by forgoing the point of rest that gives purpose to our union. In self-defence – which in this case means defence of our shared self-building – I may destroy your good. I may fight against your career, your friendships, your activity – everything, in short, that gives you the chance to live happily without me. (This is what Blake meant by saying that love 'joys in another's loss of ease'.)

Hence, as we have seen, I may rejoice in your faults, since they may be the sign of your dependence. At the same time, these faults must be tolerable to me. I may be pleased that others find them disheartening; but even in erotic love I must be able to regard them, not as great moral failings, but as weaknesses, and as qualities which endear you to me. For I must be able to accept your weaknesses as part of my practical reasoning. I can make allowances for your laziness, your selfishness, your lack of essential refinements. For these do not place you outside the reasoning whereby I conduct my life. But can I make allowances for your cowardice, your viciousness, your character, say, as a murderer or rapist?

The answer is surely 'no'. But it is a qualified 'no'. If I cannot condone your vice, then it must inevitably erode my love for you, since it introduces calculations that cannot enter my reasoning as they enter yours. (He who freely and happily loves a criminal is always capable of being himself an accomplice in crime.) If this does not seem to be so, it is because of the tension that is contained within the project of love. My desire to be with you may have formed habits and bonds that are too resistant to be easily sundered. In the case of erotic and filial love the relation always has this inevitable character. In such cases, the conflict between love and esteem – or rather, between the need to be with you and the need to 'incorporate' your projects – may be severe, and could never be resolved without pain. Erotic love, like maternal love, may generate a fierce internal conflict. And here too, where love wars with esteem, love may predominate.

The same considerations explain the phenomenon of 'hatred in love'. This is no more surprising a phenomenon than self-hatred: the conflict which ensues when my nature is recalcitrant to my purposes. In love – and especially in love of an erotic or filial kind – there is a core of attachment which resembles my attachment to myself: something given, unquestionable, rooted in my 'empirical condition' as a dying animal. My devotion to you is nourished upon an idea of mutual aid. But my attachment remains, even when it enters into conflict with your disobedience to my idea of your good. I then rebel against the intolerable compulsion of this attachment; but it prevails, and, being forced to live in intimacy with it, I inevitably begin to hate it and wish for its destruction. Thus it frequently happens that erotic love, which begins in the idealisation of the beloved, turns to a systematic disappointment. Because of the attachment against which it vainly struggles, this disappointment seems more like hatred than like friendship.

The course of love

In Chapter 4 I argued that the intentionality of sexual desire, like the intentionality of any other social attitude, involves several distinct stages of development, or 'moments', to use the Hegelian term. The initial aim – sexual union – has to be defined in terms of 'the course of desire'. The further project which emerges from this aim – sexual intimacy – is one of which I have given an implicit description. But I have said little about the fulfilment of desire: about the condition which answers desire, as vindication and repentance answer anger. I have suggested, however, that this 'moment' of intentionality must be described in normative terms. In delineating the fulfilment of a state of mind, one is recommending a long-term project, which will resolve the tensions, and fulfil the ancillary wishes and needs, that arise in the expression of the basic intentional structure. It is evident that I have already begun to identify this project as erotic love. Erotic love provides the lover with the justification of his desire, and, if reciprocated, with the inner peace that rewards the trouble of desire. Erotic love is, however, like desire, in that its aim must be described in terms of its 'course'.

One may describe the course of love as a kind of 'mutual self-building', in something like the way that the course of desire is a 'mutual arousal'. I want you to be worthy of my love, behind which desire lies, always compelling me. And I too want to be lovable, so that you may reciprocate my affection. Hence we begin to enact a cooperative game of self-building. I identify you as something wholly free, wholly responsible, all of whose states, including your desire, express the unspoiled 'self-identity' that is yours. And I seek to attain in your eyes the same integrity that I attribute to you. By virtue of this mythopoeic enterprise, our focusing each upon the other gains a special kind of coherence. Everything you do you do for my eyes, seeking to acquire by reflection the unity, virtue and integrity which you attribute ineluctably to me. Thus, in the common metaphor, we become 'involved'. I build myself upon a conception of your perspective, and its transcendental continuity, from which all that is spirit in you flows. I cannot do without the sight of you; I need the renewed experience of your embodiment. This perception is the food of a necessary myth, and anything which threatens it threatens my existence. (Hence Milton's words, discussed earlier, 'smiles from reason flow, and are of love the food'.)

Such considerations help to explain the peculiar helplessness of the victim of erotic love. Everything that he is and wants has come to depend upon another's cooperation. With that cooperation he has everything; without it nothing. Love that is unrequited is therefore desperate, and love that is cut short by death is tragic. Such facts reflect a feature of human love that might be called 'nuptiality'.[32] Human love involves an inevitable tendency to seek out and be with the other, to involve one's destiny completely and inseparably with his. Love seeks, not a promise of affection, but a *vow* of loyalty. Vows are more than promises: they involve the complete surrendering of one's future to a present project, a solemn declaration that what one now is, one will always be, in whatever unforeseeable circumstances. This is the substance of Ferdinand's vow to Miranda:

> As I hope
> For quiet days, faire issue, and long life,
> With such love as 'tis now, the murkiest den,
> The most opportune place, the strongest suggestion
> Our worser Genius can, shall never melt
> Mine honor into lust.
> [*The Tempest*, IV.i]

Lovers are not always taken in by their own mythopoeia, nor do they necessarily imagine that their impetuous vows are to be literally interpreted. Often, even in the most powerful flux of love, a man may stand back from his own illusions, recognising the intricate impossibility of the necessary myth which governs him. But in doing so, he only confirms the commitment that lies at the heart of love, while lamenting the fact that it will remain unfulfilled. W. H. Auden has captured the experience in lines which deserve quotation, since, while seeming to deny what I have said in this section, they elaborately confirm it, laying bare the acknowledged impossibilities towards which love itself propels us:

> Lay your sleeping head, my love,
> Human on my faithless arm;
> Time and fevers burn away
> Individual beauty from
> Thoughtful children, and the grave
> Proves the child ephemeral:
> But in my arms till break of day
> Let the living creature lie,
> Mortal, guilty, but to me
> The entirely beautiful.
> Soul and body have no bounds:
> To lovers as they lie upon
> Her tolerant enchanted slope
> In their ordinary swoon,
> Grave the vision Venus sends
> Of supernatural sympathy,
> Universal love and hope;
> While an abstract insight wakes
> Among the glaciers and the rocks
> The hermit's sensual ecstasy.
>
> Certainty, fidelity
> On the stroke of midnight pass
> Like vibrations of a bell.

The existence of this vow – which is a hidden vector within the intentionality of love – helps to provide further explanation of jealousy. We can see why jealousy is an expression of love, even though it focuses, not on the love of another, but on his desire. Desire involves the beginnings of that exclusive intentionality which is transformed, in my own fictive enthusiasm, into the project of love. I build myself upon that love, and upon the idea of your reciprocal loyalty. I am therefore jeopardised by the discovery that this process, so necessary to me, is not necessary to you. You did not justify your desire in terms of an ideal of me. I then feel, not disappointed, but betrayed, since my love for you involved the thought of you as bound by a vow.

The course of true love perhaps does not run smooth. But it is not the course of desire. Love has a tendency to grow with time, while desire has a tendency to wither. The course of love, therefore, leads of its own accord to the state which the Platonists recommend to us. Eventually desire is replaced by a love which is no longer erotic, but based in trust and companionship. The trouble of desire is then at an end. The problem is, how to shut out the third party who will begin it again, how to prevent the calm love of nuptial union from being shattered by the turbulence of a new desire. Not only how, but whether. That question, which is a fundamental question of sexual morality, must for the moment remain unanswered.

The expression of love in desire

Let us return, instead, to the more fundamental question. How can desire be an expression of love, and in what way is love modified by desire? We have already said something in answer to the second part of the question, but we still need to say something more specific in answer to the first.

The term 'express' is ambiguous.[33] It can mean 'evince', 'give evidence for' or 'manifest'. In this sense a cry may express pain, as silence may express anger. Alternatively, it may mean 'capture' or 'convey'. In this sense, behaviour expresses by virtue of its power to communicate a state of mind – to embody it, and to reveal it to another. This is something more than giving evidence: it is part of the *constitution* of the mental state in behaviour. We need to consider, not whether desire provides evidence of love – for, taken alone, I do not believe that it does – but whether the characteristic gestures of desire can be 'filled with love', in the way that a melody may be 'filled with grief' or a speech 'filled with anger'.

A remnant of puritanism may persuade us that, while love is compatible with desire, and perhaps reinforced by it, it is nevertheless not expressed through it. To some people, it is strangely embarrassing to mingle desire and love so closely, and much of the 'medicinal' language of the modern sex educationist and of the literature of Kinseyism can be seen as an expression of this embarrassment.[34] And yet who can doubt the sincerity of Héloïse, who crowns her expression of a still warm love for Abelard, with the expression of an equally warm desire?

> God knows I never sought anything in you except yourself; I wanted simply you, nothing of yours. I looked for no marriage-bond, no marriage portion, and it was not my own pleasures and wishes I sought to gratify, as you well

know, but yours. The name of wife may seem more sacred or more binding, but sweeter for me will always be the word mistress, or, if you will permit me, that of concubine or whore.[35]

Pope, in his brilliant transformation of Héloise's letter, imitates this passage conscientiously, until he encounters the crucial word. His paraphrase of what Héloise means in this one word occupies him for eight lines:

> Not Caesar's empress would I deign to prove;
> No, make me mistress of the man I love;
> If there be yet another name more free,
> More fond, than mistress, make me that to thee!
> Oh happy state! when souls each other draw,
> When love is liberty, and nature, law:
> All then is full, possessing, and possess'd,
> No craving void left aking in the breast:
> Ev'n thought meets thought, ere from the lips it part,
> And each warm wish springs mutual from the heart.
> This sure is bliss (if bliss on earth there be)
> And once the lot of Abelard and me.

Curiously, Héloise's word dimly survives in the rhyme of the line where it should have occurred. Perhaps Pope contemplated this:

> Oh happy state! To be my lover's whore,
> And love in liberty, by nature's law.

Héloise's words are not the words of flippant self-deception, but the plain truth about an experience in which love and desire have been inseparable, the second being the final expression of the first. How is that possible?

You might say that there is no problem here. For after all, does not desire express itself in glances, caresses and kisses, and may not these be 'filled with love' in just the way that our words are filled with love? But the problem lies deeper than that suggests. Looking, caressing, and kissing are voluntary actions, and may be filled with love, because the agent himself can *mean* love in them. Such actions can be given all the structure of intentional communication; I may gaze at you with the intention that you recognise my love, by recognising that such is my intention. Sexual desire, however, is not voluntary, and its principal expression – sexual arousal – is not an intentional act. It is something suffered, not something done. If sexual desire could become an expression of love only by being expressed through voluntary gestures which are not themselves special to desire, then Plato's question remains. It is open to someone to argue that it is the gestures alone which convey love, not by virtue of, but in spite of, their association with desire. Hence the Augustinian condemnation focuses always on the taint of sexual arousal, in which I am *overcome* by my body, and my will is set aside.

The answer to Plato's question can be found, nevertheless, precisely in the nature of arousal. A kiss or a caress may become an expression of love through the epistemic character which it shares with sexual arousal. Although voluntary actions, kisses and caresses are also responses to the thought of another's perspective. In kissing him, I imprint on his flesh the sign of my own good feelings for him, and the pleasure lies in the immediate sense that he perceives me thus. For a moment, during the glance, caress or kiss of love, our separateness is extinguished, and our perspectives invaded by the sense of another's desire. In a similar way, the experience of arousal may extinguish all the forces that divide us, so that, in this experience, your aims and interests are also mine.

To see how this comes about, it is instructive to turn again to aesthetics. Aesthetic interest, while it is based in sensory experience, is the prerogative of the 'cognitive' senses – of the eye and the ear.[36] These senses present us with experiences whose sensory quality is inseparably bound to an epistemic content. The pleasures of taste, touch and smell – at least those that we share with the animals – have a large sensory component. The pleasures of the eye and the ear, however, are intentional pleasures – pleasures of contemplation. Hence 'the eye is not satisfied with seeing, nor the ear filled with hearing.'

The literature of love praises the sight of the beloved, as the symbol of his sensory presence. The neo-Platonist Renaissance philosopher Leone Abravanel argues that the senses of sight and hearing – unlike the 'lower' senses whose pleasures stem from our animal nature – serve the interest of the individual, and not the interest of the species. These senses are the vehicles of knowledge and understanding; the lower senses, however, are the vehicles of desire. Abravanel recognises in this contrast a crucial difficulty for the philosophy of love, and so responds to the resonance of Plato's question.[37] If sexual love were based in sight alone, there would be no difficulty in understanding the union of love and desire. It would be a special case of the intentional unity which constitutes the core of aesthetic pleasure. When I hear the melancholy *in* the music, a thought takes auditory shape before me, and at the same time accommodates itself to the intentional constraints of hearing: this, for me, is the *sound* of melancholy. In just such a way, the neo-Platonist seems to argue, the sight of my beloved conveys and restricts my thought of him. I see him as himself, and understand him in terms of what I see. Hence my love may reverberate in my experience, just as my experience displays the thought of *him*.

However, sexual desire is not a matter of sight alone. Its ecstasies belong to touch, to taste and to smell. To invoke these 'lower' senses is to speak or write desirously:

> How fair is thy love, my sister, my spouse,
> How much better is thy love than wine!
> And the smell of thine ointments than all spices!
> Thy lips, O my spouse, drop as the honeycomb,
> Honey and milk are under thy tongue:
> And the smell of thy garments is like the smell of Lebanon. . . .
>
> My beloved put his hand by the hole
>   ['of the door' (AV) but not in the Hebrew]
> And my bowels were moved for him.
> I rose up to open to my beloved:
> And my hands dropped with myrrh,
> And my fingers with liquid myrrh,
> Upon the handles of the lock.
>   [the last three words no doubt also an idea of the AV]
> [*Song of Songs*, 4: 10–11, 5: 4–5]

Such a concentration of gustatory, olfactory and tactile imagery creates an intoxicating sense of the body's *Untergang* in desire, and of the true meaning of 'sensuality'. At the same time, the familiar – but in truth extremely obscure – distinction that I have been rehearsing, between the cognitive and the non-cognitive senses, enables us to understand what is required by the present enquiry. Plato's question would be answered, provided that we could show that the unity of thought and experience which occurs in aesthetic pleasure can also occur in the tactual experiences of desire. Can the experience of sexual contact be a vehicle of love, in the way that the sight of the beloved is a vehicle of love? Can I experience in my sexual organs the same synthesis of experience and thought that I experience in visual perception? And can this unity serve to unite my pleasure with my love for you, to bind them in the same intimate knot that binds my aesthetic pleasure in a work of art with my apprehension of its moral content?

The answer, I believe, is yes. Expression depends not on the experience of the one expressing, but on the experience of the other to whom his expression is addressed. Can this experience be *received* as an expression of another's love – can love be felt in it, as it can be seen in your eyes or heard in your voice? (Cf. the problem of expression in aesthetics: to show that music expresses emotion, for example, is to show, not that the composer is able to put his emotion into the work, but that the listener is able to hear it there.)[38] If the sexual experience can be received as an expression of love, it can also be used by the lover to express his love, since he can intend his love through it. This alone makes the experience into a vehicle of love. The experience of sexual arousal – which is the essential precondition of sexual pleasure – conforms to this requirement. Arousal is a form of openness to your perspective (cf. the words of the Shulamite quoted above). Love can be felt *in* the experience of arousal, so that love becomes the arousal, as love becomes the caress, the kiss or the glance. That is what is meant by tenderness: the lover caresses and kisses his beloved, intending thereby to produce the perception of love. Such tenderness is an end in itself. The expressive gesture is a revelation of what I am and mean, and as such it is complete. All I can do is to repeat it – which may be exactly what you want:

> *da mihi basia mille, deinde centum,*
> *dein mille altera, dein secunda centum,*
> *deinde usque altera mille, deinde centum.*

The kiss of love, so pathetically evoked by Catullus,[39] is the resolution of the conflict in desire. Here the project of desire comes to rest.

This tenderness is so much a natural outcome of desire, and so obviously pivotal in forming our moral sentiments, that we react with shock to the suggestion that it might be absent. At the same time, its absence is a powerful object of obscene thoughts. To abolish tenderness is to create the image of a pure, impersonal desire, a pure lust, which by emphasising the life of the species shields us from the dangerous intimacies of love. Such obscene thoughts are prefigured in a highly significant image of popular culture – the girl spy, who seeks to trap the hero (James Bond), and whose treachery must be circumvented, even in the sexual act. The total danger which the partners present to each other negates every possibility of tenderness. It makes a clearing around their desire, displaying it in all its imperious impersonality. For those who lack a serious understanding of sexual arousal, that fantasy describes, not the perversion, but the norm of desire. For such people, Plato's question exists in its most intransigent form, as an impassable barrier between 'lust and love'. This is one of the most important consequences, indeed, of the theories of desire espoused by the Freudian and Kinseyan sexologists, summarised in the following words by the neo-Freudian, Theodor Reik:

sex is an instinct, a biological need, originating in the organism, bound to the body. . . . It can be localised in the genitals and other erogenic zones. Its aim is the disappearance of a physical tension. It is originally objectless. Later on the sexual object is simply the means by which the tension is eased.

None of these characteristics can be found in love.... [Love] is not a biological need, because there are millions of people who do not feel it and many centuries and cultural patterns in which it is unknown. We cannot name any inner secretions or specific glands which are responsible for it. Sex is originally objectless. Love certainly is not. It is a very definite, emotional relationship between a Me and a You.[40]

Plato may have deserved Byron's dismissive accusations: but how much more pernicious has been the puritan response to Plato's question, exemplified so vividly in that passage.

Beauty

Two features of erotic love distinguish it from friendship: the sense of compulsion, and the absolute focus on the physical nature of the other. These features are both contributed by desire, and both are in turn modified by the 'course of love' — by the project of self-building. The components of erotic love stand in so intimate a relation to each other that the physical attributes of the other are 'moralised' in the very act of perceiving him. And the compulsion of desire is also moralised; I feel it as a movement of sympathy towards the friend whose warmth will eventually console me. La Rochefoucauld has a cynical maxim, that there is no woman whose merit survives her beauty. His point is not that a woman's merit *consists* in her beauty; but rather that it persists just so long as others trouble to compel her to display it, and that they will do this just so long as they can *see* her merit in her countenance.

It is a universal habit to employ the idea of beauty in describing this intricate confluence of attractions. Does this use of the term involve an employment of the very same concept that is involved in the assessment of art? It is worth saying something in answer to that question. It is necessary to dismiss all attempts at a 'realist' analysis of the beautiful — an analysis which holds the adjective 'beautiful' to denote a property of the object that is correctly so described. No such analysis could do justice to the role of the term 'beautiful' in evaluation, to the range of its application, or to the 'sincerity conditions' which govern its use.[41] 'Beautiful' is not a descriptive, but an expressive term, whose main function is to designate an item as the object of a certain kind of interest. In other words, the rules governing the use of 'beautiful' refer, not to material conditions of the object described, but to the intentional structure of the state of mind expressed. (The same must also be said of certain other adjectives – notably 'affective' terms such as 'moving', 'disgusting', 'exciting' etc.) 'Beautiful' would be genuinely ambiguous were it habitually used to convey incongruent states of mind. Conversely, it would be univocal were the various states of mind conveyed by it to have a common intentional structure. Clearly the latter hypothesis is to be preferred, given the universal tendency to use the terms 'beautiful', '*beau*', '*bello*', '*schön*', '*gözel*', '*krásný*', '*piękny*' and so on, equally of the object of aesthetic pleasure and of the object of desire.

I have already suggested (Chapter 5, pp. 108–9) that the 'beautiful' is the proper object of any attitude that is attentive, non-transferable and immediate. Aesthetic interest and sexual desire correspond to those conditions. But, it might be objected, if that is as far as the similarity goes, it could hardly offset the enormous difference between aesthetic interest and desire. The first is purposeless, the second purposeful; the first unrestricted in its object, the second interpersonal. To argue that the three common structural features are sufficient foundation for a unified concept of beauty is surely to detract from the importance of the resulting category.

However, we have seen that there is a further similarity which, added to the given three, sufficiently explains the need for a unitary concept of the beautiful. Although sexual desire is not reason-based, it lends itself to, and typically forms part of, another attitude, erotic love, which is. Erotic love sees *meaning* in the appearance of the other, and seeks to ground its existence in the meaning that it sees. At the same time it retains the immediacy of desire. Only what is revealed in your appearance can feed my emotion. It is the meaning that I hear *in* your words and tone of voice, and that shines *in* your movements and features, which provides the foundation for my erotic feelings. This exactly parallels the case of aesthetic interest, which is both immediate and reason-based, and which seeks to justify itself in terms of a 'revealed meaning' that may be heard or seen in the aesthetic object. (Hence the principal objects of aesthetic interest are works of art, since works of art invite interpretative perception.)

That is only a sketch. But it points the way to important conclusions. In particular, we may suggest that erotic love, like aesthetic interest, is essentially evaluative. The object of the evaluation in question is not the character of the other, abstractly conceived, but the concrete embodiment of that character in an individual human frame, the binding together, in the here and now of bodily presence, of the outlook and responsibility that constitutes the self-conscious person. Erotic love is therefore the most vivid reminder that we exist as centres of value *here and now*, in the condition of mortality. This recognition is, like erotic love itself, compelled from us, and we inevitably surrender to it. The object of *erōs* has a unique tutelage over us. Without it we should appreciate less vividly the fundamental premise of morality: that the repository of infinite value which is the other self, exists not in some Platonic supersphere, but here in the flesh. This infinitely precious thing actually *is* the animal: it is identical with the fragile body which bears the human attributes that I admire.

This experience of embodiment, under the exacting regimen of erotic love, is to some extent echoed in our experience of the beautiful fragility of children. But only in erotic love does it become clear to me that it is precisely the moral agent in you who is the object of my care towards your embodied form. This experience lies at the root of our awe at the human frame. Without that awe nobody could perceive the true horribleness of murder, torture and rape. To defend with reasons the judgements that condemn those crimes is always to fall short of their true atrociousness. Only in the experience of erotic love is this atrociousness revealed to us, and made an immovable part of our moral intuitions. That is the principal reason, I believe, why we must finally reject both the Kantian view, which asks us to see *erōs* as lying outside the area of true respect, and also the Platonic view, which sees value as residing, not in the embodied individual, but in the discarnate universal. If my intuition is right, the erotic becomes fundamental to a full understanding of what it is for persons to be 'ends in themselves'.

New problems

All that I have said concerning 'the course of desire' and 'the course of love' depends upon an idea of normality. I have described a norm of human conduct, and it will naturally be argued that I have no right to this concept of 'normality' – even that I have committed myself to a way of thinking which, in these enlightened times, is morally unacceptable. I must therefore attempt to justify the idea of sexual normality, and to give a genuine philosophical basis to a concept which I believe we cannot avoid in our day-to-day understanding of sexual conduct – the concept of perversion. To this topic I turn in Chapter 10.

But there is another and more urgent problem which now must be confronted. It may be conceded that, by linking sexual desire and erotic love in the above manner, I have solved Plato's problem. But only by creating another problem, equally serious, about the nature of sex itself. I have situated desire so firmly in the realm of the interpersonal as to close the gap between desire and love. But in doing so I have opened another gap, that between desire and sex, between the project of sexual union and the progenitive act. What has *sex* to do with the intentionality of desire on my account? I have made desire a part of love, only by describing it in terms which make little or no reference to the procreative impulse. So perhaps what Plato *meant* may still be correct. It is still a problem, to understand how our nature as sexual beings – with sexual impulses, sensations and equipment – enters into the workings of desire. Only if we understand that will we be able finally to close the gap, between the 'spiritual' world of the interpersonal attitudes and the 'animal' world of the human organism: the gap between the self and the body. It is to this problem that we now must turn.

9

SEX AND GENDER

Men reproduce sexually, and, biologically speaking, reproduction is the function of the sexual act. That platitude has enormous consequences for our subject and two will be of particular concern to us. First, it is sometimes argued that the reproductive function of the sexual act is part of its nature *as an act*.[1] Hence sexual performance severed from its reproductive consequences – as in homosexual or contracepted intercourse – is a different act, intentionally and perhaps also morally, from the sexual act allied to its biological function. According to that view, reproduction is not only a biological but also a spiritual feature of the sexual act.

In the present chapter I shall consider another, related thought, suggested by the biological destiny of human desire. It is evident that there are things which are not persons, with neither self-knowledge nor responsibility, which also reproduce sexually, and which are therefore compelled by whatever urge induces them to engage in the act of copulation, and rewarded by whatever pleasure accompanies its performance. We must surely be subject to the same urges, and the same pleasures, as govern the reproductive activities of other sexual beings. Why is that not the basic fact of sexual experience? There may indeed be interpersonal attitudes of the kind that I have described – attitudes of love and desire, attached by whatever cultural process to the basic urge to copulate. Nevertheless it is the urge which is fundamental, and which reveals the truth of our condition.

That is the residual content of what I have called 'Plato's question'. The objection raises in its widest form the general subject of the relation between our erotic lives as persons and our sexual lives as animals. It therefore bears once again on the vexed question of embodiment: the question, how can one and the same thing be both a person and an animal?

I shall argue that there is indeed a biological basis to our sexual conduct; but I shall reject the implication that it provides the core of sexual experience. The best way to understand the position for which I shall argue is in terms of an analogy. A tree grows in the soil, from which it takes its nourishment, and without which it would be nothing. And it would be almost nothing *to us* if it did not also spread itself in foliage, flower and fruit. In a similar way, human sexuality grows from the soil of the reproductive urge, from which it takes its life, and without which it would be nothing. Furthermore, it would be nothing *for us*, if it did not flourish in personal form, clothing itself in the flower and foliage of desire. When we understand each other as sexual beings, we see, not the soil which lies hidden beneath the leaves, but the leaves themselves, in which the matter of animality is intelligible, only because it has acquired a personal form. Animal and person are, in the end, inextricable, and just as the fact of sexual existence crucially qualifies our understanding of each other as persons, so does our personal existence make it impossible to understand sexuality in 'purely animal' terms.

Sex and gender

I have conducted the entire discussion until this point without explicitly mentioning sex – the fact, that is, of sexual differentiation. The reader might reasonably wonder what *sex* has to do with the interpersonal attitude that I have been describing. Of course, sexual desire does not occur only between people of different sex: an account of sexual desire that could not be extended to homosexuality would be ludicrous in itself and also totally ineffective as a basis for coherent moral judgement. It is surely one of the vital questions of sexual morality, whether homosexual is morally distinguishable from heterosexual intercourse. If the first is not an expression of desire, it would be difficult to see in what terms this question could be posed, let alone answered.

Even in homosexuality, however, the fact of sexual differentiation is a prominent, and indeed immovable, part of the experience. The male homosexual desires the other (in the first instance) *as a man*; the female homosexual desires the other (in the first instance) *as a woman*. Of course there are complexities here: I may, for example, desire you as a man, but only on condition that you also play at being a woman. Nevertheless, the complexities are no different from those which attend the sex-lives of heterosexuals. It is integral to both heterosexual and homosexual experience that the object is a sexual being, and a representative of the particular sex that is his. It is only on this assumption, I shall argue, that the phenomena of homosexual love become intelligible.

Such thoughts already alert us to a vital distinction – that between the material and the intentional concepts of sexuality. The material concept of sexuality is the concept of a division between natural kinds – the division, in most cases, between male and female. In the material sense, it is for science to determine what it is to be male or female, and to describe the biological and functional characteristics of sexual union. In this sense, it is clear that we have discovered much about sexuality; indeed, it could be said that no one knew very much about it until a century ago.

In the intentional sense, however, people knew as much before the Darwinian revolution as after it. (Indeed, they probably knew more.) The intentional concept of sexuality is of a perceivable division within the world of phenomena, which incorporates not only the distinct observable forms of man and woman, but also the differences in life and behaviour which cause us selectively to respond to them. I shall refer to this intentional distinction as that between masculine and feminine *gender* – thereby giving a respectable use to a term that has a disreputable history.

In addition to the concept of gender, it is also important to acknowledge the varying *conceptions* and the varying ideals which have been associated with it. To the extent that you and I both distinguish the masculine and the feminine in the immediate objects of experience, and identify the same central examples of each, then we share a concept of gender. But you may associate with that concept a variety of beliefs about men and women which I reject; in which case we have separate conceptions of the distinction. Likewise, I may have an ideal of masculine conduct, or of feminine conduct, which is repugnant to you. And both of us may disagree in our conceptions and ideals, while agreeing not only in our possession of the concept of gender, but also in our possession of the concept of sex. We may even have identical *conceptions* of sex – accepting the same body of scientific reports and theories about the real distinction between woman and man. The separation of concept, conception and ideal is familiar to philosophers. But it is important to refer to it at the outset, before entering a terrain that is fraught with moral and intellectual dangers.

Failure to distinguish sex and gender – to distinguish the material base from the intentional superstructure – is responsible for many interesting confusions, and in particular for the once popular attempt to identify a masculine and a feminine character, and to associate these characters with the separate physiological conditions of man and woman. Thus Otto Weininger, writing in 1903, attempted to give a comprehensive biological theory of the moral distinction between man and woman, the tone of which is well illustrated by his remarks concerning the 'emancipated woman':

> Emancipation, as I mean to discuss it, is not the wish for an outward equality with man, but what is of real importance in the woman question, the deep-seated craving to acquire man's character, to attain his mental and moral freedom, to reach his real interests and his creative power. I maintain that the real female element has neither the desire nor the capacity for emancipation in this sense. All those who are striving for this real emancipation, all women who are truly famous and are of conspicuous mental ability, to the first glance of an expert reveal some of the anatomical characters of the male, some external bodily resemblance to a man. Those so-called 'women' who have been held up to admiration in the past and present, by the advocates of woman's rights, as examples of what women can do, have almost invariably been what I have described as sexually intermediate forms.[2]

Few would now wish to express themselves in Weininger's terms. Nevertheless, his is an interesting example of a global theory of sexuality, which tries to trace the entire moral phenomenon of gender to a biological basis. Confronted with the obvious fact that the moral division is far from absolute, Weininger is therefore forced to believe that the difficult cases of gender are, for that very reason, difficult cases of sexual identity, intelligible, however, to the 'first glance of an expert'. The very implausibility of Weininger's theory should alert us to the real distinction between sex and gender – and also to the shifting character of our conceptions of both, which have clearly changed so much since 1903 as to render the thought that a famous woman must for that reason have a masculine temperament as well as an 'intermediate sexuality', wildly implausible.

I propose, in what follows, to explore the concept of gender, and to show its place in focussing the experience of sexual union. It has been argued that distinctions of gender are entirely arbitrary, and may be either abolished or constructed in any way, depending upon the social conventions, prejudices and ideological purpose of the person who makes them. Such, at any rate, is a frequent claim of feminists, as well as of certain exponents of 'gay liberation'. For such thinkers, there is no such thing as a 'natural' distinction of gender, even though there is a natural distinction between the sexes. Sometimes the language in which this thesis is expressed may confuse the issue, by using 'sex' to mean 'gender' – as in the following passage:

there is no natural sex or sexuality (the only thing that might conceivably be called 'natural' is the reproduction of the species but that too is to run the risk of abstracting from culture and ending up by essentializing – exactly naturalizing – some particular social organization: reproduction might be natural, mothers and fathers never are). There is no natural sex or sexuality; sexuality is not some absolute and eternal entity at the beginning of an underlying human being – it simply does not exist. Or rather, its only existence is as specific construction, specific definition of the sexual.[3]

But what the writer means, in this evocation of a 'specific construction, specific definition', is what I mean by gender, as opposed to what I have called 'sex'. (Sex is the underlying material fact which the writer sums up in the knotty reference to reproduction.) The tone of the passage indicates the depth of sentiment by which it is motivated. Clearly this issue is a provocative one. Feminists have an interest in proving that distinctions of gender are arbitrary, and perhaps eliminable. So too do certain defenders of homosexuality, who wish to argue, with Guy Hocquenghem, that the very description of a certain desire as 'homosexual' is the expression of an ideological stance, and that, in truth, desire is neither homosexual nor heterosexual, but merely personal.[4] The 'homo' or 'hetero' element is *imposed* by our divisions of gender, and cannot be made intelligible independently.

Gender construction

Gender denotes, in my usage, an intentional classification: an order elicited in reality by our way of seeing and responding to it. But in this case we are also the object of our classification, and have a consuming interest in the facts which it records. Hence the existence of the classification changes the thing described: we match reality to our perception, and so justify the intentional understanding that is expressed in it. The phenomenon perceived through the concept of gender is also to some extent the product of that concept.

The term 'gender' therefore verges on ambiguity – or, at least, it has two semantic levels. It expresses the concept which informs our intentional understanding of sex; it also denotes the artefact which we construct in response to that understanding, and whereby we embellish, exaggerate or conceal our sexual nature. In such a case, to parody Frege, sense does not merely *determine* reference; it also changes it. In what follows, therefore, I shall use the term 'gender' to denote both a way of perceiving things and a particular artificial feature of the thing perceived (its 'gender construction').

There are other concepts belonging to our intentional understanding which have this effect of changing the reality to which they are applied. One such is the concept of the person. By seeing ourselves as persons, we also motivate ourselves to *become* persons – to reconstruct ourselves according to the requirements of a fundamental perception. I shall suggest that we cannot engage in this 'personal construction' without engaging in gender construction too.

Kantian feminism

In so arguing, I shall be expressly opposing the philosophical picture behind the claims considered above. I shall describe this picture in its clearest form, as the 'Kantian feminist' theory of gender. According to this theory, what I really and fundamentally am, for myself and for another, is a person. My nature as a person establishes completely and exclusively all my claims to be treated with consideration, and is the true basis of every interpersonal reaction to me. Although I am incarnate, my being so is, so to speak, the instrument of my 'realisation', in the public world of personal emotion. My personality is distinct from its bodily form, and is the true locus of my rights, my privileges, my values, my choices and – to use the Kantian term – my 'freedom'. Features of my body, which distinguish my body from yours, cannot give reasonable ground for any judgement as to my nature as a person. If I am crippled, or black, or handsome, I am as much a person as you, who are whole, white and ugly. The category 'person' is a unity: there is only *one* kind of thing that falls under it, and distinctions between persons are simply distinctions among accidental personal properties – distinctions expressed and revealed in free choices. There is no real distinction between the masculine and the feminine, except in so far as human freedom has been bent in certain directions, by whatever social pressures, so as to take on two contrasting forms. Distinctions of gender cannot lie in the *nature of things*. For, while there may be two kinds of human body – the male and the female – there cannot be two corresponding kinds of human *person*. For that would mean attributing these bodily distinctions to the 'freedom' of the persons which they divide, in the way that the racist attributes the race or skin colour of another to his responsibility. Although the enslaved black wears the character induced by his slavery, he is, in himself, something independent of the social conditions which produced him. To say that he wears his personality *by nature* – as in the Aristotelian defence of slavery – is to say that his physiological distinction from his white master is the outward sign of a distinct moral identity. The Kantian feminist argues that it is as absurd and wicked to suppose that persons are fundamentally masculine or feminine as that they are fundamentally enslaved or free. Such *natural* differences as there are, are *merely* bodily – the difference between the male and the female, the difference between the Caucasian and the Negro. All differences of personality are the outcome of social conditions which, because they are the product of choice, might also be freely altered.

That argument – which has been given eloquent expression in recent years by Simone de Beauvoir[5] – is undeniably appealing. I have given it in what is perhaps its most popular form, as a corollary of the categorical imperative, expressed in terms of the Kantian notion of freedom. However, it can be re-expressed in the language of my previous argument, as follows: the distinction between the sexes lies in the nature of things, and, although there may be odd cases of sex change, the basic division between male and female is one between two separate natural kinds. The kind 'person' is not, however, a natural kind, and divisions within the natural kind 'human animal' do not imply divisions in the 'social' kind 'person'. On the contrary. The kind 'person' owes its existence to our sense that human beings are alike in respect of their rationality, and that the possession of this attribute is sufficient to found a distinct pattern of response towards them. The kind 'person' ranges indifferently across all beings with a capacity for rational response, and the 'deep' characteristics of the person – the possession of a first-person perspective, and of the attitude towards agency that I have called responsibility – are exemplified by every specimen, or at least are possessed alike by men and women. Hence, there is no inference from the sexual distinction within the natural kind 'human being', to the gender distinction within the social kind 'person'. The latter is artificial, changeable and in any case not of the essence, while the former is natural, unchangeable and essential to the nature of the things which display it.

There are other kinds of feminism, and if I choose to discuss the Kantian variety, it is only on account of its intellectual purity, and its consequent ability to display what is really at stake, and not because it is intrinsically plausible. The Kantian feminist position, I contend, must be criticised on three counts. First, it assigns an implausible role to the concept of gender. Secondly, it fails to take seriously the fact of embodiment: it is at war with the truth that we *are* our bodies, and, in separating personal freedom entirely from biological destiny, it is misled by a transcendental illusion. Finally, Kantian feminism fails to recognise that, in the sense that distinctions of gender are 'artificial', so too is the human person.

The role of gender

The feminist claims that concepts of gender have no validity outside the attitudes which they serve to convey. There is no *fact of the matter* about gender, only distinctions of attitude that can be redrawn at any time. To put it another way: the idea of gender is purely intentional; it neither engages with the material distinction between the sexes, nor does it have any explanatory purpose that would lead us to assign an independent reality to the division that it records.

That would be plausible only if the deep division between man and woman (the division of natural kind) were such that it did not intrude into our intentional understanding. To *assume* that it does not intrude is, however, to beg the question. The anti-feminist claims that the distinction between man and woman *determines* distinct responses towards the two natural kinds, and that we employ concepts of gender so as to focus those responses upon the relevant features of their objects. For the feminist, the distinction of sex is hidden, in the way that the distinction between onyx and porphyry is hidden. The two stones can be made to look very different; they can also be made to look very similar. We are interested in their similarity, and therefore we classify them together, despite the vast distinction of natural kind. Likewise, the feminist argues, men and women, considered as *persons*, can be made to seem very similar, or they can be made to seem very different. It depends upon our interests. If we choose, we can reconstruct the social world, so that the two sexes appear equally as persons. And in such a world we should have no use for the concept of gender.

The anti-feminist will argue, however, that sex is more *apparent* than that suggests, and hence that our conceptions of gender embody an attempt, not merely to project our attitudes, but to understand the inward constitution of reality. They are responsive to the *deep* facts about man and woman, in the way that the concept 'ornamental marble' is not responsive to the deep facts about stones. Even if we have no knowledge of the science of sex, we may yet be responsive to the facts of sex. And one of our responses to these facts is our formation of a concept of gender. To some extent, therefore, our conceptions of gender may record the underlying facts of sexual differentiation. Indeed, if they did not, it would be difficult to see how we could describe them as conceptions of gender. They can be such only if they aim to distinguish man from woman, and the masculine from the feminine, in terms which convey the intentional content of responses that would be meaningless but for the underlying distinction of sex.

It is difficult to determine *a priori* which of those views is correct. The best we can do is to study, first, what *might* be true concerning the capacity of sex to intrude into our sexual experience, and secondly, what *is* true of the experience itself – and, in particular, how the distinction between man and woman is *seen*.

Man and woman

It is widely recognised that the biological distinction between the sexes is not as absolute in reality as it tends to be in our thoughts. While sexuality is not exactly a matter of degree, there is a scale upon which male and female characteristics may be placed. There are also cases which cannot be placed on this scale: cases such as hermaphroditism, in which characteristics of both sexes are exhibited, and neuterism, in which neither sex seems properly to have emerged, and the creature is endowed either with no reproductive organs at all, or with only atrophied organs, incapable of carrying out any serious sexual task. The existence of these cases leads us to an idea of sexual normality – of the man or woman, in whom everything relevant to the reproductive function is also optimally suited to it. This way of seeing sex is so natural, and relies on facts that are so vivid and so interesting to us, that it would not be surprising to find that it has permeated our conceptions of gender. In gender too, we recognise masculine and feminine characteristics, and ambiguous or puzzling cases which seem to defy classification. We also recognise a scale of masculine and feminine – although, as I shall argue below, it is a scale that is unlike other polarities. Finally our ideas of gender are saturated with a conception of normality which, while it only partly corresponds to the idea of sexual normality, contains an essential reference, if not to the function of the sexual act, at least to the nature of desire.

Far more important than the sexual scale, however, is the sexual distinction itself. Men and women differ in their bodily appearance and in their bodily capacities. They develop according to a different rhythm, and seem to possess different intellectual aptitudes.[6] There are lessons to be drawn about the genetic constitution of men and women from the observation that they are *socially* so distinct. Men and women differ in their powers, in their energies and in their approach to practical problems. But in nothing do they differ so much as in their sexual dispositions and experiences. For women may become pregnant; and their bodies have a rhythm, and a destiny, that are conditioned by the fact of childbirth.

From the genetic point of view, the distinction between the sexes is a deep characteristic, determined from the earliest stages of foetal development by a chromosome mechanism. In a thousand ways, the development of the male is minutely different from the development of the female, and we can expect these differences to survive in enduring dispositions and biologically determined habits. But what are the implications for our idea of gender? Here it is instructive to engage in a piece of *a priori* sociobiology. The relentless struggle of the gene to perpetuate itself, which – according to the sociobiologist – is the root cause of sexual union, is furthered by distinct behaviour in the male and the female. The male helps his genes to the extent that he impregnates females, and ensures that his own offspring have a better chance of survival than their competitors. The female perpetuates her genes to the extent that she is impregnated, and is able to nourish her offspring. The genes of the male are benefited, therefore, by his determination to assert exclusive sexual use of the females whom he has impregnated, while the genes of the woman are benefited by her determination to secure the enduring cooperation of a strong, reliable male, in the maintenance of her life and the support of her offspring. These two functions are not incompatible – indeed, they form, for the sociobiologist, the true material reality that underpins the marriage contract. But they indicate that the genetic ambitions of male and female would be furthered by distinct psychological dispositions. Suppose we were to allow ourselves a little imaginative licence, and attempt to describe, from sociobiological premises, the psychological dispositions of man and woman that would be most favourable to the perpetuation of their genes. We might paint the following picture:

The man is active in the pursuit of women; he does not confine his attentions to one woman only, but moves on restlessly after new conquests, and attempts to exclude other men from enjoying their favours. Moreover, his jealousy has a peculiar focus. He is pained, not so much by the attempt by other men to help and support his woman, as by their attempt to unite with her sexually. Indeed, it is the thought of her copulating with another which causes him the greatest outrage. (Our imaginary sociobiologist would not be surprised by the tribe (described by Buffon)[7] who close the maiden vagina with a ring, and who on marriage replace that ring with another that may be opened, although with a key guarded by the husband.) At the same time, he has a disposition to provide for her, and to seek food and shelter that will facilitate the nourishment of his children.

The woman is not active in the pursuit of men, but modest and retiring. She thereby guarantees that she can be obtained only at the cost of effort and determination, and so ensures that her genes will unite with the strongest available strain, thus furthering their chances of survival. Once possessed, she does her utmost to secure the services of the man, and to bind him to her, so as to enjoy the fruits of his protection during the times ahead. She is jealous of other women, but her jealousy focusses not so much on the sexual act – provided it is performed in a spirit of indifference – as on the enduring relationships which threaten her own protection. She is frightened more by the thought that her man's love may be enticed away from her than by the thought of his copulating with another. To prevent what she fears, she provides comforts for him that will bind him to their common home.

The disparity between the genetic requirements of man and woman is reflected also – according to the imaginary portrait that I am offering – in the structure of male and female desire. The man will be attracted to those features in the woman which promise healthy offspring and easy childbirth. He will be moved by her youth, vitality and regular features; by her readiness for domestic life, and by her modesty. He will value chastity, and even virginity: the harbingers of his own genetic triumph. And he will try to win her by a display of strength and competence.

She, however, will respond to the man who promises the greatest protection to her offspring. She is impressed less by his youth than by his power. Everything that promises security is capable of arousing her affections, and even a far older man may excite her, provided there is, in his look, his smell, his conversation or his social manner, the necessary virtues of a father. The authoritative glance, the resolute action, the confident enjoyment of social pre-eminence: all such qualities will be as important in the woman's eyes as her youth, freshness and vitality are important in the eyes of a man. At the same time, she will not be indifferent to a man's physical character, and – like him – will be turned away by evident deformities, and by the signs of intellectual or emotional decay.

Of course, it is stretching the imagination beyond the bounds of probability to suppose that real human beings would behave like that. If sociobiology implies that they do, so much the worse for sociobiology. As a matter of fact, however, sociobiology can hardly fail to have some such implication. For it is committed to the view that reproductive behaviour is to be explained functionally, in terms of its capacity to further the propagation of the genes of those who engage in it. Moreover, it is not only sociobiology that is guilty of this horrendous description of the difference between man and woman. It seems to be a received idea of the literature of love, from Theocritus to D. H. Lawrence. Almost all agree in distinguishing male desire from female desire, male jealousy from female jealousy and male love from female love, in ways that are already suggested in my piece of *a priori* sociobiology. *Tantum imaginatio potuit suadere malorum!*

Suppose, however, that such a picture – which I have presented in the broadest outline – were true to our biological condition, and to the psychological dispositions that are rooted in it. Would this not have the greatest imaginable implications for our ideas of gender? In particular, would it not suggest that the traditional conception of gender, according to which men and women have different characters, different emotions, and different social and domestic roles, is neither a biological accident nor a social superfluity? May it not even refute the view that gender distinctions have been manufactured 'for the convenience of the male', and 'at the expense of the female', by a society in which men have been peculiarly dominant? (If we do not think that it refutes that view, we must explain *why* men have been so dominant. We will then be forced to suppose just the kind of biological differentiation that is being questioned.)

It is certainly true that, until recently, almost every writer on sex has recognised a difference of tendency, and a difference of focus, between male and female desire, and many have attempted to explain this in terms of some piece of *a priori* biology, of the kind that I have offered. As an example, it is perhaps sufficient to quote Senancour:

> *La beauté des femmes ne se soutient pas durant plus de la moitié de la vie, comme la force des hommes; le temps de l'amour sera moins long chez elles, et sera encore abrégé par des intérruptions, les unes fréquentes, les autres considérables. Il en résulte que l'imagination de l'homme suppose assez généralement la possession de plusieurs femmes. Entraîné par un grand besoin de mouvement, et se sentant destiné à vivre peut-être dans les climats divers, il*

se dit qu'il formera des liaisons conformes à l'instabilité de sa fortune. Mais une femme se borne plus volontiers à un seul attachement.[8]

The explanation is feeble. And many doubt the fact explained. Indeed, it is increasingly forbidden to affirm it, and a writer who dares to do so may be greeted with a flood of intolerant abuse.[9] Fortunately, it is not necessary to my argument either to assert or to deny the conclusion which Senancour espouses. It is necessary only to recognise that there would be nothing surprising should male and female desire show such marked differences of tendency and structure.

Embodiment

At this point the reader might reasonably object that I am failing to acknowledge one of my own persistently reaffirmed premises: that the intentional and the material are conceptually distinct, and that the first is determined at best only by our *conception* of the second. Why cannot our conception of gender take whatever form is required by our moral understanding, without regard for the scientific truth concerning sexual differentiation? For, after all, this 'truth' is a comparatively recent 'discovery' – perhaps even a recent invention – and more like a scientistic apology for an old ideology than a scientific basis for a new one.

While there is some force in that objection, I have already suggested that it fails to be wholly persuasive. Our conceptions of gender are permeable to our conceptions of sex, and the facts of sex are sufficiently important, and sufficiently vivid, to make an indelible impact upon our experience. We recognise the biological division between man and woman, and it is resurgent in our perceptions. But we also recognise other distinctions, not so obviously biological, which we perceive in conjunction with the biological reality. It is an integral part of the experience of sexual desire that we regard the subject as overwhelmed, in that moment, by his *sex*. It is this bodily condition which comes to the surface, and which takes command of him. And in this moment all that is associated with his existence as a sexual being – everything from his tone of voice to his social role – is gathered into his sexuality and made part of it. Gender is an elaborate social prelude; when the curtain rises, what is disclosed is not gender, but sex.

There is no doubt that we are never so revealed as animals as in the sexual act. The physical reality of the body is exposed in this act, and becomes the object of exploration and curiosity. Precisely those parts which distinguish the sexes take on the most overwhelming significance. Our perception of the animal basis of our existence is therefore shot through with our knowledge of sexual differentiation. All our attempts to elaborate or diminish the distinction, to give it social and moral identity, to redeem it from the stigma of the 'merely animal', end by confirming the ultimate fact – that our nature as incarnate animals is revealed precisely in the physiology which divides us. In the final surrender to desire, we experience our incarnate nature; we know, then, the 'truth' of gender: which is that, as embodied creatures, we are inseparable from our sex.

The experience of embodiment in sexual desire is, then, one of the root responses that are focussed by our concept of gender. What happens in the sexual act enforces upon us a sense of our 'gender identity', while compelling us to experience the embodiment of gender in sex. At the same time, very little of the observed distinction of gender could be explained by 'reference back' to the sexual act. Our perception of gender is responsive to our experience of intercourse, but far from determined by it. If the roles adopted by man and woman in the sexual act seem to explain the social distinction of gender, this is partly because the sexual act is performed under the influence of a conception of gender. In sexual intercourse I experience, not only the embodiment of my *self*, but also the incarnation of a 'moral kind'.

What, then, is the origin of that 'moral kind'? Clearly, people attempt to signal their sex in their social behaviour, and to signal their fitness for desire. The basic differences between the sexes – hair, skin, voice, form and movement – are redeemed from their arbitrariness by being represented as integral to a moral condition. In this way, both the creation of gender and its rooting in sex become parts of a common social enterprise.

That exercise is, indeed, 'culturally determined'. Even if gender distinctions are in some sense natural – perhaps even inevitable – consequences of our experience of sexual embodiment, it does not follow that there is some *one* distinction of gender which every society must attempt to construct or obey. The universality of gender is, however, confirmed by the evidence of anthropologists, whose findings are summarised in the following terms by Margaret Mead:

> In every known society, mankind has elaborated the biological division of labour into forms often very remotely related to the original biological differences that provided the original clues. Upon the contrast in bodily form and function men have built analogies between sun and moon, night and day, goodness and evil, strength and tenderness, steadfastness and fickleness,

endurance and vulnerability. . . .

. . . . we know of no culture that has said, articulately, that there is no difference between men and women except in the way they contribute to the next generation.[10]

Nor is the social construction of gender confined to heterosexuals. Although the homosexual's conception, both of his sex and of his gender, must inevitably reflect his predilections, he is as active in the affirmation of his gender as any heterosexual. Indeed, we may agree with Hocquenghem[11] that if it were not for gender homosexuality would be unintelligible. The thesis of the 'effeminacy' of the homosexual, once so popular, and especially among those who wished, like Weininger, to give a biological theory of homosexual behaviour, is now rightly repudiated. Although there are homosexuals who cultivate the habits and manners of the opposite sex, they are the exception rather than the rule, and in any case seldom advance beyond a state of transparent theatricality, designed to draw attention, at one and the same time, and often in a single gesture, both to their posture as a representative of one sex, and to their reality as a member of the other. We should not be surprised, therefore, at the enhanced effort of gender construction exhibited by the homosexual, whose consciousness of his own sex is magnified by his own attraction towards it. (Consider, for example, the 'sun and steel' ethos of Mishima.)[12] But the process which the homosexual exhibits at its most developed is displayed also by the rest of humanity.

The artefact of gender is not merely one of display. Men and women develop separate characters, separate virtues, separate vices and separate social roles. The modern consciousness is less disposed to admit those facts than was Aristotle, say, or Hume.[13] Nevertheless, it cannot be denied that, whatever men and women *ought* to do, they have persistently conspired to create an effective 'division of moral labour', with the virtues and aptitudes attributed to the one sex being complemented, but by no means always imitated, by the other. Hence it has often been held that a single disposition might be a virtue in one sex and a vice, or a neutral attribute, in the other. The case of chastity – mentioned in this connection by Hume – is perhaps too emotive to bear consideration. A more bearable instance is that of gossiping. This is regarded by many people as a harmless and indeed justifiable extension of woman's desire to break down the barriers of privacy and create a common social world, so blocking the secret paths to violence and immorality. The same disposition, however, is frequently regarded as the most scandalous vice in a man – indeed as a paradigm of 'unmanliness', on a par with the disposition to flee from enemies or to abandon one's wife and child.

As I earlier remarked, however, this practice of 'gender construction' may well be 'culturally determined'. If Margaret Mead is to be trusted,[14] there are societies in which gossiping is regarded as a male prerogative, and in which women are assigned the arduous duties of organised labour, in order that men should be free to lie in the shade, discussing the great concerns of human destiny and also the trivial titbits of the hearth. The important point is not whether a particular *conception* of gender is a human universal, but whether the *concept* of gender is such: whether human beings must experience the world according to this artificial fracture. The argument that I have given suggests at least that something integral to the experience of sex is missing without it. Without gender, sex ceases to play a part in human embodiment, and the sexual act, far from being liberated from its 'mere animality', is in fact detached from its most natural moral interpretation.

Embodiment and gender construction

Our embodiment is no more 'natural' than the phenomena that are expressed in it. It is a result of the social process which transfigures us from animal to person. Hence embodiment expresses both the compulsions and the choices which that process involves. Just as we attach our interpersonal attitudes to our bodily reality, so do we remake the body, in order that it should be a more effective vehicle for the meanings which it is instructed to reveal. The most striking example of this is provided by clothing, which dramatises the sexuality of the body in the act of concealing it. Sex is hidden, so that it might be revealed as gender. Men and women are able to perceive each other sexually in the veils which hide their sex. Thus the most daring thought of another's sexual nature may take up peaceful residence in a perception of his clothes, as when Herrick transforms his desirous perception of Julia:

> When as in silks my Julia goes,
> Then, then (me thinks) how sweetly flows
> The liquefaction of her clothes.

The representation of the body in the clothes that cover it is matched, in Western art, by a reciprocal representation of the clothes in the body. Anne Hollander has persuasively argued that the tradition of Western erotic painting, in which the naked form provides the object of a sustained and contemplative interest, represents the body as 'unclothed' – i.e. as *lacking* the clothes which 'belong' to it.[15] It is a tradition, in Kenneth Clark's terms, of the naked rather than the nude.[16] Painters have frequently accomplished this, Hollander adds, by representing the body in terms of the shapes and movements of the garments which have been peeled from it. Hence is captured, in a single visual image, both the desirable body and the process of unveiling which disclosed it. The body unclothed (*desnuda*) is the visible record of a sexual transaction.

Clothes have to some extent lost that representational function. But the function has not been lost. Instead it has been transferred to the body itself. Through weight-lifting, sun-bathing, massage and dieting, the modern person attempts to express his gender in his body, to achieve a *direct* embodiment, without the mediation of clothes – to establish before our eyes the living identity of sex and gender, in a manner that hides nothing of sex. The result admits of much moral commentary. Let us only note the enormous loss of freedom that is entailed when sexual embodiment must be achieved by such painful means. How much more lightly could one wear one's gender when one wore it in one's clothes!

I have argued that gender distinctions are artificial, but only in the way that persons are artificial. At the same time, I have conceded that they are more variable, and more easily changed, than many other features in which our ideas of personality are rooted. Hence there inevitably arises the question of justification. How ought the gender distinction to be constructed? The remainder of this book gives no more than an implicit and disputable answer to that question. To understand it, however, it is necessary to have some idea of the *process* of gender construction. We must identify the precise occasions for change; for these will be the places where justification *counts*.

The distinction between man and woman is a distinction of sphere, of activity, of role and of responses; it is also a distinction within the structure of desire. We may fight against these distinctions; we may wish to remodel them, even to destroy them altogether. But they exist, and not a few philosophers have drawn extraordinary conclusions which depend, for their plausibility, upon our acceptance of the given gender identities as natural. Witness Hegel:

> Woman – the eternal irony in the heart of the community – changes by intrigue the universal end of government into a private end, transforms its universal activity into the work of a specific individual, and perverts the universal property of the State into a possession and ornament for the family. Thus she turns to ridicule the grave wisdom of maturity, which, being dead to mere particulars (pleasure, satisfaction and actual activity), attends only to what is

universal; she makes this wisdom a laughing stock before the malice of wanton youth, as something unworthy of their enthusiasm. She holds up as principally valuable the strength of youth – of the son, lord of the mother who bore him, of the brother as the man who is equal to the sister, of the youth, through whom the daughter is freed from dependence, so as to find the satisfaction and dignity of wifehood.[17]

The incantatory quality of Hegel's remark is indicative of the phenomenon to which he refers: we construct the distinction between the masculine and feminine partly by *aligning* the distinction of sex with distinctions of a similar resonance: inner and outer, private and public, passive and active, even (for Hegel) 'subjective and objective'. We are dealing, not with a given polarity within human experience, but with a 'synthesis of opposites', whose opposing quality is an invention of our own.

Hegel's view of women is exaggerated, to say the least. Nevertheless, it is right in one particular, which is that gender distinctions are to be explained partly in political terms. We are educated into gender as we are educated into personality, by institutions which we collectively create and sustain. And in epochs of high civilisation this effort of gender construction is enhanced, in the intuitive recognition that the nervous energy of society – its ability to sustain elaborate artifice – is dependent upon the excitement created between the sexes in their coming together.[18]

The principle is well illustrated by the education of the sexes in France's golden age. The convent in eighteenth-century France served as the school, the retreat, the asylum, the hotel and the *point de repère*, the place equally of prayer and of gossip, of devotion, education and social ease, for the aristocratic lady.[19] In such an epoch, the education of the woman, like that of the man, was an exercise in exaggeration (the kind of exaggeration that was subsequently to make Hegel's view of the matter seem like a profound explanation of something thoroughly familiar). Each feminine trait was rescued from nature and reconstituted as artifice, as the blush is remade with rouge. The effect was to make womanhood itself into a property of the will, although by no means of a free will. (And the same was true of manhood.)

In such epochs an enormous sacrifice is made for the sake of gender: the sacrifice involved in exchanging the comfort of a fully private existence for the exhilarating danger of display. By surrendering himself to play, the aristocrat frees his life from the taint of utility. The ideal of gender that he traces in decorative outline is an aesthetic ideal. Man and woman become objects of contemplation, their being and appearance wholly absorbed into the single task of sexual embodiment. Molière's *précieuses ridicules* are ridiculous only because their gender has become a matter of *politesse*. They have ceased to display in their gender the real, urgent and tragic finitude of their being. Gender, for them, is no longer a living principle. The true aristocrat also plays with his gender, but only because he plays with his life.

Nevertheless play is ancillary to the real business of existence, a model to be imitated, a comic rendering of our tragic flutter towards extinction. The display of the aristocrat must therefore find its meaning elsewhere, in a surrounding world that does not partake of it. The rest of mankind pillages the wardrobe of aristocratic disguises – so as to be a real gentleman or a real lady, if only once. Aristocratic frippery therefore provides a model for common courtship, in which each party strains to exaggerate his usefulness and attractiveness to the other, by representing the perfect complementarity of their manners.

But the disguise has worn thin. In an aristocratic civilisation, the display of gender invades the whole life of those who take part in it. For their lives are public, conducted behind open doors, through which petitioners, scandal-mongers, politicians and whores are constantly welcomed and dismissed. To take on the burden of a public life merely for the sake of display is no longer possible. The privileged minority which once made that sacrifice exchanged all hope of repose for a vague promise of fleeting gaieties. And their liaisons foundered on the reef of *méchanceté* by which the isle of Cythaera is surrounded. The conditions no longer obtain, in which people can willingly undertake that hazardous existence. Audacity, snobbery, contempt for the 'common' – all such responses exist, now, only in forms which are painfully theatrical.

Without the glory of display the labour of gender construction is a burdensome labour, whose rewards seem dim and inconclusive. At the same time there is a crucial moment – the moment of courtship – when the need for play, and for the concentration of gender into a demonstrative act, is still felt with all its traditional urgency. The courting couple still need to be 'purposeful without purpose', and therefore still dress up and dance, even though dancing, like so much else, has partly retreated into itself, to become a merely 'private' exercise.

The traditional social dance differs radically from the formless vibration of the body that now passes for dancing. Each dancer had to obey the formation, and from time to time change partners so as to dance with someone whom he did not choose. He must confine his seductive gestures to those little nuances which are all the more pleasurable for their resemblance to the innocent smiles and touches of the dance. The excitement lies in coordinated movement, in which a shared skill provides the foundation for a common pleasure. In such a dance the sexual motive is neutralised, precisely so that the construction of gender may be enhanced. The young couple who enter the dance with desire in their souls conceal it or reveal it just as they would in any other social congress. The dance is not a prelude to sexual union, but a baptism in the creative spring of gender, in which each refreshes his sense of embodiment and sports it to the world. Such dancing is a supreme expression of our rationality, and also an integral part of moral education. Moreover, it shows us something which the aristocratic culture of display conceals: that gender construction is a pleasure, and perhaps one of the largest pleasures that we know.

Dressing up is naturally associated with dancing, and, like dancing, its 'purposiveness' is without purpose, available to anyone, whatever his age, sex, outlook and desire. It is an activity of social display, which imposes uniformity, so as to permit interesting divergence from a norm. (Thus, Philippe Perrot argues, following a familiar idea of Saussure's, in fashion, as in language, meaning is produced not by the likenesses but by the differences which they engender.)[20] Since fashion is so important a device of gender construction, it cannot be passed over without remark: what I say, however, will do scant justice to the subject.

Fashion is a cooperative activity, whereby men and women – and especially women – attempt to make gender new and surprising. The meaning of fashion resides almost entirely in gender construction. A new fashion remodels and revitalises the universal truth of gender, by creating a form that may be shared. Fashion displays what is common to every woman, so as to permit her individuality to shine forth from the frame of her gender, as the thing that is truly desired in it. Hence a fashion is never schematic: it is complete with the completeness of human life; it prescribes a total appearance, a total vocabulary of expressions and gestures, a community of friends and rivals, a pool of common resources and common actions – even a language of its own. And all of those things are expressly ephemeral, encapsulating in their brief glory the evanescence of life itself. Because fashion is so evidently a human action, a deliberate reconstruction of the body, it serves as a collective defiance of our destiny, a gesture of revolt against the implacable law of embodiment. That which is outside our control – the body, its sex and the procreative yearning that lurks there – is recuperated as a conscious achievement, a light-hearted gesture flung in the face of the gods. Fashion pierces the opacity of the body, and overcomes its *eeriness*. Whatever is most weird or astonishing is no longer in face and limbs, but in clothes and manners – i.e. in that which we can alter, that which bears the mark of 'something done'. Hence fashions must constantly change, precisely in order to renew the changeless reality of gender.

The labour of gender construction is still expended in fashion – although, as I earlier remarked, fashion now afflicts not clothing only, but also the body itself. The labour continues unabated, sometimes exaggerating the distinction between the sexes – sometimes (as now) narrowing it, so that the only real distinctions should reside in the body itself, which is carefully outlined by tightly fitting clothes.

Fashion reminds us again of the extent to which gender arises, not only through education and segregation, but also through play. It is precisely in play that our deepest social needs and perceptions are articulated. To change distinctions of gender is to learn different games. To the question of whether we should do that, I offer only an implicit answer. It is important to remember, however, that the energy released when man and woman come together is proportional to the distance which divides them when they are apart.

Personal kinds

The result of gender construction is that we perceive the *Lebenswelt* as subject to a great ontological divide. Not only is there an intentional distinction between person and thing, there is another between the masculine and the feminine, which is initially a distinction among persons. But this second ontological divide, while it takes its sense from our understanding of persons, is not confined to the personal realm. On the contrary, it reaches through all nature, presenting us with a masculine and a feminine in everything. A willow, a Corinthian column, a Chopin nocturne, a Gothic spire – in all these one may receive the embodied intimation of femininity, and someone who could not understand the possibility of this is someone with impoverished perceptions. Thus the intentional world reflects back to us the ontological division which we exemplify. We absorb and reabsorb the ideas of the masculine and the feminine, as intentional contents, already impressed with the mark of human sexuality and human desire. Gender thereby becomes an inescapable feature of our world, none the less real through being our own creation.

Although gender is an artefact, it is also, in another sense, as natural a feature of the *Lebenswelt* as the human person himself. No person can easily refrain from thinking of himself as 'of' a certain sex, and of rationalising that thought in a conception of gender. The experience of sexual embodiment, which so compromises and diverts our projects, forces us to be aware of our sex as a channel through which will and consciousness flow. Gender is the concept whereby sex *enters* our lives, giving a persistent and reasoned form to otherwise inchoate projects. It is hard to avoid this way of identifying myself, since it is hard to avoid the impulse which prompts me to see myself in sexual terms. My sexual desire stems, not from some accidental part of me, but from my *self*. Hence, I think, not of my body, but of *myself*, as being of a certain sexual kind. However I may divest my 'inner' self of attributes, I find it hard to divest it of this one. Even those pure 'first-person perspectives' – the gods who move in transcendental spheres – are identified in terms of their gender. The most abstract religion will attribute a gender to its god: not to do so is to cast in doubt the whole *style* of God's agency. (Thus the God of Islam has a gender, despite his wholly discarnate nature; and this gender is made explicit, even when the Koran is translated into a gender-free language, such as Turkish.)

If Kantian feminism were correct, it would be impossible to think of myself as a man, rather than as a person with a man's body. Yet it is precisely to the self that we attribute the feature which bears most overwhelming witness to our incarnate condition. Confirmation is to be found in a case which at first might seem to refute the claim – the case of the 'sex change'. So persuasive is the idea that gender is an artefact, and so immovable is the human prejudice that sex is nothing but gender, that the theory has arisen of sex, too, as an artefact.[21] It suffices to make a few adjustments to the physical constitution of the body, and any child could be brought up indifferently as a boy or as a girl: the social relativity of his gender is tantamount to the social relativity of his sex. Such ideas are biological nonsense.[22] But this has not prevented them from being extremely influential, or from nurturing the fantasy that each person may have a 'real sex', which is belied by his bodily form, but which is revealed in his own conception of his gender. The sex-change patient undertakes this hazardous operation, not in order to change his 'real sex', but in order to change his *body*, to the sex that is really *his*. In other words, he identifies his sex through his gender, and his gender not through his body but through his conception of himself. His body, he feels, belongs to a kind to which he himself does not belong. It is on this ground that sex-change operations are both desired by those who undergo them and justified by those who perform them. No more vivid example exists of the human determination to triumph over biological destiny, in the interests of a moral idea.

A similar conclusion is suggested by the case of hermaphroditism, as recorded by the pathetic Herculine Barbin.[23] Mlle Barbin's sexuality underwent genuine changes, causing the most intolerable anguish in the mind of the victim, and leading at last to suicide. The spiritual uncertainty, which grows from biological uncertainty, shows the intense drama of an individual soul, as it tries to fit a necessary idea of gender onto a seemingly fluctuating attribute of sex. Herculine Barbin's reflections show, indeed, just how far a human being will go – even to the point of losing sight of his own existence – in order to spiritualise his private parts and to gather up the attribute of sex within a personal conception.

It is tempting to conclude, therefore, that there is a *real distinction* of gender: that 'man' and 'woman' denote two kinds of person, whose biological distinction is gathered up within a division of kinds. This is intimated, at least, by our habits of self-identification, and in particular by our identification of ourselves in and through our gender. At the same time, it might be held that, since distinctions of gender are distinctions, not among natural, but among 'phenomenological' kinds, there can be no sense to the idea of a *real* distinction. Since these kinds are in some sense created by us, how can we speak of a 'real essence' which unites whatever is included by them? In which case, what is the content of our belief that men and women are two kinds of person?

Superficially, such a question is easy to answer. We have only to refer to the analogy with secondary qualities. The distinction between red and green, is an objective distinction, even though it is, in Colin McGinn's words, 'subjectively constituted'.[24] It is the nature of the objects themselves which causes us to perceive some as red and some as green. The distinction between the objects of experience is here as real as the distinction between the experiences. To establish a 'real distinction' of gender, therefore, it would be sufficient to show that our experience of persons contains gender as part of its content.

But the question has another, and less superficial, component, and one which led to the reference to a 'real essence' of each personal kind. The Kantian feminist may accept that gender distinctions are inescapable – or at least escapable only at intolerable cost – and yet hold that they are also inherently trivial. Such distinctions do not in any way touch upon the moral reality of the persons themselves. Certainly there is no such thing as a 'real essence' of men, distinct from the 'real essence' of women, when the terms 'man' and 'woman' are taken to denote two kinds of *person*.

But here we encounter what is perhaps the most serious objection to Kantian feminism, which is that, in precisely the sense that gender is an artefact, so too is the human person. It is inevitable that human beings, in social conditions, will develop into persons, and be described by each other in personal terms. Hence all human beings must possess a concept of the person. *Conceptions* of the person, however, vary from culture to culture and from tribe to tribe. In just the same way, all human beings in social conditions inevitably develop into men and women, and describe each other by means of those categories. Hence all human beings possess a concept of gender. But *conceptions* of gender vary from place to place and from time to time. And it is plausible to suppose that the two processes go hand in hand: that the evolution of the person, and his fitting into a gender, are two aspects of a single history.

Artificial kinds may have 'real essences'. It is an essential property of a person that he has a first-person perspective. It is a peculiar feature of the Kantian theory of morality that it attributes the moral nature of a person entirely to modifications of two of his essential properties – freedom and reason. But there are reasons for being dissatisfied with the Kantian view: in particular, it neglects the third essential property of the human person – that of embodiment – and fails to recognise that there are moral qualities which involve our embodiment *essentially*, such as warmth of heart and liveliness. All such qualities belong, for Kant, merely to the empirical aspect of human nature and not to the rational core. Kantian philosophy must say the same of gender. However, this seems to be just as implausible. First, there is a marked disposition to regard gender as an essential property: to regard genuine changes of *gender*, as opposed to changes of sex, as 'transsubstantiations', in which one individual is abolished and replaced by another. We find it as implausible to suppose that Zeus could seduce Callisto by appearing as the huntress Diana as that he could seduce Leda by appearing as a swan. The gender transformation in the first case is as much a barrier to imagination as the species transformation in the second. The other's being a man, say, is inseparable from his existence as a person, and although I may sometimes entertain in imagination the thought of him as belonging to the other sex, the possibility of this thought is precisely what is excluded by all my normal interpersonal responses to him. It is an essentially 'literary' thought, such as afflicted the drunken Bloom in Night-town.

I have no argument for the conclusion that gender *is* an essential property of whatever possesses it: such arguments are always hard to produce, and always inconclusive. But even without that strong conclusion, we can surely accept that gender is a morally *significant* property of whatever possesses it, and hence that the Kantian feminist position, which banishes gender to the periphery of human freedom, is mistaken.

For it is precisely the existence of gender that serves to unite our sexual nature to the moral life that grows from it. Gender – in my analogy – is the trunk through which the flower and foliage of desire are nurtured. To understand this is both to reject the feminist claim and to answer the Platonic question.

Plato's question and the root of desire

Given the existence of gender, we can no longer assume that the sexual act between humans is the *same* act as that performed by animals. Every feature of the sexual act, down to its very physiology, is transformed by our conception of gender. When making love I am consciously being a man, and this enterprise involves my whole nature, and strives to realise itself in the motions of the act itself. Although the man who enters a woman, or the woman who encloses a man, are satisfying a primitive urge, and experiencing whatever sensations and palpitations may accompany the fulfilment of that urge, this is not a description of 'what they are doing' in the act of love. Even if they are acutely conscious of the process – and it is to be supposed that their thoughts abound in fantasies which direct them constantly to the source of their physical pleasure – it is not the physical process, described as such, which constitutes the object of their intention. They are intending to 'make love', that is, to unite as sexual beings, in an experience guided by the concept of gender. It is 'man uniting with woman' rather than 'penis entering vagina' which focusses their attention. The latter episode is perceived simply as a 'moment' in the former, which provides its indispensable context.

Hence the physical performance, in becoming a human action, is lifted out of its biological circumstance. It is adapted to the morphological requirements of sexual desire, by being reconstituted in terms of gender. The pleasurable exercise of copulation is moralised by the concept of gender, and made into something distinctively human, just as the pleasurable exercise of skipping and jumping is moralised by the idea of the dance. Animals can skip and jump and feel the corresponding pleasure. But they cannot dance, for they cannot perceive their movements in the way required by dancing – as things significant in themselves. Hence, though they can experience the pleasure of skipping, they cannot experience the pleasure of dancing. Nor, for similar reasons, can they experience the pleasure of sex, in which the movements of copulation embody a moral idea of sex-membership, and are engaged in, not simply by impulse, but because of what they mean.

However, in the words of James Thurber – is sex necessary? I mean, is it necessary for sexual desire, with its peculiar interpersonal intentionality, to lead us into precisely *this* predicament? Of course, we should not call it *sexual* desire if it habitually and normally expressed itself in some other way. But that is merely a verbal matter. What is it about the intentionality of desire that requires its attachment to the sexual act?

The introduction of sex into desire is not without the most far-reaching consequences. In particular, it introduces an element of universality into the object of desire. He or she is desired *as* a man or *as* a woman, and it is from this thought that much of the phenomenology of desire arises – a point that I have already tried to illustrate in discussing shame and jealousy. The universality in question is, however, not that of sex, but that of gender. The other appears to me, even in the sexual act, not as the naked animal, but as a person, clothed in the moral attributes of his gender. In desiring him I see him as essentially embodied, and his body as essentially ensouled; the gap between soul and body is closed for me by my desire. It is hard to imagine this utter unity in the intentional object arising from a non-sexual motive. Interpersonal union which culminates in swimming together, walking together, talking together, does not focus upon the reality of the other's body in quite the way of the sexual act. It is only when kisses and caresses become part of the aim of interpersonal union, and the true source of pleasure, that we are forced to see the other's body as truly him, and contact with his body as contact with him. Sexual desire must therefore involve such activities as kissing and caressing if it is to fulfil its fundamental aim. It is surely obvious, therefore, that the natural culmination of these activities – the sexual act – should become incorporated into the intentional content of desire. Desire both exploits and confirms our concept of gender, by refusing to countenance the separation between a person and his body. The sexual act is, both biologically and intentionally, the culmination of a process of physical intimacy, in which a person is joined to another through his body. None of our bodily functions is so well fitted to this union as is the sexual function, provided that sex is perceived under the aspect of gender – perceived, in other words, as a personal attribute, rather than as a merely biological fact.

Hence we find enormous difficulty in envisaging true sexual desire between fishes and other creatures which reproduce sexually but without sexual contact. The female mackerel may deposit an egg which is later fertilised and guarded by a male. But what, in this solitary action, bears the aspect of desire? Not only physical contact, but every conceivable mutuality, has been extruded from the sexual process, which in consequence cannot be seen, by any stretch of the imagination, as a form of desire. How much easier is it to see desire in the copulation of dogs, or even that of insects. (Thus, whatever else it is, artificial insemination is never adultery.)

It seems, therefore, that, so long as sex is perceived as gender, there is an intrinsic fittingness which unites the sexual act to the interpersonal attitude of desire. Hence, just as the intentionality of desire takes root in the pleasures of sexual congress, so does an idea of gender enter into the intentional content of desire, determining the 'kind of thing' which is its proper object. The individual is always pursued under the aspect of his gender, as one instance of a sexual kind.

Beauty and gender

It is worth returning at this point to the discussion of beauty. Almost anything in the world belongs to some kind, specimens of which appear beautiful to us. There are beautiful pens, horses, stones, clouds, houses, proofs and sounds. There are also beautiful characters and souls – that is to say, people whose moral attributes we do not merely praise, but also contemplate with pleasurable emotion. This raises the question whether 'beautiful' is an 'attributive' adjective[25] in the sense made familiar by Geach. The proposition that 'X is beautiful' does not *have* to be expanded into 'X is beautiful as an F' in order to be fully intelligible. At the same time, at a less grammatical level, the beautiful is every bit as attributive as the useful and the good. The sincere *judgement* of beauty depends always upon an understanding of the kind of thing that is judged. What is beautiful in a horse may not be beautiful in a partridge, and James may be beautiful as a horse, while being profoundly ugly as a garden ornament.

This 'kind-relatedness' in the idea of beauty is perhaps not surprising. It is somewhat more surprising, however, to find that, in the case of persons, beauty is relative not to personality but to gender. You are beautiful as a man or as a woman, but not, as a rule, as a person. The reference to 'beautiful people' is usually understood either inclusively (to cover both beautiful men and beautiful women) or as a reference to moral, rather than physical, qualities. People do not possess some attribute – personal beauty – independent of their beauty or ugliness as a member of their sex.

It is true that we speak freely of a 'beautiful child', meaning not to raise the question of its sex. But this is because its sex has not developed to the point where we consider it fitting to take an interest in it. As soon as sex becomes prominent, our judgements of human beauty respond at once to the concept of gender. A physically beautiful person is beautiful as a woman or as a man, and his beauty is thoroughly qualified by the distinguishing attributes of his sex. There are of course men of feminine beauty, and women of masculine beauty – but our very disposition so to describe them indicates that we attach beauty, even in these cases, to an idea of gender, and cannot perceive it in other terms.

I have already argued that the concept of beauty is univocal – that its application to the object of aesthetic contemplation and the object of desire involves no real ambiguity. Hence we should not be surprised to find that the types of human beauty correspond to the types of human desire: in particular, they exemplify the same division of the object according to gender. By 'rooting' itself in sex, desire also raises sex from its animal purposes, and incorporates it into a moral idea of gender. It is this idea which finds its 'sensuous embodiment' – to use Hegel's expression[26] – in the experience of human beauty.

It is hard to summarise in simple terms the many ideas that are condensed into our experience of the human body – the emotions which lead us to see the human body as so peculiarly luminous among the objects of our experience. But it is through watching, caressing and outlining the human form that we come to understand the full richness of human companionship. Without these experiences, all visions of heavenly bliss would be seriously impoverished. Mahomed has often been mocked for peopling his paradise with desirable women, and inviting us to long for their caresses. But surely he was responding to a natural and healthy instinct, which finds in the contemplation of a beautiful body, not only the stimulus to desire, but also the satisfaction of a deeper yearning. We yearn, in fact, to *justify* the human body, to give grounds for our feeling that this is God's image. And in this yearning is expressed our real knowledge that we are our bodies and that they are we.

What, then, of 'Plato's question'? My argument implies that to search for the roots of sexual experience in the biological function is to search too low. It is to look, not at the basis of our sexual perceptions, but below that basis. Gender, then, gives way to sex. But the concept of sex does not, in itself, describe the contours of our *Lebenswelt*. Everything about our sexual activity, including the act of love itself, is gathered up into our interpersonal perceptions. Although it is true that desire is rooted in sex, sex in turn reaches its true flowering in desire, and only there, in its *telos*, is its essence revealed, as a phenomenon in the world of human experience, and as an object of that intentional understanding whereby we make sense of our world.

In the course of arguing for that conclusion, I have acknowledged the existence of gender distinctions, as real features of our interpersonal universe. Distinctions of gender incorporate both the artificial and socially determined distinctions that arise between the sexes, and also the natural and biologically determined distinctions which condition the perceived surface of human conduct. The rooting of desire in sex leads also to the rooting of gender, and to the enriching of the biological distinction with inbuilt moral commentaries. Whether we should rewrite those commentaries, embellish them or reduce them are matters of concern. But it should not be thought that the decision here is a simple one, or that any particular recommendation can be either readily acted upon or fully understood. Furthermore, distinctions of gender will reflect the separate structures of male and female desire. To the extent that these structures have their roots in natural and biologically determined distinctions, it is both futile and dangerous to tamper with them. Part of the function of our conceptions of gender lies in the need to accept the underlying biological differences, to lift them out of the realm of animal destiny, and to dignify them with the costumes of morality.

Homosexuality and gender

All the features of our sexual perception that I have referred to in this chapter, from the bare distinction of biological kinds to the high point of aesthetic contemplation, serve to emphasise not only the distinction between the sexes, but also the otherness of the other sex, and the familiarity of one's own. Kantian feminism has tended to assume – with Simone de Beauvoir – that it is only *one* sex that has perceived the other in terms of its 'otherness'.[27] In that very observation, however, is revealed the covert recognition that man is as much the 'other' for woman as woman is the 'other' for man. Man is the 'other' whose otherness resides in his 'creation' of woman's otherness. If Kantian feminism were true, it would be impossible to think of men, as a class, engaged in this supposedly false representation and in its associated oppressive action. Only individual persons – who happen to be male – could be responsible for such a crime. But, *ex hypothesi*, their maleness, not being a feature of their personality, would have no part to play in their responsibility. In which case it could never be said that the division of the world into genders, and the erection of a myth of the 'other' sex, was the doing of men, or in any other way an upshot of masculine dominion. To put it shortly, if the claims made by Kantian feminists were true, Kantian feminism would be false.

For the Kantian feminist, the *enracinement* of the person in the soil of animal activity is a single phenomenon, exemplified alike by man and woman. One and the same person might have taken root in either soil. If this were so, there can be no moral difference between homosexual and heterosexual desire. The body's sex would be irrelevant to the inter-personal emotions that are displayed in it; just *this* person might have had just *this* desire, whatever his sex. Otherwise we must say that desire is not, after all, an interpersonal attitude, but simply a residue of bodily experience, indicating not the person but his biological destiny, in the manner of sensory pleasure and sensory pain. In other words, Kantian feminism has radical moral consequences. Either it denies the moral distinction between heterosexual and homosexual desire – and, along with it, the idea of a sexual 'normality' answerable to our nature as sexually reproducing beings. Or else it forces us to accept the Platonic view of desire as 'merely animal'. Neither view is acceptable.

Casanova tells the story of his meeting with Bellino, a castrato singer whom he believes to be a man, but whom he desires *immediately*, on the uncertain hypothesis that he is a woman. Bellino comes to dinner in woman's clothes, and Casanova stares at him desirously, remarking that 'ma nature vicieuse me faisait trouver une douce volupté à le croire d'un sexe *dont j'avais besoin qu'il fut*' (my emphasis).[28] At the same time, Casanova feels within himself a profound revulsion towards homosexual love; when he discovers Bellino to be a man, he continues to think of him desirously, but only as the woman whom he had previously imagined him to be. And then, at last, he discovers Bellino to be a woman, and rushes at once to the consummation of his desire. This, surely, is an accurate description of the role of gender in the genesis of desire. For the Kantian feminist, Casanova's problem was entirely artificial: he *could* have desired Bellino with *just this* desire, while believing him to be a man. But Casanova's desire was extinguished by that thought: he could no longer desire Bellino as he believed him to be, but only as he once thought that he was.

However, it is not easy to give a full explanation of Casanova's anguish. Why does he hesitate so much before the threshold of homosexual desire? I shall conclude with a brief suggestion, to which I return in the chapter which follows.

The plain fact is that, because we live in a world structured by gender, the other sex is forever to some extent a mystery to us, with a dimension of experience that we can imagine but never inwardly know. In desiring to unite with it, we are desiring to mingle with something that is deeply – perhaps essentially – not ourselves, and which brings us to experience a character and inwardness that challenge us with their strangeness. (Such is, of course, the prevailing theme of D. H. Lawrence's novels: and, in *The Rainbow* at least, Lawrence vindicates his vision.)

This might imply that there is a distinction between homosexual and heterosexual desire. The heterosexual ventures towards an individual whose gender confines him within another world. The homosexual unites with an individual who does not lie beyond the divide which separates the world of men from the world of women. Hence the homosexual has a peculiar inward familiarity with what his partner feels. His discovery of his partner's sexual nature is the discovery of what he knows. Like Verlaine, he may make sport of this, savouring the doubleness of a single experience:

> *Et tu te réjouis, petit,*
> *Car voici que ta belle gaule,*
> *Jalouse aussi d'avoir son rôle,*
> *Vite, vite, gonfle, grandit,*
>
> *Raidit. . . . Ciel! la goutte, la perle*
> *Avant-courrière, vient briller*
> *Au méat rose: l'avaler,*
> *Moi, je le dois, puisque déferle*
>
> *Le mien de flux.*

Or, more explicitly, and in dreadful prose:

> While I give I am given. The same storm, the same upheaval. One never has this with a man, his experience hidden as mine is. But two women have the same nerves. The merest flick of my finger on her clitoris hidden like a pearl in its folds alerts its head and my own throbs touched as surely as by a hand. [Kate Millet, *Flying*]

Are there moral consequences to be drawn from this dissimilarity between heterosexual and homosexual desire? In particular, is this the true basis of the frequent (whether or not erroneous) condemnation of homosexuality? As a preliminary to discussing that question, we must arm ourselves with a concept of sexual perversion.

10

PERVERSION

Talk of sexual perversion is rejected, both by those who see it as a threat to their sexual practices and by those who believe it to rely upon a discredited concept of normality. Is there anything to be said about the idea of sexual 'normality', other than that it records a double confusion – between human sexual desire and animal 'tumescence', and between the norms of biological existence and the obligations of the moral life? Certainly, contemporary writing on the subject of perversion has often shown little awareness of what is at stake. Freud, for example, describes as perverted any sexual impulse which is diverted from the 'biologically normal' aim of sexual union – i.e. the aim which, in favourable circumstances, leads to procreation.[1] Hence all acts which do not involve or tend towards the insertion of the penis into a female vagina are, for Freud, 'abnormal', and the disposition to perform them 'aberrant', 'deviant' or 'perverted'. Freud refrains from drawing any moral conclusions from this description, aware of the moral fragility of the concept that is expressed in it. In which case, it could fairly be said that he has not really introduced a concept of perversion at all, but merely a concept of variety. For is it not part of human nature to go beyond the limited repertoire of conduct which is instilled in us by our simian instincts? In other words is not Freud's 'abnormality' precisely what is normal, in beings like us?

Clearly, the first task for any theory of perversion is to analyse the idea of normality. This idea has an important place in biological science, enabling us to draw a vital distinction without which the concept of a species would be of dubious explanatory value: the distinction between the normal and the average. Suppose all lions were smitten with a plague which caused them to lose their manes. The average lion would then be without a mane. But the normal lion would still retain one – despite lacking the privilege of existence. In such circumstances all existing lions would be abnormal. The normal lion is the one which typifies leonine nature – the one which lives, flourishes and declines, in accordance with the laws of its kind. The concept of a species is already definitive, therefore, of a biological norm.

If our idea of sexual normality is governed by biological thinking, we shall indeed agree with Freud in limiting normal sexual performance to the straightforward act of heterosexual copulation, together with its preliminaries and sequels. In which case, we shall have to describe many acts which occur quite naturally and spontaneously between heterosexual couples as abnormal. Fellatio, for example, and cunnilingus, both of which have immense symbolic significance, and neither of which can be excluded from the natural lyricism of the kiss. Consider Thomas Carew on the subject of cunnilingus:

> And, where the beauteous region doth divide
> Into two milky ways, my lips shall slide
> Down those smooth alleys, wearing as I go
> A tract for lovers on the printed snow;
> Thence climbing o'er the swelling Appenine
> Retire into thy grove of eglantine,
> Where I will all those ravished sweets distill
> Through love's alembic, and with chemic skill
> From the mixed mass one sovereign balm derive,
> Then bring that great elixir to thy hive.
> ['A Rapture']

Of course fellatio or cunnilingus performed in isolation from the rest of love-making – by someone for whom this is the *only* means of sexual expression – is a very different act from fellatio conducted 'in the course' of normal desire. And it is also true that this uniting of the face – symbol of the self-conscious perspective – with the sexual organ – symbol of the body's ultimate dominion – has a moral significance which changes the meaning of our sexual stratagems. Nevertheless, to exclude these acts from the exercise of normal desire for those reasons alone is to deprive the idea of normality of any truly human significance.

As a matter of fact, one could quite reasonably refuse to use the concept of perversion of animal activity. Consider anal intercourse – a practice certainly not unknown in the animal kingdom, whether between male and female, or between male and male. Such a phenomenon surely demands no special explanation, and certainly no explanation in terms of the 'perversion' of an instinct. That an animal should desire to insert his member into this particular orifice – or indeed into any orifice – is profoundly unsurprising, given his propensity to insert it into that orifice which is its 'natural' home. For, judged from the point of view of animal perception, the two orifices are alike: warm, passive, toothless and reeking of 'species life'. It is not even necessary to assume the existence of a mistake, in order to explain this 'natural' buggery.

It is only when we consider human intercourse that these innocent pastimes of the animals begin to require special explanation. For human sexual intercourse is mediated by, and expressive of, a conception of itself. Hence it demands explanation in intentional terms. Practices which are unavailable to the animal – practices involving elaborate fantasies, such as foot fetishism – are available to the human. And the innocent gambols of the animals here become as susceptible to judgement as the unfamiliar practices with which human ingenuity has embellished them. To the sociobiologist there can be nothing abnormal in the following behaviour, which, on one interpretation, displays the exemplary concern of a set of genes for the resources necessary for their survival. Imagine, however, a concept of perversion that did not apply to its human equivalent!

> The mantis is almost the only insect with a neck; the head does not join the thorax immediately, the neck is long and flexible, bending in all directions. Thus, while the male is enlacing and fecundating her, the female will turn her head back and calmly eat her companion in pleasure. Here is one headless, another is gone up to the corsage, and his remains still clutch the female who is thus devouring him at both ends, getting from her spouse simultaneously the pleasures *ac mensa ac thoro*, both bed and board from her husband. The double pleasure only ends when the cannibal reaches the belly: the male then falls in shreds and the female finishes him on the ground. Poiret has witnessed a scene perhaps even more extraordinary. A male leaps on a female and is going to couple. The female turns her head, stares at the intruder, and decapitates him with a blow of her jaw-foot, a marvellous toothed-scythe. Without disconcertion the male wedges up, spreads himself, makes love as if nothing abnormal had happened. The mating took place, and the female had the patience to wait for the end of the operation before finishing her wedding breakfast.[2]

To put the matter shortly, what is biologically 'normal' is governed by the demands of the species. But this may be neither 'normal' conduct for a rational being nor compatible with what is so. Norms of rational conduct and norms of animal activity may in fact be totally incommensurable. It is, for example, conceivable that all straightforward sexual activity might be described as perverted. Plato certainly came near to describing ordinary heterosexual intercourse in such a way. And later writers – St Paul and St Jerome among them – were inclined to think the same of any sexual activity whatsoever, on grounds to which I have already referred.

There is, however, a strong tradition – represented at its most serious in the teachings of the Roman Catholic Church – which recognises that the concept of perversion can be legitimately applied only to the conduct of a rational being, and also argues that it is to be explained in terms of the *animal* process of biological reproduction. The tradition has recently been defended by Elizabeth Anscombe, who argues roughly as follows.[3] The normal sexual act is intrinsically generative. This fact is a datum, upon which the intention of those who make love is (in the normal case) founded. Because the generative character of the act belongs to its very nature, it constitutes part of the 'description under which' it is intended. Not that the normal act is always the expression of an intention to have children; rather that it is the expression of an intention to perform an intrinsically generative act. And this fixes the moral character of the action: this is what normal sexual intercourse *is*, from the moral point of view. All other forms of sexual intercourse are therefore essentially deviant; and, Anscombe adds, condemnable on account of their deviance.

It is fair to say that few philosophers have found Anscombe's argument satisfactory.[4] It seems to have the consequence that not only contraceptive intercourse, but also heterosexual intercourse with someone known to be infertile, are deviant (and also condemnable) *in the same way, and for the same reason as*, homosexual intercourse: a result which is extremely counter-intuitive, even for someone who believes all three kinds of intercourse to be morally wrong. Moreover, the argument, if valid, would imply that the sexual act performed by people ignorant of the facts of human reproduction is intrinsically deviant, while homosexual acts performed in the mistaken hope of inducing pregnancy in a male are perhaps not. Now it is equally true that our *knowledge* of the consequences of what we do is an important part of our doing it – both because it modifies our intentions and because it changes the description of the act. And it is certainly true that our disposition to divorce the sexual act from reproduction has brought about a vast, and morally significant, change in the project of love-making. Clearly, practices which remove the likelihood that new and wholly overwhelming personal responsibilities will issue from an act can change the moral nature of the act. (Thus Germaine Greer has argued, vaguely but not implausibly, that contraception has induced a widespread 'demystification' of the human body.)[5] But to use such insights as the sole basis for the complex morality of sexual conduct, and to assume that they generate an idea of 'normality' that would be useful in the description and explanation of human sexual behaviour, is to hang too complex a moral argument on too fragile a conceptual peg. Whatever conclusions are to be drawn about the morality of 'infertile' acts must depend upon far wider assumptions about human nature, and cannot be derived from the fluctuating intentionality of infertile intercourse.

We must look elsewhere, too, for an account of the 'norm' of sexual conduct. For it is seriously to be doubted that a theory which implies that contraception is a perversion, perhaps as much a perversion as bestiality or necrophilia, will really enable us to capture what is repellent in those latter vices. Can we derive a concept of perversion that achieves that purpose, while resting upon foundations as objective as those that we can give to the idea of the biologically normal? As I have emphasised throughout this work, human nature is dual: we are both animals and rational persons. And it is quite clear that in many of its employments reason determines norms which govern its own activity. For many of the activities of reason – logic, mathematics, scientific inference and so on – there is clearly no room for the suggestion that these norms are 'subjective', in a way that the norms of biology are not. However, matters become immensely more complex when we address ourselves, not to rational argument, but to the nature of the rational being himself. The rational being is a personal being, characterised not only by his ability to reason but also by his possession of a first-person perspective, responsibility and the rich interpersonal emotional life which those entail. Is there room for a serious idea of normality, that will distinguish those who flourish according to the laws of this 'personal' existence from those who do not?

In attempting to give an affirmative answer to that question, I shall be following a path trodden by Aristotle, in his *Nicomachean Ethics* and elsewhere. I shall be attempting to give a theory of human nature which will be sufficiently rich to give grounds for distinguishing the flourishing from the declining varieties. In the present chapter I shall confine myself to a discussion of the normality inherent in sexual desire. In the chapter which follows I shall incorporate my remarks into a wider theory of human virtue, which will show, I hope, that the Aristotelian approach to these questions succeeds in providing the objective basis for what is, in effect, a moral doctrine.

The human person is a human artefact, the product of the social interaction which he also produces. He can exist only in those conditions which permit the emergence of a first-person perspective – in other words, only when attached to the public linguistic practices which give sense to the concept of the self. He is by nature, therefore, a social being, not merely in the sense of being made for society, but in the stronger sense of being made *by* society. Hence we must count among his most important motives the interpersonal attitudes which express his recognition of his social nature. As I shall show more fully in the next chapter, these attitudes are not merely necessary to our happiness; they are also constitutive of our personal existence. A person who lacks them is, in a real sense, 'depersonalised'. In other words, these attitudes are elements of normal human nature, and to lack them is to be a deviant. (If there is any basis to the idea of a 'psychopath' it lies in this lack of interpersonal response.)

It is this fact which makes it useful to introduce a concept of perversion into our description of human desire. Sexual desire involves the marshalling and directing of animal urges towards an interpersonal aim, and an interpersonal fulfilment. It is, moreover, a powerful and all-consuming motive. Our life-projects coalesce about it, and are little able to place obstacles in its path. Hence we think of sexual desire as at one and the same time an animal force which overtakes us, and a personal choice whose direction expresses our will. In desire we experience the unity of our animal and personal nature, and our sense of the first as governed by an objective norm transmits itself to our perception of the second. I believe that the concept of perversion which explains the sense that perversion is morally contaminated is also that which has the greatest explanatory value: the concept which describes as perverted all deviations from the unity of animal and interpersonal relation. We may, whether or not wittingly, detach the sexual urge from its interpersonal intentionality, and reconstitute it in impersonal, and purely 'bodily', terms. This is not just a case of bad manners: it is not like the habit of the gluttonous eater who, overcome by animal compulsion towards the food that lies before him, ignores the presence of his companion, and sets to like a pig at a trough. In sexual desire the companion is also the *object* of what is felt, and what is done is done *to* him. The complete or partial failure to recognise, in and through desire, the personal existence of the other is therefore an affront, both to him and to oneself. Moreover, in so divorcing sexual conduct from the impulse of accountability and care, we remove from the sphere of personal relations the major force which compels us to unite with others, to accept them and to compromise our lives on their account. In other words, we remove what is deepest in ourselves – our life – from our moral commerce, and set it apart, in a realm that is free from the sovereignty of a moral law, a realm of curious pleasure, in which the body is both sovereign and obscene. This, I believe, is the major structural feature of perversion, and the feature which justifies the moral condemnation of perverted desire, and also introduces a distinction that facilitates the explanation of its nature.

Before going on to illustrate those remarks, it is worth distinguishing the theory prefigured in them from that given by Thomas Nagel, in his article on sexual perversion.[6] While the suggestions made by Nagel agree in outline with what I have written, they differ in one crucial detail. Nagel considers perversion to involve 'truncated or incomplete versions of the complete configuration'.[7] In other words, perversion has to be seen as a limitation or distortion of sexual development. Since Nagel describes this development in terms of the interpersonal nature of desire, his suggestion is very close to mine. However, the reference to a natural 'development' introduces an extraneous element. It could equally be said that the sexual impulse *naturally* develops in the way that I have called perverted. It might even be said that some forms of perversion are fully achieved, and by no means truncated, versions of the sexual impulse. The important feature is not their 'potential' and 'unrealised' nature, but rather their successful realisation of a divorce between the animal and the personal: their successful dividing of our personal existence from that force which most powerfully expresses the fact that we are alive. (Thus his reading of Kant's moral philosophy, which seems to argue for such a division, led D. H. Lawrence, in a letter, to condemn Kant as 'one of the great perverts'.)

As Nagel points out, however, a perversion is not an act but a disposition – in other words, a motive from which actions spring. Many otherwise normal people have on occasion experimented with sexual novelties: only the acquisition of a disposition can justify the judgement that a particular desire is perverted. For only in such a case can we see a fundamental turning away of the sexual impulse from its normal goal of union with another. Only in such a case is it appropriate to consider that the direction and focus of sexual desire has changed. (Compare the lover who, in an access of passion, bites his beloved, with the lover whose sexual pleasure is entirely focused in this act.)

At the same time, it should be recognised that people cannot easily see their sexual behaviour as a sequence of isolated acts. On the contrary, any encounter may seem to be 'revelatory' of an otherwise hidden inclination. A person can seldom give way 'just once' and think no more of it. A particular encounter, which involves the heights of sexual arousal, may reverberate through one's life, gathering to itself the significance of every subsequent longing. The experience is recorded by Cavafy, in a poem entitled 'One Night':

> And there, on that ordinary, plain bed,
> I had love's body, I had the lips,
> The delicious red lips of drunkenness,

Red lips of such drunkenness that now,
As I write – after so many years –
In my lonely house, I am drunk again.

The poet had, not a particular human body, but 'love's body' (*to sōma tou erōtos*), and the experience has no detail beyond its drunkenness (*methē*), and the red lips, which breathlessly compel us through the verse to the point where drunkenness returns (*methō xana*). This 'emotion recollected in anxiety' is the present tribute to a desire which found its goal. Always, in the willing sexual encounter, the act absorbs and troubles the agent, and provides the motive and the desire for its own repetition. Were it otherwise, Anna Karenina should have had no reason to fear Vronsky, or to warn him that, should she fall, it would be without hope of a remedy.

To illustrate my meaning, I shall consider certain standard examples of sexual desire that have been called 'perverted', and ask whether, and, if so, how, they deserve this label. I shall consider bestiality, necrophilia, paedophilia, sadism, masochism, homosexuality, incest, fetishism and masturbation. While all these have been frequently condemned as immoral, not all are now considered perverted, and not all are everywhere condemned or, where condemned, condemned for the same reason. All, however, repay examination, since between them they illustrate the major problems which must be confronted by any attempt to derive a morality of sexual conduct.

Bestiality

Unless the victim of delusions, the person who copulates with an animal is aware, first, that this act cannot have, for the animal, the significance that it has for him, and secondly, that the animal can make no moral demands on him, can feel neither shame nor embarrassment, can respond with no assumption of responsibility and no personal commitment. The bestial person may not share the thoughts that I have tried to convey – he may not recognise, for example, that animals cannot be aroused – but he will know that what he is doing with this animal could not be done, in the same frame of mind, with another human. Or if he does not know this, it is because the distinction between the animal and the personal has been abolished for him. In one of the most impressive descriptions of bestiality – Ovid's account of Pasiphaë's desire for the bull – the poet recognises, in fact, that the distinction between the animal and the personal has been momentarily abolished. Pasiphaë, observing the natural sexual habits of her lord, is moved to jealousy of the cow which sports before him in the field, and slightingly refers to its foolish belief that it is more beautiful than she:

> Aspice, ut ante ipsum teneris exultet in herbis:
> Nec dubito, quin se stulta decere putet.
> [Ars Amatoria, 315–16]

In her fury Pasiphaë orders the offending cow to be dragged from the herd and submitted, undeserved, to a feigned sacrifice. The poet's description of Pasiphaë at the altar, holding in exultant hands the entrails of her fancied rival, conveys a most penetrating image of the absurdity of Pasiphaë's desire, which has caused her to regard, not only a bull, but the whole species to which he belongs, in personal terms, and to attribute to a cow the human responsibility without which this jealousy and this exultation would be incoherent.

It might be said that, precisely because Pasiphaë has translated her lover from animal to person, her desire is no longer bestial. The truly bestial desire remains locked in the sense of the *merely* animal nature of its object. For the truly bestial person, jealousy would indeed be impossible, as would shame before the object of desire. All the 'trouble' of desire is vanquished in his mind, with the abolition of the conditions which create it. Here lie both the appeal of bestiality and the real source of the common revulsion which it inspires. The bestial person sees himself as he sees the object of desire: a 'mere' animal, acting in a realm where no moral idea troubles the senses, a realm from which the crippling awareness of the other's perspective has been removed. This realm, where responsibility is no longer recorded in the intentional structure of experience, is safer than the human world. He who enters it is untroubled by the sacred, and unafflicted by the knowledge that, in joining his body to another, he has compromised his self.

But it is precisely in that loss of 'trouble' that he proves offensive. His act is a 'pollution' – a violation of the body's sanctity. His act is abhorrent, not *merely* because it denies the interpersonal intentionality of desire, but, specifically, because it does so by being *obscene*. It voids the body of the spirit which distinguishes it, and exchanges the trouble of human intercourse for the curious pleasure of a palpitating gland. The sexual act is detached from its meaning and reduced to a spasm of the flesh.

Bestiality provides, in fact, a paradigm of perversion: of the sexual act set outside the current of interpersonal union, and at the same time poisoned by an obscene thought. Note that there are two related aspects to the phenomenon: loss of interpersonal intentionality, and obscenity. Perversion illustrates the true moral danger of obscenity, which, by polluting the sexual act, in effect renders it *unusable* as a form of personal union. All thought and emotion stop at the act itself, and at the body as it is revealed in the act: defiant, spiritless and decaying. The body becomes *opaque* to the person who is embodied in it, and all union with him must therefore bypass sexual congress and establish itself in other terms. The conditions for the generation of erotic love have been destroyed. (Hence shame, which forbids obscene perception, is the shield of love.)

Bestial desire cannot, therefore, be an expression of love. It is at best ancillary to love. For although men may love animals, they cannot love them *through* desire.[8] If they seem to do so, it is because, like Pasiphaë, they have come to believe that the object of desire is also a person. The legend which would have Zeus disguise himself as a swan, in order to satisfy his desire for Leda, is no legend of human love. Nor could Zeus have satisfied, through this metamorphosis, the desire which prompted it. His desire was to induce love for *himself*, and thereby to cause arousal. But, if Leda believed the creature which mounted her to be a swan, it becomes ridiculous to think that her desire was also a form of love. If she loved the swan, it was not through her desire, but in spite of it. This is perhaps why Yeats describes the scene as one of rape:

> A sudden blow: the great wings beating still
> Above the staggering girl, her thighs caressed
> By the dark webs, her nape caught in his bill,
> He holds her helpless breast upon his breast.
> How can those terrified vague fingers push
> The feathered glory from her loosening thighs?

This detachment from erotic love is a mark of all perversion. And in bestiality the sharpest severance exists between the emotional possibilities which lie before the person and the life of sexual expression through which he might have focussed them.

This severance also provides a clue to the explanation of bestiality. Bestiality is a kind of moral disability, a fear of confrontation with the perspective of another, a fear of being sexually *known*. Such a fear is by no means easy to describe: but it is a common occurrence, and we are all, to some extent, acquainted with it.

Necrophilia

Precisely the same explanation may apply to the case in which the 'object' of desire (if it can be so described) is neither animal nor person, but the dead relic of both. In a sense necrophilia shows the process of perversion at its most accomplished, with the separation between sexual impulse and interpersonal emotion made absolute by death, and by the consequent extinction of the other's perspective. Moreover the body has been made opaque by death: it is repulsive to us precisely as it is repulsive when obscenely perceived. Its warmth and vitality have vanished, and nothing remains but flesh, which has no destiny besides decay. Congress with this body pollutes the body that touches it, and renders it obscene. It also pollutes the body of the dead, for it displays obscenely that which we must still perceive, if we can, as the image of a human soul. (Hence necrophilia used to be called 'corpse prophanation'.)[9]

It is said of James I that he would, when hunting, command the newly slaughtered stags to be cut open so that he could insert his member into the smoking entrails. It is difficult to say whether this act is more, or less, perverted than the usual practice of the necrophiliac, who expends his energies on a human body. But it should be said that such a necrophiliac does, in a sense, desire a person. However, it is an extinguished person, one who now has no knowledge of what is happening to his body. Once again, it is necessary to distinguish true necrophilia from its false simulacrum. A grieving lover will naturally clasp the dead body of his beloved and give kisses to what lacks the life to welcome them. The agony of grief may go further, in response to what Keats described as 'love; cold – dead indeed, but not dethroned':

> In anxious secrecy they took it home,
>   And then the prize was all for Isabel:
> She calm'd its wild hair with a golden comb,
>   And all around each eye's sepulchral cell
> Pointed each fringed lash; the smeared loam
>   With tears, as chilly as a dripping well,
> She drench'd away: – and still she comb'd, and kept
>   Sighing all day – and still she kiss'd and wept.
> [*Isabella*, LI]

But clearly such passion is the pathetic survival of an unsatisfiable desire, and perverted, if at all, only in the imaginations of those who see it so. In true necrophilia, the subject wants the other not to exist – he may even rejoice in his non-existence. For the removal of the other's perspective is a necessary condition of the necrophiliac's desire. The necrophiliac's embrace is a safe version of the stolen kiss, in which all danger of discovery has been neutralised. (Hence necrophilia is prefigured in sexual intercourse with a drugged or somnolent person: cf. Kleist's *Die Marquise von O.*)

The appeal of necrophilia, like that of bestiality, lies in the freedom from the anxiety of personal knowledge. However, the necrophiliac is not necessarily bestial: he may not wish to see the other as an animal; but may wish him to retain the distinctive marks of humanity, so as to satisfy himself upon a body which *might* have responded with a personal desire. He is then able to enjoy the phantom of sexual satisfaction, by breathing into the other's body the imaginary life which, because it issues from his will, presents no obstacles to his will, and represents no perspective other than his own.

We can see an important distinction emerging in the realm of sexual perversion, between the perversion that is mediated by a fantasy object and the perversion that is not. The second – the 'pure' perversion – involves the total abolition of the other, and, for that very reason, is hard to understand. For what could possibly be the pleasure in a pure necrophilia, which might not be better and less shamefully provided by a leather jerkin? It is the 'impure' necrophilia which fits best with our sense of what the necrophiliac is 'up to'. We can understand his act, to the extent that we can see it as a *substitute* for human intercourse, in which the subject fills the gap between his action and its meaning with fantasies of another's arousal. Thus he restores at the level of imagination some of the intentionality of desire. At the same time, his body, engaged in an act of depersonalised intercourse, displays that separation between the interpersonal and the sexual which is the mark of perverted desire and the natural focus of obscene perception.

Paedophilia

Necrophilia is the most absolute form of perversion, in which the other's existence is regarded as a threat to the sexual endeavour. In other perversions, the other is wanted, not in absent, but in diminished, form. The paradigm case is paedophilia, in which the other is wanted, not in spite of the fact that he is a child, but *because* he is a child. There is a natural instinct to cherish what is young, and to vent our desires upon what is fresh and beautiful. The paedophile, however, directs his attentions not to a 'young human being', but to a 'child'. The difference here parallels that between sex and gender. The idea of the childlike belongs not to material, but to intentional, understanding. It records our sense that the life of the person is divided into two episodes, the one a prelude to the other. The child is the creature – however developed in physical form – whose personal nature is as yet unformed, who cannot bear the full weight of interpersonal responses, and in particular who is regarded as only partly responsible for what he says and does. The child is the prelude to the person, and with a child full reciprocity is neither possible nor desirable. In the tenderness of desire it is natural to wish to protect the other as one protects a child. But this feeling is no more than a premonition of the ultimate privacy of the sexual bond, and of its domestic fulfilment – its fulfilment *apart from* the world:

> Tree you are
> Moss you are,
> You are violets with wind above them.
> A child – *so* high – you are,
> And all this is folly to the world.
> [Ezra Pound, 'A Girl']

When the childhood of the other plays a constitutive role in desire, desire is deflected from its interpersonal aim. Like the bestial man and the necrophiliac, the paedophile cannot surrender himself to the full challenge of another perspective, but must confine his attentions to that which he can also control.

It would be a mistake, however, to think that paedophilia is *one* thing. The paedophile may indeed be moved by the unformed personality of the object of his desire. But he may also be moved by a more subtle emotion. There is, in all our dealings with children, a disposition to consider the child as 'innocent' – innocent, that is, of the polluted motives which govern the lives of adults. We look on children in two incompatible ways. On the one hand, they are pre-moral, unable to do wrong because unable to do right. On the other hand, they are 'innocent', acting always from pure motives which justify our praise. The truth of the matter is simple: children are partially moral, and act sometimes rightly, sometimes wrongly, but never with full responsibility for what they do. This is a truth that we put out of mind. By looking on the child as innocent, we connive at our own desire to make him so. We protect him from evil motives by supposing that he cannot have them.

One of the most important ingredients in this idea of innocence is that of sexual unreadiness. For reasons that I shall consider more fully in the next chapter, our perception of sexual development involves an image of 'initiation'. This image is sometimes given objective reality in a ceremony, conducted perhaps by a priest. But, even in the absence of such ceremonies, the image persists, playing an important role in the traditional conception of marriage, and also in the less institutionalised modern form of commitment. The divide between virgin and non-virgin is one that we seek to align with that between child and adult, and, even if this alignment is without ultimate justification, it causes us to establish, as a legal principle, that sexual intercourse ought not to occur before the 'age of consent'. This legal fiction denotes the age of responsibility, the age when the person is complete.

Sexual initiation abolishes the inhibition that postpones the habit of intercourse. We desire that initiation should not occur before the 'age of innocence' has expired, since we desire sexual expression to be withheld until it can exist as an interpersonal response. Our perception of the moral innocence of the child is therefore combined with a powerful interdiction: not to awaken in the child an interest in these things which are forbidden to him. This interdiction – which the Freudians call a 'tabu' – is something more than an irrational prejudice. And it is precisely what excites the greatest transport in the paedophile, who seeks to relive the child's experience of forbidden things, so as to recreate the excitement of uncovering them. He re-enacts the primal curiosity, when certain parts of the body, certain words, certain actions, attracted a magic quality of forbidden pleasure, and when the 'unveiling' of sexual arousal was prefigured in the 'naughtiness' of the sexual game. Although elements of this prurience survive into adult life, becoming a source of humour and of the gestures whereby some people overcome the embarrassing preludes to desire, we do not hesitate to describe the adult whose sexual impulses remain fixated upon the world of childish 'naughtiness' as perverted – even though the child, who lives in that world, is not. The adult looks upon that world from a mature perspective which it cannot contain – the perspective of one who knows. His curiosity is really 'knowingness', a leering familiarity with actions whose naughtiness he wishes to preserve, in the form of an obscene perception. For the responsible being, there cannot be naughtiness in the sexual act, even though there can be sin. The pursuit of the naughty is simply another way of refusing to enter the sexual encounter with one's responsibility engaged, while relishing the obscene opacity of the body.

The Freudian 'discovery' of childhood sexuality has no real relevance to the above account of paedophilia. It is true that children feel sexual urges, and attach these urges to this or that object of affection. But the resulting emotion cannot have the intentional structure of desire. A child can be sexually excited by an adult, and can obtain sexual pleasure. But the result will not be desire for the adult, nor will it express knowledge of, and consent towards, the adult's own desire. The child's feeling may, in the course of time, grow into desire, as he grows into personhood. But the desire will be poisoned by the memory of its origins. Like the desire of Lara for Komarovsky in *Dr Zhivago*, it will be felt as a compulsion, a defilement, a 'vileness', and hence as an obstacle to sexual fulfilment.

Sado-masochism

As I have already argued in Chapter 6, sado-masochism must be understood as a relatively normal part of the canon of sexual possibilities, in which an intelligible moral relation between effective equals finds embodiment in a sexual act. Nevertheless, sado-masochism also has its perverted form. Here the perversion consists, not so much in a failure to confront the other as a person, but in the failure to acknowledge him. To understand the perverted nature of sadism, however, one must understand the moral character of slavery, of which it is a sexual embodiment.

Only rational beings can be enslaved, and only rational beings are enslavers. The domestic horse is trained into unnatural habits of conformity, but, having acquired them, he exists equably within their constraints, the victim of no injustice and the object of no abuse.[10] Slavery is a particular solution to the problem of human conflict. By conferring stable dominion on one party and subjugating the other, it gives a single, and non-paradoxical, answer to the questions of collective choice.[11] In a famous passage Hegel argued that enslavement is the first resolution of something which he called the 'life and death struggle'[12] with the other. This life and death struggle results from the self's need to affirm itself against others, and to compel their recognition of its freedom. Without this recognition, Hegel argues, the self is essentially incomplete, being without 'self-certainty' – without the sense of its objective reality as a free and estimable agent in the public world. In resolving the life and death struggle by a trial of strength, one side wins the power to deprive the other of life. To kill the other, however, is to destroy the possibility of compelling the recognition that is sought – it is to forswear precisely the self-certainty that was the aim of conflict. Hence the victor must content himself with enslaving the vanquished. By presenting him at every instance with the unanswerable demands of his master's will, the master compels the slave's acknowledgement.

This project, Hegel argues, is essentially paradoxical. Precisely in the act of enslaving, the master relinquishes the power to obtain what he desires. For what he desires is not bare power, but *freedom*, in a particular, and 'positive'[13] sense of this term, according to which freedom presupposes a certain kind of social existence. Freedom in this sense is not simply the ability to obtain what one desires; it is the ability to value what one can also obtain, and to find in it confirmation of one's significance as a rational being. However, not every social order can confer this freedom upon those who belong to it. Consider the 'freedom' enjoyed by the inhabitants of Aldous Huxley's *Brave New World*, who can obtain all that they desire, and differ from us only in this: that their desires, implanted in them by those who seek to control them, add no significance to their moral life. They cannot say whether it is worthy or unworthy, wise or foolish, to possess or fulfil them. In such desires, the self of the agent is not engaged: to satisfy them is not to express oneself in an act of self-realisation, nor is it to exercise the freedom which is proper to our rational nature. The sense of oneself as present in and confirmed through one's desires requires a specific kind of social context – one in which a sense of validity can form the ground of self-esteem.

The enslavement of the other renders him incompetent to provide this context and this validity. Precisely in being compelled to respect, the slave ceases to respect. The master, hungry for recognition, cries out for it tyrannically; without it, he has power but no authority, and the slave's servile obedience is no more than an irksome reminder of the moral emptiness which his power conceals. At the same time, released from the need to labour for his advantages, the master enjoys another kind of freedom: freedom from necessity. But this freedom is the freedom of the consumer, who seeks in vain for that which will assure him of the value of his actions, and whose gratification is always abolished in the moment of attaining it.

To understand the master's predicament, we must understand also the predicament of the slave. Hegel argues that we can do this only if we first understand two fundamental components of the human world: labour and the fear of death.[14] (In what follows, as in what I have already said, I am of necessity paraphrasing radically.) It is the nature of rational activity to possess an end or purpose, and to seek to change the world so as to realise that purpose. The final end of every rational being is the building of the self – of a recognisable personal entity, which flourishes according to its own autonomous nature, in a world which it partly creates. The means to this end is labour, in the widest sense of that term: the transformation of the raw materials of reality into the living symbols of human intercourse. By engaging in this activity, man imprints on the world, in language and culture as well as in material products, the marks of his own will, and so comes to see himself reflected in the world, an object of contemplation, and not merely a subject whose existence is obscure to everyone including himself. Only in this process of 'imprinting' can man achieve self-consciousness. For only in becoming a publicly recognisable object (an object for others) does a man become an object of knowledge for himself. Only then can he begin to see his own existence as a source of value, for which he takes responsibility in his actions, and which creates the terms upon which he deals with others who are free like himself. ('Labour' is, in effect, the means to our embodiment.)

It is not my purpose in this work to give full cogency to those ideas, although I have said much that, if true, must serve to make them attractive. Notice that there are two distinct theses contained there: first, the thesis defended in Appendix 1, that self-consciousness is created by a shared public practice tantamount to language, and by the forms of life which are implied in that. Secondly, the thesis touched upon at various points in this work, that the major expression of self-consciousness is in the projection of relations of responsibility which tie one's present self to one's future self, and both to the objective world which they affect and transform. Hegel argues that the power of the master cannot amount to freedom, since it contains no active engagement with the world. The master has only a diminished sense of his own reality as a responsible agent. The slave, by contrast, does not lack that sense. On the contrary, he becomes increasingly aware of it, and aware, too, of the unjust usage which deprives him of the power to do for himself what he has the mental and physical resources both to undertake, and to value, on behalf of another. Of necessity, therefore, the slave must grow to resent his position, while the master must cease to find value in the dominion which he enjoys. The first acquires the desire to overthrow the power that oppresses him, the second loses the will to retain it. Their relation contains the seeds of its own collapse. And as it develops, the inner contradiction gradually bursts their unstable intercourse asunder, and places the slave in the master's shoes, and the master in the slave's. Thus, by the very labour which is compelled from him, the slave achieves the capacity for inner freedom; and by the very power which he exercises, the master loses all sense of value and, with it, the inner freedom that is granted to the slave. The slave embodies himself, while the master becomes subject to his body.

The outcome of this 'dialectic' – this to-ing and fro-ing of power between master and slave – is, according to Hegel, the eventual 'overcoming' of the contradiction which binds them. The relation of master and slave is transcended into that of equals, in which the partners cease to treat each other as means, and begin instead to treat each other as ends in themselves. Then, at last, in the emergence of an 'ethical' relation, the contradiction is resolved. Each now has the whole of freedom – the power to exercise it, and the social recognition that makes its exercise worthwhile. The 'recognition' that led to the original conflict requires just this resolution: it is *this* – the acknowledgement of the personal autonomy and individual right of the other – that confers the true recognition that was sought. Thus Hegel argues for the thesis that true freedom and true fulfilment necessitate obedience to the moral law and in particular to that fundamental axiom upon which morality is founded – the Kantian 'respect for persons'.

Hegel's argument is expressed in the quasi-parabolic form of the 'dialectic'. But its force is undeniable. In all human relations, there seems to be both an element of conflict – a desire to compel the other to give what is required – and a compulsion towards agreement, towards the mutual recognition that only what is given can be genuinely received. All relations which deny the *ethical* reality of the human encounter deny also the value that is sought in it, and constitute a falling away from truly personal existence. All such relations show a diminution in the personal responsibility, and personal existence, of those who engage in them.

It is, therefore, part of our nature as persons that our relations toward one another should tend of their own accord in the direction which Hegel indicates – towards mutual respect, in which each desires the other to change only through his own consent, and in which the offering of reasons takes precedence over the brandishing of force. We may now transfer this thought to the case of sado-masochism. Here too there is an intrinsic paradox in the master's (the sadist's) position. He wishes to possess the other, but also to be recognised by the other as a person and accepted accordingly. Without that recognition – without the sense of *himself* as an object in the other's perspective – the stratagems of his desire are self-defeating, and he might as well relieve himself on a dummy or a corpse. In order to become something for the other, and to force the recognition that is not freely granted, he has recourse to suffering. Through causing pain he comes to *count* in the other's perspective. This strategy has, I believe, both a normal and an abnormal course. In the normal course, the aspect of pain inflicted and endured becomes incorporated into the love-play of the partners, and is thereby transcended. It gains a symbolic force in the physical tumult of the sexual act, and the masochist, by wanting his affliction, redeems the sadist from the guilt of inflicting it. Both can take pleasure in the other's desire, without reducing the other to a mere instrument of desire. In this 'normal' course, the sado-masochistic impulse is incorporated into an interpersonal relation, and so transcended in the affirmation of mutual respect.

In the perverted form of sado-masochism, however, the element of slavery remains untranscended. The sexual act expresses a perduring relation of moral bondage. The extreme form of sadism is indifferent to the other's consent, and perceives the sexual encounter as outside consent altogether, reducing the other to a state of servitude in which his existence as a free being is systematically negated. Indeed, this negation is an essential part of the sadist's aim. Both the sadist and his victim are bound together in a relationship that is essentially 'pre-personal', in the manner of Hegel's master and slave. Hence desire is experienced as a move out of the interpersonal sphere into another and darker realm. Sadism is perverted, in that it seeks to abolish the personal object of desire from the sexual act and replace him with a compliant dummy. The victim is erased from the sadist's intentionality and replaced by a fantasy of the sadist's own devising. The sadist, like the necrophiliac, the paedophile and the rapist, can accept the other only on terms that are dictated by himself. In an important sense he creates the other in the sexual act, writing upon the *tabula rasa* of his body the lines of a secret drama. The other's body is the means to accomplish a private ceremony. Through pain the sadist hopes to animate this body, to make it obedient to the fantasy with which he 'ensouls' it. But pain can produce only the dull refusal to recognise the right of the tyrant, the negating stare of resentment, which Sartre discerns in the dying eyes of Faulkner's Christmas.[15] Thus the project of sadism, in negating the other, negates itself, and is left in the end with nothing but the obscene contemplation of the body's triumph.

Similar observations apply to masochism, which, like sadism, may exist in perverted or in unperverted form. Freud describes masochism as 'sadism turned against itself'.[16] The description is plausible, though perhaps no more plausible than the description of sadism as 'masochism turned against itself'. The desire to enslave the body of the other may be matched by the other's desire to see his own body in just such terms. Equally, the desire to be seen as the inflictor of pain may be matched by a desire to see the tormentor as 'beyond morality', a creature in the grip of destructive frenzy, a kind of punishing machine, such as that devised by the officer in Kafka's *Penal Settlement*. This explains the dominant character of the obscenities of sado-masochism, in which parts of the body are as it were detached by pain, becoming isolated lumps of flesh, attended to with a close, tender relish for the painful sensation contained in them. H. S. Ashbee, the Victorian collector of pornographic curiosities, quotes an interesting description from *Venus School Mistress*:

'The machine represented in the frontispiece to this work, was invented for Mrs Berkley to flog gentlemen upon, in the spring of 1828. It is capable of being opened to a considerable extent, so as to bring the body to any angle that might be desirable. There is a print in Mrs Berkley's memoirs, representing a man upon it quite naked. A woman is sitting in a chair exactly under it, with her bosom, belly and bush exposed: she is *manualizing* his *embolon*, whilst Mrs Berkley is birching his posteriors.'[17]

The detailed psychology of sado-masochism is of course far more complicated than I can here display. There is frequently an aspect of punishment: the sadist's punishment of the other for failing to return his desire or for failing to play sincerely the role that the sadist has devised for him; the masochist's desire for punishment, which relieves him of the burden of a culpable desire. The masochist may indeed receive the strokes of the whip as a kind of 'permission' – a reassurance that he is paying here and now for his sexual transgression, and that the claims of conscience have been satisfied. Again, Ashbee provides a useful illustration:

'Fear and shame were both gone: it was as though I were surrendering my person to the embraces of a man whom I so loved I would anticipate his wildest desires. But no man was in my thoughts; Martinet was the object of my adoration, and I felt *through the rod* that I shared her passions. . . . When the rods were changed, I continued to jump and shout, for she liked that, but – believe me or not – I saw my nakedness with her eyes, and exulted in the lascivious joy that whipping me afforded her.'[18]

However, such a masochism – through and through saturated by a moral idea – is far from obviously perverted. The girl is thinking *lascivious* thoughts, but they are not obscene thoughts: on the contrary, they form part of a sincere erotic giving of herself to another. In such examples we see the reciprocity that can emerge between sadist and masochist. The concentration is not on the body and its sufferings but on the moral idea of chastisement. Such sado-masochism is the extreme case of the 'normal' sado-masochism – the 'lover's pinch' – that I described in Chapter 6.

Perverted sado-masochism is not without its intimacies and *petits soins*. But they are the intimacies and cares of contempt and hatred. The person who truly desires the *suffering* of another, and for whom this is not just an erotic game, is at war with the truth which he perceives in his victim's eyes, the truth that the other will not, and cannot, be made anew, in accordance with the desires of his tormentor. The true sadist seeks to appropriate the flesh of the other, to remake it through pain, to sculpt from its compliant matter the perfect object of possession. And such an attitude – which transgresses the most fundamental laws of morality – can stop at nothing. Like the sadism portrayed in the novels of de Sade, it leads irresistibly to murder, and can be restrained from murder only by timidity or force.

The 'benign' forms of sado-masochism, like the transgressive forms, show the operation of the Hegelian paradox – the paradox of servitude. They also show, however, that this paradox is a normal feature of the human condition. Any human relation may collapse into a relation of servitude, and so lose the ethical dimension through which it might be resolved. Commenting on Hegel's argument, Robert Solomon describes the normal case of anxiety between those who love:

> Each person would like to be *certain* of the approval of the other, but to be certain of the other is already to lose that sense of the other as an independent judge. I want you to say 'I love you', but the last thing I would want to do is to ask you, much less to force you, to say it. I want you to say it freely, and not because I want you to or expect you to. But then, you know that I do want you to say it, and I know that you know that I want you to say it. So you say it; I don't really believe you. Did you say it because you mean it? Or in order not to hurt my feelings? And so I get testy, more demanding, to which your response is, quite reasonably, to become angry or defensive, until finally I provoke precisely what I feared all along, – an outburst of abuse. But then, I feel righteously hurt; you get apologetic. You seek forgiveness; I hesitate. You aren't sure whether I will say it or not: I'm not sure whether you mean it or not, but I say, 'I forgive you'. You wonder whether I'm really forgiving you or just trying to keep from hurting your feelings, and so you become anxious, testy, and so on.[19]

That homely summary of familiar predicaments serves to remind us of the pervasiveness in our lives of the Hegelian transition – the transition from the ethical relation to the relation of bondage, and from bondage back to mutual freedom. Poised always on this boundary, we face both ways, and, in our sexual life as in our day-to-day encounters, we may lean in either direction. What I have called the 'normal' form of sado-masochism is a strategy designed to rectify a dangerous disequilibrium, to grasp the threat of bondage and to conquer it through play. The perverted form, however, involves the collapse of personal relation, and the incorporation of the sexual act into an achieved exercise of mutual annihilation.

Homosexuality

A common modern response to the suggestion that homosexual conduct is perverted is to dismiss it as a piece of defunct ideology. Homosexual desire, it will be said, like heterosexual desire, may exist equally in perverted and in normal form, and if it is perverted it is in the same circumstances and for the same reasons that heterosexual desire is perverted. For the only difference lies in the fact that, while in heterosexual love the partners are of different sex, in homosexual love they are of the same sex. And how can *that* matter so very much, when the standard of normality derives, not from our nature as animals, but from our nature as persons?

However, while the conclusion is plausible, it is necessary to reconsider the argument which leads to it. For this argument confuses sex and gender. In so far as homosexuality has been considered to be a distinct phenomenon, it is because people have recognised, and judged to be morally significant, the disposition to desire those who are of the same *gender* as oneself. The masculine and the feminine denote two distinct kinds of person, and the experience of gender plays a significant part in determining the intentional content of desire. Homosexual desire may retain the interpersonal intentionality that is normal to us; but there may yet be a moral difference between homosexual and heterosexual conduct. The correct position, I believe, is this: homosexuality is perhaps not in itself a perversion, although it may exist in perverted forms. But it is *significantly* different from heterosexuality, in a way that partly explains, even if it does not justify, the traditional judgement of homosexuality as a perversion. I say this with extreme tentativeness, and knowing that it may be received as an outrage. My purpose, however, is not to condemn, but to elucidate, and if the truth is uncomfortable, this will not be the only occasion of its being so.

Traditional Roman Catholic teaching condemns homosexuality and pronounces it to be perverted, at least partly on account of its procreative sterility. This reversion to a 'biological' idea of perversion is, as I have argued, wholly unsatisfactory, even if it shows a difference of moral character between the sexual relations of man and woman and the sexual relations of man and man or woman and woman. The reference to procreation is best understood as a kind of shorthand for a complex, and partly institutional, conception of human commitment, in which the sexual act gains its moral significance from its place in the formation of conjugal and filial ties. It is easy to find an *explanation* in these terms for the hostility towards homosexual conduct. The sociobiologist might argue (again, with Schopenhauer's vivid support)[20] that homosexual acts are condemned because of the threat that they pose to the survival of the genes which compel them. But the 'because' here is merely causal, and to explain is not necessarily to justify. The question is whether we can distinguish the intentional content of homosexual from that of hetero-sexual desire, so as to justify the judgement that the first has a distinct moral character, and perhaps also to justify the judgement that it diverges from the norm of interpersonal relations in the direction of obscenity.

In the last chapter, I argued that the division between the sexes has – when construed under the aspect of gender – a certain mysterious quality. The other sex is regarded as having a 'moral domain': a sphere of actions, emotions and responses which is peculiar to it, and which defines it as a 'moral kind'. And in the sexual act, the sexes confront each other through an experience that is opaque to their enquiry, involving perceptions and stratagems which are inseparable from the gender-identity of the subject who possesses them. In awakening the other's sexual feeling, you take responsibility for a transformation whose inner workings are in an important sense unknowable to you. Your own gender, which is part of your habit of self-identification, is experienced as through and through familiar to you. It has a first-person presence in you, and its inner workings are appropriated by your first-person perspective. You act, feel and respond as a woman or as a man. This appropriation of gender is nowhere more imposed upon you than in the sexual act, and in the surrounding context of desire. Precisely when most compelled to see yourself *as* a woman or *as* a man, you are confronted with the mystery of the other, who faces you from across an impassable moral divide. What you are awakening in the other is something with which you are *not* through and through familiar: you are subjecting him to a force of which you do not have first-person awareness, and yet which forms and transforms his responsibilities, with the same imperious energy as the desire which governs you. Respect for the other requires a peculiar delicacy of negotiation: each tries to express in his words and gestures his preparedness to take responsibility for the effects of this unknown thing – else he remains at least partly indifferent to the other's freedom, and indifferent to the liabilities of a personal tie. The observation was made in forthright terms by Michelet, in his fulsome encomium of womanly virtue:

> . . . the religious duo [of man and woman], in which each plays a different and most delicate role, each fearing to wound the other. For they have no common knowledge of how much they really are in accord with each other. Hence that tremulous feeling of the way, those hesitations full of anxieties, that gentle

debate between two souls which in reality are but one.[21]

The opening of the self to the mystery of another gender, thereby taking responsibility for an experience which one does not wholly understand, is a feature of sexual maturity, and one of the fundamental motives tending towards commitment. This exposure to something unknown can resolve itself, finally, only in a mutual vow. Only in a vow is the trust created which protects the participants from the threat of betrayal. Without the fundamental experience of the otherness of the sexual partner, an important component in erotic love is therefore put in jeopardy. For the homosexual, who knows intimately in himself the generality that he finds in the other, there may be a diminished sense of risk. The move out of the self may be less adventurous, the help of the other less required. In an important sense it is open to the homosexual to make himself less vulnerable and to offer, because he needs, less support.

I do not suggest that such an observation is always and everywhere valid. Nevertheless, there may be a significant absence from homosexual partnership of that aspect of erotic love which might be summarised as the 'force of destiny' – the sense that one is being compelled to put one's whole being at risk. A sociobiologist will of course say that this is nothing more (nor less) than the reflection in consciousness of the procreative urge – of the law of 'species-life' which subjects our individual choices to the imperious needs of our genes. (And there too lies the partial truth of the Catholic doctrine.) But this does not alter the fact that the intentional understanding cannot overlook the element of mystery, and of danger, which surrounds the heterosexual union.

At the same time, it should be recognised that male and female homosexuality are significantly different, just as male and female desire are different. The need for a lasting partnership takes precedence in a woman's sentiments over the immediacy of sexual excitement (or rather, sexual excitement tends to be inseparable from the feeling of dependence), while the male impulse towards new encounters may lead to promiscuity on a remarkable scale. The 'flitting' nature of Greek pederasty is beautifully conveyed by the poems included in Strato's *Musa Puerilis*, and in particular by those of Meleager, who laments that his eyes (*paidōn kunes* – 'boy-hunting hounds') repeatedly betray his soul into the trap of Aphrodite. In his incomparable description of the sexual encounter between M. de Charlus and Jupien, Proust shows the dramatic reality of a desire which knows no *inner* constraint, while being subject to an immense *outward* interdiction. The two partners recognise each other's need immediately, observe only those proprieties that are necessary to conceal their mutual desire, accomplish their union, and separate, all the while entertaining towards each other an outlook of indifference, contempt or at best (in Jupien's case) curiosity (*Sodome et Gomorrhe*).[22] The possibility of such an encounter is, I believe, enhanced by the sense that no barrier divides one from the sex of the other, that his desire is already intimately known and as ready for fulfilment as one's own. This, combined with the natural predatoriness of the male, constitutes the danger inherent in male homosexuality, and is one of the major reasons for its traditional interdiction. It also partly explains the Greek attitude to male homosexuality. As the amphorae illustrate, the phallic component is uppermost in the appeal of the *erōmenos*, a fact which is greatly relished by Sir Kenneth Dover in his trivialising book on the subject.[23] And in one poem, Meleager delights in the vision of five boys ministering to a single throbbing penis (no. 95 of Strato).

The case of female homosexuality is remarkably different – at least in so far as it has been sensitively recorded. There is not the same emphasis on the sexual organs and on the moment of sexual excitement; instead there is an extremely poignant, often helpless, sense of being at another's mercy. The lesbian knows that she desires someone who will not typically make those advances that are characteristic of a man, even if she wants to; nor can she make these advances herself without compromising the gender-identity which (she wishes to believe) is integral to her own attractiveness. She can only wait, and wish, and pray to the gods, with the troubled fervour captured by Sappho in her hymn to Aphrodite: *poikilothron athanat' Aphrodita.*

To compare the passage of Proust with the poem of Sappho is to bring together works so disparate in style and meaning as to cast doubt on any conclusion that might be drawn from the comparison. Nevertheless, the two works contain, in intensest possible form, the distillation of two complementary experiences. In the one, sexual desire is revealed as an imperative force, stayed only by social barriers and rushing forward quickly to its satisfaction as soon as these are breached. In the other, an inner hesitation, a sense of the whole personality as risked in desire, leads to the appeal for divine intervention, which will sow the seeds of love. If there is truth in the traditional attitude to homosexuality, it is partly this: the promiscuous impulse of the first of those desires is neutralised and turned against itself when it is brought into contact with the second. And the self-regarding hesitations which poison the second are swept away by its contact with the insistence of the first. Some such thought has been orthodoxy through the ages: if true, it signals an important element in heterosexual desire, which is its 'complementarity'. Desire directed towards the other gender elicits not its simulacrum but its complement.

Male desire evokes the loyalty which neutralises its vagrant impulse; female desire evokes the conquering urge which overcomes its hesitations. Often, of course, this complementarity can be re-created, either momentarily, in play, or permanently, between members of the same sex. (To signal this, Genet describes his suffering inverts in the feminine gender and uses the masculine gender for the rough criminals who excite their self-indulgent loyalty.)

I have emphasised the partly artificial nature of desire, and argued that gender distinctions, while necessary, are also socially constructed. The construction of these distinctions is not, however, arbitrary, but forms part of an attempt to understand the biological distinction between the sexes, as this affects and is revealed in social behaviour. It is impossible to establish, by philosophical argument, that the gender distinctions which we know are also inevitable. It is impossible to rule out the possibility that any 'masculine' feature of desire, and any 'feminine' feature, may disappear, without losing the fundamental tendency towards union with the other sex. Hence, it will always be possible to argue that the 'complementarity' that I have just referred to is an arbitrary or vanishing phenomenon, and that, as it vanishes, the impulse of heterosexual desire will approximate ever more closely to that of homosexual desire. But if this happens another change must also happen along with it, namely, 'the decline in the sentiment of sex'. The fact of sexual difference becomes ever less important as desire roams freely over the two sexual kinds. The idea of the moral indistinguishability of homosexual and heterosexual desire is made possible by the gradual evaporation of gender distinctions, and the construction of a new order of desire, in which what is sought in desire is not the complement, but the simulacrum, of the present feeling.

There is a traditional Christian argument against homosexuality which condemns it, not for the insult that it offers to fecundity, but for its violation of a principle of 'complementarity'. On this view, the 'impurity' of homosexual intercourse lies (according to one eminent Protestant theologian):

> in the refusal of differences and the triumph of non-differentiation i.e. disorder. Now sexual difference . . . crowns the creative action of God: the creation of the world culminates in the creation of man as man-and-woman. The couple thus experiences in their flesh the order of differentiation which structures the world. . . . [Hence] sexuality should be lived out by the man and woman as the very meaning of all differentiation, that is, recognized as a call to a relationship that is organized and creative, like a call to arms against the constant threat of disorder and chaos, whose most insidious form is the confusion of the sexes.[24]

The account is liberal with metaphors, and implies a metaphysic of creation which it is by no means easy to accept. One might legitimately object that the 'complementarity' of the two sexes is not a reflection of some underlying natural order, but a carefully constructed human artefact. People have perceived, in the easy acceptance of homosexual mores, a threat, not to the homosexual himself, but to the institutions of heterosexual union, which have been built upon subtle compromises and carefully reinforced oppositions. Even if this threat exists, however, this provides no ground for the judgement that homosexual desire is perverted. Whatever moral implication we may wish to draw from it cannot be expressed through so simple a conception.

At best, the argument from complementarity shows the presence of a *fault* in the content of homosexual desire – an imbalance which, if left uncorrected, threatens the course of love. Homosexuality could be shown to be perverted only if the homosexual act were shown to be intrinsically depersonalised or intrinsically obscene.

Now it is undeniable that many people *see* homosexual acts in that way. What horrifies them is not so much the destiny of this desire (its remoteness from an ideal of complementarity) as the fleshly quality of the act which satisfies it: the contact in arousal of woman and woman or man and man. Moreover, this perception is not centred on any particular act – buggery say – in which the parts of the body are used unusually.[25] The kiss of passion between man and man is enough to provoke it: the obscenity is seen in the arousal of the flesh by its own sexual kind.

But is homosexuality really perverted in the way that bestiality and necrophilia are perverted? Bestiality and necrophilia are *proper* objects of obscene perception: not to perceive these acts as obscene is to misperceive them. It is to have an aberrant experience, either of human embodiment or of the body itself – an experience in which the tension between them is no longer recognised. (This tension is not recognised by the most plausible natural science of man; hence the person who misperceives human sexuality frequently boasts that his is the truly scientific view: he may be right in this, and wrong only to boast of it.)

Is there anything in the homosexual act which is the *proper* object of obscene perception? A positive answer to that question must rely, I believe, on the strangeness of the other gender – on the fact that heterosexual arousal is arousal by something through and through other than oneself, and other as *flesh*. In the heterosexual act, it might be said, I move out *from* my body *towards* the other, whose flesh is unknown to me; while in the homosexual act I remain locked within my body, narcissistically contemplating in the other an excitement that is the mirror of my own. Such a suggestion is no more than that, and certainly far from a proof. Nevertheless, it connects with a key argument of the previous chapter: the argument that gender distinctions play a constitutive role in the sexual act and provide part of the 'description under which' the act is done. It is not possible to assume that the radical revision of gender perception required by the homosexual act will leave the act unchanged, and in particular that it will leave unchanged the perceived relation of the participants to their bodies. Equally, it is not possible to assume the opposite, and in particular that the changed perception involves a move towards obscenity. Of course, the obscene perception of homosexual acts has been an important part of our culture: but that neither justifies nor condemns it. The real question is, by what is this perception compelled? And it is a question which defies a simple answer.

Incest

There are many psychological explanations of what has become known as the 'incest tabu'. Interestingly enough, however, the two most popular – that of Freudian psychology and that of the sociobiologist – are in flat contradiction. For the sociobiologist, the purposes of sexual selection can be fulfilled only in a species which looks beyond its 'genetic circle' for its mating partner. There is a survival value attached to the loathing of incest; in the long run, therefore, it will emerge as a dominant psychological trait. For the Freudian, however, the incest tabu, far from expressing an innate loathing, is an acquired reaction to an innate desire. The tabu is the interiorisation of a parental edict, and masks forbidden yearnings which – in the sexual life of the mature adult – find expression in purified form, when the parent is re-created in the figure of a permitted substitute. Freud's theory is prefigured by Paley, who – in one of the few existing attempts to give a philosophical underpinning to common sexual morality – sees the forbidding of incest as a necessary caution against the evil consequences of an over-strong desire.[26]

All such theories are for us without importance. We must again remember the distinction between explanation and justification, and the power of moral thinking to breach not only social but also biological laws. If the partners love each other, and fulfil their love in the sexual act, what, asks the romantic moralist, can conceivably be wrong? The act of love is a matter of individual responsibility; one is answerable to one's partner, and not to one's genes. So where lies the fault? And what conceivable justification could there be for the judgement that incest is perverted? A mere social convention – even if it is dressed up as a law of nature – is no match for the force of love. How easy it is, therefore, to take sides with Wotan against the outraged 'moral law' of the nagging Fricke:

> *Was so schlimmes schuf das Paar,*
> *das liebend einte der Lenz?*
> *Der Minne Zauber entzückte sie:*
> *wer nüsst mir der Minne Macht?*

However, we must remember one of the vital features of the situation of the pair to whom Wotan refers. They had been separated forcibly at an early age, and had since experienced the greatest unhappiness in their relation with the 'normal' world – the world of social convention which is ruled by the law of Fricke. Biologically they are indeed brother and sister, but not socially. Indeed, they do not know at first that they are blood relations. In the place of the domestic tie of brotherhood they have only the bond of mutual 'recognition'. Their circumstances make it inescapable that their recognition should embody itself in a glance of love. In the love-glance a person submits to his destiny, as the subject of erotic emotion. The moral relation of brother and sister has there been sundered, and its fragments built anew in erotic form. The result is incest only in an abstract sense – a sense that has no immediate bearing on our moral intuitions.

Conversely, we should consider a case which has all the moral character of incest, without any risk to the genes of those involved: the case of child and step-parent. Perhaps the greatest of all tragedies of erotic love – Racine's *Phèdre* – testifies to the horror with which this union may be regarded. Phèdre herself is in no doubt about the correct description of her passion:

> *C'est moi qui, sur ce fils chaste et respectueux,*
> *Osai jeter un oeil profane, incestueux.*

And what gives credence to this description is Hippolyte's reaction to his step-mother's passion, which offends and horrifies him, precisely as the passion of someone to whom he owes loyalty of another, and incompatible kind. Nor is it merely the bond of marriage between Phèdre and Thesée that creates this feeling – as though Phèdre's passion were merely adulterous. There is an additional moral quality contained in it, by virtue of the familial relation between the partners. It is the awareness of this relation and its meaning that Hippolyte expresses in his shame. A like shame, overcome and redoubled by desire, is that of Lara, at the beginning of *Doctor Zhivago*, as she vainly struggles with her feelings for her mother's lover Komarovsky, whose base seduction seems almost as great an intrusion into domestic innocence as the intrusion of Phèdre into the honourable emotions of Hippolyte.

The important feature of these cases is also present in the normal case of 'true' incest: the violation of a domestic tie. In this violation the moral nature of incest is revealed. When a father (or step-father) seduces the girl who has grown up in his care, he does indeed violate Fricke's law: the law of the hearth. He destroys the existing filial relation and superimposes upon its ruins another, which is incompatible with it. In other words, he violates, through his desire, the responsibilities that are integral to parental love.

The threat posed by incest is a threat to the members of the household and also to the very conception of the household, as a place of open cooperation between people whose relations are settled by the mere fact of their coexistence. It is a gesture of rejection towards the *penates*, and the effective dissolution of the bond that holds the family together: the bond of piety. The obligations of erotic feeling stem from the exercise of choice – from the 'choice of love' by which we unite ourselves to the object of desire. They are bonds, not of piety, but of personal obligation. The bonds of piety which come to replace them in the family have, as their central feature, the fact that they have not been chosen. Although perhaps you chose to have a child, your obligation to *him* was not chosen in the course of your relations. Indeed it preceded his existence; it was no more chosen than was his reciprocal obligations to you who bore and nurtured him. This is not the place to explore the logical and moral peculiarities of the bond of piety. Suffice it to say that the only modern philosophy that has directed itself with any seriousness to the importance of the family in the development of the political animal – that of Hegel[27] – provides overwhelming reason for thinking that the private life of the individual must be formed around one or another form of 'natural piety'.

What then of incest? Is it a perversion? If it is, it might be argued, it is a perversion, not of the sexual act, but of the *familial* relationship. For incest builds upon a pre-established interpersonal relation that is in fact incompatible with it. It can be expressed only by destroying the most sacred of all the responsibilities that encumber the life of the rational being. Its impact on the personal life of those who engage in it is therefore essentially negative. It destroys the interpersonal relation that exists between them, while offering no commitment in its place. It works essentially *against* the development of personal feeling, and to the extent that it flourishes, it both poisons the home and impedes its dissolution: for the father who is in love with his daughter will feel jealousy at every impulse of sexual desire between his daughter and another man.

On that account, the case is distinct from that of paedophilia (the daughter may be desired only when she is an adult, and only *as* an adult), and at the same time *analogous* to paedophilia. It involves an intrusion into the innocence of at least one of the parties, and of the relation that hitherto prevailed between them. Even if we hesitate to call incest perverted, therefore, its object is not a proper object of desire. Something of intense personal value is, in this case, *threatened* by desire. The threat extends beyond the individuals in question to the whole institution of the household. If incest is a crime, therefore, it is also a political crime – one whose proliferation threatens a fundamental change in the basis of political order. Those who welcome incest may also welcome this change in the political order. But, as I shall suggest in Chapter 12, they are wrong.

If that theory is acceptable, incest is a perversion only in an attenuated sense. The threat that it poses to interpersonal relations is circumstantial, and does not reside in the act itself. In particular, incest does not have any essential reference to obscene perception. Once again, however, we must note that common morality runs counter to the suggestion. The quoted lines from Racine bear witness to the fact that incest is regarded as in itself obscene: Phèdre feels that she pollutes the chaste body of Hippolyte by the very fact of her desire. People who have lived together in domestic intimacy feel a peculiar revulsion at the thought of sexual contact between them – almost every intimacy between them may seem natural and consoling, save the intimacy that proceeds from arousal. The thought of sexual union is, for them, strange and repugnant. (Cf. Fromentin's *Dominique* – a novel concerning the love of cousins: 'to me the very idea of marrying someone whom I knew as a baby is as absurd as that of coupling two dolls'.) The case is not unlike that of homosexuality, in which a moral danger is foreseen and pre-empted by a perception of its obscenity – a perception, however, which is by no means necessary to the thing perceived.

This perception arises whenever one member of a family is forced to dwell in thought on the sexual desire of another member. Perhaps the tragedy of Hamlet ensues from such a thought, precipitated by the perception of his mother's desire. Her transference of passion, from his father (who has the moral authority of a disembodied ghost) to a man of flesh, awakens in Hamlet the sense of her body as polluted. He assails her with this perception, painting her life 'in the ranke sweat of an enseamed bed, / Stew'd in Corruption; honying and making love / Over the nasty Stye'. His own flesh appears obscenely – for it is her flesh, corrupted by the act which engendered it:

Oh that this too too solid Flesh would melt,
Thaw and resolve it self into a Dew.

The Quarto has 'sallied' (presumably 'sullied') for 'solid': a reading that places Hamlet, in this first soliloquy, firmly within the radius of obscene perception. And it is with such a perception that he later assails Ophelia, raging against the woman in her, by forcing her to see her body in depersonalised terms ('faire thought to ly between Maid's legs'). Ophelia's flesh is sullied by Hamlet's diatribes, and – before she purifies it in the water that extinguishes her – she too, in her madness, gives utterance to strange obscenities.

The poison of Hamlet's thought shows the natural history, and the catastrophe, of obscenity, and the absolute need, contained in every bond of piety, to forbid its image. One may disagree with the Freudian interpretation of the play, as a drama of covert incest, and still recognise the truth contained in it: that incest implants in the life of the family the 'invisible worm' of obscene perception.

Fetishism

The high tragedy of incest is to some extent balanced by the low comedy of fetishism – the most harmless and amusing of all perversions, and the one which (unless combined with some disposition to hurt or humiliate others) can most safely be left to the individual's discretion. That fetishism is a perversion almost goes without saying – for what could be further from a personal object than a shoe, a handbag or a brassière? But it is precisely the remoteness of the fetish from the normal object of desire that casts doubt on the idea that fetishism is perverted. It seems to be less a perverted form of sexual desire than a form of something else. In order for fetishism to look like sexual desire *at all*, an elaborate story has to be told. The activity (whatever it might be) involving the fetish must be connected by some intelligible link to the activity of sexual intercourse. Theories of fetishism are, for the most part, theories of the 'missing link'. And they divide into two broad kinds: causal and symbolic. According to the causal theory, the fetish gains its power by *association*. For example, some genuine occasion of desire (recognisable as such by normal criteria) involved the fetish in some interesting or dramatic way: thereafter the subject feels the stirrings of sexual excitement through contemplating the fetish alone, consciously or unconsciously conjuring the scene of its former employment. (Thus Sacher-Masoch, if he is to be believed, was particularly moved by the fur coat of the lady who so excited him by beating him as a child, and thereafter was moved in a similar way by fur coats, whether or not they happened to enclose a lady, and whether or not that lady was disposed to extend a disciplinary hand.)

According to the symbolic theory, the fetish acquires its power not because it is associated with sexual activity, but rather because it symbolises or represents it. The fetish stands to the object of desire, on this theory, rather as the religious image stands to the god who is worshipped or the saint who is implored. It is not, in itself, the object of desire, any more than the image is the object of worship. It serves to direct attention to, and to focus feeling upon, the *real* object of desire, which may be provided by some former or imaginary sexual episode of a wholly normal kind.

The difference between the two theories is not always noticed. Thus the Freudian theory of substitution, according to which the objects of sexual feeling may substitute for one another and desire become attached, through whatever emotional charge, to new and peculiar objects, is really a form of causal theory. It tries to explain how sexual feeling survives through the most extraordinary *change* of object. It is presented by Freud and many of his followers, however, as a symbolic theory, according to which the fetish is a symbol of something else that is the true object of desire. The symbolism is 'unconscious', but this does not alter the fact that it is, nevertheless, a form of symbolism.

The symbolic theory has the consequence that fetishism is not perverted, or not perverted in the way that its overt form suggests. For it implies that the fetish is *not* the object of desire. The object of desire, according to this theory, is not the fetish itself, but rather a fantasy object. In caressing the shoe I am caressing, in my fantasy, the woman who wears it, and my sexual excitement is directed towards her, just as my excitement on reading an erotic novel is directed towards the scene which it describes, or perhaps towards some particular person who is contained in that scene. Now it is of course undeniable that the *form* taken by fetishistic representation is peculiar. But if the purpose of the fetish is *purely* symbolic, the fetish is not the object of the sexual passion that it evokes.

Only the causal theory gives a clear picture of the *perverted* quality of fetishism. And it is this theory that was suggested when the term 'fetish' was originally borrowed from the description of primitive religion.[28] The religious fetish is itself supposed to possess the supernatural powers that are wielded by means of it. The fetish is more like an incarnation than a representation. Likewise the shoe itself possesses the sexual magic that attracts the fetishist. He caresses the shoe because he wishes to caress *it*, and because he finds his pleasure *there*.

However, it is only a being with the *power* of symbolism that can obtain this pleasure. In the rutting season stags may rub their sexual parts against the trunks of trees and bring themselves to the point of orgasm. No one would call this a 'fetishistic' impulse or think of the tree-trunk as the object of a sexual urge. It is only in people that the impulse to rub against a tree-trunk could be given such a meaning. The reason is obvious: the stag's excitement in no way depends upon his knowledge that it is a *tree* that he is rubbing against. The fetishist's excitement, by contrast, is dependent upon the thought that this, in his hand, is a *shoe* (and the very word may be breathlessly uttered as he confesses it). Here we see a structural similarity with normal sexual conduct that might lead us to describe the fetishist's impulse as one of sexual desire, and, therefore, as perverted. For he seems to focus on the shoe 'for its own sake', with just the same kind of individualising intentionality, and perhaps even a parody of the tenderness, that normal people direct towards their lovers.

If that is the true character of fetishism, however, there is no doubt that the causal theory, while being in the main correct, falls far short of explaining the fetishist's *pleasure*. From the intentional point of view, the whole activity is now shrouded in mystery. What the fetishist is *doing* with the shoe becomes utterly foreign to us and utterly opaque. And maybe that is all that mere philosophy can say.

Masturbation

The above discussion brings us to a familiar, and widely practised, form of sexual release: masturbation, accompanied, as a rule, by sexual fantasy. Masturbation exists in two forms; one, in which it relieves a period of sexual isolation, and is guided by a fantasy of copulation; the other, in which masturbation replaces the human encounter, and perhaps makes it impossible, by reinforcing the human terror, and simplifying the process, of sexual gratification. On one plausible view, only the second of these could reasonably be described as perverted, for only the second shows a bending of the sexual impulse away from interpersonal union – a bending, however, that occurs under the pressure of fantasies of sexual union.

To understand this second form of masturbation we must look a little closer at the subject of sexual fantasy. I wrote somewhat loosely above of the 'representation' of the sexual object. In order to understand the operation of sexual fantasy, however, it is necessary to distinguish representation from substitution. Something which appears to be a representation might in fact be a surrogate or substitute. For example, someone who desires to satisfy his curiosity concerning the appearance of Sophia Loren may be contented with a waxwork simulacrum. This object would be, for him, a perfect substitute. Another person, who did not wish merely to see the static form of Miss Loren, but also to observe her movements, would require a more complex device – a holograph, say. But he too could be satisfied by a substitute. Another, who desired Miss Loren, would be content with nothing short of the woman herself.

In sexual fantasy, an object is represented, often by means of a picture. But the aim is to approach as nearly as possible to a substitute for the absent object: though a substitute that is free from danger. (Hence the necrophiliac's need for the dead body of another, the body which can no longer *discountenance* him.) Sexual fantasy feeds upon modes of representation which are more like substitution than representation proper: photographs (which present what *really happened*); video films; key-hole visions; or simply mental images. Serious erotic art, which moves by suggestion, and by the interposition of thought between audience and object, is hostile to surrogates. It is concerned to excite an imaginative involvement in a genuinely erotic predicament, but not to present fantasy objects for sexual gratification. The response to erotic art is an imaginative identification with the sexual activity of another. Hence although, in a sense, it involves the invocation of fantasy, the fantasy is controlled by the artistic medium and made continuous with, and an example of, genuine sexual feeling. In particular, the danger of the sexual encounter is in no way minimised: being imaginary, it may also be realistically displayed.[29]

When critics distinguish erotic art from pornography, they often have some distinction in mind such as that between representation, which is addressed to the creative imagination and bound by a principle of truth, and substitution, which is addressed to the sexual fantasy and bound only by the requirement of gratificatory power. The latter must always offend against the proprieties of art, while the former may remain obedient to them.[30]

In some such way one might also distinguish the thoughts of the 'normal', from those of the 'perverted', masturbator. The latter uses representations which are purged of their imaginative challenge, and of all the dangers and difficulties that surround the sexual encounter.[31] The sexual activity of the 'normal' masturbator is, primarily, a re-creation in memory or imagination of the act towards which his body tends. The 'perverted' masturbator, by contrast, uses images as a substitute for the real thing: realistic representations of the human body, purged of the dangers and difficulties presented by the human soul. Thus Kant considered masturbation to be the archetype of all perversion, precisely because it replaces the real object of desire by a fantasy that is self-created and therefore obedient to the will:

> Lust is called *unnatural* if man is aroused to it, not by its real object, but by his imagination of this object, and so in a way contrary to the purpose of the desire, since he himself creates its object.[32]

The imaginings of such a masturbator are not personal but corporeal, perhaps explicitly phallic. They exhibit the structural trait of obscenity. They exist precisely in order to facilitate sexual gratification *without* the trouble of the human encounter, in order to turn the subject away from the pains and the rewards of interpersonal desire, towards an alternative that – while easy in itself – displays the defining feature of perversion.

But if the thoughts of the 'perverted' masturbator are obscene, so too is the act of masturbation, even in the 'normal' case. For masturbation involves a concentration on the body and its curious pleasures: even when it is not itself a 'perversion', it cannot be witnessed without a sense of obscenity. (The cynic Diogenes is reported to have masturbated in public, as he ate in public, arguing that, if there is no evil in eating, the act cannot change its moral character simply because other people observe it.[33] In a sense Diogenes was right: but that which cannot be witnessed without obscene perception is itself obscene. The moral character of our private acts may be determined by the experience of those who should never observe them.)

Thus, when masturbation intrudes into the sexual act, it has precisely that freezing character which turns us from perversion. Consider the woman who plays with her clitoris during the act of coition. Such a person affronts her lover with the obscene display of her body, and, in perceiving her thus, the lover perceives his own irrelevance. She becomes disgusting to him, and his desire may be extinguished. The woman's desire is satisfied at the expense of her lover's, and no real union can be achieved between them. The incipient obscenity of masturbation threatens the intentionality of desire, and brings us constantly to the verge of perversion. Hence it is wholly natural to us to perceive our own flesh as 'forbidden territory', like the flesh of our family. (Such is the thought behind the traditional education of children in the ways of 'moral hygiene', and, laughable though its literature may now appear to us, with its lurid stories of premature death and wan survival, we should not discount the moral intuition upon which it was founded.)

Chastity

The above brief summary of certain standard cases of perversion, or what is sometimes alleged to be perversion, raises two important questions. First, is chastity a perversion? Secondly, is perversion necessarily reprehensible?

True chastity is not a perversion – for it involves, not the deflection of desire from its personal object, but either the overcoming of desire or the control of its overt expression. The unchaste soul may be unable to perform the sexual act. He may like Klingsor still live in the world of desire, motivated by it in everything, not fulfilled but frustrated in his loneliness. True chastity involves a devotion to projects which do not require desire – a setting of desire to one side, not by denying its interpersonal nature, but by forbidding its motivating power. This need not destroy desire: indeed, popular wisdom and popular morality invite us to see it as an important prelude to desire, and the normal condition of the person who has no genuine attachment to another. Desire may, in the end, be overcome, or 'sublimated' (a description which, however, suggests explanations that are at best contentious); but it is not perverted by a process which aims precisely to safeguard its interpersonal intentionality and to free it from obscenity. This is, I believe, the correct way to understand chastity – or, if you prefer, 'true' chastity, as opposed to the false chastity of Klingsor. Chastity is a project designed to restrain the sexual impulse and to safeguard it against obscene abuses, so that the full intentionality of desire may grow from it and, in due course, be released towards its goal and fulfilment. Chastity may also, in certain cases, be an end in itself. But then it is never obviously admirable, unless the outcome of a vow: unless, that is, it is an act of renunciation which is the inverse and the image of the vow of love, and which has its own troubles and ecstasies. Then, indeed, chastity is the clear mirror of erotic life, and like the chastity of St Teresa, so acutely portrayed in Bernini's sculpture, it shows itself in an ecstasy which is the intensest form of embodiment.

By now it should be clear that our discussion has led to the heart of the problems of sexual morality, and nothing further can be said about perversion – whether it be reprehensible or harmless – until the foundations of sexual morality have been laid.

11

SEXUAL MORALITY

The subject of this chapter is of such importance that my treatment must inevitably limit itself to first suggestions. I hope that those who disagree with my conclusions will at least find, in the supporting arguments, a procedure whereby to refute them. My purpose is not to provide a comprehensive philosophy of morals, but to show how a plausible account of moral reasoning may, when combined with the foregoing theory of sexual desire, lead to an intuitively persuasive sexual morality.

Morality, in its fundamental meaning, is a condition upon practical reasoning. It is a constraint upon reasons for action, which is felt by most rational beings and which is, furthermore, a normal consequence of the possession of a first-person perspective. Morality must be understood, therefore, in first-person terms: in terms of the reasoning that *leads* to action.

Our life is limited by what is forbidden, and fulfilled in what is valuable. Kantian philosophy, which subsumes both those facts under the idea of duty, has been of enormous appeal, partly because it imposes a coherent and unified structure on moral thought, and partly because it shows moral thinking to be a necessary consequence of rational agency, and an expression of the first-person perspective that defines our condition. It is now evident, however, that Kant's attempt to derive morality from the categorical imperative, and the categorical imperative from the first-person perspective (the perspective that forces on us the idea of a 'transcendental freedom'), is unlikely to succeed. For Kant, the sympathy that we feel for the virtuous, and the benevolent emotions that prompt us to do what virtue commands, are not genuine expressions of morality, but merely 'empirical determinations', which intrude into the realm of practical reason only to deflect it from its categorical purposes. Many have entirely rejected Kant's theory on account of this, while others have tried to modify it, reinterpreting the categorical imperative, either as a special kind of *thought* contained within the moral emotions,[1] or as a kind of normative emotion, which may perhaps grow from human sympathy, but which spreads its charge over the whole human world.[2] Those modifications of Kant's view retain what I believe to be its central idea: that moral reasoning expresses the view of ourselves which is imposed on us by our existence as persons, and by our interaction with others of our kind. Moral reasoning is the formal recognition of the strictures placed upon us by our interpersonal attitudes, from which in turn our existence as persons derives.

The position expressed in that last sentence owes much to Kant, and much to Hegel and Bradley.[3] There is also another central tenet of Kant's theory, which must be accepted in something like its original form: the idea that moral reasons close the subject's mind to alternative courses of action. Whether we wish to analyse this 'closing of the mind' as a kind of inner force,[4] as an internal property of moral reasons,[5] as the result of a 'barrier to information',[6] or perhaps as a mere blindness, it yet seems evident that it exists, and that it is one of the most striking characteristics of the moral being. *Because* the moral being is rational, there are certain courses of action which he cannot consider. If Kant is right, it is man's very rationality that leads him to close his mind to actions for which a thousand prudential reasons might be given.

How are such extraordinary constraints on practical reasoning to be justified, and which? For Kant, the problem of morality is posed always from, and within, the immediate first-person point of view, in response to the question 'why should I do *that*?' To step outside that point of view is to lose the perspective from which practical questions must be asked, and hence to lose the hope of answering them. The question what to do is either mine or no one's, and the significance of the categorical answer – the answer embodied in an *ought* – is that it addresses itself to me as agent, and also lays claim to a validity that transcends all that is merely mine. Hence, for Kant, the standard of validity in moral reasoning must be internal to it: it must at the same time provide a motive for *me* to act, and also lay down a universal law.

Kant was aware of the enormous difficulties that beset such a view. It seems impossible to derive a *standard of validity* which is also, at the same time, a first-person reason for action. If there is such a standard, then, by its very universality, it must avoid all mention of *me*; in which case, how can it have the motivating force required by a genuine first-person reason? Conversely, if it is such a reason – a reason which motivates *me* – its claim to universal validity must be doubted. This conflict emerges at a metaphysical level, in the divide between the transcendental and the empirical self. The first is a kind of abstract ego, released from the constraints of concrete existence, and with no *principium individuationis* that would enable us to identify it with an 'empirical self'. It is the empirical self who must act, and only the transcendental self that can listen to instructions. Their non-relation (indeed, the strict *inconceivability* of a relation between them) provides an immovable obstacle to Kantian ethics.

The conflict emerges also at the level of practical reasoning itself, between the motive that prompts me here and now, and which grows from my empirical circumstances, and the claim to validity which, because it must abstract from all that is merely mine towards a universal law, removes me from the circumstances which motivate my action. The conflict stems from the contradictory requirements of abstraction and concretion – the requirements that I be removed from my circumstances, and that I be identified with them.

Modern Kantians, such as Rawls in his *A Theory of Justice*, encounter some equivalent of the same objection. Rawls, for example, affirms that 'the self is prior to the ends which are affirmed by it,'[7] meaning that our values and aims belong to our individual (one might say, empirical) circumstances, and cannot therefore be considered by any theory of justice that is to be universally applied. The correct theory of justice must attain its standard by abstraction – by winnowing away the features which distinguish persons one from another, so as to approach the hypothetical position in which agents have no other basis for their choice than the fact of choice itself. (This procedure, whereby almost everything that matters to a person is discounted, is part of what Rawls means by 'fairness'.) The abstracted chooser who occupies Rawls's 'original position' is still a self, who retains whatever is necessary freely to enter a 'social contract' with similar 'disprivileged' beings. As Michael Sandel has argued,[8] however, this is to suppose precisely the same metaphysical vision as is supposed by Kantian ethics: the vision of a purely noumenal self, who, while being detached from all empirical constraints, may yet have, through his reason, the motive to choose. In abstracting from my values, my everyday aims and preferences, from all that constitutes my contingent condition, I abstract also from the circumstances of my act – and, in particular, from the desires and interests which initially raised for me the question of action.

Kant's approach is the most beautiful and thorough of all the theories which try to find the basis of morality in the first-person perspective, and its failure must serve as a warning. We should, I believe, follow the path of those philosophers – notably Aristotle – who have looked for the grounds of first-person practical reason outside the immediate situation of the agent. Kant's principal opponent – Hume – was such a philosopher. But his scepticism, and his grotesque caricature of the human mind, render him a doubtful authority. I propose, like Hume's predecessors, Shaftesbury and Hutcheson, to return to the philosophical intuitions of Aristotle, and to refurbish them for the needs of a modern moral perspective.

The weakness of the Kantian position lies in its attribution of a 'motivating force' to reason – in its denial of Hume's principle that reason alone cannot be a motive to action.[9] The Aristotelian position involves no commitment to the idea of a 'pure practical reason'. It recognises that practical reasoning concludes in action only because it begins in desire. The 'practical syllogism' has a practical premise, and to the agent with evil desires no reason can be given that will, by its sheer force as a reason, suffice to make him good.[10]

It might seem that, from such a realistic premise concerning the nature of practical reasoning, only moral subjectivism could emerge. For the premise suggests that practical reasoning does not change, but merely realises, the desires of the agent, and hence that it can concern itself only with means and never with ends. And indeed, from the immediate first-person point of view – the point of view of my present motives – such a conclusion is unavoidable. However, there is also the long-term point of view, and it is the distinctive feature of Aristotelian ethics that it makes this point of view central to its argument. It develops a kind of third-person reasoning which, while containing its own incontrovertible claim to validity, may also be applied by each agent to himself, so becoming practical, by transforming his desires.

The model for this reasoning is the practice of moral education. In educating a child I am concerned, not merely with what he does, but with what he feels and with his emerging character. Feeling and character, which provide his motives, determine what he will do. In moulding them, I mould his moral nature. I know that my child's desires will, if he is rational, determine his behaviour – for I know the truth enshrined in Aristotle's practical syllogism, according to which rational action is the realisation of desire. Moreover, I know that my child has (in normal circumstances)[11] reason to be rational, for no other gift can compensate for the lack of this one. Hence I must, if I care for him, devote myself to the education both of his reason and of his desires.

Of course, given his present childish nature, I cannot easily persuade him to change in the preferred direction: only his love and my authority may elicit in him the disposition to do willingly that which is in his long-term interests. However, unlike him, I take an overview of his future life. I see that there is reason for him to have some desires rather than others, even if he cannot at present appreciate this fact. What, then, will guide me in his moral education?

We must note that the practical syllogism, which arises from the concrete circumstances of action, cannot be anticipated. I cannot solve now the specific practical problems that will encumber my child's existence. Nevertheless, I can anticipate, in a general way, the difficulties which any rational being must encounter on life's way, and I can consider the character which might generate fulfilment. To engage in such reflections is to invoke an idea of happiness, or *eudaimonia*.

Aristotle's strategy, in the *Nicomachean Ethics*, is not easy to grasp, and is open to many interpretations. The strategy I shall propose may or may not be identical with Aristotle's; at least, it is inspired by Aristotle's and leads to similar conclusions. I suggest that Aristotle's invocation of happiness, as the final end of human conduct, is essentially correct. Happiness is the single final answer to the question 'why do that?', the answer which survives the conflict with every rival interest or desire. In referring to happiness we refer, not to the satisfaction of impulses, but to the fulfilment of the person. We all have reason to want this fulfilment, and we want it reasonably, whatever our other desires, and whatever our circumstances. In moral education this alone is certain: that the child ought to be happy, and hence that whatever disposition is essential to happiness is a disposition that he has reason to acquire.

But what is happiness? Kant dismissed the idea as empty: happiness, he argued, simply stands for the generality of human desires: it means different things for different people, and provides no coherent motive of its own. Following Aristotle, however, I shall propose an idea of happiness as a kind of 'flourishing'. A gardener who tends a plant has reason to see that it flourishes. The unflourishing plant is one that tends towards non-existence. Flourishing pertains to the *being* of the plant, and to care for the plant is to care for its flourishing.

As a plant flourishes when it has what it needs, so does my child flourish when he has what is necessary to him. To act in order to flourish is always to act in accordance with what is reasonable, since to act otherwise is to destroy the possibility of being moved by reason at all. From the parental point of view, therefore, I must secure at least this for my child. At this point, the theological and secular moralities tend to diverge. Some say that man flourishes only in proximity to God, and only when he walks in God's ways. Others say that he flourishes here and now, in accordance with a law of his own. I shall argue for the second view, but my conclusions would also follow, I think, from the first — although by a more roundabout route.

Obviously my child is not a plant; nor is he just any kind of animal. So it remains to determine what 'flourishing' means in his case. This is exactly the same question as the question of his nature. For flourishing is the activity of his *essence*: it is the successful employment of those capacities that are integral to his being. (An essence is that which cannot be lost without ceasing to be.) Aristotle himself defines *eudaimonia* as 'an activity of the soul in accordance with virtue',[12] and once again I believe it is instructive to follow him.

My child is essentially (but also only potentially) a rational being or person. He may flourish or decline as such, and his potential for being such may not be realised: he may grow up as a mere animal, an instance of *homo faber*, nurtured by some gentle wolf. Supposing, however, that his potential for rational conduct is realised; what then constitutes his flourishing? We may divide the answer to that question into two parts: health and happiness. Health is the state in which I flourish as an animal; happiness the state in which I flourish as a person. And it is an important feature of the ontological dependence of personhood – of its need to find *embodiment* in an animal life – that health is such an important precondition of happiness. But health is not everything; happiness requires that we flourish as rational beings. We must exercise our rational capacities successfully: we must be fulfilled as persons, through the decisions which guide our lives.

It is clear that, if I have reason to do anything, I have reason to be successful in what I do. But success is not merely a matter of choosing the right means to my ends; it is also a matter of rightly choosing the end itself. Consequently, there is a distinction between virtue (which involves the disposition to make appropriate choices of ends) and skill (which involves mastery of the means whereby to accomplish them). This is the origin of Aristotle's distinction between *aretē* and *technē*.

Virtue is the disposition to choose those courses of action which contribute to my happiness: which cause me to flourish as a rational being. In educating my child I am educating his habits, and it is clear therefore that I shall always have reason to inculcate a habit of virtue, not for my sake, but for his own. At least, that is so provided we accept that my main concern is what matters for *him*, in the future to which *he* is destined. At the same time, I do not think of virtue as a *means* only: it consists in the right choice of end.

Consider friendship. To say that an action was done out of friendship is already to describe an end. Indeed, there is a sense in which there cannot be a further end which is still compatible with this motive. To say that I

327

was friendly to John because of the advantage that I hoped to gain from him is to imply that I was not moved by *friendship*. Nevertheless, one may justify both the general disposition to friendship (which Aristotle was not alone in believing to be one of the rewards of virtue) and the individual friendship for John, by pointing to the connections between these dispositions and the happiness of the person who possesses them. Hence there is no contradiction in saying that a person values what he does (when acting out of friendship) as an *end*, and that there is also a further reason for doing it, namely, that such is the way to happiness.

Virtue, like friendship, is a disposition to intentional action. It is the disposition to want what is justified or reasonable, in the face of the natural impulse to act in despite of reason. Consider the classical virtue of courage. All human beings have rooted in their animal nature two rival instincts: that of aggression and that of fear. In the case of threat one instinct prompts to attack, the other to flee. The conflict between them may resolve itself without reasoned calculation, purely on the basis of their relative strengths. At the same time, however, the rational being wants to do what reason commands. In particular, he wants to take into account those 'unconditional' imperatives which the Kantian rightly emphasises as the true forms of moral constraint. He wants to do what he judges to be right or honourable, even in the occasion of mortal fear. To have this disposition is to be (to some degree) courageous.

Note that this disposition to want to do what is right in the face of danger is a disposition to act for a reason. It overcomes the instinct of fear, but not as the instinct of aggression may overcome it. As John Casey has argued,[13] courage does not enter the situation as one competing desire among others. It enters through a decision, which is not balanced against fear as one force against another, but which discounts fear as a factor irrelevant to the present course of action. The courageous man does not pit his rage against his fear and become thereby a battle-ground for conflicting humours. He acts in defiance of fear: his action is not the victory of a force, but the conquest of all forces, a subduing of animal nature. The resulting action is therefore attributed to *him*, as springing from his nature as a rational being. There are, of course, false virtues: the foolhardiness of the raging man, which may be mistaken for courage; the meanness and self-love of the prudish man, which might be taken for temperance. There are those circumstances in which:

> Patience hardens to a pittance, courage
> unflinchingly declines into sour rage,
> the cobweb-banners, the shrill bugle-bands

and the bronze warriors resting on their wounds.
[Geoffrey Hill, *The Mystery of the Charity of Charles Péguy*]

But those are circumstances, not of virtue, but of the vice which imitates virtue, and into which virtue declines.

Aristotle's doctrine of the mean has proved, in this regard, especially confusing. It may seem as though the virtue is a disposition to choose a course of action between two extremes. But the course of action between the two extremes dictated by fear and anger is not a course of action at all: it is a state of paralysed inertia, such as may indeed afflict an animal but which has nothing to do with the motives of the courageous person. The mean is simply that which reason commands, despite the prompting of fear and anger.

It is clear that virtue is a part of rational fulfilment. For without the disposition to want what is reasonable, there is no such thing as an *exercise* of reason. And while this may seem a rather trivial assertion, it is, in the context, far from trivial. For if I have reason to aim at anything, I have reason to acquire the dispositions that enable me to fulfil my aims. I therefore have a reason to acquire courage – and perhaps other virtues too. I will also try to inculcate these dispositions in my child, since whatever his desires his long-term fulfilment will depend upon his acquisition of the habits which prevent their frustration. And these habits will constrain his desires, so that he will learn to want what is reasonable.

That sketch of the Aristotelian strategy enables us to draw an interesting conclusion. The reasoning that justifies a given course of moral education may underpin and justify the present ends of conduct, even when they seem to entail pain and disaster for the agent. Consider the courageous man in battle: he will expose himself to risk and may die as a result, where the coward escapes with his life and prospects. In what way is the courageous man more rational? How can it be rational to do knowingly that which leads to the extinction of life and reason? The answer is obvious. Both the coward and the brave man act in a way which is, from the immediate first-person point of view, wholly rational. The first desires to save himself and acts accordingly; the second desires to do what is right and honourable, and he too chooses the course appropriate to that end. The question which of their ends is appropriate is, however, not to be settled from a consideration of the present moment, nor does it depend upon their first-person reasons for action: their present motives. It can be settled only by rehearsing again the arguments of the moral educator. These arguments dwell, not on the specific occasion of choice, but on the overall structure of a rational life. It is more in the interests of the rational being to have the disposition of courage than to be at the

329

mercy of fear. The view of the moral educator justifies the disposition which, in the peculiar circumstances of battle, subjects the agent to a mortal danger. In so far as there is a rational justification of the *ends* of conduct, it is the courageous man, and not the coward, who acts in accordance with reason, even if he dies.

I can take the same overall view of my own nature and fortune as I take of my child's, and endeavour to inculcate in myself those virtues which I would wish on my child. This endeavour is, of course, necessarily enfeebled by the urgency of present desires; but it will always engage with one of my desires – the desire to be happy. Moral education is important, since, while I have little control over my own corrupted temperament, I may still control the unformed temperament of my child. However hopeless my own situation, however sunk in vice I may be, I may yet judge the wretchedness of my condition and seek to ensure that others do not share in it. For the Aristotelian, the real question of morality is not whether I, here and now, can be persuaded to alter my course, but whether there are reasons why another, who may yet be corrected, should alter *his* course.

The Aristotelian approach offers hope to those who seek for a secular morality of sexual conduct. Not only does it place in the forefront of moral thinking the crucial practice through which sexual morality arises – the practice of moral education; it also gives cogency to prohibitions and privations – something that a secular morality seems otherwise incompetent to do. Thus, in the same way as the sacrifice of the brave man in battle may be shown to be supremely reasonable, so too might we justify such peculiar practices as chastity, modesty and sexual hesitation. Although these block the road to present pleasure, and seem, from the immediate first-person point of view, wholly irrational, they may yet be justified in terms of the disposition from which they spring. It may be in the long-term interests of the rational agent that he acquire just this kind of control over his sexual impulses. Thus Sidgwick regarded the function of sexual morality as twofold: the maintenance of a social order believed to be most conducive to the prosperous continuance of the human race, and 'the protection of habits of feeling in individuals believed to be generally most important to their perfection or their happiness'.[14] We could interpret the second of those functions as the one to which the Aristotelian strategy is directed. (The first is arguably not part of morality at all, even if it is a foreseeable offshoot of moral conduct that our genes will be the ultimate beneficiaries.)

In order to settle the question, whether any such thing be true, we must return to the idea of happiness or fulfilment which underlies the

Aristotelian strategy. Fulfilment here means fulfilment of the person, and, in order to describe it, we must delve a little more deeply into the obscure regions of the self. That is, we must attempt to make sense of the first-person perspective, as it is revealed in practical reasoning. For it is in this – the defining feature of persons – that the reality of human fulfilment will be found. The thought of a person is self-conscious thought, expressing a rational conception of the world and of his place within it; his action is self-conscious action, stemming from practical reason. The 'self' is a name for these distinctive thoughts and feelings, and in what follows I shall refer to 'self-fulfilment', in order to denote the fulfilment of the rational being – the being with a first-person perspective.

In Chapter 3 I referred to two closely related features of the first-person perspective: privileged access and responsibility. Both have been frequently invoked in the subsequent discussion, and the first is to some extent accounted for in Appendix 1. In dealing with rational fulfilment, however, we are more concerned with the second feature, which defines the relation of the person to his own past and future. Responsibility denotes a pattern of thought and feeling, whereby a person anchors himself, not in the moment, but in the stretch of time which is his 'life'. Derek Parfit has argued that personal identity ought not to matter in our practical reasoning: what matters, or ought to matter, he believes, is something else, which has been confused with identity on account of a metaphysical illusion.[15] In what follows I shall be arguing that, from the first-person point of view, it is *precisely* identity that matters, for it is by virtue of a self-identifying thought that my practical reason engages with the future at all. This thought is, perhaps, an illusion. But so, as we have seen, is much else that informs our first-person view of ourselves.

I begin by introducing the 'minimal self'. This is a creature who has command of language, and in particular of the first-person case, sufficient to obey the rules of self-attribution concerning his present mental states. The difference between animality and selfhood is one of kind, and admits of no degrees: either a creature grasps self-attribution or he does not, and the conditions on grasping it are fairly stringent. However, the transition – which can be described, in Hegelian idiom, as the transition from object to subject – is built up of certain stages or 'moments'. That which begins in self-attribution leads towards intention and responsibility – towards the 'maximal self' who projects himself forward and backward in time, and lives according to the logic of a human biography.

As we have seen, the minimal self is already the repository of authority. His voice is not the observer but the expression of his present mental state. He has a unique and irreplaceable authority in all matters relating to his own mental condition. Hence he may reveal himself to others, and also hide himself from them. He can pretend, just as he can be honest. He can also be argued with and learned from. All this creates, as I have argued, the foundation of interpersonal existence, by providing distinct responses and reactions, the subject and object of which are creatures with the first-person point of view.

Let us consider, now, the various attitudes that the minimal self may have towards his past and future. It is clear that, without a conception of my identity through time, many of my mental states would be strictly unintelligible to me. I cannot attribute to myself beliefs of a theoretical character, or moral beliefs, without also supposing that I endure long enough for such beliefs to make a difference in my behaviour. An instantaneous monad, who is no sooner born into the world than taken from it, has no time for serious belief, and to the extent that we see ourselves as theoretical and enquiring creatures, to that extent must we inevitably think of ourselves as enduring in time. The minimal self exists fully in the present, therefore, only by also asserting his identity over time. He attributes to himself both a past and a future, and although he may be mistaken in this attribution (as he may perhaps be mistaken in any assertion of identity over time)[16] it is part of his nature to make it. On the basis of this attribution of self-identity, the present self may take up a variety of attitudes towards both past and future.

Consider, for example, remorse. If I say sincerely, 'I am remorseful over what happened,' not only do I assert my identity with a preceding person, I also incorporate the actions and omissions of that person into my own present accountability towards the world – my present sense of my debts and liabilities. The case should be contrasted with the sincere assertion 'I regret what happened,' which is more like a statement of wish, and makes no essential reference either to my own previous existence or to my present responsibility.

Now clearly it is possible to feel either regret *or* remorse for one and the same occurrence: a person who never felt anything stronger than regret would have a different attitude to his past from one who also felt remorse. Suppose John had desired Lucy's death and in pursuit of that desire had brought it about that Lucy died. With hindsight John might reflect on what happened and say, 'I regret Lucy's dying; moreover I see that she died as a direct result of my desire that she should do so: my desire was the real cause of her death.' If that is all there is to it, it is clear that John is in some way dissociating himself from his past. He is supposing that he, the present self, is not answerable for the actions of that previous self, in the manner of the gentleman in *The Jew of Malta*, who reports that it was in a foreign country, and besides, the wench is dead.

John's case should be contrasted with that of Harold, who, perceiving that his own desire for Lucy's death was also the cause of her death, is stricken by remorse. (Where John says, 'My desire caused her death,' Harold says, '*I* caused her death' — and the intrusion of the 'I' into the centre of thought is the mark of responsibility.) The very feeling of remorse contains an affirmation of unity with the previous self — a sense that his actions belong to me, and form the ground of my present liability. Remorse links the present self to its past, in a self-conscious bond. It constitutes an *inner* link, one that depends for its strength precisely upon the present capacity to feel it. In this feeling the minimal self enlarges himself, enriching his mental content with a lived sense of his own duration.

Suppose Harold, having expressed his remorse, goes on to say, 'but of course, I have no intention to avoid or refrain from such things in future; what will be will be.' We should at once doubt the sincerity of his previous expression of feeling. To take responsibility for one's past is also to project that responsibility forward into the future. To feel remorse is to acquire a motive to refrain. Indeed, in the normal case, remorse involves something like a decision: a resolve that, in future, things will be otherwise.

However, just as a self-conscious being may have distinct attitudes to his past, so too may he have distinct attitudes to his own future. His outlook on the future ranges between two contrasting poles — which we may name, following Hampshire's seminal discussion,[17] predicting and deciding. He may see himself in the future merely as the vehicle of impersonal forces which act through him but not from him, or else as an irreplaceable agent, the originator of actions of his own. As many philosophers have argued, intention involves a kind of certainty about one's future. In deciding, I lay claim now to a future event, and to the extent that I am sincere I must be certain that it will occur. An expression of the form 'I intend to do it but I do not know if I will' cannot be sincere — unless it amounts to no more than the admission that I may change my mind.

Imagine now someone who never made decisions: the extreme case of the predictive person. We could never affect what he will do simply by arguing with him: no change of his view of the world will introduce a decision to alter it, and therefore nothing we say to him can give us grounds for thinking that he will do one thing rather than another. (After all, his *predictions* are no better than ours.) We cannot treat him as having any particular authority concerning his future conduct, nor will our desire to influence his conduct be furthered by consulting his expressed interests. If we are to engage with his future at all, it is only by steering him towards it independently of any expressed plan, intention or resolve. Just as he sees himself in the future as the helpless vehicle of impersonal forces, so must we *treat* him as such: as a means whereby those forces seek expression and not as an 'end in himself'. So if he sees himself as an object, so too must we. (There begins a proof of a fundamental Hegelian and Marxian contention, that alienation from self is alienation from other.)

The example shows us how the self-conception of the minimal self may be enriched. In acquiring a decisive attitude towards his own future, as in acquiring a responsible attitude to his own past, the minimal self ceases to be merely a vehicle for the transmission of impersonal forces and becomes instead an active subject, whose relation to the world is one of freedom. He now *belongs* where he was previously an observer. However, there is more to the transition than the passage from predicting to deciding. He could make that transition merely by a few decisions, about matters of no importance. This alone will not amount to that full sense of the responsibility for his own future which is required of the mature rational agent. The truly decisive person also reasons about the future, and takes upon himself in the present the task of his remaining life.

How do we characterise this fully responsible being? One suggestion is that we suppose him, not merely to *have* desires, but also to stand in a critical relation towards them. We suppose him to engage in the reasoned criticism of desires, selecting those whose influence he would wish to prevail. Some philosophers have considered, therefore, that we should characterise the rational agent as the possessor of 'second-order' desires.[18] He desires some things, and desires to desire others. But again, it would be odd, and incomplete, if this were seen by the agent himself as simply another personal peculiarity, that he not only desired health, say, but also desired to desire it. Why should this new desire suffice to change his image of himself from that of a thing acted on to that of an agent who takes full responsibility for his future life?

What is required, I believe, is not a new order of desire, but a new conception of the object of desire – a conception that attributes to the object a specific importance, over and above the fact of being desired. In short, the subject should not only desire the object, but *see it as desirable*. He must attribute to it a *claim* over his desire, so that it becomes *right* to desire it. He must perceive the object of desire under the aspect not of desire only, but also of value.

Many philosophers have argued that values are not objective properties of things but subjective colourings, or (more usually) human artefacts.[19] Such arguments are irrelevant to our purpose. They also tend to be based on peculiar assumptions: nobody ever thought that because a temple is an artefact it is therefore unreal. It does not matter that values are artefacts: what matters is that something vital to self-consciousness is omitted by those who fail to construct them. Whether there are rules (as Kant supposed) which constrain us to construct our values according to a certain pattern is a philosophical question that we may be unable to answer. But, to the extent that we have reason to pursue self-consciousness in its fullest form – and so enlarge the realms of subjectivity beyond those occupied by the minimal self – to that extent do we have reason to manufacture values. A world without values is one in which all activity has an ending, but no activity has an end. Consider the difference between the man who desires x, which he values, and the man who just desires x. The latter might satisfy his desire with no sense of improving his lot. He had a desire; now he has abolished it, and, if he is lucky, quietus falls. The first man, however, had a desire and, in abolishing it, obtains something of value – something which ministers to his sense of well-being. His lot has significantly improved; had it not improved, this would signify a change in his values.

To recognise the object of desire as desirable is to attribute to one's desire a new role in deliberation. In pursuing what he holds to be desirable, the agent is engaged, not merely in the calculation of means, but also in the rational choice of ends. It is this kind of deliberation that enables the present self to incorporate its own future into its practical reasoning, so as to pursue, not merely that which is presently desired, but also that which is conducive to satisfaction.

If values are artefacts, it is from the stuff of interpersonal emotion that they are constructed. Consider the emotion of pride. Someone who, upon obtaining the object of desire, feels proud of it, shows thereby that he regards it as desirable. The characteristic thought of such a person is that to obtain this object casts *credit* on himself. This thought grows from the personal interaction that leads us constantly to compare the actions of those around us with our own. In pride, as in remorse, the self is viewed from outside, as one among many social objects, defined in part by his relation to his kind. Implicit in these emotions is the idea of a rational community – the Kantian 'Kingdom of Ends' to which all rational beings by nature belong.

It thus seems plausible to suppose that the minimal self advances towards responsibility for its past and future only by also enlarging its perspective, so as to confront itself as the object of interpersonal attitudes, one member of the class of beings who may be praised, blamed and

335

criticised. Let us now pose the Aristotelian question: would it be better for my child to be a minimal or an 'enlarged' self? Would it be better for him, overall, to avoid the sense of responsibility that causes him to answer now for his past and future, or to acquire it? The answer, I believe, is evident. In advance of any knowledge of the particular circumstances of his future, I must surely wish to inculcate in him the faculty of choice, and the outlook on himself that permits him, not only to desire things, but also to find fulfilment in obtaining them. For without such gifts my child cannot conceivably flourish according to his nature – which is that of a rational person.

This means, however, that I must wish also to prepare my child for interpersonal relations, and to inculcate in him the dispositions – pride, remorse, admiration, contempt – which are involved in constructing a concept of the desirable. The 'maximal' self must not only acquire this concept, but also give it the place in practical reasoning necessary to secure an active attachment to his past and his future. Finally, he must learn to see as desirable only that which, in general human conditions, is the occasion of fulfilment. When he has learned that, he has learned virtue.

That brief sketch raises, of course, as many questions as it answers. But it suffices to suggest a way out of the impasse presented by Kantian ethics: a way of circumventing the paradoxes of the first-person case, while retaining the fundamental Kantian intuition that practical reason is built upon a concept of the self and its freedom. The Aristotelian strategy presents us with a view upon the self from a point of view outside it, and then derives conclusions – which, in principle at least, are of universal validity – concerning the well-being of that which it observes. This strategy provides us, I believe, with an important insight into the foundations of morality. It implies that the first-person perspective is fulfilled only when the world is seen in terms of value. On the Aristotelian principle, that *to telos phusis estin* (the end is the essence), we might say that morality belongs to the *nature* of the self. The argument also implies that the building of the first-person perspective comes about precisely through the exercise of interpersonal responses – through a developing third-person perspective on the attitudes of others, which leads us to perceive both them and ourselves as belonging to a single moral kind, distinguished by the 'self-hood' which makes this perception available. The building of the self is the building of a social context, in which the self takes its place beside the other, as object and subject of the universal attitudes of praise and blame – the attitudes which encapsulate the reality of 'respect for persons'. Thus the Aristotelian perspective that led us to seek for the grounds of morality in the third-person perspective of the moral educator leads us back to the Kantian subject, as the locus of moral existence.

We must now attempt to apply the Aristotelian strategy to the subject-matter of this book, and ask whether there is such a thing as sexual virtue, and, if so, what is it, and how is it acquired? Clearly, sexual desire, which is an interpersonal attitude with the most far-reaching consequences for those who are joined by it, cannot be morally neutral. On the contrary, it is in the experience of sexual desire that we are most vividly conscious of the distinction between virtuous and vicious impulses, and most vividly aware that, in the choice between them, our happiness is at stake.

The Aristotelian strategy enjoins us to ignore the actual conditions of any particular person's life, and to look only at the permanent features of human nature. We know that people feel sexual desire; that they feel erotic love, which may grow from desire; that they may avoid both these feelings, by dissipation or self-restraint. Is there anything to be said about desire, other than that it falls within the general scope of the virtue of temperance, which enjoins us to desire only what reason approves?

The first, and most important, observation to be made is that the capacity for love in general, and for erotic love in particular, is a virtue. In Chapter 8 I tried to show that erotic love involves an element of mutual self-enhancement; it generates a sense of the irreplaceable value, both of the other and of the self, and of the activities which bind them. To receive and to give this love is to achieve something of incomparable value in the process of self-fulfilment. It is to gain the most powerful of all interpersonal *guarantees*; in erotic love the subject becomes conscious of the full reality of his personal existence, not only in his own eyes, but in the eyes of another. Everything that he is and values gains sustenance from his love, and every project receives a meaning beyond the moment. All that exists for us as mere hope and hypothesis – the attachment to life and to the body – achieves under the rule of *erōs* the aspect of a radiant certainty. Unlike the cold glances of approval, admiration and pride, the glance of love sees value precisely in that which is the source of anxiety and doubt: in the merely contingent, merely 'empirical', existence of the flesh, the existence which we did not choose, but to which we are condemned. It is the answer to man's fallen condition – to his *Geworfenheit*.[20]

To receive erotic love, however, a person must be able to give it: or if he cannot, the love of others will be a torment to him, seeking from him that which he cannot provide, and directing against him the fury of a disappointed right. It is therefore unquestionable that we have reason to acquire the capacity for erotic love, and, if this means bending our sexual impulses in a certain direction, that will be the direction of sexual virtue. Indeed, the argument of the last two chapters has implied that the development of the sexual impulse towards love may be impeded: there are sexual habits which are vicious, precisely in neutralising the capacity for love. The first thing that can be said, therefore, is that we all have reason to avoid those habits and to educate our children not to possess them.

Here it may be objected that not every love is happy, that there are many – Anna Karenina, for example, or Phaedra – whose capacity for love was the cause of their downfall. But we must remind ourselves of the Aristotelian strategy. In establishing that courage or wisdom is a virtue, the Aristotelian does not argue that the possession of these virtues is in every particular circumstance bound to be advantageous. A parable of Derek Parfit's, adapted from T. C. Schelling,[21] adequately shows what is at stake: Suppose a man breaks into my house and commands me to open the safe for him, saying that, if I do not comply, he will begin to shoot my children. He has heard me telephone the police, and knows that, if he leaves any of us alive, we will be able to give information sufficient to arrest him if he takes what the safe contains. Clearly it is irrational in these circumstances to open the safe – since that will not protect any of us – and also not to open it, since that would cause the robber to kill my children one by one in order to persuade me of his sincerity. Suppose, however, I possess a drug that causes me to become completely irrational. I swallow the pill, and cry out: 'I love my children, therefore kill them'; the man tortures me and I beg him to continue; and so on. In these changed circumstances, my assailant is powerless to obtain what he wants and can only flee before the police arrive. In other words, in such a case, it is actually in the interests of the subject to be irrational: he has overwhelming circumstantial *reason* to be irrational, just as Anna Karenina had an overwhelming circumstantial *reason* to be without the capacity for love. Clearly, however, it would be absurd, on these grounds, to inculcate a habit of irrationality in our children; indeed no *reason* could be given, in the absence of detailed knowledge of a person's future, for acquiring such a habit. In so far as reasons can be given now, for the cultivation of this or that state of character, they must justify the cultivation of rationality before all else – for how can I flourish according to my nature as a rational agent if I am not at least rational?

In like manner, it is not the particular personal tragedy but the generality of the human condition that determines the basis of sexual morality. Tragedy and loss are the rare but necessary outcomes of a process which we all have reason to undergo. (Indeed, it is part of the point of tragedy that it divorces in our imagination the right and the good from the merely prudential: that it sets the value of life against the value of mere survival.) We wish to know, in advance of any particular experience, which dispositions a person must have if he is successfully to express himself in sexual desire and to be fulfilled in his sexual endeavours. Love is the fulfilment of desire, and therefore love is its *telos*. A life of celibacy may also be fulfilled; but, assuming the general truth that most of us have a powerful, and perhaps overwhelming, urge to make love, it is in our interests to ensure that love – and not some other thing – is made.

Love, I have argued, is prone to jealousy, and the object of jealousy is defined by the thought of the beloved's desire. Because jealousy is one of the greatest of psychical catastrophes, involving the possible ruin of both partners, a morality based in the need for erotic love must forestall and eliminate jealousy. It is in the deepest human interest, therefore, that we form the habit of fidelity. This habit is natural and normal; but it is also easily broken, and the temptation to break it is contained in desire itself – in the element of generality which tempts us always to experiment, to verify, to detach ourselves from that which is too familiar in the interest of excitement and risk. Virtuous desire is faithful; but virtuous desire is also an artefact, made possible by a process of moral education which we do not, in truth, understand in its complexity.

If that observation is correct, a whole section of traditional sexual morality must be upheld. The fulfilment of sexual desire defines the nature of desire: *to telos phusis estin*. And the nature of desire gives us our standard of normality. There are enormous varieties of human sexual conduct, and of 'common-sense' morality: some societies permit or encourage polygamy, others look with indifference upon premarital intercourse, or regard marriage itself as no more than an episode in a relation that pre-exists and perhaps survives it. But no society, and no 'common-sense' morality – not even, it seems, the morality of Samoa[22] – looks with favour upon promiscuity or infidelity, unless influenced by a doctrine of 'emancipation' or 'liberation' which is dependent for its sense upon the very conventions which it defies. Whatever the institutional forms of human sexual union, and whatever the range of permitted partners, sexual desire is itself inherently 'nuptial': it involves concentration upon the embodied existence of the other, leading through tenderness to the 'vow' of erotic love. It is a telling observation that the civilisation which has most tolerated the institution of polygamy – the Islamic – has also, in its erotic literature, produced what are perhaps the intensest and most poignant celebrations of monogamous love, precisely through the attempt to capture, not the institution of marriage, but the human datum of desire.[23]

The nuptiality of desire suggests, in its turn, a natural history of desire: a principle of development which defines the 'normal course' of sexual education. 'Sexual maturity' involves incorporating the sexual impulse into the personality, and so making sexual desire into an expression of the subject himself, even though it is, in the heat of action, a force which also overcomes him. If the Aristotelian approach to these things is as plausible as I think it is, the virtuous habit will also have the character of a 'mean': it will involve the disposition to desire what is desirable, despite the competing impulses of animal lust (in which the intentionality of desire may be demolished) and timorous frigidity (in which the sexual impulse is impeded altogether). Education is directed towards the special kind of temperance which shows itself, sometimes as chastity, sometimes as fidelity, sometimes as passionate desire, according to the 'right judgement' of the subject. In wanting what is judged to be desirable, the virtuous person wants what may also be loved, and what may therefore be obtained without hurt or humiliation.

Virtue is a matter of degree, rarely attained in its completion, but always admired. Because traditional sexual education has pursued sexual virtue, it is worthwhile summarising its most important features, in order to see the power of the idea that underlies and justifies it.

The most important feature of traditional sexual education is summarised in anthropological language as the 'ethic of pollution and taboo'.[24] The child was taught to regard his body as sacred, and as subject to pollution by misperception or misuse. The sense of pollution is by no means a trivial side-effect of the 'bad sexual encounter': it may involve a penetrating disgust, at oneself, one's body and one's situation, such as is experienced by the victim of rape. Those sentiments – which arise from our 'fear of the obscene' – express the tension contained within the experience of embodiment. At any moment we can become 'mere body', the self driven from its incarnation, and its habitation ransacked. The most important root idea of personal morality is that I am *in* my body, not (to borrow Descartes' image) as a pilot in a ship, but as an incarnate self. My body is identical with me, and sexual purity is the precious guarantee of this.

Sexual purity does not forbid desire: it simply ensures the status of desire as an interpersonal feeling. The child who learns 'dirty habits' detaches his sex from himself, sets it outside himself as something curious and alien. His fascinated enslavement to the body is also a withering of desire, a scattering of erotic energy and a loss of union with the other. Sexual purity sustains the *subject* of desire, making him present as a self in the very act which overcomes him.

The extraordinary spiritual significance accorded to sexual 'purity' has, of course, its sociobiological and its psychoanalytical explanations. But what, exactly, is its *meaning*, and have people been right to value it? In Wagner's *Parsifal*, the 'pure fool' is uniquely credited with the power to heal the terrible wound which is the physical sign of Amfortas's sexual 'pollution'. He alone can redeem Kundry, the 'fallen' woman, whose sexual licence is so resistant to her penitent personality, that it must be confined to another world, of which she retains only a dim and horrified consciousness. That other world is a world of pleasure and opportunity, a world of the 'permitted'. It is governed, however, by the impure eunuch Klingsor, whose rule is a kind of slavery. Wagner finds the meaning of Christian redemption in the fool's chastity, which leads him to renounce the rewards of an impure desire for the sake of another's salvation. Parsifal releases Amfortas from the hold of 'magic', from the 'charm' which tempts Szymanowski's King Roger towards a vain apotheosis.[25] Parsifal is the harbinger of peace and freedom, in a world that has been enslaved by the magic of desire.

The haunting symbols of this opera owe their power to feelings that are too deep to be lightly dismissed as aesthetic artefacts. But what is their meaning for people who live unsheltered by religion? The answer is to be found, not in religious, but in sexual, feeling. The purely human redemption which is offered to us in love is dependent, in the last analysis, upon public recognition of the value of chastity, and of the sacrilege involved in a sexual impulse that wanders free from the controlling impulse of respect. The 'pollution' of the prostitute is not that she gives herself for money, but that she gives herself to those whom she hates or despises. This is the 'wound' of unchastity, which cannot be healed in solitude by the one who suffers it, but only by his acceptance into a social order which confines the sexual impulse to the realm of intimate relations. The chaste person sustains the ideal of sexual innocence, by giving honourable form to chastity as a way of life. Through his example, it becomes not foolish but admirable to ignore the promptings of a desire that brings no intimacy or fulfilment. Chastity is not a private policy, followed by one individual alone for the sake of his peace of mind. It has a wider and more generous significance: it attempts to draw others into complicity, and to sustain a social order that confines the sexual impulse to the personal sphere.

Chastity exists in two forms: as a publicly declared and publicly recognised role or policy (the chastity of the monk, priest or nun); or as a private resolution, a recognition of the morality that lies dormant in desire. Thus Hans Sachs, in *Die Meistersinger*, who has the opportunity to fulfil his desire, chooses rather to renounce it, knowing that it will not be reciprocated. Sachs is loved and admired for the irreproachable aloneness which makes him the property of all. He is the buttress of Nuremberg, whose satisfactions are public satisfactions, precisely because his own seed has not been sown. His melancholy and bookish contemplation of the trivialities of progenerative man are in one sense a sigh from the genetic depth: the species is alive in this sigh, just as the individual dies in it. In another sense, however, his melancholy is the supreme affirmation of the reality of others' joys: the recognition that desire must be silenced, in order that others may thrive in their desire.

The child was traditionally brought up to achieve sexual fulfilment only *through* chastity, which is the condition which surrounds him on his first entering the adult world – the world of commitments and obligations. At the same time, he was encouraged to ponder certain 'ideal objects' of desire. These, presented to him under the aspect of an idealised physical beauty, were never *merely* beautiful, but also endowed with the moral attributes that fitted them for love. This dual inculcation of 'pure' habits and 'ideal' love might seem, on the face of it, to be unworthy of the name of education. Is it not, rather, like the mere *training* of a horse or a dog, which arbitrarily forbids some things and fosters others, without offering the first hint of a reason why? And is it not the distinguishing mark of education that it engages with the rational nature of its recipient, and does not merely mould him indifferently to his own understanding of the process? Why, in short, is this moral education, rather than a transference into the sexual sphere – as Freud would have it – of those same processes of interdiction that train us to defecate, not in our nappies, but in a porcelain pot?

The answer is clear. The cult of innocence is an attempt to *generate* rational conduct, by incorporating the sexual impulse into the self-activity of the subject. It is an attempt to impede the impulse, until such a time as it may attach itself to the interpersonal project that leads to its fulfilment: the project of union with another person, who is wanted not merely for his body, but for the person who *is* this body. Innocence is the disposition to avoid sexual encounter, except with the person whom one may fully desire. Children who have lost their innocence have acquired the habit of gratification through the body alone, in a state of partial or truncated desire. Their gratification is detached from the conditions of personal fulfilment and wanders from object to object with no settled tendency to attach itself to any, pursued all the while by a sense of the body's obscene dominion. 'Debauching of the innocent' was traditionally regarded as a most serious offence, and one that offered genuine *harm* to the victim. The harm in question was not physical, but moral: the undermining of the process which prepares the child to enter the world of *erōs*. (Thus Nabokov's Lolita, who passes with such rapidity from childish provocativeness to a knowing interest in the sexual act, finds, in the end, a marriage devoid of passion, and dies without knowledge of desire.)

The personal and the sexual can become divorced in many ways. The task of sexual morality is to unite them, to sustain thereby the intentionality of desire, and to prepare the individual for erotic love. Sexual morality is the morality of embodiment: the posture which strives to unite us with our bodies, precisely in those situations when our bodies are foremost in our thoughts. Without such a morality the human world is subject to a dangerous divide, a gulf between self and body, at the verge of which all our attempts at personal union falter and withdraw. Hence the prime focus of sexual morality is not the attitude to others, but the attitude to one's own body and its uses. Its aim is to safeguard the integrity of our embodiment. Only on that condition, it is thought, can we inculcate either innocence in the young or fidelity in the adult. Such habits are, however, only one part of sexual virtue. Traditional morality has combined its praise of them with a condemnation of other things – in particular of the habits of lust and perversion. And it is not hard to find the reason for these condemnations.

Perversion consists precisely in a diverting of the sexual impulse from its interpersonal goal, or towards some act that is intrinsically destructive of personal relations and of the values that we find in them. The 'dissolution' of the flesh, which the Marquis de Sade regarded as so important an element in the sexual aim, is in fact the dissolution of the soul; the perversions described by de Sade are not so much attempts to destroy the flesh of the victim as to rid his flesh of its personal meaning, to wring out, with the blood, the rival perspective. That is true in one way or another of all perversion, which can be simply described as the habit of finding a sexual release that avoids or abolishes the *other*, obliterating his embodiment with the obscene perception of his body. Perversion is narcissistic, often solipsistic, involving strategies of replacement which are intrinsically destructive of personal feeling. Perversion therefore prepares us for a life without personal fulfilment, in which no human relation achieves foundation in the acceptance of the other, as this acceptance is provided by desire.

Lust may be defined as a genuine sexual desire, from which the goal of erotic love has been excluded, and in which whatever tends towards that goal – tenderness, intimacy, fidelity, dependence – is curtailed or obstructed. There need be nothing perverted in this. Indeed the special case of lust which I have discussed under the title of Don Juanism, in which the project of intimacy is constantly abbreviated by the flight towards another sexual object, provides one of our paradigms of desire. Nevertheless, the traditional condemnation of lust is far from arbitrary, and the associated contrast between lust and love far from a matter of convention. Lust is also a habit, involving the disposition to give way to desire, without regard to any personal relation with the object. (Thus perversions are all forms of lust even though lust is not in itself a perversion.) Naturally, we all feel the promptings of lust, but the rapidity with which sexual acts become sexual habits, and the catastrophic effect of a sexual act which cannot be remembered without shame or humiliation, give us strong reasons to resist them, reasons that Shakespeare captured in these words:

> Th'expence of Spirit in a waste of shame
> Is lust in action, and till action, lust
> Is perjur'd, murdrous, blouddy, full of blame,
> Savage, extreame, rude, cruell, not to trust,
> Injoyd no sooner but dispised straight,
> Past reason hunted, and no sooner had,
> Past reason hated as a swollowed bayt,
> On purpose layd to make the taker mad:
> Mad in pursuit and in possession so,
> Had, having, and in quest to have, extreame,
> A blisse in proofe, and prov'd, a very woe,
> Before a joy proposd, behind, a dreame,
>   All this the world well knowes, yet none knowes well
>   To shun the heaven that leads men to this hell.

In addition to the condemnation of lust and perversion, however, some part of traditional sexual education can be seen as a kind of sustained war against fantasy. It is undeniable that fantasy can play an important part in all our sexual doings, and even the most passionate and faithful lover may, in the act of love, rehearse to himself other scenes of sexual abandon than the one in which he is engaged. Nevertheless, there is truth in the contrast (familiar, in one version, from the writings of Freud)[26] between fantasy and reality, and in the sense that the first is in some way destructive of the second. Fantasy replaces the real, resistant, objective world with a pliant substitute – and that, indeed, is its purpose. Life in the

344

actual world is difficult and embarrassing. Most of all it is difficult and embarrassing in our confrontation with other people, who, by their very existence, make demands that we may be unable or unwilling to meet. It requires a great force, such as the force of sexual desire, to overcome the embarrassment and self-protection that shield us from the most intimate encounters. It is tempting to take refuge in substitutes, which neither embarrass us nor resist the impulse of our spontaneous cravings. The habit grows, in masturbation, of creating a compliant world of desire, in which unreal objects become the focus of real emotions, and the emotions themselves are rendered incompetent to participate in the building of personal relations. The fantasy blocks the passage to reality, which becomes inaccessible to the will.

Even if the fantasy can be overcome so far as to engage in the act of love with another, a peculiar danger remains. The other becomes veiled in substitutes; he is never fully himself in the act of love; it is never clearly *him* that I desire, or *him* that I possess, but always rather a composite object, a universal body, of which he is but one among a potential infinity of instances. Fantasy fills our thoughts with a sense of the obscene, and the orgasm becomes, not the possession of another, but the expenditure of energy on his depersonalised body. Fantasies are private property, which I can dispose according to my will, with no answerability to the other whom I abuse through them. He, indeed, is of no intrinsic interest to me, and serves merely as my opportunity for self-regarding pleasure. For the fantasist, the ideal partner is indeed the prostitute, who, because she can be purchased, solves at once the moral problem presented by the presence of another at the scene of sexual release.

The connection between fantasy and prostitution is deep and important. The effect of fantasy is to 'commodify' the object of desire, and to replace the law of sexual relationship between people with the law of the market. Sex itself can then be seen as a commodity:[27] something that we pursue and obtain in quantifiable form, and which comes in a variety of packages: in the form of a woman or a man; in the form of a film or a dream; in the form of a fetish or an animal. In so far as the sexual act is seen in this way, it seems morally neutral – or, at best, impersonal. Such criticism as may be offered will concern merely the dangers for the individual and his partner of this or that sexual package: for some bring diseases and discomforts of which others are free. The most harmless and hygienic act of all, on this view, is the act of masturbation, stimulated by whatever works of pornography are necessary to prompt the desire for it in the unimaginative. This justification for pornography has, indeed, recently been offered.

As I have already argued, however, fantasy does not exist comfortably with reality. It has a natural tendency to realise itself: to remake the world in its own image. The harmless wanker with the video-machine can at any moment turn into the desperate rapist with a gun. The 'reality principle' by which the normal sexual act is regulated is a principle of personal encounter, which enjoins us to respect the other person, and to respect, also, the sanctity of his body, as the tangible expression of another self. The world of fantasy obeys no such rule, and is governed by monstrous myths and illusions which are at war with the human world – the illusions, for example, that women wish to be raped, that children have only to be awakened in order to give and receive the intensest sexual pleasure, that violence is not an affront but an affirmation of a natural right. All such myths, nurtured in fantasy, threaten not merely the consciousness of the man who lives by them, but also the moral structure of his surrounding world. They render the world unsafe for self and other, and cause the subject to look on everyone, not as an end in himself, but as a possible means to his private pleasure. In his world, the sexual encounter has been 'fetishised', to use the apt Marxian term,[28] and every other human reality has been poisoned by the sense of the expendability and replaceability of the other.

It is a small step from the preoccupation with sexual virtue, to a condemnation of obscenity and pornography (which is its published form). Obscenity is a direct assault on the sentiment of desire, and therefore on the social order that is based in desire and which has personal love as its goal and fulfilment. There is no doubt that the normal conscience cannot remain neutral towards obscenity, any more than it can remain neutral towards paedophilia and rape (which is not to say that obscenity must also be treated as a *crime*). It is therefore unsurprising that traditional moral education has involved censorship of obscene material, and a severe emphasis on 'purity in thought, word and deed' – an emphasis which is now greeted with irony or ridicule.

Traditional sexual education was, despite its exaggerations and imbecilities, truer to human nature than the libertarian culture which has succeeded it. Through considering its wisdom and its shortcomings, we may understand how to resuscitate an idea of sexual virtue, in accordance with the broad requirements of the Aristotelian argument that I have, in this chapter, been presenting. The ideal of virtue remains one of 'sexual integrity': of a sexuality that is entirely integrated into the life of personal affection, and in which the self and its responsibility are centrally involved and indissolubly linked to the pleasures and passions of the body.

Traditional sexual morality has therefore been the morality of the body. Libertarian morality, by contrast, has relied almost entirely on a Kantian view of the human subject, as related to his body by no coherent moral tie. Focussing as he does on an idea of purely personal respect, and assigning no distinctive place to the body in our moral endeavour, the Kantian inevitably tends towards permissive morality. No sexual act can be wrong merely by virtue of its physical character, and the ideas of obscenity, pollution and perversion have no obvious application. His attitude to homosexuality is conveniently summarised in this passage from a Quaker pamphlet:

> We see no reason why the physical nature of the sexual act should be the criterion by which the question whether it is moral should be decided. An act which (for example) expresses true affection between two individuals and gives pleasure to them both, does not seem to us to be sinful by reason *alone* of the fact that it is homosexual. The same criteria seem to apply whether a relationship is heterosexual or homosexual.[29]

Such sentiments are the standard offering of the liberal and utilitarian moralities of our time. However much we may sympathise with their conclusions, it is not possible to accept the shallow reasoning that leads up to them, and which bypasses the great metaphysical conundrum to which all sexual morality is addressed: the conundrum of embodiment. Lawrence asserts that 'sex is *you*', and offers some bad but revealing lines on the subject:

> And don't, with the nasty, prying mind, drag it out from its deeps
> And finger it and force it, and shatter the rhythm it keeps
> When it is left alone, as it stirs and rouses and sleeps.

If anything justifies Lawrence's condemnation of the 'nasty, prying mind', it is the opposite of what he supposes. Sex 'sleeps' in the soul precisely because, and to the extent that, it is buried there by education. If sex is you, it is because you are the product of that education, and not just its victim. It has endowed you with what I have called 'sexual integrity': the ability to be *in* your body, in the very moment of desire.

The reader may be reluctant to follow me in believing that traditional morality is largely justified by the ideal of sexual integrity. But if he accepts the main tenor of my argument, he must surely realise that the ethic of 'liberation', far from promising the release of the self from hostile bondage, in fact heralds the dissipation of the self in loveless fantasy: th'expence of Spirit, in a waste of shame.

12
THE POLITICS OF SEX

Sexual desire is a social artefact. Like language, and like morality, it is born from the social relations between human beings, and adds to those relations a structure and a firmness of its own. It does not follow from this, however, that sexual desire is 'merely conventional', or not a part of human 'nature'. For some artefacts are natural to human beings: in particular, all those which stem directly from social existence and which form the basis for the construction of personality. We could, indeed, imagine a human being 'outside society', but this *homo faber* would be, not a natural phenomenon, but a freak – a creature in whom the normal human potential has been frozen or destroyed. *Homo faber* would be without sexual desire, and without morality. He would also not be a person – or at least, he would be a person only *in potentia*, like a foetus or a new-born child. Not the least damaging of the Rousseauist fantasies that have dominated the moral thinking of our age is the belief that, by shaking off the 'conventions' of 'society', man achieves sexual 'liberation': he returns to a state of pure and guiltless desire, untroubled by the conflict between innocence and knowledge. If my argument is right, there is no sense to the idea that sexual fulfilment or sexual desire are located *outside* society, in a state of nature to which we must, in the sexual act, return. On the contrary, outside society there is nothing distinctively human, and all values are annulled.

Sexual desire is as natural an artefact as the human person. There could, perhaps, be human beings without this response. But the collective endeavour which paints our face on the blank of nature also generates desire, as one of the fundamental links between embodied persons. The building of personality and the building of desire are the same process, conceived under different aspects. There is no normal human sexual development which avoids the predicament of desire, and no normal development as a person which avoids the acquisition of a 'gender'.

348

Persons are essentially desirous, and desire essentially personal.

If that is so, however, we have every reason to fear the corruption of desire. Any widespread loss or perversion of this characteristic involves a threat to the human person. Sexual disintegration entails personal disintegration, and the loss of desire will entail the gradual erasure from nature of the human face which covers it. 'Mere' nature then confronts us, in all its senseless impersonality. The fear of this result, and the recognition that it might already be occurring, has been one of the impulses behind both the humanistic phenomenology of the later Husserl and the social and cultural criticism of such writers as Eliot, Lawrence and Leavis. For the phenomenologist, meaning[1] belongs only to the world as lived. It is a feature, not of the 'objective' world of natural science, but of the *Lebenswelt* with which we engage through our spontaneous thought and action. Value is a part of meaning, and, along with value, obligation. Our sense of obligation irradiates the world with a peculiar 'numinosity', which Rudolf Otto calls 'the holy',[2] and which I shall refer to, in slightly less tendentious terms, as the 'sacred'. Meaning is embedded in the given, since it is inseparable from the conceptions whereby the world is grasped. At the same time, argue such Husserlians as Heidegger and Patočka, meaning can be lost: the *Lebenswelt* then falls apart, and persists only in fragmented form.[3] Being threatened, then, by an unmediated confrontation with a merely 'objective' world, we find our existence as subjects jeopardised or denied.

The theme is, of course, older than phenomenology, and older than modern literary and cultural criticism. It should be traced back, in fact, to Kant's *Critique of Practical Reason*, where it is presented as the theme of the incommensurability between our vision of ourselves as free beings, in a world that is 'open to our agency', and our vision of ourselves as part of nature, subservient to the laws of causality of which science alone provides knowledge. In this work I have dealt with a phenomenon which lies at the intersection of these two points of view, which may be seen, now as the 'individualising' bond which ties one person to another in a relation of responsibility, now as the outcome of bodily impulses which operate according to the meaningless laws of the natural world. The 'sexual integrity' which I recommended as the true ideal of virtue can be seen as a bastion against the 'objective' and 'senseless' view of ourselves. Take away that bastion and nothing remains in the spectacle of human sexuality, but a comic vision of a tragic enslavement, in which the human soul is 'instrumentalised' by the body, and the sexual act is a matter only of technique. The true meaning of 'Kinseyism' is to be found in this: it is the device whereby the sexual act is given back to objective nature and rid of its meaning. It is the device whereby all that is 'inner', 'subjective', 'value-laden' in our sexual experience is discounted. It is a mark of our alienation that we are so often tempted to see the resulting description of our acts, not as utterly mendacious, but as profoundly true.

As I have mentioned, many writers and philosophers have looked for the solution to this 'alienated', 'reified' or 'fetishised' perspective, by recommending a state of nature. Marcuse, Fromm, Reich, Norman O. Brown and countless other disenchanted moralists have seen the route to a rediscovered sexuality in the ethic of 'liberation' – in the casting off of social garments.[4] Like Rousseau, they propose, not savagery, but a 'higher' civilisation as their preferred 'natural' state: a new society based on free association, often without institutions, without laws, without any constraints other than those that bind consenting adults to one another by an unforced promise.

That search for a meaning outside society – or in a society of the future which we neither understand concretely nor know how to bring about – is but another expression of the alienation that it condemns, and an attempt to dress up the outlook of the alienated individual in the attributes of virtue. Alienation becomes prophecy, and those who still seek their consolation in the actual are seen merely as slaves of the impure institutions which they support. In truth, however, there is no way back to sexual integrity which does not involve the care of institutions, and the attempt to restore to the actual social order the concrete marks of a public morality. Only this can imbue the world of man with a meaning that is greater than his immediate purposes, and so enable him to find himself as a subject, unthreatened by the senselessness of a merely objective world. Sexual morality must, therefore, have its political aspect, and – even if it is impossible or dangerous to formulate the politics of sex as a programme – we cannot complete the description of desire without reviewing the nature and function of sexual institutions.

It is undeniable that sexual institutions have changed, and may even have entered a state of crisis. The fate of political institutions is but one aspect of the fate of persons, and the fate of persons is inseparable from the history of the institutions which form and nurture them. The erosion of the integrated viewpoint, of the long-term perspective, of the individual responsibility not just for the here and now, but for the past and future of oneself and of the social order to which one belongs – these are facts. And such facts are both personal and political in their implications. Recognition of the interdependence between the individual and the institutions of the *polis* has been the major theme of conservative political thought from Aristotle to modern times, and it has been a distinguishing feature of modern conservatism that – wittingly or not – it has sought to found its picture of political order and legitimate government upon a perception of the nature of domestic relations and of the erotic bond which underlies them.[5] In this chapter I shall make a few very brief remarks that will show why this attempt is important, and why it might provide conservatism with a surer political foundation than its critics have supposed.

The human self requires the social structure that will sustain both desire and the love which grows from it. This in turn requires that we live in conditions that nourish the long-term view of things – the view which enables us to live beyond the realm of the 'minimal self', and to assert responsibility for the past and future into which our concerns extend. In love, as in hatred, we rejoice in the view of one another as unified and transcendental beings, whose identity and activity are governed by different principles from those which govern the identity and the unity of the body. At the same time, we identify the 'transcendental' with the 'empirical' self, and see the body as identical with that pure core of agency which defines each person's perspective, and which remains infinitely free, infinitely capable and infinitely to blame. The beloved object who shatters this illusion – who acts without consistency, without integrity and as though propelled by his body regardless of his self – confuses and destroys our love. We would rather he were faithless, so that we could hate him, than that his thoughts and feelings should lie beyond human grasp, exhibiting no pattern or order that is indicative of anything more persistent than a minimal self. There exists, however, an enduring public need to create the conditions of responsible agency and the expectations that nurture our sense of ourselves as answerable not only for our present actions, but for our lives as a whole, and able to project that answerability onto those whom we encounter. We have reason, in other words, to create the maximal self, which mediates in all our dealings. The maximal self does not exist in the state of nature, but only in society, and is sustained by customs, habits and beliefs that are easily destroyed and which we destroy at our peril.

The ability to spread oneself in time, and to answer now for past and future, is what Patočka called 'historicity' (*dějinnost*).[6] At times of crisis, Patočka argued, man experiences the disappearance of his historical attachments. He does not find the public world in which the 'care of the soul' is a recognised state of being: his *polis* can exist, if at all, only inwardly.[7] The public world then contains only the routine technicalities of 'everyday life' (*každodennost*) – a life from which meaning has been expunged, and in which the only important value is life itself, the intricate

351

task of daily survival. In response to this, man may take refuge in exultation. That is, he may excite himself into a kind of dionysiac frenzy, in which all consciousness of his situation is destroyed. For it is easier to close one's mind to the *Lebenswelt* than to confront its fractured form and to see through that fracture the meaningless reality of the everyday. Exultation may take many forms, but its characteristically modern form is revolutionary politics: the extinguishing of all scruples, all *care*, in the tumult of an uncomprehended purpose. This is the final, insensate, substitution of the 'morality of goals' for the 'morality of sense'.[8] For us, Patočka argued, historicity involves acquiring what the exulted person also acquires – a separation between the present self and everyday life. But it is a separation achieved, not at the cost of consciousness, but *through* consciousness. Hence, it involves, not the loss, but the gain of the 'care of the soul' which exists in the ideal *polis*.

For Patočka, the return from exultation is by two well-worn paths: philosophy, which teaches us to care for the soul through the love of truth; and the *polis*, which surrounds us with the institutions by which meaning is perpetuated in the public world. Patočka's turning to philosophy was a result of his despair at the modern state – a despair which, in his circumstances, may well have been justified.[9] But philosophy is a minority pursuit. It is able to bring comfort to the intellectual and to neutralise his dangerous propensity to exultation, but it has no real meaning for the common man. Meaning, for common humanity, lies in a constant confrontation with the sacred. And in this confrontation man rehearses the transcendental illusion, that his personal existence in the world is possible only because he is not of the world.

In the *Critique of Practical Reason* Kant argued that the truths of religion may be justified through the exercise of *practical* rather than theoretical reason, and so escape the strictures against rational theology that he had made in the first *Critique*. Most commentators are dissatisfied by these 'practical proofs' of God's existence, but many feel that they carry a profound suggestion as to the nature of religious belief. The suggestion, I believe, is this: the first-person perspective imposes habits of intentional understanding. We see the world as 'open to agency'; we find *room* in the world for the self and its works, and we see our freedom as reflecting a real order of events. To perceive the world 'under the aspect of freedom', however, is to perceive it in sacral terms. For the world then bears the mark of will, and is also open to will.

For primitive man this sense of belonging is unquestionable. Nature itself has will; its movements are the movements of spirits, which inhabit the trees and the waters as we inhabit our bodies. Everywhere about him primitive man encounters the reality of embodiment and the order of agency. His own embodiment is no more puzzling to him than the embodiment of the perspectives that look on him with such hostile or protective eyes from every grove and thicket. In a similar manner, however, the belief in a transcendental order enables less primitive people to sustain the vital sense of belonging. The world which would otherwise overwhelm them with its merely causal order, and which threatens to crush their small attempts at responsible living, is rendered friendly and submissive. Men are redeemed from their *Geworfenheit*, and restored to the transcendental illusion upon which their happiness depends. By believing the soul to be immortal, outside nature and in eternal relation with the perspectiveless first-person of God, I gain moral security. As Kant saw, this security comes, not from the belief that God commands us to be good, but from the sense that our transcendental identity and freedom arc not illusory but real. The world has opened to the *subject*; its steely objectivity has been breached.

In the ideal *polis*, therefore, religion has always had its place, and carried with it the lamp of the sacred. No better way has ever been devised of giving substance to human vows and human values than the belief in a transcendental order, and in the eternal presence of the dead. But a belief can survive only so long as we are persuaded by it, and without belief the exercise of virtue may appear hollow or vain. The restoration of meaning, which Patočka looked for in philosophy, comes easier through religion, and with the decline of religion (however temporary) the institutions of the *polis* seem to stand on less solid ground.

It is evident that, while there may be *reasons* for the belief in God and immortality, they are not the normal *causes* of those beliefs (a fact which certain philosophers would regard as discrediting the claims of faith and doctrine).[10] Religious faith is the upshot of social practices – ritual, ceremony, custom – which fill the vacuum in the heart of things with a transcendental meaning. Nature abhors a vacuum, and the voiding of religious meanings has not emptied the world of superstition. The 'disenchantment' described by Weber[11] has indeed occurred; but in the place of religious ideas our world presents us with the ludicrous superstitions of the exultant – the belief in 'progress', in utopia, in 'liberation' and in a purely secular redemption (through sex, politics or psychoanalysis) from the burden of original sin. Those beliefs too are no more caused by the reasons which support them than the beliefs of old-fashioned religion, and one can be forgiven for thinking that, in comparison, they are both spiritually empty and morally incompetent. Nevertheless, they arise almost inevitably from a social condition in which custom, ceremony and deference are no longer the norm.

The 'restoration of the sacred' may be a political hope, but it cannot be a political task: to make it one is to risk the most violent cataclysm and the collapse of liberal political institutions. But it is necessary to draw the moral from those brief reflections and to face up to the – perhaps unpalatable – truth which they contain. The experience of the sacred is, I have implied, a fundamental component in our sense of the world as 'open to agency', as containing within it the mark of the first-person perspective by which we live. The loss of that experience threatens the life of the subject, and the *Lebenswelt* in which he may recognise himself. In particular it threatens the pattern of thought which I have identified as integral to traditional moral education, and which centres upon a conception of 'sexual innocence'. The perception of the child as innocent, of the virgin as sacrosanct, of sexual abuse as a 'pollution' – these 'survivals' of the ethic of 'pollution and taboo' – are also our most immediate experiences of the sacred, and are threatened by the disappearance of the customs and rituals by which the idea of the sacred is nurtured. Well might Yeats have asked

> How but in custom and in ceremony
> Are innocence and beauty born?

The loss of innocence is an affair, not of individuals, but of institutions and customs, and, in perceiving the damage inflicted upon those social artefacts, we see the true extent to which sexual morality has been jeopardised. At the same time, sexual integrity is a condition of stable relations between those who love, and the foundation of the cheerful fecundity upon which social continuity depends. It has become fashionable to lament the disparaging of fecundity and the rise of sexual customs which endorse and even celebrate sterility as a human good.[12] But it is more important to see what is lacking from a society in which the bond of desire has been rendered fragile and impermanent by the loss of innocence. Such a society is threatened, not merely in its continuity, but in its very existence, by the sexual alienation of its members. To the extent that this alienation is an index of institutional decline, sexual morality inevitably requires a politics of sexual institutions.

'Spontaneous social order' is an illusion, fed upon the fairy-tales of anthropologists and upon the fables of Adam Smith and Friedrich von Hayek.[13] The 'invisible hand' which directs our collective well-being is not the spontaneous upshot of human cooperation, but the elaborate artefact of centuries of institution-building. Erotic love is like private property in many things: in its closeness to the self, in its exclusiveness and in the new dimension of freedom which it opens to those who are bound by it. But it is no more a gift of nature than private property is a 'natural right': both are the products of institutions which sustain them, and both grant their benefits, not as rights, but as achievements and privileges. If we wish to guarantee the survival of either, it is not sufficient to leave their future to the 'spontaneous social order' of the neo-conservatives. We must sustain the institutions which protect them, and which may not be the offshoot of every social order at every time. In a sequel to this volume I shall consider the nature of such institutions in more detail. In what follows I shall deliver only the barest sketch.

In emphasising the role of the sacred in the ideal *polis*, I have made a large institutional demand. In particular, I have implied that sexual integrity will flourish in a society in which religious institutions and customs also flourish and retain their authority. And my discussion has implied much else about the character of civil society in the virtuous *polis*. Civil society, however, is nothing without the state, which is its 'realised' form.[14] The state protects and ratifies the institutions of civil society, by endowing them with legal and moral personality. By casting over all social arrangements the protective mantle of sovereignty and law, it removes the arbitrariness from custom and agreement. Associations, such as the family, the club, the firm, the government and the state itself, cease to be mere contracts between private people for purposes of their own and become instead recognisable entities – artificial persons, with rights, duties and liabilities, which present an intelligible face to the world and can be understood in personal terms. By associating himself with such collectives the individual expands his own capacity for action, and acquires also an expanded image of himself, as a bearer of functions and roles. No civil society can persist in stable form, unless these collective entities become institutions, with personality, agency and the capacity to survive their present membership, and to acquire a history and an identity of their own. One of the principal functions of the state is to provide the legal and political framework within which that transaction can occur. And in doing so, the state is inevitably selective, providing protection for some institutions (for example, for the family), and removing it from others (for example, from the private army).

Liberalism is the natural philosophy of the 'desacralised' world. For the liberal conscience, obligations do not surround us in the *Lebenswelt*, but are created by our individual choices. 'There is', said Hobbes, 'no obligation on any man which ariseth not from some act of his own'.[15] Hence there can be no obligation between you and me without an agreement which binds us. With a little strain, many social arrangements can be seen in those terms, as 'voluntary associations', arising out of the common consent, and common expectations, of their members. At the same time, however, there is something extremely artificial about the liberal way of seeing things, even when formulated in the sophisticated manner of Rawls, who sees the obligations of civil society as founded, not in an actual, but in a hypothetical contract.[16] Men join an association not as a rule because they seek agreement with existing members, but either because they have no choice, or because they seek to be part of the association itself, as an entity which is something more than a mutual promise. People are expanded and set free by association, precisely because associations transcend their capacities to 'agree on terms'. And the two most important of all human associations – the family which nurtures us, and the state which governs us from birth to death – are not, and could not be, founded in a 'social contract'.[17]

One should not be surprised, therefore, if at every important juncture in civil association – every point at which a decision of *membership* has to be made – we find, not just associations, but also institutions. People worship and pray together, but through the institution of church or mosque; they compete and play, but through clubs and local societies; they learn and teach, but through educational institutions which exert the widest possible influence over those who attend them. And their sexual union too seems to crave for its institutional realisation – for the publicly recognisable form whereby it is enlarged into something other than a mutual agreement.

Such a form is marriage, which imposes on the bond of erotic love the non-contractual and pious arrangement of the home. Marriage is a public endorsement of the passion which separates lovers from their surroundings. It is the public acceptance of their exclusive privacy. In entering a marriage they do not merely exchange promises: they pass together into a condition that is not of their own devising, and which contains the deposits of countless previous experiences of intimacy. Marriage, like every worthwhile institution, is also a tradition – a smooth handle on experience, which has been passed from generation to generation, and, in the passing, slowly worn itself into the shape required by human nature. It has a story attached to it: its comic and tragic aspects are a familiar part of popular culture; its hardships and joys can be anticipated and also shared; it has the respect and the understanding of others. Moreover, it translates itself into legal forms, and endeavours to reconstitute as legal rights the many and mysterious obligations which arise from domestic proximity. In many societies a marriage is a 'legal person' in itself, with agency and answerability that are not those of the partners. If there is an 'ethical idea of marriage',[18] it lies at least partly in this subsumption of the 'merely private' bond of love under laws that are open, disputable and a matter of moral and legal right.

The marriage ceremony is therefore one of the most important of human ceremonies, and one which marks a transition from one state of existence to another. At such moments, man is confronted with his fragility and dependence. As at the moments of death and birth, he is beset by awe. This feeling is a recognition of the sacred: of the intrusion into the human world of obligations that cannot be created by an act of choice, and which therefore demand a transcendental meaning. The sacred is 'the subjectivity of objects' – the presentation, in the contours of day-to-day things, of a meaning that sees 'from I to I'. Out of the mute objectivity of the surrounding world, a voice suddenly calls to me, with a clear and intelligible command. It tells me who I am, and enjoins me to enter the place that has been kept for me. In marriage I 'undertake' an obligation that precedes my choice, and which resides in the scheme of things. Not surprisingly, therefore, marriage is a religious 'sacrament', comparable to the sacraments of baptism and extreme unction. The universal participation of religions in the marriages of believers is testimony to the shared perception of this sacred quality. And like all sacred matters, marriage presents different aspects to the participant and to the observer. The sacred is a personal concept, one that features in the intentional understanding of the person who *participates* in a certain social practice. From the scientific point of view, however, there is no such reality as that of the sacred. At best there is, in anthropological language, an 'initiation rite', in which the transition of a person from one state of social existence to another is confirmed by the mass participation of the tribe.[19]

In order to understand the marriage obligation in its full political meaning, it is necessary to distinguish the ceremony of marriage from the institution which is created by it. The first is an attempt to embody, in publicly intelligible form, the experience of a sacred obligation. It represents marriage as a point of *transition*, which, like death, permits of no return, but which, unlike death, establishes a new life in this world for those who undergo it. 'To apprehend / The point of intersection of the timeless / With time, is an occupation for the saint,' wrote Eliot. His sentiment was, however, heretical. This point of intersection is apprehended in every experience of the sacred. Matrimony, as Eliot reminds us, is a 'dignified and commodious sacrament', and if every true marriage yearns for ceremony, it is in order to record this fact, and to confirm the apprehension of sacred things by making them matters of public knowledge and public concern.

The institution of marriage is, however, something more than the ceremony with which it begins. And it is as necessary for the state to join in the institution as it is for the church to join in its beginning. For marriage is a moral and legal reality, which takes its meaning from the two most fundamental forms of human love: erotic love, and love between parent and child. Both loves have their natural history; both vary from the intensity of passion to the serenity of day-to-day assurance. But both demand recognition, not only from those who are bound by them, but also from the surrounding world, which might otherwise threaten their exclusiveness, or rebel against the unfair privilege which every love contains. If marriage survives it is because people seek public recognition for their intimacies. Only an institution which imposes a single, invariable obligation on all who elect to join it can create this public recognition, by making clear that the meaning of the individual action is to be found, not in the private desire which prompted it, but in the public custom which gives it form. Hence the bond of marriage, even in the secular state, has a 'transcendental' meaning – one that cannot be summarised in terms of contract or consent. The obligations of marriage are not contracted between the partners, but imposed by the institution, which endeavours to translate into articulate form the constant upsurge of new responsibilities between those who have entered it together. The greatest threat to marriage – as indeed to all institutions which permit the enlargement of the human spirit – is the 'ideology of contract': the view that no man can be bound except by terms to which he has consented. Who, when faced with his wife's fatal illness, can justify divorce on the ground that this was not an eventuality that he had foreseen, or a duty that he had willingly undertaken? It is of course true that a man 'takes responsibility' for another's life in marriage. But this 'taking responsibility' is not to be summarised in a promise. For its terms cannot be stated, nor can its duties be foretold. Thus it is that the transition from private passion to public institution gives substance to the 'vow' of erotic love. To remake marriage as a personal contract, with conditions and terms, is in fact to abolish it, and thereby to threaten both the obligations which it protects and the state of mind which dares to confront them. (Hence sentences of the ecclesiastical courts, which release the parties *à vinculo matrimonii*, are not releases from a 'marriage contract', but declarations that a marriage never existed.) The world of the 'consenting adult', the world remade in accordance with the 'social contract' of the enlightened liberal conscience, is, in the last analysis, a world too timid for love.

It might be argued that, if the obligations of love are private, they need no public institution to protect them. But to argue thus is, I believe, to make a serious mistake about the character of civil society. It is to suppose that social relations can simply sustain themselves, without the complicity of the social world. On the contrary, however, social existence is 'existence under observation'. It involves activities which place us continually before the curious, envious or condoning eyes of others. The moral sense itself arises from the habit of turning upon ourselves the eyes which we turn on other persons. Their eyes on us direct our eyes also. And if we develop the capacity for the vow of love, it is because we see ourselves reflected in this public observation, as objects of judgement that can make no exceptions in their own favour, and who must take life as it is offered. This public pressure on the individual is made bearable by marriage, which instructs others to avert their eyes and to create the legitimacy of a life lived privately. The division between the public and the private *creates* the private, by creating the space from which others are excluded. In doing so, it brings to a resolution that dialectical anxiety of lovers, who wish constantly to be assured of love, but who cannot demand it. (Cf. the passage from Robert Solomon, quoted on p. 304.) Marriage brings inquisition to a close, and fills the resulting silence with an unspoken answer.

It is perhaps unnecessary to contrast the unhappy condition of the adulterer, who must be secret in all his works and for whom the privacy demanded by love is a rare achievement, no sooner enjoyed than threatened with discovery. However, it is not only the adulterer who is in this predicament. The element of generality in our sexual feelings – the element which leads us to look on people as 'fair game' – leads to a curiosity about the sexual lives of others, and a nascent jealousy, that can be extinguished only by the closing of doors. Marriage, which is legitimate exclusion, creates a peculiar safety and inwardness between lovers. One philosopher has even written of 'the domestic' as a separate 'phenomenological category'.[20]

Stani, a character in Hofmannsthal's *Der Schwierige*, utters the outrageous opinion that women are of two kinds: those you marry and those you love.[21] There are many reasons for marriage apart from love; why, therefore, does marriage not pollute love with considerations that are unworthy of it? Marriage has an economic and also a philo-progenitive meaning. Marriage may be a means to something else, and valued for no intrinsic reason. Love, however, is never a means, and contains its virtue intrinsically. In comparison with marriage – *le ron-ron monotone du pot-au-feu conjugale*, as Sardou described it – adultery seems more exciting, and often more pure: as indeed it was for the medieval expositors of the ethic of courtly love.[22] It may even seem as though *only* adultery is worthy of the higher transports of erotic love, since only adultery can show that it is love alone which creates its obligations, and not the external morality of a public institution polluted by others' purposes and others' needs.

That Tristanian justification of adultery is also, however, a plea for the public acceptance of marriage, as the necessary background for these forbidden pleasures. The adulterer trades security for excitement, and intimacy for a precarious exposure to jealousy and pain. The desire of the adulterer is greater, just as the desire for food is greater in the hungry man. The value of marriage lies, however, not in the heightening of desire, but in the fulfilling of it. Marriage creates thereby the objective conditions for the genesis of desire, and if desire sometimes strays towards the forbidden and the fruitless, this is made possible only because it also has a normal course which sustains its wayward intensities.

It is a small step from the institution of marriage to that of private property. The exclusive erotic relation fights also for its exclusive territory; for the right to close a door. Within that territory everything is 'shared', and since only what is privately owned can be privately shared, the sphere of marriage and of the family is one of private ownership. Moreover, ownership of the home (in the wide sense of 'tenure' as this concept has been developed in English law) is ownership of a stake in the means of production. The home is not merely the 'means of consumption', as the Marxists would have us believe. It is a place of collective labour, where things are not only consumed but also *made* for consumption. Agricultural produce may be grown and sold; carpets and clothes may be sewn and embroidered; the home itself may be improved and passed on. In short, the home has a natural tendency to realise itself as capital, and will do so upon the death of parents, unless some political system exists which prevents the transition from residence to sale. Hence, as Hegel wrote:

> The family, as person, has its real external existence in property; and it is only when this property takes the form of capital that it becomes the embodiment of the substantial personality of the family.[23]

That passage serves to remind us of a deep and important truth. The institutions of the world into which we were born have the appearance of political contrivances; they may seem, under the impact of this or that revolutionary theory, to be no more than passing phases of man's historical condition. But those appearances may also be mistaken. It may be that human nature, which enjoins us to love, imposes upon us the religious, civil and legal institutions that abounded everywhere in the world, until exultant intellectuals decided that the time had come to dispense with them. No account of erotic love will be either politically innocent or politically neutral. And it will be the greatest error of a political system that it overlooks the demands of love. This error was made, I believe, by the nineteenth-century communists, in their demand for a society without exclusive relations either between people or between people and things: a kind of dance of death, performed by indistinguishable noumenal selves.

This book ends, however, with the defence of marriage. All that I have said about other institutions is no more than a hint, and must await wider argument. In place of that argument, I here give only a gesture. Many social and political changes have swept the world clean of the apprehension of sacred things: the rejection of custom and ceremony; the conversion of marriage into a defeasible contract; the relaxing of the laws governing, sexual conduct and obscenity; the decline of faith and saintliness. As those changes take their effect, the experience of erotic love becomes dangerous and uncertain in its outcome. Our responsibility retreats further from the confused terrain of sexual experience, and threatens even to void it of desire.

Hence, it might be said, my ability to reflect, in so neutral and philosophical a fashion, on the nature of this phenomenon is perhaps already an index of its decline: of the fact that desire does not, now, have the importance for us that formerly caused men to conceal it in poetry or overcome it through prayer. What we understand of our condition may also pass from us in the act of understanding. For we were never meant to have knowledge of this thing; we were meant only to be subject to its command. No phenomenon, perhaps, illustrates more profoundly the great poetical utterance of Hegel; that

> When philosophy paints its grey in grey, then has a shape of life grown old. By philosophy's grey in grey it cannot be rejuvenated but only understood. The owl of Minerva spreads its wings only with the gathering of the dusk.

On the other hand, it is a century and a half since Hegel wrote those words, and life goes on.

EPILOGUE

In a recent work, Michel Foucault asks the following question:

> Why does sexual behaviour, and why do the activities and pleasures which pertain to it, form the object of a moral preoccupation? Why this ethical concern, which, at least at certain moments, in certain societies, or in certain groups, appears more important than the moral attention paid to other domains equally essential to individual and collective life, such as the supply of provisions, or the accomplishment of civic duties? . . . Why this 'problematisation'? And after all, it is the task of a history of thought, in contrast to the history of behaviour or of representations, to define the conditions in which the human being 'problematises' what he is, what he does, and the world in which he lives.[1]

Foucault supposes his question to be historical. He assumes that there could be societies in which this 'problematisation' of the sexual did not occur. I have argued, however, that there could be neither arousal, nor desire, nor the pleasures that pertain to them, without the presence, in the very heart of these responses, of the moral scruples which limit them. What Foucault assumes to be an historical fact is no such thing, but rather an *a priori* truth concerning the human person. No history of thought could show the 'problematisation' of sexual experience to be peculiar to certain specific social formations: it is characteristic of personal experience generally, and therefore of every genuine social order.

At the same time, however, my conclusions are by no means morally neutral. Nor do they express intuitions common to all people at all times. In a certain sense my method has been descriptive: I have been concerned to analyse a feature of our intentional understanding. But the concepts that I have considered transform the experience of those who apply them. Moreover they are permeable to the moral sentiments which grow within our culture, and which focus our activities in historically variable ways. Inevitably, therefore, my analysis has included a large prescriptive

362

component. Since I have given what is, in effect, a defence of 'bourgeois marriage', I shall certainly provoke the charge that my conclusions could not possibly be valid outside the historical circumstances that have engendered them. Such would certainly be said by those historians for whom the 'bourgeois' is a distinct social category.

I shall not answer the charge, except to say that my examples have been taken from Greek and Latin literature, from medieval chivalry and nineteenth-century morality, from the court literature of Japan and the decadent pages of the French *fin-de-siècle*. I have expressly ranged across as many articulations of sexual experience as are familiar to me, and my final defence of the 'bourgeois' order is intended to apply to every civilised society – every society in which the human person may emerge as a distinct phenomenon. Once we have rejected the schoolboy history of *The Communist Manifesto* (a history to which Foucault himself shows an obstinate attachment),[2] little substance remains to the claim that my preferred social order is bourgeois. The same might be said of the order defended by Aristotle in the *Politics*, by Shakespeare in *The Winter's Tale* and *Measure for Measure*, by Homer, Chaucer, Hesiod and Dante; by Langland, Goldsmith, Thackerary and Dickens; by Joyce, Conrad and Lawrence – in short, by every writer who has seen the natural *telos* of desire in the creation of a moral unity between persons. There are 'non-bourgeois' philosophies of desire. But the principal example – that given by Plato – has been the target of my argument throughout. And if bourgeois society is the answer to Plato, *vive la bourgeoisie!*

APPENDIX I
THE FIRST PERSON

As it is now generally understood, phenomenology involves two root ideas. One is the exploration of the *Lebenswelt*. The other is the attempt to provide a purely 'intentional' description of experience, which makes no assumptions about the 'objective' world, and which records the immediate content of self-awareness.[1] In Chapter 1 I avoided that second idea, and skirted around the problems generated by Husserl's attempt – in *Cartesian Meditations* and elsewhere – to combine a theory of the 'transcendental subject' with an endorsement of Descartes' method of doubt. My purpose was first to relate my argument to ideas which have gained understandable currency, and secondly to allay any anxiety concerning the incompetence of analytical philosophy, either to discuss the complexities of individual experience, or to resolve the 'phenomenological problems' which are generated by the attempt to describe it. In what followed I encapsulated my observations concerning the first person, within the limits imposed by a third-person point of view. In particular, I considered the first-person perspective as a publicly recognisable and socially generated property of language-using creatures, the moral and metaphysical meaning of which is contained not in some exclusively 'subjective' realm, but in the overt reality of linguistic practice. This first-person perspective indicates no mystery in the human condition. Those phenomenologists who disclose such a mystery are victims of an illusion; what they think to have discovered they have in fact created.

In this appendix I give a more technical exposition of the philosophy which underlies my treatment of the first-person case. This philosophy is not necessary for an understanding of my argument, but it is important for those who wish to ponder the metaphysical consequences of the views put forward in the body of this text. I shall be concerned to expose what I shall call the 'first-person illusion'. This is the view that the essential quality of every mental state lies in what is immediately 'given' to consciousness: in what is grasped by the subject, in the very moment of experience, and which could not be grasped by any observer simply from the standpoint of a 'third-person' perspective. The essential quality of a sensation lies in 'how it feels', rather than in any physical circumstance that causes or evinces it. The essential quality of a belief lies in a 'given' content which the subject grasps in the act of believing. And so on. On such a view, the essential quality of sexual desire would lie in what is 'given' to the first-person perspective. Hence there could be no enquiry into the nature of sexual desire that was not, in the end, an enquiry into *what it is like* to undergo or enjoy it.

But how should I answer the question 'what is it like?' How should I answer it, that is, by appeal only to what is given to *me*? No words seem quite to capture the truth of the matter; indeed, in the end, words fail. The experience alone seems able to contain an answer. Philosophical description – description upon which I could found an account of the human subject and his position in the world – seems neither necessary nor possible. To 'know what it is like' is to share in an experience: it is to have passed over from the condition of the observer, for whom there can indeed be the 'knowledge by description' which captures a truth in words, to the condition of the subject, for whom the given is inseparable from the experience itself. No description can take me from the first of those conditions to the second. The best it can do is to stimulate my imagination, so enabling me, if not to know, at least to imagine 'what it is like'. But this 'imagining what it is like' is itself an experience, not to be captured in terms of information that may be as well contained in words.[2] Or rather it can be contained in words, but only metaphorically. The less the intellectual content of an experience, the more does this metaphorical character of its first-person description become prominent – as is evinced, for example, in the description of wine, ironically recorded by Evelyn Waugh, in a nonsense dialogue between drunken adolescents:

> '. . . It is a little, shy wine, like a gazelle.'
> 'Like a leprechaun.'
> 'Dappled, in a tapestry meadow.'
> 'Like a flute by still water.'
> '. . . And this is a wise old man.'
> 'A prophet in a cave.'
> '. . . And this is a necklace of pearls on a white neck.'
> 'Like a swan.'
> 'Like the last unicorn.'
> [*Brideshead Revisited*]

Indeed the final recourse of a writer who wishes to convey experience to the inexperienced is poetry – the language of the imagination. In poetry, however, words are bent to the task of conveying, not information only, but an individual experience which, whether or not it depends on information, could never be reduced to it.

Intellectual states of mind are less obviously 'phenomenological'. It seems implausible to speak of 'what it is like to believe that p', or to suppose that there is a subjective aspect of belief that is captured by this phrase. Of course, a thought may carry a penumbra of emotion. There is, for example, a penumbra about the thought of human imperfection – a sense of changeless change and fickle constancy – which gives sense to the words of one who doubts that he knows what it is like to have that thought. He may cease to doubt when the appropriate metaphor is provided:

O saisons, O châteaux!
Quelle âme est sans défaut!

However, the need for metaphor is dictated, not by the thought, but by the experience. Imagine someone saying: 'I know what it is like to believe that Chlorine is an element, but I cannot imagine what it would be like to believe that Chlorine is a compound.' What possible difference could he have in mind, other than the evident difference in content? However, even beliefs, the phenomenologists argue, are to be understood subjectively. It is only to the first person that the content of a belief is immediately known, and only subjectively that this content is affirmed, in a mental act that must be studied in its 'inward' manifestation. Such a study will be as much a study of the 'given', and as much in need of metaphorical embellishment, as the study of the 'inner' aspect of experience.

Some philosophers, motivated by an enterprise of Husserl's, have sought to remedy what they have taken to be the defective condition of natural language: that it can speak of the subjectively 'given' only in metaphorical terms. They have tried to develop a language of philosophical technicalities, which will capture the 'inner' essence of thought and experience, the subjective core which remains when all outer reference has been 'bracketed'.[3] The result has been, either a technical language whose field of reference can never be specified, or else a new kind of metaphor – exemplified in the phenomenological works of Heidegger and Sartre – instances of which have occurred throughout this work. Not only is that true as a matter of fact; it is also true, I believe, as a matter of necessity. There are no literal truths of 'pure phenomenology', and it is therefore no deficiency in a language that it is unable to present them. To think otherwise is to suffer from the first-person illusion.

It is not only phenomenologists who have suffered from that illusion. It has provided the pivotal thought of many philosophical theories, including the Cartesian theory of the mind, the standard empiricist and positivist theories of knowledge (for example, the constructivist conception of reality expounded by Carnap in *The Logical Structure of the World*),[4] and the Husserlian concept of consciousness, as a purely immanent 'noetic structure', containing the clue to everything that can be known of an objective world which is itself 'constituted . . . purely within the transcendental ego'.[5] For all such theories the world becomes, in Husserl's words, 'a universal problem of egology.'[6] The first-person illusion is thus the philosophical elaboration, and the transformation into metaphysical theory, of the 'transcendental illusion' which haunts our interpersonal emotions.

It is to Wittgenstein, I believe, that we owe the argument which destroys this illusion – destroys it by showing that what seems most certain to its victim is precisely that which he has greatest reason to doubt. The argument against the possibility of a private language has had many interpreters, and has been given many applications. I do not suggest that the version which I shall expound represents either Wittgenstein's intentions or the most far-reaching of the many consequences which flow from his remarks. My interest in the argument is an interest purely in its validity, and, although I believe that it corresponds to much of Wittgenstein's meaning in the *Philosophical Investigations*, §§243ff., it is of no great importance that this or that commentator may seek to interpret those sections differently. All further discussion of what *Wittgenstein* meant I hereby consign to a note.[7]

The argument begins from the idea of first-person knowledge. I have privileged access to my present conscious states: I know, immediately, incorrigibly and certainly, various facts about my present condition – that I am in pain, say. This privileged access does not extend beyond the present moment. I can therefore make mistakes about my past and future consciousness. For the same reason, I can make mistakes in any judgement of my present condition which involves some *hypothesis* about the past or future. For example, I can be mistaken in thinking that I am in love, or jealous, or desperate. My first-person privilege extends no further than my present consciousness. My belief that I am in pain is self-guaranteeing, incorrigible and also immediate, based in no observation of my own condition. Following Wittgenstein, I shall take sensations as the paradigms of such 'objects of immediate knowledge'. It should be remembered that this is a device of convenience only, and that what I go on to say will apply equally to any other conscious content. In particular it will apply to the immediate contents of thought and to the associated 'noetic' structures, which are the preferred objects of analysis for Husserlian phenomenology.

The first-person illusion arises in the following way. My immediate awareness of *my* pain contrasts with the mediate, fallible and hypothetical belief that I have concerning *yours*. There is an epistemological asymmetry between first-person and third-person awareness. Hence – it is supposed – while I can know my sensations, I cannot really know yours. Your sensations are accessible to you, but not to me. Thus a sensation is an essentially 'private' item, something with an 'inner' or 'phenomenal' essence, which is revealed to no one besides the subject. The 'inner' episode is contrasted with every 'outer' manifestation. The 'sensation itself' is not publicly identifiable and is therefore distinct from anything that *is* so identifiable. In particular, it is distinct from every condition of the body and from every item of behaviour through which the sensation may find 'expression'. We may summarise the illusion, therefore, in the following terms:

A sensation is a 'private object' – one whose nature and existence is connected only contingently with any 'publicly identifiable' state of affairs, and whose 'inner' nature is therefore knowable only to the subject. By 'object' here I mean 'object of knowledge' or 'object of reference'. I do not mean that the private object is a 'reidentifiable particular', rather than, say, a property, a state, an event or a process. A 'private object' is an item about which only one person can have genuine knowledge – an item with features that are revealed to no one but him.

It is necessary to explain the term 'publicly identifiable'. An item is publicly identifiable if more than one person can obtain sufficient evidence of its existence and properties. 'Sufficient' here means sufficient to establish a rule of reference, such that, by using the rule, any person could refer to the item and know exactly what he was referring to. (I give here a necessary condition, and not a sufficient condition, for 'public identifiability', since no more is required.) Thus any physical object is publicly identifiable, and so too are the changes and processes that occur in physical objects. Theoretical entities are also publicly identifiable, even though they may be observed only through their effects.

The demolition of the first-person illusion proceeds by showing that no private object could be an object of knowledge, since no such object could be referred to. It is useful to begin – as Wittgenstein begins – by asking the question 'how do words refer to sensations?' (The strategy is to show that we *do* refer to sensations, that we *cannot* refer to private objects, and therefore that sensations are not private objects.) In order to answer our question we must disregard the first-person case, which is only one special case of the use of sensation language, and attend to the third-person usage of terms like 'pain'. How could we establish, in a natural language, a practice of communication in which that term is used referringly?

The first condition which such a practice must meet is that of teachability. It must be possible to teach a newcomer how to engage in it, and this means that it must be possible publicly to correct him when he makes mistakes. If the practice is one of reference, it follows immediately that the items referred to must be publicly identifiable. For it must be possible for the teacher to know – within normal limits of error – whether the circumstances referred to obtain. If he cannot know this, he cannot know whether the pupil is proceeding rightly or wrongly. In which case, whatever seems right to the pupil *is* right. Which is just another way of saying that there is no longer a genuine rule of reference, placing independent constraints upon the pupil's use of words. Whatever his words may do in these circumstances, they do not refer.

Hence, if there is to be a genuine, learnable, third-person use of sensation language, we must connect words like 'pain' with publicly identifiable circumstances which govern their application. Wittgenstein tends to describe these circumstances as the 'natural expression' of sensation. But there is no need to pre-empt the question (nor indeed did Wittgenstein really do so) as to how these circumstances are to be finally described. The 'expression of sensation' might be understood by both teacher and pupil as the 'sign' of something else. Provided that the 'something else' is publicly identifiable, it may be here understood as the true object of reference. (This 'something else' might, for example, be a process in the nervous system.)

Supposing such a sensation language is introduced. How, then, do we understand its first-person use? In Chapter 3 I gave an indication of how the first-person case might be explained, consistently with the view that the third-person use of sensation language is prior. Roughly speaking, I argued that first-person privilege is a grammatical feature of the public language – a shadow cast in the language by the fact that speakers may on occasion apply mental predicates to themselves. This grammatical feature is generated by and in the course of a practice in which sensation words are used primarily to describe the condition of other people.

'But I can't be in error here; it means nothing to doubt whether I am in pain!' – That means: if anyone said 'I don't know if what I have got is a pain or something else', we should think something like, he does not know what the English word 'pain' means.[8]

The theoretical basis to that remark of Wittgenstein's can be found above, in Chapter 3. Here we must concern ourselves with two important consequences: First, the privilege of the first person is an offshoot of the public 'language-game' with such words as 'pain'. In other words, my privileged access is not to 'private objects', but to such things as *pains*, where the word 'pain' is understood in its public language sense, as referring to a publicly identifiable phenomenon.

Second, in ascribing sensations to myself (in the public language sense of 'sensation') I need, as Wittgenstein puts it, no 'criterion of identity', no criterion which tells me that I am here using the word 'pain' as I always use it, to refer to pain. My understanding of the word here guarantees its reference – but only because its reference is publicly intelligible and publicly taught.

On the basis of that complex premise, we can construct an argument against the 'private object', in a manner corresponding to Wittgenstein's procedure in the sections following on from §243 in the *Philosophical Investigations*. It seems to me that the argument is persuasive, and inherently far more plausible than any argument that can be given for the existence of private objects. It has the following overall structure:

(1) How do words refer to sensations? The answer given above implies that sensations (in the public language sense of that term) are publicly identifiable.

(2) Suppose that there were 'private objects'. Then by (1), they would not be sensations (in the commonly understood sense of this term).

(3) Nevertheless, could we refer to 'private objects'? If we could, it would be impossible for you to refute my assertion that this, which I now have, is such an object.

(4) We cannot refer to private objects in a public language, for no private object can, in these circumstances, be identified by a learnable rule of reference.

(5) Nor can we refer to them in a private language, for such a language is not a coherent possibility.

(6) Nor is there any other means of referring to them.

(7) Hence the private object is not a possible object of reference.

The three crucial steps in this argument – (4), (5) and (6) – can be spelt out at great length, and indeed might well occupy a treatise in themselves. But I believe that a relatively brief exposition will suffice to show their inherent plausibility.

Step (4) is the subject-matter of Wittgenstein's justly celebrated argument concerning the beetle in the box:

> If I say to myself that it is only from my own case that I know what the word 'pain' means – must I not say the same of other people too? And how can I generalize from the *one* case so irresponsibly?
> Now someone tells me that *he* knows what pain is only from his own case!
> – Suppose everyone had a box with something in it: we call it a "beetle". No one can look into anyone else's box, and everyone says he knows what a beetle is only by looking

at *his* beetle. – Here it would be quite possible for everyone to have something different in his box. One might even imagine such a thing constantly changing. – But suppose the word "beetle" had a use in these people's language? – If so it could not be used as the name of a thing. The thing in the box has no place in the language-game at all; not even as a *something*: for the box might even be empty. – No, one can 'divide through' by the thing in the box; it cancels out, whatever it is.

That is to say: if we construe the grammar of the expression of sensation on the model of 'object and designation' the object drops out of consideration as irrelevant.[9]

In order not to be misled by the image, one must remember that, in the phrase, 'no one can look into anyone else's box', 'can' means 'can logically'. Moreover the last sentence, which is capable of many interpretations, is directly pertinent to our theme, just so long as 'object' (*Gegenstand*) is understood in the way implied in the preceding paragraph – as meaning what I have called a 'private object', knowable to the subject alone. The argument seems to establish that such objects are, by their very nature, irrelevant to the application of any referential term in a public language. The correct use of such a term could not possibly be made to depend upon the presence or absence of a private object, which therefore 'drops out of consideration as irrelevant'. The private object has no place in the rule governing the use (and therefore the meaning) of any sentence designed to refer to it, and therefore 'a nothing would serve just as well as a something about which nothing could be said'.[10]

Of the responses made to that argument, two in particular deserve consideration, since they express doubts which have deep philosophical roots, and which do not depend upon rejecting the major premise of the private language argument (the premise that first-person privilege is not a private but a public phenomenon). The first response[11] argues thus: it is indeed true that the rule governing the use of a term in a public language must be publicly intelligible and therefore applicable in publicly identifiable circumstances. But this is a stricture, not on the reference of such a word, but on its *sense*. And it is surely possible for a term with a public sense to have a private reference. Not to acknowledge this possibility is to ignore a distinction which, since Frege, has been one of the cornerstones of philosophical analysis.[12]

The objection is ill-conceived, for the following reason. Suppose that we accept Frege's distinction, and accept that the rule governing the use of a word directly governs, not its reference, but its sense. It does not follow that no limits are placed by that rule on the reference of the term. On the contrary, if the term is itself referential – if it is designed to pick out something in reality – then its sense must determine its reference. The sense of a term, as Frege argued, is the 'route' to its reference, and therefore cannot be specified in such a way that the reference becomes irrelevant to its use.[13] In Wittgenstein's example, the beetle (or private object) might as well not exist – it could still be correct to use the word which supposedly refers to it. But if that is so, the sense given is not a route to *that* reference. And the example is clearly of general application, implying that no word with a public sense *could* have a private reference. Even if something private occurs every time the word is used, the word does not (in the public language) *refer* to that private thing. The private object simply drops out of consideration as irrelevant.

The second objection raises issues of great complexity, and I shall have to content myself with what is no more than the sketch of an answer. The rule for the use of the word 'beetle', this objection argues, is not a rule determining the *truth* of such assertions as 'There is a beetle in my box'. It is a rule determining their 'correctness' or 'assertability', a rule framed within the context of what has come to be known[14] as an 'anti-realist' theory of meaning. It is simply a general fact about public language that it falls short of guaranteeing reference to such entities as the beetle, and not a specific fact about their 'private' nature. For no rule in a public language can really be attached to an idea of *reference*; the best that we can do is to lay down conditions for the assertability or correctness of our sentences.

However, suppose we accept the basis of that objection – accept that the fundamental aim of a rule of use is to establish standards not of truth but of assertability. This cannot really upset the conclusion of the argument, which is that, while we can speak in a public language about publicly identifiable things, we cannot speak in such a language about private objects. Anti-realism implies simply that we must here give a new interpretation of the word 'about', an interpretation based, not in the idea of correspondence to reality, but in the idea of assertability. But this reinterpretation will run through *all* language, and be absorbed, as it were, into the very structure of public utterance. It makes no real difference to any *particular* argument, about any *particular* kind of thing. It therefore does nothing to change the validity of the conclusion that assertions in a public language can be about what is publicly identifiable, but not about private objects. Anti-realism changes only the general, meta-linguistic interpretation of our sentences and of their supposed attachment to the world. For our purposes, such a theory is irrelevant.

Besides, it seems to me extremely tendentious to advance from the view that, in learning language, we learn 'rules of correctness', to the conclusion that it is therefore correctness, and not truth, which is the primary semantic idea. Surely, we understand the 'rules of correctness' only because we respond to them as the rules of a common enterprise (or language-game); and the purpose of this enterprise is not to establish agreement with others, come what may, but to inform each other about an independent reality. (Of course it may be that we could not do that, unless agreement – in use, in judgements, in 'forms of life' – were the normal condition.) A rule such as that mentioned in the case of the beetle in the box should be seen as part of an attempt to connect language with reality. The question was, could it also connect language in the requisite way (the way of 'reference') to a private object? And the answer was that it could not.

But this brings us to the private language argument. It could be replied that we may nevertheless refer to private objects in a language designed especially for that purpose, just so long as we jettison the requirement that language should be publicly intelligible. At least I, the inventor and user of the language, could know what I mean; and that should suffice. For me, at least, the 'private object' will not 'drop out of consideration as irrelevant'. For I can, so to speak, see that it is there.

Several arguments have been proposed in recent literature, based more or less on Wittgenstein's later writings, for the conclusion that such a 'private language' is impossible. In giving one such argument, I do not wish to reject the other arguments that have been proposed. On the contrary, I shall be arguing towards a conclusion that many have found persuasive, for many different (but related) reasons.

In this appendix, and in Chapter 3, I have affirmed the self-guaranteeing nature of the 'first-person case'. The guarantee – which makes it absurd for me to question whether I am now in pain – is bestowed upon me by the grammar of our public language. It also creates the first-person illusion; the illusion that, in my own case, something is 'given' to me, which only I can know. This special feature of public language is to be seen, I have argued, as an epiphenomenon, a 'grammatical' consequence of the extension to my case of predicates learned in the public forum, where they are governed by the third-person point of view. It cannot be supposed that such a feature will survive the destruction of the conditions which make language publicly intelligible. If we remove those conditions, therefore, we shall require procedures for applying the predicates of our language, rules which specify the conditions under which referential words are correctly applied. To use the idiom of Wittgenstein: if we 'abrogate the normal language-game with the expression of sensation,' we shall need a 'criterion of identity', something which tells the user of the private language that he really *is* referring, as he intended, to a private object: 'and then the possibility of error exists.'[15]

In other words, the guarantee which governs my first-person ascriptions in the public language, and which upholds my claim to know immediately and incorrigibly that this, which I now have, is a pain, cannot guarantee my claim that this, which now confronts me, is a private object. I could be wrong in thinking so. For, after all, this 'privacy' is not a property that an object wears on its face: it is not an 'immediate' feature of something that it is connected only contingently with the world of public objects. The 'Cartesian' character of an object is not 'given' to 'consciousness'. (Nor is it right to assume that 'consciousness' – which is, after all, a word of our public language, obedient to the conditions that have been 'abrogated' – denotes the relation between the private language speaker and the object that he is seeking to describe.)

Let us suppose that the speaker of the private language is entitled, for whatever reason, to assume that *something* occurs whenever he uses the given sign 'S'. He wishes that sign to refer to a private object. He must therefore have some guarantee that this, which occurs, *is* such an object. What guarantee can he obtain? How can he test his hypothesis, that this, which now confronts him, is not publicly identifiable?

The temptation is to reply as follows. The speaker of the language, who is acquainted directly with this thing, is in a position to know that it is private. For he is able to know *something* about this present occurrence (for example, that it occurs). And is that not more than is publicly available? Is not the object therefore already private, or at least, so to speak, with private parts?

The answer is no. The most that is implied is that it now *seems* to him as though he confronts a private object. The hypothesis that no one else can know about it is a hypothesis to which he is not entitled. For this fact (if it is a fact) is not 'given' to him. On the contrary, it is no more than a philosophical speculation, and one, moreover, for which there may be no conceivable grounds. The temptation is to say that he can simply *know*, without evidence, that this is a private object. But it is a temptation that must be resisted. Even if we allow that something is 'given' to the private language user, we cannot infer that the something is a private object. On the contrary, the only plausible examples that we have of the 'given' – sensations, thoughts, experiences – are publicly identifiable phenomena, which we describe without trouble in a public language. Given the abrogation of the normal conditions which govern 'privileged access', we cannot suppose that anything is guaranteed for the user of the private language by his sense that *now* is the occasion to use the word 'S'. What seems to him right is right. But that means that the rule which he appears to be following is no better than the appearance of a rule.

We seem forced to the conclusion that the private language speaker does not succeed in establishing a rule of reference. The supposition that the word 'S' denotes a private object remains, for him, a mere supposition that could be true or false without making any difference to his linguistic practice. Neither he nor anyone else can have the slightest reason to think that he *is* referring to a private object. And here one is tempted to agree with Wittgenstein, that 'a wheel which can be turned, though nothing else moves with it, is not part of the mechanism'.[16]

Our strategy may now be completed by turning to stage (6) of the argument: the proposition that there is no language in which private objects can be referred to. It needs only a short consideration to see that this is so. A language is public just so long as its rules of reference identify their subject-matter in ways accessible to more than one. It does not matter if only one person *happens* to speak the language.[17] If the field of reference is publicly identifiable, the language is publicly learnable. A language which is not publicly learnable must be a language whose field of reference cannot be publicly defined. And such a language would fall under precisely the same criticism that I have levelled against private languages – the criticism that, in these circumstances, no rule of reference could be established. Moreover, the attempt to refer to a private object will always be tantamount to the attempt to establish a private language. Hence, given the impossibility of that attempt, we may conclude that no private object can be referred to.

But, it will be objected, have you not already referred to private objects, throughout the very argument which purported to deny that this was possible? What else were you talking about? How can you deny, not just the existence, but, as it were, the very speakability of something? How can you formulate the proposition that a certain kind of thing cannot be referred to, without at the same time referring to it?

There is something oppressively Hegelian about that objection, which argues that it is impossible to draw limits to reference, since every attempt to draw limits ends by extending them. At the same time, the objection reminds us that our arguments about reference are not so much linguistic as epistemological: they concern, not what can be said, but what can be thought. And here it is useful to turn from Wittgenstein to his predecessor, Kant, whose 'transcendental idealism' came across precisely the same difficulty and for precisely the same reasons. Kant tried to draw limits, not explicitly to our powers of reference, but to the understanding (the faculty of judgement). But the difference between Kant and Wittgenstein is one of emphasis. A judgement, for Kant, is that which can be true or false: that which purports to state a fact, or to refer to the world. Hence, an exploration of the limits of the human understanding, in Kant's sense, is also, for that very reason, an investigation into the limits of reference.

Kant's theory may be summarised as follows. We have knowledge of phenomena, which are 'objects of possible experience' i.e. objects known to *us*, and which therefore conform to our mental capacities. Such objects must satisfy certain *a priori* conditions. In particular, they must be situated in space and time, and must exemplify the categories, including the categories of substance (which implies that objects of experience also endure) and of cause (which implies that nothing exists which is not the effect of something else). Phenomena include the theoretical entities postulated by natural science,[18] objects known to us only by inference from their effects,[19] and the everyday objects with which we come into physical contact. All such objects are bound by the conditions contained in the idea of 'possible experience'. The human understanding cannot advance beyond those conditions, and the attempt to think outside them is fraught with paradox. Suppose there were an object inaccessible to experience – an object entering into no empirical relation with any possible observer, and which therefore does not conform to the categories. Such an object would be inaccessible to the understanding; no judgements could be made about it. It would be, in Kant's terms, a 'noumenon': a something whose existence and nature had no correlate in human experience, and which could enter into no causal relation with anything that we might observe. To such an object one might well apply the dictum of Wittgenstein, that a nothing would serve as well as a something about which nothing could be said.

Clearly there is a very important similarity between the conclusions of Kant and those of Wittgenstein. Kant's argument implies that we can refer to objects only if they are 'objects of possible experience' (in the wide sense given to that phrase by the detailed theory of the categories). Wittgenstein's argument implies that we can refer to objects only if they are 'publicly identifiable'. These two restrictions on reference are, if not identical, at least closely similar. Wittgenstein completes an argument already hinted at in 'The Refutation of Idealism' and 'The Paralogisms of Pure Reason' in the first *Critique*. He reaches the extraordinary conclusion that the item postulated by so many philosophers as the most immediately known of all empirical phenomena – the 'private object' of Cartesian and empiricist epistemology – is in fact not a phenomenon at all, but a noumenon, about which nothing intelligible can be said.

To return now to the objection. We should answer it in the manner suggested by Kant, who argued that the concept of the noumenon was legitimate only in its negative employment. It could be used to draw a limit to the understanding, but not to transcend that limit. To employ the concept positively is to employ an 'idea of reason', leading inevitably to paradox and self-contradiction. In the negative use of the concept of a noumenon, we make no assertions about what exists, but say merely: that way lies nonsense. Likewise with the concept of a private object. The argument I have given shows that any *application* of the concept of a private object, in order to identify an item in the world, will be no more than the apparent application of a concept (or the application of an apparent concept). There is no way of using the idea of a private object in order to denote some constituent of reality. All that can be said is that this idea – the idea of a thing, state, event or process knowable in principle only to one person – has no application. To say as much is not to apply the concept, but to refuse to apply it, as Kant (in his more consistent moments) refused to apply the concept of a noumenon.

The reference to Kant reminds us of another problem – that of abstract and mathematical entities. One reason for Kant's peculiar theory of mathematics, as describing *a priori* 'forms of sensibility', was to avoid the conclusion that mathematical entities, such as numbers, are noumena. We certainly refer to numbers. And yet they seem to lie outside space and time, and enter into no causal relations with the world of phenomena. Indeed they enter into no causal relations whatsoever. Of course, it is the fact that I put three apples and not two on the balance that caused the balance to swing. But that is not a peculiar causal achievement of the number three. For in what way was the number three itself affected by this change? And is it not odd, and counter to all our intuitions about causality, that an object should participate in change and yet remain forever unaffected by it? Furthermore, why do we say that it was the number three that caused the change, and not the number six – for there were six half-apples in the balance? (And so on, through all the numbers.) Those, and related, considerations suggest that, if numbers are genuine independent entities, they do not 'conform to the categories', and are not 'objects of possible experience'.

But those facts – while they caused an evident problem for Kant – do not cause a problem for the private language argument. For they do not imply that numbers and other mathematical objects are not 'publicly identifiable.' On the contrary, it is the attempt to understand *how* mathematical entities may be identified, as objects of reference in a public language, which has motivated much of the philosophy of mathematics, and in particular the 'constructivist' theories advanced by Brouwer and accepted in part by the later Wittgenstein.[20] The idea of public identifiability is wider than the Kantian concept of a 'phenomenon'. For an item to be publicly identifiable it is sufficient that a procedure exist whereby a teacher can know (within normal limits of error) that a pupil is referring to *that* object, rather than to another, or to no object at all.

Moreover, whatever they are, numbers are not private objects. Like all abstract entities, they exist as a problem within the realm of public reference. They are publicly identifiable – of that we are sure. But we do not know how. They cannot affect the validity of the argument that I have given, and can be safely reimmersed in their problematic existence.

The upshot of the discussion in this appendix is this. The first-person case, with its privileged access and the perspective that grows therefrom, is a publicly identifiable phenomenon. It does not create, nor does it testify to, a distinct 'inner' realm. There is no 'transcendental subject', no 'Cartesian ego', no 'inner essence', which could provide the subject-matter of a purely phenomenological enquiry. Whatever the peculiarities of the first-person case, they can provide no grounds for the illusion that I know something about myself which shows me to be inaccessible in principle to you.

The ontological consequences are enormous. Not only must we abandon the Cartesian view of the mind; we are also, I believe, led ineluctably towards the view that the mind, like any object of reference, is publicly identifiable. It is therefore a part of nature, and, if we wish to express that thought in the (misleading) modern idiom, we should say that the mind is a physical thing.[21] For us, however, the interest of the argument is not so much ontological as methodological. For it implies that there can be no such thing as a 'pure phenomenology'. The attempt to capture the essence of a mental state, by concentrating upon its first-person manifestation, is doomed to failure. Furthermore, the first-person illusion – the illusion that what I am for myself, I am not, and can never be, for you – is without foundation. It is an illusion to which I am inevitably prey. But it is also no more than an 'idea of reason', which represents me to be something that I cannot be, either for another or for myself.

APPENDIX 2
INTENTIONALITY

The laws of physics, which govern the behaviour of atoms and the movements of the stars, govern also the conduct of rational beings. And yet:

> Being is still enchanted for us; in a hundred
> Places it remains a source – a play of pure
> Powers, which touches no one, who does not kneel and wonder.

> Words still go softly forth towards the unsayable.
> And music, always new, from palpitating stones
> Builds in useless space its godly home.
> [Rilke, *Sonnets to Orpheus*, 11]

This enchantment – revealed to us in the constant intimation of sacred things – belongs, not to the world of physical science, but to the *Lebenswelt*, which we ourselves construct through our collusive actions. The 'scientific realist' sees only a disenchanted world; and what he sees is real. But within reality we also make our home, and in doing so we provide the meaning that is lacking from the world of science. I have tried to display the workings of this 'intentional understanding' in the creation of an important human experience. But nothing that I have said has the slightest tendency to contradict the 'physicalist' ontology, or to suggest that the human reality defies the laws of nature. In the previous appendix I attacked the persistent superstition that the existence of a 'subjective' viewpoint provides the refutation of the scientific world-view. A proper understanding of what is meant by the thesis that the mental is 'publicly identifiable' will lead us in the physicalist's direction, towards the view that we *are* the organisms in which we are embodied. As I have argued at several points, this truth constantly intrudes upon our moral sense, and forces us to recognise that meaning and value lie, not in the Platonic super-sphere, but here and now, in these eyes, these words, this face and this body.

I have relied on a fairly intuitive understanding of 'intentionality', a term used to denote the 'directedness' of mental states, and I here replace that intuitive understanding by the sketch of a theory. My purpose is twofold: first, to dispel the impression that intentionality provides an obstacle to the kind of physicalism that I have assumed; secondly, to analyse 'intentional understanding'. Many of my

377

arguments are familiar from recent literature, and I shall summarise them in the briefest possible form. I again present a third-person study of the first-person case (a piece of 'hetero-phenomenology', as Dennett has called it).[1] But this emphasis on the third-person will yet allow the conclusion that the *Lebenswelt* is partly constituted by our attitudes and powers.

The concept of intentionality was reintroduced into the philosophy of mind by Brentano, who argued that:

> every mental phenomenon is characterised by what the scholastics of the Middle Ages called the intentional (and also mental) inexistence [*Inexistenz*] of an object [*Gegenstand*], and what we could call, although not quite unambiguously, the reference to a content, a direction upon an object (by which we are not to understand a reality in this case) or an immanent objectivity.[2]

The obscurity of this passage is matched by its extreme hesitancy. It is further compounded by Brentano's description of intentionality as the mark which distinguishes mental *phenomena* from physical *phenomena*, the latter being described, not as objective features of the natural world, but as appearances. In later editions of *Psychology from an Empirical Standpoint* Brentano described intentionality as a property of 'mental activity', and characterised it as a kind of 'mental reference'.[3] But at no point in his writings is it really clear what property he had in mind.

Brentano's obscurity was inherited by his pupil Husserl, whose method of 'phenomenological reduction' was supposed to isolate the intentional component (or 'noetic structure') of every state of mind, by 'bracketing' all reference to the material world.[4] By this method Husserl argued that there are important and intricate 'phenomenological problems' – problems concerning the 'direction' or 'reference' of our states of mind. To these problems other philosophers – notably Merleau-Ponty and Heidegger – made substantial additions.[5] But neither Husserl nor his disciples have shown what these problems are really about, or why we need to solve them in order to gain an understanding of the human mind. For in every case, it has been assumed that we know precisely what is being referred to as the 'object' of a state of mind, and precisely what is meant by such words as 'of', 'about', 'towards', in the description of human thoughts and responses.

Matters have been made worse by the attempt to find, in Brentano's discussion, a 'criterion of the mental'. Among analytical philosophers this attempt has had a peculiar slant to it. It has been supposed that we should look for a property, not of the mental *per se*, but of the mental *as described*. The search has been for a grammatical feature of sentences referring to mental states. For example, it has been suggested that 'mental contexts' (contexts in which some mental item is identified) always include a term which occurs without reference, or with reference of an oblique or distorted kind. Thus if John believes that $F(a)$, and $a = b$, it seems not to follow that John believes that $F(b)$. This property of such contexts as 'John believes that . . .', 'John thinks of . . .', and so on, is a property of beliefs and thoughts themselves, only in the sense that these items are (or, more interestingly, must be) referred to in such a way. Brentano argued that '[the immanent object's] being an object . . . is merely the linguistic correlate of the person thinking *having* it as object,'[6] thereby implying that the 'grammatical' feature of intentionality is secondary. Analytical philosophers have, on the whole, tended to make it primary, on the understanding that 'mental reference' is inscrutable until captured in language, and that what is shown to be true of every genuine identification of a 'mental object' must be true of the object itself.

This concentration on grammar has been thought to fulfil a useful philosophical function. If it can be shown that contexts employed in referring to physical processes need not possess 'intentionality', whereas contexts employed in referring to mental processes must possess it, then this (it is hoped) would be an effective argument against any theory which held that mental statements are translatable into equivalent statements about the physical world.[7] (Behaviourism is such a theory.) It might even be some kind of argument against physicalist theories which are less overtly 'reductionist' than behaviourism – which argue, not for a logical equivalence between mental and physical descriptions, but merely for an identity of reference.

However, a moment's reflection shows the futility of this hope. Suppose someone claimed to have arrived at a satisfactory definition of 'intentionality', as a term denoting some property possessed by all and only those contexts which refer to mental items. What tells us that the definition *is* satisfactory? The usual test has been that it should fit exactly to our previous notion of the mental: the defined property is said to belong to all and only contexts in which a mental item is identified. In other words the procedure is extensional. The least that is required, however, is a proof that mental items *must* be identified in intentional contexts.

However, even if such a proof could be supplied, it is difficult to see what follows. Donald Davidson, for example, has argued for the thesis (which he explicitly associates with the Kantian theory of rival 'empirical' and 'transcendental' points of view upon our own mentality) that to identify an object *as* mental is to identify it in 'intentional language' – language which resists translation into the discourse of physical science.[8] Nevertheless, he contends, what follows from this is not the 'non-physical' nature of mental items, but the 'anomalous' character of mental descriptions: their uselessness in the formulation of causal laws. We cannot conclude that there is not some *other* way of referring to mental items, so as to identify them as the subject-matter of causal laws. Indeed, Davidson argues, there *must* be causal laws governing the interaction between the mental and the physical, so that mental events *must* be identifiable in this other way. For Davidson, therefore, the thesis of the 'intentionality of the mental' provides an argument *for* some kind of monism, not against it. Furthermore, Dennett and others have argued[9] that there could be machines which are 'intentional systems', whose behaviour may be usefully (if perhaps not finally) explained by the reference to propositional attitudes. This suggests that there might be true causal laws, the statement of which involves the use of 'intentional' language, and the subject matter of which consists in purely physical (and, moreover, inorganic) processes.

The moral of such arguments is simple. We should refrain from drawing any general conclusions, either about the ontological status of mental items, or about the epistemological perspective that we must maintain upon them, from the premise that some or all of them are identified in 'intentional' contexts. At the same time, intentionality presents an intractable problem for the philosophy of mind, and for the attempt to map the relation between the world and our response to it from a point of view which is not that of the subject himself. I shall therefore sketch a theory of what Brentano called 'mental reference',[10] and what more recent philosophers have sometimes called 'mental representation'.[11]

Brentano's quoted definition refers to the 'intentional inexistence of an object' – the existence of an object internal to the 'mental act'. This has been widely interpreted to mean the following: there are mental items which have objects, such that (a) it does not follow that there is any 'real' object outside the mind; (b) if there is such a real object, then it does not follow that it is as it appears to be, or appears to be as it is; (c) the 'internal object' may be indeterminate – in other words, it may be no *particular* object, but just an object of some particular kind. Thus, if I fear a lion, it does not follow either that there is a lion which I fear, or that the lion which I fear is as it appears to be (it may be wounded and unable to charge), or that there is any *particular* lion to which my fear is directed (I may have been told to watch out, since there are lions around).

If we translate this suggestion into a definition of intentional contexts – rather than a characterisation of the items described in them – then we find that there is a strong resemblance between intentionality and the logician's concept of non-extensionality (or 'intensionality').[12] Non-extensionality means the failure of extensionality, i.e. of the law that the extension of a complex expression is determined by the extension of its parts, in the way that the reference of 'the father of John' is completely determined by the reference of 'John' and the reference of 'the father of'. 'John' refers to a man, and 'the father of' to a function which maps every person onto his father. Those two rules enable us to understand indefinitely many referring expressions in English: for example, 'the father of the father of the father of John' – hence we need not lament, as did Scott's Antiquary, that the English language has no express term for this relation to which we so often have cause to refer.

Under the influence of Frege, the 'law of extensionality' has been thought to be a cornerstone of logic, and its breakdown has been treated as a matter of concern. Developments in the semantics of natural language, in modal logic and in the logic of 'intentionality' have therefore often involved an attempt, either to dismiss non-extensionality as a merely 'surface' phenomenon, or to provide a semantics for intensional contexts in a purely extensional meta-language.[13] The ancestor of the first of those enterprises is Frege's own theory, which tried to show that the failure of extensionality in contexts such as 'John believes that . . .' is only apparent. The effect of such contexts is to *change* the extension of terms occurring within them. Terms denote, not their normal reference, but their 'oblique' reference, which is their normal sense.[14] Frege's suggestion is now widely thought to be unsatisfactory;[15] indeed, it is increasingly accepted that the law of extensionality is neither true nor a necessary foundation of semantic analysis.[16]

Nevertheless, the suggestion is associated with an important insight. Frege argued that extension (*Bedeutung*) is a unitary concept, which applies equally to singular terms, to complex referring expressions, to predicates and relations, and to sentences as a whole. The extension of a sentence, according to Frege, is a truth-value. Only this (at first sight, counter-intuitive) thesis is compatible with a unified theory of extensionality, which will show just *how* it is that the assigning of extensions to the parts of a sentence leads to an interpretation of the whole. In order to understand what is correct in Frege's thesis, we must see extension, not in terms of some intuitive idea of reference, but in terms of substitutivity. The theory of extension is the theory of substitution *salva veritate*, and the theory of intensionality is the theory of substitutional failure.

The proof of Frege's thesis then goes as follows. We first define extensionality. $C(\ )$ (where the gap is filled by a singular term) is extensional if and only if it obeys the following law:

$$(a = b) \rightarrow (C(a) \equiv C(b)).$$

For various reasons which do not concern us,[17] the '$\rightarrow$' here must denote a stronger relation than material implication. In this case, failure of extensionality is what Quine has called 'referential opacity'.

$C'(\ )$ (where the gap is filled by a predicate), is extensional if and only if it obeys the following law:

$$(x)\, (F(x) \equiv G(x)\,) \rightarrow (C'(F) \equiv C'(G)\,).$$

$C''(\ )$ (where the gap is filled by a sentence) is extensional if and only if it obeys the following law:

$$(p \equiv q) \rightarrow (C''(p) \equiv C''(q)\,).$$

We could establish that these three conditions define three applications of the same concept by showing that, necessarily, they are satisfied together. It is obvious, first, that every context which is extensional for sentences is also extensional for predicates and referring expressions. (Suppose $C(\ )$ is extensional for sentences. Then if $p \equiv q$, $C(p) \equiv C(q)$; but if $a = b$, $F(a) \equiv F(b)$; hence 'a' can be substituted for 'b' in $C(\ )$ *salva veritate*.) It is also the case that contexts which are extensional for singular terms are extensional for sentences. The result may be proved in a variety of ways,[18] but is perhaps most simply expressed as follows:

We first assume that the context $C(F(\ )\,)$ is extensional for singular terms, i.e. that if $C(F(a))$ and $a = b$, then $C(F(b))$. We also assume that $C(\ )$ permits the substitution of logical equivalents, i.e. that if $C(p)$ and $p \equiv_\square q$, then $C(q)$. Suppose now that:

(1) $C(p)$.

Now every proposition is logically equivalent to the proposition that its truth-value is identical with the true. Hence:

(2) $p \equiv_\square$ (tv of $p = $ T).

Therefore:

(3) $C(\text{tv of } p = \text{T})$.

Take any proposition q, such that $p \equiv q$. Then:

(4) tv of p = tv of q.

Since C is extensional for singular terms, (4) permits us to substitute in (3), yielding:

(5) $C (\text{tv of } q = \text{T})$.

But, repeating the argument for (2):

(6) $(\text{tv of } q = \text{T}) \equiv_\square q$.

Hence, by (5), (6) and the assumption that $C(\ \ )$ permits the substitution of logical equivalents:

(7) $C(q)$.

In other words, extensionality for singular terms entails extensionality for sentences, provided that we can assume the substitutability of logical equivalents. This assumption has indeed been questioned by those who wish to reject Frege's view (frequently supported by versions of the above argument) that sentences *refer* to their truth-values, in just the way that names refer to objects.[19] But, for the purpose of establishing a theory of intensional contexts, it can be accepted, as explicating an intuitive idea of substitutivity whose limits we are trying to fix.

Let us now return to the property of intentionality, construed, in modern manner, as a property of contexts in which mental items are identified. Three properties have been singled out as defining this property, and it can be seen by inspection that they correspond fairly closely to the three intuitive ideas mentioned above as implied by Brentano's own discussion:

(A) Non-extensionality (in all three forms). (Condition (b) above.)
(B) Lack of an existence commitment: Neither the completed sentence $C(a)$, nor its contradictory, implies that there is, or is not, anything to which the object expression 'a' applies. (Condition (a).)
(C) Indeterminacy of the object. For example, if I look for an honest man, there may be no particular honest man that I am looking for. (Contrast, 'I met an honest man'.) (Condition (c).)

Those features are spoken of as 'criteria' of intentionality. But this cannot mean that they are mere indications of a property that they do not completely identify; for how else *are* we to identify the property? Accordingly, (A), (B) and (C) must be taken either as separately necessary (jointly sufficient) conditions, as separately sufficient conditions, or as what Mackie has called INUS conditions.[20]

(A), (B) and (C) are features of contexts which 'take an object' in the grammatical sense. The object expression is said to identify the 'intentional object' of the mental item referred to by the completed context as a whole.

Understood in this way, it is clear that intentionality, if it is to reflect the properties of mental states obliquely indicated by Brentano, will always involve non-extensionality. Human fallibility will always ensure that substitution of extensional equivalents cannot be licensed in a description of the content of our thoughts.

Quine argues that it is not in general legitimate to quantify into opaque contexts.[21] From: I believe that $F(a)$, for example, it is not possible to infer that: $(\exists x)$ (I believe that $F(x)$). For in the quantified sentence, the 'description under which' the object of belief is presented no longer serves to identify it. Hence opaque contexts do not obey the law: $F(a) \equiv (\exists x) (x = a \,.\, F(x))$, as can be seen by inspection.

Of course, matters are not so simple as that implies. For there are also *de re* beliefs, beliefs whose content must be specified in relation to some actually existing item 'outside the mind'. In other words, there are beliefs which are correctly reported as follows: $(\exists x)$ (John believes that $F(x)$). Moreover, it has been argued that the content of some thoughts simply cannot be specified without such 'quantifying in'.[22] I shall leave these cases aside for the present and concentrate only upon examples of indisputable 'inexistence'.

Quine's argument suggests an explanation of condition (C) in terms of condition (A): for (C) follows at once from the failure of quantification into intensional contexts. It might also be thought that the same consideration would serve to explain (B) – the lack of an existence commitment. If that is so, a useful result immediately follows, namely, that, if (A), (B) and (C) are separately *necessary* conditions for intentionality, they all reduce to one: (A). In other words, intentionality is simply intensionality. However, that conclusion is too hasty. (B) does not state the requirement that quantification should fail, but the stronger requirement that there should be no existence commitment. For example, quantification into 'It is necessary that $F(a)$' is not generally permissible, since the truth of this sentence may depend upon the 'description under which' a is presented. On the other hand, the sentence, even in its *de dicto* reading, implies that $(\exists x) (x = a)$. Likewise for some mental contexts. From: John knows that $F(a)$ it cannot be inferred that: $(\exists x)$ (John knows that $F(x)$), although it can be inferred that: $(\exists x) (x = a)$.

It could be retorted that, in the case of psychological contexts, such as 'John knows . . .', 'John perceives . . .', there is a covert affirmation of two propositions, only one of which is about the *content* of a mental item. When I say that John knows that $F(a)$, I mean both that there is a mental act of John's in relation to the proposition that $F(a)$, and that $F(a)$ is true. The psychological component in what I say does lack an existence commitment, and here the indifference to existence is of a piece with the failure of quantification. It is therefore arguable that the three conditions still *in effect* reduce to one. At least, this is the suggestion which I shall consider, as giving the most plausible available account of intentionality.

The account develops a theory of 'propositional attitudes' – mental states like belief, with a 'representational content', or 'thought' (in Frege's sense), which might be true or false. Any context used to identify such attitudes will include (explicitly or implicitly) some sentence in indirect speech (whether *oratio recta* or *oratio obliqua*),[23] designed to capture the mental content. And indirect speech leads to a failure of extensionality, since it reports an utterance which it does not affirm. The truth-value of the report depends neither upon the truth-value of the sentence reported, nor upon the extension of any term contained in it. Modern theories of intentionality therefore centre upon the idea of a propositional attitude, and account for the intentionality of mental language in terms of the intensionality of reported speech.

There are two major obstacles to the development of such a theory. First, there are intentional contexts which do not seem to contain, even implicitly, any sentential clause: 'John thinks of . . .', for example, which is completed by a singular term, but which implies nothing about any proposition that is 'before John's mind' in the act of thinking. Secondly, the content of our mental states does not seem to depend only upon what is 'before the mind'. It may also depend upon *the way the world is*, and therefore be inadequately captured by a purely intensional idiom. This possibility is illustrated by the semantic properties of indexicals, proper names and 'natural kind' terms. The most frequent example cited of the difficulty that these terms present for theories of 'mental represent-ation' is Putnam's case of 'twin earth'.[24] A planet (twin earth) exists, which is as near as possible a duplicate of our earth, containing replicas of all people, things, places and events on earth, but with one difference: in place of H_2O there is another substance XYZ, indistinguishable in all its normally observable properties from water, but chemically distinct. Twin-earth dwellers call this substance 'water', and my beliefs about water are exactly mirrored by my twin-earth counterpart's beliefs about XYZ. But while my beliefs are about *water*, his are not, and while we are both in the psychological state that would naturally be expressed in the affirmation of the sentence 'Water is H_2O', my belief is true, whereas his is false. Such examples (which are of course immensely contentious in almost every particular) have been held to suggest that the *content* of a propositional attitude may vary with the surrounding circumstances, precisely because the sense of terms occurring within the sentence which identifies that attitude are determined by their reference. How then can we account for mental representation, and the meaning of the crucial word 'about', in terms of the content of the subject's mind alone? And how can we capture that content in reported speech?

Both difficulties connect with one of the underlying problems of this book: the problem of 'individualising intentionality'. What is it about John's thought that makes it a thought *of* an individual – of Mary, say? How, in particular, is the individualising intentionality of attitudes like love and desire to be accounted for? Some philosophers argue – on the strength of examples like Putnam's – that the individualising component of a thought belongs to it by virtue of a real relation with something outside the mind. What makes John's thought a thought of *Mary*, rather than of 'twin-Mary', is the fact that it is caused by Mary herself. In establishing precisely which individual is 'intended' by a mental act, therefore, we must adopt the third-person perspective, so as to look outside the 'given' mental content.

Similarly with desire and love. Gareth Evans presents an imaginary case of a man in love with one of a pair of identical twins.[25] There is nothing 'in the mind', Evans argues, which could make this love into the love of one twin rather than the other. Even if *God* looked into the subject's mind, He could not tell, from the information contained there, which of the twins is the object of the man's affections. The answer is available *only* from the third-person viewpoint. As Putnam puts it, in such cases, 'the world takes over', and completes the task which our mental activity merely initiates – the task of focussing on an individual item in reality.

In my discussion of desire I stressed the importance of individualising thoughts. I also suggested that the belief that our *thoughts* may be sufficient, by virtue of their content, to individuate their objects, might be an illusion. In fact, however, it does not matter if that is so. It may be that we should accept the view of Putnam, that the individualising character of a thought belongs to it by virtue of a 'real relation' with an existing individual. Alternatively, it may be more plausible to agree with his opponents (such as Searle)[26] that a thought may be *intrinsically* 'particular'. The theory of intentionality as a form of representation is compatible with either view.

The answer to the above difficulties is to be found not by rejecting the 'indirect speech' theory of intentionality, but by refining it. First, indirect speech may identify something less than a complete utterance – as when I say, for example, that Michael *mentioned* John. Secondly, terms used to describe the object in such reported speech may also be used referentially. Suppose I say that Michael mentioned John, do I imply that John exists? And, if John is the Mayor of Kensington, do I imply that Michael mentioned the Mayor of Kensington? Clearly, there is a temptation to deny both of those implications, and therefore to admit the 'intentionality' of non-sentential descriptions of reported speech. There is also, however, a temptation to affirm both implications, for the very reasons emphasised by Putnam. The question is one of construction. We may, for example, believe that proper names – even in reported speech – spread a peculiar semantic nimbus over the contexts in which they occur. For example, we may believe that names occur always with maximum *scope* within every sentence.[27] On this reading, the sentence should be rewritten: 'It is true of John, that Michael mentioned him.' 'John' occurs in that sentence with normal referential use: the sentence implies both that John exists, and (if John is the Mayor of Kensington) that the Mayor of Kensington was mentioned by Michael. To give this interpretation is simply to say that, whenever I use a proper name to report the content of another's utterance, I also use that name to refer to its bearer.

The sentence 'Michael referred to John', so construed, performs two separable functions: (a) it refers to Michael, and also to John; (b) it refers to an utterance of Michael's, and asserts that *it* refers to John. If I wished *merely* to report Michael's utterance, I should say 'Michael mentioned someone whom he called John' – or even 'Michael mentioned "John"' – from which it does not follow either that

John exists, or that Michael mentioned the Mayor of Kensington. The *reporting* of Michael's speech does, therefore, create an opaque context, even though, in the act of reporting, I may make a reference of my own, which, so to speak, erases the opacity.

The same considerations govern my description of Michael, not as mentioning, but as thinking of, or desiring, John. These contexts too, despite being non-sentential, are intensional for singular terms. And once again, they seem to admit of two constructions. We might wish to say that the context 'John is thinking of . . .' has an existence commitment; or we might wish to deny it. Which we say will depend upon the semantic properties of the term which the context encloses. If the term is a proper name, and if names always carry maximum scope, it will be used referentially here, as everywhere. Nevertheless, whatever intentionality the context possesses, it possesses by virtue of the facts which explain the intensionality of reported speech – namely, that reports of a reference to x do not necessarily refer to x.

The second difficulty should be tackled in a similar spirit. As Colin McGinn has argued,[28] our assignment of content to the psychological state of others involves two separate enterprises. We wish both to explain behaviour in terms of the internal structure of the mental states which compel it, and also to *assess* those mental states, according to the exacting canons of the true and the false. Hence we view beliefs both as mental states which express themselves in conduct and as items with referential truth-conditions. We should not be surprised, therefore, by such examples as that of twin earth. As McGinn puts it, we should expect 'that beliefs may have the same truth-conditions and different explanatory role, and the same explanatory role accompanied by different truth-conditions'.[29] And the important fact about representations – the fact which explains both their explanatory role and the intensionality of the language used to report them – is their *fallibility*: hence 'it cannot be that some state of a creature should qualify as a representation and yet be logically guaranteed to represent reality correctly.'[30]

We should expect, therefore, that the contexts used to report propositional attitudes should diverge in certain predictable ways from the paradigm of intensionality. In particular we should expect them frequently to carry an existence commitment, despite the opacity of the contexts in which the relevant terms occur. This commitment, far from refuting, in fact confirms the theory that intentionality is a special case of reported utterance.

Recent theories of 'mental representation' have considered two broad questions. First, is there a unitary account of all representational states? In particular, can a single explanation be provided for the 'intentionality of perception' and the intentionality of belief?[31] Secondly, can there be mental representation without language? The second question is of particular import-ance for those who wish to give a third-person theory of intentionality. Some philosophers, arguing from the premise that thoughts can be individuated only through their linguistic expressions, are sceptical of the view that thoughts may be attributed to unspeaking animals. Representation, they argue, is a property of language, and of mental states only in so far as they are expressible in language.[32]

Others have taken the opposing position, arguing that language is represent-ational only if given a representational *use*, and that means a use in the expression of a representational state of mind.[33] As I have suggested in Chapter 3, the opposition between these two views may not be as clear as it seems. But whatever its outcome, we can assume, for the sake of this appendix, that mental representation and representation in language are a single phenomenon, which can be examined in either form. Moreover, there is no obstacle to a third-person study of intentionality: on the contrary, we need only study the behaviour of terms in intentional contexts, so avoiding the complex mental contortions involved in Husserl's 'bracketing'. Nor does the phenomenon of intentionality provide us with any grounds for rejecting a physicalist theory of the mind.

We can now turn to the idea of intentional understanding, which has played such an important role in the argument of this book. The first-person approach of the phenomenologists has gained plausibility from the systematic disparity between two kinds of utterance: the utterance of the agent and the utterance of the observer. The agent, whose language is designed to focus and guide his activity towards the world, employs classifications that are entirely foreign to the thought of the observer. The observer's language is the language of science, bent towards the task of explanation and prediction, and employing theoretical concepts that might be profoundly revisionary of our ordinary ways of thought. It might therefore be supposed that the *Lebenswelt* – the world as presented to the agent – could be studied only from the first-person point of view. However, I have already argued that that supposition is mistaken. Not only is it impossible to carry out the desired first-person description (the description of what remains when the objective world has been 'bracketed'); it is also unnecessary. The *Lebenswelt* is just as much a public object, and just as much susceptible to third-person description, as is the world of science.

However, a difficulty arises. How, it might be asked, can there be a gap between the real and the apparent *Lebenswelt*? The *Lebenswelt* is not an independent reality: on the contrary, it is constructed by our way of understand-ing it. How then can we apply to it the concepts of truth and reference? With what, in the application of such concepts, is our mental representation to be compared?

To answer that question we must turn again to the case of 'secondary qualities'.[34] It is argued that, in an important sense, qualities like colour are contributed to objects by those who perceive them. The theory of colour explains why things appear coloured to creatures with certain perceptual capacities, without mentioning colour as an independent feature of reality. However, while, from the scientific point of view, no object is really red or green, objects may nevertheless be truly or falsely classified as red or green. The test of something's being red is indelibly marked with the epistemological condition of those who apply it: nevertheless it is publicly accessible, publicly learnable and publicly applied. It may therefore be misapplied. Hence, when I say of Michael that he sees the book as, or thinks it to be, red, I leave room for the possibility of a 'representational defect'. What I say allows for the possibility that Michael's application of the tests for redness should have gone astray: hence, in describing how he sees things, I use a colour predicate bound by an intensional clause.

Things really are coloured, even though nothing has colour. We can make mistakes about colours, despite the fact that colour is essentially 'for' us, and depends for its existence upon our capacity to perceive it. The paradox dissolves, once we see that our attributions of colour do not really contradict the findings of science. For science simply *remains silent* concerning the colours of objects, and none of our colour judgements need lead us into serious conflict with scientific truth. In this respect our common-sense judgements about secondary qualities are more secure than those about primary qualities, which are constantly revised under the impact of scientific discovery – as when we learn that ordinary things are not, as we thought, solid.

The case of secondary qualities is familiar to analytical philosophers. Somewhat less familiar are the cases that I have touched on in this work, in which properties are singled out by classifications that cut across sensory and scientific boundaries in response to practical and emotional imperatives. Consider again the concept of an ornamental marble. It seems that there is a real distinction between ornamental marbles and other kinds of stone. People can make mistakes in their use of this classification, wrongly believing, for example, that a certain piece of stone can be used for ornamental purposes. At the same time, science recognises no such distinction among stones as that between ornamental marbles and the rest.

The case is analogous in one respect to that of secondary qualities. It employs a classification which does not compete with those employed by the science of stones. The responses that are focussed in this classification are directed towards the surface of the world, and contain no explanatory hypothesis that reaches to the depths. At the same time, the case is significantly unlike that of secondary qualities. The classification 'red' is relative to sensory experience, and records a distinction that may be observed by any creature with the requisite sensory capacity. The classification 'ornamental marble' is relative to a highly complex pattern of responses, activities and feelings. It denotes a discrimination that is beyond the competence of all but the most sophisticated creatures. The classification serves to focus activities that are integral to our lives as rational beings and which have no place in the lives of animals.

Such classifications raise an important question for the theory of intentionality – the question: which comes first, belief or attitude? Consider fear – a mental attitude which we share with the animals. Fear is like many mental states, in possessing a 'formal object'.[35] There is a characteristic belief upon which fear is founded, the belief that the object threatens harm. Thus all objects of fear must be thought to satisfy a certain description: 'harmful'. It is evident, however, that fear does not usually create, still less is it constituted by, the belief that something threatens harm. An object can be thought to threaten harm by someone who does not fear it. This obvious point may be obscured by the failure to distinguish the formal from the proper object of fear. The formal object is given by the description under which something must be represented if it is to be feared – it is what *can* be feared. The proper object is not what *can* be feared, but what it is right, proper or justified to fear. The harmful is the formal object of fear; its proper object is the fearful. To justify the description 'fearful' is to justify fear: it is to justify, not a belief only, but the whole response, and in particular the pattern of activity that expresses it.

Confusion between formal and proper objects leads many – including Sartre[36] – to consider emotions to be a kind of judgement. Fear then becomes the recognition of the fearful, anxiety the recognition of the *angoissant*, amusement the recognition of the amusing, and so on. It begins to seem as though nothing of the emotion remains, beyond this act of (admittedly passionate) appraisal. The characteristic of a formal object is that someone may think something to be an instance of it, and yet feel no prompting toward the emotion that it partially identifies. The formal object is given by a description which falls short of embodying the peculiar emotional characteristics which it serves to focus.

If one were to ask for the meaning of the classification 'fearful', therefore, it would not be sufficient to offer the truth-conditions of a belief: this classification must be understood *in terms of* the emotion that it commemorates, and not in terms of some belief upon which the emotion is founded. To put the matter more directly: to justify the description 'X is fearful' is to give, not theoretical, but practical reasons. It is to justify, not a classification, but a response. The response comes first, and the classification is then explained in terms of it. This fact is, I believe, extremely important for an understanding of the intentionality of the moral emotions.[37] It is also relevant to the consideration of love, desire and the other interpersonal attitudes. Such attitudes, because they have persons as their object, are 'justification hungry'. The subject feels judged in his own eyes by his lusts and loves, and seeks to present himself, through these activities, as worthy of the sympathy and respect of all who might challenge them. Love and desire, therefore, are inevitably mediated and disciplined by conceptions of the lovable and the desirable – classifications subordinate to the vicissitudes of our emotional life and to the demands of practical reason.

Even such classifications, however, may cross the gap between appearance and reality. It is essential to practical reason that we *think* its claims to be objectively binding, and this indispensable thought resurges in the concepts and classifications which have practical reasoning as their base. The lovable and the desirable are distinguished in our thought from the merely apparently lovable and the merely apparently desirable. Even these classifications, therefore, create the risk of epistemological failure. John may be misled in his judgement that Mary is lovable, so that the true report that he rejoices in her lovable nature implies nothing about Mary's nature, and certainly not that she is lovable or that she is beautiful, trustworthy and kind (assuming that last description to be coextensive with 'lovable').

Returning now to our marbles, we can draw the following tentative conclusions:

(1) The classification 'ornamental marble' embodies a certain 'intentional understanding'. That is, it denotes a 'perceived similarity', which may not

be the index of any deep material similarity between the substances described.

(2) The perceived similarity is important to us, since it lies at the point of intersection of various actions, emotions and responses which collectively assign an interesting role in our lives to ornamental marbles.

(3) New classifications emerge from those actions and emotions which denote not their foundation in belief, but their justified occasions.

(4) These new classifications express not beliefs, but emotions and activities, and the practical reasoning which supports them. Nevertheless, they reinforce the more literal classifications mentioned in (1), by adding a new dimension of authority to the 'perceived similarity' which underlies them. Thus the classification 'ornamental' – which is consequent upon the habit of ornament – lends support to the perceived similarity which guides the hand of the sculptor and the architect. In itself, however, it is an unstable classification, denoting not a secondary quality, but at best a 'tertiary' quality or aspect,[38] with no reality independent of the changing responses which govern it.

Interpersonal responses also exhibit this multi-faceted intentionality. This might lead someone to doubt the independent content of the classifications exhibited by them. For example, a philosopher might argue – following a suggestion made by Strawson[39] – that interpersonal attitudes like resentment, blame, forgiveness and gratitude, far from being founded upon the belief that others are responsible for their actions, are themselves the true foundation for the classification of acts as 'responsible'. This classification does not precede, but follows, the 'reactive' attitudes which are endorsed by it, in the manner of such classification as the 'lovable' and the 'fearful'. A philosopher might go further (in the spirit of those who regard the idea of the person as a 'forensic' concept)[40] and argue that the classification which seems to be most fundamental to our interpersonal responses – the classification of certain natural (and perhaps also supernatural) phenomena as persons – is to be accounted for, not as the foundation, but as the consequence of those responses in which it most prominently figures. The principal ground for such an argument would be this: that a creature without interpersonal responses really does not see the world as containing persons. For him, the world of nature is no more than the world of nature, and although it contains complicated and awkward animals which present special obstacles to his strategies, it no more contains persons than the world of the horse contains holiness or virtue.

Authority for such a view might again be found in the writings of Kant, who argued that human beings are persons in that they are *to be treated* in a certain way (namely, as ends, and not as means only); in other words human beings are persons *relative* to a certain capacity that we have to respond to them. If some such thing were true, we should expect the 'intentional understanding' characteristic of interpersonal responses to be yet more fragile than that involved in the attribution of secondary qualities, and yet more susceptible to be wiped off the surface of things by the busy hygiene of natural science. However, such a view is extremely implausible. At least the *core* of our concept of the person can be separated from the responses that express it, and attached to the world independently. For this core consists in the two related properties of first-person privilege and responsibility – the properties that I have subsumed under the title of the 'first-person perspective'. And, while it may be natural, and perhaps even inevitable, for a creature with such a perspective to respond interpersonally to other members of his kind, this does not seem to be a matter of logical necessity. The first-person perspective is the foundation of interpersonal feeling, but it does not logically compel it.

At the same time, however, the argument of this book has implied that there is a peculiar metaphysical theory lying dormant within our interpersonal attitudes. Like the aesthetic responses rooted in the classification of stones, interpersonal attitudes build upon the 'perceived similarity' which grounds them, and introduce, through their own hunger for justification, new layers of intentional understanding. Some of these layers – like the concept of the sacred discussed in Chapter 12 – are historically conditioned and liable to disease and decay. Others are more permanent features of the *Lebenswelt*, such as the transcendental self or soul, which is forever resurgent in our loves, hatreds and desires. This concept, like that of the sacred, is indispensable to our flourishing and also the embodiment of a metaphysical illusion. If that is so, then the intentional understanding from which the *Lebenswelt* is constructed contains a vast metaphysical flaw. It is not merely that we see the world decked out in secondary qualities – qualities which science repudiates as insubstantial. We also see it in terms which have, because they could have, no genuine application.

Again, however, we should not regard this fact as vitiating the account that I have given of intentionality. Although there are such faulty layers in our intentional understanding, there is still a difference in reality between those objects which can, and those which cannot, sustain the transcendental illusions which are built upon them. Hence there is exactly the same possibility here as elsewhere of a lack of correspondence between inner state and outer reality. And it is this possibility which generates the 'intentional inexistence' of the object of love and desire.

My argument has tended to the conclusion that the concepts exhibited by our intentional understanding (and therefore the *Lebenswelt* which those concepts help to create) are very much more complex than is often supposed, and give rise to problems that cannot be resolved by scientific enquiry. This returns me to the opening remarks of this book. There are, indeed, questions which science is incompetent to answer. And these questions – the questions of philosophy and criticism – are nearer to us, and more important to our happiness, than any of the questions of natural science. One such question has been the subject-matter of this book, and, in answering it by the method of 'conceptual analysis', I have been describing, not concepts only, but a form of life.

NOTES

1 The problem

1 I. Kant, *Lectures on Ethics*, tr. L. Infield, new edn, New York, 1963, pp. 164ff., and *Foundations of the Metaphysic of Morals*, Prussian Academy edition, p. 399 (tr. L. W. Beck, New York, 1959, p. 15). See also *Kant's Philosophical Correspondence: 1759–99*, ed. and tr. Arnulf Zweig, Chicago, 1967, p. 235, where Kant refers to marriage as an agreement between two people for the 'reciprocal use of each other's sexual organs'. Kant's views are discussed below, Chapter 4.

2 G. W. F. Hegel, *The Philosophy of Right*, tr. and ed. T. M. Knox, Oxford, 1942, addition to para. 158. J. P. Sartre, *Being and Nothingness*, tr. Hazel E. Barnes, New York, 1956, book III, ch. 3. Sartre's views are discussed below, Chapter 5.

3 Arthur Schopenhauer, *The World as Will and Representation*, tr. E. J. F. Payne, Indian Hills, Colorado, 1958, vol. II, pp. 549ff. Schopenhauer's views are discussed below, Chapter 7.

4 Plato, *Symposium*. Plato's views are discussed below, Chapter 8. It is of course important to recognise that Plato himself changed his mind about many fundamental questions during the course of his creative life, and, although the *Symposium* is a comparatively mature work, it is nevertheless true that it does not offer Plato's last word on the subjects of love and desire.

5 Augustine's thoughts on the erotic are scattered throughout the *Confessions*, *De Nuptiis et Concupiscentia* and the *City of God* (esp. book XIV, chs 16–26). Boethius' best-known statement on the philosophy of love is contained in the *Consolation of Philosophy*. The medieval sources are typified by Chaucer, *The Parliament of Fowles* and *The Knight's Tale*; Cavalcanti, *Canzone* and *Sonnets*; Dante, *La Vita Nuova* and the *Convivio*; Boccaccio *La Visione Amorosa* and the *Teseïde*; and the troubadour Arnault Daniel, whose major poems have been collected in Hugh Kenner (ed.), *The Translations of Ezra Pound*, London, 1953.

6 On the possible sources of conflict between phenomenology and conceptual analysis, see Appendix 1.

7 See especially the fragmentary work gathered together as vol. VII of Dilthey's *Collected Works* (ed. B. Groethuysen, Leipzig, 1914), excerpts of which are available (under the title 'The Construction of the Historical World in the Human Studies'), tr. and ed. H. P. Rickman, in *Dilthey, Selected Writings*, Cambridge, 1976, pp. 168–245. The work to which I refer in modern philosophy of science centres around the discussion of natural kind concepts (see H. Putnam, 'The Meaning of "Meaning" ', in *Philosophical Papers*, vol. II: *Mind, Language and*

Reality, Cambridge, 1975, and S. Kripke, *Naming and Necessity*, Oxford, 1978.)

8 See Putnam, 'The Meaning of "Meaning" ', and Kripke, *Naming and Necessity*. The term 'natural kind' derives obliquely from J. S. Mill, *A System of Logic*, 10th edn, London, 1879, book 1, ch. vii. Mill refers to Kinds, which have an existence in nature, and thereafter retains the capital 'K' in order to denote this kind of kind. The observation that our classifications are frequently functional or analogical and therefore misrepresent the nature of that to which they are applied is of course far older than Mill, inspiring Locke's distinction between 'real' and 'nominal' essence (*Essay Concerning Human Understanding*, book III, ch. 3, § 15), and Buffon's method in the *Histoire Naturelle*, in which he explicitly rejects our ordinary habits of classification, since they try 'to divide nature at points where she is indivisible'.

On the distinction between natural and functional kinds, see David Wiggins, *Sameness and Substance*, Oxford, 1980, pp. 171ff. The idea of a functional kind is perhaps less familiar than that of a natural kind; some such idea is, however, necessary, if we are to make sense of 'functionalism' as a theory of the mental. Functionalism has been expounded at length by D. C. Dennett, in the articles collected in his book *Brainstorms*, Brighton, 1978.

9 This view – that description and explanation are continuous parts of a single process – has been sustained by a variety of writers, including W. V. Quine, *Word and Object*, Cambridge, Mass., 1960, and Wilfred Sellars, *Science, Perception and Reality*, London, 1963.

10 The distinction between primary and secondary qualities is at least as old as Pierre Gassendi; nevertheless, it has never ceased to be problematic: for a glimpse of the modern discussions, see Appendix 2.

11 Husserl referred to the world of human experience as the 'natural world' (*Naturwelt*), a term taken up by several of his disciples (e.g. by Patočka, in his *Přirozený Svět jako Filosofický Problém* (The Natural World as a Philosophical Problem), Prague, 1933 – a book which subsequently proved fertile in suggesting a role for philosophy in the interpretation of human experience that would be distinct from the role of science). Husserl's later preferred designations – *Umwelt* ('surrounding world') and *Lebenswelt* – indicate a belated recognition that it is precisely by *contrast* to a certain view of 'nature' that the world of human experience should be characterised. The term *Lebenswelt* has an older ancestry. It occurs in Dilthey and in the works of certain theorists of *Einfühlung* (such as Lipps); it also occurs in phenomenological sociologists like Alfred Schutz, and is related to the vocabulary of the Hegelian art historians (e.g. Wölfflin). (See Dilthey, *Collected Works*, vol. VII. Dilthey's preferred expression is, however, more Hegelian: 'objectifications of life'. Also Alfred Schutz, *The Phenomenology of the Social World*, tr. G. Walsh and F. Lehnert, Portland USA 1967; Heinrich Wölfflin, *Renaissance and Baroque*, tr. K. Simon, London, 1964, pp. 77ff.)

12 Cf. Heidegger's idea that, for me, 'things' are essentially 'to be used': *Being and Time*, tr. J. Macquarrie and E. S. Robinson, New York, 1962, pp. 96ff.

13 Cf. the distinct but complementary arguments presented against 'rationalism' in politics, by Michael Oakeshott (*Rationalism in Politics*, London, 1968) and F. A. von Hayek (*Studies in Philosophy, Politics and Economics*, London, 1967).

14 Dilthey, *Collected Works*, vol. VII; Max Weber, 'The Nature of Social Action', in W. G. Runciman (ed.), *Weber, Selections in Translation*, Cambridge, 1978. See below, Chapter 7, note 10.

15 I return to this point in Chapter 12, where I say more about what I mean by 'meaning,' and its connection with the viewpoint of the human subject, who is always, in the end, at war with the 'impersonality' of science. For some interesting Czech speculations on this theme, see V. Bělohradský, *Krize Eschatologie Neosobnosti*, Munich, 1982, and the penetrating, doctoral speech of Václav Havel sent to the University of Toulouse, 'Politics and Conscience', *Salisbury Review*, 3 (2), 1985.

16 See R. A. D. Grant, review of S. R. Letwin, *The Gentleman in Trollope*, *Salisbury Review*, 1 (1), 1982, pp. 41–2.

17 The Marxian theory of ideology has its origins in K. Marx and F. Engels, *The German Ideology*, 1846. The contrast between ideology and science – vital to the Marxian theory of history, and to the Marxian critique of philosophy – is now so well established that one commentator is able to say that 'it is a defining property of ideology that it is unscientific' (G. A. Cohen, *Karl Marx's Theory of History, a Defence*, Princeton, 1978, p. 46).

18 E. Husserl, *Die Krisis der europäischen Wissenschaften und die transzendentale Phänomenologie*, ed. W. Biemel, The Hague, 1976, part 2.

2 Arousal

1 Alfred C. Kinsey, W. B. Pomeroy, C. E. Martin *et al.*, *Sexual Behaviour in the Human Male*, London and Philadelphia, 1949; *Sexual Behaviour in the Human Female*, London and Philadelphia, 1953.

2 This theory is discussed below, in Chapter 7, in which Freudian and pre-Freudian sources are given.

3 On the classification of mental states, in terms of these formal distinctions, see my *Art and Imagination*, London, 1974, part II.

4 That we might distinguish aim, gratification, fulfilment and resolution for a single mental state is a point that I discuss more fully in Chapter 4.

5 Procopius, *Secret History*, book ix, 20.

6 G. Deleuze and F. Guattari, *L'Anti-Oedipe*, Paris, 1972.

7 See the discussions of the glance by J. P. Sartre, *Being and Nothingness*, tr. Hazel E. Barnes, New York, 1956, pp. 379f., and by T. Nagel, 'Sexual Perversion', in *Mortal Questions*, Cambridge, 1979.

8 *Being and Nothingness*, book III, ch. 3. Sartre's theory is discussed below, Chapter 5.

9 R. A. D. Grant, 'The Politics of Sex', *Salisbury Review*, 1 (2), 1983, p. 5.

10 H. P. Grice, 'Meaning', *Phil. Rev.*, vol. 66 (1957), pp. 377–88; J. R. Searle, *Speech Acts*, Cambridge, 1970; D. K. Lewis, *Convention*, Cambridge, Mass., 1969.

11 Nagel, 'Sexual Perversion'.

12 See Grice, 'Meaning', and the argument given by P. F. Strawson in 'Intention and Convention in Speech Acts', *Phil. Rev.*, 1964, reprinted in *Logico-Linguistic Papers*, London, 1971.

13 John Aubrey, *Brief Lives*, ed. V. L. Dick, London, 1949, p. 138.

14 Hannah Arendt, *The Human Condition*, Chicago, 1958.

15 *Being and Nothingness*, book IV, ch. 2, iii, esp. pp. 605–12.

16 Michel Foucault, *Histoire de la sexualité*, 3 vols, Paris, 1976, 1984.

3 Persons

1 W. V. Quine, *Word and Object*, Cambridge, Mass., 1960, ch. 1; *Ontological Relativity and Other Essays*, New York, 1969.

2 This may be one of the motives behind Aristotle's claim that the word 'flesh' is used only homonymously of dead flesh – of flesh from which the *psuchē* has flown: *De Generatione et Corruptione*, 390a; *De Generatione Animalium*, 734b; and elsewhere.

3 I mean, the idea of substance which seems to underlie the use of this term by Descartes, Spinoza and Leibniz, according to which a substance is both the bearer of attributes and an entity capable of independent existence. See W. Kneale, 'The Notion of a Substance', *Proceedings of the Aristotelian Society*, vol. XL (1939–40).

4 *Ethics*, book III, prop. 7.

5 Sir Ernest Barker, *Principles of Social and Political Theory*, Oxford, 1951, book IV.

6 See, for example, the essays on reasons for action and intention contained in Donald Davidson, *Essays on Actions and Events*, Oxford, 1980, section 1, and Davidson's 'Rational Animals', *Dialectica*, 36 (1982).

7 See for example, J. F. Bennett, *Rationality*, London, 1964. The thesis is qualified in the same author's *Linguistic Behaviour*, Cambridge, 1976.

8 The (real or apparent) conflict between expressive and representational theories of linguistic understanding now focusses upon the rival merits of the 'intention and use' theory of H. P. Grice ('Meaning', *Phil. Rev.*, vol. 66 (1957), pp. 377–88), and the 'semantic analysis' theory of Donald Davidson ('Truth and Meaning', *Synthèse*, VII (1967) pp. 304–323). The view that the two approaches are incompatible is increasingly doubted. But see J. R. Searle, *Speech-Acts*, Cambridge, 1970.

9 Such would be the approach of Davidson; see 'Thought and Talk', in S. Guttenplan (ed.), *Mind and Language*, Oxford, 1975.

10 Such is the approach of J. R. Searle, e.g., in *Intentionality*, Cambridge, 1982.

11 This thesis could be said to be one of the main conclusions of Kant's 'The Paralogisms of Pure Reason', in *The Critique of Pure Reason*, (1781, 1787), tr. Norman Kemp Smith, London, 1929, in which Kant criticises the inference from the purely 'formal' unity presupposed in self-consciousness (the 'transcendental unity of apperception') to the 'substantial unity' required for the rationalist theory of the soul.

12 These two absurdities are discussed and explained by Kant in the extremely unsatisfactory first part of *The Critique of Pure Reason*, the 'Transcendental Aesthetic'.

13 My argument at this point is influenced by Douglas Gasking, 'Avowals', in R. J. Butler (ed.), *Analytical Philosophy, First Series*, Oxford, 1968, and also by unpublished work by M. J. Budd.

14 The term 'self-intimation' comes from Gilbert Ryle, *The Concept of Mind*, London, 1955.

15 G. E. M. Anscombe, 'The First Person', in Guttenplan, *Mind and Language*.

16 See, for example, the essays by Anthony Kenny and Norman Malcolm in C. Diamond and J. Teichman (eds), *Intention and Intentionality*, Brighton, 1979.

17 The phrase comes from S. Shoemaker, 'Self-Reference and Self-Awareness',

Journal of Philosophy, vol. LXV (1968), pp. 555–67. See also the discussion of this subject in Gareth Evans, *The Varieties of Reference*, ed. J. McDowell, Oxford, 1982, pp. 179–92, in which Evans alters the phrase slightly.

18 L. Wittgenstein, *Philosophical Investigations*, tr. G. E. M. Anscombe, Oxford, 1952, part I, section 244, and part II, section xi, p. 223.

19 The attempt has been made, in two contrasting ways, by D. C. Dennett, *Content and Consciousness*, London, 1969, esp. pp. 100ff. and by H. P. Grice, 'Method in Philosophical Psychology', Presidential Address to the American Philosophical Association, 1974–5.

20 See *Philosophical Investigations*, part I, sections 172ff.

21 Some philosophers have drawn radical conclusions from the generality of Wittgenstein's arguments; see, for example, S. Kripke, *Wittgenstein on Rule-Following and Private Languages*, Oxford, 1982.

22 See for example, the seminal paper by S. Hampshire and H. L. A. Hart, 'Decision, Intention, and Uncertainty', *Mind*, vol. LXVII (1958), pp. 1–12. Also Hampshire's *Thought and Action*, London, 1956, ch. 2.

23 See the arguments in H. P. Grice, 'Intention and Uncertainty', *Proc. Brit. Acad.*, 1974.

24 G. E. M. Anscombe, *Intention*, Oxford, 1957.

25 Michael Oakeshott, 'The Voice of Poetry in the Conversation of Mankind', in *Rationalism and Politics*, London, 1968; and *On Human Conduct*, London, 1974.

26 The increasing emphasis on the concept of responsibility, rather than that of freedom, has been fruitful in understanding the assignment of legal liability. See the essays in H. L. A. Hart, *Punishment and Responsibility*, Oxford, 1968. My contention, that the legal and moral concepts can be understood in terms of the more basic idea of responsibility that I invoke in this section, is probably as old as Aristotle's *Nicomachean Ethics*.

27 See Kant, 'The Paralogisms of Pure Reason'.

28 See, however, the cases discussed by T. Nagel, 'Brain Bisection and the Unity of Consciousness', in *Mortal Questions*, Cambridge, 1979, in which Nagel gives reason to doubt this 'atomistic' quality of the self, although little reason to think that we could replace it by anything more cogent.

29 See the considerations offered by Derek Parfit in *Reasons and Persons*, Oxford, 1984, part III.

4 Desire

1 Mary Midgley, *Beast and Man*, London, 1979.

2 On the theory of 'embodiment', see Maurice Merleau-Ponty, *The Phenomenology of Perception*, tr. C. Smith, London, 1962, part 1. Merleau-Ponty's book contains a chapter on 'The Body in its Sexual Being', which is, however, surprisingly unhelpful in relation to the problems that I discuss.

3 Brian O'Shaughnessy, *The Will*, Cambridge, 1980, vol. 1, pp. liii–liv.

4 Charles Darwin, *The Expression of the Emotions in Man and Animals*, London, 1872, p. 310.

5 Christopher Ricks, *Keats and Embarrassment*, Oxford, 1976, p. 50.

6 *Ibid.*, p. 54.

7 See Havelock Ellis, *Studies in the Psychology of Sex*, vol. I: *On Modesty*, 3rd edn, Philadelphia, 1923, p. 73.

8 St Augustine, *City of God*, book XIV, ch. 23.

9 The operation and its emotional consequences are discussed by Thomas Szasz, *Sex: Facts, Frauds and Follies*, London, 1981, p. 84.

10 See A. Danto, 'Basic Actions', in A. R. White (ed.), *The Philosophy of Action*, Oxford, 1968.

11 This thesis, a subtle variant of which was given by Aristotle in one of his greatest passages (*De Anima*, 403 a–b), has been defended in a variety of ways by recent philosophers. See especially Bernard Williams, 'Are Persons Bodies?', in *Problems of the Self*, Cambridge, 1973.

12 Helmuth Plessner, *Lachen und Weinen*, 3rd edn, Bern, 1961; tr. James Spencer Churchill and Marjorie Grene, *Laughing and Crying: A Study of the Limits of Human Behaviour*, Evanston, 1970.

13 A. Schopenhauer, *The World as Will and Representation*, tr. E. J. F. Payne, Indian Hills, Colorado, 1958, vol. II, p. 543.

14 See *Salmond on Jurisprudence*, 12th edn, ed. P. J. Fitzgerald, London, 1966, ch. 10, esp. section 73.

15 See Derek Parfit, *Reasons and Persons*, Oxford, 1983.

16 *The Kinsey Report* (Alfred C. Kinsey, W. B. Pomeroy, C. E. Martin *et al.*, *Sexual Behaviour in the Human Male*, London and Philadelphia, 1949; *Sexual Behaviour in the Human Female*, London and Philadelphia, 1953); but the view is at least as old as Freud: see the passage from Freud quoted in the preface to this book.

17 T. Nagel, 'Sexual Perversion', in *Mortal Questions*, Cambridge, 1979; Nagel criticises what he calls the 'received radical view' of sexual experience – roughly the view indicated in my previous paragraph – while Sartre (*Being and Nothingness*, tr. Hazel E. Barnes, New York, 1956), criticises more generally the assimilation of sexual desire to appetite.

18 *The Kama Sutra of Vatsyayana*, tr. Sir R. Burton and F. F. Arbuthnot, London, 1963, pp. 168–9.

19 The various views concerning names, all of which have the implication that individuating reference is achieved in some other way than by virtue of the *content* of our thought, are discussed further in Appendix 2. Kripke's view of names, as 'rigid designators', is expounded in *Naming and Necessity*, Oxford, 1978. A rival way of arguing for partially similar conclusions is provided by Michael Dummett, *Frege: Philosophy of Language*, London, 1973, appendix to ch. 5.

20 My argument here parallels Nagel's ('Sexual Perversion', at pp. 42–3).

21 Bishop Butler, *Sermons*, London, 1726, sermon 1, 'On the Social Nature of Man'.

22 For a partial, but interesting critique of the ethologist's thesis, see Konrad Lorenz, *On Aggression* (1963), tr. M. Latzke, London, 1966, ch. ix. The thesis criticised may be found in Mary Midgley, *Beast and Man*.

23 Sartre, *Being and Nothingness*, pp. 387f.

24 I. Kant, *Lectures on Ethics*, tr. L. Infield, new edn, New York, 1963, p. 164.

25 *Ibid.*, p. 166.

26 See, for example, the case of *Fairclough* v. *Whipp* (1951) 35 Cr. App. R. 138.

27 On the 'iron law of oligarchy', see Roberto Michels, *Political Parties*, Basle,

1915, tr. Eden and Cedar Paul, London, 1921.

28 Roberto Michels, *Sexual Ethics, a Study of Borderland Questions*, New York, 1914, p. 34.

29 Alexis de Tocqueville, *De la démocratie en Amérique*, Paris, 1835.

5 The individual object

1 Schopenhauer: 'The quite special and individual passion of two lovers is just as inexplicable as is the quite special individuality of any person, which is exclusively peculiar to him: indeed at bottom the two are one and the same; the latter is *explicite* what the former was *implicite*' (*The World as Will and Representation*, tr. E. J. F. Payne, Indian Hills, Colorado, 1958, vol. II, p. 536).

2 See Hegel's paradox of the master and the slave, discussed in Chapter 10, below.

3 S. Kierkegaard, *Either/Or*, tr. W. Lowrie, New York, 1959, vol. II: *The Aesthetic Validity of Marriage*, pp. 111–14.

4 See R. M. Hare, 'Universalisability', *Proceedings of the Aristotelian Society*, vol. LV (1954–5), reprinted in *Essays on Moral Concepts*, London, 1972.

5 On the distinction between love and esteem, see I. Kant, *Foundations of the Metaphysic of Morals*, Prussian Academy edition, pp. 395ff. For the distinction between the rational and the pathological, see *ibid.*, 399. Kant also argues, however, that 'love . . . is an indispensable supplement to the imperfection of human nature, as a free assumption of the will of another under one's own maxim': *Das Ende aller Dinge*, Prussian Academy edition, vol. VIII, p. 337.

6 I have argued elsewhere for the view that in moral judgement, precisely because the crucial component is not a belief but an attitude, the belief in reasons is inexhaustible: 'Attitudes, Beliefs and Reasons', in John Casey (ed.), *Morality and Moral Reasoning*, London, 1971.

7 G. E. M. Anscombe, *Intention*, Oxford, 1957, section 37.

8 *Ibid.*

9 E.g. D. W. Hamlyn, 'The Phenomena of Love and Hate', in *Perception, Learning and the Self*, London, 1983.

10 Blaise Pascal, *Pensées* (no. 306 of the Penguin translation by J. M. Cohen, Harmondsworth, 1961).

11 E. B. de Condillac, *Traité des sensations et des animaux*, in *Oeuvres complètes*, Paris, 1821, vol. 3, p. 90.

12 This view exists in many variants: in particular in the versions due to Kant (*Critique of Judgement*, 1790, tr. J. H. Bernard, New York, 1951), and those due to Croce (*Aesthetic*, 2nd edn., tr. D. Ainslee, London, 1923). For a discussion of these views, and a defence of a particular one of them, see my *Art and Imagination*, London, 1974, ch. 9.

13 I argue for this in *Art and Imagination*, and in *The Aesthetics of Architecture*, London, 1979, ch. 5.

14 G. E. M. Anscombe, *Intention*.

15 See my *Art and Imagination*, ch. 1, and also 'Photography and Representation', in *The Aesthetic Understanding*, London, 1983.

16 This fallacy is fundamental to Croce's theory of art, as given in his *Aesthetic*, and also to the derivative view presented by R. G. Collingwood, in his *Principles of Art*, Oxford, 1937. Analytical philosophers are not immune from the mistake.

See in particular P. F. Strawson's paper, 'Aesthetic Appraisal and Works of Art', in *Freedom and Resentment and Other Essays*, London, 1974, in which Strawson argues that works of art are distinguished by a peculiar criterion of identity – one which in effect makes all their aesthetically relevant features into essential properties.

17 See, for example, S. Hampshire, 'Logic and Appreciation', in W. Elton (ed.), *Aesthetics and Language*, Oxford, 1954.

18 See F. A. Hayek, *Studies in Philosophy, Politics and Economics*, London, 1967, and Michael Polanyi, *Personal Knowledge*, London, 1958, ch. 7.

19 A. G. Baumgarten, *Reflections on Poetry*, 1735.

20 This thesis has been upheld in countless ways. See, for example, Kant, *Critique of Judgement*, section 32, and, for a particularly influential modern restatement, F. N. Sibley, 'Aesthetic Concepts', *Phil. Rev.*, 1957, and 'Aesthetic and Non-Aesthetic', *Phil. Rev.*, 1965.

21 The confusion has been well set out and criticised by P. F. Strawson in *The Bounds of Sense*, London, 1966, and also by R. Walker, *Kant*, London, 1978, ch. IV.

22 See note 5 above.

23 On the 'pernicious' character of this idea, see D. Wiggins, *Sameness and Substance*, Oxford, 1980, p. 120.

24 We should not be surprised therefore that the greatest of all sustained attempts to give sense to the idea of an individual essence – that of Spinoza – tends naturally to the conclusion that there is only one thing, and that thing is God.

25 Wiggins, *Sameness and Substance*.

26 P. F. Strawson, *Individuals, an Essay in Descriptive Metaphysics*, London, 1959.

27 See especially Bernard Williams, *Descartes, The Project of Pure Enquiry*, London, 1978, on the Cartesian 'absolute' conception of the world. Pertinent criticism of this conception, in a version of it attributed to Leibniz, can be found in Strawson, *Individuals*, ch. 4.

28 In *The Critique of Pure Reason* (1781, 1787), tr. Norman Kemp Smith, London, 1929, 'Transcendental Dialectic'.

29 J. G. Fichte, *The Science of Knowledge*, tr. and ed. P. Heath and J. Lachs, Cambridge, 1982, second Introduction.

30 T. Nagel, 'Subjective and Objective', in *Mortal Questions*, Cambridge, 1979.

31 I. Kant, *Lectures on Philosophical Theology*, tr. Allen J. Wood, R. Gertrude, M. Clark, Ithaca and London, 1978, p. 150. The notion of an 'intellectual intuition' was regarded as of great importance in this connection by several of Kant's followers, and notably by Fichte in *The Science of Knowledge*.

32 See Z. Vendler, 'A Note on the Paralogisms', in G. Ryle (ed.), *Contemporary Aspects of Philosophy*, Stocksfield, 1976.

33 See the references to Shoemaker and Evans in note 17 of Chapter 3.

34 G. Evans, *The Varieties of Reference*, ed. J. McDowell, Oxford, 1982, chs. 6 and 7.

35 'The Paralogisms of Pure Reason', and also 'The Amphiboly of the Concepts of Pure Reason', in *The Critique of Pure Reason*.

36 The 'selflessness' of Spinoza's metaphysics is one of its most remarkable features. There is no proposition remotely equivalent to Descartes' *cogito* until book 2, proposition XI of the *Ethics*, in which it is asserted that 'the first thing which constitutes the actual being of the human mind is nothing else than the idea

of an individual thing actually existing' – a proposition that makes the individual existence of the human mind dependent upon an *idea* of individuality. And Spinoza's detailed theory of human individuality in book 3 makes it clear that there is no identity to the self other than that which can be ascribed to the body: that which is detachable from the body is not the individual self but the eternal attribute of reason which partakes of the nature of God.

37 Thus Kant, who argues (in the *Critique of Judgement*) that in the judgement of beauty we understand the harmony between our own faculties and the world of objects, and in consequence read into the works of nature an idea of finality which is understood from our activity and nature.

38 *Being and Nothingness*, tr. Hazel E. Barnes, New York, 1956, book III, ch. 3.

39 *Ibid.*, pp. 384–5.

40 *Ibid.*, p. 396.

41 *Ibid.*, p. 404.

42 *Ibid.*, p. 399.

43 See the argument concerning sadism in Chapter 10, below.

44 G. W. F. Hegel, *The Philosophy of Right*, tr. and ed. T. M. Knox, Oxford, 1942, addition to para. 158.

45 See my *Art and Imagination*, ch. 11.

46 Aurel Kolnai, *Sexualethik, Sinn und Grundlagen der Geschlechtsmoral*, Paderborn, 1930, p. 66.

47 See St Augustine, *De Nuptiis et Concupiscentia*, and the encyclical of Pope Innocent III, *De Miseria Humanae Conditionis*. The views of the present pontiff, while in line with the Augustinian tradition, show a marked Kantian influence, which approximates them to the theories expounded in this work: 'The exchange of the gift of the person constitutes the real source of the experience of innocence . . . . [By contrast] the extorting of the gift from the woman by the man, or vice versa, and reducing him or her in one's own mind to a mere object, marks exactly the beginning of shame' (Pope John Paul II (Karól Woytila), *Love and Responsibility*, 1960, tr. H. J. Willetts, London, 1981, quoted in Paul Johnson, *Pope John Paul II and the Catholic Restoration*, London, 1982. The passage is intended as a commentary on Genesis 2: 25 – 'And they were both naked, the man and his wife, and were not ashamed' – a verse that is crucial to the Christian theories of embodiment).

48 *De Hominis Opificio*, ch. 17, tr. H. A. Wilson, in *Gregory of Nyssa, Dogmatic Treatises etc.*, Oxford, 1893.

49 Bella Millett (ed.), *Hali Meidhad*, Oxford (Early English Text Society), 1982, p. 4. My translation captures none of the strenuous alliteration of the original.

50 St Augustine, *The City of God*, book XIV, ch. 19.

51 *Ibid.*

52 *Ibid.*, ch. 23.

53 *The World as Will and Representation*, vol. I, book 3, section 51.

54 On the interpretation of this poem, see J. A. W. Bennett, *The Parliament of Fowls, an Interpretation*, Oxford, 1957. I am particularly indebted to Victoria Rothschild, 'The Parliament of Fowls, Chaucer's Mirror up to Nature?', *The Review of English Studies*, vol. XXXV, (1984), pp. 164–84.

6 Sexual phenomena

1 This kind of laughter – though not every kind – is agreeably characterised by Henri Bergson, *Le Rire*, 23rd edn, Paris, 1924; *Laughter*, Philadelphia, 1970.

2 Henry James, *Notebooks*, ed. T. Matthieson, p. 124, and Preface to *The Bostonians*.

3 Havelock Ellis has a nice discussion concerning the hiding of the face in shame. See *Studies in the Psychology of Sex*, vol. I: *On Modesty*, 3rd edn, Philadelphia, 1923, pp. 58–9. The Moslem habit of the veil is an index of shame and modesty. As Moslem women often point out, the more you hide, the more vulnerable becomes the last remaining surface that is not yet hidden. The eyes, hands and ankles of the covered woman become peculiarly exciting, and also peculiarly vulnerable to any concupiscent glance. Often it seems as though a woman's hands react spontaneously to the stare which focusses them, even when the man has not been observed.

4 *Ibid.*, vol. I.

5 T. Carlyle, *Sartor Resartus*, Everyman Edition, 1908, p. 30.

6 The evidence is conveniently summarised in Ellis, *Studies in the Psychology of Sex*, vol. I.

7 Aurel Kolnai, *Sexualethik, sinn und Grundlagen der Geschlechtsmoral*, Paderborn, 1930, p. 13: 'Die Kategorie der Schmutzer kommt primar und unmittelbar nur in sexuellen Bezirk der Ethos vor; nur hier ist "moralisch unsauberer Ding" als wirklich dinglicher, massiver Realitätsbestandteil vorhanden.' I provide a defence of this observation in Chapter 11.

8 Nicolas Restif de la Bretonne, *M. Nicolas*, Paris, 1827, vol. 1, p. 94.

9 The story is given in L. Lombroso and G. Ferrero, *La Femme prostituée*, Paris, 1893, p. 590.

10 Camille Mélinaud, 'La Psychologie de la pudeur', *La Revue*, no. 10, p. 397.

11 Max Scheler, *Über Scham und Schamgefühl*, in *Schriften aus dem Nachlass*, 2nd edn, ed. Maria Scheler, Bern 1957, p. 80.

12 For example, in *De Generatione Animalium*, 725b.

13 Aristide Bruant, *Dictionnaire français-argot*, Paris, 1901, entry for *coït*.

14 Wayland Young, *Eros Denied*, London, 1965, ch. 1.

15 J. P. Sartre, *Being and Nothingness*, tr. Hazel E. Barnes, New York, 1956, p. 397.

16 Leopardi, '*A sè stesso*'. I discuss the meaning of this poem in *The Aesthetic Understanding*, London, 1983, pp. 237–40.

17 The painting is partially described in Wayland Young, *Eros Denied*, pp. 95–6.

18 Havelock Ellis, *Studies in the Psychology of Sex*, vol. I, p. 82.

19 E. P. de Senancour, *De l'amour*, Paris, 1834, vol. i, p. 209.

20 Georg Simmel, *The Philosophy of Money*, tr. T. Bottomore, D. Frisby and K. Maengelberg, London, 1978, pp. 376–7.

21 Bernaldo de Quiros y Llanas Aguilaniedo, *La Mala Vida da Madrid*, Madrid, 1901, p. 204.

22 In his examination of the ethos of consumerism, Jean Baudrillard has little to say about prostitution, but much about the sexual significance of dolls, and the 'fetishising' of the body, so as to make it doll-like and therefore the subject of a process of 'simulation and restitution': *La Société de consommation*, Paris, 1970, pp. 235ff.

23 The phrase 'moral economy' is used by E. P. Thompson in 'The Peculiarities of the English' (in *The Poverty of Theory*, London, 1978), in order to describe the arrangements which, in his view, were swept away by the Industrial Revolution and the voiding of the countryside.

24 I refer here to the ideal types of 'primitive communism', 'slavery', 'feudalism', 'capitalism', 'socialism' and '(full) communism' as these are described in *Capital* and elsewhere. I use the expression 'ideal type' in the sense given to it by Weber: see my *Dictionary of Political Thought*, London, 1982, entry for *ideal type*.

25 Pauline Réage, *Histoire d'O*, Sceaux, 1954.

26 P. H. Wicksteed, *An Introduction to Political Economy*, London, 1910.

27 G. Garibaldi, *Memorie autobiografiche*, 7th edn, Florence, 1888, p. 56.

28 Stendhal, *De l'amour*, Paris, 1891.

29 Georg Simmel, 'Die Koketterie', in *Philosophische Kultur, Gesammelte Essais*, ed. J. Habermas, Berlin, 1983 (original, Potsdam, 1923).

30 *Ethics*, book 3, proposition XXXV.

31 *La Fugitive*, Pléiade edn, pp. 545–6.

32 *Ethics*, book 3, proposition XXXV.

33 Stendhal, *De l'amour*, book II, ch. 59; Denis de Rougemont, *Passion and Society*, tr. M. Belgion, revised edn, London, 1956.

34 Søren Kierkegaard, 'The Immediate Stages of the Erotic', in *Either/Or*, tr. W. Lowrie, New York, 1959, vol. I.

35 *Ibid.*, pp. 98–9.

36 *De l'amour*, vol. ii, pp. 229–30.

37 Letters of Lord Byron, ed. Leslie Marchand, vol. 6, London, 1976.

38 The phrase 'objective correlative' is taken from T. S. Eliot's essay on *Hamlet* ('Hamlet and his Problems'), in *The Sacred Wood*, London, 1920.

39 Cf. the Freudian characterisation of this episode given by Pierre-Jean Jouve, *Le Don Juan de Mozart*, Paris, 1952.

40 Ellis, *Studies in the Psychology of Sex*, vol. III.

41 *Ibid.*, pp. 137ff.; C. Féré, *Revue de Medecine*, 1900.

42 Charles Cornevin, *Archives d'anthropologie criminelle*, 1896, cited, Ellis, *Studies in the Psychology of Sex*, vol. III, pp. 137–8.

43 *Ibid.*, p. 160.

44 Richard Freiherr von Krafft-Ebing, *Psychopathia Sexualis*, tr. (as *The Aberrations of Sexual Life*) by A. V. Burbury, London, 1951.

45 See M. Foucault, *Surveiller et punir*, Paris, 1975.

46 Sartre, *Being and Nothingness*, p. 404.

47 *Ibid.*, p. 403.

48 De Sade, *La Nouvelle Justine*, ch. 1, suffices to illustrate the idiom.

49 Georges Bataille, *L'Érotisme*, Paris, 1957.

7 The science of sex

1 Montaigne, 'Upon Some Verses of Virgil', in *Essays*, tr. J. Florio, vol. 3, p. 192.

2 G. W. Peckham, quoted in Havelock Ellis, *Studies in the Psychology of Sex*, 3rd edn, Philadelphia, 1923, vol. III, p. 35.

3 See Appendix 2.

4 This is simply one aspect of what is sometimes known as the 'Quine–Duhem' thesis, according to which observation and theory are interdependent; *what* you observe is genuinely observed only when theory guarantees the observation. (See P. M. M. Duhem, *The Aim and Structure of Physical Theory*, tr. P. P. Wiener, Princeton, 1954, and W. V. Quine, *Word and Object*, Cambridge, Mass., 1960.)

5 Edward O. Wilson, *Sociobiology, the New Synthesis*, Cambridge, Mass., 1975, p. 320. A readable summary of sociobiological theories of sex and reproduction is contained in D. P. Barash, *Sociobiology and Behaviour*, 2nd edn, London, 1982, chs 10 and 11.

6 The inherent incompleteness of Darwinian explanation has important consequences for the philosophy of evolution: in particular, it is unclear *what* needs to be added to the Darwinian account in order to make non-trivial predictions concerning the evolution of the species. The *easiest* way to complete Darwinian explan~tion is to add a theory of genetic development, and to assume that all features which contribute to the survival of the species are themselves genetically determined. This might be contentiously expressed by saying that what matters is not the survival of the species, but the survival of the *gene*. The sociobiologist usually takes this position, and argues that social behaviour, *because* it adapts itself to ensure species-survival, must *therefore* be genetically determined. The conclusion is wholly unwarranted in itself, and is usually supported by a question-begging analogy between human society and the 'societies' of insects, in which none of the adaptability of human behaviour is displayed. (See, for example, E. O. Wilson, *The Insect Societies*, Cambridge, Mass., 1971.) In the insect world, *everything* is genetically programmed. And an honest scientist would go on at once to say: and look how *different* it is from our world!

7 This objection is made, for example, by Sir Edmund Leach, in *Social Anthropology*, London, 1982.

8 E. O. Wilson, *On Human Nature*, Cambridge, Mass., 1978, pp. 139–40.

9 The sense of the difference between the two patterns of activity – that imposed by a genetic programme and that derived from the creative acts of rational cooperation – is responsible for Henri Bergson's distinction between instinct and intellect: *Creative Evolution*, tr. A. Mitchell, London, 1911. An impressive description of the complex social habits of bees has been given by Karl von Frisch, *The Dancing Bees, an Account of the Life and Senses of the Honey Bee*, tr. D. Ilse, London, 1954. Von Frisch's account is discussed fruitfully by Jonathan Bennett in *Rationality*, London, 1964. Bennett shows that the complexity of the bees' behaviour, however remarkable, cannot justify the description of it as a language; and without language there is neither rationality nor genuine 'cooperation', of the kind familiar in the human world.

It is important to emphasise that the behaviour of the higher animals is unlike that of the insects in exhibiting learning, and is therefore infinitely adaptable to the receipt of *new information*. Bergsonians, who use the term 'instinct' to cover both insect behaviour and certain types of behaviour in higher animals, obscure this vital distinction.

10 This term, introduced to the social sciences by Dilthey, and adopted by Weber, is designed to capture a familiar, but elusive, intellectual act, whereby we understand the behaviour and thoughts of others through a partial identification with their point of view. See the article on *Verstehen* in my *Dictionary of Political*

Thought, London, 1982.

11 I refer here to Desmond Morris, *The Naked Ape, A Zoologist's Study of the Human Animal*, London, 1967, and also to Alex Comfort, *Sex in Society*, 1950, revised London, 1963 in which a wholly revisionary description of the sexual act is attempted, in order to present its pleasures in appetitive terms.

12 *On Human Nature*, p. 109.

13 Pierre van den Berghe, quoted in Wilson, *ibid*., pp. 109–10.

14 *Ibid*., p. 142.

15 A. Schopenhauer, *The World as Will and Representation*, tr. E. J. F. Payne, Indian Hills, Colorado, 1958, vol. II, ch. 44, 'The Metaphysics of Sexual Love.'

16 *Ibid*., p. 549.

17 *Ibid*., p. 537.

18 *Ibid*., p. 537.

19 *Ibid*., p. 559.

20 Plato, *Symposium*, 192c.

21 Eduard von Hartmann, *Philosophy of the Unconscious*, tr. W. C. Coupland, London, 1884, p. 223.

22 *Ibid*., p. 232.

23 *Ibid*., p. 238.

24 Melanie Klein, *Envy and Gratitude, a Study of Unconscious Sources*, London, 1957; Wilhelm Reich, *The Function of the Orgasm*, 1968, tr. V. R. Carfagno, New York, 1973, London, 1983.

25 The precise kind of theory that Freud hoped for is a matter of some dispute. A plausible candidate is discussed by Richard Wollheim, *Sigmund Freud*, Modern Masters, London and New York, 1971.

26 This functionalist idea of myth is familiar from the writings of Georges Sorel (especially *Réflexions sur la violence*, Paris, 1908); its application to psychoanalysis seems to be implicit in Wittgenstein's discussion in *Lectures and Conversations on Aesthetics, Freud, and Religious Belief*, ed. C. Barrett, Oxford, 1966.

27 'Three Essays on Sexuality' (1905), reprinted in the Penguin Freud Library, vol. 7: *On Sexuality*, ed. J. Strachey and A. Richards, Harmondsworth, 1977, p. 60.

28 *Ibid*., p. 61.

29 *Ibid*., p. 83.

30 *Ibid*., p. 83.

31 I discuss the meaning of this term more fully below. See also note 44.

32 'Three Essays', p. 94.

33 See especially the painstaking reconstruction in Peter Madison, *Freud's Concept of Repression and Defence, its Theoretical and Observational Language*, Minneapolis, 1961.

34 S. Freud, *Beyond the Pleasure Principle*, standard edition of the works of Freud, ed. J. Strachey, London, 1955, vol. XVIII, pp. 29–30.

35 Sir Karl Popper, *Conjectures and Refutations*, London, 1963, ch. 1, pp. 34–5; Ernest Nagel, 'Methodological Issues in Psychoanalytic Theory', in S. Hook (ed.): *Psychoanalysis, Scientific Method, and Philosophy*, New York, 1959, pp. 38–56.

36 Freud, 'Three Essays', p. 119.

37 'On the Universal Tendency to Debasement in the Sphere of Love' (1912), in

On Sexuality, pp. 243–60.

38 For example, in the 1915 edition of the 'Three Essays'.

39 See, for example, 'Analysis Terminable and Interminable' (1937), in *Collected Papers*, tr. J. Riviere, New York and London, 1924–50, Vol. V, p. 344.

40 Melanie Klein, *Envy and Gratitude*.

41 'Three Essays', p. 139.

42 *Ibid.*

43 Wilhelm Reich, *The Function of the Orgasm*; Norman O. Brown, *Life Against Death*, London, 1959.

44 E. Chambard, *Du somnambulisme*, Paris, 1881. See the discussion in Havelock Ellis, 'The Doctrine of Erotogenic Zones', *Studies in the Psychology of Sex*, vol. VII, Philadelphia, 1928, pp. 111–20.

45 Freud, 'Three Essays', p. 84.

46 *Ibid.*, p. 99.

47 Hume's theory that an 'idea' (i.e. any intellectual mental content) is, and must be, the faded remainder of an 'impression' is given in the *Enquiry into the Human Understanding*, 1748, section 2. The disastrous effect of this theory, in obliterating the distinction between sensory and intellectual processes, and in effectively removing the possibility of explaining the intentionality of the latter, has been a matter of frequent philosophical comment, ever since Kant first effectively demolished it in *The Critique of Pure Reason* (1781, 1787), tr. Norman Kemp Smith, London, 1929.

48 'Three Essays', p. 125.

49 *Ibid.*, p. 98.

50 *Ibid.*, p. 130. It is evident that there is a distinction between sensations in the eye, and perceptions by means of the eye. Some philosophers argue that perception does not involve, and is therefore not a form of, sensation (e.g. D. M. Armstrong, *Bodily Sensations*, London, 1962). Even if we disagree with this (see, for example, Christopher Peacocke, *Sense and Content*, Oxford, 1983), we must recognise that a *pleasure* of perception is a radically different thing from a *pleasure* of sensation. As Aquinas argues persuasively, the first can include aesthetic pleasures (the pleasures involved in the recognition of beauty), while the second cannot (*Summa Theologica*, 1a, 2ae, 27, 1). I discuss this point further in Chapter 8.

51 'Three Essays', p. 157.

52 *Ibid.*, p. 69.

53 *Ibid.*

54 Thus, among the thirteen standard criteria of 'resistance' to analysis, Madison (*Freud's Concept of Repression and Defence*, p. 69), lists the following: 'expressing an intellectual opposition to the theory of psychoanalysis on scientific grounds'; 'feelings of unpleasure experienced during therapy'; and even, 'developing a theoretical interest in psychoanalysis, and wanting to be instructed in the theory by the therapist'!

55 *New Introductory Lectures on Psychoanalysis*, New York, 1933, pp. 126–7.

56 Wittgenstein, *Lectures and Conversations*, p. 18.

57 Cf. John Casey, 'The Autonomy of Art', in *Philosophy and the Arts*, Royal Institute of Philosophy Lectures, vol. VI, London, 1973.

58 It should perhaps be pointed out that, for psychoanalysis, all these moral feelings are, in the end, systematically discounted. In an influential and pharisaic

exposition of psychoanalytic morality J. C. Flugel writes: 'What we might call *rational restraint* on the part of the individual is . . . another substitute for taboo' (*Man, Morals and Society*, 1945; Peregrine Edition, Harmondsworth, 1962, p. 163).

8 Love

1 Andreas Capellanus, *The Art of Courtly Loving*, tr. and ed. J. J. Parry, New York, 1941, p. 28.

2 Dante, *Vita Nuova*, ch. 2.

3 On this theme, see the exaggerated theories of Denis de Rougemont in *Passion and Society* , tr. M. Belgion, revised edn, London, 1956; and *Comme toi-même*, Paris, 1961, tr. as *The Myths of Love*, by R. Howard, London, 1964.

4 This idea is emphasised by Abravanel (Leone Ebreo), *The Philosophy of Love* (*Dialoghi d'amore*), tr. F. Friedburg-Seeley and J. H. Barnes, introduction by C. Roth, London, 1937, p. 41.

5 D. Hume, *Treatise of Human Nature*, book II, ch. 2, section xi.

6 *Ibid.*

7 Plato, *Symposium*, 211B–212A.

8 Aristotle, *Nicomachean Ethics*, book VIII.

9 R. G. Collingwood, *Principles of Art*, Oxford, 1938, ch. V.

10 B. Croce, *Aesthetic*, 2nd edn., tr. D. Ainslee, London, 1923, ch. XII.

11 The search for an objectivist theory of virtue is now regarded with some suspicion, for reasons some of which are given in Bernard Williams, *Morality*, London 1973, pp. 69–76.

12 See S. Hampshire, 'Logic and Appreciation', in W. Elton (ed.), *Aesthetics and Language*, Oxford, 1954.

13 I. Kant, *Foundations of the Metaphysic of Morals*, Prussian Academy edition, pp. 399ff.

14 This emphasis on the connection between self-consciousness and a sense of identity over time is central to many of the arguments in Kant's *Critique of Pure Reason* (1781, 1787), tr. Norman Kemp Smith, London, 1929.

15 See the now familiar arguments of Sidney Shoemaker in *Self-Knowledge and Self-Identity*, Ithaca, 1963.

16 Cf. M. Merleau-Ponty's theory of the intentional understanding directed towards the other's 'embodiment', in *Phenomenology of Perception*, tr. C. Smith, London, 1962.

17 G. Lessing, *Laocoon*, 1766, ch. IV.

18 A. Schopenhauer, *The World as Will and Representation*, vol. I, book 3, section 51.

19 Montaigne, *Essays*, book 1, ch. XXVII.

20 Martin Buber, *I and Thou* (1922), tr. R. G. Smith, New York, 1958.

21 J. M. E. McTaggart, *The Nature of Existence*, Cambridge, 1927, vol. II, ch. 41, p. 151. A similar account is given by Max Scheler, *The Nature of Sympathy*, tr. P. Heath, London, 1954, p. 121: 'Nothing shows better [that the object of love is an "unspecified particularity"] than the extraordinary perplexity which can be seen to ensue when people are asked to give "reasons" for their love.' And cf. Montaigne, 'Of Friendship' (*Essays*, book 1, no. xxvii): 'If a man urge me to tell

wherefore I loved him I feele it cannot be expressed, but by answering: Because it was he, because it was my selfe' (John Florio's translation).

22 McTaggart, *The Nature of Existence*, p. 152.

23 S. Kierkegaard, *Either/Or*, tr. W. Lowrie, New York, 1959, vol. II, p. 46.

24 Vol. 1, ostensibly concerned with the 'aesthetic' way of life, contains the harrowing 'Diary of a Seducer', to which vol. 2, concerned with the 'ethical' way of life, offers a kind of answer, in a quiet and solemn analysis of marriage.

25 F. Nietzsche, *The Will to Power*, tr. W. Kaufman and R. J. Hollingdale, ed. W. Kaufman, New York, 1967, no. 964.

26 J. P. Sartre, *Saint-Genet, comédien et martyr*, Paris, 1955.

27 Stendhal, *De l'amour*, Paris, 1891, book I, ch. 2: *'il suffit de penser à une perfection pour la voir dans ce qu'on aime.'*

28 I have defended this thesis in detail in *The Aesthetics of Architecture*, London, 1979, chs 5–9.

29 The breaking up of the lines here, in order to expose the internal rhyme, is due to Ezra Pound: see Hugh Kenner (ed.), *The Translations of Ezra Pound*, London, 1953, in which the *canzone* is printed with a facing translation. Pound gives another, more beautiful and more personal translation in Canto XXXVI.

30 Robert Solomon, *Love: Emotion, Myth and Metaphor*, New York, 1981, esp. p. 48.

31 *Ibid.*, p. 5.

32 Pope John Paul II has spoken of the 'nuptiality' of the human body (*Love and Responsibility*, 1960, tr. H. J. Willetts, London, 1981). His words derive from Max Scheler, although I have not been able to locate the relevant passage.

33 See Virgil C. Aldrich, *Philosophy of Art*, Englewood Cliffs, 1963, ch. 1.

34 See the devastating critique of the literature of sex education, and its anti-love ideology, in Thomas Szasz, *Sex: Facts, Frauds and Follies*, Oxford, 1981.

35 *The Letters of Héloise and Abelard*, ed. and tr. Betty Radice, Harmondsworth, 1974, p. 113.

36 I argue the point in *Art and Imagination*, London, 1974, ch. 9.

37 Abravanel, *The Philosophy of Love* , p. 53.

38 I have tried to establish this in 'Understanding Music', in *The Aesthetic Understanding*, London, 1983.

39 Catullus' lines are imitated by Josephus Secundus: *'Centum basia centies, / Centum basia millies, / Mille basia millies, / Et tot millia millies, / Quot guttae siculo mare, /* etc.' The passage is quoted in Robert Burton's *Anatomy of Melancholy*, part III, section 2.

40 Theodor Reik, *Of Love and Lust*, New York, 1957, ch. 1.

41 I have tried to defend this claim in *Art and Imagination*, parts I and II.

9 Sex and gender

1 See G. E. M. Anscombe, 'Contraception and Chastity', in *The Human World*, vol. II (1972).

2 Otto Weininger, *Sex and Character*, English edition, London, 1903, p. 65.

3 Stephen Heath, *The Sexual Fix*, London, 1982, p. 145.

4 Guy Hocquenghem, *Le Désir homosexuel*, Paris, 1972, p. 12.

5 Simone de Beauvoir, *Le Deuxième Sexe*, Paris, 1949, tr. as *The Second Sex* by H. M. Parshley, London, 1953:

> Now, what peculiarly signalises the situation of woman is that she – a free and autonomous being like all human creatures – nevertheless finds herself living in a world where men compel her to assume the state of the Other. They propose to stabilise her as object and to doom her to immanence since her transcendence is to be overshadowed and for ever transcended by another ego (*conscience*) which is essential and sovereign. The drama of woman lies in this conflict between the fundamental aspirations of every subject (ego) – who always regards the self as the essential – and the compulsions of a situation in which she is the inessential. [Penguin edn, p. 29]

6 Some of the evidence for this claim – hotly disputed, for example, by Anne Oakley in *Sex, Gender and Society*, London, 1972 – is collected by Jo Durden-Smith and Diane de Simone in *Sex and the Brain*, London, 1983. The authors draw attention to the extensive censorship, and the almost universal censorious-ness, exercised by feminists towards established scientific facts.

7 'De la puberté', 1749, in *L'Histoire naturelle* (selections, ed. J. Varloot, Paris, 1984, p. 87).

8 E. P. de Senancour, *De l'amour*, Paris, 1834, vol. i, pp. 72–3.

9 See above, note 4.

10 Margaret Mead, *Male and Female*, New York, 1950; Harmondsworth, 1962, pp. 30–1.

11 Guy Hocquenghem, *Le Désir homosexuel*.

12 Yukio Mishima, *Sun and Steel*, tr. J. Bester, London, 1971. See also the description of homosexual desire in Mishima's *Forbidden Colours*, tr. A. H. Marks, New York, 1968.

13 The distinction between male and female virtues is of course far older than Aristotle. Hume distinguishes male and female virtues at *Treatise of Human Nature*, book III, ch. 2, section xii. However, since he regards the virtues over which men and women most differ (chastity and courage) alike as 'artificial' virtues, it is possible that he might have agreed with the feminist claim that the virtues might have been constructed in the same form for either sex.

14 Margaret Mead, *Coming of Age in Samoa*, New York, 1927. Margaret Mead's findings have been vigorously, if crudely, questioned by Derek Freeman, *Margaret Mead and Samoa*, Cambridge, Mass., 1983.

15 Anne Hollander, *Seeing Through Clothes*, New York, 1978.

16 Kenneth Clark, *The Nude, Study of Ideal Form*, New York, 1956.

17 G. W. F. Hegel, *The Phenomenology of Spirit* (1807), ed. J. Hoffmeister, Hamburg, 1952, section 475 (my translation).

18 Ruskin, in a fervent, sentimental tract, advocates separate education for men and women, in terms which betray this excitement at every juncture: 'The perfect loveliness of a woman's countenance can only consist in that majestic peace, which is founded in the memory of happy and useful years, – full of sweet records; and from the joining of this with that yet more majestic childishness, which is still full of change and promise; – opening always – modest at once, and bright, with hope of better things to be won, and to be bestowed' (*Sesame and Lilies*, London, 1865, section 71).

19 See Edmond et Jules de Goncourt, *La Femme au 18ᵉ siècle*, Paris, 1862.

20 Philippe Perrot, *Les Dessus et le dessous de la bourgeoisie*, Paris, 1980.

21 The issue of the relation between sex and gender is usefully discussed in the judgement of Ormrod J. in *Corbet* v. *Corbet* [1970] 2 All E.R. 1, at 33–51, the divorce case precipitated by April Ashley's decision to 'become' the woman whom she already felt herself to be. As the judge remarks, the distinction is of considerable legal importance, since many adjudicable matters require the gender of the parties to be determinate, even when the sex is not. (Passports, for example, must be unambiguous as to gender.) See also the sentimental self-torturings of Jan Morris in *Conundrum*, London, 1974.

22 See, generally, Robert Gray and Bruce McEwen, *Sexual Differentiation of the Brain*, Cambridge, Mass., 1980, and in particular John Money and Mark Schwartz, 'Biological Determinants of Gender Identity Differentiation and Development', in J. B. Hutchinson (ed.), *Biological Determinants of Sexual Behaviour*, New York, 1978.

23 Herculine Barbin's recently discovered memoirs have been published, translated by R. McDougall with an introduction by Michel Foucault, by the Harvester Press, Brighton, 1980.

24 Colin McGinn, *The Subjective View*, London, 1983.

25 P. T. Geach, 'Good and Evil', in P. Foot (ed.), *Theories of Ethics*, Oxford, 1967.

26 *Lectures on Aesthetics*, tr. T. M. Knox, Oxford, 1974, Introduction.

27 Jacques Casanova de Seingalt, *Mémoires*, Paris, 1930, vol. 2, ch. 1.

28 See the quotation from Simone de Beauvoir in note 5 above.

10 Perversion

1 See, 'Three Essays on Sexuality' (1905), reprinted in the Penguin Freud Library, vol. 7: *On Sexuality*, ed. J. Strachey and A. Richards, Harmondsworth, 1977, especially no. 1, 'The Sexual Abberations'.

2 Rémy de Gourmont, *The Natural Philosophy of Love*, tr. Ezra Pound, London, 1926, new edn 1957, pp. 91–2 (originally *Essai sur l' instinct sexuel*, Paris, 1904). Recent research has suggested that this peculiar feature of the mantis's amatory behaviour is *not* in fact natural, but an effect of being watched by prurient entomologists.

3 G. E. M. Anscombe, 'Contraception and Chastity', in *The Human World*, vol.II (1972).

4 See the replies to Anscombe's article from P. Winch, B. Williams and M. Tanner, in *ibid*. The controversy has been discussed by Jenny Teichman, 'Intention and Sex', in C. Diamond and J. Teichman (eds), *Intention and Intentionality*, Brighton, 1979.

5 Germaine Greer, *Sex and Destiny*, London, 1984, p. 101.

6 Thomas Nagel, 'Sexual Perversion', in *Mortal Questions*, Cambridge, 1979.

7 *Ibid.*, p. 48.

8 Féré has an interesting account of what he calls 'zoophilia', the love of animals which, while not in itself a perversion, may precede the development of bestial desire. The implication is that, in such a case, desire grows from love (C. Féré, *Evolution and Dissolution of the Sexual Instinct*, 2nd edn, Paris, 1904, p. 181). The implication is also contained in J. R. Ackerley, *My Dog Tulip*, London, 1956. But, as Ackerley makes clear, desire is made possible here only because the dog is perceived entirely in personal terms.

9 The expression is used by Henry Spencer Ashbee ('Pisanus Fraxi'); see Peter Fryer (ed.), *Forbidden Books of the Victorians*, London, 1970 (H. S. Ashbee's bibliographies of erotica).

10 Cf. Céline's descriptions of the behaviour of horses in war: '*les chevaux ont bien de la chance eux, car s'ils subissent aussi la guerre, comme nous, on ne leur demande pas d'y souscrire, d'avoir l'air d'y croire*' (*Voyage au bout de la nuit*, Paris, 1952, p. 45).

11 The 'paradoxes of collective choice' are many and varied – ranging from those arising from the search for a 'social welfare function' (for example, 'Arrow's Theorem', 'Sen's Paradox of the Paretian Liberal') to the quasi-moral paradox of democracy ('why ought I to accept a majority decision to do something which I think ought not to be done?'). In almost all cases these paradoxes disappear, just so soon as one individual can dictate the outcome of the collective choice. (The relevant sections of Arrow and Sen are contained in Frank Hahn and Martin Hollis (eds), *Philosophy and Economic Theory*, Oxford, 1979.)
It was typical of Hegel's genius that he should have shown that the very solution which seems to pre-empt these paradoxes places the individual in a deeper contradiction, of an ontological, rather than a theoretical, kind.

12 See G. W. F. Hegel, *The Phenomenology of Spirit* (1807), tr. A. V. Miller, Oxford, 1977, B. IV. A, sections 178–196.

13 See Sir Isaiah Berlin's distinction between 'positive' and 'negative' freedom, in 'Two Concepts of Liberty', in *Four Essays on Liberty*, Oxford, 1969.

14 *Phenomenology of Spirit*.

15 J. P. Sartre, *Being and Nothingness*, tr. Hazel E. Barnes, New York, 1956, p. 406.

16 S. Freud, 'Instincts and their Vicissitudes', 1915, and 'The Economic Problem of Masochism', 1924, in *Collected Papers*, tr. J. Riviere, New York and London, 1924–50, vols II and IV.

17 Fryer, *Forbidden Books of the Victorians*, p. 24.

18 *Ibid.*, p. 178.

19 Robert Solomon, *In the Spirit of Hegel*, Oxford, 1983, pp. 448–9.

20 A. Schopenhauer, *The World as Will and Representation*, tr. E. J. F. Payne, Indian Hills, Colorado, 1958, vol. II, pp. 565–6. An interesting twist to the sociobiologist's argument is given by Michael Levin, who contends that the genetic abnormality of the homosexual act must also be a source of unhappiness – even when not recognised as such – just as our failure to take exercise is a source of unhappiness: 'Why Homosexuality is Abnormal', *The Monist*, 1984.

21 Jules Michelet, *La Femme* (1859), ed. Thérèsa Moreau, Paris, 1981, p. 286.

22 Pléiade edn, Paris, 1954, vol. 2, pp. 601–13.

23 Sir Kenneth Dover, *Greek Homosexuality*, London, 1978.

24 Eric Fuchs, *Sexual Desire and Love*, tr. M. Daigle, Cambridge, and New York, 1983 (original: *Le Désir et la tendresse*, Geneva, 1979), p. 216.

25 Michael Levin, 'Why Homosexuality is Abnormal', tries to account for the 'abnormality' of the homosexual act by the suggestion that the participants are using their sexual organs for what they are not *for* – and gives a functionalist theory of what he means by this. The result is not only absurd in itself, but also deeply misleading in the suggestion that the moral character of homosexual is no different from that of heterosexual buggery.

26 William Paley, *Moral and Political Philosophy*, 1785, book III, part III, ch. 5.

27 G. W. F. Hegel, *The Philosophy of Right*, tr. and ed. T. M. Knox, Oxford, 1942.

28 Charles de Brosses, *Du Culte des dieux fétiches*, Paris, 1760. The term had begun to acquire its distinctive modern meaning in Kant's *Religion within the Limits of Reason Alone* (1793), tr. T. M. Greene and H. H. Hudson, Chicago, 1934, book 4, part 2, section 3.

29 I have discussed this matter further in 'Fantasy, Imagination and the Screen', in *The Aesthetic Understanding*, London, 1983.

30 *Ibid.*

31 See R. A. D. Grant, 'The Politics of Sex', *Salisbury Review*, 1 (2), 1982.

32 Kant, *Metaphysic of Ethics*, Prussian Academy edition, part II, pp. 423–4 (tr. M. J. Gregor, as *The Doctrine of Virtue*, New York, 1964, pp. 87–8).

33 Diogenes Laertius, VI, 2, 46.

11 Sexual morality

1 See John McDowell, 'Reason and Virtue', *The Monist*, 1979, and 'Are Moral Requirements Hypothetical Imperatives?', *Proceedings of the Aristotelian Society, Supplementary Volume*, 1978.

2 R. Scruton, 'Attitudes, Beliefs and Reasons', in J. Casey (ed.), *Morality and Moral Reasoning*, London, 1971.

3 I. Kant, *Critique of Practical Reason*, 1788, tr. L. W. Beck, Chicago, 1949; G. W. F. Hegel, *Phenomenology of Spirit* (1807), tr. A. V. Miller, Oxford, 1977 F. H. Bradley, *Ethical Studies*, Oxford, 1876.

4 Cf. Hare's view that moral imperatives are distinguished partly by their 'overriding' quality – R. M. Hare, *Freedom and Reason*, Oxford, 1963, ch. 9, pp. 168f.

5 McDowell, 'Reason and Virtue'; see also Mark Platts, 'Moral Reality and the End of Desire', in M. Platts (ed.), *Reference, Truth and Reality*, London, 1980.

6 The suggestion is made by Armatya Sen, 'Informational Analysis of Moral Principles', in Ross Harrison (ed.), *Rational Action*, Cambridge, 1979.

7 John Rawls, *A Theory of Justice*, Oxford, 1971, p. 560.

8 Michael Sandel, *Liberalism and the Limits of Justice*, Cambridge, 1982.

9 I spell out this suggestion in more detail in the Appendix to *The Meaning of Conservatism*, 2nd edn, London, 1984.

10 On the structure of the practical syllogism, see G. E. M. Anscombe, *Intention*, Oxford, 1957, §§33–5.

11 There are abnormal and unforeseeable circumstances, in which someone may have good reason to be irrational; see below, pp. 338–9.

12 Aristotle, *Nicomachean Ethics*, 1098b.

13 John Casey, 'Human Virtue and Human Nature', in J. Benthal (ed.), *On Human Nature*, London, 1973.

14 Henry Sidgwick, *The Methods of Ethics*, London, 1879, 7th edn, 1907, p. 359.

15 D. Parfit, *Reasons and Persons*, London, 1984. Parfit implies that criteria of personal identity over time are unattainable, and also unnecessary. Very similar

arguments have been used (e.g. by Hume, *Treatise of Human Nature*, bk. I, ch. 4, ii) to show that criteria for the identity of *any* object over time are unobtainable, and likewise unnecessary.

16 Hume's argument (*Treatise of Human Nature*, book I, ch. 4 section ii) purports to show that assertions of identity over time *always* go beyond the evidence which we have for making them. The consideration underlying Hume's argument (that there are only contingent connections between events at separate times) also underlies many of the arguments given by Parfit. Some philosophers have maintained that there are some judgements of identity over time which *cannot* be mistaken – specifically, certain kinds of first-person memory claim. See S. Shoemaker, *Self-Knowledge and Self-Identity*, Ithaca, 1963.

17 S. Hampshire, *Thought and Action*, London, 1956, ch. 3.

18 The suggestion derives from H. Frankfurt, 'Freedom of the Will and the Concept of a Person', *Journal of Philosophy*, vol. 68 (1971), pp 5–20, and is fruitfully explored by D. C. Dennett, in 'Conditions of Personhood', in A. O. Rorty (ed.), *The Identities of Persons*, Los Angeles, 1976.

19 See, for example, J. L. Mackie, *Ethics, Inventing Right and Wrong*, Harmondsworth, 1977.

20 'Thrown-ness' – Heidegger's term for the condition in which the agent first confronts the objective world (*Being and Time*, tr. J. Macquarrie and E. S. Robinson, New York, 1962). The term describes the agent's situation as *perceived*: before I have taken responsibility for my existence, my being has a quality of arbitrariness which afflicts me with anxiety.

21 Parfit, *Reasons and Persons*, pp. 12–13, drawing on T. C. Schelling's *Strategy of Conflict*, Cambridge, Mass., 1960.

22 See again the criticisms offered to Margaret Mead by Derek Freeman, *Margaret Mead and Samoa*, Cambridge, Mass., 1983.

23 Cf. the love poetry of Hafiz, of Omar Khayam, and of the Divan poets; and also the tales of faithful love in the *Thousand and One Nights*.

24 See Mary Douglas, *Implicit Meanings*, London, 1975, and *Purity and Danger*, London, 1966, for a study of the phenomena of disgust and pollution among African tribes.

25 *King Roger* is, I believe, an important expression of a certain vision of the erotic, which is seen as essentially *outside* society, chthonic, unintelligible and subversive of established things. I have discussed the opera and its meaning in 'Between Decadence and Barbarism: the Music of Szymanowski', in M. Bristiger, R. Scruton and P. Weber-Bockholdt (eds), *Karol Szymanowski in seiner Zeit*, Munich, 1984, pp. 159–78.

26 'Formulations Regarding the Two Principles in Mental Functioning' (1911), in *Collected Papers*, tr. J. Riviere, New York, 1924–50, vol. IV.

27 An eccentric and politicised, but frequently perceptive, critique of this 'commodification' of sex is contained in Stephen Heath, *The Sexual Fix*, London, 1982.

28 Karl Marx, *Capital*, tr. S. Moore and E. Aveling, ed. F. Engels, London, 1887, vol I, part I, ch. 1, section 4.

29 A. Heron (ed.), *Towards a Quaker View of Sex*, London, 1963, quoted in Ronald Atkinson, *Sexual Morality*, London, 1965, p. 148.

12 The politics of sex

1 I use 'meaning' here as a translation of German *Sinn* (and Czech *smysl*), to capture what Husserl and Patočka regarded as the true subject-matter of the 'human' sciences. The term has many technical meanings. My use is not to be confused with those which belong to the philosophy of language (e.g. Frege's use of *Sinn*), even though there may be independent reasons for thinking that linguistic meaning is a special *case* of what I mean by meaning. I have in mind the meaning of 'meaning' in 'the meaning of life', where the meaning of life is at least partly distinguished from the purpose of life. In the English tradition, the study of this kind of meaning has been regarded as the concern of the literary critic, rather than the philosopher. There is, indeed, considerable similarity between the Husserlian idea of the task of philosophy and the Leavisite conception of cultural criticism. In denying that there can be *two* cultures, and that science can be a culture, Leavis argues, in effect, for the priority and autonomy of the *Lebenswelt*, and for the need to approach it with interests and conceptual tools other than those of scientific explanation. (See F. R. Leavis, *Nor Shall my Sword*, London, 1973.) The critic's study is not explanatory but *comparative*; it involves an attempt to discern the significance, for morally motivated agents, of the works of man and of nature.

2 Rudolf Otto, *The Idea of the Holy*, tr. J. W. Harvey, Oxford, 1923.

3 See Heidegger's study of care (*Sorge*) and anxiety (*Angst*), in *Being and Time*, tr. J. Macquarrie and E. S. Robinson, New York, 1962. The relevant work of Patočka's is *Dvě Studie o Masarykovi*, Toronto, 1980. It has unfortunately not yet been translated.

4 H. Marcuse, *Eros and Civilisation, A Philosophical Enquiry into Freud*, new edn, Boston, Mass., 1966; Erich Fromm, *The Art of Loving*, New York, 1960; Wilhelm Reich, *The Function of the Orgasm*, 1968, tr. V. R. Carfagno, New York, 1973, London, 1983; *The Sexual Revolution*, London, 1951; and Norman O. Brown, *Life Against Death*, London, 1959.

5 Aristotle's attack on Plato's ideas of marriage, private property and the rearing of children is the ancestor of a tradition of conservative thinking, according to which political allegiance stems ultimately from the domestic bond. The master of this way of thinking is Hegel, in *The Philosophy of Right*, tr. and ed. T. M. Knox, Oxford, 1942.

6 See J. Patočka, *Kacířské eseje o Filosofii Dějin* (Heretical Essays on the Philosophy of History), Munich, 1980, tr. Erika Abrams, *Essais Hérétiques*, Paris, 1980.

7 See J. Patočka, *Platon a Evropa* (private lectures of 1973), Prague, 1973. This is a *samizdat* text, which has been translated into French by Erika Adams, as *Platon et L'Europe*, Paris, 1983.

8 *Dvě Studie o Masarykovi*, pp. 83ff.

9 Patočka died in 1977, after brutal interrogation from the Czech secret police. This interrogation resulted from his position as spokesman of Charter 77. Seen by the outside world as a movement for 'human rights', Charter 77 is better understood from within, as demanding the re-establishment of *political*, as opposed to coercive, order, in countries subjected to the impersonal tyranny of communism.

10 See the remarks on the genesis of moral belief, in G. Harman, *The Nature of*

Morality, New York, 1977, and the general tenets of 'scientific realism' as expounded by J. J. C. Smart in *Philosophy and Scientific Realism*, London, 1966.

11 Weber's term is *Entzauberung*. See *Wissenschaft als Beruf*, tr. as 'Science as a Vocation', in *From Max Weber*, ed. and tr. H. H. Garth and C. Wright Mills, London, 1947.

12 The lament is given in verbose and florid form by Germaine Greer, in *Sex and Destiny*, London, 1983.

13 Adam Smith, *The Wealth of Nations*, 1776. Hayek's views are derived in part from Ludwig von Mises, *Socialism*, 1923, but have a distinctive philosophical character, to be seen at its most ostentatious in *Law, Legislation and Liberty*, London, 1973–9, vol. 1: *Rules and Order*, 1973.

14 This thought is Hegelian: I try to translate it into acceptable political language in *The Meaning of Conservatism*, 2nd edn, London, 1974.

15 Thomas Hobbes, *Leviathan*, II.

16 John Rawls, *A Theory of Justice*, Oxford, 1971. Pertinent criticism of this idea is offered by Ronald Dworkin, in 'The Original Position', in Norman Daniels (ed.), *Reading Rawls*, Oxford, 1975, reprinted as ch. 6 of *Taking Rights Seriously*, London, 1977.

17 See Hegel, *The Philosophy of Right*. The essential contrast, in terms of which the Hegelian view of political order is to be expressed, is that between piety and justice. The first, which consists in the ability to accept and be bound by obligations that were never chosen, is denounced by the liberal conscience as mere superstition. I have defended piety in my *Meaning of Conservatism*.

18 The phrase is Kierkegaard's: see *Either/Or*, tr. W. Lowrie, New York, 1959, vol. II.

19 Telling anthropological studies of 'initiation rites' include M. Fortes and G. Evans-Pritchard, *African Political Systems*, Oxford, 1940; and J. Beattie, *Other Cultures*, London, 1964.

20 E. Husserl, *Die Krisis der europäischen Wissenschaften und die transzendentale Phänomenologie*, ed. W. Biemel, The Hague, 1976.

21 Cf. Demosthenes, *Against Naicea*: 'mistresses we keep for the sake of pleasure, concubines for the daily care of our person, but wives to bear us legitimate offspring, and to be faithful guardians of the hearth.'

22 See Chapter 8, and especially the work by Capellanus there referred to.

23 *The Philosophy of Right*, section 169.

Epilogue

1 Michel Foucault, *L'Usage des plaisirs*, Paris, 1984, p. 16.

2 See Roger Scruton, 'Thinkers of the Left: Michel Foucault', *Salisbury Review*, 1(3), 1983, reprinted in *Thinkers of the New Left*, London, 1985.

Appendix 1 The first person

1 The two ideas are treated separately by Husserl in his later work. See especially *Die Krisis der europäischen Wissenschaften und die transzendentale Phänomenologie*, ed. W. Biemel, The Hague, 1976, part 3, section 34: 'Exposition des Problems einer Wissenschaft von der Lebenswelt'.

2 On this point, see my *Art and Imagination*, London, 1974, chs 7 and 8.

3 This 'bracketing' (*epochē*), by which all reference to outer objects is discounted in the description of a mental state, provided, for Husserl, one of the principal moves in phenomenological analysis. See his *Ideas, General Introduction to Phenomenology*, 1913, tr. W. R. Boyce Gibson, London, 1931.

4 Rudolf Carnap, *Der logische Aufbau der Welt*, Berlin, 1928.

5 E. Husserl, *Cartesian Meditations*, tr. D. Cairns, The Hague, 1960, reissued 1969, p. 52.

6 *Ibid.*, p. 53.

7 Interpretations of Wittgenstein's argument include the following:

i The argument is directed against the possibility of 'private ostensive definition'. (G. E. M. Anscombe in conversation, and A. J. Kenny, in *Wittgenstein*, London, 1973.)

ii The argument concludes that I cannot refer to 'private sensations', but only to the public circumstances that attend them. (This interpretation is familiar from many of the earlier critics – see the articles in O. R. Jones (ed.), *The Private Language Argument*, London, 1971.)

iii The argument is the corollary to a more general thesis about language and, in particular, to the view that has come to be known as 'anti-realism', according to which the meaning of a sentence is determined not by the conditions for its truth, but by the conditions for its justified assertion. (S. Kripke, *Wittgenstein on Rule-Following and Private Language*, Oxford, 1982, following M. Dummett, *Truth and Other Enigmas*, London, 1978, Preface, esp. pp. xxxiv–xxxvii.)

The second interpretation seems to me to be wholly mistaken. At the beginning of the argument Wittgenstein asks the question 'How do words refer to sensations?', and proceeds to offer 'one suggestion' in answer. The whole tenor of the argument is directed towards the conclusion that, because we *do* refer to sensations, sensations cannot be 'private'. The third interpretation I have criticised elsewhere (in a review article of Kripke, *Mind*, vol. XCIII (1984), pp. 592–601). It seems to me that Wittgenstein's argument does not depend upon anti-realism, and that, if it did, it would be as unpersuasive as anti-realism itself. The first interpretation is difficult to grasp, since it seems not to say what it is about 'inner processes' that makes their 'ostension' impossible. However, it may be that the argument that I give is compatible with this interpretation.

The argument begins at section 243, where a supposition is made that sensations are 'immediate private' objects. The argument goes on to show the absurd consequences of that supposition. From which it follows that the supposition is wrong, and that sensations are *not as described* in this section. Wittgenstein proceeds to affirm that words *do* refer to sensations, and makes a suggestion as to how this is so. The suggestion at once obliges him to examine the peculiarities of the first-person case, since these peculiarities indicate that his suggestion might be wrong. He argues (sections 246–50) that the first-person case is misinterpreted by his opponent, so as to beg the question in favour of the 'private object'. He goes on to consider the evident fact that we can speak of two people having the *same* sensation, and offers suggestions as to the functioning of the public language-game of 'identity' that would show how this is so. He then, at section 256, introduces the private language argument, in its various versions.

Section 258 (the diary argument) seems to me to be weak as it stands, and open to the objections that Ayer and others have made to it. (See the articles in Jones, *The Private Language Argument*.) But it is only a gesture, and the argument returns in a stronger and more devastating form at section 288 – and it is this subsequent version that I have drawn on. The intervening sections provide the basic observations in support of a theory of the publicity of sense, which will accommodate the case of sensation words. In the interpretation that I give I have been much influenced by conversations with Malcolm Budd.

8 L. Wittgenstein, *Philosophical Investigations*, tr. G. E. M. Anscombe, Oxford, 1952, section 288.

9 *Ibid.*, section 293.

10 *Ibid.*, section 304.

11 This is the response, e.g., of Don Locke, in *Myself and Others*, Oxford, 1963.

12 G. Frege, 'On Sense and Reference' (irritatingly retranslated as 'On Sense and Meaning'), *The Philosophical Writing of Gottlob Frege*, tr. and ed. P. T. Geach and M. Black, Oxford, 1952.

13 See the discussion in M. Dummett, *Frege, Philosophy of Language*, London, 1973. Dummett interprets the idea of a 'route' to reference in epistemological terms, i.e. as a procedure for discovering the reference of a term. This is clearly not necessary. See D. C. Dennett, 'Beyond Belief', in A. Woodfield (ed.), *Thought and Object, Essays on Intentionality*, Oxford, 1982.

14 See Dummett, *Frege, Philosophy of Language*, and Kripke, *Wittgenstein on Rule-Following*.

15 *Philosophical Investigations*, section 288.

16 *Ibid.*, section 271.

17 *Pace*, e.g., A. J. Ayer ('Can There be a Private Language?', in Jones, *The Private Language Argument*), who argues that Wittgenstein's proof, if valid, would prevent Robinson Crusoe from learning his language in isolation.

18 I. Kant, *Critique of Pure Reason*, (1781, 1787), tr. N. Kemp Smith, London, 1929, A 442 (B 470).

19 *Ibid.*, A 496 (B 524).

20 There is no doubt that Wittgenstein's *Remarks on the Foundations of Mathematics* (ed. G. H. von Wright, R. Rhees and G. E. M. Anscombe, tr. G. E. M. Anscombe, Oxford, 1956) show him to be in part persuaded by the constructivist approach. I believe that he was motivated, not by an 'anti-realist' theory of meaning generally, but by the desire to account for the peculiarities of mathematical truth – in particular, its *a priori* and necessary character.

21 See Appendix 2 below.

Appendix 2 Intentionality

1 D. C. Dennett, 'Beyond Belief', in A. Woodfield (ed.), *Thought and Object, Essays on Intentionality*, Oxford, 1982.

2 F. Brentano, *Psychology from an Empirical Standpoint*, 2nd edn, ed. Oskar Kraus, Leipzig, 1923, tr. A. C. Rancurello, D. B. Terrell and L. L. McAlister, London, 1973, book II, ch. 1, section 5, pp. 88–9. (I have slightly amended the translation.)

3 *Ibid.*, Supplementary Remarks, pp. 271ff. See also Oscar Kraus, Intro-

duction to the second edition of Brentano's work (included as a postscript to the English text), esp. section II, pp. 373ff.

4 See E. Husserl, *Ideas, General Introduction to Phenomenology*, 1913, tr. W. R. Boyce Gibson, London, 1931.

5 But, as Wittgenstein points out, in his pertinent *Remarks on Colour* (ed. G. E. M. Anscombe, tr. L. L. McAlister and M. Schattle, Oxford, 1977), 'there is no such thing as phenomenology, although there are indeed phenomenological problems' (section 53).

6 F. Brentano, *The True and the Evident*, ed. O. Kraus, tr. R. Chisholm, London, 1966, p. 78.

7 See R. Chisholm, in H. N. Castañeda (ed.), *Intentionality, Minds and Perception*, Detroit, 1967.

8 D. Davidson, 'Mental Events', in *Essays on Actions and Events*, Oxford, 1980.

9 D. C. Dennett, 'Intentional Systems', *Journal of Philosophy*, vol. 68 (1971), reprinted in *Brainstorms*, Brighton, 1978.

10 *Psychology from an Empirical Standpoint*, Supplementary Remarks.

11 See, for example, Colin McGinn, *The Character of Mind*, Oxford, 1982.

12 See W. Kneale, 'Intensionality and Intentionality', *Aristotelian Society Supplementary Volume*, vol. XLII (1968).

13 Hence the emergence of 'possible world' semantics, in the theory of modal logic. See G. E. Hughes and M. J. Creswell, *An Introduction to Modal Logic*, London, 1968, pp. 75–80.

14 G. Frege, 'On Sense and Reference' (retranslated as 'On Sense and Meaning'), *The Philosophical Writing of Gottlob Frege*, tr. and ed. P. T. Geach and M. Black, Oxford, 1952.

15 For example, identity of sense will not permit substitution in such contexts as 'John believes that . . .'. If John is ignorant of the identity of sense between 'p' and 'q', he may believe that p, and yet not believe that q.

16 See Martin Davies, *Meaning, Quantification and Necessity*, Themes in Philosophical Logic, London, 1981.

17 See C. Lewy, *Meaning and Modality*, Cambridge, 1976, ch. 1.

18 See, for example, A. Church's devastating review of Carnap's *Introduction to Semantics* in *Philosophical Review*, vol. LII (1943), and W. V. Quine's 'Ways of Paradox', in *Ways of Paradox and Other Essays*, New York, 1966. Church and Quine choose not truth-values but sets as their preferred objects of singular reference, thus avoiding the suspicion that questions might be begged in Frege's favour by the assumption that truth-values are 'objects'.

19 'Situation semantics', which rejects the idea that sentences *refer* to truth-values, rejects also the principle that logical equivalents can be substituted *salvo denotato*: see Jon Barwise and John Perry, *Situations and Attitudes*, Cambridge, Mass., 1983. However, that does not affect the question whether they can be substituted *salva veritate*, and hence leaves the discussion of intentionality untouched.

20 J. L. Mackie, 'Causes and Conditions', in Ernest Sosa (ed.), *Causation and Conditionals*, Oxford, 1978.

21 See 'Reference and Modality' in *From a Logical Point of View*, 2nd edn, Cambridge, Mass., 1961.

22 See David Kaplan, 'On Quantifying in', in D. Davidson and J. Hintikka (eds),

Words and Objections, Dordrecht, 1969; H. Putnam, 'The Meaning of "Meaning" ', in *Philosophical Papers*, vol. II: *Mind, Language and Reality*, Cambridge, 1975.

23 The *oratio recta* theory derives from R. Carnap, *The Logical Syntax of Language*, tr. A. Smeathon, London, 1937, pp. 240ff. The *oratio recta* theory for mental contexts might be expressed in terms of P. T. Geach's notion of 'saying in one's heart'; see *Mental Acts*, London, 1957, pp. 79ff.

24 Putnam, 'The Meaning of "Meaning" '.

25 Gareth Evans, 'The Causal Theory of Names', *Aristotelian Society, Supplementary Volume*, vol. XLVIII (1973), pp. 187–208.

26 See J. R. Searle, *Intentionality*, Oxford, 1983, pp. 62ff.

27 M. Dummett, *Frege, Philosophy of Language*, London, 1973, appendix to ch. 5.

28 Colin McGinn, 'The Structure of Content', in Woodfield, *Thought and Object*.

29 *Ibid.*, p. 211.

30 *Ibid.*, p. 212.

31 This issue is discussed by C. Peacocke, in *Sense and Content*, Oxford, 1983.

32 Such would appear to be the line taken by Donald Davidson, in a variety of papers, e.g. 'Thought and Talk', in S. Guttenplan (ed.), *Mind and Language*, Oxford, 1975.

33 For a vigorous defence of this position, see J. R. Searle, *Intentionality*.

34 I am indebted to the discussion of secondary qualities in C. McGinn, *The Subjective View: Secondary Qualities and Indexicals*, Oxford, 1983. See p. 123.

35 For an explanation of this term, see A. J. Kenny, *Action, Emotion and Will*, London, 1963, p. 189.

36 J. P. Sartre, *Sketch for a Theory of the Emotions*, tr. P. Mairet, preface Mary Warnock, London, 1962.

37 I have argued for this in 'Attitudes, Beliefs and Reasons', in J. Casey (ed.), *Morality and Moral Reasoning*, London, 1971.

38 Among tertiary qualities, I include aspects, emotional qualities (the gloominess of a landscape), affective qualities (being moving, depressing and so on), and aesthetic qualities. For a theory of tertiary qualities, see my *Art and Imagination*, London, 1974, part II.

39 P. F. Strawson, 'Freedom and Resentment', in *Freedom and Resentment and Other Essays*, London, 1974.

40 The expression, and the idea, come from John Locke, *Essay Concerning Human Understanding*, book II, ch. 27, §26: 'Person ... is a forensic term appropriating actions and their merit'.

INDEX OF NAMES

INDEX OF SUBJECTS